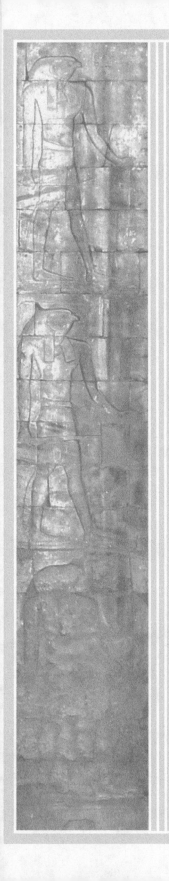

THE RISE AND FALL
OF ANCIENT EGYPT

THE RISE AND FALL OF
ANCIENT EGYPT

TOBY WILKINSON

RANDOM HOUSE · NEW YORK

Published in the United States by Random House, an imprint of
The Random House Publishing Group, a division of Random
House, Inc., New York.

RANDOM HOUSE and colophon are registered trademarks of Random House, Inc.

Originally published in the United Kingdom by Bloomsbury Publishing, Plc., London, in 2010.

All images reproduced in the insert sections are courtesy of the
Werner Forman Archive, with the exception of the pectoral of
Princess Mereret, which is reproduced courtesy of Sandro
Vannini/Corbis.

LIBRARY OF CONGRESS CATALOGING-IN-PUBLICATION DATA
Wilkinson, Toby A. H.
The rise and fall of ancient Egypt / Toby Wilkinson.
p.   cm.
Includes bibliographical references and index.
ISBN 978-0-553-80553-6
eBook ISBN 978-0-679-60429-7
1. Egypt—History—To 332 B.C.   2. Egypt—History—
332–30 B.C.   I. Title.
DT83.W658   2011   932—dc22   2009047322

Printed in the United States of America on acid-free paper

www.atrandom.com

9 8 7 6 5 4 3 2 1

FIRST U.S. EDITION

Maps by John Gilkes
Book design by Simon M. Sullivan

FOR BEN AND GINNY

"My name is Ozymandias, king of kings:
Look on my works, ye Mighty, and despair!"
Nothing beside remains. Round the decay
Of that colossal wreck, boundless and bare,
The lone and level sands stretch far away.

—Percy Bysshe Shelley, "Ozymandias"

CONTENTS

Timeline   *xiii*

Author's Note   *xxiii*

Introduction   *xxv*

PART I: DIVINE RIGHT (5000–2175 B.C.)   1

  1. IN THE BEGINNING   5

  2. GOD INCARNATE   25

  3. ABSOLUTE POWER   40

  4. HEAVEN ON EARTH   57

  5. ETERNITY ASSURED   77

PART II: END OF INNOCENCE (2175–1541 B.C.)   99

  6. CIVIL WAR   103

  7. PARADISE POSTPONED   124

  8. THE FACE OF TYRANNY   140

  9. BITTER HARVEST   162

PART III: THE POWER AND THE GLORY (1541–1322 B.C.)   179

  10. ORDER REIMPOSED   183

  11. PUSHING THE BOUNDARIES   202

  12. KING AND COUNTRY   222

  13. GOLDEN AGE   240

  14. ROYAL REVOLUTION   257

PART IV: **MILITARY MIGHT** (1322–1069 B.C.)   279

    15. MARTIAL LAW   283

    16. WAR AND PEACE   301

    17. TRIUMPH AND TRAGEDY   323

    18. DOUBLE-EDGED SWORD   341

PART V: **CHANGE AND DECAY** (1069–30 B.C.)   361

    19. A HOUSE DIVIDED   365

    20. A TARNISHED THRONE   383

    21. FORTUNE'S FICKLE WHEEL   399

    22. INVASION AND INTROSPECTION   420

    23. THE LONG GOODBYE   444

    24. FINIS   465

Epilogue   483

Acknowledgments   487

Notes   489

Bibliography   539

Index   579

All dates are B.C. The margin of error is within a century or so circa 3000 B.C. and within two decades circa 1300 B.C.; dates are precise from 664 B.C. The system of dynasties devised in the third century B.C. is not without its problems—for example, the Seventh Dynasty is now recognized as being wholly spurious, while several dynasties are known to have ruled concurrently in different parts of Egypt—but this system remains the most convenient method for subdividing ancient Egyptian history. The broader periods are more modern scholarly conventions.

PERIOD/DYNASTY/KING	DEVELOPMENTS: IN EGYPT	OUTSIDE EGYPT

EARLY DYNASTIC PERIOD, 2950–2575

First Dynasty, 2950–2750		Newgrange chambered tomb built in Ireland
NARMER	Unification of Egypt	
AHA		
DJER		
DJET		
DEN		
ANEDJIB		
SEMERKHET		
QAA		
Second Dynasty, 2750–2650		
HETEPSEKHEMWY		
NEBRA		
NINETJER		Emergence of Elamite
(several ephemeral kings)		kingdom
PERIBSEN		
KHASEKHEM(WY)		Earliest evidence of silk-weaving in China

PERIOD/DYNASTY/KING	DEVELOPMENTS: IN EGYPT	OUTSIDE EGYPT
Third Dynasty, 2650–2575		
NETJERIKHET (DJOSER),		
2650–2620	Step Pyramid at Saqqara	
SEKHEMKHET		
KHABA		
SANAKHT		
HUNI, 2600–2575		Emergence of Indus civilization
OLD KINGDOM, 2575–2125		
Fourth Dynasty, 2575–2450	Zenith of pyramid building	
SNEFERU, 2575–2545		
KHUFU, 2545–2525	Great Pyramid at Giza	
DJEDEFRA		
KHAFRA	Great Sphinx completed	
(ephemeral unnamed king)		
MENKAURA		
SHEPSESKAF		
Fifth Dynasty, 2450–2325		
USERKAF	Sun temples	
SAHURA		
NEFERIRKARA KAKAI		
SHEPSESKARA IZI		
NEFEREFRA		
NIUSERRA INI		
MENKAUHOR		
DJEDKARA ISESI		Kingdom of Akkad founded by Sargon
UNAS, 2350–2325	Pyramid Texts compiled	
Sixth Dynasty, 2325–2175		
TETI		
USERKARA		
PEPI I, 2315–2275		
MERENRA		
NEFERKARA PEPI II,	Harkhuf's expeditions to	
2260–2175	Nubia	
Eighth Dynasty, 2175–2125		
Eighteen ephemeral kings,		
including:		
NEMTYEMSAF II	Decline in royal authority	

PERIOD/DYNASTY/KING	DEVELOPMENTS: IN EGYPT	OUTSIDE EGYPT

NEITIQERTY SIPTAH
IBI
NEFERKAURA
NEFERKAUHOR
NEFERIRKARA

FIRST INTERMEDIATE PERIOD, 2125–2010

Ninth/Tenth Dynasty,
2125–1975   Rise of the Osiris cult
Several kings, including:
KHETI I
KHETI II
MERIKARA

Eleventh Dynasty, 2080–1938
INTEF I   Civil war begins   Main phase of Stonehenge
INTEF II   Emergence of Minoan
                                                   civilization on Crete; col-
                                                   lapse of Indus civilization

INTEF III

MIDDLE KINGDOM, 2010–1630

MENTUHOTEP II, 2010–1960   Civil war ends; Egypt
                            reunified
MENTUHOTEP III, 1960–1948
MENTUHOTEP IV, 1948–1938

Twelfth Dynasty, 1938–1755   Literature flourishes
AMENEMHAT I, 1938–1908
SENUSRET I, 1918–1875   Nubian fortresses built
AMENEMHAT II, 1876–1842   Earliest evidence for domes-
                                                   tic horses in Central Asia

SENUSRET II, 1842–1837
SENUSRET III, 1836–1818
AMENEMHAT III, 1818–1770   Land reclamation in the   Code of Hammurabi
                            Fayum   compiled
AMENEMHAT IV, 1770–1760   Traditional date for the
                                                   foundation of the Shang
                                                   Dynasty in China, 1766

SOBEKNEFERU, 1760–1755

PERIOD/DYNASTY/KING	DEVELOPMENTS: IN EGYPT	OUTSIDE EGYPT

Thirteenth Dynasty, 1755–1630
At least fifty kings, including:
SOBEKHOTEP III

Asiatic immigration into the
delta
Foundation of the Hittite
Kingdom

SECOND INTERMEDIATE PERIOD, 1630–1539

Fourteenth Dynasty
Several ephemeral kings,
beginning with:
NEHESY

Political fragmentation

Fifteenth (Hyksos) Dynasty, 1630–1520
Six kings, including:
KHYAN, 1610–1570
APEPI, 1570–1530   Civil war with Thebes
KHAMUDI, 1530–1520

Sixteenth Dynasty
Numerous ephemeral kings, including:
NEFERHOTEP III
MENTUHOTEPI

Seventeenth Dynasty, 1630–1539
Numerous kings, including:

Emergence of Mycenaean
civilization in Greece;
Babylonia sacked by the
Hittites

RAHOTEP
NUBKHEPERRA INTEF
SOBEKEMSAF II
SEQENENRA TAA, 1545–1541   Battles against the Hyksos
KAMOSE, 1541–1539

NEW KINGDOM, 1539–1069

Eighteenth Dynasty, 1539–1292
AHMOSE (I), 1539–1514   Hyksos defeated and expelled
AMENHOTEP I, 1514–1493   Valley of the Kings inaugurated
THUTMOSE I, 1493–1481   Conquest of Nubia
THUTMOSE II, 1481–1479

PERIOD/DYNASTY/KING	DEVELOPMENTS: IN EGYPT	OUTSIDE EGYPT
THUTMOSE III, 1479–1425 and HATSHEPSUT, 1473–1458	Battle of Megiddo, April 1458	Mycenaean conquest of Crete, end of Minoan civilization
AMENHOTEP II, 1426–1400	Egyptian empire in Levant	
THUTMOSE IV, 1400–1390		Linear B script
AMENHOTEP III, 1390–1353	Monumental buildings at Thebes	
AMENHOTEP IV/AKHENATEN, 1353–1336	Foundation of Akhetaten, 1349	
NEFERNEFERUATEN, 1336–1333		
SMENKHKARA, 1336–1332		
TUTANKHAMUN, 1332–1322		
AY, 1322–1319		
HOREMHEB, 1319–1292	Army rises to prominence	Height of Olmec civilization in Mexico

Nineteenth Dynasty, 1292–1190

RAMESSES I, 1292–1290		
SETI I, 1290–1279		
RAMESSES II, 1279–1213	Battle of Kadesh, May 1274	
MERENPTAH, 1213–1204	Libyan invasion, 1209	Hittite capital sacked
SETI II (SETI-MERENPTAH), 1204–1198		
AMENMESSE, 1204–1200		
SIPTAH, 1198–1193		
TAWOSRET, 1198–1190		

Twentieth Dynasty, 1190–1069

SETHNAKHT, 1190–1187		
RAMESSES III, 1187–1156	Battle against the Sea Peoples	Traditional date for the fall of Troy, 1184
RAMESSES IV, 1156–1150		Collapse of Mycenaean civilization
RAMESSES V, 1150–1145		
RAMESSES VI, 1145–1137		
RAMESSES VII, 1137–1129		
RAMESSES VIII, 1129–1126		
RAMESSES IX, 1126–1108	Tomb robberies begin	
RAMESSES X, 1108–1099		
RAMESSES XI, 1099–1069		

PERIOD/DYNASTY/KING	DEVELOPMENTS: IN EGYPT	OUTSIDE EGYPT

THIRD INTERMEDIATE PERIOD, 1069–664

Twenty-first Dynasty, 1069–945
NESBANEBDJEDET, 1069–1045
(HERIHOR, 1069–1063)
(PINEDJEM I, 1063–1033)
AMENEMNISU, 1045–1040
PASEBAKHAENNIUT I, 1040–985
AMENEMOPE, 985–975
(PINEDJEM II, 985–960)
OSORKON THE ELDER, 975–970
SIAMUN, 970–950
PASEBAKHAENNIUT II, 950–945

Formal division of Egypt — Composition of the *Rig Veda* in India

Twenty-second Dynasty, 945–715

SHOSHENQ I, 945–925	Egyptian conquest of Judah	Death of Solomon, division of Hebrew Kingdom into Israel and Judah
OSORKON I, 925–890		Rise of Assyrian Empire
SHOSHENQ II, 890		
TAKELOT I, 890–874		
OSORKON II, 874–835	Secession of Thebes	
SHOSHENQ III, 835–793		Traditional date for the foundation of Carthage, 814
SHOSHENQ IV, 793–783		Emergence of Etruscan civilization in Italy
PAMAY, 785–777		Earliest recorded Olympic Games, 776
SHOSHENQ V, 777–740		Traditional date for the foundation of Rome, 753
PADIBASTET (II), 740–730		Homer composes *The Iliad* and *The Odyssey*
OSORKON IV, 735–715		

Twenty-third Dynasty, 838–720

TAKELOT II, 838–812	Civil war in Thebes	
PADIBASTET (I), 827–802		
IUPUT I, 812–802		
SHOSHENQ VI, 802–796		
OSORKON III, 796–768		
TAKELOT III, 773–754		
RUDAMUN, 754–735	Kushite conquest of Thebes	
INY, 735–730		
PEFTJAUAWYBAST, 730–720		

PERIOD/DYNASTY/KING	DEVELOPMENTS: IN EGYPT	OUTSIDE EGYPT

Twenty-fourth Dynasty, 740–715
TEFNAKHT, 740–720
BAKENRENEF, 720–715

Twenty-fifth (Kushite) Dynasty, 728–657

PIANKHI, 747–716	Kushite conquest of Egypt, 728	
SHABAQO, 716–702		Capital of Assyria moved to Nineveh, 705
SHABITQO, 702–690		
TAHARQO, 690–664	Assyrian invasions	
TANUTAMUN, 664–657		

LATE PERIOD, 664–332

Twenty-sixth (Saite) Dynasty, 664–525

PSAMTEK I, 664–610	Reintegration of Thebes	Babylonian conquest of Assyria; Nineveh sacked, 612
NEKAU II, 610–595		Jews exiled to Babylon; earliest Mayan pyramids built
PSAMTEK II, 595–589		
WAHIBRA, 589–570	Babylonian invasion repulsed	Persian conquest of Babylonia, 539; birth of the Buddha and Confucius
AHMOSE II, 570–526	Greek trading center at Naukratis	
PSAMTEK III, 526–525		

Twenty-seventh Dynasty (First Persian Period), 525–404

CAMBYSES, 525–522	Persia conquers Egypt	
DARIUS I, 522–486	Ancient Suez Canal built, 497	Roman republic founded 509; Athens adopts democracy, 509–507
XERXES I, 486–465		Battle of Thermopylae, 480; deaths of the Buddha and Confucius
ARTAXERXES I, 465–424		Completion of the Parthenon in Athens, 432; Peloponnesian War, 431
DARIUS II, 424–404		Deaths of Euripides and Sophocles, 406

PERIOD/DYNASTY/KING	DEVELOPMENTS: IN EGYPT	OUTSIDE EGYPT

Twenty-eighth Dynasty, 404–399

AMENIRDIS, 404–399 — Rivalry between delta dynasts — Execution of Socrates, 399

Twenty-ninth Dynasty, 399–380

NAYFAURUD I, 399–393
HAGAR, 393–392
PASHERMUT, 392–391
HAGAR (restored), 391–380
NAYFAURUD II, 380

Thirtieth Dynasty, 380–343

NAKHTNEBEF, 380–362 — Egypt hires Spartan mercenaries
DJEDHER, 365–360
NAKHTHORHEB, 360–343 — — Death of Plato, 347

Thirty-first Dynasty (Second Persian Period), 343–332

ARTAXERXES III, 343–338 — Persia reconquers Egypt
ARSES, 338–336
DARIUS III, 335–332

MACEDONIAN DYNASTY, 332–309

ALEXANDER III (THE GREAT), — Alexander visits Siwa oracle
  332–323
PHILIP ARRHIDAEUS
  (PHILIP III OF MACEDON),
  323–317
ALEXANDER IV, 317–309

PTOLEMAIC PERIOD, 309–30

PTOLEMY I, 304–282 — Alexandria Library founded
PTOLEMY II, 285–246 — Pharos completed, 280 — Outbreak of First Punic War, 264

PTOLEMY III, 246–221 — Theban rebellion, 205–186 — Outbreak of Second Punic
PTOLEMY IV, 221–204 — — War, 218; Hannibal crosses the Alps

PTOLEMY V, 204–180
PTOLEMY VI, 180–145 — Rome intervenes to save Egypt — Outbreak of Third Punic War, 149; Rome destroys Carthage, 146

PTOLEMY VIII AND
  CLEOPATRA II, 170–116
PTOLEMY IX, 116–107
  and CLEOPATRA III, 116–101

PERIOD/DYNASTY/KING	DEVELOPMENTS: IN EGYPT	OUTSIDE EGYPT
PTOLEMY X, 107–88		
PTOLEMY IX (RESTORED), 88–80		
PTOLEMY XI and BERENIKE III, 80		
PTOLEMY XII, 80–58	Temple of Horus consecrated, 70	
CLEOPATRA VI, 58–57 AND BERENIKE IV, 58–55		
PTOLEMY XII (restored), 55–51	Cleopatra meets Antony, 55	Caesar lands in Britain, 55
CLEOPATRA VII, 51–30 and PTOLEMY XIII, 51–47	Cleopatra meets Caesar, 48	
and PTOLEMY XIV, 47–44		Assassination of Caesar, 44
and PTOLEMY XV CAESARION, 44–30		Rome conquers Egypt

AUTHOR'S NOTE

PROPER NAMES

Names of ancient Egyptian people and places have been given in the form most closely approximating the original usage (where this is known), except when the classical form of a place-name has given rise to a widely used adjective. Therefore, "Memphis" (and "Memphite") are used instead of "Mennefer" or the earlier "Ineb-hedj," "Thebes" ("Theban") rather than "Waset," "Sais" ("Saite") instead of "Sa," and "Herakleopolis" ("Herakleopolitan") instead of "Nen-nesut." For ease of reference, the modern equivalent is given in parenthesis after the first mention of an ancient place-name in the text, and the ancient equivalents are given for classical toponyms.

For reasons of accessibility, the names of the Persian and Greek rulers of Egypt in the sixth to first centuries B.C. have been given in their classical and anglicized forms, respectively: for example, Darius instead of Dariyahavush, Ptolemy rather than Ptolemaios, Mark Antony instead of Marcus Antonius.

The Roman numerals (e.g., Thutmose I–IV, Ptolemy I–XV) are a modern convention, used to distinguish between different kings in a sequence who shared the same birth name. Throughout most of Egyptian history, the kings were referred to principally by their throne names; these are formulaic, often long-winded, and generally unfamiliar except to Egyptologists.

DATES

All dates are B.C., except in the Introduction and Epilogue or unless explicitly stated. For dates before 664 B.C., there is a margin of error that ranges from ten to twenty years for the New Kingdom to as much as fifty to a hundred years for the Early Dynastic Period; the dates given in the text represent the latest scholarly consensus. From 664 B.C. onward, sources external to Egypt make a precise chronology possible.

Two hours before sunset on November 26, 1922, the English Egyptologist Howard Carter and three companions entered a rock-cut corridor dug into the floor of the Valley of the Kings. The three middle-aged men and one much younger woman made an unlikely foursome. Carter was a neat, rather stiff man in his late forties, with a carefully clipped mustache and slicked-back hair. He had a reputation in archaeological circles for obstinacy and a temper, but was also respected, if somewhat grudgingly, for his serious and scholarly approach to excavating. He had made Egyptology his career but, lacking private means, was dependent on others to fund his work. Fortunately, he had found just the right man to bankroll his current excavations on the west bank of the Nile at Luxor. Indeed, his patron was now beside him to share in the excitement of the moment.

George Herbert, fifth earl of Carnarvon, cut a very different figure. Raffish and debonair, even for his fifty-six years, he had led the life of an aristocratic dilettante, as a young man indulging his love of fast cars. But a driving accident in 1901 had nearly cost him his life; it had left him weakened and prone to rheumatic pain. To spare himself the cold, damp air of English winters, he had taken to spending several months each year in the warmer, drier climate of Egypt. So had begun his own, amateur interest in archaeology. A meeting with Carter in 1907 inaugurated the partnership that was to make history. Joining the two men on this "day of days"—as Carter was later to describe it—were Carnarvon's daughter, Lady Evelyn Herbert, and Carter's old friend Arthur "Pecky" Callender, a retired railway manager who had joined the excavation only three weeks earlier. Although a novice to archaeology, Callender had a knowledge of architecture and engineering that made him a useful member of the team. His carefulness and dependability appealed to Carter, and he was well used to Carter's frequent mood swings.

Howard Carter and the governor of Qena province greet Lady Evelyn Herbert and Lord Carnarvon on their arrival at Luxor station, November 23, 1922. SOURCE UNKNOWN

Just three days into the excavation season (which was due to be the last season—even Carnarvon's fortune was not inexhaustible), workmen had uncovered a flight of steps leading downward into the bedrock. Once the staircase had been fully cleared, an outer blocking wall had been revealed, covered with plaster and stamped with seal impressions. Even without deciphering the inscription, Carter had known what this meant: he had found an intact tomb from the period of ancient Egyptian history known as the New Kingdom, an era of great pharaohs and beautiful queens. Was it possible that beyond the blocking wall lay the prize for which Carter had been striving for seven long years? Was it the last undiscovered tomb in the Valley of the Kings? Always a stickler for correctness, Carter had put decorum first and ordered his workmen to refill the flight of steps, pending the arrival from England of the expedition's sponsor, Lord Carnarvon. If there was a major discovery to be made, it was only proper that patron and archaeologist should share it together. So on November 6, Carter sent a telegram to Carnarvon: "At last have made wonderful discovery in Valley; a magnificent tomb with seals intact; re-covered same for your arrival; congratulations."

After a seventeen-day journey by ship and train, the earl and Lady Evelyn arrived in Luxor, to be met by an impatient and excited Carter.

The very next morning, work to clear the steps began in earnest. On November 26, the outer blocking wall was removed to reveal a corridor, filled with stone chips. From the pattern of disturbance running through the fill, it was clear that someone had been there before: robbers must have entered the tomb in antiquity. But the seal impressions on the outer blocking wall showed that it had been resealed in the New Kingdom. What might this mean for the state of the burial itself? There was always the possibility that it would turn out in the end to be a private tomb, or a cache of funerary equipment collected from earlier robbed tombs in the Valley of the Kings and reburied for safety. After a further day of strenuous work, in the heat and dust of the valley floor, the corridor was emptied. Now, after what must have felt like an interminable wait, the way ahead was clear. Carter, Carnarvon, Callender, and Lady Evelyn found themselves before yet another blocking wall, its surface also covered with large oval seal impressions. A slightly darker patch of plaster in the top left-hand corner of the wall showed where the ancient robbers had broken in. What would greet this next set of visitors, more than three and a half thousand years later?

Without further hesitation, Carter took his trowel and made a small hole in the plaster blocking, just big enough to look through. First, as a safety precaution, he took a lighted candle and put it through the hole, to test for asphyxiating gases. Then, with his face pressed against the plaster wall, he peered through into the darkness. The hot air escaping from the sealed chamber caused the candle to flicker, and it took a few moments for Carter's eyes to grow accustomed to the gloom. But then details of the room beyond began to emerge. Carter stood dumbstruck. After some minutes, Carnarvon could bear the suspense no longer. "Can you see anything?" he asked. "Yes, yes," replied Carter, "wonderful things." The following day, Carter wrote excitedly to his friend and fellow Egyptologist Alan Gardiner, "I imagine it is the greatest find ever made."

Carter and Carnarvon had discovered an intact royal tomb from the golden age of ancient Egypt. It was crammed, in Carter's own words, with "enough stuff to fill the whole upstairs Egyptian section of the B[ritish] M[useum]." The antechamber alone—the first of four rooms entered by Carter and his associates—contained treasures of unimaginable opulence: three colossal gilded ceremonial beds, in the shapes of fabulous creatures; golden shrines with images of gods and goddesses; painted jewelry boxes and inlaid caskets; gilded chariots and fine archery equipment; a magnificent gold throne, inlaid with silver and precious stones; vases of beautiful translucent alabaster; and, guarding the right-hand wall, two life-size figures of the dead king, with black skin and gold accoutrements. The royal name on many of the objects left no doubt as to the identity of the tomb owner: the hieroglyphs clearly spelled out Tut-ankh-Amun.

By curious concidence, the breakthrough that had allowed ancient Egyptian writing to be first deciphered, and had thus opened up the study of pharaonic civilization through its numerous inscriptions, had occurred exactly a century before. In 1822, the French scholar Jean-François Champollion published his famous *Lettre à M. Dacier*, in which he correctly described the workings of the hieroglyphic writing system and identified the phonetic values of many important signs. This turning point in the history of Egyptology was itself the result of a long period of study. Champollion's interest in ancient Egyptian writing had been prompted when he'd first learned about the Rosetta Stone as a boy. A royal proclamation inscribed in three scripts (Greek, demotic characters, and hieroglyphics), the stone had been discovered by Napoleonic troops at el-Rashid (Rosetta) during the French invasion of 1798, when Champollion was eight years old, and it was to provide one of the main keys to the decipherment of Egyptian hieroglyphics. Champollion's early genius for languages had enabled him to become proficient in Greek and, crucial in this endeavor, Coptic, the liturgical language of the Egyptian Orthodox Church and a direct descendant of ancient Egyptian. Armed with this knowledge, and with a transcription of the Rosetta Stone, Champollion correctly translated the hieroglyphic version of the text and so began the process that was to unlock the secrets of ancient Egyptian history. His grammar and dictionary of the ancient Egyptian language, published posthumously, allowed scholars, for the first time, to read the words of the pharaohs themselves, after an interval of more than two thousand years.

At the same time that Champollion was working on the mysteries of the ancient Egyptian language, an Englishman, John Gardner Wilkinson, was making an equally important contribution to the study of pharaonic civilization. Born a year before Napoléon's invasion, Wilkinson traveled to Egypt at the age of twenty-four and stayed for the next twelve years, visiting virtually every known site, copying countless tomb scenes and inscriptions, and carrying out the most comprehensive study of pharaonic monuments undertaken to that point. (For a year, in 1828–1829, Wilkinson and Champollion were both in Egypt, traveling and recording, but it is not known if the two ever met.) On his return to England in 1833, Wilkinson began compiling the results of his work and published them four years later. The three-volume *Manners and Customs of the Ancient Egyptians*, together with the two-volume *Modern Egypt and Thebes* (published in 1843), was and remains the greatest review of ancient Egyptian civilization ever accomplished.

Wilkinson became the most famous and most honored Egyptologist of his age, and is regarded, with Champollion, as one of the founders of the subject. Just a year before Wilkinson died, Howard Carter was born, the man who was to take Egyptology—and the public fascination with ancient Egypt—to new heights. Unlike his two great forebears, Carter stumbled into Egyptology almost by accident. It was his skill as a draftsman and painter, rather than any deep-rooted fascination with ancient Egypt, that secured him his first position on the staff of the Archaeological Survey at the age of seventeen. This brought Carter the opportunity to train under some of the greatest archaeologists of the day—including Flinders Petrie, the father of Egyptian archaeology, with whom he excavated at Amarna, the capital city of the heretic pharaoh Akhenaten and the probable birthplace of Tutankhamun. By copying tomb and temple scenes for various expeditions, Carter became intimately acquainted with ancient Egyptian art. His firsthand knowledge of many of the major archaeological sites would, no doubt, have been supplemented by reading the works of Wilkinson. So it was that, in 1899, Carter came to be appointed inspector general of monuments of Upper Egypt, and four years later of Lower Egypt. But his hot temper and stubbornness brought his promising career to an abrupt end when he refused to apologize after an altercation with some French tourists, and he was promptly sacked from the Antiquities Service (then under French control). Returning to his roots, Carter earned his living for the next four years as an itinerant watercolorist, before joining forces with Lord Carnarvon in 1907 to begin excavating, once again, at Thebes.

After fifteen long, hot, and none-too-fruitful years, Carter and his sponsor finally made the greatest discovery in the history of Egyptology.

After sunset that November day in 1922, the astonished party made its way back to Carter's house for a fitful night's sleep. It was impossible to take in everything that had happened. They had made the greatest archaeological discovery the world had ever seen. Nothing would be the same again. But one final question nagged at Carter. He had found Tutankhamun's tomb, and the bouquets of flowers left over from the royal funeral, but did the king himself still lie, undisturbed, in his burial chamber?

The new dawn brought with it a feverish rush of activity, as Carter began to appreciate the immensity of the task that lay before him. He realized he would need to assemble—and quickly—a team of experts to help photograph, catalogue, and conserve the vast number of objects in the tomb. He started contacting friends and colleagues, and informed the Egyptian antiquities authorities about the spectacular discovery. A date of November 29 was agreed upon for the official public opening of the tomb. The event would be covered by the world's press, the first major archaeological discovery of the media age. Thereafter, it would be impossible for Carter to retain control of the situation. If he wanted to solve the mystery of the king's final resting place, quietly, and in his own time, he would have to do so before the official opening, and go behind the backs of the antiquities officials.

On the evening of November 28, a matter of hours before the press were due to arrive, Carter and his three trusted companions slipped away from the crowds and entered the tomb once more. His instinct told him that the black-skinned guardian figures framing the right-hand wall of the antechamber had to indicate the location of the burial chamber. The plaster wall behind them confirmed as much. Once again Carter made a small hole in the plaster wall, at ground level, just big enough to squeeze through, and with an electric flashlight this time instead of a candle, he crawled through the opening. Carnarvon and

Lady Evelyn followed; Callender, being a little too portly, stayed behind. The three inside found themselves face-to-face with an enormous gilded shrine that filled the room. Opening its doors revealed a second shrine nested within the first . . . then a third, and a fourth shrine concealing the stone sarcophagus. Now Carter knew for certain: the king's burial lay within, having been undisturbed for thirty-three centuries. After squeezing back out into the antechamber, Carter hastily, and rather clumsily, disguised his unauthorized break-in with a basket and a bundle of reeds. For another three months, no one else would see what Carter, Carnarvon, and Lady Evelyn had seen.

The public unveiling of Tutankhamun's tomb made newspaper headlines around the world on November 30, 1922, capturing the public's imagination and generating a wave of popular interest in the treasures of the pharaohs. But there was more to come. The official opening of the burial chamber on February 16, 1923, was followed a year later by the lifting of the one-and-a-quarter-ton lid from the king's immense stone sarcophagus—a feat expertly accomplished by Callender with his engineering background. Inside the sarcophagus, there were yet more layers protecting the pharaoh's body: three nested coffins, to complement the four gilded shrines. The two outer coffins were of gilded wood, but the third, innermost coffin was of solid gold. Inside each coffin there were amulets and ritual objects, all of which had to be carefully documented and removed before the next layer could be examined. The whole process, from lifting the lid of the sarcophagus to opening the third coffin, took more than eighteen months. Finally, on October 28, 1925, nearly three years after the discovery of the tomb and two years after Carnarvon's untimely death (not from the pharaoh's curse but from blood poisoning), the moment was at hand to reveal the boy king's mummified remains. Using an elaborate system of pulleys, the lid of the innermost coffin was raised by its original handles. Inside lay the royal mummy, caked in embalming unguents that had blackened with age. Standing out from this tarry mess, and covering the king's face, was a magnificent funerary mask of beaten gold in the image of the young monarch. Above his brow were the vulture and cobra goddesses, and around his neck was a broad collar of inlaid glass and semiprecious stones. Carter and Tutankhamun had come face-to-face at last.

Howard Carter cleaning Tutankhamun's second coffin.
© GRIFFITH INSTITUTE, UNIVERSITY OF OXFORD

The mask of Tutankhamun is perhaps the most splendid artifact ever recovered from an ancient civilization. It dazzles us today as it did those who first beheld it in modern times, almost a century ago. During the 1960s and '70s, it formed the highlight of the traveling Tutankhamun exhibition, drawing crowds of millions around the world, from Vancouver to Tokyo. Although I was too young to visit the show when it came to London, the book published to accompany the exhibition was my first introduction to the exotic world of ancient Egypt. I remember reading the book on the landing at home, at age six, marveling at the jewels, the gold, the strange names of kings and gods. The treasures of Tutankhamun planted a seed in my mind that was to grow and flourish in later years. But the ground had already been prepared. A year earlier, at the age of five, while leafing through the pages of my first childhood encyclopedia, I had noticed an entry illustrating different writing systems. Never mind the Greek, Arabic, Indian, and Chinese scripts: it was the Egyptian hieroglyphics that captured my imagination. The book gave only a few signs, but they were enough to allow me to work out how to write my own name. Hieroglyphs and Tutankhamun set me on the path to becoming an Egyptologist.

Indeed, writing and kingship were the twin cornerstones of pharaonic civilization, the defining characteristics that set it apart from other ancient cultures. Despite the efforts of archaeologists to uncover the rubbish dumps and workshops that would reveal the daily lives of ordinary citizens, it is the abundant written record and the imposing edifices left behind by the pharaohs that continue to dominate our view of ancient Egyptian history. In the face of such powerful testimonies, perhaps it is not surprising that we are inclined to take the texts and monuments at face value. And yet the dazzling treasures of the pharaohs should not blind us to a more complex truth. Despite its spectacular monuments, magnificent works of art, and lasting cultural achievements, ancient Egypt had a darker side.

The first pharaohs understood the extraordinary power of ideology—and of its visual counterpart, iconography—to unite a disparate people and bind them in loyalty to the state. Egypt's earliest kings formulated and harnessed the tools of leadership that are still with us: elaborate trappings of office and carefully choreographed public appearances to set the ruler apart from the populace; pomp and spectacle on grand state occasions to reinforce bonds of loyalty; patriotic fervor expressed orally and visually. But the pharaohs and their advisers knew equally well that their grip on power could be maintained just as effectively by other, less benign means: political propaganda, an ideology of xenophobia, close surveillance of the population, and brutal repression of dissent.

In studying ancient Egypt for more than twenty years, I have grown increasingly uneasy about the subject of my research. Scholars and enthusiasts alike are inclined to look at pharaonic culture with misty-eyed reverence. We marvel at the pyramids, without stopping to think too much about the political system that made them possible. We take vicarious pleasure in the pharaohs' military victories—Thutmose III at the Battle of Megiddo, Ramesses II at the Battle of Kadesh—without pausing too long to reflect on the brutality of warfare in the ancient world. We thrill at the weirdness of the heretic king Akhenaten and all his works, but do not question what it is like to live under a despotic, fanatical ruler (despite the modern parallels, such as in North Korea, that fill our television screens). Evidence for the darker side of pharaonic civilization is not lacking. From human sacrifice in the First Dynasty to a peasants' revolt under the Ptolemies, ancient Egypt was a society in which the relationship between the king and his subjects was based on coercion and fear, not love and admiration—where royal power was absolute, and life was cheap. The aim of this book is to give a fuller and more balanced picture of ancient Egyptian civilization than is often found in the pages of scholarly or popular works. I have set out to reveal both the highs and the lows, the successes and the failures, the boldness and the brutality that characterized life under the pharaohs.

The history of the Nile Valley lays bare the relationship between rulers and the ruled—a relationship that has proved stubbornly immutable across centuries and cultures. The ancient Egyptians invented the concept of the nation-state that still dominates our planet, five thousand years later. The Egyptians' creation was remarkable, not only for its impact, but also for its longevity: the pharaonic state, as originally conceived, lasted for three millennia. (By comparison, Rome barely managed one millennium, while Western culture has yet to survive two.) A key reason for this remarkable survival is that the philosophical and political framework first developed at the birth of ancient Egypt was so well attuned to the national psyche that it remained the archetypal pattern of government for the next one hundred generations. Despite prolonged periods of political fragmentation, decentralization, and unrest, pharaonic rule remained a powerful ideal. A political creed that harnesses itself to a national myth can embed itself very deeply in the human consciousness.

It is extremely difficult to engage with a culture so remote in time and place from our own. Ancient Egypt was a sparsely populated tribal society. Its polytheistic religion, its premonetary economy, the low rate of literacy, and the ideological dominance of divine kingship—all these defining characteristics are utterly alien to contemporary Western observers, myself included. As well as a familiarity with two centuries of scholarship, the study of ancient Egypt thus requires a huge leap of imagination. And yet, our common humanity offers a way in. In the ca-

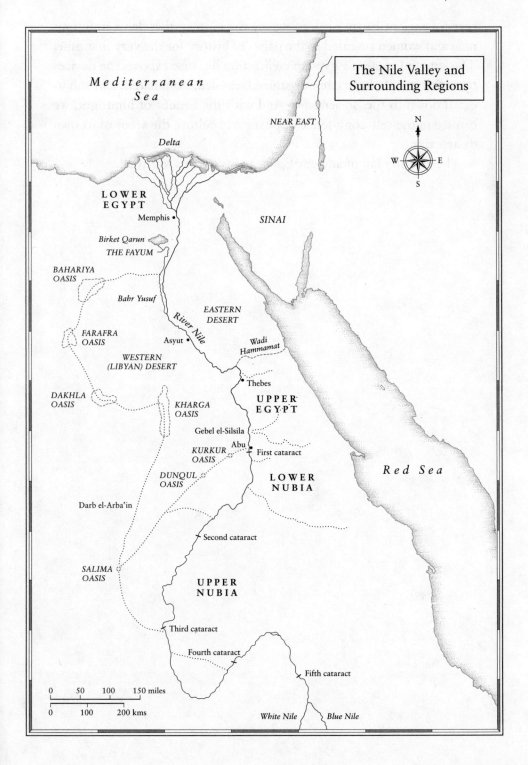

The Nile Valley and Surrounding Regions

Mediterranean Sea

NEAR EAST

Delta

LOWER EGYPT

Memphis

SINAI

Birket Qarun
THE FAYUM

BAHARIYA OASIS

Bahr Yusuf

EASTERN DESERT

FARAFRA OASIS

Asyut

River Nile

Wadi Hammamat

WESTERN (LIBYAN) DESERT

DAKHLA OASIS

KHARGA OASIS

Thebes

UPPER EGYPT

Gebel el-Silsila

KURKUR OASIS

Abu

First cataract

DUNQUL OASIS

LOWER NUBIA

Darb el-Arba'in

Red Sea

Second cataract

SALIMA OASIS

UPPER NUBIA

Third cataract

Fourth cataract

Fifth cataract

| 0 | 50 | 100 | 150 miles |
| 0 | 100 | 200 kms |

White Nile *Blue Nile*

reers of ancient Egypt's rulers, we see the motives that drive ambitious men and women revealed in the pages of history for the very first time. The study of ancient Egyptian civilization likewise exposes the devices by which people have been organized, cajoled, dominated, and subjugated down to the present day. And with the benefit of hindsight, we can see in the self-confidence of pharaonic culture the seeds of its own destruction.

The rise and fall of ancient Egypt holds lessons for us all.

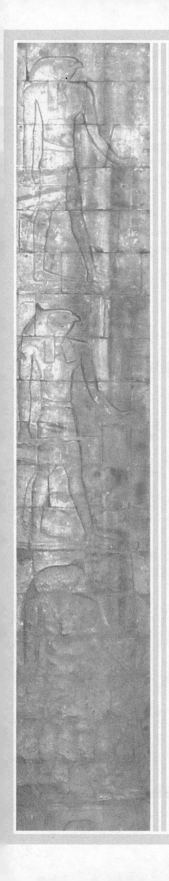

PART I
DIVINE RIGHT
(5000–2175 B.C.)

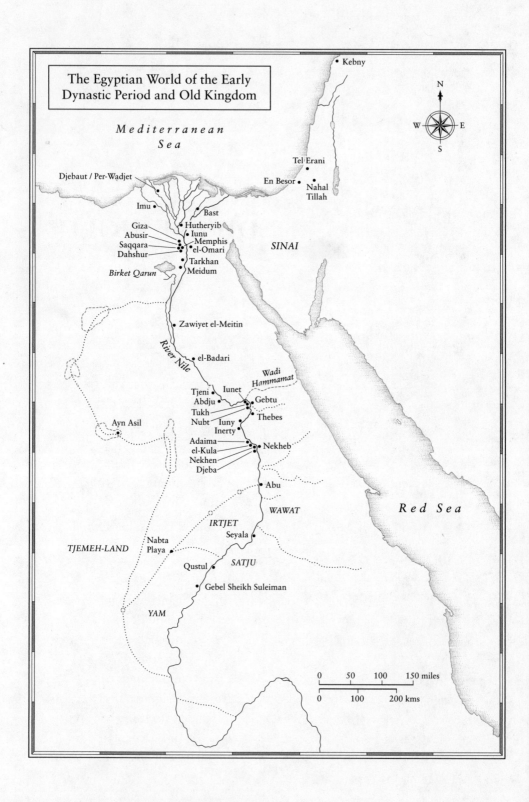

The Egyptian World of the Early Dynastic Period and Old Kingdom

Mediterranean Sea

N
W E
S

• Kebny

Tel Erani •

Djebaut / Per-Wadjet

En Besor •
Nahal Tillah

Imu •

Bast •

SINAI

Giza
Abusir
Saqqara
Dahshur

Hutheryib •
Iunu •
Memphis
el-Omari •
Tarkhan •
Meidum •

Birket Qarun

Zawiyet el-Meitin •

River Nile

el-Badari •

Wadi Hammamat

Tjeni •   Iunet
Abdju •   • Gebtu
Tukh •
Nubt •   • Thebes
         Iuny
         Inerty
Adaima •
el-Kula •   • Nekheb
Nekhen •
Djeba •

Ayn Asil •

• Abu

WAWAT

IRTJET

Nabta
Playa •
        Seyala •

TJEMEH-LAND

SATJU

Qustul •

• Gebel Sheikh Suleiman

YAM

Red Sea

| 0 | 50 | 100 | 150 miles |
| 0 | 100 | 200 kms |

THE PYRAMIDS OF GIZA ARE THE DEFINING SYMBOL OF ANCIENT Egypt. In historical terms, they mark the first great flowering of pharaonic culture, the Old Kingdom. Yet the pyramids and the sophisticated culture they represent did not spring into existence fully formed without a long period of gestation. The origins and early development of civilization in Egypt can be traced back to at least two thousand years before the pyramids, to the country's remote prehistoric past.

Over a period of many centuries, communities living in the fertile Nile Valley and the dry grasslands to the east and west developed the main cornerstones of Egyptian culture, their distinctive outlook shaped by their unique natural environment. As competing territories were forged, through trade and conquest, into the world's first nation-state, the pace of social development accelerated, and by the advent of Egypt's first dynasty of kings, all the main elements were in place.

The subsequent eight centuries witnessed the emergence of a great civilization, and its fullest expression is in those most iconic of monuments on the Giza plateau. Yet, as the Egyptians themselves knew only too well, order and chaos were constant bedfellows. As quickly as it had blossomed, the overstretched state withered under pressures at home and abroad, bringing the Old Kingdom to an inglorious end.

Part I of this book charts this first rise and fall of ancient Egypt, from its extraordinary birth to its cultural zenith at the height of the Pyramid Age, and its subsequent decline—the first of many such cycles in the long history of the pharaohs. If there is one defining feature of this period, it is the ideology of divine kingship. The promulgation of a belief in a monarch with divine authority was the most significant achievement of Egypt's early rulers. The belief embedded itself in the Egyptian consciousness so deeply that it remained the only acceptable form of government for the next three thousand years. For sheer longevity, this type of monarchy ranks as the greatest political and religious system the world has ever known. The belief in this system was expressed through art, writing, ceremony, and, above all, architecture, such expression providing both the inspiration and the justification for massive royal tombs.

The officials who served the king and whose administrative genius built the pyramids left their own monuments, too, their lavishly decorated sepulchres a testament to the sophistication and resources of the court. But there was also a darker side to royal government. The appropriation of land, forced labor, a scant regard for human life—these were characteristics of the Pyramid Age as much as grandiose architecture was. The ruthless exploitation of Egypt's natural and human resources was a prerequisite for achieving the state's wider ambitions, and it set the scene for the following centuries of pharaonic rule. While kings ruled by divine right, the rights of their subjects interested them little. This would be an abiding theme in the history of ancient Egypt.

CHAPTER 1

IN THE BEGINNING

THE FIRST KING OF EGYPT

IN A TALL GLASS CASE IN THE ENTRANCE HALL OF THE EGYPTIAN MUseum in Cairo stands an ancient slab of fine-grained greenish-black stone, about two feet high and no more than an inch thick. Shaped like a shield, it is carved on both sides in low relief. The scenes, though still crisp, are difficult to make out in the diffuse, hazy light that filters down through the dusty glazed dome in the museum ceiling. Most visitors barely give this strange object a second glance as they head straight for the golden riches of Tutankhamun on the floor above. Yet this modest piece of stone is one of the most important documents to survive from ancient Egypt. Its place of honor at the entrance to the Egyptian Museum, the world's greatest treasure-house of pharaonic culture, underlines its significance. This stone is the object that marks the very beginning of ancient Egyptian history.

The Narmer Palette, as it is known to Egyptologists, has become an icon of early Egypt, but the circumstances of its discovery are clouded with uncertainty. In the winter of A.D. 1897–1898, the British archaeologists James Quibell and Frederick Green were in the far south of Egypt, excavating at the ancient site of Nekhen (modern Kom el-Ahmar), the "city of the falcon" (classical Hierakonpolis). The nineteenth century was still the era of treasure seeking, and Quibell and Green, though more scientific in their approach than many of their contemporaries, were not immune from the pressure to discover fine objects to satisfy their sponsors back home. So, having chosen to excavate at Nekhen, a site eroded by countless centuries and largely devoid of major standing monuments, they decided to focus their attentions on the ruins of the local temple. Though small and unimpressive by comparison with the great sanctuaries of Thebes, this was no ordinary provincial shrine. Since the dawn of history, it had been dedicated to the celebration of Egyptian kingship. The local falcon god of Nekhen, Horus, was the patron deity of the Egyptian monarchy. Might the temple, therefore, yield a royal treasure?

The two men worked away, and their initial results were disappointing: stretches of mud brick wall; the remains of a mound, faced in stone; a few worn and broken statues. Nothing spectacular. The next area to be investigated lay in front of the mound, but here the archaeologists encountered only a thick layer of clay that resisted systematic excavation. The city of the falcon seemed determined to keep its secrets. But then, as Quibell and Green struggled their way through the clay layer, they came upon a scatter of discarded ritual objects, a motley collection of sacred paraphernalia that had been gathered up and buried by the temple priests some time in the remote past. There was no gold, but the "Main Deposit"—as the archaeologists optimistically called it—did contain some interesting and unusual finds. Chief among them was a carved slab of stone.

There was no doubt about what sort of object they had found. A shallow, circular well in the middle of one side showed it to be a palette, a grindstone for mixing pigments. But this was no workaday tool for preparing cosmetics. The elaborate and detailed scenes decorating both sides showed that it had been commissioned for a much loftier purpose, to celebrate the achievements of a glorious king. Beneath the benign gaze of two cow goddesses, a representation of the monarch himself—shown in the age-old pose of an Egyptian ruler, smiting his enemy with a mace—dominated one side of the palette. The archaeologists wondered who he was and when he had reigned. Two hieroglyphs, contained within a small rectangular panel at the very top of the palette, seemed to provide the answer, spelling out the monarch's name: a catfish (*"nar"* in the Egyptian language) and a chisel (*"mer"*)—Narmer. Here was a king previously unknown to history. Moreover, the style of the carvings on the Narmer Palette pointed to a very early date. Subsequent research showed that Narmer was not just *an* early king; he was the very first ruler of a united Egypt. He came to the throne around 2950, the first king of the First Dynasty. In the mud of Nekhen, Quibell and Green had stumbled upon ancient Egypt's founding monument.

The Narmer Palette   WERNER FORMAN ARCHIVE

While Narmer may be the first historical king, he is not the beginning of Egypt's story. The decoration of his famous palette shows the art of the Egyptian royal court and the iconography of kingship already in their classical forms. However, some of the palette's stranger motifs, such as the intertwined beasts with long serpentine necks and the bull trampling the walls of an enemy fortress, hark back to a remote prehistoric past. On his great commemorative palette, Narmer was explicitly acknowledging that the cornerstones of Egyptian civilization had been laid long before his own time.

THE DESERT BLOOMS

AS THE NARMER PALETTE DEMONSTRATES ON A SMALL SCALE AND FOR an early date, the Egyptians achieved a mastery of stone carving unsurpassed in the ancient, or modern, world. Diverse and abundant raw materials within Egypt's borders combined with great technical accom-

plishment to give the Egyptians a highly distinctive medium for assert-
ing their cultural identity. Stone also had the advantage of permanence,
and Egyptian monuments were consciously designed to last for eternity. The origin of this obsession with monumentality was in the Western Desert, near the modern border between Egypt and Sudan. The
remote spot is known to archaeologists as Nabta Playa. Today, a paved
main road carves through the desert only a mile or two away, bringing
construction traffic to Egypt's New Valley project. But until very recently, Nabta Playa was as far away from civilization as it was possible
to get. Its main distinction was as a pit stop on the cross-country route
between the desert springs of Bir Kiseiba and the shores of Lake
Nasser. The flat bed of an ancient, dried-up lake—or playa—together
with a nearby sandy ridge, certainly make Nabta an ideal spot for an
overnight camp. There is, however, much more to the site than a casual
first glance would suggest. Scattered throughout the landscape are
large stones—not naturally occurring boulders but megaliths that had
been hauled from some distance away and set up at key points around
the edge of the playa. Some stand in splendid isolation, as sentinels on
the horizon; others form a linear alignment. Most remarkable of all, on
a slight elevation a series of stones has been set out in a circle, with
pairs of uprights facing each other. Two pairs are aligned north to
south, while two more point toward the midsummer sunrise.

Previously unknown and entirely unexpected, Nabta Playa has
emerged from obscurity as the ancient Egyptian Stonehenge, a sacred
landscape dotted with carefully placed stone structures. Scientific dating of the associated sediments has revealed a startlingly early date for
these extraordinary monuments, the early fifth millennium b.c. At that
time, as in even earlier periods, the Sahara would have been very different from its current arid state. On an annual basis, summer rains
would have greened the desert—filling the seasonal lake, and turning
its shores into lush pasture and arable land. The people who migrated
to Nabta Playa to take advantage of this temporary abundance were
seminomadic cattle herders who roamed with their livestock across a
wide area of the eastern Sahara. Large quantities of cattle bones have
been excavated at the site, and traces of human activity can be found
scattered over the ground: fragments of ostrich eggshells (used as water
carriers and, when broken, for making jewelry), flint arrowheads, stone

axes, and grindstones for processing the cereals that were cultivated along the lakeshore. With its seasonal fertility, Nabta offered semi-nomadic people a fixed point of great symbolic significance, and over generations they set about transforming it into a ritual center. Laying out the stone alignments must have required a large degree of communal involvement. Like their counterparts at Stonehenge, the monuments of Nabta show that the local prehistoric people had developed a highly organized society. A pastoral way of life certainly needed wise decision-makers with a detailed knowledge of the environment, close familiarity with the seasons, and an acute sense of timing. Cattle are thirsty animals, requiring a fresh supply of water at the end of each day's wandering, so judging when to arrive at a site such as Nabta and when to leave again could have been a matter of life and death for the whole community.

The purpose of the standing stones and the "calendar circle" seems to have been to predict the arrival of the all-important rains that fell shortly after the summer solstice. When the rains arrived, the community celebrated by slaughtering some of their precious cattle as a sacri-

Prehistoric rock art in Egypt's Eastern Desert TOBY WILKINSON

fice of thanks, and burying the animals in graves marked on the ground with large, flat stones. Under one such mound, archaeologists found not a cattle burial but a huge sandstone monolith that had been carefully shaped and dressed to resemble a cow. Dated, like the calendar circle, to the early fifth millennium B.C., it is the earliest known monumental sculpture from Egypt. Here are to be found the origins of pharaonic stone carving—in the prehistoric Western Desert, among wandering cattle herders, a millennium and more before the beginning of the First Dynasty. Archaeologists have been forced to rethink their theories of Egypt's origins.

On the other side of Egypt, in the Eastern Desert, equally remarkable discoveries have been made, confirming the impression that the arid lands bordering the Nile Valley were the crucible of ancient Egyptian civilization. Thousands of rock pictures pecked into the sandstone cliffs dot the dry valleys (known as wadis) that crisscross the hilly terrain between the Nile and the Red Sea hills. At some locations, usually associated with natural shelters, overhangs, or caves, there are great concentrations of pictures. One such tableau, by a dried-up plunge pool in the Wadi Umm Salam, has been likened to the Sistine Chapel. Its images constitute some of the earliest sacred art from Egypt, prefiguring the classic imagery of pharaonic religion by as much as a thousand years. Like their sculpture-loving counterparts at Nabta Playa, the prehistoric artists of the Eastern Desert seem also to have been cattle herders, and pictures of their livestock—and the wild animals they hunted out on the savanna—feature heavily in their compositions. But instead of using megaliths to signify their deepest beliefs, they exploited the smooth cliff faces offered by their own environment, turning them into canvases for religious expression. Gods traveling in sacred boats, and ritual hunts of wild animals, are key themes in the pharaonic iconography first attested in the Eastern Desert rock art. The inaccessible and inhospitable character of the region today belies its pivotal role in the rise of ancient Egypt.

GATHERING SPEED

ONGOING SURVEY AND EXCAVATION AT SITES ACROSS THE WESTERN and Eastern deserts is revealing a pattern of close interaction between desert and valley peoples in prehistory. Rather unexpectedly, the semi-nomadic cattle herders who roamed across the prehistoric savanna seem to have been more advanced than their valley-dwelling contemporaries. But in a lesson for our own times, the cattle herders' vibrant way of life was made extinct by environmental change. Beginning in about 5000, the climate of northeast Africa began to undergo a marked shift. The once predictable summer rains that for millennia had provided cattle herders with seasonal pasture away from the Nile became steadily less reliable. Over a period of a few centuries, the rain belt moved progressively southward. (Today the rains, when they fall at all, fall over the highlands of Ethiopia.) The savannas to the east and west of the Nile began to dry out and turn to desert. After little more than a few generations, the desiccated land was no longer able to support thirsty herds of cattle. For the herders, the alternative to starvation was migration—to the only permanent water source in the region, the Nile Valley.

Here, the earliest settled communities, along the edge of the floodplain, had been established in the early fifth millennium B.C., broadly contemporary with the megalith builders of Nabta Playa. Like the cattle herders, the valley dwellers had also been practicing agriculture, but in contrast to the seasonality of rainfall in the arid regions, the regime of the Nile had made it possible to grow crops year-round. This would have given the valley dwellers the incentive and the wherewithal to occupy their villages on a permanent basis. The way of life the valley dwellers developed is known to Egyptologists as the Badarian culture, after the site of el-Badari, where this lifestyle was first recorded. The local vicinity was ideally suited to early habitation, with the juxtaposition of different ecosystems—floodplain and savanna—and excellent links to a wider hinterland. Desert routes led westward to the oases, while a major wadi ran eastward to the Red Sea coast. It was through these avenues that the Badarian way of life was strongly influenced by the early desert cultures.

One such influence, an interest in personal adornment, stayed with the ancient Egyptians throughout their history. Another development with long-term ramifications was the gradual stratification of society into leaders and followers, a small ruling class and a larger group of subjects. This was a system that owed much to the challenging lifestyle faced by pastoral seminomads. These external stimuli and internal dynamics began to transform Badarian society. Over many centuries, gradual changes took root and began to accelerate. The rich grew richer and began to act as patrons to a new class of specialist craftsmen. They, in turn, developed new technologies and new products to satisfy their patrons' ever more sophisticated tastes. The introduction of restricted access to prestige goods and materials further reinforced the power and status of the wealthiest in society.

The process of social transformation, once started, could not be stopped. Culturally, economically, and politically, prehistoric society became increasingly complex. Egypt was set on a course toward statehood. The final drying-out of the deserts around 3600 must have injected further momentum into this process. A sudden increase in population—when those living in the deserts migrated to the valley—may have led to greater competition for scarce resources, encouraging the development of walled towns. More mouths to feed would also have stimulated more productive agriculture. Urbanization and the intensification of farming were responses to social change but were also a stimulus to further change.

Under such conditions, communities in Upper Egypt began to coalesce into three regional groupings, each probably ruled by a hereditary monarch. Strategic factors help to explain the early dominance of these three prehistoric kingdoms. One kingdom was centered on the town of Tjeni (near modern Girga), a site where the floodplain narrowed and allowed the town's inhabitants to control river traffic. This area was also where trade routes from Nubia and the Saharan oases met the Nile Valley. A second territory had its capital at Nubt ("the golden," modern Nagada), which controlled access to gold mines in the Eastern Desert via the Wadi Hammamat, on the opposite bank of the river. A third kingdom had grown up around the settlement of Nekhen, which, like Tjeni, was the starting point for a desert route to the oases (and thence to Sudan) and, like Nubt, controlled access to important Eastern Desert gold reserves, in this case the more southerly deposits reached via a wadi directly opposite the town.

The rulers of these three territories did what all aspiring leaders do: they sought to demonstrate and enhance their authority by political, ideological, and economic means. Their unquenchable thirst for rare and valuable objects, whether gold and precious stones from the deserts of Egypt or exotic imports from far-off lands (such as olive oil from the Near East and lapis lazuli from Afghanistan), stimulated internal and external trade. The authority to remove such items permanently from circulation was a particularly powerful statement of wealth and privilege, so the burials of the elite became increasingly elaborate and richly furnished, building upon a tradition of grave goods that stretched back to Badarian times. The development in all three territories of special burial grounds, set aside for the local ruling class, is a sure sign of strongly hierarchical societies. With three kingdoms vying for dominance, the inevitable clash was not long in coming.

The precise train of events is hazy, for this was an era before written texts. However, by comparing the size and magnificence of tombs in the three localities, we can get some indication of who was winning the battle for supremacy. Certainly, the burials at Nekhen and Abdju (classical and modern Abydos, the necropolis serving the town of Tjeni) outstrip their counterparts at Nubt. The later reverence shown to Nekhen and Abdju by Narmer and his successors—in contrast to their relative lack of interest in Nubt—points in the same direction.

An intriguing recent discovery, once again in the Western Desert, may even record the moment at which Tjeni eclipsed Nubt. The desert between Abdju and Nubt is crisscrossed by tracks, many of which have been in use for thousands of years. These overland paths happened to offer a quicker, more direct route than the river, because of the wide bend the Nile describes at this point in its course. Next to the principal route between Abdju and Nubt, a rock-cut tableau seems to record a victory by the prehistoric ruler of Tjeni, perhaps against his rival. Winning control of the desert routes certainly would have given Tjeni a decisive strategic advantage, allowing it to outflank its neighbor and cut it off from access to trade with areas farther south.

It can be no coincidence that, during exactly the same period, a ruler of Tjeni built the largest tomb of its time anywhere in Egypt, in the elite cemetery at Abdju. The tomb was designed to resemble a miniature palace, and its unparalleled size and contents—which included an ivory scepter and a cellar of the finest imported wine—mark it out as a true kingly burial. Furthermore, its owner was clearly a ruler whose economic influence spread far beyond his Nile Valley homeland. Among the most remarkable finds from the tomb were hundreds of small bone labels, each inscribed with a few hieroglyphic signs. Each label was once attached, by means of a cord, to a box or jar of supplies for the royal tomb. The inscriptions record the quantity, nature, provenance, or ownership of the contents, demonstrating—from the very dawn of writing—the ancient Egyptians' predilection for record keeping. Not only are these labels the earliest Egyptian writing yet discovered, but the places they mention as the sources of commodities include the shrine of Djebaut (in modern Tell el-Fara'in) and the town of Bast (modern Tell Basta) in the Nile delta, hundreds of miles north of Abdju. The ruler of Tjeni who built this impressive sepulchre was well on the way to becoming the king of all Egypt.

One monarch ruling from Tjeni with control over the Nile delta, another based at Nekhen with access to sub-Saharan trade: there were now just two players left in the game. It is frustrating that there is virtually no evidence for the last phase of the struggle, but the preponderance of martial motifs on decorated ceremonial objects from the period, and the construction at Nubt and Nekhen of massive town walls, strongly suggests that military conflict was involved. So does the incidence of cranial injuries among the late predynastic population of Nekhen.

The final outcome was certainly clear-cut. When the dust settled, it was the line of kings of Tjeni that claimed victory. Their control of two-thirds of the country, combined with access to seaports and to the lucrative trade with parts of the Near East (modern Syria, Lebanon, Israel, and Palestine), proved decisive. Around 2950 B.C., after nearly two centuries of competition and conflict, a ruler of Tjeni assumed the kingship of a united Egypt—the man known to us as Narmer. To symbolize his conquest of the delta—perhaps the final battle in the war of unification—he commissioned a magnificent ceremonial palette, decorated with scenes of triumph. In a gesture of homage to his erstwhile rivals (or perhaps to rub salt into their wounds), he dedicated the object in the temple at Nekhen . . . where it lay until its retrieval from the mud 4,900 years later.

GIFT OF THE NILE

GIVEN THE ARCHAEOLOGICAL AND SCHOLARLY EFFORT INVOLVED IN rediscovering Narmer, it is humbling to acknowledge that his relatively recent identification as the first king of ancient Egypt merely confirms the account given by the Greek historian Herodotus, writing twenty-four centuries ago. For the father of history, there was no doubt that Menes (another name for Narmer) had founded the Egyptian state. It is a salutary lesson that the ancients were often far cleverer than we give them credit for. Herodotus also made another fundamental observation about Egypt, which still captures the essential truth about the country and its civilization: "Egypt is the gift of the Nile."[1] Flowing through the Sahara, the Nile makes life possible where otherwise there would be none. The Nile Valley is a linear oasis, a narrow strip of green hemmed in on either side by a vast and arid desert, boundless and bare. The rise of ancient Egypt is to be traced as much in the river and its character as in the archaeology of graves, rock pictures, and megaliths.

The environment of the Nile Valley has always had a profound effect on its inhabitants. The river molds not only the physical landscape, but also the way in which the Egyptians think about themselves and their place in the world. The landscape has influenced their habits and customs, and from an early period it imprinted itself upon their collective psyche, shaping over the course of generations their most fundamental philosophical and religious beliefs. The symbolic force of the Nile is a thread that runs through pharaonic civilization, starting with the Egyptians' myth of their own origins.

According to the most ancient account of how the universe was formed, in the beginning there was nothing but a watery chaos, personified as the god Nun: "The great god who creates himself: he is water, he is Nun, father of the gods."[2] A later version of the creation myth described the primeval waters as negative and frightening, the embodiment of limitlessness, hiddenness, darkness, and formlessness. Yet despite being lifeless, the waters of Nun nevertheless held the potential for life. Although chaotic, they held within them the possibility of created order. This belief in the coexistence of opposites was characteristic of the ancient Egyptian mind-set, and was deeply rooted in their distinctive geographical surroundings. This view was reflected in the contrast between the arid desert and the fertile floodplain, and in the river itself, for the Nile could both create life and destroy it—a paradox inherent in its peculiar regime.

Until the construction of the Aswan Dam in the early twentieth century A.D. and its larger twin, the Aswan High Dam, in the 1960s, the Nile performed an annual miracle. The summer rains falling over the Ethiopian highlands swelled the Blue Nile—one of two great tributaries that join to form the Egyptian Nile—sending a torrent of water downstream (in this case, north). By early August, the approaching inundation was clearly discernible in the far south of Egypt, both from the turbulent sound of the floodwaters and from a noticeable rise in the river level. A few days later, the flood arrived in earnest. With an unstoppable force, the Nile burst its banks, and the waters spread out over the floodplain. The sheer volume of the flood caused the phenomenon to be repeated along the entire length of the Nile Valley. For several weeks, all the cultivable land was underwater. But as well as destruction the inundation brought with it the potential for new life: a layer of fertile silt deposited by the floodwaters over the fields, and the water itself. Once the flood retreated, the soil emerged again, fertilized and irrigated, ready for the sowing of crops. It was thanks to this annual phenomenon that Egypt enjoyed such productive agriculture—when the Nile flood was sufficient but not too powerful. Deviations from the norm, both "low Niles" and "high Niles," could prove equally catastrophic, leaving crops to desiccate with insufficient water or drown in waterlogged fields. Fortunately, in most years the inundation was moderate and the harvest bountiful, providing a surplus beyond the immediate subsistence needs of the population and allowing a complex civilization to develop.

In fact, Egypt was doubly blessed by its geography. Not only did the river bring the annual miracle of the inundation, but the river's shaping of the valley's topography also proved highly beneficial to agriculture. In cross section, the Nile Valley is slightly convex, with the highest land lying immediately next to the river—the remnants of old levees—and lower-lying areas located at the edges of the floodplain. This made the valley especially suitable for irrigation, both by the natural floodwaters and by artificial means, since water would automatically come to rest, and remain longest, in the fields farthest from the riverbank—potentially the very areas most prone to drought. Moreover, the long, narrow floodplain naturally divides into a series of flood basins, each compact enough to be managed and cultivated with relative ease by the local population. This was an important factor in the consolidation of early kingdoms, such as those based at Tjeni, Nubt, and Nekhen.

The fact that Egypt was unified under Narmer instead of remaining a series of rival power centers or warring city-states—the situation in many neighboring lands—can likewise be attributed to the Nile. The river has always provided an artery for transport and communication, serving the whole country. All life in Egypt ultimately depends on the life-giving waters of the Nile, so in ancient times no permanent valley community could have survived more than a few hours' walk from the river. This proximity of the population to the Nile allowed a dominant authority to exercise economic and political control on a national scale with relative ease.

As the country's defining geographical feature, the Nile was also a powerful metaphor for all Egyptians. For this reason, Egypt's rulers gave the river and its annual inundation key roles in the state ideology that they developed to underpin their authority in the eyes of the population at large. The political value of religious doctrine can be seen most strikingly if we look at one of the earliest creation myths, developed at Iunu (classical and modern Heliopolis). According to the story, the waters of Nun receded to reveal a mound of earth, just as dry land would appear from the floodwaters after the inundation. This story underscored the ever present potential for creation in the midst of chaos. The primeval mound then became the setting for the act of creation itself, with the creator god emerging at the same time as the mound, sitting upon it. His name was Atum, which, characteristically, means both "totality" and "nonexistence." In Egyptian art, Atum was usually represented wearing the double crown of kingship, identifying him as the creator not just of the universe but also of ancient Egypt's political system. The message was clear and unambiguous: if Atum was the first king as well as the first living being, then created order and political order were interdependent and inextricable. Opposition to the king or his regime was tantamount to nihilism.

A slightly different version of the creation myth explained how a reed grew on the newly emerged mound, and the celestial god, in the form of a falcon, alighted on the reed, making his dwelling on earth and bringing divine blessing to the land. Throughout the long course of pharaonic history, every temple in Egypt sought to emulate this moment of creation, siting its sanctuary on a replica of the primeval mound in order to re-create the universe anew. The rest of the myth recounts the origins of the essential building blocks of existence: the male and female principles; the fundamental elements of air and moisture; the earth and sky; and, finally, the first family of gods, who, like the waters of Nun from which they arose, embraced both orderly and chaotic tendencies. In total, Atum and his immediate descendants numbered nine deities, three times three expressing the ancient Egyptian concept of completeness.

The essential interest of the story, apart from its philosophical sophistication and its subtle legitimation of royal government, is that it demonstrates the force with which the Egyptians' unique environment—the combination of regularity and harshness, dependability and danger, and an annual promise of rebirth and renewal—imprinted itself on the people's collective consciousness and determined the pattern of their civilization.

THE TWO LANDS

THE NILE WAS NOT JUST THE CAUSE AND INSPIRATION OF ANCIENT Egyptian culture; it was also the unifying thread running through Egyptian history. It witnessed royal progresses, the transport of obelisks, the processions of gods, the movement of armies. The Nile Valley and delta—"the Two Lands" in the Egyptians' own terminology—are the backdrop to the rise and fall of ancient Egypt, and their particular geography is key to understanding Egypt's long and complex history.

There are no surviving maps of Egypt in ancient times, but if there were, one startling difference would leap off the page. The ancient Egyptians oriented themselves to the south, because it was in the south that the Nile rose, and it was from the south that the annual inundation arrived. In the ancient Egyptian mind-set, south lay at the top of their mental map, north at the bottom. Egyptologists perpetuate this unorthodox view of the world by calling the southern part of the country Upper Egypt and the north Lower Egypt. In accordance with this orientation, the west lay to the right (the two words were synonymous in ancient Egyptian), the east to the left. Egypt itself was known affec-

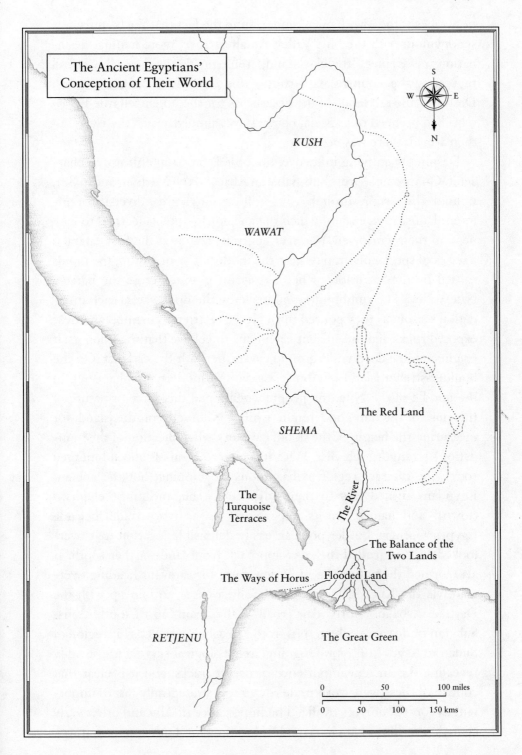

The Ancient Egyptians'
Conception of Their World

KUSH

WAWAT

The Red Land

SHEMA

The River

The
Turquoise
Terraces

The Balance of the
Two Lands

The Ways of Horus   Flooded Land

RETJENU

The Great Green

0   50   100 miles

0   50   100   150 kms

tionately as "the Two Banks," underlining the fact that the country was synonymous with the Nile Valley. An alternative, more familiar designation was Kemet, "the black land," referring to the dark alluvial soil that gave the country its fertility; this was often contrasted with Deshret, "the red land" of the deserts. As for the Nile itself, the Egyptians had no need of a special name: it was simply Iteru, "the river." In their world, there was no other.

Despite its unifying influence, the Nile is far from uniform in character. On its course from sub-Saharan Africa to the Mediterranean Sea, it molds the terrain through which it flows into a great diversity of different landscapes, each of which the ancient Egyptians learned to harness. In their worldview, the river began its course at the first cataract, a series of spectacular rapids near the modern city of Aswan, the rapids caused by the intrusion of hard, resistant granite across the narrow Nile Valley. The rumbling sound made by the floodwaters each inundation season, as they poured through the restricted channels and over exposed rocks, led the ancient Egyptians to believe that the flood itself originated in a deep underground cavern beneath the cataract. On the boulder-strewn island of Abu (classical and modern Elephantine), in the middle of the Nile, the people worshipped this force of nature in the guise of the ram god Khnum, while a Nilometer on the island, for measuring the height of the flood, gave an early indication of the inundation's strength each year. With its dangerous rapids and submerged rocks, the cataract region is hazardous to shipping, but the ancient Egyptians turned this to their advantage. Abu, meaning "elephant (town)" and named for its importance in the ivory trade, became Egypt's southern border post, an easily defensible location that overlooked and controlled the river approach from lands farther south. It also formed the natural point of departure for caravans heading overland, via the Kurkur, Dunqul, and Salima oases, to join up with the Darb el-Arba'in ("forty days road"), the main north-south trans-Saharan trade route, which runs from El Fasher in the Darfur region of Sudan to Asyut in Egypt. Ongoing archaeological surveys are steadily revealing the ancient importance of desert tracks, and it is clear that control of these well-worn trade routes was strategically just as important as control of river traffic. The importance of Abu and other early centers was due to their favorable location for both types of travel.

Throughout ancient Egyptian history, Abu and the first cataract region marked the beginning of Egypt proper. When Egyptian ships sailing north from conquered territories passed Biga Island, at the head of the cataract, their crews must have rejoiced, for they knew they were home at last.

North of Abu, the Nile Valley is at its narrowest, flowing between cliffs of hard Nubian sandstone. Here, the strip of agricultural land on either side of the river is extremely compressed—no more than a couple of hundred yards wide in some places—and, as a result, this part of southern Upper Egypt never supported a large population. But it has other natural advantages that the ancient Egyptians were swift to exploit. In particular, wadis lead from both banks of the Nile deep into the surrounding deserts, providing access to trade routes and to the sources of valuable raw materials such as gemstones, copper, and gold. These factors compensated for the relative scarcity of agricultural land and made the southern Nile Valley a major center of economic—and hence political—developments throughout Egyptian history, from Nekhen in prehistoric times to nearby Apollonopolis Magna (modern Edfu) in the Roman Period.

A major transition in the geology of the Nile Valley occurs at Gebel el-Silsila, forty miles north of Abu, where Nubian sandstone gives way to the softer Egyptian limestone. The towering sandstone cliffs that extend to the water's edge at this point were obvious markers for boats plying up- and downriver. The cliffs also provided a readily accessible quarry for large sandstone blocks, supplies for major building projects in the later phases of pharaonic civilization.

Beyond Gebel el-Silsila, the landscape is gentler, the cliffs lining the valley lower and more eroded, and the floodplain wider. With greater agricultural potential, the region is able to sustain a larger population than areas farther south. This was a key factor in the rise and steady growth of Thebes, the largest city in Upper Egypt for most of ancient Egyptian history. The main centers of habitation were always situated on the east bank of the Nile, where the floodplain is at its widest, while the dramatic cliffs of the west bank and the broad expanse of low desert at their foot offered ideal locations for burial—close enough to the city for convenience, yet far enough away to maintain an essential separation. Thebes was thus divided, both geographically and ideologically, into a city of the living (where the sun rose) and a city of the dead (where the sun set). The city also benefited from the extensive network of desert tracks behind the hills of the west bank. Keenly contested, control of these cross-country express trails conferred a major strategic advantage, and played a decisive role at important moments of Egyptian history. In addition, they allowed Thebes to regulate access to Nubia from the north.

As the Nile enters the great "Qena bend," it swings to the east, bringing it closer to the Red Sea than at any other point in its course. The east bank was therefore the obvious point of departure for expeditions into the Red Sea hills—with their gold mines and stone quarries—and beyond to the shores of the Red Sea itself. Throughout pharaonic times, the Egyptians sent trading expeditions to the distant and fabled land of Punt (coastal Sudan and Eritrea)—expeditions that left from Red Sea ports. In the Ptolemaic and Roman periods, the Red Sea offered the quickest maritime route to India, and the deserts to the east of the Qena bend were a hive of commercial and military activity.

Continuing northward past the Qena bend, the Nile Valley changes character again, becoming much wider, with only distant vistas of age-eroded bluffs. Ironically, although it is one of the most agriculturally productive parts of the country, northern Upper Egypt generally remained something of a backwater, because of its comparative isolation from the main centers of political power. A notable exception was the prominence of Tjeni during the prehistoric period and early dynasties, which probably resulted from its command of the shortest route from the Nile to the oases. In later periods, the great antiquity of Abdju as a royal burial ground gave it a religious significance, and it became the most important pilgrimage site in the whole of Egypt, a status it retained throughout pharaonic times. In the civil war that followed the collapse of the Old Kingdom state, Abdju was a key prize, and the surrounding region would be fought over many times in the periodic conflicts that erupted between rival power centers in the north and south of Egypt.

Continuing downstream, there is a marked constriction in the Nile Valley at the modern city of Asyut. The name Asyut is derived from the ancient Egyptian place-name Sauty, meaning "guardian," and the moniker is well chosen, for Asyut guards both the northern approach to the riches of Upper Egypt, and, from the other direction, the southern approach to the capital city and the Mediterranean ports. Hence, Asyut was always a natural "break point" in the territorial integrity of Egypt: when the country split into northern and southern halves, as it did during various periods, the border was generally drawn at Asyut. The city also guards the Egyptian terminus of the Darb el-Arba'in, the forty days road, so Asyut is a place of huge strategic importance.

North of Asyut, the lush, expansive fields resume, imparting a serene and timeless beauty to the stretch of valley sometimes called Middle Egypt. Once again, desert routes from the west bank provide easy access to the Saharan oases and thence to Sudan. However, the most notable feature here is not the valley itself but the large, fertile depression of the Fayum, fed by a subsidiary Nile branch, the Bahr Yusuf, which leaves the main river at Asyut. Birket Qarun, the vast freshwater body at the heart of the Fayum, brings life to the surrounding Sahara. In ancient times the area would have teemed with wildlife, and the lake's shores supported abundant vegetation and productive agriculture. From the very beginning of pharaonic history, the Fayum was a popular location for royal retreats and summer palaces. In the Middle Kingdom and Ptolemaic Period in particular, it was the focus of major irrigation and land reclamation activities, which in effect created "another Egypt" in the Western Desert.

Strategically, the most important location in the whole of Egypt is the point where the Nile Valley broadens out and the river divides into many distributaries as it flows toward the Mediterranean Sea. This region formed the junction between Upper and Lower Egypt, and the ancient Egyptians called the area "the balance of the Two Lands"; after unification, it was the obvious location for the capital city, since it commanded both parts of the country. Home to ancient Memphis and modern Cairo, the apex of the delta has remained the administrative hub of Egypt for more than five millennia. Its importance in pharaonic times is underscored by the pyramids that line the edge of the desert escarpment west of Memphis for a distance of nearly twenty miles.

In ideological and political terms, the ancient Egyptians gave Lower Egypt and Upper Egypt equal prominence; yet our modern understanding of the delta still lags far behind that of the Nile Valley. The main reasons are the steady accumulation of silt over centuries, burying many of the ancient remains, and the area's difficult and uncompromising terrain. The contrast with the narrow, well-defined valley could not be greater. The delta comprises great expanses of flat, low-lying land, stretching to the horizon, interrupted only by the occasional stand of palm trees. Hazardous marshes and a multitude of small waterways make cross-country travel particularly difficult. The delta offers fertile grazing land and bountiful agriculture, but it is marginal land, at perennial risk from the inundation or the sea. (The ancient Egyptians clearly recognized this, referring to Lower Egypt as Ta-Mehu, "flooded land.") It was also Egypt's exposed northern flank, with the western delta prone to incursion by Libyans and the east prone to migration and attack by people from Palestine and beyond. The fringes of the delta were surrendered to foreign domination during periods of national weakness, and were fortified at times of strong central government—as a buffer zone against attack and as a base for military campaigns to defend and widen Egypt's borders. At the end of pharaonic history, the delta rose to prominence because of its Mediterranean links and its proximity to the other centers of power in the ancient world, notably Greece and Rome.

As the Nile nears the end of its course, the marshlands of Lower Egypt give way to brackish lagoons fringing the coast, and the sandy shores of the Mediterranean. This is a shifting landscape, poised between dry land and sea, and it served as a further reminder to the ancient Egyptians of the precarious balance of their existence. Their whole environment seemed to emphasize that the maintenance of created order relied upon the balance of opposites: the fertile black land and the arid red land, the east as the realm of the living and the west as the realm of the dead, the narrow Nile Valley and the broad delta, and the annual struggle between the chaotic floodwaters and the dry land.

If the geography of Egypt molded the psyche of its inhabitants, it was the particular genius of the country's early rulers to cast the king as the linchpin who alone could maintain the forces in equilibrium.

CHAPTER 2

GOD INCARNATE

LONG LIVE THE KING

THE UNIFICATION OF EGYPT IN 2950 CREATED THE WORLD'S FIRST nation-state. Today, this form of political and social unit seems both natural and inevitable: our prosperity (or poverty), our rights and duties, our freedoms (or lack of them) are all profoundly affected by our nationality. With the exception of Antarctica, the entire surface of our planet is divided up into countries, numbering more than two hundred. Yet it was not always so. Before the late fourth millennium B.C., there were no such states. Identity and loyalty were based instead on family, community, or region. The concept of a nation-state—a political territory whose population shares a common identity—was the invention of the ancient Egyptians.

Beginning with Narmer, Egypt's early kings found themselves the rulers of an entirely new form of polity, one bound together as much by governmental structures as by shared values. It was an unprecedented challenge: to foster a sense of nationhood among diverse people, spread out over an area extending from the first cataract to the shores of the Mediterranean Sea. The creation of a distinctive sense of Egyptianness ranks as one of the greatest achievements of Egypt's early rulers. At its heart lay a large measure of self-interest. The doctrine of divine kingship defined pharaonic civilization, produced such iconic monuments as the pyramids, and inspired the great tombs and temples that stand to this day.

The dominance of monarchy in ancient Egyptian culture and history is underlined by the system we use for dividing up the three-thousand-year span between the reign of Narmer and the death of Cleopatra. Rather than focusing on cultural achievements (such as Stone Age, Bronze Age, Iron Age), Egyptian chronology employs a scheme based on dynasties of kings. In a way that seems particularly appropriate for one of the most conservative of all ancient cultures, the basic system we use today remains the same as that devised by Manetho, an ancient Egyptian priest and historian who lived twenty-three hundred years ago. Looking back at the history of his own country, and assisted by temple records, Manetho divided Egypt's kings into thirty ruling houses, or dynasties. His scheme started with Menes (the king we know as Narmer) as the founder of the First Dynasty (circa 2950), and ended with Nectanebo II (Nakhthorheb) as the last king of the Thirtieth Dynasty (360–343 B.C.). For historical completeness, modern scholars have added a Thirty-first Dynasty, comprising the Persian conquerors who briefly ruled Egypt between the demise of Nakhthorheb and the conquest of Alexander the Great. The Macedonian and Ptolemaic dynasties, founded by Alexander and Ptolemy respectively, were not included within Manetho's original scheme. Although these dynasties comprise kings of non-Egyptian origin and represent, to some extent, a break with the pharaonic system of government, they do emphasize the continued importance of dynastic kingship in the later history of ancient Egypt.

In keeping with the ancient Egyptian ideal, perpetuated in temple reliefs and inscriptions, Manetho's dynasties emphasized a single, unbroken succession of kings stretching back to "the time of the gods" and ultimately to the moment of creation itself. In turn, this ideal reflected the doctrine promulgated by the pharaonic court. According to this doctrine, the creator god Atum set the pattern for kingship at "the first time," and each subsequent ruler was the legitimate inheritor of a divinely sanctioned form of government. The reality, of course, was rather different. At times of national disunity, several rulers based in different parts of the country were able to claim royal titles and rule concurrently. Hence, our modern understanding of Egyptian history regards Manetho's Twenty-second, Twenty-third, and Twenty-fourth dynasties as at least partially overlapping. Recent scholarship has shown some of his dynasties (such as the Seventh) to be wholly spurious, the result of a misunderstanding of the ancient temple records, while the Ninth and Tenth dynasties seem to represent only one ruling family, not two. These corrections and modifications aside, Manetho's system has proved impressively robust and durable. Above all, the fact that it remains the most convenient way of dividing up ancient Egyptian history underlines the centrality of monarchy to his—and our—understanding of pharaonic civilization.

Indeed, as a form of government, kingship was quintessentially Egyptian. Among the early civilizations of the ancient world, only Egypt embraced this particular mode of rule from the very beginning of its history. In Mesopotamia (modern Iraq), city-states based their identity on their local temples, so it was the high priests who wielded the greatest political and economic power. Only later did a monarchical system develop, and it was never as thoroughgoing or omnipotent as its Egyptian counterpart. In the Nile Valley, kings seem to have ruled the people from prehistoric times. Recent excavations in the early royal burial ground at Abdju have uncovered graves dating back to around 3800. One of them contained a pottery beaker painted with perhaps the earliest image of a king. It shows a tall figure with a feather in his hair, holding a mace in one hand, and in the other, a rope binding three captives. The subjugation of enemies and the distinctive combination of feather headdress and mace—which is also found in the prehistoric rock art of the Eastern Desert—identify the scene as royal, even though the ruler in question probably controlled only a limited territory. Kingship also seems to have developed elsewhere in Upper Egypt at about the same time, as suggested by a fragment of pottery from Nubt decorated with a crown, and by a monumental complex of pillared halls in the desert close to Nekhen.

By around 3500 the unmistakable iconography of kingship was given full expression in a tomb at Nekhen known as the Painted Tomb. One of the inside walls of this burial chamber was plastered and painted with a frieze showing a royal figure taking part in various ritual activities. The decoration is dominated by a spectacular procession of boats, but in one corner of the scene the king is shown smiting three bound captives. This motif, already prefigured on the Abdju vase, became the defining image of Egyptian kingship. We see it repeated on the Narmer Palette and thereafter on temple walls until the very end of pharaonic civilization. The imagery of early kingship was as enduring as it was violent.

CROWN AND SCEPTER

DURING THE PROCESS OF STATE FORMATION, THE ARTISTIC EXPRESSION of royal rule underwent rapid development, to keep pace with the changing notion of kingship itself. We can trace the changes in a series of ceremonial objects and commemorative inscriptions. Particularly striking is the so-called Battlefield Palette, an object similar to the Narmer Palette but dating to a century or so earlier. Whereas Narmer's monument gives pride of place to an image of the king in human form, the older palette shows the ruler instead as a huge lion, trampling and goring his enemies who lie prostrate on the field of battle. The intention was to present the king as a force of nature. In a similar vein, a contemporary inscription carved at Gebel Sheikh Suleiman, near the second Nile cataract in Nubia, shows the victorious Egyptian king as a giant scorpion, holding in its pincers a rope that binds the defeated Nubian chief. From Narmer's own time, an ivory cylinder shows the king as a vicious Nile catfish, beating rows of prisoners with a large stick. The message was clear: the king was not just a mere mortal who ruled by virtue of his descent and leadership abilities; he also embodied the strength and ferocity of wild animals, superhuman powers granted to him by divine authority. Elevating themselves above their subjects, Egypt's prehistoric rulers were intent on acquiring godlike status.

These trends culminate in the Narmer Palette. Its very form harks back to a time when wandering cattle herders lived a seminomadic existence, carrying everything they needed with them and using their own bodies as canvasses for their art. In such a society, face paint played a central role in the ritual life of the community, and cosmetic palettes were a favorite and prized possession. But by Narmer's time, the palette had been transformed into a vehicle for proclaiming the omnipotence and divinity of the king.

The decoration of the Narmer Palette likewise spans two worlds and two ages. The shallow well that betrays the object's practical origins is formed by the entwined necks of two fabulous creatures, held on leashes by attendants. These "serpopards" (leopards with serpentine necks) are not Egyptian in origin. They come from the artistic canon of ancient Mesopotamia. Their presence on an early Egyptian artifact points to a period of intense cultural exchange between two of the great cultures of late prehistory, when ideas and influences from the valleys of the rivers Tigris and Euphrates reached the distant banks of the Nile. Egypt's predynastic rulers were intent upon promoting their own authority and influence. To do so, they needed tried and trusted means to display their power, and they were quite happy to borrow ideas from abroad, if the ideas served the purpose. So, for a few generations, Egyptian elite culture adopted a range of Mesopotamian imagery, especially artistic motifs to represent complex or difficult concepts, such as the notion of kingship itself (a rosette) or the reconciliation of opposing forces by the ruler (two intertwined beasts). But once the borrowed ideas had achieved the desired effect, they were discarded just as quickly, in favor of indigenous cultural expressions—the only exception being the Mesopotamian-inspired style of architecture adopted for the king's palace and other royal buildings. The Narmer Palette captures this pivotal moment in cultural history: Mesopotamian motifs appear on one side, exclusively Egyptian motifs on the other. Egyptian civilization had come of age and was finding its own voice.

Prehistoric and historic modes of expression are likewise reflected in the depiction of Narmer himself. On one side he is shown as a wild bull, tearing down the walls of a rebel stronghold and trampling the hapless enemy underfoot. Turn the palette over, and the representation of the ruler as a wild animal has been relegated to the past. The image of the victorious king in human form now dominates. The ideology of royal authority had not changed, but its representation was undergoing a profound transformation. From now on, it was not thought appropriate to depict the king as an animal. His newly acquired divinity required a more elevated and sophisticated representation.

Monarchs throughout history have adopted elaborate trappings to distinguish themselves from their subjects. Royal regalia encodes the different attributes of kingship, providing a kind of visual shorthand for a complex underlying ideology. In Christian monarchies a crown surmounted by a cross symbolizes that the king's temporal power is subject to a greater, divine authority (the orb reinforces the same message), while a scepter stands for power tempered by justice. In ancient Egypt, regalia was similarly used to convey the nature of royal authority. Once again, many of the elements have prehistoric origins. The earliest symbol of office yet discovered in Egypt dates back to 4400, more than fourteen centuries before the foundation of the dynastic tradition. It is a simple wooden staff, about a foot long, with knobbed ends, found buried next to its owner in a grave at el-Omari, near modern Cairo.

Wielding a big stick is, of course, the most basic expression of authority, and a wooden staff remained the identifying badge of high office throughout ancient Egyptian history. Monarchy, however, has a tendency to elaborate. So early in the development of Egyptian kingship, the simple stick evolved into a more complex object, a scepter. As we have seen, an ivory scepter in the shape of a shepherd's crook survives from a predynastic royal tomb at Abdju, and the crook became so closely identified with sovereignty that it was adopted as the hieroglyphic sign for the word "ruler." Together with the flail or goad—a stick with knotted cords or strings of beads attached to one end—it came to symbolize the office of kingship, more specifically the monarch's duty to both restrain and encourage his flock. These two key items of royal regalia betray the prehistoric origins of Egyptian civilization. They recall a past where livelihoods were dominated by animal husbandry, where the man wielding the crook and flail—the man controlling the herds—was the leader of his community. A similar echo is heard in the peculiar item of regalia worn by Narmer on both sides of his palette, a bull's tail. This was intended to demonstrate that the king embodied the power of the wild bull, perhaps the most awesome and ferocious of ancient Egyptian fauna, and the tail provided a subconscious link between the dynastic monarchy and its predynastic antecedents.

A crown is the quintessential emblem of monarchy. Sovereigns have always distinguished themselves by wearing a special form of headdress that, at its most basic level, elevates the wearer above the populace (literally and metaphorically). Like the concept of the nation-state, crowns seem to have been an ancient Egyptian invention. And in keeping with the Egyptians' worldview, their kings wore not one but two distinctive crowns, to symbolize the two halves of their realm. From earliest historic times, the red crown was associated with Lower Egypt. It consisted of a squat, squarish cap with a tall tapering projection rising from the back, and attached to the front of this projection was a curly protuberance reminiscent of a bee's proboscis. Its counterpart, the white crown—tall and conical with a bulbous end—was the symbol of Upper Egypt. This neat equation shows the Egyptians' love of binary divisions, but it is also an artificial creation. Archaeological evidence from the prehistoric period suggests that both crowns originated in Upper Egypt (the crucible of kingship), the red crown at Nubt and the white crown farther south, beyond Nekhen. Following the unification of the country, it made perfect sense to recast the northern red crown as the symbol of northern Egypt, keeping the southern crown as the symbol of the south. The ancient Egyptians were particularly good at inventing traditions. In the middle of the First Dynasty, about a century after Narmer, the royal iconographers took the obvious step of combining the red and white crowns into a single headdress, the double crown, to symbolize the ruler's dual dominion. Thereafter he had a choice of three distinct headpieces, depending upon which aspect of his authority he wished to emphasize.

If art could be used to project the king's authority, how much more effectively could architecture do the same, but on a monumental scale. Like other totalitarian rulers throughout history, Egypt's kings had an obsession with grand buildings, designed to reflect and magnify their status. From the very beginning of the Egyptian state, the monarchy showed itself adept at using architectural vocabulary for ideological purposes. It chose to emphasize one particular style of building as the visible expression of kingship. A façade composed of alternating recesses and buttresses—which create a highly effective pattern of light and shade in Egypt's sunny climate—had first been developed in Mesopotamia, in the middle of the fourth millennium B.C. Like other cultural borrowings during the period of state formation, this distinctive architectural style, known as palace-façade architecture, found a receptive audience among Egypt's early rulers. It was both exotic and imposing: ideal as a symbol of royal power. So it was swiftly adopted as the architecture of choice for the king's palaces, including the royal compound in the capital city of Memphis, which served as the principal seat of government. With its whitewashed exterior, this building known as White Wall must have been a dazzling sight, comparable in its symbolism to the White House of a modern superpower. Other royal buildings throughout the land were consciously modeled on White Wall, and an architectural motif of foreign origin rapidly became one of the hallmarks of the Egyptian monarchy.

TITLE ROLE

THROUGHOUT PHARAONIC HISTORY, ICONOGRAPHY AND ARCHITECTURE retained important roles in projecting the desired image of kingship to the people. Iconography and architecture were especially effective in a country such as Egypt, where up to 95 percent of the population was illiterate. But in the ancient world, the main threat to a king rarely, if ever, came from the masses. The people a monarch needed to keep on his side, above all, were his closest advisers. The small group of literate high officials who ran the administration were in a better position than most to pose a threat to the reigning king. Of course, such individuals generally owed their position, status, and wealth to royal patronage, and therefore had a vested interest in maintaining the status quo. However, Egypt's masterful royal propagandists devised a subtle means of bolstering kingship among the literate class. In the process, they raised the office to a position of virtual unassailability.

The solution lay not in iconography but in writing. Hieroglyphs were first developed in the late prehistoric period for a rather prosaic purpose, to facilitate record keeping and enable economic control over a geographically extensive territory. But the ideological potential of writing was swiftly realized. On the Narmer Palette, for instance, signs are used to identify the main protagonists (the king, his followers, and his enemies) and to label the principal scenes. Words could just as easily be employed to convey the fundamental essence of kingship through royal titles. In the contemporary Western world, titles have generally lost their former potency, although some, such as "commander in chief" and "defender of the faith," still carry echoes of a former age of deference and rigid hierarchies. In ancient Egypt, names and titles were highly significant, and the early development of the royal titulary, the royal protocol of titles, exploited this to the full.

The most ancient of all royal titles, in use even before Narmer's time, was the Horus title. It explicitly identified the king as the earthly incarnation of the supreme celestial deity, Horus, who was worshipped in the form of a falcon. This made a statement as bold as it was uncompromising. If the king was not just the gods' representative on earth but an embodiment of divinity, his office could not be challenged without destroying the whole of creation. The message was reinforced at every available opportunity. The king's seal, stamped on commodities to mark royal ownership, or carved in stone on royal monuments, showed the falcon god standing on top of a rectangular frame containing the king's Horus name, the name which expressed the king's identity as the earthly incarnation of Horus. The frame was designed to resemble a gate in the royal compound. The not so subliminal message was that the king within his palace operated under divine sanction and was himself a god incarnate. As a statement of monarchical rule, it was direct and unanswerable.

A second royal title, attested from the reign of Narmer's successor, took royal propaganda a stage further. It was written with the signs of a vulture and a cobra, representing two goddesses. Nekhbet the vulture was associated with Nekheb (modern Elkab), a town opposite Nekhen in the heart of Upper Egypt. Wadjet the cobra was the goddess of Dep, one of the twin towns that made up the important delta city of Per-Wadjet (modern Tell el-Fara'in); she therefore stood for Lower Egypt. Choosing two ancient deities to symbolize the two halves of the country, and making both goddesses joint protectors of the monarchy, was a clever move, creating from strands of local belief and custom a national theology, centered on the person of the king. The adoption of the red and white crowns was part of the same process. So was the prominence given to the delta goddess Neith in the names of early royal wives. Narmer's wife, for example, was called Neith-hotep, "Neith is satisfied." From the marshes of the north to the southernmost Nile Valley, all the major cults—and their followers—were drawn into the ideology of kingship. It was a brilliant demonstration of the unite-and-rule concept, a theological takeover of the entire country.

The third royal title, adopted at the same time as the double crown, represented a further elaboration and definition of the king's role. It comprised two Egyptian words, *"nesu bity,"* literally translated as "he of the reed and bee" but more elegantly rendered "dual king." While the precise derivation is obscure—on one level, the reed may have symbolized Upper Egypt and the bee Lower Egypt—the meaning was wide-ranging and sophisticated. It embraced the many pairs of opposites over which the king presided and which he alone kept in balance: Upper and Lower Egypt, the black land and the red land, the realms of the living and the dead, and so on. The title also reflected the most fundamental dichotomy at the heart of Egyptian kingship, the contrast be-tween the sacred office (*nesu*) and the secular function (*bity*). The *nesu bity* title reminded the king's followers that as well as head of state he was also god on earth—an irresistible combination.

POMP AND CIRCUMSTANCE

RULERS OF ALL KINDS, BUT ESPECIALLY HEREDITARY MONARCHS, HAVE instinctively recognized the cohesive power of ceremony and display, the capacity of public ritual to generate popular support. The ancient Egyptians were masters of royal ceremony, and from an early period. An elaborately decorated stone mace head, found alongside the Narmer Palette at Nekhen, shows an earlier king (known to us as Scor-pion) performing an irrigation ceremony. The king uses a hoe to open a dike while an attendant, stooping before the royal presence, holds a basket ready to receive the clod of earth. Fan bearers, standard-bearers, and dancing women add to the sense of occasion. In this vivid tableau from the dawn of history, we get a flavor of early royal ceremonies: rit-ually charged events that emphasized the king's role as guarantor of prosperity and stability.

Another mace head from the same cache records a different, though equally resonant, ceremony. This time the presiding king is Narmer, enthroned on an elevated dais under an awning, wearing the red crown and carrying the crooklike scepter. Beside the dais stands the custom-ary pair of fan bearers, accompanied by the king's sandal bearer and chief minister. Behind them are men wielding big sticks—even a sacral monarchy needed security. The ceremony, too, has a militaristic flavor, its main act being the parade of captured booty and enemy prisoners before the royal throne. In a stark analogy, three captive antelope in-side a walled enclosure are shown next to the parade ground. The ide-ological connection between warfare and hunting, between the unruly forces of nature and the king's opponents, remained potent through Egyptian history.

A recent reexamination of the early town at Nekhen, including the place where Narmer's palette and mace head were discovered, offers a further, tantalizing insight into the practice of early kingship. The area

"King Scorpion" performs an irrigation ceremony. WERNER FORMAN ARCHIVE

hitherto identified as a temple to the local falcon god Horus may not have been a temple at all, but instead an arena for royal ceremony. According to this interpretation, the mound in the center of the walled enclosure may have been a raised dais for the king's formal appearances. The open ground in front of the mound could have been used for rituals like a parade of prisoners. If so, the Narmer mace head may picture the actual scene at such an event. Certainly, the objects found at Nekhen seem to reflect a cult of monarchy. Decorated ivories from the Main Deposit depict large mace heads erected on poles in an enclosure, so perhaps the Narmer and Scorpion mace heads were originally used to identify and demarcate a royal arena. Looking beyond Nekhen to the rest of Egypt, buildings previously identified as shrines may be reinterpreted in the same way, as centers of the royal cult. Certainly, the king and his deeds dominate the written and artistic record of the early dynasties, with other deities playing only supporting roles. The question of where the gods are in early Egyptian culture may have an unsettling answer: in early Egypt, the kings *were* the gods. Monarchy was not just an integral part of religion; the two were synonymous.

This would remain the dominant theme of pharaonic civilization until the very end, but it had a dark side. Looking again at the Narmer and Scorpion mace heads, the objects themselves—setting aside their decoration—tell us something about the character of Egyptian monarchy. Mace heads were symbols of authority from prehistoric times, for obvious reasons—a person wielding a mace was met with respect and obedience. The fact that mace heads were adopted as symbols of kingly power speaks volumes about the nature of royal authority in ancient Egypt. The scenes on the Narmer Palette are a further reminder of the brutality that underpinned Egyptian kingship. On one side of the palette, the king is shown with a mace, ready to smite his enemy. On the other side, Narmer has not only defeated his adversaries, but dealt them utter humiliation. He is shown inspecting rows of decapitated bodies that have suffered the added indignity of having their genitals cut off. The victims' heads and penises are placed between their legs; only one of the dead has been allowed to retain his manhood. Uncomfortable as it may be, we must assume that the ancient Egyptians of Narmer's time routinely humiliated their defeated enemies in this way.

At the pinnacle of Egyptian society, the king embodied this ruthless streak. While on the one hand he was keen to portray himself as the unifier of the country, a divine presence on earth who maintained created order, royal iconography also made it abundantly clear that defending creation meant meting out destruction to the king's enemies, be they from outside or inside his realm. Narmer and his predecessors had won power by violent means, and they would not hesitate to use violence to retain power. The visual propaganda employed to promote the monarchy—the king as a lion, a giant scorpion, a fierce catfish, a wild bull, or a mace-wielding superhero—was unashamedly brutal. It was both a promise and a warning.

In this context, one of the most jarring scenes from early Egypt is the band of decoration around the top of the Scorpion mace head. The tableau consists of a series of royal standards, each symbolizing a different aspect of the king's authority. But they are not just standards; they are also gallows. From each one hangs a crested bird with a rope around its neck. In hieroglyphic writing, the lapwing (*"rekhyt"* in ancient Egyptian) symbolized the common people, as opposed to the small circle of royal relatives (*pat*) who wielded power. On the Scorpion mace head, the common people have been hanged on the gibbets of royal power. It is a message that would be repeated later in Egyptian history. For example, the base of a statue of King Netjerikhet (also known as King Djoser), builder of the first pyramid, is decorated with archery bows (denoting foreigners) and also lapwings—so that the king could trample underfoot his subjects as well as his enemies. Egyptologists have recoiled at the underlying symbolism of such scenes, but it is inescapable. Autocratic regimes live and die by force, and ancient Egypt was no exception.

The most chilling example of this tendency can be seen in the tombs of Egypt's early rulers. At Nubt, an elite burial dating to around 3500 contained more than the expected array of grave goods. Around the walls of the tomb, the excavators found a series of human long bones, and in the center a collection of skulls. The dismembered bodies of several individuals had clearly been interred with the tomb owner. At Nekhen, bodies in the predynastic cemetery show frequent evidence of scalping and decapitation. At nearby Adaima, two individuals had had their throats slit before being decapitated. The archaeologist who found them thought they might have been early examples of self-sacrifice, loyal retainers killing themselves in order to accompany their master to the grave. But the First Dynasty royal tombs at Abdju suggest a different, more sinister, explanation.

Under Narmer's successors of the First Dynasty, the royal tomb itself was accompanied by a series of subsidiary graves for members of the court. In one case, the king's afterlife companions were all in the prime of life when they died, with an average age of twenty-five years or younger. In another royal tomb from the end of the First Dynasty, a single roof covered the servants' graves as well as the king's chamber. Both examples provide unequivocal evidence for the sacrifice of retainers, since it is impossible that an entire retinue would conveniently die at the same time as its monarch. However, this could have been self-sacrifice: perhaps the bonds of loyalty were so strong that servants willingly took their own lives when their master died. Recently, however, closer inspection of the subsidiary graves has swept away this explanation, for the bodies show evidence of death by strangulation. The conclusion is as grim as it is shocking: Egypt's early kings had the power of life and death over their subjects and did not hesitate to use it to demonstrate their own authority. To be a member of the common people meant a life of subjugation; to be a member of the king's inner circle meant a life of fear. Neither can have been particularly pleasant.

Retainer sacrifice peaked at a relatively early stage: the tomb of Djer, third king of the First Dynasty (circa 2900), was surrounded by 318 subsidiary burials. It seems as if Egypt's rulers, having acquired absolute power, were eager to try it out. Those buried around the king, to serve him faithfully in the afterlife, included his pets alongside his human attendants. The fact that the same mortuary provision was considered appropriate for both dogs and concubines speaks volumes about the status of royal servants at the early Egyptian court. After the reigns of Djer and his successor Djet, the practice of retainer sacrifice seems to have declined before stopping abruptly at the end of the First Dynasty. But one cannot help wondering if it was economic rather than ideological reticence that put an end to the practice. After all, eliminating an entire entourage at the end of each reign was hugely wasteful of talent, and the ancient Egyptians were nothing if not practical.

Human sacrifice is also depicted on labels from the royal tombs. Some of these dockets, which were originally attached to jars and boxes

Human sacrifice in the First Dynasty DR. KATE SPENCE

of supplies, are inscribed with scenes of royal activities. Two such labels, evidently commemorating the same event, show a man kneeling down with his arms tied behind his back. In front of him, on the floor, there is a large basin. Its purpose is gruesomely clear, for another man stands over the victim with a long knife, ready to plunge it into his chest. There is no written text to shed further light on this scene, but there can be little doubt that it involved the ritual killing of a human prisoner as part of a ceremony of kingship.

By means of the objects buried within it and the servants interred around it, the royal tomb was designed to enable the king to continue presiding at royal ceremonies for all eternity. As such, the tomb was the essential guarantor of kingship and, from the rise of ancient Egypt until the demise of the pharaohs, the most important construction project of each reign. The preparation of the king's burial must have absorbed huge effort and expenditure, in labor, materials, and human life. It is often argued that the people of Egypt made the investment willingly, as their side of a contract that guaranteed the prosperity and survival of the country. Of course the person advancing that ideology was the king himself. It was in the monarchy's own interests to promote its role in national unification. In reality, the king's motivation was self-interest. The First Dynasty royal cemetery at Abdju, with its hierarchy of the king's tomb surrounded by the burials of his retainers, was simply a concrete manifestation of Egyptian society—a state totally dominated and controlled by one man. The creation and implementation of this ideology helped to fashion pharaonic civilization, but at a price. With the rise of ancient Egypt, the relentless march of state control had begun in earnest.

CHAPTER 3

ABSOLUTE POWER

COMMAND ECONOMY

IDEOLOGY IS NEVER ENOUGH, ON ITS OWN, TO GUARANTEE POWER. To be successful over the long term, a regime must also exercise effective economic control to reinforce its claims of legitimacy. Governments seek to manipulate livelihoods as well as lives. The development in ancient Egypt of a truly national administration was one of the major accomplishments of the First to Third dynasties, the four-hundred-year formative phase of pharaonic civilization known as the Early Dynastic Period (2950–2575). At the start of the period, the country had only just been unified. Narmer and his immediate successors were faced with the challenge of ruling a vast realm, stretching five hundred miles from the heart of Africa to the shores of the Mediterranean. By the close of the Early Dynastic Period, the government presided over a centrally controlled command economy, financing royal building projects on a lavish scale. Just how this was achieved is a story of determination, innovation, and, above all, ambition.

Among the great inventions of human history, writing has a special place. Its transformative power—in the transmission of knowledge, the exercise of power, and the recording of history itself—cannot be overstated. Today, it is virtually impossible to imagine a world without written communication. For ancient Egypt, it must have been a revelation. We are unlikely ever to know exactly how, when, and where hieroglyphics were first developed, but the evidence increasingly points toward a deliberate act of invention. The earliest Egyptian writing discovered to date is on bone labels from a predynastic tomb at Abdju, the burial of a ruler who lived around 150 years before Narmer. These short inscriptions already used fully formed signs, and the writing system itself showed the complexity that would characterize hieroglyphics for the next three and a half thousand years. Archaeologists dispute whether Egypt or Mesopotamia should take the credit for inventing the very idea of writing, but Mesopotamia, especially the southern city of Uruk (modern Warka), seems to have the better claim. It is likely that the *idea* of writing came to Egypt along with a raft of other Mesopotamian influences in the centuries before unification—the concept, but not the writing system itself. Hieroglyphics are so perfectly suited to the ancient Egyptian language, and the individual signs so obviously reflected the Egyptians' particular environment, that they must represent an indigenous development. We may imagine an inspired genius at the court of one of Egypt's predynastic rulers pondering the strange signs on imported objects from Mesopotamia—pondering them and their evident use as encoders of information, and devising a corresponding system for the Egyptian language. This may seem far-fetched, but the invention of the Korean script (by King Sejong and his advisers in A.D. 1443) provides a more recent parallel, and there are few other entirely convincing explanations for the sudden appearance of fully fledged hieroglyphic writing.

Whatever the circumstances of its invention, writing was swiftly embraced by Egypt's early rulers, who recognized its potential, not least for economic management. In the context of competing kingdoms expanding their spheres of influence, the ability to record the ownership of goods and to communicate this information to others was a marvelous innovation. Straightaway, supplies entering and leaving the royal treasury began to be stamped with the king's cipher (his Horus name). Other consignments, destined for his tomb, had labels attached to them, recording not just ownership but other important details such as contents, quantity, quality, and provenance. Having been developed as an accounting tool, writing found an enthusiastic reception among bureaucratically minded Egyptians. Throughout ancient Egyptian history, literacy was reserved for a tiny elite at the heart of government. To be a scribe—to be able to read and write—was to have access to the levers of power. That association was evidently formed at the very start.

Writing certainly transformed the business of international trade. Many of the labels from the royal tombs at Abdju—whose miniature scenes of royal ritual serve as an important source for early pharaonic culture—were originally attached to jars of high quality oil, imported from the Near East. An upsurge in such imports during the First Dynasty can be associated with the establishment of Egyptian outposts and trading stations throughout southern Palestine. At sites such as Nahal Tillah and Tel Erani in present-day Israel, imported Egyptian pottery (some stamped with the cipher of Narmer), locally made pottery in an Egyptian style, and seal impressions with hieroglyphs testify to the presence of Egyptian officials in the heart of the oil- and wine-producing region. At the springs of En Besor, near modern Gaza, the Egyptian court established its own supply center, for revictualing trade caravans using the coastal route between Palestine and the Nile delta.

Under state sponsorship, Egypt's international relations entered a new period of dynamism—not that you would have guessed it from the official propaganda. For domestic consumption, the Egyptian government maintained a fiction of splendid isolation. According to royal doctrine, the king's role as defender of Egypt (and the whole of creation) involved the corresponding defeat of Egypt's neighbors (who stood for chaos). To instill and foster a sense of national identity, it suited the ruling elite—as leaders have discovered throughout history—to cast all foreigners as the enemy. An ivory label from the tomb of Narmer shows a Palestinian dignitary stooping in homage before the Egyptian king. At the same time, in the real world, Egypt and Palestine were busy engaging in trade. The xenophobic ideology masked the practical reality. This should serve as a warning for the historian of ancient Egypt: from earliest times, the Egyptians were adept at recording things as they wished them to be seen, not as they actually were. The written record, though undoubtedly helpful, needs careful sifting, and must always be weighed against the unvarnished evidence dug up by the archaeologist's trowel.

Whereas Egypt's relationship with the Near East was, from the start, contradictory and complex, its attitude toward Nubia—the Nile Valley south of the first cataract—was far more straightforward . . . and domineering. Before the beginning of the First Dynasty, when the predynastic kingdoms of Tjeni, Nubt, and Nekhen were rising to prominence in Egypt, a similar process was under way in lower (northern) Nubia, centered on the sites of Seyala and Qustul. With a sophisticated culture, kingly burials, and trade with neighboring lands, including Egypt, lower Nubia displayed all the hallmarks of an incipient civilization. Yet it was not to be. The written and archaeological evidence tell the same story, one of Egyptian conquest and subjugation. Egypt's early rulers, in their determination to acquire control of trade routes and to eliminate all opposition, moved swiftly to snuff out their Nubian rivals before they could pose a real threat. The inscription at Gebel Sheikh Suleiman, discussed in the previous chapter, which shows a giant scorpion holding in its pincers a defeated Nubian chieftain, is a graphic illustration of Egyptian policy toward Nubia. A second inscription nearby, dating to the threshold of the First Dynasty, completes the story. It shows a scene of devastation, with Nubians lying dead and dying, watched over by the cipher (hieroglyphic marker) of the Egyptian king. The prosperous city-states of the Near East, which were useful trading partners and geographically separate from Egypt, could be allowed to exist, but a rival kingdom immediately upstream was unthinkable. Following Egypt's decisive early intervention in lower

The Palermo Stone MUSEO ARCHEOLOGICO REGIONALE DI PALERMO, ITALY/
GIRAUDON/THE BRIDGEMAN ART LIBRARY

Nubia, this stretch of the Nile Valley—though it would remain a thorn in Egypt's side—would not rise again as a serious power for nearly a thousand years.

TAXATION WITHOUT REPRESENTATION

SECURE IN ITS BORDERS, WITH HEGEMONY OVER THE NILE VALLEY AND flourishing trade links, the early Egyptian state witnessed a marked rise in overall prosperity, but the rewards were not evenly spread across the population. Cemeteries that span the period of state formation show a sudden polarization of grave size and wealth, a widening gap between rich and poor, with those who were already affluent benefiting the most. The greatest beneficiary by far was the state itself, for the practical effect of political unification was to convey all land into royal ownership. While individuals and communities continued to farm their land as they had before, they now found themselves with a landlord who expected rent in return for their use of his property. The First Dynasty government lost no time in devising and imposing a nationwide system of taxation, to turn the country's agricultural productivity to its own advantage. Once again, writing played a key role. From the very beginning of recorded history, the Egyptian government used written records to keep accounts of the nation's wealth and to levy taxes. Some of the very earliest ink inscriptions—on pottery jars from the time of Narmer—refer to revenue received from Upper and Lower Egypt. It seems that, for greatest efficiency, the country was already divided into two halves for the purposes of taxation.

The government's ambition to control every aspect of the national economy is underlined by two measures introduced in the First Dynasty. Both are attested on the Palermo Stone, a fragment of royal annals that were compiled in the Fifth Dynasty, around 2400, and stretched back to the beginning of recorded history. The earliest surviving entry, for a First Dynasty king, probably Narmer's immediate successor, Aha, concerns an event called the "Following of Horus," which evidently took place every two years. Most probably, it consisted of a journey by the king and his court along the Nile Valley. In common with the royal progresses of Tudor England, it would have served several purposes at once. It allowed the monarch to be a visible presence in the life of his subjects; enabled his officials to keep a close eye on everything that was happening in the country at large, implementing policies, resolving disputes, and dispensing justice; defrayed the costs of maintaining the court, and removed the burden of supporting it year-round in one location; and, last but by no means least, facilitated the systematic assessment and levying of taxes. (A little later, in the Second Dynasty, the court explicitly recognized the actuarial potential of the Following of Horus. Thereafter, the event was combined with a formal census of the country's agricultural wealth.) From the third reign of the First Dynasty, the Palermo Stone also records the height of the annual Nile inundation, measured in cubits and fractions of a cubit (one ancient Egyptian cubit equals 20.6 inches). The reason why the court would have wished to measure and archive this information every year is simple: the height of the inundation directly affected the level of agricultural yield the following season, and would therefore have allowed the royal treasury to determine the appropriate level of taxation.

When it came to collecting taxes, in the form of a proportion of farm produce, we must assume a network of officials operated on behalf of the state throughout Egypt. There can be no doubt that their efforts were backed up by coercive measures. The inscriptions left by some of these government officials, mostly in the form of seal impressions, allow us to re-create the workings of the treasury, which was by far the most important department from the very beginning of Egyptian history. Agricultural produce collected as government revenue was treated in one of two ways. A certain proportion went directly to state workshops for the manufacture of secondary products—for example, tallow and leather from cattle; pork from pigs; linen from flax; bread, beer, and basketry from grain. Some of these value-added products were then traded and exchanged at a profit, producing further government income; others were redistributed as payment to state employees, thereby funding the court and its projects. The remaining portion of agricultural produce (mostly grain) was put into storage in government granaries, probably located throughout Egypt in important regional centers. Some of the stored grain was used in its raw state to finance court activities, but a significant share was put aside as emergency stock, to be used in the event of a poor harvest to help prevent widespread famine. Whether this represented genuine altruism or practical self-interest on the part of the state depends on one's point of view. The people as a whole certainly benefited from this national insurance policy, but at a cost to themselves. This, of course, is the enduring truth about taxes.

With a national system in place for assessing, collecting, and redistributing taxes, Egypt's early kings could turn their attention to increasing productivity, both in agriculture and in the machinery of government. Administrations develop their own momentum, bureaucracies their own priorities, and while the Egyptian populace may have benefited indirectly from enhancements to the nation's political and economic infrastructure, it is difficult not to see the enhancements as essentially self-serving on the part of the ruling elite. In ancient Egypt an increase in national prosperity facilitated the construction of yet more sumptuous monuments celebrating the king—not the provision of facilities for the masses or the amelioration of their living conditions.

The government's focus on the elite is especially apparent under King Den, whose reign in the middle of the First Dynasty (circa 2850) marks an important milestone in the rise of ancient Egypt. In his three or four decades on the throne, innovations were introduced in many different spheres, from the royal titulary to the design of the royal tomb. (The introduction of an entrance stairway, to facilitate access to the burial chamber, seems obvious in retrospect, but the stairway revolutionized the provisioning of the tomb and paved the way for much larger funerary monuments in due course.) Changes were also afoot beyond the narrow confines of the court. An entry on the Palermo Stone records the reorganization of agricultural lands in the delta, possibly involving the relocation of entire communities to allow for the establishment of royal estates. The government, it seems, was not a particularly benevolent landlord.

The redesignation of whole tracts of Lower Egypt as "crown land" was the precursor to wider administrative reforms. To allow for more effective political control of the regions, the state introduced a system of local government that divided the Nile Valley and delta into forty-two provinces (nomes), each governed by a centrally appointed official (the nomarch) answerable to the king. The Upper Egyptian provinces seem to have been based upon traditional community boundaries, themselves reflecting the irrigation basins of prehistoric times. In the delta, by contrast, there was no such template, and here the newly created provinces seem to have been more arbitrary, no doubt working around the location of royal estates. Either way, replacing an earlier system of allegiance with a new, systematic pattern of provincial administration gave the king and his government much tighter control.

Governmental reforms continued during the latter half of the First Dynasty. A rise in the number of high officials who were granted a lavish burial, paid for by the state, indicates an expansion and professionalization of the administration. At North Saqqara, the main court cemetery serving Memphis, the highest functionaries in the land built huge mud brick tombs (known by the Arabic term "mastaba") along the edge of the escarpment. Facing the sunrise and overlooking the capital city, these imposing monuments promised their occupants both rebirth and a continuation of their earthly status. The façades of the tombs, modeled on White Wall at Memphis, provided a visual demonstration of their owners' royal connections. For the king was the ultimate fount of authority, and most, if not all, high officials at this period were royal relatives.

One such tomb was built at North Saqqara for a man named Hemaka, who served under King Den as chancellor, at the head of the treasury. Among his grave goods was a small inlaid wooden box containing two rolls of papyrus—the earliest examples yet discovered. There could be no better illustration of the close connection between writing and power in early Egypt. Indeed, the earliest "autobiographical" inscription from the Nile Valley is written on the gravestone of one of Hemaka's successors. Merka served under the last king of the First Dynasty, and his particular combination of titles and appointments reveals the nature of high office in early Egypt. Despite holding a number of positions connected with the royal household, including director of the royal barque (the king's state boat) and controller of the audience chamber, Merka gained his exceptional status from an ancient religious office associated with the cult of divine kingship. For him and his contemporaries, the king was the only route to career advancement. Merka's motley collection of administrative, courtly, and religious titles reflects an administrative system that was, on the whole, rather loosely organized. Except perhaps in the treasury, there was no precise demarcation of responsibilities. Proximity to the king was all that mattered.

The tombs constructed at North Saqqara for Hemaka, Merka, and other high officials were not just rewards for loyal service, however. They also served as a bold and highly visible statement of the government's authority, silhouetted against the skyline. At sites found along the length and breadth of the Nile Valley, from Giza and Tarkhan in the north to Inerty (modern Gebelein) and Iuny (modern Armant) in the south, the unification of the country and the resulting royal omnipotence were announced in the same way. The sudden appearance of imposing tombs in the palace-façade style, dominating their local communities, must have had a profound effect on the population at large. The impact must have been comparable to that felt after the construction of motte and bailey castles throughout England after the Norman conquest, and the message was the same: the whole country was now ruled by the king and his appointees. The tentacles of government reached into every province. A new order had arrived.

A final, telling example of how the early Egyptian state imposed its control can be found at the country's southern frontier, on the island of Abu. Here, at the very beginning of the First Dynasty, the government lost no time in building a massive fortified customs post, to monitor and regulate the movement of people and goods across the border with Nubia. The fact that the chosen location for the fortress—an elevated part of the island, overlooking the main channel for shipping—also cut off access to the local shrine was evidently of no concern to the national authorities. Economic and political control were far more important considerations than local sensibilities. From the dawn of history, the state's arrogance in its dealings with the population set the scene for the next three thousand years. For the ancient Egyptians, the price of national unity, effective government, and a successful economy was authoritarian rule.

NEW DIRECTIONS

THE DEATH OF QAA, LAST KING OF THE FIRST DYNASTY, AROUND 2750, was marked with the usual obsequies in the ancestral royal burial ground at Abdju. The king's funeral cortège made its way slowly from his palace of eternity, a huge mud brick enclosure near the town, to his remote burial place among the tombs of his forebears. The chosen spot was aligned with a prominent cleft in the cliffs, which the Egyptians believed to be an entrance to the underworld. The king's body was placed in his burial chamber, accompanied by a host of supplies to sustain his spirit in the afterlife. So that his unfortunate attendants could cater for his every need, their bodies were interred around him in subsidiary graves. Then the chamber was sealed, the process watched over by Qaa's heir, the new king, Hetepsekhemwy. A smooth transition of power had been effected, a new reign had begun. There was little to suggest that Hetepsekhemwy would inaugurate a very different era of Egyptian history. Yet later chroniclers identified him as the first king of a new dynasty. The reason lies in his dramatic decision to abandon Abdju—where kings had been buried for more than three centuries—and found an entirely new royal burial ground hundreds of miles to the north. The site he chose was Saqqara, overlooking the capital city of Memphis.

The reasons behind the move to Saqqara are obscure. Perhaps Hetepsekhemwy had family ties to the region, or perhaps he calculated that a monument as symbolically charged as the king's tomb should stand at the very balance of the Two Lands, not in an Upper Egyptian province. Whatever the motive, the radical location of his tomb was matched by its design. It was aligned to true north, rather than to the local geography. It was cut into the rock rather than built of mud brick. It was arranged as a series of long galleries opening off a central corridor, rather than as a burial chamber surrounded by storerooms. And it terminated in a suite of rooms resembling the private quarters of a contemporary house. Hetepsekhemwy was concerned that his spirit should be provided with every necessity for the hereafter—not just food and drink, but all modern conveniences, including a bedroom and bathroom.

His two successors, Kings Nebra and Ninetjer, maintained his innovations and built their tombs at Saqqara, but the Second Dynasty's outward stability masked rising tensions in the country at large. In the middle of Ninetjer's reign (circa 2700), civil unrest seems to have broken out. An obscure entry on the Palermo Stone speaks of "hacking up Shem-ra and the north." If Lower Egypt was trying to secede from central control, it might explain why the two or three kings after Ninetjer are unknown in the south of the country. Perhaps the First Dynasty's focus on Upper Egypt had led to simmering resentment among Egypt's northern population. The latter half of the Second Dynasty provides further tantalizing clues that hint at a political breach. Three or four generations after it had been abandoned, Abdju was promptly reinstated as the royal burial ground. The decision was taken by a king who—unique in the history of ancient Egypt—cast himself as the earthly incarnation not of Horus (celestial god and patron deity of kingship) but of Seth (god of the deserts, and local god of Nubt). The reasons for such a radical move can only be guessed at. The Upper Egyptian focus on the Seth cult may have appealed to a king whose authority seems to have been greatest in the south of the country. Yet, despite his unprecedented titulary, the Seth king, Peribsen (circa 2680), seems to have taken great pains to adopt the other trappings of traditional Egyptian monarchy. His tomb at Abdju was consciously modeled on its First Dynasty precursors, deliberately harking back to the early years of the pharaonic state. Peribsen was also the first king since Qaa to build a separate funerary palace at Abdju.

All in all, the written and architectural evidence from the middle of the Second Dynasty suggests a period of turmoil. The hard-won unity of the early Egyptian monarchy was weakened and undermined, and the institution of kingship itself was under greater stress than at any time since the wars of unification. What the state needed was another strong leader in the mold of Narmer, someone with the charisma, strength, and determination to rebuild the edifice of power before all was lost. Step forward, Khasekhem.

Ancient Egyptian civilization may never have progressed beyond its formative stage, may never have developed its distinctive pyramids, temples, and tombs, had it not been for the last ruler of the Second Dynasty (circa 2670). Khasekhem's very name, "the power has appeared," announced his intentions, and he lived up to them. He is a pivotal figure in ancient Egyptian history, bridging the transition between an older culture, essentially derived from prehistoric forms, and a new, quintessentially pharaonic civilization with a bolder vision.

Like Peribsen, Khasekhem seems to have come from Upper Egypt, and his power base, too, was in the south. He lavished particular attention on Nekhen, dedicating statues and stone vessels in its cult center and starting work on a massive enclosure behind the town. His so-called fort is the oldest standing mud brick structure in the world, its walls still towering thirty-four feet high more than four and a half thousand years after they were built. Khasekhem's intention to reign as a traditional king was likewise signaled by his restoration of the traditional royal titulary, announcing himself as the incarnation of the sky god Horus.

It was crucial for Egypt's destiny that these outward displays of authority were matched by Khasekhem's resolve to reunify the country and bring the whole of the Two Lands under his sway. Two life-size statues of the king from Nekhen show him wearing the tight-fitting robe of the royal jubilee, one of the most ancient celebrations of kingship. Their bases are inscribed not with the king's titles but with scenes of war dead in contorted positions. The accompanying hieroglyphs read "47,209 northern enemies." Khasekhem's stone vessels from the same shrine are also carved with scenes of triumph: the Upper Egyptian vulture goddess, Nekhbet, stands on a ring containing the word "rebel," while an inscription reads "the year of fighting the northern enemy." These ancient documents seem to record the launch of an offensive by Khasekhem's forces. His intention was to reconquer rebellious Lower Egypt and forcibly reannex it to the crown. It was a bold vision, but under Khasekhem's leadership it was swiftly realized. The king marked his successful reunification of Egypt by subtly changing his name and titles. Khasekhem became Khasekhemwy, "the two powers have appeared," supplemented by the epithet "the two lords are at peace in him." The Horus falcon was joined by the Seth animal atop the royal cipher. Conflict had been resolved, harmony restored, and opposing forces reconciled in the person of the king.

Once again, national unity ushered in a period of economic activity and cultural renaissance. And once again, the basis was tight central control of the country's resources. The Palermo Stone records the reinstatement of a regular census, only this time it was a "census of gold and fields," encompassing both the mineral and agricultural wealth of Egypt. With the government coffers full again, Egypt reestablished trading contacts with the Near East. Its particular interest was no longer southern Palestine, as in the past, but the port of Kebny (classical Byblos, modern Jubayl, north of Beirut). The king even presented the local temple with an inscribed stone vessel, to cement the bond of friendship. For their part, the traders of Kebny supplied Egypt with two of the most important raw materials it coveted, cedar and tin. Cedar logs were essential for shipbuilding, since Egypt lacked its own supply of good quality timber, and large seagoing ships were an imperative for trade contacts with the rest of the eastern Mediterranean. An entry on the Palermo Stone for the seventeenth year of Khasekhemwy's reign (circa 2655) refers to shipbuilding, and the results of the tin trade are evident in his burial at Abdju: a ewer and basin from the royal tomb are the earliest bronze vessels from the Nile Valley.

The superior technology of bronze, together with an increase in trade income, facilitated an upsurge in state construction projects, and Khasekhemwy was by far the most prolific builder in Egypt's early history. He dedicated new temple buildings throughout Upper Egypt and completed his cult enclosure at Nekhen before turning his attention to Abdju. Following in the footsteps of his immediate predecessor, he chose the ancient burial ground of kings for his own funerary monuments. His enclosure at Abdju dwarfed even its counterpart at Nekhen, and dominates the surrounding area to this day. As for the royal tomb, the king's architects chose an entirely new design, combining elements from First Dynasty and early Second Dynasty traditions. It was as if he were announcing that all the developments of Egyptian civilization up to that point were being brought together under his leadership. And he was looking to the future, too. His burial chamber was lined with carefully dressed blocks of limestone, on a scale that had never been attempted before. It was a taste of things to come.

It used to be thought that Khasekhemwy confined his building projects to Upper Egypt. But recent survey and excavation suggest that he decided to make his mark in the north as well. Far out in the desert at Saqqara, beyond the modern tourist trail, beyond even the reach of the camel drivers, lie the remains of a truly vast enclosure. It is most easily visible in aerial photographs; on the ground its walls are discernible only as a low ridge. The dimensions are staggering: it measures a quarter of a mile wide by nearly half a mile long. No wonder its local Arabic name is Gisr el-Mudir, "the enclosure of the boss." Partial excavation of the walls shows that they were built of huge stone blocks laid in sloping courses, while the corners are of solid masonry construction. No inscriptions have yet been found to confirm the date of the Gisr el-Mudir, but it looks increasingly likely that it was built by Khasekhemwy—a third monumental enclosure of his reign. In its finished state, it would have been by far the biggest and most impressive royal monument Egypt had ever seen. Khasekhemwy had brought the country to the threshold of a new age.

PYRAMIDS AND POLITICS

TODAY, THE GISR EL-MUDIR IS BUT A SHADOW OF ITS FORMER SELF. The reason is not that it was left unfinished, nor that it was poorly built. The explanation lies within view, on the skyline of Saqqara—the Step Pyramid of King Netjerikhet. The builders of Egypt's first pyramid did what their successors would do throughout Egyptian history: they looked around for a ready source of building stone and found it in a nearby monument. Rather than going to the trouble of quarrying new stone, they simply dismantled the Gisr el-Mudir and reused its

The Step Pyramid at Saqqara   WERNER FORMAN ARCHIVE

blocks to build something even grander. The result, the Step Pyramid, dominates our view of the Third Dynasty (2650–2575) just as it dominates the landscape. The ruler for whom it was built was Khasekhemwy's immediate heir and chosen successor. But if Netjerikhet inherited his father's predilection for grand designs, he was equally determined to eclipse Khasekhemwy's achievements. He would take the visible expression of absolute power to new heights—literally as well as metaphorically.

The Step Pyramid started life ambitiously enough, as a huge mastaba tomb, built in stone to last for eternity. It rose in one single step, towering above the king's burial chamber, a mountain of stone to replicate the primeval mound of creation. In a brilliant flash of inspiration, the two elements of the earlier royal burials at Abdju—a tomb and a separate funerary enclosure—were combined into a single monument, by constructing a huge wall around the mastaba. From the outside, it resembled White Wall at nearby Memphis and thus announced its royal associations. The space inside the enclosure was filled with a collection of dummy buildings, for this was the grandest of all stage sets, designed as an eternal backdrop for the ceremonies of kingship.

For the first time in history, the brilliant conception and execution of a royal monument can be attributed to a known individual. His name echoes down the centuries as the epitome of ancient Egyptian wisdom and learning: Imhotep. A statue base from the entrance colonnade of the Step Pyramid—where it could be seen by all those entering the enclosure—bears his name together with that of his king. Although Imhotep bore a string of titles (royal seal bearer, first under the king, ruler of the great estate, member of the elite, greatest of seers, and overseer of sculptors and painters), he is nowhere explicitly named as the architect of the Step Pyramid. Yet it was as the pyramid's architect that he achieved posthumous fame, and he is the only plausible candidate. Nobody else held such a prominent position at the court of King Netjerikhet, nobody else was immortalized within the Step Pyramid complex itself. Imhotep's extraordinary vision saw the development of the royal tomb from a single-stepped mastaba to a four-stepped pyramid and finally to a six-stepped form, the tallest building of its time. The idea for the stepped shape may already have been latent within Egyptian ideology, but the translation of this idea into stone, on a monumental scale, was Imhotep's lifetime achievement. His innovation marks the beginning of the Pyramid Age, and it had far-reaching effects.

The administrative effort required for pyramid building was greater than anything Egypt had developed to date. A step change in government organization was needed, and one of the first moves was the creation of the post of vizier, a single individual in overall charge of the government machine, reporting directly to the king. The vizier was hence Egypt's chief minister, with the added power that came from direct access to the monarch. Netjerikhet's inner circle of trusted lieutenants—who are better known than any of their predecessors—likewise exemplify the increasing professionalism of the court: Ankh and Sepa were district administrators; Ankhwa was the controller of the royal barque; Hesira was master of the royal scribes, perhaps the leading civil servant; and Khabausokar was the controller of the royal workshops. The old system of royal relatives holding a portfolio of unrelated offices was being replaced by a more structured bureaucracy, opened up, for the first time, to career professionals drawn from a wider section of society and promoted on merit. As Egypt embarked on pyramid building, the pyramids were building Egypt.

This quiet revolution in government is particularly well illustrated by the career of Metjen. His tomb inscription from Saqqara includes the earliest extensive autobiographical text, and it charts his rise from humble storehouse clerk to a position in local government, followed by promotion to the governorship of several delta provinces. At the end of his career, as a trusted courtier, Metjen was appointed controller of the king's pleasure palace in the Fayum. It was a pattern of advancement that would be followed for many centuries to come. From now on, the history of ancient Egypt would be made by private individuals as well as their royal masters.

The reign of Netjerikhet (2650–2620) and the achievements of his court were so impressive that his successors in the Third Dynasty pale into insignificance by comparison. Most are little more than obscure names in the historical record—Sekhemkhet, Khaba, and Sanakht. None left a monument even approaching the Step Pyramid in scale (although several tried). Only when we reach the end of the Third Dynasty and the reign of King Huni (2600–2575) do the advances of the

Pyramid Age manifest themselves. Yet, unless a ruined pyramid at Meidum has been misattributed, Huni did not indulge in pyramid building
on a lavish scale. His greatest contribution to the future glories of
pharaonic civilization was far more prosaic, but no less significant—its
architectural manifestation not one gigantic pyramid but a series of
small ones, scattered throughout the provinces of Egypt. From those
monuments discovered so far, a clear building program emerges. The
southernmost pyramid was constructed on the island of Abu, always a
favored location for statements of royal power. This monument and its
associated palace were named "the diadem of Huni." Moving downstream, the king commissioned another pyramid at Djeba (modern
Edfu); a third at el-Kula, near Nekhen; a fourth at Tukh, near Nubt;
and a fifth at Abdju. Further monuments in the series have been identified at Zawiyet el-Meitin, in Middle Egypt; Seila, at the entrance to
the Fayum; and Hut-heryib (modern Tell Atrib), in the delta. Each of
the locations was either a provincial capital or an important regional
center. Abu was the capital of the first province of Upper Egypt, Djeba
the capital of the second, and Nekhen the capital of the third. Huni's
intention seems to have been to erect a visible marker of royal power in
every province. And, to judge from the Abu pyramid, collection centers
for the royal treasury were also part of the plan. The monuments were
not just *symbols* of the king's authority throughout the country; they
were also practical *instruments* of that authority in the central management of the economy. For the local population, the small step pyramid
in their midst would have served as a constant reminder of their economic duty to the state: a duty to pay their taxes to support the court
and its projects. From the state's point of view, the monuments and
their associated administrative buildings—with one facility in each
province—made the collection of revenue both easier and more systematic.

At the end of the Third Dynasty, the monarch and his administration had achieved their ultimate goal: absolute power. The stage was
set for the greatest royal project the world had ever seen.

CHAPTER 4

HEAVEN ON EARTH

GRAND DESIGNS

THE PYRAMIDS AT GIZA ARE THE SOLE SURVIVING WONDER OF THE AN-
cient world. The Hanging Gardens of Babylon have disappeared without a trace; the Temple of Diana at Ephesus lies in ruins; but the
pyramids stand, as awesome and enduring today as when they were first
built four and a half thousand years ago. Of the three pyramids built by
successive generations of kings in the Fourth Dynasty, it is the oldest
and biggest, the Great Pyramid of King Khufu, that attracts the most
attention—and deservedly so. It is truly vast, built from 2.3 million
blocks of stone, each weighing on average more than a ton, and covering an area of thirteen acres. A simple calculation reveals that the
builders would have had to set one block of stone in place every two
minutes during a ten-hour day, working without a pause throughout
the year for the two decades of Khufu's reign (2545–2525). Once completed, at 481 feet high, the Great Pyramid remained unsurpassed in
scale until modern times. For forty-four centuries, until the completion of the Eiffel Tower in A.D. 1889, it was the tallest building in the
world. Yet despite its massive size, it is engineered and aligned with
breathtaking precision, its orientation to true north diverging by only
one twentieth of one degree. More than any other monument in the
world, the Great Pyramid seems to defy rational explanation. Little
wonder that it has attracted wild speculation about its construction,
meaning, and purpose. Theories range from the unorthodox (its blocks
are made of an ancient type of concrete) to the downright dotty (the
blocks were moved by sound waves), and a whole host of otherworldly
builders have been invoked to account for its bewildering size and perfection, including refugees from Atlantis and visitors from another
planet. The truth is, if anything, even more amazing. The Great Pyra-

mid was, indeed, the product of something extraordinary: not extraterrestrial intelligence but a superhuman authority. This radical new projection of royal power had a profound significance for ancient Egyptian civilization as a whole, and to understand its origins, we need to go back a generation before the Great Pyramid, to the reign of Khufu's father.

The Egyptians' penchant for monumentality can be traced back to prehistoric times at Nabta Playa; the construction of a vast edifice of stone was first fully realized during the reign of Khasekhemwy, at the end of the Second Dynasty; and the first pyramid was built for his successor, Netjerikhet, at the beginning of the Third. But the advent of the true, geometrical pyramid during the reign of Sneferu (2575–2545), first king of the Fourth Dynasty and father of Khufu, marked something quite new—not just the perfection of an architectural form or a change in the concept of the royal afterlife, but the transformation of the relationship between the king and his people. As was so often true in ancient Egyptian history, the new order was initially proclaimed in the king's titles. For his Horus name, the most ancient and symbolically most significant element of the royal titulary, Sneferu took the phrase *"neb maat."* The common translation, "lord of truth," scarcely does it justice. In ancient Egyptian ideology *"maat"* was the embodiment of truth, justice, righteousness, and created order—in short, the divinely ordained pattern of the universe. The word *"neb"* meant not just "lord," but "possessor," "owner," and "keeper." Sneferu was announcing nothing less than a new model of kingship. For him, the exercise of power was no longer confined to dispensing justice. It meant having a monopoly on truth. The king's word was the law because the king himself was the law. If this smacked more of divine than human authority, that was the point.

To reinforce this blunt message, Sneferu adopted a new title, *netjer nefer.* It meant, simply, "the perfect god." Is that really how his subjects saw him? Throughout history, megalomaniacs and tyrants have used such epithets—"father of the nation," "dear leader"—but the terms usually have a hollow ring. Modern experience suggests that the titles are more about brainwashing and subjugation than the expression of popular acclaim. And yet, when it comes to ancient Egypt, scholars still balk at such an interpretation. A leading expert on the Pyramid Age has written that "support for the system was genuine and widespread" and that "coercive state mechanisms, such as police, were conspicuous by their absence."[1] Unless Fourth Dynasty Egypt was a utopian society, never again experienced in human history, this rose-tinted view seems highly unlikely. When the head of state is "the perfect god," opposition becomes not just unwise but unthinkable. When the king also controls the written record, it is hardly surprising that accounts of repression or brutality are absent. Archaeology, however, reveals something more of the truth.

Throughout the first three dynasties, Egyptian society retained much of its prehistoric character. The material culture was largely dominated by forms (of pottery, stone vessels, even statuary) derived from predynastic antecedents. The major regional centers were still those from the period of state formation, places such as Inerty, Nekheb, Tjeni, Nubt, and Nekhen. Beyond the immediate confines of the royal court, society, too, seems to have been organized along ancient, traditional lines, dominated by family, regional, and perhaps tribal loyalties. All that seems to have changed at the beginning of the Fourth Dynasty. New styles of pottery and sculpture were promulgated by the court to be produced in state workshops. New towns were founded by the state to replace the earlier centers of power—Iunet (modern Dendera) displaced Tjeni as the regional administrative capital, Thebes grew at the expense of Nubt, and Djeba eclipsed Nekhen. It is tempting to see these phenomena as parts of a deliberate and coordinated government policy designed to snuff out local autonomy and replace it with a new, absolute dependency on central authority. Even in the mortuary sphere, the king's commanding presence held sway. Anyone with any position whatsoever in the vast machinery of government now sought to be buried in the court cemetery, founded by the king and dominated by his own gigantic funerary monument, rather than being interred in their local burial ground, hallowed by age and ancestral ties.

The first of these new court cemeteries grew up at Meidum, a rather remote site near the entrance to the Fayum. The choice of location was significant in itself. By breaking with tradition and eschewing the existing royal burial grounds of Abdju and Saqqara, Sneferu was distancing *himself* from his ancestors, too. His was an avowedly forward-looking

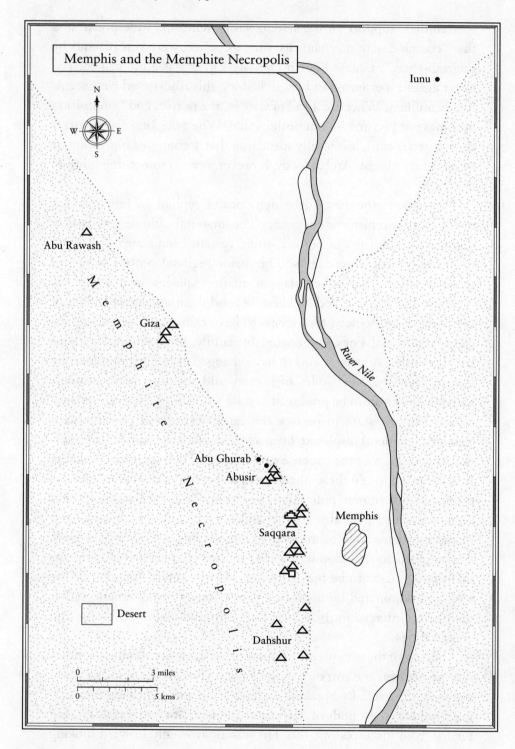

Memphis and the Memphite Necropolis

Iunu

Abu Rawash

Giza

Abu Ghurab

Abusir

Saqqara

Memphis

Dahshur

River Nile

Memphite

Necropolis

Desert

0 _____ 3 miles

0 _____ 5 kms

age, in which power would be independent of inheritance. As such, the age demanded a bold, new architectural statement. So Sneferu's engineers and builders set to work on a monument designed to surpass anything that had been attempted before. Although it followed the basic form of Netjerikhet's Step Pyramid, the Meidum pyramid was altogether grander in scale, rising up in eight giant steps (against Netjerikhet's six), and was half again as high as its predecessor. In a further break with tradition, the complex of buildings surrounding the Step Pyramid was abandoned in favor of an elongated plan, with the various architectural elements laid out along an axis. This led eastward from the pyramid itself, via a small temple and a stone causeway to a valley temple on the edge of cultivation. The east-west orientation, replacing the northern alignment of Third Dynasty royal monuments, was no accident either—Sneferu's final journey would consciously mirror the sun's course across the heavens, from its rising in the east to its setting in the west. As "the perfect god," the king was publicly associating himself with the supreme divinity and source of all life.

But even this was not enough for a ruler of Sneferu's vaunting ambition. After about a decade on the throne, with the Meidum pyramid all but complete, the king embarked upon an even more audacious project. Once again, he chose a virgin site (modern Dahshur) at the southern end of the great necropolis of Memphis. Perhaps deliberately, his chosen spot was within sight of Netjerikhet's Step Pyramid, but—as if to drum home the message that his was a new era—Sneferu had plans for an entirely new form of monument: Egypt's first true geometric pyramid. The subtle solar symbolism of the Meidum complex would be replaced by the overt representation of a shaft of sunlight, rendered in stone on a monumental scale. The name of the Dahshur pyramid, Appearance, used the same word as the rising of the sun. A new age had truly dawned. An eight-and-a-half-acre site was cleared for construction, and the plans were for the most majestic pyramid yet, with sides rising at a steep angle of 60 degrees to a height of nearly five hundred feet. A subsidiary pyramid for the king's *ka* (eternal spirit), a small side chapel, a long stone causeway, and a valley temple for the celebration of the royal mortuary cult were laid out at the same time, as part of a single grand design.

To fund this massive project, and ensure a perpetual supply of commodities for the king's cult, an equally vast administrative effort was required. An entry on the Palermo Stone for the fourteenth year of Sneferu's reign records the creation of thirty-five royal estates (complete with their human workforces) and 122 cattle farms. Many of these new foundations were located in the wide expanses of the delta, and one of them, in the western delta, subsequently grew to a considerable size. Imu (modern Kom el-Hisn) demonstrates the extent to which government policy shaped the demography of Old Kingdom Egypt. Although cattle seem to have been reared in large numbers at the site, the local population did not enjoy the fruits of their labors. Their diet was unusually low in beef and cattle products, suggesting that most of the livestock was sent straight to the royal palace and cult centers near Memphis, leaving the cattle keepers themselves to survive on more meager fare. Even the cereals grown at Imu seem to have been fed preferentially to the cattle rather than to their human attendants. Once again, we see the essentially self-interested nature of the ancient Egyptian monarchy. This was not so much enlightened despotism as despotism, pure and simple.

While the extensive low-lying fields of the delta provided ideal grazing for vast herds of cattle, the royal estates in Upper Egypt concentrated on grain production. The staple crop was barley, which provided the basic ingredient for both bread and beer. Egypt's climate and the annual regime of the Nile favored arable farming. As soon as the floodwaters receded, in early autumn, seed was broadcast over the newly irrigated and fertilized fields, and it germinated quickly. The main growing season coincided with the cooler months of winter, and this was followed by the onset of summer, which ripened the grain and allowed harvesting to take place in ideal conditions, before the inundation arrived to start the annual cycle over again. In such a favorable environment, it was relatively easy to produce a surplus; easy, too, for the state to siphon off a significant percentage of agricultural production, by way of taxation, to fund its own projects. The end product of all this economic activity is illustrated in reliefs from the Dahshur valley temple. In a frieze around the walls, a line of female offering bearers, each personifying a different royal estate, is shown bringing supplies for the royal cult. The king was letting it be known that his pyramid was a national enterprise, involving the whole country—whether the populace liked it or not.

Sneferu may have been able to command his people and their livelihoods, but he could not control the forces of nature. As his massive pyramid at Dahshur reached the halfway point, geology rudely intervened. Cracks started appearing in the outer casing, the telltale signs of subsidence. The underlying sands and shales were simply not strong enough to support the vast weight of the growing pyramid, and the ground had begun to give way. As an emergency measure, extra blocks of stone were laid around the base of the pyramid, reducing the angle of the sides to 54 degrees, but it was too little, too late. Fissures started to open up in the internal corridors and chambers. The architects tried everything from plaster repairs to a new stone lining. They even used expensive imported logs to shore up the ceilings (an entry on the Palermo Stone records the arrival of forty ships from Kebny, laden with coniferous timber), but to no avail. Finally in a desperate attempt to salvage the pyramid—and their own careers—from complete ruin, the architects implemented a radical change of plan. For the upper half of the pyramid, the angle of incline was reduced still further, to 43 degrees. Smaller blocks of stone were employed, and they were laid in

The Bent Pyramid at Dahshur WERNER FORMAN ARCHIVE

horizontal courses, rather than the inward-sloping courses used previously, which had unintentionally contributed to the stresses and strains at the base. The result would be a completed pyramid, but a seriously botched job. Though it would ultimately reach 346 feet in height, the "Bent Pyramid" was hardly fit to serve as the eternal resting place of the perfect god. Exhausted and humiliated, Sneferu's engineers, architects, and builders were left in no doubt about what they had to do—start again from scratch.

Work continued on the Bent Pyramid—although now useless, it nevertheless had to be completed. An unfinished disaster would be the ultimate disgrace. Eventually the focus of attention and activity shifted toward preparations for a third great monument. This time, the lessons learned from bitter experience were rigorously applied. A site was chosen with stable underlying geology; the monument was planned, from the outset, with a reduced angle of slope (the same 43 degrees used for the upper part of the Bent Pyramid); and the stone blocks would all be laid in horizontal courses. Resources and manpower were mobilized as never before, for the only commodity in short supply was time. Sneferu had already been king for twenty years, and his monument for eternity had to be finished before he died. As an insurance policy, the royal builders returned to Meidum to convert the king's eight-stepped pyramid into a true pyramid by casing it with additonal masonry. For a time, major construction work was taking place on three different monuments simultaneously, an unprecedented commitment of manpower and resources.

The accelerating pace of construction was extraordinary. In the first decade of Sneferu's reign, during initial work at Meidum, his builders had laid around 46,000 cubic yards of stone per year. In the second decade, as the Bent Pyramid was taking shape, the rate was increased to 105,000 cubic yards per year. In the king's third decade on the throne, with work taking place on three fronts, between 130,000 and 200,000 cubic yards of stone were laid each year. It is unlikely that this work rate was ever surpassed, even a generation later during the construction of Khufu's Great Pyramid at Giza. Remarkably, it has been calculated that Sneferu's third pyramid, known today as the Red Pyramid (from the color of its core limestone blocks), could have been built in as few as ten and a half years. The extra effort involved in hauling blocks higher and higher up the pyramid was compensated for by the sharply reducing volume of the monument toward its apex. The first eleven courses of masonry (out of 157) accounted for 20 percent of the pyramid's total volume. By the time the builders laid the sixty-sixth course (less than halfway up), they had accomplished 80 percent of the work by volume. In such a way, with an unrelenting pace and enormous effort, the Red Pyramid was finished in good time. The greatest pyramid builder in Egyptian history finally had a monument worthy of the name. (Indeed, the name Appearance was transferred to the Red Pyramid while the Bent Pyramid was rather embarrassingly renamed Southern Appearance.) Not only was it perfect in outward form, but its interior chambers also showed a new sophistication of design, with elegantly corbeled roofs producing pyramid-shaped spaces to reflect the building as a whole. Two of the rooms stood at ground level, but the third, perhaps destined to be the king's burial chamber, was placed higher up in the body of the pyramid. In death as in life, the king would be elevated above the mundane, closer to heaven than to earth.

THE GREATEST SHOW ON EARTH

IF THE ART OF PYRAMID BUILDING WAS GRADUALLY PERFECTED UNDER Sneferu, it was taken to new heights by his son. Virtually nothing is known about Khufu the man, and the events of his reign are sketchy. But it seems likely that he grew up in his father's shadow, his young life shaped by the court's obsession with pyramid building, and that he resolved to outdo even Sneferu by commissioning the ultimate in funerary monuments. The Great Pyramid at Giza marks the zenith not just of ancient Egyptian kingship but of the universal tendency for absolute power to project itself in grandiose architecture. At its most stark, the structure represents the untrammeled exercise of political and economic control; at its most inspirational, it represents a unique episode in human history. It is this combination of the sinister and the dazzling that gives Khufu's monument its enduring fascination.

From the outset, it was designed to set new standards that would remain unsurpassed. Khufu chose the site carefully, the Giza plateau (like Dahshur) being visible from Saqqara, yet virgin ground. The underlying geology—a strong seam of limestone called the Mokattam

Formation—was ideally suited to bear the weight of a gigantic monument. The local availability of building material in vast quantities was a further advantage, and during the inundation, boats could reach the base of the plateau, facilitating deliveries to the construction site from all over Egypt.

The king also chose wisely when appointing the man who would oversee the entire project. For most of the Fourth Dynasty, the highest offices of state were reserved exclusively for senior male members of the royal family, in what seems to have been a deliberate policy to concentrate all power in the hands of the king. For the greatest undertaking of his reign, therefore, Khufu chose a trusted royal relative. Hemiunu was probably the king's nephew. His membership in the king's inner circle undoubtedly gave him opportunities for advancement, but he must have possessed innate ability as well, for his rise to a position of great eminence was rapid. In his prime, he held a combination of courtly, religious, and administrative offices, ranging from elder of the palace to high priest of Thoth (the god of writing and wisdom). The unusual title "director of music of the south and the north" may reflect one of Hemiunu's private interests, but the offices that conferred the greatest responsibility were those directly connected with the business of government: overseer of royal scribes (in other words, head of the civil service) and overseer of all construction projects of the king. Of all Khufu's construction projects, none was more important than his Great Pyramid, and Hemiunu was responsible for the entire operation, from provisioning and organizing the workforce to quarrying and transporting the stone, from building and maintaining the construction ramps to marshaling the surveyors, architects, and supervisors. Hemiunu's life-size statue from his tomb at Giza shows a man in full enjoyment of the benefits of high office, his pronounced corpulence emphasizing his wealth and privilege. With an aquiline nose and strong jaw, his facial features project an air of self-confidence and determination. Notwithstanding his impeccable royal connections, these were qualities he would have needed in large measure as he stood on the Giza plateau for the first time, at the beginning of his uncle's reign, contemplating the immense challenge that lay before him.

The first—and in many ways the most crucial—stage of building a pyramid involved laying out and preparing the site. The extraordinary

Hemiunu—the man behind the Great Pyramid © ROEMER–UND PELIZAEUS MUSEUM HILDESHEIM,
GERMANY/PHOTO: SHAHROK SHALCHI

precision with which the Great Pyramid is aligned to the points of the
compass indicates that a method of orientation involving the stars must
have been used. Solar methods are simply not accurate enough. The
precise technique that the Egyptians used is not certain, but it may well
have involved a pair of stars that circle the celestial north pole; when
the two are in a direct vertical alignment (easily checked with a simple
plumb line), the line of sight toward them marks true north. We may
imagine this alignment ceremony being carried out with great solemnity, in the presence of priests, with Hemiunu and perhaps the king
himself looking on, for the efficacy of the pyramid as a means of resur-
recting the king after his death depended on the accuracy of its
orientation—as we shall see later.

Once the site had been laid out, and the ground cleared and leveled—

probably by using channels cut into the surface of the rock and filled with water—it was time for the construction itself to begin. The scale of the project seems almost overwhelming today, but to the government machine of Khufu's reign, with the benefit of a generation's experience in the construction of vast pyramids, it may have appeared less daunting. The ancient Egyptian approach to any large-scale undertaking was to divide it up into a series of more manageable units. When it came to pyramid building and the organization of a vast workforce, this proved both efficient and highly effective. The basic unit of the workforce was probably a team of twenty men, each with its own team leader. This kind of organization would have produced a team spirit, and a sense of friendly rivalry between teams would have encouraged each to try and outdo the others. This was certainly the case with larger units of the workforce, as surviving inscriptions testify. Ten teams formed a two-hundred-strong division, known today by the Greek term "phyle." Five phyles, each with its own leader and identity, made up a gang of a thousand workers. And two gangs, again with distinctive and often jokey names (such as "the king's drunkards"), made a crew, the largest unit of men. The pyramid-shaped structure of the workforce reflected the monument itself. Like the regiments, battalions, and companies of an army, the organizational arrangement engendered a strong sense of corporate identity and pride at different levels of the system. Team vied with team, phyle with phyle, and gang with gang to be the best and to win recognition. This structure was a simple and ingenious solution to a massive task, and it ensured that motivation was maintained.

It needed to be. Throughout the two decades it took to build the Great Pyramid, the construction work was hot, unrelenting, exhausting, and dangerous. The conditions must have been particularly unpleasant down in the main quarry, a few hundred yards south of the pyramid itself. Choking clouds of limestone dust, the blinding glare of the quarry face, the constant din of chisels, swarms of flies, and the stench of sweated labor: it was not a pleasant environment. The rawest of recruits had to serve their time here, earnestly hoping for promotion—and working hard to achieve it. Not that the alternative was any less strenuous. Hauling the vast stone blocks from quarry face to construction site was backbreaking work. Each block, weighing a ton or more, had to be levered onto a wooden sledge, then dragged by ropes along a carefully prepared track. At the end of its journey, it had to be taken off the sledge and moved carefully into position, ready for shaping and finishing. And all this at the pace of one block every two minutes, for ten hours a day.

Despite its superhuman scale, Khufu's monument was nevertheless a profoundly human achievement, and well within the capacity of the ancient Egyptians. Calculations and practical experiments have shown that just two crews, or four thousand men, would have been sufficient to quarry, haul, and set in place the more than two million stone blocks used to build the pyramid. Perhaps the same size of workforce again would have been required to construct and maintain the vast ramps leading from the main quarry to the pyramid and up the sides of the monument as it grew steadily in height. Another army of workers toiled behind the scenes to keep the whole operation going: carpenters to make the sledges for dragging huge blocks of stone; water carriers to lubricate the passage of the sledges along wood and mud tracks; potters to make the jars for the water carriers as well as the day-to-day ware for storage, cooking, and eating; smiths to forge and repair copper chisels for the quarrymen; bakers, brewers, and cooks to supply the entire workforce. Even so, the number of people employed at any one time on the Great Pyramid project may not have risen much beyond ten thousand.

Only a relatively small contingent of specialist quarrymen, surveyors, engineers, and craftsmen, together with their wives and children, lived at the pyramid site year-round. The majority of the workers were temporary employees, serving for a period of a few months before returning to their families in towns and villages throughout Egypt. The pyramid town in which these ordinary workmen were quartered reveals fascinating details of their daily lives. During the construction of the Great Pyramid, the main settlement, called Gerget Khufu ("settlement of Khufu"), was located near the cultivation, close to Khufu's valley temple. Large quantities of broken pottery, charcoal, ash, and animal bones indicate a hive of activity, focused primarily on feeding the thousands of workers. Farther south, at the edge of the Giza plateau, an even larger pyramid town flourished during subsequent reigns. The town illuminates the meticulous organization and planning that went into pyramid building. Separated from the sacred necropolis by a massive stone wall, thirty feet high and thirty feet thick at the base, the town was carefully laid out. Its various components all point to a rigidly hierarchical arrangement mirroring and reinforcing the management pyramid of the workforce.

The men slept in fairly primitive conditions, on rough earth beds ranged along the walls of barrack blocks. Each long, narrow unit could have housed two teams of twenty workers. At the back of each unit, more spacious living quarters were probably reserved for the team supervisors. The overseer in charge of the entire operation—not an individual of Hemiunu's rank but the official who supervised day-to-day activity at the construction site—lived in even greater comfort in a large detached villa. Directly opposite, a columned hall could have served as a communal dining facility. Eating together would certainly have helped to reinforce bonds of community and friendship among the workforce. The hard manual labor of pyramid building demanded a diet rich in protein, and up to eleven cattle and thirty sheep and goats were slaughtered every day in the town, providing meat to supplement the abundant rations of dried fish. At the same time, dozens of bakeries were kept busy producing the ancient Egyptian staples of bread and beer. As the most important dietary ingredient, grain was carefully rationed and its distribution was kept under close supervision. The silos and granaries were situated within a royal administrative complex, set within its own double enclosure wall at the edge of the town for added security. Despite the friendly camaraderie among the workforce, there was no forgetting whom they served.

Perhaps the most intriguing question surrounding Khufu's monumental construction project related to its purpose. What inspired such a feat of architecture, engineering, and sheer administrative effort? Why would ten thousand men toil for twenty years to build an artificial mountain of stone? The easy answer, favored by Egyptologists, cites the ideology of divine kingship—the notion that the monarch was the sole arbiter between the people and the gods, the defender of created order and the guarantor of Egypt's continued stability and prosperity. In such a system, the population would surely have labored willingly on a vast royal project in order to honor and maintain the covenant between them and their ruler. Perhaps. But even if pyramid building *was* a form of social security, providing employment for a large proportion of the population, especially during the months of the inundation when the fields were underwater; even if the workers were reasonably well housed and fed, not the slaves of popular myth; even if the overseers impressed upon their recruits the noble nature of the task at hand—the fact remains that the conditions were uncomfortable (at best) and the work compulsory. When royal officials came to a village to draft its men for state service, there is unlikely to have been much rejoicing. Workers sustained frequent injuries on the Giza plateau, their skeletons showing evidence of broken bones, severe lower back stress, and painful arthritic joints. Accidents must have been frequent, often resulting in fatalities. The official record is predictably silent about how many died building the Great Pyramid.

So, if the pyramid was not exactly a national project in which the whole country could take part and feel pride, what was it? The uncomfortable answer is that it was the ultimate projection of absolute power. Despots throughout history have been attracted to colossal buildings, from Nicolae Ceauşescu's Palace of the People in Bucharest to tin-pot dictator Félix Houphouët-Boigny's vast (and ridiculous) basilica in the jungles of Ivory Coast. The Great Pyramid of Khufu is merely the most audacious and enduring of such *folies de grandeur*. Little wonder that its royal builder gained a posthumous reputation as a megalomaniac tyrant with scant regard for human life. The Greek historian Herodotus, writing in the fourth century B.C., declared that Khufu "brought the country into all sorts of misery. He closed all the temples, then, not content with excluding his subjects from the practice of their religion, compelled them without exception to labour as slaves for his own advantage." Herodotus added that "the Egyptians can hardly bring themselves to mention [him], so great is their hatred."[2] The symbolism of the Great Pyramid has not been lost on more recent dictators. After his invasion of Egypt in A.D. 1798, Napoléon Bonaparte made straight for Giza and camped his soldiers at the foot of the plateau, before rallying them with the words "Soldiers of France, forty centuries gaze down upon you."

The Great Pyramid is not only the epitome of monumentality and indestructibility. What makes it unique are its unparalleled accuracy and complexity. Its precise orientation to true north has already been commented upon. Most extraordinary of all are the narrow shafts that lead upward and outward from the burial chamber (and the chamber below it), through the solid masonry, to the outer edge of the pyramid, stopping just short of the world beyond. Erroneously dubbed air shafts, they had a purpose that was altogether loftier and more transcendent, for they pointed to the stars—more specifically to the culminations of Sirius (the dog star), a star in the constellation Orion, and two of the circumpolar stars that rotate around the celestial north pole. The ancient Egyptians were accomplished astronomers, and stars played an important part in state religion, especially in beliefs about the king's afterlife. The circumpolar stars were a particular source of fascination. They alone remained permanently visible in the night sky, never setting, and were thus the perfect metaphor for the king's eternal destiny—a place in the great cosmic order of the universe that would endure forever. Khufu's pyramid was nothing less than a way of uniting heaven and earth for the everlasting well-being of the king.

SON OF THE SUN

THE PYRAMIDS OF GIZA ARE AN APPROPRIATE SYMBOL OF ANCIENT Egyptian society in the Fourth Dynasty (2575–2450). Just as the tombs of courtiers and workmen clustered around the king's own funerary monument (or as close as the tomb's owner's status allowed), so the country at large showed a similar dependence on royal power. Members of the ruling class chose to have themselves depicted as lowly scribes, emphasizing their service to the king. Autobiographical inscriptions written on tomb walls further reinforced this culture of servitude. It is no coincidence that one of the longest lasting of all ancient Egyptian funerary formulae first appeared in the early Fourth Dynasty. Written in tomb chapels, on offering tables, and later on coffins, it expressed the notion that all provisions for the tomb and the owner's mortuary cult depended upon royal largesse, constituting "an offering which the king gives." The elevation of the king found further expression in the appearance and growing popularity of personal names where the name of a god was replaced with the name of the reigning monarch. Children given names such as Khufu-khaf, "Khufu, he appears," might well have grown up wondering if there was any practical difference between the king and the sun god. The conscious modeling of the royal mortuary temple on the shrines of the gods further blurred the distinction.

This profound change in the relationship between the king and his subjects reflected an aggrandizement of monarchy that is seen not just at Giza, the epicenter of royal authority, but in the furthest reaches of the Egyptian realm. Inscriptions among the inhospitable mountains of Sinai, to the northeast, and on an isolated rocky outcrop in the southwestern desert bear witness to the state-sponsored expeditions sent by Khufu and his successors to the remotest corners of Egypt. The purpose of the expeditions was to bring back precious stones for the royal workshops, materials that could be transformed into statues, jewelry, and other costly objects to project and enhance the king's authority. The opulence—even decadence—of Khufu's court is most evident in two tombs excavated close to the Great Pyramid. One belonged to a dwarf called Perniankhu, whose job was to entertain the king and members of the royal family, perhaps by dancing and singing—the ancient Egyptian equivalent of a medieval court jester. We may imagine the scenes of feasting and revelry that took place in the royal palace, while the king's subjects bedded down in their cramped barracks at the end of yet another day of toil on the Giza plateau.

The second tomb contained equipment prepared for the king's own mother, and it provides revealing insights into the lifestyle of Fourth Dynasty royalty. Hetepheres was the wife of one great pyramid builder (Sneferu), the mother of another, and very probably a king's daughter to boot. As befitted her exalted status, she lived a life of luxury and ease, borne from place to place in a gilded carrying chair with ebony panels. Its gold inlaid hieroglyphs spelled out her many titles: mother of the dual king; follower of Horus; director of the ruler; the gracious one, whose every utterance is done for her. If these epithets are to be believed, it seems that Khufu took orders from only one person, and that was his mother. The impression of a peripatetic royal family, moving from one palace to another, is reinforced by the other items in Hetepheres's tomb equipment, which included a bed with a separate canopy and two low chairs. The furniture was lightweight and highly portable, easily dismantled and reerected. Its simplicity and elegance of design, combining exemplary craftsmanship and sumptuous materials, encapsulates the self-confidence and restrained opulence of the Fourth Dynasty. Hetepheres's most treasured possessions were her jewelry boxes, one of which was specially designed to hold twenty silver bracelets. A figure of the queen on her carrying chair shows her wearing fourteen of these bracelets at once, all along her right arm. At this period of Egyptian history, silver (which had to be imported from distant lands) was much more valuable than gold, and the bracelets were further enhanced by inlaid decoration in turquoise, lapis lazuli, and carnelian. All in all, Hetepheres must have presented a dazzling spectacle of an African queen, appropriate for the mother of an all-powerful king.

But even Khufu could not defy mortality. Around 2525 he died, and was buried with proper pomp and solemnity in his Great Pyramid, the funeral ceremonies presided over by his son and heir, Djedefra. The new king seems not to have inherited his father's penchant for lavish monuments; he built a much smaller pyramid in an entirely new site on the northernmost edge of the great Memphite necropolis. Perhaps he realized he could not compete at Giza. A more symbolic reason for the novel choice of location was that it faced the town of Iunu, principal cult center of the sun god Ra. Djedefra was clearly fascinated by the solar deity, and the sun's life-giving brilliance presented an eminently suitable metaphor for an omnipotent, resplendent monarchy. Djedefra decided to harness this symbolism, to forge a bond between king and god that would achieve, in theological terms, what his father had achieved through monumental architecture. Djedefra's very name, meaning "Ra, he speaks," was a public statement of the sun god's supreme authority. The king went further, adding a new title to the royal collection by calling himself "son of Ra." It was a decisive break with earlier tradition, which had emphasized the primacy of the celestial falcon god Horus, and it underlined the Fourth Dynasty's independence from the past, their determination to establish a new model for kingship. Under royal patronage, the cult of Ra rapidly became the most powerful in the land, and the god himself rose to a position of unassailability in the Egyptian pantheon.

The twin strands of Fourth Dynasty royal ideology—pyramid building on a massive scale and a close association with the sun god—came together in the reign of Djedefra's successor and younger brother,

Khafra (beginning circa 2500). For his funerary monument he returned to Giza, siting his pyramid next to Khufu's, but he cleverly
chose a slightly more elevated spot. This meant that, even though the
pyramid was not quite as high as its neighbor (474 feet as opposed to
482 feet), it appeared bigger—an inspired combination of deference
and self-assertion. An impressive causeway led down the plateau to the
valley temple, which was sheathed in polished slabs of red granite, a
stone with strong solar connotations. Around the temple's inner hall,
which was paved with dazzling white calcite (symbolic of purification),
stood twenty-three life-size statues of Khafra. They showed the king
enthroned in majesty with the falcon god and traditional patron of
kingship, Horus, perched behind his head, offering him protection.
Each statue was carved from a single block of gneiss, a spectacular
banded black-and-white stone brought hundreds of miles from a remote quarry in the Western Desert. The total effect, enhanced by carefully controlled light levels, must have been mesmerizing. Had there
ever been a more imposing representation of kingship? But Khafra had
not finished. His coup de grâce was to order the transformation of an
imposing knoll of rock that rose from the ground next to his valley
temple. Under the masons' chisels, it was transmogrified into a giant
recumbent lion, its human head bearing a royal countenance. The
Great Sphinx symbolized nothing less than Khafra's unification with
the sun god. Guardian of the Giza necropolis, it reoriented the whole
site around Khafra's own monument. Khufu's second son had not only
trumped the Great Pyramid; he had effectively appropriated it as well.

Three generations of huge investment—human, material, and administrative—in pyramid building transformed Egypt but proved an
unsustainable drain on its resources. Khafra's successor, Menkaura, was
the last king to build a pyramid at Giza, and it was on a much reduced
scale, reaching only 216 feet in height and only one-tenth of the volume of the Great Pyramid. The architects tried hard to compensate
with an extravagant use of red granite, brought by barge all the way
from the first cataract region, and by an enlarged pyramid temple,
where Menkaura's funerary cult continued to be celebrated for centuries after his death. But the era of massive pyramids was over. Later
kings would have to find new ways of projecting their power.

An Arabic proverb states "man fears time, but time fears the pyramids." The Great Pyramid was perhaps the most ambitious construction project of the ancient world. Its royal builder bestrode his era like a colossus. Yet—in one of the greatest ironies of archaeology—the only certain image of Khufu to have survived from his own time is a tiny thumb-size statuette of ivory. Discovered in the ruins of the temple at Abdju, it measures just three inches high. The regalia of kingship are clear enough in the statuette—the king is shown enthroned, wearing the red crown and holding the royal flail—but the scale is diminutive. An autocrat during his lifetime and a tyrant in later tradition, history has finally cut Khufu down to size.

CHAPTER 5

ETERNITY ASSURED

THEM AND US

IN ONE VERY CRUCIAL SENSE, THE APPARENT STABILITY OF THE PYRA-mid Age was an illusion. Behind the veil of glorious majesty, there were ripples of dissent within the royal family. In response to a series of dynastic crises at the height of the Fourth Dynasty (hushed up, but no less real for that), the rulers of the later Old Kingdom took conscious steps to regain control of the succession. These steps, in turn, laid the foundations for a very different style of monarchy—and a different model of society—in the three centuries after the masons' chisels fell silent at Giza.

Given that ancient Egyptian kings were invariably polygamous, it is not altogether surprising that sons born of different wives (and the wives themselves) should have jostled for influence and power. Factional quarrels are never explicitly mentioned in the written record—these quarrels hardly supported the picture of a serene and unchallengeable monarchy that the kings wished to present—but they can be guessed at from tantalizing clues: fleeting reigns in the midst of apparent dynastic stability (like Khafra's ephemeral successor, whose name is not even preserved), and sudden, unexplained departures in royal policy, such as the relocation of the royal burial ground from Giza to Saqqara at the end of the Fourth Dynasty.

After the lackluster reign of Menkaura's successor, Shepseskaf—notable only for his singular funerary monument that, in a radical departure from recent tradition, was shaped like a giant sarcophagus instead of a pyramid—a new dynasty, the Fifth (2450–2325), came to power in the person of King Userkaf. From the outset, he was eager to make a fresh start, presenting himself as the founder of a new age, a new model of government, and a new concept of kingship. The first and most public statement of his intent was his choice of tomb. Ignoring Shepseskaf's bizarre innovation, he reverted to the traditional pyramid model. What's more significant, however, is that he chose to build it at the corner of Netjerikhet's great Step Pyramid enclosure, by now a venerable two-hundred-year-old monument. He was thus explicitly associating himself with one of the great kings of the past. Just as the reign of Netjerikhet had marked a new beginning, so, too, would the reign of Userkaf.

But whereas Netjerikhet's massive pyramid—and those of his Fourth Dynasty successors—had projected an uncompromising image of the king's political power, Userkaf chose a different path, emphasizing instead the sacred character of his office. While his pyramid was a rather small affair (at only 161 feet in height, it was the smallest royal pyramid to date), far greater resources were devoted to a monument quite separate and distinct from the king's tomb. This was a sun temple, built at the site of Abusir, midway between Saqqara and Giza. It was an innovation as bold and epoch-making, in its own way, as the Step Pyramid. Comprising a walled stone enclosure with a symbolic mound at its center, Userkaf's monument—called Nekhen-Ra, "Ra's stronghold"—was designed, above all, to underline the king's unique relationship with the sun god. Sacrifices were made in its open court, under the rays of the sun, and consecrated to Ra upon an altar in front of the mound. If contemporary hieroglyphic representations are to be believed, the mound may even have been topped with a wooden perch, for the convenience of the sun god in his falcon form. As befitted a monument dedicated to the preeminent deity, the sun temple was endowed with its own land and personnel, and was at least as important an institution as the royal pyramid. Indeed, supplies destined for the king's mortuary temple were often delivered via the sun temple, which acted as a sacred filter, giving the goods used in the celebration of the king's own cult an extra, divine stamp of approval.

The sun temples built by Userkaf and his Fifth Dynasty successors were a bold attempt to rebrand Egyptian kingship. No longer able to bear the economic burden of colossal pyramids, the monarchy had to find a new way of projecting itself and underlining its position at the apex of ancient Egyptian society. It did so by removing the king even further from the mortal sphere, linking him more closely than ever with the realm of the divine. In the first three dynasties, royal ideology had stressed the king's position as the earthly incarnation of the ancient sky god Horus. In the Fourth Dynasty, Djedefra had taken the step of calling himself "son of Ra," adding the sun god to the web of royal associations. Building upon these developments, Userkaf gave concrete expression to his relationship with the solar deity, and he would be remembered in later folk tradition as the very offspring of Ra—subtle theology in place of naked displays of power. Psychology had replaced tyranny as the favored tool of royal propaganda.

The deliberate distancing of the king from his subjects took other forms, too. While the tombs of bureaucrats had clustered tightly around the Fourth Dynasty pyramids at Giza—proximity to the royal monument reflecting rank at court—in the Fifth Dynasty a marked separation was enforced between the divine king and mere mortals. Royalty and the common people would be carefully demarcated in death as well as in life. A necropolis for high-ranking officials was established at Saqqara (less prominent individuals had to make do with a tomb at Giza, now abandoned as the main center of royal activity), but the royal pyramid kept its distance, moving even farther away, to Abusir, under Userkaf's successors. Nor were the officials themselves as closely connected to the royal family as they had been in times past. From the dawn of Egyptian history until the late Fourth Dynasty, the highest offices of state had been reserved for the king's relatives. Without exception, every vizier from the reign of Sneferu to the reign of Menkaura had been a royal prince, and most of the overseers of works as well. In a dramatic and far-reaching departure, Userkaf opened up the top jobs in the administration to men of nonroyal birth. The motives for such a radical shift of policy seem to have been both ideological and pragmatic. It allowed the king and his family to rise above the nitty-gritty of government. Just as important, by removing political power from the hands of (often quarrelsome) princes, Userkaf no doubt hoped to avoid the internal wranglings that so often threatened the stability of the monarchy.

The result was a new class of professional bureaucrats, men who achieved power as much by their own abilities as by their royal connections. At the same time, the administration expanded to reflect increased job specialization. Whereas it might have worked for a prince to hold a diverse portfolio of responsibilities, connected only by the fact of his royal blood, a full-time, professional administrator could scarcely be expected to excel at a dozen different roles simultaneously. From now on, career officials, not royal relatives, would be the backbone of the ancient Egyptian government machine. And without the aura or status of royalty, they would have much more to prove.

An expanded professional bureaucracy composed largely of commoners, and the establishment of a new necropolis in which they could build their eternal resting places without reference to—and without being overshadowed by—the king's pyramid: these interlinked developments set the scene for the defining monuments of the later Old Kingdom—the tombs of the courtiers. For the first time in Egyptian history, they allow us to enter the world of the king's subjects—with often surprising results.

KEEPING UP APPEARANCES

Above all, the private tombs of the Fifth and Sixth dynasties (2450–2175) are extraordinary works of art. The sophistication of their painted reliefs testifies to the skills of ancient Egyptian craftsmen, skills that had been honed over many generations in the royal cemeteries of Dahshur and Giza. With space to build larger monuments and ambitious peers to impress, the high officials of the later Old Kingdom took the business of tomb construction and decoration very seriously. It swiftly became a competitive activity, and a bureaucrat would wait as long as he dared before commencing work on his monument, hoping for one final promotion that would enable him to lord it over his contemporaries (and their descendants) in appropriately grand architectural fashion. Officials lavished particular attention on their tomb chapels, the public rooms or suites of rooms aboveground where family members and other visitors would come after the owner's death to present offerings to his statue. By contrast, the burial chamber itself, belowground and out of sight, rarely received more than the most cursory decoration. "If you've got it, flaunt it" would certainly have struck a chord with the ancient Egyptians.

As for the decoration, certain themes were de rigueur. Although an elaborate tomb was an essential piece of one-upmanship in the competitive world of the Old Kingdom civil service, its more fundamental purpose—to protect and nurture the undying spirit of the deceased for all eternity—could neither be forgotten nor neglected. So the most important tomb scenes were those that depicted the manufacture and presentation of offerings, ranging from the basics of life (bread and beer) to the finer accoutrements of privilege, such as furniture, jewelry, and

A statue of Mereruka emerges from its niche to receive offerings from visitors to his tomb. WERNER FORMAN ARCHIVE

wine. Incidentally, such scenes provide a wealth of information about the techniques of agriculture, craft production, and food preparation, but recording daily life was not their primary purpose. Rather, they were an artistic insurance policy: according to Egyptian beliefs, if the actual grave goods buried with the body were ever exhausted or destroyed, the scenes would come to life in the tomb and ensure a continuous supply of every requirement by magical means. The lines of painted offering bearers, marching incessantly toward the false door that communicated with the burial chamber below, would similarly become animated by magic and never fail to deliver their bounty to the tomb owner.

Given the twofold purpose of a tomb chapel—to proclaim the owner's status and guarantee him a comfortable afterlife—it is not surprising that the decoration presents a highly idealized view of life in ancient Egypt. The sculptors and painters were required to depict things not as they really were but as the client wished them to be. Decoration was designed, above all, to reinforce the established social order. For example, while the owner stands tall, dominating every scene, his servants—and, indeed, his wife and children—are more often shown as diminutive figures, sometimes barely reaching his knees. This principle of hierarchical scaling, so strange to modern eyes, perfectly reflects the Egyptians' obsession with rank. Another feature of tomb decoration is its deliberate timelessness. There is little or no sense of narrative progression. Scenes appear as if suspended in space and time. The key moments in the owner's life, such as his childhood, marriage, and promotion to high office, are conspicuous by their absence, for to have included them in the decoration would have perpetuated them for eternity. Only the endpoint—the peak of achievement, wealth, and status—was deemed appropriate to immortalize in art.

Although tomb scenes may not be reliable evidence for the realities of daily life, they do allow us to enter into the fantasies of the ancient Egyptian elite. The pleasures of the idle rich are meticulously recorded: hunting in the desert, fishing and fowling in the marshes, and a range of indoor pursuits. Mereruka, a vizier of the early Sixth Dynasty, is shown painting and playing board games. In another scene, members of his household staff prepare his bed, arranging the mattress, headrest, and canopy; Mereruka then relaxes on his four-poster while his wife entertains him by playing the harp. When, from time to time, he had to bestir himself and actually do some work, he could at least enjoy traveling from place to place in the comfort of a shaded palanquin, borne on the shoulders of servants. Such activities were, of course, a world away from the harsh realities of life in rural Egypt (ancient and modern). The bureaucrats of the later Old Kingdom may have been commoners, but once they had climbed the greasy pole of career advancement, they were more than content to shut themselves off from the rest of the population and wallow in pampered luxury—or at least the promise of it after death. Very occasionally, a glimpse of the world beyond the silken veil is allowed to intrude, but only to emphasize a point. In Mereruka's tomb, his life of leisure is contrasted with the brutal punishment meted out to tax defaulters over whom he exercised authority. An unpleasant fate indeed awaited the head man of a village found in arrears. After being frog-marched to the local tax office, he could expect to be lashed naked to a whipping post and flogged with wooden sticks, while scribes stood by recording the offense and the punishment. Away from the cloistered lives of the hunting and fishing set, life was mean and miserable.

Nowhere is this disparity better illustrated than in matters of health. The upper echelons of society were able to call upon the services of doctors, dentists, and other medical specialists. In their tombs, the elite are always depicted in vigorous good health, the men fit and virile, the women nubile and graceful. By contrast, skeletons and mummified remains—as well as the occasional tomb scene—confirm that the peasantry suffered from a range of debilitating and painful diseases, many of them still prevalent in Egypt today. Schistosomiasis, a parasitic disease transmitted by water snails in canals, ditches, and stagnant pools, caused blood in the urine, sometimes leading to anemia, and must have been a common cause of ill health and early death. Tuberculosis seems to have been prevalent, often leading to deformation of the spine (Pott's disease), and similar symptoms were no doubt a common result of unremittingly hard physical labor. Tumors, too, are attested on Old Kingdom skeletons, while three depictions in contemporary tombs may represent individuals suffering from hernias. Apart from adding a little color to scenes of peasants at work, disease, deformity, dirt, and dissent had no place in the artisocratic ideal of the ruling elite.

The impression of a governing class badly out of touch with the rest of the population is only reinforced when we look at the jobs of these tomb owners. To be sure, some of them, such as Mereruka and his predecessor Kagemni, were viziers and held important government offices. But others seem to have had little or no administrative responsibility, instead deriving their exalted status purely from their proximity to the king. Irukaptah, the head of palace butchers, undoubtedly had a central part to play in the provisioning of the royal court, but the splendor of his tomb at Saqqara (complete with scenes of butchery) suggests that the king cared rather more about what he ate for dinner than about how his ministries were run. In a similar vein, the twin brothers Niankhkhnum and Khnumhotep, joint heads of palace manicurists, were rewarded for their devoted attention to the royal fingernails with a beautifully decorated tomb. The vizier Khentika owed his promotion not to his experience of sound administration but to his varied roles in the king's personal service, which included controller of the robing room, overseer of clothes, administrator of every kilt, chief of secrets of the bathroom, and even overseer of the king's breakfast. At an effete royal court steeped in pampered privilege, the most sumptuous of all Fifth Dynasty tombs at Saqqara was built not for a chancellor or overseer of works but for the head of palace hairdressers. Ty's magnificent edifice comprises a vast open courtyard with pillars forming a shady portico on all four sides, a long corridor leading to a further two rooms, and a separate chamber to house his statue. He demonstrates the extent to which royal favor was still the main passport to wealth and status. The administration had indeed been opened up to commoners, but old habits died hard.

This age-old method of advancement is exemplified in the career of Ptahshepses (circa 2400), owner of the largest known Fifth Dynasty private tomb in all Egypt. The major turning point in his career was his second marriage, when he took the hand of the king's own daughter. Becoming a royal son-in-law gained Ptahshepses access to the innermost circle at court. His newfound status prompted a major enlargement of his funerary monument, including the addition of a grand columned entrance. But such dizzying success came at a price. He seems to have been forced to disinherit his eldest son, born of an earlier marriage, in favor of the children from his second, royal marriage.

Loyalty to the monarch counted for more than loyalty to one's own family.

The reforms of the early Fifth Dynasty, which had been designed to distance the royal family from the business of government, unintentionally resulted in an overstaffed, overpaid, and overbearing bureaucracy. By the middle of the dynasty, government jobs—and the highfalutin titles that went with them—had multiplied to such an extent that a special system of ranking titles was introduced, to help distinguish between different degrees of privilege. But the growing influence of high officials had begun to threaten the king's monopoly on power and could not be allowed to continue unchecked. Toward the end of the dynasty (circa 2350), the monarchy implemented a major reorganization of the administration, to reduce the number of bureaucrats and curb their powers. A central plank of these reforms was the delegation of responsibilities to officials based in the provinces. While the intention was to restrict the influence of the ambitious men at court, the unintended consequence was a weakening of central government itself, with far-reaching and long-lasting repercussions for the stability of the Egyptian state. Officialdom, once given a taste of power, would not be easily muted. The bureaucrats whose careers defined the later Old Kingdom would, in the end, be responsible for its demise.

TEMPLES AND TEXTS

WHILE THE RULING CLASS WAS LEAVING ITS MARK IN A SERIES OF LAVishly decorated tombs, the kings of the Fifth Dynasty (2450–2325) concerned themselves with their own architectural legacy: pyramids and sun temples. Userkaf's five successors paid homage to the sun god Ra in their names (Sahura, Neferirkara, Shepseskara, Neferefra, and Niuserra) and erected their pyramids at Abusir, in the vicinity of Userkaf's sun temple. While nowhere near as large or as solidly built as Fourth Dynasty pyramids, these Fifth Dynasty counterparts were beautifully and extensively decorated in keeping with the fashion of the time. Sahura's pyramid complex alone contained an estimated twelve thousand square yards of relief carving. The decoration included several new genres, such as scenes of gods presenting foreign captives to the king, or a goddess suckling the monarch. The sophisticated taste of the court is also evident in the deliberate and careful use of contrasting types of stone: Sahura's valley temple had a dado and columns of red granite (the latter shaped like palm fronds), a floor of black basalt, and upper walls of fine white limestone, while the roof was painted dark blue with golden stars, to resemble the night sky. The covered causeway leading up the escarpment was decorated with reliefs along its whole length, and further decoration covered the walls of the mortuary temple next to the pyramid proper. The whole effect must have been spellbinding.

The mortuary temple was not merely the inner sanctum of the whole complex; it also housed the king's statue, which was the focus of cult activity during his reign and—he hoped—for eternity. (Needless to say, every monarch was to be frustrated in this hope, and few cults were maintained for more than a few generations after their founders' deaths.) Remarkably, archives of papyrus documents have survived from two mortuary temples at Abusir, the temples attached to the pyramids of Neferirkara and Neferefra, and they give unrivaled information about the day-to-day operation of a royal funerary cult in the Old Kingdom. They reveal a system obsessed with bookkeeping, but a mind-set that was more concerned with processes and protocols than standards.

The personnel of Neferirkara's temple served on a monthly rota, and at the beginning of each thirty-day period the members of staff coming on duty were required to carry out a thorough inspection of the temple and its contents. The building itself was examined for damage, and each piece of furniture or equipment was checked against a detailed inventory, arranged systematically by material, shape, and size. One sheet of papyrus lists items made from stone and flint. Under the heading "crystalline stone," subheading "bowls," category "white," an inspector has noted "various repairs to rim and base, and to sides." A blade of flint is recorded as having "chips missing, having been dropped," while a small silver offering table was found in an equally parlous state, "badly split; loose joints; corroded." The fact that these inspections took place just fifty years after Neferirkara's death shows how quickly items of temple equipment could become damaged. Apparently, regular inspection and recording was more important than actually looking after the items in question. Style over substance, impression over action—an all-too-common phenomenon in societies hamstrung by bureaucracy.

Deliveries of foodstuffs and other supplies were also meticulously recorded, but here again there were systemic failures that even the most assiduous record keeping could not mask. Among the commodities due each day at Neferirkara's sun temple were fourteen consignments of special bread. During one year, none arrived on the first day of the month, none on the second, and none on the third or fourth, until on the fifth day of the month seventy batches were delivered in one go. The next six days' supplies failed to materialize at all and seem to have been written off. By contrast, the next eleven days' deliveries were received on time. Apparently even a society as structured and prescribed as ancient Egypt could not ensure the regular delivery of the most basic commodities being transported from one royal foundation to another. It is a surprising revelation, at odds with the outward impression of a well-ordered, confident, and efficient civilization. Perhaps the Old Kingdom governmental machine was not as robust as its monuments liked to suggest, even in times of peace and plenty, let alone in the face of serious political or economic turbulence. Those who dared to look beyond their own rhetoric might have seen that the seeds of collapse had not only been sown, they were already germinating.

Not that Unas, the last king of the Fifth Dynasty (2350–2325), was outwardly concerned with such problems. He was far too busy reinventing traditions, adding new and innovative elements to the already weighty edifice of royal ideology. Like Userkaf before him, he chose a site for his pyramid at one corner of Netjerikhet's Step Pyramid enclosure. And it was not only the pyramid's location that announced Unas as a renaissance ruler. The most radical innovation was reserved for the chambers underneath the monument. Eschewing the stark simplicity of earlier undecorated walls, Unas commissioned an altogether more elaborate resting place for his afterlife. His coffin was painted black to symbolize the earth, while the ceiling of the burial chamber was studded with golden stars against a dark blue background to mimic the night sky. Around the sarcophagus, the walls of the burial chamber were lined with white alabaster, grooved and painted to resemble an enclosure made from a wooden frame and reed matting, representing the type of primitive shrine that the ancient Egyptians believed had existed at the dawn of creation. The whole ensemble was designed to be nothing less than a microcosm of the universe.

The greatest novelty of all was the decoration on the walls of the burial chamber and anteroom—column after column of texts, painted blue to recall the watery abyss of the underworld. The so-called Pyramid Texts constitute the earliest surviving body of religious literature from ancient Egypt, and the only large corpus of inscriptions from the Old Kingdom. They are a motley collection of prayers, spells, and hymns, all designed to assist the king in his afterlife journey into the cosmic realm to join the indestructible circumpolar stars. The language and imagery of some utterances suggest that they date back many centuries, perhaps even to the dawn of Egyptian history. Others were surely composed anew at the end of the Fifth Dynasty.

Spells, incantations, and prayers must have played a part at all royal funerals and in all royal mortuary cults. Yet the idea of inscribing them permanently on the walls of the king's tomb, to serve for eternity, was an innovation of Unas's reign. They were not simply carved, willy-nilly, on any available surface. Rather, the careful disposition of texts on different walls was designed to reinforce the symbolic geography of the pyramid itself. Texts explicitly concerned with the underworld were concentrated in the burial chamber, while the antechamber was identified as the horizon, the place of rebirth where the king might rise into the heavens. In this way, hieroglyphs and architecture complemented and strengthened each other, enhancing the magical power that was designed to guarantee Unas's resurrection.

But there was more to it than mere magic. The king could look forward to a glorious rebirth because he commanded absolute obedience—from deities as well as mere mortals. As far as the king's relationship with the gods was concerned, he had might, as well as right, on his side. This rather shocking presumption is given voice in one of the most chilling of Unas's Pyramid Texts. Dubbed "the Cannibal Hymn," its graphic imagery has made it (in)famous. A brief extract gives the flavor:

> Unas is he who eats people, who lives on the gods . . .
> Unas is he who eats their magic, swallows their spirits:
> Their big ones are for his morning meal,
> Their middle ones for his evening meal,
> Their little ones for his night meal,
> Their old males and females for his burnt offering.[1]

The king's theologians and hymnographers had excelled themselves in conveying the starkest of messages: Unas was omnipotent because he had literally consumed and assimilated the powers of the divine realm in all their manifestations. Nothing and no one could stand in his way of achieving cosmic immortality.

Such a tyrannical attitude toward the gods did not bode well for the king's relationship with his mortal subjects. The reign of Unas has left little in the way of evidence for historic events—a battle scene showing Egyptians fighting Asiatics is a rare exception—but one particular series of scenes from his pyramid causeway suggests a grim episode with dreadful human consequences. The images of famine, rendered in excruciating detail, are horribly familiar to modern audiences, who are accustomed to scenes of misery and degradation emanating from the African continent. On the Unas causeway, the tableau is just as harrowing: a man on the verge of death is supported by his emaciated wife, while a male friend grips his arm; a woman desperate for food eats the lice from her own head; a little boy with the distended belly of starvation begs a woman for food. The mental and physical anguish is real enough, yet there are no inscriptions to identify the starving people. It is scarcely conceivable that they were supposed to be native Egyptians, since the whole purpose of art in a funerary context—especially in the king's pyramid complex—was to immortalize an ideal state of affairs. The only logical conclusion is that the famine victims are desert tribespeople, the descendants of Egypt's prehistoric cattle herders, who continued to eke out a precarious existence in the arid regions to the east and west of the fertile Nile Valley. Their parlous state was illustrated to contrast with the good fortune of the Egyptians; the miserable wretchedness of those living beyond Unas's rule served both as a stark reminder and as a warning to his own subjects. For all the outward piety of the Fifth Dynasty kings, an older model of despotic monarchy had never entirely gone away.

CRACKS IN THE EDIFICE

ALL THE PROPAGANDA OF ART AND ARCHITECTURE, OF TEXT AND IMAGE, might buy the king immortality, but it could not bring him an heir. Mocking Unas's self-promotion as the founder of a new age, fate de-

Famine victims WERNER FORMAN ARCHIVE

creed that he should die without a son to inherit his kingdom. The throne passed instead to a commoner, a man called Teti, who swiftly married his predecessor's daughter to secure his legitimacy. So began the Sixth Dynasty (2325–2175), in an atmosphere of uncertainty, court intrigue, and barely managed crisis that was to haunt it until the very end.

With his rather tenuous claim to the kingship, Teti needed to surround himself with trusted lieutenants. Their magnificent, decorated tombs at Saqqara, nestling close up against the royal pyramid, testify once again to the critical importance of royal patronage for career advancement, but also to the claustrophobic oligarchy of Teti's court. The vizier Kagemni exercised unrivaled authority as the king's right-hand man. His successor, Mereruka, enjoyed great wealth and status, and luxuries unimaginable to the majority of the population. He could indulge his palate with haute cuisine of the most exotic kind: the scenes of animal husbandry in his tomb go beyond the normal depictions of cattle rearing to include semidomesticated antelopes eating from mangers, cranes being force-fed (it seems foie gras was on the menu in Sixth Dynasty Egypt), and—most bizarre of all—hyenas being fattened for the table.

Such refined pleasures were the reward for ultraloyal service to the king, and were designed to ensure that Teti's closest advisers were also his strongest supporters. Yet the greatest danger to his crown, and indeed his life, came not from his chief ministers but from disgruntled royal relatives, especially the male offspring of minor wives. For them, an attemped coup, however risky, was the only alternative to a life of idle frustration. If the historian Manetho is to be believed, Teti suffered just such a fate, succumbing to assassination in a palace plot. The contemporary evidence, too, points to a hiatus in the succession, with an ephemeral king, Userkara, ruling for the briefest of periods after Teti's demise and not deemed worthy of mention in biographies of the time. Little wonder, perhaps, that when Teti's chosen heir, Pepi I, finally achieved his birthright and was enthroned as king, he pursued a policy of extreme caution. He placed an unusual degree of trust in a very few high officials, notably his own mother-in-law—whom he appointed vizier for Upper Egypt—and brother-in-law, Djau. Pepi pursued a vigorous policy designed to reassert royal prestige by commissioning cult chapels dedicated to himself at important sites throughout the land, from Bast, in the central delta, to Abdju and Gebtu (modern Qift), in Upper Egypt. (By contrast, temples dedicated to local gods were still virtually unknown in a country where public works focused entirely on kingship.) But while such bold architectural statements of the king's power might have convinced the populace, the statements were less effective at stifling dissent among his entourage.

Our best insight into palace politics during Pepi's forty-year reign (2315–2275) comes from the tomb autobiography of a career courtier named Weni. He rose from the humble position of storehouse custodian to a financial position in the palace administration. Proximity to the king duly brought opportunities for advancement, and Weni was promoted to overseer of the robing room and head of the palace bodyguard, becoming a key confidant of the monarch. As a measure of the trust placed in him by his sovereign, Weni was given responsibility for sensitive judicial matters: "I heard a case alone with the vizier, in complete confidence. [I acted] in the name of the king for the royal harem."[2] The royal harem, comprising the households of the king's female relatives and minor wives, was an important institution in its own right. It owned land and operated workshops (notably for textile manufacture), and was thus a potential power base for an ambitious rival to the reigning king. Throughout ancient Egyptian history, palace intrigue and attempted coups would often originate inside the harem. It was therefore vitally important for the king to have someone on the inside he trusted implictly, someone who could provide surveillance and report back to his royal master. In Weni the king had chosen well. Thanks to his diligence, a plot against Pepi I was discovered before it could achieve its seditious aims. To keep the lid on such a dangerous act of treason, the matter had to be investigated and the perpetrators brought to justice quickly and quietly. Weni duly obliged:

> When secret proceedings were launched in the royal harem against the "great of sceptre" [that is, the queen], His Majesty sent me to judge on my own. There was no judge, no vizier, no official there, only myself alone. . . . Never before had one like me heard a secret of the royal harem; but His Majesty made me judge it, for I was excellent in His Majesty's heart, more than any [other] official of his, more than any noble of his, more than any servant of his.[3]

Weni's rewards were commensurate with his loyal service: promotion to the rank of "sole companion" and a stone sarcophagus, a token of status usually reserved for members of the royal family. The great monolith was transported "in a great barge of the residence together with its lid, a false door, an offering table, two jambs, and a libation table"[4] by a company of sailors under the command of a royal seal bearer. This show of royal favor must have been a signal honor. Being responsible for the king's safety had its compensations.

But in the uncertain world of the Sixth Dynasty, the dangers to an Egyptian ruler came not only from his own palace. Beyond the borders of Egypt, too, less fortunate peoples—those very nomads so mercilessly caricatured in Unas's reliefs—were starting to view the Nile Valley's wealth with increasingly greedy eyes. These "sand dwellers," as the Egyptians disparagingly called them, now rebelled against centuries of domination, provoking an immediate and savage response. Weni was put in charge of the operation to suppress the insurgency. Swapping the gilded opulence of the royal robing room for the dusty field of battle, he led an army of Egyptian conscripts and Nubian mercenaries through the delta to engage the rebels in their desert homeland of southern Palestine. Using a classic pincer movement, Weni ordered half of the army to proceed by boat, landing in the enemy's rear, while the other half marched overland to launch a frontal attack. This strategy carried the day for the Egyptians, but the nomads were no pushovers. Weni boasted, rather shallowly, that "His Majesty sent me to lead this army on five occasions, to crush the land of the sand dwellers every time they rebelled."[5]

ECLIPSE

THE USE OF MERCENARIES FROM NUBIA TO BOLSTER A CONSCRIPT ARMY showed a renewed interest by Egypt's rulers in the lands to the south of the first cataract. And for once Egyptian concern was not merely directed at exploiting Nubia's human and mineral resources. Along the upper reaches of the Nile, new powers were beginning to stir—powers that, if left unchecked, might disrupt the trade routes with sub-Saharan Africa and threaten Egypt's economic interests. The Egyptian government responded to the growing risk with a raft of policy initiatives. A fortified outpost of the central administration was established in the distant Dakhla Oasis, a key point along the desert route between Egypt and Nubia. The town of Ayn Asil was provided with strong defensive walls and garrisoned with soldiers under the oasis commander. As part of the same military infrastructure, all major access routes into and out of the oasis were guarded by a network of watch posts. Situated on hills, within signaling distance of one another, and supplied directly from the Nile Valley, the guard stations allowed Egyptian security personnel to keep an eye on all movements of people and goods entering or leaving the area. By such means, Egypt could both safeguard its crucial trade routes and help to prevent infiltration by hostile Nubians.

Under Pepi I's successor, Merenra, Weni was appointed governor of Upper Egypt, the first commoner to hold this strategically important post. Weni gave the king eyes and ears in the far south of the country, the better to monitor developments across the border in Nubia. Merenra even made a personal visit to Egypt's southern border to receive a delegation of Nubian chiefs. By this unprecedented gesture he hoped, no doubt, to secure their continuing loyalty to Egyptian overlordship or, failing that, at least a promise to refrain from outright hostility. However, a one-off royal visit and second- or thirdhand reports from a local official were scarcely a good enough basis for deciding matters of national security. What was needed was firsthand intelligence from Nubia itself. This would form the third plank of the government's new policy toward its restive southern neighbor.

The frontier town of Abu was Egypt's gateway to Nubia. Its inhabitants knew the upper Nile better than any of their compatriots, and many had close economic or family links with the Nubian population just over the border. Government-sanctioned expeditions into Nubia had been taking place sporadically since the reign of Teti, at the beginning of the Sixth Dynasty. The time had come to place these reconaissance missions on a more systematic footing, and of all the people in Abu none was better qualified to undertake such a mission than the chief of scouts. He, after all, was the government official responsible for maintaining security and for ensuring that the peoples of Nubia and beyond delivered a steady supply of exotic products to the royal treasury. On Merenra's orders, the chief of scouts, a man named Harkhuf, set out with his father, Iri, on an epic journey. His ultimate destination was the distant land of Yam, far up the Nile, beyond the limits of Egyptian control. The one-thousand-mile return trip took seven months, at the end of which Harkhuf and Iri returned safely to Egypt, laden with exotic goods for their sovereign.

Just as valuable must have been the intelligence they brought with them about political developments in Nubia. So troubling were the reports that Harkhuf was sent to Yam a second time. Abandoning the pretense of a trade expedition, the intrepid traveler acknowledged the true purpose of his eight-month mission: "I returned through the region of the realm of the ruler of Satju and Irtjet, having opened up those foreign lands."[6] What Harkhuf reported back to his master was an alarming development in the political geography of lower Nubia. The local population, for so long subservient to the Egyptians, was showing signs of wishing to reassert its autonomy. The coalescence of districts such as Satju and Irtjet was a dangerous warning sign that Egypt could not afford to ignore.

Taking account of these new political realities on his third expedition to Yam, Harkhuf studiously avoided the river valley, following instead the Oasis Road. On arrival at Yam, Harkhuf discovered to his dismay that its ruler had left to fight his own battle against the Tjemeh people of southeastern Libya. Old political certainties were crumbling, and across northeast Africa, lands were in a state of flux. Undeterred, Harkhuf set out immediately in pursuit of the Yamite chief, following him to Tjemeh land. The rendezvous accomplished, the two men concluded their negotiations to mutual satisfaction. Harkhuf embarked on the journey home "with three hundred donkeys, laden with incense, ebony, precious oil, grain, panther skins, elephant tusks, throw sticks— all good tribute."[7] However, the situation in lower Nubia was now more hazardous than ever for an Egyptian envoy. Harkhuf swiftly discovered that the chief of Satju and Irtjet had added the whole of Wawat (lower Nubia north of the second cataract) to his growing territory. Such a powerful chief was not about to allow Harkhuf and his considerable booty to pass unhindered. Only the presence of an armed escort provided by the Yamites allowed Harkhuf to continue his journey unmolested.

Suddenly, Egypt was no longer the only serious power in the Nile Valley. Under its very nose, upstart Nubian chiefs had taken control, threatening Egypt's centuries-old domination. It was a dramatic reversal of fortune for the most prosperous and stable nation of the ancient world. Only decisive leadership might hope to restore Egyptian hegemony. Yet soon after Harkhuf's return, Merenra died, leaving the throne to a boy of six. The infant king, Neferkara Pepi II, was not in a position to offer any kind of guidance to his beleaguered country. At home, government was exercised by a regency council, headed by the king's mother and uncle. As for foreign affairs, the inexperienced advisers seem to have decided to maintain a semblance of continuity by sending Harkhuf on his fourth (and final) journey to Yam. But gone, it seems, was the intelligence-gathering motive of earlier missions. Instead, this was to be an old-fashioned trade expedition, its objective to bring back exotic tribute for the new sovereign. This act of homage would serve publicly to proclaim Egypt's continued authority over neighboring lands, even as that authority ebbed away. It was the ancient Egyptian equivalent of fiddling while Rome burned.

Harkhuf abided loyally by his new orders and found just the trophy to delight his six-year-old monarch: "a pygmy of the god's dances from the land of the horizon dwellers."[8] News of this dancing pygmy from the ends of the earth reached the boy king back in Egypt. Pepi II hurriedly penned an excited letter to Harkhuf, urging him to hurry back to the royal residence with his precious human bauble:

> Come northward to the residence immediately! Hurry and bring this pygmy with you . . . to delight the heart of the Dual King Neferkara, who lives forever. When he goes down with you into the ship, appoint excellent people to be around him on both sides of the ship, lest he fall into the water! When he lies down at night, appoint excellent people to lie around him in his hammock. Inspect ten times per night! My Majesty wants to see this pygmy more than the tribute of the Sinai and Punt![9]

Receiving personal correspondence from the king (albeit a boy of six) was the ultimate accolade for an Egyptian official. Harkhuf had the complete text of the royal letter inscribed on the façade of his tomb, in pride of place next to the account of his four epic expeditions. It was to stand as an eternal testament to his sovereign's favor.

Pepi II's boyish exuberance may have touched the heart of an old retainer, but it was hardly an effective remedy for a country beset by problems, internal and external. In Nubia, the coalition of states first reported by Harkhuf in the reign of Merenra grew increasingly powerful and increasingly troublesome to Egyptian interests. One of Pepi's senior officials, the chancellor Mehu, was killed by hostile locals while on an expedition to Nubia, and his body had to be retrieved by his son in the course of a difficult mission. Although the Egyptian presence remained strong in the Dakhla Oasis, Egypt had effectively lost control of events in Nubia.

At home, too, authority was slipping from the government's grasp.

The devolution of political power to provincial officials, instigated in the late Fifth Dynasty, had proved both unwise and unstoppable. Local bigwigs—some now calling themselves "great overlord" of their province—were amassing ever more authority, arrogating to themselves a combination of civil and religious offices. When a mere local magistrate like Pepiankh of Meir could revel in a list of dignities that covered an entire wall of his tomb—member of the elite, high official, councilor, keeper of Nekhen, head man of Nekheb, chief justice and vizier, chief scribe of the royal tablet, royal seal bearer, attendant of the Apis, spokesman of every resident of Pe, overseer of the two granaries, overseer of the two purification rooms, overseer of the storehouse, senior administrator, scribe of the royal tablet of the court, god's seal bearer, sole companion, lector-priest, overseer of Upper Egypt in the middle nomes, royal chamberlain, staff of commoners, pillar of Kenmut, priest of Maat, privy to the secret of every royal command, and favorite of the king in every place of his—then, clearly, the system was out of control. Officials were now so busy feathering their own nests and ensuring their own eternal existence that they neglected the future well-being of the Egyptian state. In matters of traditional royal patronage, too, the central government seems to have lost its way. Outwardly, Pepi II's pyramid was the model of a Sixth Dynasty royal monument, complete with Pyramid Texts. But much of the decoration of the pyramid temple was slavishly copied from Sahura's complex at Abusir. With artistic creativity stalled, looking back to an earlier golden age was an easy refuge for an administration that had lost its way.

To compound the difficulties caused by a weak administration headed by an ineffectual king, a prolonged period of low Nile floods wreaked havoc with Egypt's agricultural economy. So marked was the drought that the level of Birket Qarun dropped alarmingly, forcing the abandonment of the nearby basalt quarries that had supplied the state's building projects throughout the Old Kingdom. The lakeshore was now simply too far from the quarry site to make the transportation of huge granite blocks practicable. The inadequate inundations caused widespread crop failure and economic stress on a national scale. In happier times, an effective government could have taken action to alleviate hardship, releasing stocks of grain from the state granaries to feed its hungry population. But Pepi II's regime seems to have been unable to respond adequately, crippled by inaction. In later periods, Pepi II would be remembered in scurrilous stories as a weak, ineffectual, effeminate ruler, sidetracked from the business of government by a clandestine affair with his army general.

In truth, much of the problem did indeed lie with the king—not his sexual preferences but his sheer longevity. Usually, a long reign was the sign of a stable dynasty. But Pepi II's six or more decades on the throne (2260–2175) caused major problems for the succession. Not only did the king see ten viziers come and go, but he outlived so many of his heirs that the royal family struggled to find a single candidate who could command widespread support. Egypt was set on an unstoppable course toward political fragmentation. The young monarch full of boyish exuberance had become a frail old man. In theory immortal (and he must increasingly have seemed so to his subjects), in practice he had gone on too long. His passing, when it finally came, marked both the end of a life and the end of an era. The Old Kingdom had run its course.

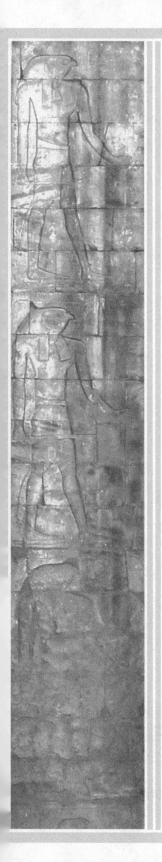

PART II

END OF INNOCENCE

(2175–1541 B.C.)

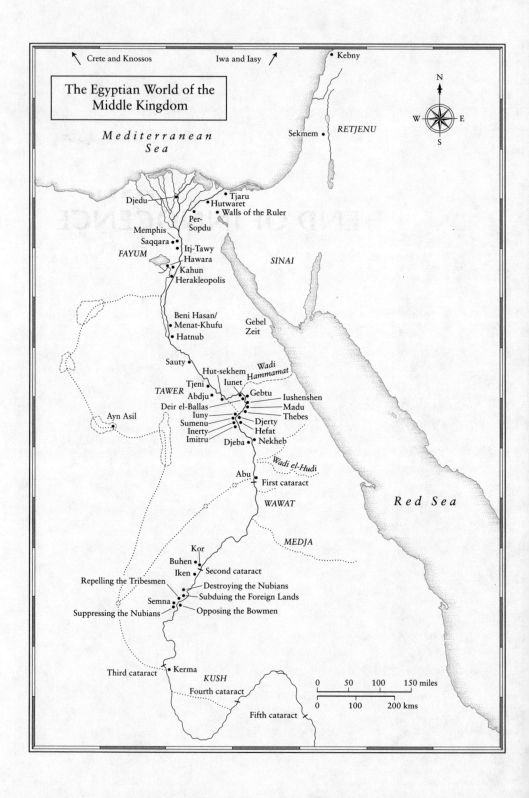

↖ Crete and Knossos   Iwa and Iasy ↗   • Kebny

The Egyptian World of the Middle Kingdom

Mediterranean Sea

N
W   E
S

Sekmem •   *RETJENU*

Djedu •
• Tjaru
• Hutwaret
Per-Sopdu •   • Walls of the Ruler

Memphis •
Saqqara •   • Itj-Tawy
FAYUM   • Hawara
• Kahun
• Herakleopolis

SINAI

Beni Hasan/
• Menat-Khufu
• Hatnub

Gebel Zeit

Sauty •

Hut-sekhem
Wadi Hammamat
Tjeni •   Iunet
TAWER   Abdju •
Deir el-Ballas •   • Gebtu   • Iushenshen
Iuny •   • Madu
Ayn Asil   Sumenu •   • Djerty   • Thebes
Inerty •   • Hefat
Imitru •   Djeba •   • Nekheb

Wadi el-Hudi

Abu •   ✝ First cataract

WAWAT

MEDJA

Red Sea

Kor •
Buhen •
Iken •   Second cataract
Repelling the Tribesmen   Destroying the Nubians
Subduing the Foreign Lands
Semna •   Opposing the Bowmen
Suppressing the Nubians

Third cataract   • Kerma   *KUSH*
Fourth cataract

Fifth cataract ✕

0   50   100   150 miles
0   100   200 kms

OUR VIEW OF ANCIENT EGYPT IS PROFOUNDLY SHAPED BY THE surviving monuments. The Old Kingdom with its pyramids and the New Kingdom with its temples and tombs loom large in the popular imagination, while the centuries in between, largely devoid of monumental architecture, are barely acknowledged, a forgotten dark age. Yet the social and political developments that took place during this neglected period had a deep and lasting effect on the trajectory of ancient Egyptian history. The weaknesses of a hereditary monarchy, the threat posed by climate change, the dangers of uncontrolled immigration, and the unforeseen consequences of closer foreign ties—all were brought home to the Egyptians in harsh lessons that would test their civilization to the breaking point.

Amid this chaos, however, Egypt witnessed a second great cultural flowering. The Middle Kingdom was the golden age of literature, when many of the great classics were composed. From the heroic *Tale of Sinuhe* to the rollicking yarn of *The Shipwrecked Sailor,* from the overtly propagandist *Prophecies of Neferti* to the subtle rhetoric of *The Eloquent Peasant,* and from the metaphysical *Dispute Between a Man and His Soul* to the burlesque *Satire of the Trades,* the literary output of the Middle Kingdom reveals ancient Egyptian society at its most complex and sophisticated. Archaeological evidence is prosaic and unsentimental, whereas the surviving writings of the ancient Egyptians allow us to enter into their imaginations, to see the world as they saw it. For this reason the Middle Kingdom seems more immediate, more tangible than many other periods of Egyptian history. For once, we can taste its flavor.

It was also a time of unrivaled craftsmanship in jewelry and statuary, of international trade and conquest. The city of Thebes rose from provincial obscurity to a position of national prominence. Much of

Nubia was conquered and annexed. Egypt emerged on the world stage, foreshadowing its later imperial expansion. The end of the Pyramid Age and the collapse of central authority in the First Intermediate Period might have presaged the terminal decline of ancient Egypt. In fact, they brought about a renaissance, albeit one with a harder edge.

Part II traces the extraordinary ups and downs of Egyptian civilization in the six centuries between the end of the Old Kingdom and the beginning of the New Kingdom. For the pharaonic state, court culture, and the lives of ordinary Egyptians it was a roller-coaster ride: from political fragmentation and civil war to the restoration of centralized control and cultural renewal, then foreign invasion and the threat of total extinction. In such turbulent times, the Egyptians' illusions about their place in the world were rudely shattered. Yet far from undermining pharaonic civilization, this collective loss of confidence in the old certainties proved a fertile breeding ground for new ideas.

So, too, did the rise of the regions and the influence of local traditions. Afterlife beliefs and burial customs, in particular, underwent profound changes in this climate of innovation, with concepts previously reserved for the king being adopted by the wider population, then adapted, elaborated, and codified. In an uncertain world, the promise of an afterlife for all offered a grain of comfort. The result was a set of tenets and practices that would endure for the rest of ancient Egyptian history and influence later religions, including Christianity.

In the political sphere, the shock of civil war and its lingering aftermath prompted a security clampdown and the introduction of repressive measures throughout the Nile Valley. Despotic, autocractic rule was the prevailing zeitgeist of the the Middle Kingdom. More than any other period of pharaonic history, it challenges our rose-tinted view of ancient Egypt.

CHAPTER 6

CIVIL WAR

APRÈS MOI LE DÉLUGE

THE DEATH OF PEPI II IN 2175, AFTER A REIGN OF RECORD LENGTH, provoked a dynastic crisis more serious than anything Egypt had faced since the foundation of the state, nearly a thousand years earlier. Disputes over the succession had flared up periodically during the Old Kingdom, but even in the aftermath of palace coups, the powerful forces of conservatism within the royal court had always managed to reimpose order and restore the status quo. This time it was different. Pepi's designated successor, his son Nemtyemsaf II, did indeed ascend to the throne, but his reign was short. He must have been a very old man himself by the time his centenarian father died. The next ruler, Neitiqerty Siptah, was of uncertain descent, and we cannot even be certain about gender: the name suggests a man, but later tradition identified Neitiqerty as a reigning queen! It was symptomatic of the confusion that now descended on the royal family, the government, and Egypt as a whole. State building projects ground to a halt, and so did foreign expeditions in search of booty. Preoccupied with troubles at home, the faltering government had no appetite for adventures abroad. At the remote outpost of Ayn Asil, in the Dakhla Oasis, for generations a bulwark against foreign infiltration, arson gutted the governor's palace and destroyed part of the northern town. The desert outposts were abandoned, and with them Egypt's forward defenses. The civilization of the pyramid builders had reached a nadir.

After Neitiqerty (who left no monuments or even inscriptions), the throne passed from one weak ruler to another, as almost anyone with a drop of royal blood in their veins—and no doubt several individuals who had none—pressed their claim. In a period of just twenty years, less than a generation after Pepi II's demise, Egypt saw seventeen kings come and go. Ten of their reigns together spanned a trifling six years. Little wonder that later chroniclers were heartily confused and ended up inventing a wholly spurious Seventh Dynasty. Not that the Eighth—those seventeen ephemeral "monarchs" in succession to Nemtyemsaf II—was really worthy of the title. Five of its kings tried vainly to project an air of legitimacy by adopting the throne name of Pepi II (Neferkara) as their own; one looked back to an even earlier king of the Fifth Dynasty; but all succumbed in short order to the force of rival claimants. Most of the royal inscriptions that have survived from this extraordinary phase of ancient Egyptian history are dated to the first year of a king's reign. It is as if, knowing that he was unlikely to last long in the post, each new ruler got down to business as quickly as possible, exercising what little authority remained to him before it was stolen away. So we see an otherwise unknown King Iti sponsoring a quarrying expedition to the Wadi Hammamat, to bring back stone for a pyramid that was never built. Another ruler, Iyemhotep, sent expeditions both as crown prince and as king but likewise left no permanent memorial.

The only king of the Eighth Dynasty who managed both to survive more than a year in office—two years, one month, and a day, to be precise—and to leave behind a monument of sorts was Ibi. (From the Fifth Dynasty onward, Egyptian monarchs seem to have had a curious fondness for personal names that sound babyish to our ears, from Izi and Ini to Teti and Pepi, Nebi, Iti, and Ibi. Perhaps this tells us something about the cosseted atmosphere inside the royal apartments.) We can well imagine the feverish activity that gripped the court and what remained of the royal workshops when the newly enthroned king announced his plans for a pyramid at Saqqara, traditional burial place of monarchs since the time of Netjerikhet. Recent experience showed that time was of the essence. In response to the new realities of kingship, Ibi's architects proposed a monument that might be completed before the wheel of fortune turned once more, bringing yet another ruler to power. The result was hardly a pyramid at all in the expected sense of the word. Although sited in deliberate proximity to the pyramid of Pepi II, it was diminutive by the standards of the Old Kingdom. At 103 feet (60 ancient Egyptian cubits) square at the base, and with a projected height of just 60 feet, it was the same size as the pyramids of

Pepi II's queens—quite a comedown for someone claiming to be the son of Ra. To facilitate the speediest possible construction, the core was built from mud, small stones, and chips of limestone, hardly a recipe for stability or longevity. The descending corridor and underground burial chamber were carved with selections from the Pyramid Texts, and a mud brick chapel was built against the pyramid's eastern face to serve as a mortuary temple. But the outer casing was never even started; time had caught up with Ibi. He would be the only one of Pepi II's direct successors even to attempt pyramid building.

In other ways, too, in defiance of its own impotence, the administration carried on in public as if nothing had changed. The most remarkable documents to survive from the Eighth Dynasty are a collection of royal decrees from the temple of Min at Gebtu, on the east bank of the Nile in Upper Egypt. Since prehistoric times, Gebtu had flourished as the gateway to the Eastern Desert and its abundant mineral resources. The local fertility god, Min, had been adopted as a national deity early in Egyptian history, and his cult center received royal patronage from the very beginning of the First Dynasty. Toward the end of the Old Kingdom, Pepi I and Pepi II added to the temple buildings and endowments. Their successors of the late Eighth Dynasty maintained this tradition, but to very different ends. King Neferkaura, for instance, issued three decrees for public display in the temple. Their purpose was not to augment the temple's estates or safeguard its personnel from government service, but something altogether more practical and political—to announce the promotion of a royal lackey, Shemai, to the governorship of Upper Egypt. Shemai would have responsibility for all twenty-two provinces from the first cataract to the outskirts of Memphis—and to confirm the succession of his son, Idy, as nomarch (provincial governor) of Gebtu. The weak rulers of the Eighth Dynasty needed all the friends they could muster, and were not averse to using royal privilege to honor and reward their supporters in the regions.

This debasement of monarchy was carried even further by Neferkaura's successor, Neferkauhor. In the space of a single day, probably the very day of his accession to the throne (circa 2155), the king issued no fewer than eight decrees to be displayed in the temple at Gebtu. All eight were again concerned with promoting and honoring Shemai and members of his family. Shemai himself was promoted to the office of vizier, while his son succeeded him as governor of Upper Egypt (albeit with a considerably reduced remit). Another son was appointed to a position on the temple staff, a decision commemorated in three separate decrees, one addressed to each male member of the family. A further edict assigned mortuary priests to Shemai and his wife, a privilege previously reserved only for royalty. In a similar vein, their funerary monuments were made from red granite, a material with strong solar connotations and subject to a royal monopoly. The reason for all these honors was made plain in the first of Neferkauhor's decrees, in which he stipulated the titles and dignities to be borne by Shemai's wife, Nebet. For she was none other than the king's eldest daughter and the king's sole favorite. As soon as Neferkauhor gained the throne, he clearly decided to use his brief period of power to shower his immediate relatives with awards and royal favors. It was the classic behavior of a tin-pot dictator.

The last of the Gebtu decrees, dated to the reign of Neferkauhor's successor Neferirkara, forbade anyone to damage the funerary monuments of Shemai and Nebet's son Idy (now promoted to vizier), or to diminish his offerings. Though issued from the national capital, it was the last gasp of the Memphite monarchy. Its craven favoritism signaled "the almost abject dependence of the Pharaohs at Memphis upon the loyalty of the powerful landed nobility of Upper Egypt."[1] Despite the apparent maintenance of economic stability and the associated prosperity of local cults like that of Min at Gebtu, royal power was waning fast. In the person of Neferirkara—named after an illustrious monarch of the Fifth Dynasty, but in reality a king of shreds and patches—the system of royal government that had served Egypt for a millennium had come to an inglorious end. The political elite and the country at large were totally unprepared for what might follow.

BIG MEN, BIG IDEAS

WITH THE COLLAPSE OF CENTRAL AUTHORITY, EGYPT FRAGMENTED along regional lines, returning to the pattern that had existed before the foundation of the state a thousand years earlier. As before, the geography of the Nile Valley—in particular the distribution of irrigation basins—was the main determining factor. The three southernmost provinces formed one natural unit, provinces four and five another, and so on downriver. The political and economic aggrandizement of the provincial governors (nomarchs), a process that had started centuries earlier, reached its logical conclusion as various local potentates declared de facto independence. However, kingship as a model of government was so ingrained in the Egyptian psyche that its replacement by something different was philosophically and theologically impossible. So it was inevitable that one of this new cohort of rulers, even if his authority was strictly limited in extent, would claim royal titles and be acknowledged, grudgingly, as suzerain—or, rather, first among equals—by his fellow leaders.

The strongman who achieved this recognition of sorts came from the town of Herakleopolis (modern Ihnasya el-Medina) in Middle Egypt. Named Kheti, he was said by the later Egyptian historian Manetho to have been more terrible than any previous king, this verdict reflecting, perhaps, a would-be dynast who pursued his claim to the throne by force, browbeating any opposition into submission. The house of Kheti would reign for a century and a half (2125–1975)—reign, but not rule. Even in its own realm the new dynasty was not universally acknowledged or approved. At the heart of Herakleopolitan power, a local potentate with royal pretensions, "King Khui," built a massive mud brick tomb, equal in size to many Old Kingdom pyramids—and this act of daring lèse-majesté just a stone's throw from Sauty (modern Asyut), the city most loyal to the Herakleopolitan dynasty. At the nearby alabaster quarries of Hatnub, the nomarchs dated their expeditions by the years of their own tenure, avoiding all reference to a royal reign. In their tomb autobiographies at Beni Hasan and elsewhere, officials rarely if ever mentioned the king, and were conspicuously silent about their own careers, completely out of character for an ancient Egyptian, and a sure sign of wavering loyalties. With such unpopularity in their heartland, Kheti and his descendants were living in a dream world if they imagined their nominal authority would remain unchallenged for long.

What dealt their authority a fatal blow was the dynasty's inability to carry out the most basic duty of kingship—to feed the people. A series of low Niles had weakened the state economy in the reign of Pepi II. Now, in the absence of an effective national government, the long-term effects of poor inundations started to be felt. Famine stalked the land, challenging the ability of provincial governors to look after their own citizens. Some undoubtedly played up the crisis to further their own careers. By acting the savior in a time of trouble, they won both local support and wider renown. A man named Merer boasted that "I buried the dead and fed the living wherever I went in this famine that happened."[2] A contemporary, Iti, let it be known that he fed his hometown, Imitru, "in the painful years" and "gave Upper Egyptian barley to Iuny and to Hefat, [but only] after feeding Imitru."[3]

Ankhtifi, governor of the third Upper Egyptian province, with its capital at Hefat (modern Moalla), went even further, claiming to have sent emergency aid supplies to affected areas from Abdju, in the north, to Abu, in the south. He presented himself as the natural leader of the seven southernmost provinces, the very same region that had been assigned to the governor of Upper Egypt in the dying days of the Eighth Dynasty. If he had proved himself capable of looking after the population when "all of Upper Egypt was dying of hunger,"[4] then surely he was qualified to be their political master as well. Indeed, Ankhtifi's longterm ambitions stretched far beyond his own province. In his tomb at Hefat, cut into the side of a natural hill shaped like a pyramid (the only fitting resting place for a true Egyptian ruler), he inscribed the details of his career, so that all posterity might remember his achievements.

Ankhtifi had shown an early talent for calculated maneuvers. Even before gaining high office, he had invited the council of the overseer of Upper Egypt, based at Tjeni, to carry out a visit of inspection of his province. No doubt this had given him the opportunity to curry favor with the Herakleopolitan government and, at the same time, to assess its strengths and weaknesses. Having weighed the likely opposition, Ankhtifi had begun his steady rise to power as soon as he'd succeeded as nomarch. First, he'd annexed the neighboring province of Djeba, under the pretense of rescuing it from mismanagement (always a convenient excuse for a landgrab). In his own version of events, he displaced the previous governor, Khuu, in accordance with divine providence:

Horus brought me to the province of Djeba for life, prosperity, and health, to set it in order. . . . I found the house of Khuu . . . in the

grip of tumult, governed by a wretch. I made a man embrace his father's killer, his brother's killer, in order to set the province of Djeba
in order. . . . Every form of evil that the people hate has been suppressed.[5]

Ankhtifi then proceeded to form a strategic alliance (no doubt backed
up with the threat of force) with the province of Abu, to give him effective control of the three southernmost provinces. Together, these
provinces formed the perfect springboard for his wider territorial ambitions, and all the while Ankhtifi publicly maintained his loyalty to the
king in Herakleopolis.

But while Djeba and Abu had proved relatively easy to bring to heel,
the fourth and fifth nomes, based at Thebes and Gebtu, were an entirely different proposition, not least because they had formed a defensive alliance against just such an attack. Massing his forces on his
northern border, Ankhtifi launched an assault against the province of
Thebes. His army destroyed the garrison fortress at Iuny and roamed
at will through the desert to the west of Thebes, the city's back door.
The Thebans refused to come out and engage the enemy, biding their
time. Ankhtifi took this reticence as a sign of weakness, but he could
not have been more wrong. Within a few years, all three of Ankhtifi's
provinces would fall under Theban domination. Thebes, not Hefat,
would be the launchpad for a campaign of national reunification.

THEBAN ASCENDANCY

OSTENSIBLY, THE GOVERNOR OF THE THEBAN PROVINCE, TOO, WAS
loyal to the Herakleopolitan overlord. Ankhtifi's contemporary, Intef
the Great of Thebes, publicly professed himself the beloved of the
king. He even agreed to Thebes's being represented at a great conference of nomarchs summoned by the Herakleopolitan authorities, perhaps in response to Ankhtifi's military aggression. It is significant that
Intef did not himself attend, instead sending the overseer of his army.
By participating, but not in person, Intef delivered a carefully calculated message to his fellow nomarchs and the Herakleopolitan king:
here was a ruler with a substantial private army who had better, and
more pressing, things to do with his time than sit around a table with

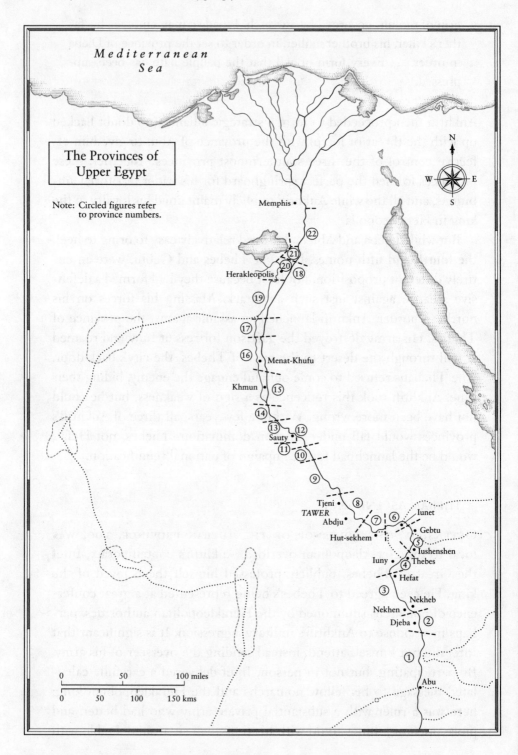

Mediterranean Sea

The Provinces of
Upper Egypt

Note: Circled figures refer
to province numbers.

N
W   E
S

Memphis •

㉒

㉑
⑳
Herakleopolis ⑱
⑲
⑰
⑯ • Menat-Khufu
Khmun • ⑮
⑭
⑬
Sauty ⑫
⑪
⑩
⑨
Tjeni • ⑧   • Iunet
TAWER ⑦ ⑥
Abdju •   • Gebtu
Hut-sekhem • ⑤ • Iushenshen
Iuny • ④ • Thebes
Hefat •
③
     • Nekheb
Nekhen • ②
Djeba • ②

①

Abu •

0   50   100 miles
0 50 100 150 kms

mere provincial governors. Protestations of fealty were easily made. They did not change the fact that Intef was busily engaged in strategic maneuvers to strengthen Thebes and position it as the head of a grand alliance. A strong signal of Intef's true intentions was his adoption of the title "great overlord of Upper Egypt," not merely of Thebes. At least one other province, that of Iunet, understood the message and threw its weight behind Intef, recognizing his authority as a regional power broker.

Iunet's defection was a serious blow to the Herakleopolitan kingdom. Ever since the rise of the house of Kheti, the province of Iunet had been steadfastly loyal to the dynasty. Its governor had ensured the continued allegiance not only of his own province, but of the two neighboring provinces as well. Now, with Theban power in the ascendant, the Herakleopolitans faced the secession of their entire southern domain. Their response was highly political and potentially incendiary: the installation of a loyal governor in the province of Gebtu, sandwiched between Thebes, to the south, and Iunet, to the north. In reality, there were few other options but to keep a tight watch on Theban ambitions. The new appointee, User, recognized the importance of his task and moved his provincial capital from the traditional seat at Gebtu to the town of Iushenshen (modern Khozam), right on the boundary with the Theban province. From here, he could literally look the enemy in the eye.

The province of Gebtu was of great strategic importance. Not only was it the gateway to the Eastern Desert, but its leaders also exercised jurisdiction over the routes through the Western Desert. These led to the Saharan oases, departing the Nile Valley from a point on the west bank directly opposite Iushenshen. User and his royal masters knew very well that Thebes had already established a military presence in the Western Desert, since the Thebans had contributed a desert garrison to the defensive alliance against Ankhtifi. It was vital that they should not be allowed to expand this toehold. If Thebes ever won control of the Western Desert routes, its rulers would be able to bypass any opposition along the Nile Valley and gain direct overland access to the holy city of Abdju, jewel in the Herakleopolitan crown and seat of the governor of Upper Egypt. Such a calamity would surely be the beginning of the end for the house of Kheti.

Responding to the situation, as ever, with a carefully calculated piece of propaganda, Intef of Thebes announced his intentions by adding yet another new title to his growing list of epithets. (He was nothing if not a typical ancient Egyptian.) By calling himself "the confidant of the king in the narrow door of the southern desert,"[6] he was directly challenging User's role as "overseer of the Eastern and Western deserts." The Thebes-Gebtu alliance, always a marriage of convenience, was formally dissolved. In its place, the two provinces now vied openly for control of the all-important desert routes. Before long, the war of words escalated into outright conflict. Thebes launched a raid across the border, destroying the town of Iushenshen. Gebtu put up stiff resistance, expelling the invaders and capturing some of their soldiers. The chief priest of Gebtu ordered the rebuilding of Iushenshen, but there could be little doubt that this was only the first salvo in what would be a protracted campaign of Theban aggression. The people of Gebtu steeled themselves for the fight they knew must come.

Prominent among the prisoners of war captured during the attack on Iushenshen were people of Medja and Wawat, Nubian mercenaries serving in the Theban army. Ever since Egypt's campaigns against the sand dwellers in the early Sixth Dynasty, Nubian recruits had played an important role in Egyptian military strategy. Nubian archers, especially, were noted for their bravery and prowess. Many a young Nubian man knew he could achieve far greater wealth and renown by joining a foreign army than by staying in his impoverished homeland. (The role of the Nepalese Gurkhas in the British Army is an instructive modern parallel.) While all factions in the conflicts of the First Intermediate Period may have employed Nubian mercenaries to a greater or lesser extent, only the Thebans made them a central element in their offensive capability. An entire colony of Nubian soldiers was established at Inerty, on the southern edge of the Theban province. While adopting Egyptian burial customs, they nevertheless retained a strong sense of their own cultural identity, an unusual exception to the normal pattern of complete assimilation. Clearly, their status in society as brave warriors was enhanced by the very fact of their Nubian ethnicity. In time of war, old prejudices were dissipating. Egyptian civilization was being transformed from the inside in unexpected ways.

Cometh the hour, cometh the man. User's successor as nomarch of

Gebtu, a man named Tjauti, was as determined a leader as his royal masters could have wished for. Tjauti's exploits in resisting Theban expansion have only recently come to light, inscribed on a remote cliffside in the Western Desert. The inscription tells of his heroic struggle to keep the desert routes open to Herakleopolitan forces, and his implacable opposition to Thebes. Styling himself "the confidant of the king in the door of the Upper Egyptian desert"[7]—a title deliberately antagonistic to Intef's own claims—Tjauti threw down a direct challenge to his Theban opponent. Both sides knew that the Western Desert routes across the great Qena bend were the key objective—in Theban hands, Abdju and all of Middle Egypt would be vulnerable to attack; in Herakleopolitan hands, the main population centers of western Thebes would be dangerously exposed. It must have come as a bitter blow to the morale of Gebtu when Intef the Great's successor as Theban leader, another Intef (the popularity of the name at this time can be decidedly confusing), seized control of an important mountaintop overlooking the main desert road, effectively closing it to traffic. Tjauti's response was immediate and inspired: he simply constructed another parallel road, a short distance to the north, with its eastern terminus safely within the territory of Gebtu. In his own words: "I have done this in order to cross this hill country that the ruler of another province sealed."[8]

But Tjauti's success was to be short-lived. Ironically, his decisive action in building a new, improved desert road was the cause of his own downfall. Just a few yards away from his commemorative inscription is another, much shorter text. It reads, simply, "the son of Ra, Intef." It marks the Theban capture of Tjauti's new road, no doubt in a swift operation launched from one of their desert garrisons. With Gebtu's control of the Western Desert swept away, nothing now stood between Thebes and Abdju, the administrative capital of Upper Egypt and the ancient burial place of kings. In this context, Intef's new title, son of Ra, is highly significant. Unlike his predecessors, he was not merely content with the style and dignity of a provincial or even regional governor. He now aspired to kingship. By claiming the ancient moniker of sovereign for himself, "King" Intef had issued a direct challenge to the house of Kheti. The prize was nothing less than the throne of Horus.

ON THE FRONT LINE

CONFIDENT THE THEBANS MIGHT HAVE BEEN, BUT THEIR OPPONENTS were not about to give up the kingship without a fight. The Egyptian civil war, once formally declared, dragged on for more than a century (2080–1970), coloring the lives of four generations. The martial character of the age is powerfully reflected in the monuments of the time: in tombs, scenes of soldiers are common; on stelae (commemorative slabs), many individuals had themselves shown with bow and arrow in hand; and grave goods often included actual weapons. Never before had Egyptian society been so militarized. It is also unusual that a number of commemorative inscriptions from both sides of the conflict allow us to reconstruct the progress of the war, with its victories and setbacks for the Thebans and Herakleopolitans alike.

Winning control of the desert routes across the Qena bend seems to have been the principal achievement of the first King Intef. In any case, his self-styled reign lasted little more than a decade, but he had at least made a decisive strategic breakthrough, providing a platform for further Theban expansion. His son and successor, Intef II, lost no time in picking up the baton and prosecuting the war with a renewed intensity. His evident charisma and leadership qualities inspired fanatical loyalty among his closest lieutenants. One, Heni, boasts of having attended his master day and night. Such devotion made for a close-knit fighting force, and brought swift success.

But before Thebes could be confident in taking on the might of the loyalist forces north of Abdju, it had to secure its southern flank. So the first objective was to consolidate Theban control over the erstwhile power base of Ankhtifi. Either late in the nomarch's life or shortly after his death the local population saw the writing on the wall and threw in their lot with Thebes. The famine, which may still have been raging, and the general impoverishment suffered by the population may have been contributory factors. The people clearly felt that their future would be more secure (or less insecure) if they were Intef II's liege men. At the same time, Thebes succeeded in expanding its control northward to encompass the three neighboring provinces of Gebtu, Iunet, and Hut-sekhem. In fulfillment of the claim made by his grandfather, Intef the Great, Intef II was now truly the great overlord of Upper

Egypt, and recognized as such throughout the "head of the south," the seven southernmost provinces from Abu to the outskirts of Abdju.

Hence, by the middle of Intef II's reign (circa 2045), the northern border of the Theban realm lay close to Abdju. Tawer (the province of Tjeni) became the new front line in the civil war, and the desert routes that gave direct access between Thebes and Abdju finally came into their own. One Theban supporter records a military expedition traveling "in the dust" to attack Tawer,[9] while another recounts the ensuing battle and the expulsion of the Herakleopolitans' loyal governor: "I descended upon Abdju, which was under [the control of] a rebel. I made him go down to his [own] realm from the midst of the town."[10] It is telling that the language of the Thebans has already shifted from rivalry to restoration. The case for Theban hegemony could be made to appear so much more compelling if the Herakleopolitan dynasty (which considered itself the legitimate successor of the Old Kingdom monarchy) were characterized as "the rebel." Theban expansion could then be cast as the removal of an affront to established order. Representing power as piety was always a favorite trick of ancient Egyptian propagandists.

To reinforce their military victory, the Thebans imposed taxes throughout Tawer and delivered the revenue back to Thebes. Buoyed by this success, Intef II used his control of Abu to strike southward into lower Nubia, reimposing Egyptian authority over the lands beyond the first cataract for the first time in more than a century. The Theban advance seemed unstoppable.

But events have a habit of turning against those who think themselves invincible. At Sauty, in Middle Egypt, a family of nomarchs with particularly close connections to the Herakleopolitan rulers now took up the loyalist banner to fight against the upstart Thebans. Back in the days before the civil war, Sauty had been governed by a man named— in honor of his sovereign—Kheti. He had been brought up in the royal circle as a pupil of the king and had even received swimming lessons with the royal children. On achieving high office, Kheti had devoted himself to improving the lot of his people, commissioning extensive irrigation works throughout his province to alleviate the worst effects of the famine. In his tomb is the inscription, "I let loose the inundation upon the old mounds. . . . Everyone who thirsted had inundation to his heart's desire. I gave water to his neighbors so that he was content with them."[11]

This Kheti's successor, Itibi, now found himself confronted by an even greater challenge, Theban aggression, and he was equally determined to triumph over adversity. So he responded to Intef II's raid on Abdju with a fierce counterattack. This achieved its primary objective of wresting back control of Tawer, but at a dreadful cost: the holy site of Abdju was desecrated during the fighting. Such an act of sacrilege was a grievous stain on the mantle of kingship, a transgression against the gods for which the Herakleopolitan monarch would repent at length. It would come to be seen in later times as the event that finally tipped the balance in favor of Thebes. But the immediate result was a victory for Itibi's forces. An attempted Theban reprisal was repulsed, and this second success gave Itibi the confidence to issue a direct communiqué to the head of the south, in which he threatened further force unless the rebellious provinces returned to the loyalist fold. Itibi's own autobiography tells the story of what happened next. The section containing his written challenge to the southern nomes was subsequently plastered over, to hide it from view and thus avoid Theban reprisals against the townspeople of Sauty for harboring such a determined opponent. Whether this tactical rewriting of history was carried out on the orders of Itibi himself or on the orders of his descendants, it suggests that, not long after his famous victories, the pendulum swung back again to Thebes's advantage.

The reversal of fortune was due, in no small measure, to Intef II's skill as a military strategist. He soon realized that Tawer was a potential quagmire for his army. Trying to capture and hold on to Abdju could easily pin down his forces for years, allowing the Herakleopolitan forces to strengthen and regroup. A flanking maneuver, bold and dangerous as it might be, was the only way to break the impasse. Once Tawer had been severed from the rest of the Herakleopolitan realm, it would be far easier to pacify. In the last decade of his long fifty-year reign, Intef II put his plan into action. Using his command of desert routes to advance around Tawer, he established a new defensive position two provinces to the north. Cut off from assistance, Tjeni and Abdju proved much easier targets and were swiftly conquered. To mark his victory, Intef sent a letter to his rival in Herakleopolis, accusing

The funerary stela of Intef II THE METROPOLITAN MUSEUM OF ART © PHOTO SCALA, FLORENCE

King Kheti of having raised a storm over Tawer. The message was clear. By failing to protect the sacred sites of Abdju, Kheti had forfeited his right to the kingship.

By contrast, Intef was determined to show that he was a just king as well as a mighty conqueror. Fierce in battle, magnanimous in victory, he demonstrated his determination to win the battle for hearts and minds by distributing food aid throughout the ten provinces of his new realm. In this way, one of his close associates could claim to be "a great provider for the homeland in a lean year."[12] Naturally, there was a good measure of psychological warfare in such pronouncements. But Intef's piety seems to have been genuine. His magnificent funerary stela, erected in his rock cut tomb at Thebes, is noteworthy not for its list of battle honors (the events of the civil war are conspicuous by their absence) but for its extraordinary hymn to the sun god Ra and to Hathor, the protector goddess who was believed to reside in the Theban hills. The verse hints at a human frailty and a fear of death lying behind the visage of a great war leader:

> Entrust [me] to the evening hours:
> May they protect me;
> Entrust [me] to early morning:
> May it put its protection around me;

I am the nursling of early morning,
I am the nursling of the evening hours.[13]

The death of a king was always a moment of great anxiety. How much more worrying it must have been for the Thebans when the king departing the throne was a war hero of the caliber of Intef II. And yet, a rare account of the moment of succession, recorded by the king's treasurer, Tjetji, suggests a calm transition from one reign to the next: "The dual king, son of Ra, Intef, who lives like Ra forever . . . departed in peace to his horizon. Now when his son had descended in his place . . . I followed him."[14] In fact, the new king, Intef III, was to enjoy but a brief reign of eight years (2018–2010). Theban overlordship of the deserts brought tribute from "the rulers upon the red land" (the desert chieftains), and the famine that had wracked Upper Egypt for more than fifty years seems to have been brought to an end. But while the economy prospered, the prosecution of the war stalled. An uneasy truce may have settled over the battlefield. Theban dominance in the eight southernmost provinces was absolute; Herakleopolitan rule over Middle and Lower Egypt remained unchallenged. And so it might easily have stayed, but for the fact that a divided nation was anathema to the ancient Egyptian worldview. Any king worthy of the name had to be lord of the Two Lands, not merely a provincial potentate.

REUNIFICATION AND REPRESSION

THE FINAL CONFRONTATION WAS NOT LONG IN COMING. INTEF III WAS succeeded by a young, dynamic ruler who had inherited his grandfather's tactical skill and determination. Indeed, the new king, Mentuhotep II, had been named after the Theban god of war, Montu, and was determined to live up to his billing. He chose as his Horus name the phrase Sankh-ib-tawy, "the one who brings life to the heart of the Two Lands." It clearly signaled his overriding aspiration to reunify Egypt.

Mentuhotep was helped enormously by unrest in the enemy's heartland. The new nomarch of Sauty, Kheti II, was encountering serious opposition within his own province. Only a show of force by the crown and the personal attendance of the Herakleopolitan king Merikara allowed the governor's installation to go ahead. The population of Sauty was starting to think the unthinkable, weighing the advantages of defection to the Theban side. Their embattled nomarch sailed southward at the head of a large fleet, partly as a show of force against the Thebans, partly to prove a point to his own restless population.

Then, in Mentuhotep's fourteenth year as king (circa 1996), Tawer—that persistent thorn in the Theban side—rebelled yet again. It was the final provocation. The Theban army swept northward, crushing Tawer and pushing onward into the Herakleopolitan heartland. Sauty was vanquished and its nomarch deposed. Nothing now stood between the Thebans and their ultimate prize, Herakleopolis itself. When Mentuhotep's army reached the capital of the house of Kheti, they gave full vent to their wrath, burning and destroying tombs in the city's cemetery. To drive home the point, the Theban king immediately installed one of his most trusted followers as his personal representative in Herakleopolis, putting him in charge of the city's most important building—its prison. That was the fate that lay in store for any "rebel" unfortunate enough not to have died in battle.

The ruthless treatment meted out by Mentuhotep to his opponents did not stop at the gates of Herakleopolis. In the heart of troublesome Tawer, he appointed an "overseer of constabulary on water and on land,"[15] suggesting a law-and-order crackdown against the inhabitants of this most unruly province. Another of Mentuhotep's henchmen boasts of taxing "Tawer, Tjeni, and [as far as] the back part of the tenth Upper Egyptian province"[16] for his master. This smacks of punitive economic sanctions against formerly hostile territory. Herakleopolitan loyalists who tried to escape retribution by fleeing to the oases were remorselessly hunted down. They had forgotten the Thebans' mastery of desert routes. The king himself addressed his victorious troops, urging them to pursue troublemakers, and moved to annex the oases and lower Nubia. A garrison installed in the fortress at Abu provided Mentuhotep with a springboard for campaigns against Wawat, while expeditions into the Western Desert were highly effective at disrupting potential enemy supply lines and mopping up any lingering resistance.

His external borders secured, the king could now turn his attention to matters of internal government. Situated on the east bank of the Nile at a place where cross-country routes through the Eastern and

Western deserts converged, the town of Thebes had first come to prominence at the end of the Old Kingdom. With excellent communication links, it made a natural capital for the whole of Upper Egypt. The role of its first family in the recent civil war had merely strengthened its claim to preeminent status. The town itself was still rather small and enclosed by a thick mud brick wall. The tightly packed streets of houses, granaries, offices, and workshops clustered in a grid pattern around the small temple of the god Amun-Ra at Ipetsut (modern Karnak). Like any provincial capital, Thebes had its own local administration. At its head was the mayor, assisted by officials responsible for such essential government tasks as land registration, irrigation and flood protection schemes, and taxation. Since Thebes was a commercial center of some importance, the quays along the river thronged with merchants, unloading their goods for purchase by government agents and private customers. Potters, carpenters, weavers, and tanners; butchers, bakers, and brewers—the backstreets of Thebes were filled with the sights, sounds, and smells of craft and food production (much like the backstreets of any Egyptian town today). Most inhabitants were peasant farmers who lived in simple mud brick dwellings and spent every day tilling the fields, as countless generations of their forebears had done, but the city also played host to a rising number of better-off families, a nascent middle class of tradesmen and lower-ranking bureaucrats with larger houses in the smarter neighborhoods. Had Thebes been any other provincial center, the inhabitants' horizons might have stayed rather limited, but with the city catapulted to national prominence, opportunities for advancement mushroomed. The good times had arrived.

Under Mentuhotep, the dynastic seat was formally established as the new national capital, and prominent Thebans were appointed to all the major offices of state. Administrative reforms were soon followed by theological ones. To mark the final phase in the civil war, the king had changed his Horus name to Netjeri-hedjet, "divine of the white crown," and he now embarked on a radical program of self-promotion and self-deification, designed to restore and rebuild the ideology of divine kingship that had taken such a battering in the years of internal strife. From Abdju and Iunet to Nekheb and Abu, Mentuhotep commissioned a series of ornate cult buildings, more often than not dedicated to himself as the gods' chosen one. At Iunet, he adopted the unprecedented epithet of "the living god, foremost of kings." Deification of the reigning king during his lifetime marked a new departure in royal ideology. Mentuhotep was clearly not a man for half measures.

He also used these monuments to send a stark political message to any remaining would-be rebels in Egypt's northern provinces. His chapel at Iunet showed him in the age-old pose of smiting an enemy, but the symbolic victim was represented as a pair of intertwined stems of papyrus, symbolizing Lower Egypt. The accompanying inscription emphasized the point, adding "the marshlands" to the traditional list of Egypt's enemies. A relief from Mentuhotep's shrine at Inerty, in his Theban heartland, was even more explicit. It showed a line of four kneeling captives, pathetically awaiting their fate of being clubbed to death by the king. First in line—in front of the expected Nubian, Asiatic, and Libyan—was an Egyptian, a representative of the "chiefs of the Two Lands." For Egypt's new king, national security began at home. After decades of war and paramilitary activity designed to snuff

Casualties of war WERNER FORMAN ARCHIVE

out all opposition, Mentuhotep felt secure enough to signal his indisputable status as ruler of a reunified Egypt. In typical Egyptian fashion, he did so by adopting a new title, a third version of his Horus name: Sema-tawy, "the one who unites the Two Lands." The factionalism and internal dissent of the time of distress had been consigned to history. Egypt could once again hold its head high as a unified, peaceable nation, ruled by a god-king. The Middle Kingdom had begun.

Mentuhotep's lasting memorial epitomizes his determination to reassert the cult of the ruler and project himself as the monarch who restored the tarnished reputation of kingship. In an embayment in the hills of western Thebes—the very same hills that had given his forebears their first military advantage—Mentuhotep ordered work to begin on a lavish funerary monument. As befitted a reunifier, a renaissance king, it amalgamated old and new ideas. The architecture cleverly combined elements from his forebears' Theban tombs and the Memphite pyramids of the Old Kingdom in a radical and innovative design. The decoration included scenes of battle alongside more traditional images of royalty. Surrounding the royal tomb, burials were prepared for the king's closest advisers and most loyal lieutenants. In a deliberate echo of the great Fourth Dynasty court cemetery at Giza, the king's courtiers would surround their monarch in death just as they had in life.

But the most poignant component of the entire mortuary complex was a simple, undecorated pit, cut into the rock within sight of the king's vast edifice. This was one of the first parts of Mentuhotep's grand design to be finished, and the pit contained the linen-wrapped bodies of sixty or more men, stacked one on top of another. In life, they had been strong and tall, with an average height of five feet, nine and a half inches, and between thirty and forty years old. Despite their strength, they had all succumbed to the same fate. The injuries on their bodies were mostly arrow wounds and traumas caused by heavy, rough objects falling from a great height. For these men had been soldiers, slain in battle while attacking a fortified town. Scars showed some to have been battle-hardened veterans. Yet what they'd faced in their final test was not hand-to-hand combat but siege warfare. The arrows and missiles raining down on them from the battlements had killed some outright, their tightly curled hair offering scant protection. Other soldiers, wounded but still alive, had been brutally dispatched on the battlefield by having their skulls smashed with clubs. In the heat of battle, bodies had been left for vultures to peck at and tear. Only after the battle had been won, and the town stormed, could the survivors gather up their dead (some already stiff with rigor mortis), strip them of their blood-soaked clothes, scour the bodies clean with sand, and bandage them with linen, making them ready for burial. No attempt had been made to mummify the corpses, and little distinction had been made between different ranks of the dead. The two officers had simply been bandaged rather more thoroughly and placed in simple undecorated coffins. Finally, before burial, the names of the deceased had been written in ink on their linen wrappings—good Theban names such as Ameny, Mentuhotep, and Intefiqer; intimate family names such as Senbebi ("Bebi's brother") and Sa-ipu ("Ipu's son"); and also names such as Sobekhotep, Sobeknakht, and Sehetepibsobek, which suggest an origin far from Thebes, close to the northern cult centers of the crocodile god Sobek. It seems probable that these slain soldiers, given the unique honor of a ceremonial war grave, had been involved in the decisive battle of the civil war, the final attack on Herakleopolis itself. Some of them may have been local men who nonetheless had supported the Theban army against their own rulers, and so had been especially honored.

For King Mentuhotep, conqueror of the Herakleopolitans and re-unifier of Egypt, erecting a national cenotaph close to his own tomb was a brilliantly calculated piece of propaganda. It would serve as a powerful reminder to his contemporaries, and to posterity, of the sacrifices that Thebes had made in the conflict. It would cause Mentuhotep to be forever remembered as a great war leader. And in a foretaste of his successors' mode of rule, it would cement the myth of the king and his band of brothers as the defenders of the nation.

The war grave was a harbinger of something else, too. In the brave new world of the Middle Kingdom, a glorious death would, for many, be a substitute for the joys of life.

CHAPTER 7

PARADISE POSTPONED

SOMETHING TO HOPE FOR

ANCIENT EGYPT SEEMS TO HAVE BEEN A CIVILIZATION OBSESSED WITH death. From pyramids to mummies, most of the hallmarks of Egyptian culture are connected with funerary customs. Yet, if we look more closely, it was not death itself that lay at the heart of the Egyptians' preoccupations, but rather the means of overcoming it. Pyramids were designed as resurrection machines for Egyptian kings. Mummies were created to provide permanent homes for the undying spirits of the dead. And if mortuary beliefs and grave goods dominate modern views of ancient Egypt, it is only, perhaps, because cemeteries located on the desert edge have survived rather better than towns and villages on the floodplain. Tombs have provided generations of archaeologists with rich and relatively easy pickings, while the excavation of ancient settlements is difficult, laborious, and decidedly less glamorous. Nonetheless, the importance of afterlife beliefs and customs to the ancient Egyptians cannot be waved away as a mere accident of archaeological preservation. Proper preparation for the next world was deemed an essential task if death was not to bring about utter annihilation.

Although the hope of an afterlife, and the necessary preparations for it, can be traced back to Egypt's earliest prehistoric cultures, the century or more of political unrest (2175–1970) following the collapse of the Old Kingdom marked a watershed in the long-term development of ancient Egyptian funerary religion. Many of the characteristic features, beliefs, and practices that would survive until the very end of pharaonic civilization were forged in the crucible of social change that accompanied the period of civil war and its aftermath. The weakening of the monarchy affected all sections of the population to a greater or lesser extent. For the vast majority of the population—the illiterate peasantry—the presence or absence of strong government changed little in the pattern of their lives. Long days of toil in the fields, sowing, hoeing, tending, and reaping, were as predictable as the rising sun. But an ineffective national administration could have devastating longer-term effects for ordinary people and their families. A breakdown in central authority left the way open for unscrupulous local officials to exact punitive levels of taxation. Neglect of the irrigation and flood-protection systems increased the likelihood of poor harvests and famine. The failure of the state to maintain stockpiles of grain took away the peasant farmers' only insurance policy. Little wonder that eyewitness accounts from the century or so following Pepi II's death speak of hunger stalking the land. For the small, literate elite at the top of the social pyramid, the effects of the political crisis were perhaps less life-threatening but longer lasting. Senior bureaucrats could be sure of their next meal but not of their next promotion. When the fount of honor dried up, careers built on loyal service to the sovereign were suddenly going nowhere. Influential local families had to look to their own resources to maintain their affluent lifestyles. Shorn of royal patronage and authority, many of them simply decided to go it alone, continuing to govern their communities as before and aggregating to themselves a host of royal prerogatives.

As old certainties fell away, so did the rigid distinctions between royal and private provision that had characterized the Pyramid Age. As daily existence grew harder and more uncertain, the need for greater certainty beyond the grave became more pressing. If necessity is the mother of invention, the grim realities of life in post–Sixth Dynasty Egypt created a particularly fertile environment for theological innovation.

In more peaceful and prosperous times, as far as we can judge from the mute record of tombs and grave goods, the ruling class had been content to look forward to an afterlife that was essentially a continuation of earthly existence, albeit stripped of the unsavory aspects. The elaborately decorated tomb chapels of the Pyramid Age reflect an era of certainty and an overwhelmingly materialistic view of life after death. The fundamental purpose of tomb decoration, indeed of the tomb itself, was to provide the deceased with all the material needs of life beyond the grave. Scenes of busy bakers and brewers, potters, carpenters, and metalworkers; of fishermen landing prodigious catches; of offering bearers bringing joints of meat, poultry, fine furniture, and luxury goods: all were designed to ensure a never-ending supply of food, drink, and other provisions, to sustain the tomb owner in an all too earthly afterlife. While the king might hope for an afterlife among the stars, at one with the forces of the cosmos, that destiny was barred to even his highest officials. In death as in life, there was one rule for the king and another for his subjects.

Such rigid distinctions weakened and eventually gave way as royal authority waned during the long reign of Pepi II and the strife that followed it. Ideas of a transcendent afterlife in the company of the gods spread through the general population, transforming funerary practices and the wider culture. Earthly success and being well remembered after death were no longer enough. The hope of something better in the next world, of transfiguration and transformation, became paramount. Notions of what lay on the other side of death were elaborated, codified, and combined in ever more inventive formulations. In the process, the ancient Egyptians devised the key concepts of original sin, an underworld rife with dangers and demons, a final judgment before the great god, and the promise of a glorious resurrection. These concepts would echo through later civilizations and ultimately shape the Judeo-Christian tradition.

AN AFTERLIFE FOR ALL

BACK IN THE DAYS OF THE GREAT PYRAMID BUILDERS, RESURRECTION in any meaningful sense was reserved for the king and depended upon him achieving divine status—even if, in the case of Unas, it meant literally consuming the gods themselves. Only the king, as earthly incarnation of the sky god Horus and son of the sun, possessed sufficient influence, knowledge, and rank to gain access to the celestial realm. The first cracks in this forbidding edifice of royal prerogative appeared in the reign of Pepi II. Ironically, the erosion of the monarch's unique privilege began inside the royal family itself. Pepi's half sister, Neith, had her own tiny pyramid inscribed with texts drawn from the collection of spells that had hitherto been the preserve of the sovereign. The ripples from this minor break with tradition soon spread out across a wider section of Egyptian society. In the remote Dakhla Oasis, far enough from the court for breaches in protocol to go unnoticed, the governor Medunefer was laid to rest surrounded by protective funerary spells culled from the Pyramid Texts. A generation later, another official went even further, decorating the walls of his burial chamber with the very anthology used in the pyramid of Unas. Before long, even minor administrators in the provinces were having their wooden coffins inscribed with extracts from the Pyramid Texts and new compositions.

Just how Pepi II's successors responded to this profound social and religious change is difficult to say. With the exception of King Ibi's tiny pyramid at Saqqara, the tombs of the Eighth Dynasty and of the Herakleopolitan rulers remain undiscovered. In all probability, these monuments incorporated new ways of distinguishing their royal owners from the common people. Yet the adoption of royal texts and images by private citizens represented a seismic shift in the underlying structure of ancient Egyptian civilization. A stark division that had existed between the king and his subjects since the dawn of history had been demolished, once and for all. Now every Egyptian could hope to attain divinity in the afterlife, to spend eternity in the company of the gods. At the same time, this blurring of the distinction between royal and private served, ironically, to underline the unique position of the king. Pictures of royal regalia painted inside private coffins gave their owners the wherewithal to achieve divine status and hence resurrection after death, but only by aping the king. At a time of political fragmentation and civil war, it may have been reassuring for people to feel that divine kingship was alive and well, and a force for good in their ultimate fate. The so-called democratization of the afterlife was anything but democratic, and in this respect was a characteristically ancient Egyptian transformation.

Just as profound as the opening up of the afterlife was the change in how the afterlife was envisaged. Many of the Pyramid Texts had stressed the age-old belief in the king's journey to the stars and his destiny among the "indestructibles," but some of the spells had also introduced a newer concept, the dead king's association with Osiris. This ancient earth god was both revered and feared as ruler of the underworld, but his victory over the decay of death offered the promise of resurrection for the king and, later, for the common people, too. Eternal life could be sought just as well in the nourishment of the earth as in the unchanging rhythm of the universe. Osiris became the champion of the dead, and his underworld kingdom their destination of choice. His chthonic realm at first joined, then ultimately displaced, a celestial setting for the Egyptians' afterlife journey.

The universal wish to be identified after death with Osiris led to important, visible changes in burial customs. From the very beginnings of mummification, its aim had been to preserve the body of the deceased in as recognizable a form as possible. By wrapping the individual limbs, fingers, and toes separately, and molding the features of the face in linen bandages, a more or less lifelike appearance could be achieved. Now that the deceased wished to be transmogrified into Osiris, the preservation of human characteristics was no longer necessary. Instead, the corpse was swathed from head to toe in a single cocoon of bandages, giving it the classic form of a mummy. With this outward appearance of transfiguration being sufficient to conjure the appropriate associations, even the process of mummification could be neglected. Corners were regularly cut, stages omitted, so that underneath the bandages many Middle Kingdom mummies are very poorly preserved. Sometimes the brain was left inside the skull or the organs inside the body, leading to putrefaction. Failure to dry the body sufficiently, or economies in the use of expensive unguents, caused rapid deterioration of the soft tissues. But now that religious concerns had largely replaced material needs at the heart of funerary beliefs, a functioning body was of lesser concern than a passport to the underworld. Being wrapped up to look like Osiris was a good start.

THE UNDISCOVERED COUNTRY

OVERCOMING DEATH, ACHIEVING A SUCCESSFUL RESURRECTION, AND navigating the many dangers that lurked in the underworld required powerful magic, and it was here that texts and images came into their own. In the royal and private tombs of the Old Kingdom, the necessary spells and pictures had been carved or painted on the walls of the burial chamber and tomb chapel. But as traditions of craftsmanship slowly withered after Pepi II's death, with the decline of the royal workshops, so tomb decoration became increasingly rare. Experienced artists were simply no longer available. Three-dimensional wooden models replaced the painted scenes of craftsmen at work. For the modern scholar, the miniature yet intricate models of bakeries, breweries, slaughterhouses, and weavers' workshops are a gold mine for reconstructing ancient technologies. For the Egyptians, they were simply a poor man's substitute for fine paintings in an era of cultural impoverishment. In the absence of decorated tombs, the coffin itself became both a focus for decoration and a canvas for the magical formulae (called, appropriately, Coffin Texts) to assist the deceased in the afterlife.

To assist the owner's resurrection, the mummified body was laid on its side, facing east, toward the rising sun—sunrise, unique among natural phenomena, offered the daily promise of rebirth after the darkness of the preceding night. A pair of magical eyes, painted on the eastern face of the coffin and carefully aligned with the mummy's face, allowed the deceased to "look out" at the sunrise toward the land of the living. These eyes deliberately recalled the face markings of a falcon, giving the deceased the all-seeing power of Horus. By means of this interlocking and overlapping symbolism, the dead person was identified with Osiris, god of the underworld, and assisted by Ra and Horus, the two most powerful celestial deities.

And so, safe inside the coffin, reborn and revivified by the sun's rays, the transfigured mummy set out on its afterlife journey. Or, rather, journeys. In typical Egyptian fashion, two different paths to paradise were imagined. These were described in *The Book of Two Ways*, the earliest of the ancient Egyptian afterlife books. This particular collection of Coffin Texts expresses two contrasting destinies, revealing two competing strands of belief that had already been articulated in the Old Kingdom Pyramid Texts. A celestial afterlife with the sun god was still very much an option, and was now accessible to all. To participate in this version of paradise, the soul of the deceased, imagined as a human-headed bird, would fly out of the coffin and up from the tomb into the heavens. Each night, as the sun sank into the underworld, the soul would return again to the mummy for safety. This concept of the soul (or *ba*) illustrates perfectly the ancient Egyptians' fondness and talent for theological elaboration. Regarded as an individual's personality, the *ba* existed as a kind of alter ego during life but came into its own after death, allowing the deceased to take part in the solar cycle. However, in order to be reborn each morning, it had to be reunited with Osiris (in the form of the mummified body) each night.

The counterpart of the *ba* was the *ka*, the eternal spirit that required the sustenance of food and drink to survive, and through which the dead person could follow the alternative path, the journey through the underworld to the abode of Osiris. From the Land of Life, the deceased set out on an epic voyage toward his ultimate destination, the Field of Offering. This mythical land, the Egyptians believed, was located close to the eastern horizon, the place of sunrise. While part of the underworld, it nevertheless held the promise of rebirth. As the *ka* traveled from west to east, it followed the nightly progress of the sun through the realm of darkness and shared in its daily renewal. But accomplishing the journey safely was no easy task. According to the Coffin Texts, the way was full of obstacles and fraught with dangers: gates to enter, waterways to cross, demons to placate, esoteric knowledge to master. In one example, the dead had to learn the various parts of a ship in order to win a place on the barque of the sun god. Spells provided the magical means for overcoming such hurdles, and some coffins were even decorated (on the inside, for the convenience of the deceased) with detailed maps of the underworld, charting the various seas, islands, watercourses, and settlements along the way to the Field of Offering. The lurid descriptions of what lay between death and salvation conjure up a Hieronymus Bosch vision of hell, reflecting the universal horror of death and the desperate wish for eternal life. The ancient Egyptians' fears ranged from the all-too-familiar afflictions of thirst and starvation to the peculiar horror of an upside-down world in which they would have to walk on their heads, drink urine, and eat excrement. The Coffin Texts show the human imagination at its most fevered.

The ultimate destination, however, was worth all the trials and tribulations. The Egyptians imagined the domain of Osiris as the elysian fields, a landscape of lush, well-watered farmland yielding record harvests; of orchards and gardens bringing forth abundant produce; of peace and plenty for all eternity. Having arrived at journey's end, the deceased could look forward to an afterlife full of satisfaction:

I shall eat in it and I shall wander in it.
I shall plough in it and I shall reap in it.
I shall have sex in it and I shall be content in it.[1]

It was an afterlife to die for. Presiding over this agricultural idyll was the god Osiris, the exemplar of resurrection and the surest source of eternal life. By battling against the odds to join Osiris, the deceased had ensured not only his own rebirth but also the continued renewal of the god. In mythological terms, the deceased had acted as Horus for his father, Osiris, and Osiris had rewarded him appropriately. It is no accident that this concept of the afterlife reflects a world in which inheritance and succession are of central importance. The Coffin Texts were composed in a milieu of powerful regional governors, and simply reflected the governors' particular concerns. The ancient Egyptians, like all peoples, projected their daily experiences onto their religious beliefs.

OSIRIS TRIUMPHANT

THE RISE OF OSIRIS FROM OBSCURE BEGINNINGS TO UNIVERSAL GOD OF the dead lay at the heart of the new religious order. As he became venerated throughout the length and breadth of Egypt, Osiris eclipsed a host of other, more ancient funerary deities, assimilating their attributes and usurping their temples. The townspeople of Djedu, in the central delta, had worshipped their local god, Andjety, for centuries, believing him to have been an earthly ruler miraculously resurrected after death. As the cult of Osiris spread outward from the royal residence, it asborbed these complementary beliefs, and Djedu eventually became the main center of Osiris worship in Lower Egypt. Andjety all but disappeared as a separate deity, becoming a distant folk memory. A similar process took place in the south of the country, at Abdju. Here, the local people worshipped a funerary god in the form of a jackal, an animal often seen prowling over the desert burial grounds. Khentiamentiu, "foremost of the westerners," was the guardian of the west (the land of the dead) and lord of the necropolis. The cult of Osiris soon laid claim to these attributes as well. By the Eleventh Dynasty (circa

2000), inscriptions in the temple at Abdju were already speaking of a hybrid god, Osiris-Khentiamentiu. A few generations later and "foremost of the westerners" was regarded merely as an epithet of Osiris. The god's triumph was total.

In the case of Abdju, the additional presence of early royal tombs gave the site a special sanctity and air of antiquity. It must have seemed preordained that the archetypal resurrected ruler, Osiris, should have his main place of worship in the place where kings had been buried since the dawn of history. So, from the period of civil war onward, Abdju became the principal center of the Osiris cult and one of the most important holy places in all Egypt. The desecration of its sacred sites during the bitter war between the Herakleopolitan and Theban dynasties was a cause of shame to the northern kings, and their ultimate defeat came to be seen as divine retribution for such a heinous act of sacrilege. The victor in the civil war, King Mentuhotep II, lost no time in demonstrating his devout credentials by beautifying the shrine of Osiris-Khentiamentiu. Under Mentuhotep's successors, the temple received further royal patronage. Abdju was transformed into a focus for national pilgrimage and a stage for elaborate ceremonies celebrating the god's resurrection.

The "mysteries of Osiris" were performed annually in the presence of a great crowd of spectators from all over Egypt. At the heart of the rites was a reenactment of the god's kingship, death, and resurrection. These three strands of the Osiris myth were reflected in three separate processions. First, the cult image of the god appeared, to signify his status as a living ruler. One of the temple priests—or, on occasions, a visiting dignitary acting as the king's personal representative—took the role of the jackal god Wepwawet, "the opener of the ways," walking at the front of the procession as the herald of Osiris. The second and central element in the drama recalled the god's death and funeral. A "Great Following" escorted the cult image, enclosed in a special barque shrine, as it was born on the shoulders of priests from the temple to the royal necropolis of the First Dynasty. En route, ritualized attacks on the barque shrine were staged to represent the struggle between good and evil. The attackers were repulsed by other participants, taking the role of the god's defenders. For all its sacred imagery, this mock-battle could at times turn nasty, religious fervor tipping over into violence and resulting in serious injuries. Pious zeal and inflamed passion are ancient bedfellows. The third and final act of the mysteries was Osiris's rebirth and triumphant return to his temple. His cult image was taken back to the sanctuary, purified, and adorned. The ceremonies over, the crowds dispersed and normality returned to Abdju for another year.

So powerful was the symbolism of the Osiris mysteries that participation, whether in person or vicariously, became a lifetime goal for ancient Egyptians, their equivalent of a pilgrimage to Jerusalem or Mecca. For most of the population, long-distance travel within Egypt was a practical impossibility. Even if they could afford the trip, leaving their land unworked for a week or more risked crop failure and disaster. Bureaucrats working in the administration were rather better off in this regard, but still needed official permission to leave their posts and go up- or downsteam to Abdju. The best option for most people was attendance by proxy. If they could have a cenotaph or stela—anything with their name on it—set up along the route of the Great Following, then they, too, could benefit from the god's resurrective power as he passed by. As a result, the sacred way leading from the temple of Osiris became the favored location for memorials great and small. Those with plentiful resources might commission statues of themselves, set within miniature chapels. The less affluent had to make do with a crude stone slab, or merely a mention on someone else's monument. Rich or poor, every devout Egyptian longed for a piece of the action. Within a few generations, the Terrace of the Great God was packed with memorials five or six deep. They occupied every available inch along both sides of the route, threatening to encroach on the sacred way itself.

For those who could not afford even the humblest presence at Abdju, there were always the Osiris festivals celebrated throughout the provinces—not as potent, nor as prestigious, but better than nothing. By recalling and celebrating the god's resurrection in their local cemeteries, the priests and people hoped that some of his magic would rub off on the poor souls interred nearby, affording them, too, the promise of eternal life. From prehistoric times, Egyptian towns and villages had played host to a plethora of different beliefs, deities, and styles of worship, reflected in the diversity of local shrines and the diversity of the votive objects deposited in them. Now, for perhaps the first time in its history, Egypt had something approaching a national religion.

As Osiris worship reached its zenith at the height of the Middle Kingdom, the Coffin Texts fell rapidly out of fashion. They were replaced by a whole host of esoteric magical objects that evidently had the same function. These objects enabled the deceased to be resurrected as Osiris, to reach the Field of Offering, and to journey with Ra in his solar barque. Some of these new objects were lifted directly from daily life but given an afterlife function. Ivory wands inscribed with the images of demons and protective deities were routinely used in Egyptian households to create a protected zone around women in childbirth, to ward off evil spirits that might harm the mother or baby. To the Egyptians' way of thinking, it seemed perfectly natural to bury such an object in the tomb. The reborn was just as vulnerable as the newborn, and needed equal protection. In a similar vein, fertility figurines, used in a household setting to promote the successful delivery and rearing of children, found a corresponding role in a funerary setting, assisting rebirth and regeneration.

Other types of magical objects, however, were manufactured specifically for the tomb. Without known parallels from daily life, they often defy easy explanation. Two of the most characteristic—yet enigmatic—are small models of hedgehogs and hippopotami made from faïence (more accurately, "glazed composition"), a blue glazed glassy material. Because these are uninscribed, and without accompanying texts, it is impossible to deduce their original symbolism, although several different theories can be proposed. This is in keeping with the multilayered nature of ancient Egyptian theology, whereby multiple explanations for a single phenomenon, even if apparently contradictory, were believed to add to the weight of evidence in favor and to confer added numinousness. Hedgehogs were known to burrow underground, and may therefore have been thought of as intermediaries between the land of the living and the underworld—ideal companions for the afterlife journey. Hedgehogs also roll themselves into balls when threatened, taking on the shape of the sun disk in the process. It is possible they were believed to offer the deceased symbolic protection and a closer relationship with the sun god. Perhaps, as denizens of the semiarid desert margins, hedgehogs and similar creatures (model jerboas were also popular) symbolized the triumph of life over the barrenness of death, a highly appropriate metaphor for the tomb. Hippos, on the other hand, were aquatic creatures, inhabitants of the watery world that led to the Field of Offering. They were known to be fierce and aggressive, expert at warding off potential attackers. A hippopotamus goddess was also the deity most closely associated with pregnant women and childbirth. The web of potential connotations is extensive, reflecting the richness and variety of ancient Egyptian religious thought. Indeed, such complexity, often contradictory to the modern logical mind, merely served, in the Egyptians' eyes, to underline the mystery and unknowability of the divine.

At about the time that hedgehogs and hippos were making their appearance among grave goods, another afterlife accessory arrived on the scene, a curious little object that encapsulates the Egyptians' genius for invention and their intensely practical attitude toward problem solving. Thanks to its rapid rise in popularity, the object in question is now ubiquitous in museum collections the world over: the funerary figurine. The ancient Egyptian term was *shabti*, perhaps derived from the word for "stick" and reflecting the rudimentary modeling of the earliest examples. But this was no ordinary stick figure. It had a far more important, magical purpose. Its origins lie in the period of civil war, and, as ideas go, it was startlingly simple. Without royal workshops full of well-trained craftsmen, or sculptors and painters to decorate their tombs, the Egyptians faced a serious dilemma. If their mummified body were destroyed, how would the *ka* be sustained, and whence would the *ba* return each night after its celestial wanderings? A substitute body was the answer, and its early form was exceptionally crude, a small sticklike figure made from mud or wax, perhaps wrapped in a few shreds of linen to represent mummy bandages, and supplied with its own miniature coffin fashioned from some scraps of wood. The quality of the finished product hardly mattered. Once in the tomb, magic would put right any deficiencies in the workmanship. So began the tradition of funerary figurines, an emergency measure in an age of unrest and uncertainty. But with the reunification of Egypt under King Mentuhotep and the subsequent flowering of court culture in the Middle Kingdom, royal workshops returned, and finely crafted statues and painted tombs became available, at least to the elite, once more. Yet the funerary figurine did not disappear. It came to represent something different but just as useful—a servant to assist the deceased for all eternity.

Shabti WERNER FORMAN ARCHIVE

With an Osirian view of the after-life now dominant, the *shabti* really came into its own. For there was one major drawback to spending an eternity in the Field of Offering. While it might be an agricultural idyll, with well-watered fields yielding abundant crops, every Egyptian knew all too well that agriculture—even in such ideal conditions—involved hard physical labor. Particularly arduous and backbreaking was the annual repair of dikes, ditches, and waterways following the inundation, essential to restoring the irrigation network to full working order. Every able-bodied individual was pressed into service for this vital communal task, excavating and carrying baskets of sand and silt from field to field—all in the hot, humid, mosquito-infested conditions that followed the retreat of the floodwaters. Would this be an inescapable chore in the afterlife, too? Surely there was some way of avoiding such unpleasantness for all eternity. The solution was a stroke of genius. The little stick figure that had previously substituted as a body for the deceased retained its basic function as a stand-in, but now, instead of providing a home for the *ka* and *ba*, it would answer the call to work on behalf of its owner. Servant figurines from the late Middle Kingdom were duly equipped with miniature agricultural implements, such as hoes and baskets, and just in case they should forget, a brief hieroglyphic text, carved on their body, reminded them of their principal duty:

> O shabti, detailed to [serve] me . . . if I am summoned or if I am detailed to do any work that is to be done in the afterlife . . . you shall detail yourself to me every time, [whether] for maintaining the fields, irrigating the banks, or ferrying sand from east to west. "Look, here I am," you shall say.[2]

When it came to life after death, a *shabti* was the perfect insurance policy.

TRUTH WILL OUT

ONE FINAL, CRUCIAL ASPECT OF THE AFTERLIFE ADVENTURE ALSO MADE its first appearance in the years following the collapse of the Old Kingdom. Like the Coffin Texts, magical objects, and servant figurines, the concept of a last judgment reflected the mixture of hope and fear that beset the ancient Egyptians in their musings about life after death. Perhaps more than any other feature of Egyptian religion, the idea of a final, inevitable reckoning before a divine judge had a profound and lasting impact on the subsequent development of pharaonic beliefs. Unlike hedgehogs, hippos, and *shabti*s, the last judgment was picked up by other religious traditions of the Near East as well, notably Christianity.

The imaginary geography of *The Book of Two Ways* began with the Island of Fire, where the wicked were consumed in flames but the good were provided with refreshing water for their arduous journey through the underworld. The concept of trial by fire is an ancient one, but this relatively simplistic notion of judgment—whereby the unrighteous dead were separated from the righteous by means of a single, swift test—was itself to be refined in the flames of social change. Once again, the shattered illusions that accompanied the breakup of the Egyptian state proved a fertile breeding ground for new ideas. In troubled times, death came to be seen not as a mere transition to another dimension of creation but as a discontinuity, a break that might prove terminal. Whether an individual achieved rebirth as a divine being or suffered a second death depended on his or her own actions during life. The literary text known as *The Instruction for King Merikara*, purportedly composed by a Herakleopolitan king, summed up this new belief:

> When a man remains after passing away,
> His deeds are set alongside him. . . .
> He who reaches [the next life] without wrongdoings
> Will exist there like a god.[3]

In this scheme of things, virtue was no longer enough—it had to be accompanied by freedom from vice. In inscriptions of the period, the boastfulness and bombast typical of Old Kingdom autobiographies are joined for the first time by notes of doubt and defensiveness. A man might enumerate his many qualities and achievements but also take pains to state "I never spoke a falsehood against any living person."[4] The negative confession, a declaration not to have committed a prescribed list of wrongful acts, became an essential component of the judgment process.

Vindication before the divine tribunal required more, however, than a mere denial of wrongdoing. It involved a fundamental assessment of a person's true worth, a weighing of their good and bad deeds in order to arrive at a balanced judgment of their character. Only those who passed this calculation of differences were deemed fit to join Osiris and live forever. On his stela from Abdju, the Eleventh Dynasty general Intef confidently proclaims that his "voice is true in the calculation of differences." In other words, he has been justified and found worthy of resurrection as a transfigured spirit. From such tentative beginnings, the concept of judgment rapidly acquired a central place in Egyptian funerary religion, to the extent that the term "true of voice" became the most common euphemism for "deceased." In a society as obsessed with bureaucracy and accountancy as ancient Egypt was, it is perhaps not surprising that theologians imagined the weighing of a person's worth taking place on a giant set of goldsmith's scales. The accuracy of the balance perfectly expressed the unerring judgment of the divine tribunal. A spell from the Coffin Texts describes the scales as "that balance of Ra on which Maat is lifted up,"[5] indicating that the judgment is authorized by Ra himself, god of the sun and of creation, and that the deeds of the deceased are to be weighed against Maat, the goddess of truth. In this ultimate assessment, there was no room for cheating. The outcome of the judgment process was visualized as all the deceased being separated into groups, the justified and the unjust, "numbering the dead and counting the blessed spirits."[6] The differing fates of the two groups were crystal clear.

With eternal survival at stake in the last judgment, the fevered Egyptian imagination swung into action. Conceiving further hurdles hand in hand with the means of overcoming them seems to have given the ancient Egyptians the courage to face the uncertainties of death. In the case of judgment before the tribunal, the greatest danger was that one's own heart—seat of the intellect, fount of emotion, and storehouse of memories—might decide to bear false witness and so tip the balance against a favorable verdict. To counter this awful risk, powerful magic was required. Somehow, the heart had to be prevented from blurting out untruths (or hidden truths) that might seal its owner's fate. The ingenious solution was a new type of amulet, first introduced into burials in the late Middle Kingdom. It took the familiar shape of a scarab beetle, a potent symbol of rebirth (because young beetles hatch from a ball of dung, emblematic of death and decay). But unlike other scarab amulets, this one had a human head and was engraved with a protective spell, addressed to the heart. After the body had undergone mummification, the heart scarab was placed over the heart, with clear instructions as to how the organ should behave at the moment of truth:

> Do not stand up against me
> Do not witness against me,
> Do not oppose me in the tribunal,
> Do not incline against me.[7]

In time the heart itself came to stand for the deceased and his deeds, and the pictorial representation of the weighing of the heart against the feather of truth became an essential image on funerary papyri, an encapsulation of the final judgment. It remains one of the most instantly recognizable, characteristic, and evocative scenes from the entire repertoire of ancient Egyptian art.

And the concept of a "dreadful day of judgment, when the secrets of all hearts shall be disclosed" is still with us, four thousand years later.

CHAPTER 8

THE FACE OF TYRANNY

BRAVE NEW WORLD

VICTOR IN THE CIVIL WAR AND REUNIFIER OF THE TWO LANDS, KING Mentuhotep was fêted by later generations of Egyptians as a great founder figure, on a par with Menes, the mythical first king of the First Dynasty. Yet fate decreed that Mentuhotep's descendants did not long enjoy his hard-won spoils. After the brief and unspectacular reigns of two more Mentuhoteps, the royal line of the Theban Eleventh Dynasty, of Intef II and Mentuhotep, faltered. In its place, a new family rose to power, to claim the throne and the prize of kingship.

The Twelfth Dynasty (1938–1755) was the most stable line of kings ever to rule over ancient Egypt. For a period of 180 years, eight monarchs, representing seven generations of a single family, governed the Two Lands. Under their firm control, Egypt prospered materially and culturally. It was the golden age of ancient Egyptian literature, when many of the classics were composed. Craftsmanship reached new heights, with craftsmen creating the most exquisite jewelry to survive from the ancient world. Egypt's reach and influence were extended more widely than ever before, and in new directions, embracing the Aegean, Cyprus, and Anatolia as well as the Red Sea coast and Nubia. And, above all, the Nile Valley and delta themselves were reordered into a unified, well-regulated, and efficient country, a recentralized state to banish the recent divisions of civil war.

This description of the Twelfth Dynasty is factually accurate. Yet it is misleading in one crucial respect—it signally fails to capture the prevailing mood of the period. Literary works focus on uncomfortable themes such as world-weariness (*Dispute Between a Man and His Soul*), national upheaval (*The Admonitions of Ipuwer*), and regicide (*The Instruction of Amenemhat I for His Son*). The glowing picture of Middle

Kingdom civilization that finds favor in some histories of ancient Egypt is jarringly at odds both with writings from that time and with the evidence for internal politics and government. From its very inception, the Twelfth Dynasty set out to change the way Egypt was ruled and the way society was organized. Its was a utopian vision—or dystopian, depending on your standpoint—of absolute order, underpinned by a rigid bureaucratic framework and by the suppression of all dissent. In the business of government, the kings of the Twelfth Dynasty displayed a ruthless streak, entirely in keeping with the policies of their Old Kingdom forebears. In their determination to establish rock-solid internal security, they outdid all their predecessors, deploying sophisticated propaganda alongside brute force, subtle persuasion backed up by terror tactics. Beneath the outward show of glittering high culture, darker forces were at work.

The prevailing tone of Twelfth Dynasty rule was established at its outset. Given that the founder of the new royal line was a commoner by birth, it is scarcely surprising that the official record does not document the manner of his accession. But there are enough hints to suggest the likely course of events. The last king of the Eleventh Dynasty, Mentuhotep IV (1948–1938), was the namesake of the great reunifier but seems entirely to have lacked his leadership qualities. He had inherited his forebear's strongly Theban outlook, but not his wider ambitions. Provincial by nature as well as by background, he left no major monuments. The principal accomplishment of his short reign was to dispatch a quarrying expedition to the Black Mountains of the Wadi Hammamat, to bring back a block of stone for the royal sarcophagus. Details of the expedition were recorded in four inscriptions, cut into the quarry face. Although they pay due reverence to the king as the mission's sponsor, and wish him (insincerely, one imagines) "millions of jubilees," they give the credit for the expedition's success to its actual leader, and the man behind the inscriptions: "the member of the elite, high official, overseer of the city, vizier, overseer of officials, lord of judgment . . . overseer of everything in this entire land, the vizier Amenemhat."[1] The next time we encounter a man named Amenemhat in high office, he is lord of the Two Lands and son of Ra, the founder of the Twelfth Dynasty. Although the transition from king's right-hand man to monarch is not explicitly attested, there can be little doubt that

Amenemhat I took full advantage of his unrivaled position at court to seize the throne when it fell vacant, or when the opportunity arose.

There are strong indications that the new dynasty came to power in lawless times, by means of a coup d'état rather than by peaceful succession. A remarkable series of inscriptions in another stone quarry, at Hatnub in Middle Egypt, give a vivid account of struggles within Egypt during Amenemhat I's reign (1938–1908). Written during the tenure of the local governor Nehri, the texts are unusually dated to his years of office, not those of the reigning king. This extraordinary assumption of the kingly prerogative by a mere provincial official suggests all was not well with the age-old model of royal government. The inscriptions themselves tell of rebellion, famine, plunder, invading armies, and civil strife. And at the heart of the unrest was the palace itself: "I rescued my town on the day of fighting from the sickening terror of the royal house."[2] There is no more chilling reference to tyrannical monarchy in all of Egyptian history. Amenemhat I had chosen his Horus name well. "He who pacifies the heart of the Two Lands" had a deliberately aggressive undertone, and the long hand of royal "pacification" reached even beyond the Nile Valley, into the vast expanses of the Sahara. An experienced desert huntsman and overseer of the Western Desert named Kay was called upon to lead a counterinsurgency operation, to seek out and round up fugitives from the new regime. On Kay's funerary stela are the words, "I reached the western oasis, I investigated all its tracks, I brought [back] the fugitives I found there."[3] Under Twelfth Dynasty rule, there would be no hiding place for rebels.

Yet opposition was not so easily crushed. The king seems to have faced attack from several quarters, including internal dissent along Egypt's two banks. A funerary stela from the time refers to a naval campaign along the Nile and a dawn raid against a landing stage, while the contemporary inscription of the regional governor Khnumhotep I, in his tomb at Beni Hasan, alludes to the same mission: "I sailed with His Majesty to the south in twenty cedar ships. Then he returned, kissing the earth [for joy], because he had driven *him* from the Two Banks."[4] The foe is deliberately left unnamed. Inscribing his name in sacred hieroglyphs would have given him the possibility of eternal life, but he was clearly a homegrown rebel, perhaps even the last king of the

Eleventh Dynasty or one of his adherents. Moreover, the reliefs in Khnumhotep's tomb (and the tombs of his immediate successors) show Egyptians attacking fellow Egyptians in full-scale urban warfare—unprecedented scenes in deeply unsettled times.

Eventually, the king's forces triumphed, and Amenemhat I lost no time in appointing his loyal lieutenants to key posts in the administration. Khnumhotep was appointed mayor of the regional capital of Menat-Khufu; elsewhere in Middle Egypt, nomarchs whose families had served under the Eleventh Dynasty were summarily dismissed, to be replaced by trusted loyalists who owed everything to the current regime. Egypt's new master was tightening his grip on the levers of government.

RENAISSANCE RULER

Bolstered by his success in repressing internal dissent, the king set about restoring the status of the monarchy. Since time immemorial, the two most important roles of the sovereign had been to uphold order and to satisfy the gods. Having done the first, it was time for the second. Amenemhat I duly ordered construction to begin on a great temple to his patron deity, the Theban god Amun. After all, Amenemhat meant "Amun is at the forefront." So nothing less than the grandest temple in the land would suffice. Before the Twelfth Dynasty, Egyptian temples had been very modest affairs—small, often irregular constructions of mud brick, with only a sparing use of stone for doorways, thresholds, and the like. The most imposing buildings in Egypt were not the temples of deities but the pyramids of kings. Amenemhat changed all that, inaugurating the tradition of monumental edifices dedicated to the major gods and goddesses. Little remains of the Middle Kingdom temple of Amun at Ipetsut (modern Karnak)—it was unceremoniously swept away by later royal builders—but it must have dominated the adjoining city, making a powerful statement of royal power. The complex measured more than 330 feet long by 214 feet broad and was enclosed by two thick perimeter walls. Inside stood the sanctuary, fronted by a magnificent stone terrace, and surrounded by a maze of corridors and storerooms. By comparison with the trifling provincial temples of the Old Kingdom, it was staggering in its scale. It was also a harbinger of things to come. Amenemhat I and his successors would show an insatiable appetite for state-planned construction, the architectural manifestation of their new order.

A penchant for grand architectural statements was characteristically Egyptian, but Amenemhat took it to new heights, with a project that dwarfed even his temple to Amun. Toward the middle of his reign, the king gave the order to commence construction of nothing less than a new capital city. A narrow focus on Thebes and its hinterland had been a fatal weakness of the Eleventh Dynasty, and Amenemhat was not about to make the same mistake. The only practical solution for governing a vast realm like Egypt was to place the capital at its geographical center, and that is exactly where the new dynastic city would be built. The location was at the very junction of Upper and Lower Egypt, the balance of the Two Lands. But, to signify his iron will, the king chose a starker name for the city: Amenemhat-Itj-Tawy, "Amenemhat seizes the Two Lands." It was a bald assertion of his modus operandi— the means by which he had gained the throne, and the way in which he intended to govern.

To mark the inauguration of his new capital, the king also adopted a new Horus name. As always, the choice reflected the monarch's personal agenda. Out went references to "pacifying the heart of the Two Lands"; that had largely been achieved, and Itj-tawy now stood as concrete proof. Instead, the king proclaimed himself the instigator of a thoroughgoing renaissance. Under Amenemhat, Egypt would be reborn, its civilization rejuvenated, and its monarchy reestablished. If the aim was to bring back the cultural zenith of the Pyramid Age, a good way to start was by building an appropriately grand royal tomb. So, for the first time in two centuries, the order went out from the royal palace to the architects, masons, and craftsmen of Egypt. The king required a pyramid. Furthermore, it had to be on the same scale as the pyramids of the late Old Kingdom. Taking its dimensions from the royal monuments of the Sixth Dynasty, Amenemhat I's pyramid started to rise on the desert plateau close to his new capital city. Nothing like it had been seen for three hundred years. To give it added legitimacy and potency, the king ordered that blocks from the greatest of all such monuments, the Great Pyramid of Khufu, at Giza, be transported to Itj-tawy and incorporated into the core of his own pyramid. Demolishing and cannibalizing the monument of an illustrious predecessor might appear sacrilegious, but it was an essential part of the renaissance plan. His successors of the Twelfth Dynasty would all follow his lead and build their own pyramids. Well might Amenemhat boast, "Kingship has become again what it was in the past!"[5]

Having quelled internal rebellion, honored the gods, and begun a pyramid, Amenemhat I might have been tempted to think that the rebirth of Egyptian civilization was assured. However, foreign incursions from Palestine and Nubia during the First Intermediate Period had taught Egypt a hard lesson: its neighbors to the north and south had greedy eyes for the Nile Valley's fertile pastures. Maintaining the country's prosperity required active defense of its territorial integrity. Alive to the threat, the king directed his zeal toward securing the nation's borders. His policy would set the scene for the following century and a half. Egypt would be turned into a fortress. The country's northeastern frontier, along the margins of the delta, presented a particular challenge. The marshy terrain, crisscrossed by river branches and canals, made it difficult, if not impossible, to establish a fixed border, or to maintain watertight control over immigration from the impoverished lands of Palestine beyond. Amenemhat's response was to order the construction of a series of fortified bases, strung out along the frontier zone, within signaling distance of each other. Regular patrols were dispatched from each garrison to monitor traffic across the border. In this way, these Walls of the Ruler might hope to prevent major incursions and could provide intelligence on any unusual movements. The emphasis on surveillance as a means of control was characteristic of the Twelfth Dynasty's security policy.

Egypt's southern flank, its border with Nubia, posed a different threat and required a different solution. Ever since the expeditions of Harkhuf in the Sixth Dynasty, it had been clear that the peoples of Wawat (lower Nubia), closest to the Egyptian border, were reasserting their autonomy and forming states of their own, in direct defiance of Egyptian hegemony. With Egypt wracked by internal strife and civil war following the collapse of the Old Kingdom, this process merely accelerated. The reliance of the Theban army on Nubian mercenaries may have bolstered still further the Nubians' own sense of nationhood. By the end of the Eleventh Dynasty, the situation could scarcely have been worse for the Egyptian king. Not only had he lost control over most of Wawat, but his very prestige was being openly challenged by local Nubian rulers who were using Egyptian royal titles. One such, styling himself "the Horus Ankhkhnumra, the King Wadjkara, the son of Ra Segerseni," even referred to the Egyptians as "the enemies," turning the established rhetoric on its head. Another, with the affrontery to call himself King Intef after the great Theban war leaders of the early Eleventh Dynasty, was confident enough to have a series of fifteen inscriptions cut into rocks at prominent locations throughout his territory. Such blatant insults to the might of Egypt could not be tolerated.

A large number of inscriptions carved in the same region by *Egyptian* expeditions bear witness to a frenzy of activity from the early years of Amenemhat I's reign. Even as he was bearing down on his opponents within Egypt, it appears his spies were at work in lower Nubia, carrying out maneuvers and gathering intelligence, in preparation for a full-scale assault. After two decades of preparations, during which order was restored at home, Egyptian forces regained control of the key site of Buhen, at the foot of the second Nile cataract, and started to turn it into a fortified base, to use as a springboard for military campaigns. By Amenemhat I's twenty-ninth year on the throne, everything was ready. An expeditionary force led by his trusted vizier Intefiqer arrived from Egypt to overthrow Wawat. In his determination to snuff out any vestige of Nubian independence and to impose absolute Egyptian control over the wayward province, the king's henchman showed no mercy to the local inhabitants, boasting:

> Then I killed the Nubians of the entire remainder of Wawat. I sailed upstream in victory, killing the Nubian upon his land; and I sailed downstream, uprooting crops and cutting down the remaining trees. I put their houses to the torch, as is done to a rebel against the king.[6]

Amenemhat's scorched-earth policy was designed not merely to punish Wawat but to send a powerful message to any other would-be insurgents. As for the unfortunate Nubians who watched from the riverbank as their land was devastated and their houses went up in flames, their fate was sealed. Before laying waste to Wawat, Intefiqer recorded that he was "busy building this compound." The enclosure in question was a holding area (the ancient Egyptians might have preferred the modern euphemism "reception center") for people conscripted for state labor. A life of servitude lay in store for the conquered inhabitants of Wawat. They and their descendants would toil to exploit the resources of their homeland for its new Egyptian masters.

MIGHTIER THAN THE SWORD

UNEASY LIES THE HEAD THAT WEARS A CROWN — THE MORE SO WHEN that crown has been won by force rather than inherited by lawful succession. Amenemhat I, founder of a new dynasty and self-proclaimed renaissance king, was acutely conscious of his nonroyal origins and of the lingering resentment felt toward his rule in parts of Egypt, never mind in conquered Nubia. Anxious, above all, to consolidate his family's grip on power and ensure a smooth succession, Amenemhat took the highly unusual, if not unprecedented, step of having his son and heir crowned king while he himself still reigned. Prince Senusret became co-regent at the end of Amenemhat's second decade on the throne (circa 1918), and the two kings ruled jointly for a further decade. A few monuments bear joint dates, although for the most part Amenemhat seems to have been content for formal inscriptions to be dated to his son's reign. The institution of co-regency became a feature of royal succession in the Twelfth Dynasty. It served its primary purpose of excluding any rival claimants to the throne until, after a further century and a half, the dynasty itself ran out of steam.

But even this ultimate contingency could not protect Amenemhat I from his regime's many enemies. He had lived by the sword and he would perish in the same manner. A remarkable and unique text composed after his death has the dead king, like Old Hamlet, recalling the manner of his assassination to his son and successor:

It was after supper and night had fallen. I was taking an hour of rest, lying on my bed, for I was weary. My mind was beginning to drift off, when weapons [meant] for defense were turned against me. I was like a snake of the desert. I awoke at the fighting . . . and found it was the guard about to strike. If I had seized weapons there and then, I would

have made the buggers retreat . . . but no one is brave in the night,
no one can fight alone.[7]

Thus did the first tyrant of the Twelfth Dynasty meet his fate. But with a co-regent already on the throne, the desperate assassins had made a terrible miscalculation. In place of the father, the son assumed full power and lost no time in continuing the same policies, but with an added twist. Where overt oppression had failed, subtler methods would be deployed to win the battle for hearts and minds.

Commissioning a work of literature on the theme of his father's regicide was a bold step for Senusret I. It threatened the very ideology of divine kingship and broke a powerful taboo against discussing crises in public. But Senusret and his advisers were playing a clever game. They realized there was more to gain by publicizing the murder than by trying to hush it up. Back in the days of the civil war, provincial leaders such as Ankhtifi had used tales of crisis to emphasize their good deeds and legitimize their power. Now the political thought of the First Intermediate Period provided the foundations for the ruling ideology of the Twelfth Dynasty. By presenting the assassination of Amenemhat I in literary form to the elite of the royal court (the very individuals who posed the greatest threat to the king's life), Senusret gave himself the perfect excuse for a crackdown. His father acquired the status of martyr, the son the role of devoted disciple. Before the Twelfth Dynasty, the Nile Valley had produced scarcely any literature worthy of the name. Ever practical, Egyptian society had had little time or space for mere wordsmiths. Now, Senusret realized, poets and authors might prove just as potent as army commanders.

The flowering of literature in the Twelfth Dynasty ranks as one of the greatest cultural achievements of the Middle Kingdom. The works composed for the royal court, some of them undoubtedly at the king's personal behest, are classics, dealing with complex themes and powerful emotions, but all in the service of the royal house. Amenemhat I had explored the possibilities of propagandist literature early in his reign, presenting himself in *The Prophecies of Neferti* as the savior of Egypt and the champion of cosmic order following a period of distress and calamity:

> A king will come from the south
> Ameny, the justified, his name . . .
> Then order will return to its [proper] place,
> And chaos will be driven out.[8]

Senusret I's litterati perfected the art with the composition of the outstanding masterpiece of ancient Egyptian literature, *The Tale of Sinuhe*. It is a fictional story of a courtier who flees Egypt on hearing of the assassination of Amenemhat I. Sinuhe finds refuge at the court of a Palestinian ruler and achieves both wealth and fame in exile. But as his life draws toward a close, he longs to return to Egypt, to embrace everything it stands for, and to be reconciled with the king, its supreme embodiment:

> May the king of Egypt be satisfied with me, that I may live at his pleasure.
> May I pay my respects to the mistress of the land who is in his palace, and hearken to her children's bidding. Then my limbs will be rejuvenated.[9]

The popularity of *Sinuhe*, which was read and reread for centuries after its composition, is due to its literary brilliance, its narrative flair, and its emotional impact. But the underlying theme of loyalty to the monarch is inextricably interwoven, running as a subliminal thread through the story. As a work both of literature and of propaganda, *Sinuhe* is exemplary.

A rather more blatant example of political literature, *The Loyalist Instruction*, made loyalty to the king the guiding commandment for righteous living, urging all Egyptians to:

> Worship the king within your bodies,
> Be well disposed toward His Majesty in your minds.
> Cast dread of him daily;
> Create jubilation for him every instant.

And, just in case that exhortation fell on deaf ears, there was a chilling reminder of the surveillance state to back it up:

He sees what is in hearts;
His eyes, they search out every body.[10]

But despite this onslaught of textual injunctions to support the monarchy, the political unrest that had destabilized Egypt during Amenemhat I's reign flared up again. A further expedition had to be dispatched into the Western Desert "to secure the land of the oasis dwellers,"[11] while in the Nile Valley itself, temples at Djerty (modern Tod) and Abu, in the south of the country, were looted and destroyed. These acts of desecration were blamed on the usual suspects (Asiatics and Nubians) but were very probably stoked or supported by home-grown insurgents. The king's forces succeeded in restoring law and order; the rebels were rounded up and executed by being burned alive as human torches. Senusret I then pointedly showered attention on local temples throughout the seven southernmost provinces of Egypt (the old "head of the south" and heartland of the Eleventh Dynasty). One of the most beautiful of his new buildings was a jubilee pavilion for the temple of Amun at Ipetsut. Its delicate reliefs, in fine white limestone, show the king and god embracing, a visual metaphor for the regime's avowed legitimacy. Yet, side by side with this lofty imagery, the pavilion also demonstrates the Middle Kingdom obsession with bureaucracy. Along the base, the forty-two provinces of Egypt are enumerated, each with its representative deity, and the geographical extent of each province is given in river units (roughly six and a half miles). In Egyptian hands, a decorative scheme intended to demonstrate the all-embracing nature of the king's rule could not resist including some purely statistical information of the kind beloved by bureaucrats.

The administrative practices honed to perfection in provincial capitals the length and breadth of Egypt came in useful, too, for governing Egyptian-controlled lower Nubia. The campaign to overthrow Wawat, prosecuted nine years into the co-regency of Amenemhat I and Senusret I (circa 1909), paved the way for the formal annexation of Nubia as far south as the second cataract. Egypt demonstrated its hegemony in characteristic fashion, by embarking on massive state building projects, in this case fortresses to consolidate its subjugation of the local population. (The castles built by Edward I of England following his conquest and annexation of Wales are a more recent example of the same phe-

The fortress of Buhen at the second cataract COURTESY OF THE EGYPT EXPLORATION SOCIETY

nomenon.) The fortifications, strung out along the river between the first and second cataracts, were designed to withstand both surprise attack and protracted siege warfare—lessons learned, perhaps, during the civil war half a century earlier. Each fortress comprised a massive rectangular mud brick wall, further strengthened with external towers along the sides and at the corners. The landward wall was guarded by a deep ditch, while on the inner side a low parapet with semicircular bastions and downward-pointing loopholes for archers provided a secondary line of defense. All in all, the Nubian forts were marvels of military architecture, and they must have made a deep impression on the indigenous inhabitants, living alongside in their clusters of mud huts. With garrisons now stationed in impregnable bases guarding strategic points along the river (not least the main route to the gold and copper mines of the Eastern Desert), long-term Egyptian control of Wawat was assured. When, in Senusret's eighteenth year on the throne, his army launched a further campaign as far as the third cataract, the general in charge, Mentuhotep, could boast with some justification of having "pacified the southerners."

FOREIGN ADVENTURES

BY THE END OF SENUSRET I'S LONG REIGN OF NEARLY HALF A CENTURY (1918–1875), the troubles surrounding the beginning of the dynasty had been consigned to history. Egypt and lower Nubia were under the firm control of the central government. The gold, copper, and precious stones that poured into the royal workshops from mines in conquered Wawat provided craftsmen with the finest materials, enabling them to create jewelry, statuary, and objets d'art to beautify the royal court, enhance royal prestige, and swell the coffers of the state still further through long-distance trade in high-value luxury goods.

Egypt's foreign relations were not only confined to trade. Confident at home, Egypt showed a new willingness to engage in military activity abroad to defend its economic interests and secure access to important sources of raw materials. Both facets of foreign policy are illustrated in spectacular fashion during the reign of Senusret I's successor, a second Amenemhat. In the temple of Djerty, near Thebes, which had been ransacked by rebels and restored during the reign of Senusret I, four copper chests were uncovered, hidden in the foundations. Each was engraved with the name of Amenemhat II, and together they contained a fabulous treasure: beads, seals, and uncut pieces of lapis lazuli; ingots, chains, a model lion, and cups, all of silver; ingots and vessels of pure gold. The hoard remains one of the richest discoveries ever made in the Nile Valley. But it was not just the wealth of the horde that excited attention. The trade networks it represented were equally impressive. The lapis lazuli came from Mesopotamia and the distant mines of Badakhshan, while the silver cups were of Minoan design and must have come from Crete or a Minoan mercantile community in Syria.

A more recent discovery has confirmed this internationalism in Egypt's outlook during the middle of the Twelfth Dynasty. A block of stone from Memphis contains extracts from the annals of Amenemhat II (1876–1842), a detailed journal of the activities of the royal court during the early years of the king's reign. Besides the expected religious festivals and dedications of new cult statues, the most surprising entries record expeditions of a military nature against distant lands. One reads, "Dispatching an expedition together with the overseer of infantry troops to hack up Asia," a raid that yielded a rich booty of silver, gold, cattle, livestock, and Asiatic slaves. A further campaign against Lebanon added similar plunder to the royal treasury, together with valuable coniferous woods and aromatic oils. Perhaps most intriguing, however, is the entry that records the return of the infantry troops "after hacking up Iwa and Iasy," lands that supplied tribute of bronze and malachite as well as wood and slaves. The otherwise unknown land of Iwa may be Ura, a site on the coast of southeastern Turkey. If so, this Twelfth Dynasty expedition would be the only known occasion on which an Egyptian army raided Asia Minor. Iasy is even more tantalizing. The fact that it supplied two copper-based materials (bronze and malachite), and the writing of the place-name itself, leads to the conclusion that Iasy is probably Cyprus. Under Amenemhat II, Egypt was evidently a major player in the power politics of the eastern Mediterranean, a full 350 years before the establishment of a formal Egyptian empire in the Near East.

According to the annals, the human cargo brought back from these foreign adventures numbered thousands of slaves. Their forcible resettlement in the Nile Valley, to work on crown lands and take part in state building projects, changed profoundly the ethnic balance of Egypt's population, with long-term, unforeseen consequences. A significant concentration of Asiatic transportees ended up building and servicing the town of Kahun, founded by Amenemhat II's successor, Senusret II, to house the personnel attached to his nearby pyramid. In its strict grid layout, functional zoning, and demarcation of residential quarters by social class, Kahun represents the zenith of centralized planning and the epitome of the structured view of society so favored by the Twelfth Dynasty. Within the massive rectangular enclosure wall (designed as much, we may suspect, to keep people in as to protect them from unwanted intruders), the town was divided into two unequal sections. In the more spacious area lived the senior bureaucrats in their impressive villas, conveniently located for easy access to the town's administrative headquarters. On the other side of the divide, in much more cramped conditions, row upon row of small barracklike dwellings, separated by narrow alleyways, housed the town's workforce. It was a bald architectural reflection of the "them and us" attitude so typical of ancient Egyptian officialdom. And in Kahun, as in occupied Wawat, a compound where people could be held under restraint was an essential element in the infrastructure of state control.

Indeed, the fact that the Twelfth Dynasty kings followed very much the same policy in Egypt as in conquered Nubia speaks volumes about their worldview: resources—human as well as material, native as well as foreign—were there to be exploited for the benefit of the crown. People were merely another commodity, to be shipped from place to place according to need. Just as the industrial processes of baking, brewing, and craft manufacture could best be accommodated in regimented barrack-like workshops, so the workforce could be housed in similar fashion. Wherever Twelfth Dynasty settlements are encountered, whether in the Nile delta or in Upper Egypt, they display the same rigid design. They often seem to have been founded on virgin sites, and so must have involved the forcible relocation of entire populations— all at the whim of the state.

HIGH SESOSTRIS

THIS DESPOTIC MODEL OF MONARCHY, OF ORDER WITH AN IRON FIST, culminated in the reign of Senusret III (1836–1818), the most widely attested member of his dynasty. Under his authoritarian rule, all the elements of Twelfth Dynasty control were brought together in one concerted program—propagandist literature, rigid state planning, centralization of power in Egypt, and conquest and military occupation in Nubia—along with a new vehicle for projecting royal power, portrait sculpture.

Beginning with the written and spoken word, Senusret's poets and scriptwriters outdid themselves in the composition of laudatory texts, extolling the king's virtues. The most extreme example is the Cycle of Hymns, intended, it seems, for recitation on the occasion of a royal visit, or perhaps in front of a statue of the king:

> How Egypt rejoices in your strong arm:
> you have safeguarded its traditions.
> How the common people rejoice in your counsel:

> your power has won increase for them.
> How the Two Banks rejoice in your intimidation:
> you have enlarged their possessions.
> How your young conscripts rejoice:
> you have made them flourish.
> How your revered elders rejoice:
> you have made them young again.[12]

And so on, and so on, for stanza after stanza. A slightly subtler approach was taken in two monumental works of "pessimistic literature," *The Complaints of Khakheperraseneb* and *The Admonitions of Ipuwer.* Following in the footsteps of the earlier *Prophecies of Neferti*, an elaborate and vivid picture of utter chaos and social turmoil provided the literary background against which the firm rule of the king could be justified as necessary and even beneficent. These highly refined compositions played on the Egyptian mind-set, which—molded by the precarious balance of existence and the sharp dichotomies of nature in the Nile Valley (flood and drought, day and night, fertile land and arid desert)— saw the world as a constant battle between order and chaos. These works were squarely aimed at the literate elite surrounding the king, who seem to have wilted under such a sustained barrage of propaganda.

Having browbeaten his inner circle into submission, Senusret III turned his attention to the powerful governors, who since the days of the civil war had exercised considerable authority in the provinces of Middle Egypt. In theory, of course, every individual held office at the king's discretion, and it would have been perfectly possible for Senusret simply to dismiss the nomarchs and refuse to appoint successors. But he was too wily an operator for such a blatant display of force against an influential political class. There was no point in risking a reawakening of the dissent that had marred the early years of the Twelfth Dynasty, not when an alternative course of action presented itself. His chosen policy was ruthless, calculated, and brilliant: he neutered the nomarchs, and their potential heirs, under the guise of promoting them. Lured away from their regional power bases by the offer of prestigious (and lucrative) positions at court, men such as Khnumhotep III of Beni Hasan moved to the royal residence to enjoy the trappings of high office, leaving their provinces to be ruled from the center. Within a generation, nomarchs had disappeared from the Egyptian political scene. And once at court, officials were brought to heel, interred in tombs provided for them by the king, arranged in a neat row in the court cemetery.

This dynastic obsession with rigid planning found outlets in the two most ambitious building projects of Senusret III's reign. The first was his pyramid town, a settlement for those who worked on his pyramid at the holy site of Abdju. Here, as at Kahun, everything was laid out mathematically, the houses made of uniformly sized mud bricks and organized in blocks one hundred cubits wide, separated by streets five cubits wide. Again, elite residences occupied the prime spot (highest up, farthest from the cultivation, with its humidity and mosquitoes), while the rest of the population had to make do with cramped conditions on the other side of town. The whole settlement was modestly named Wah-sut-Khakaura-maa-kheru-em-Abdju, "enduring are the places of Khakaura [Senusret III's throne name], the justified, in Abdju." This proved rather too much for the locals, who shortened its name for everyday purposes to Wah-sut.

The king's most impressive application of zeal and energy, however, was reserved for Nubia. His motivation was threefold: to consolidate Egyptian hegemony in Wawat and establish a new, permanent border; to control trade between upper Nubia and Egypt, for the benefit of the royal treasury; and to ward off the threat from the powerful kingdom of Kush, with its capital at Kerma, beyond the third cataract. His chosen policy was equally impressive in scope—the construction of a line of substantial fortresses throughout the second cataract region. Although the forts were designed to operate as an integrated system, each individual fort had its own particular role to play. Kor, on an island in the Nile, served as a campaign palace, a headquarters for the king during military maneuvers. Iken (modern Mirgissa) was the main trading post, sited well within Egyptian-controlled territory. Askut, given the blood-curdling name "destroying the Nubians," was the most secure of the forts. It was primarily a fortified granary but also served as a center for forced labor throughout the gold-mining region of the second cataract. As befitted an arm of state control in conquered territory, the fort was centrally staffed and supplied from distant Egypt, despite the proximity of thriving native settlements. Shalfak, called "subduing the foreign

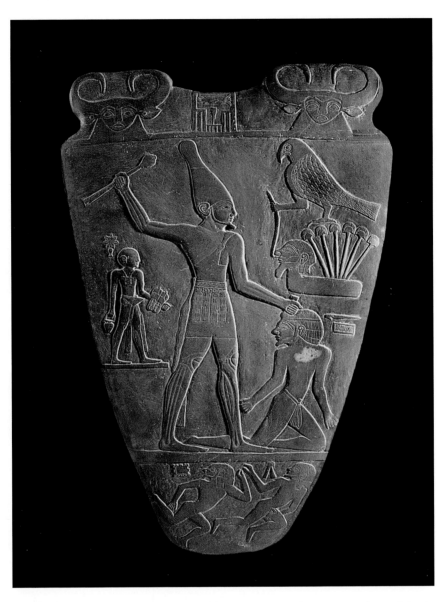

The Narmer Palette was commissioned by King Narmer (First Dynasty) to celebrate the unification of Egypt and the creation of the pharaonic state. It is ancient Egypt's founding document.

The landscape of Upper Egypt is characterized by narrow strips of cultivated land either side of the Nile River, hemmed in between towering cliffs.

The broad green fields of the Nile delta create an environment very different from the narrow valley, hence the ancient Egyptians' characterization of their country as "the Two Lands."

Royal power at the dawn of Egyptian history: the Battlefield Palette depicts the aftermath of a great battle, with a parade of captives (top section) and the king as a fierce lion, trampling the bodies of his fallen enemies (bottom section).

Ivory comb of King Djet (First Dynasty). The decoration expresses the relationship between the celestial god Horus, shown as a falcon, and his earthly incarnation, the king.

Ivory statuette of an unidentified First Dynasty king. The monarch is shown wearing the tight-fitting cloak associated with the royal jubilee festival.

Limestone statue of King Khasekhem (Second Dynasty) wearing the jubilee cloak. The statue was found at Nekhen, ancient center of Egyptian kingship.

Limestone statue of King Djoser (Third Dynasty), builder of Egypt's earliest pyramid. The statue was originally housed in a special shrine next to the Step Pyramid at Saqqara, and was intended to serve as an eternal resting place for the king's spirit.

Cedarwood barque of King Khufu (Fourth Dynasty). The boat was buried next to the king's Great Pyramid at Giza, to serve him on his afterlife journey.

Painting of red-breasted and bean geese from the tomb of Prince Nefermaat (Fourth Dynasty) at Meidum. It is one of the masterpieces of Egyptian art from the pyramid age.

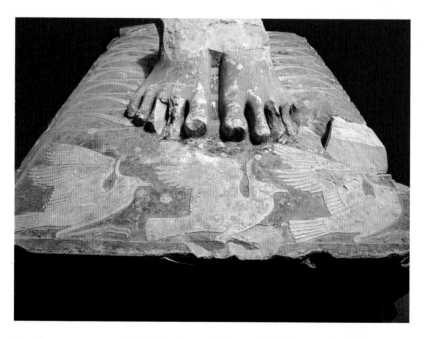

Royal supremacy: on this statue base of Djoser (Third Dynasty), the king tramples underfoot the symbols of his foreign enemies (bows) and his Egyptian subjects (lapwings).

Diorite statue of King Khafra (Fourth Dynasty), from his valley temple at Giza. The god Horus, in falcon form, perches behind the king's head in a gesture of divine protection. The statue is unsurpassed as a statement of royal authority.

The Great Sphinx of Giza (Fourth Dynasty), with the pyramid of Khufu in the background. The sphinx, with a lion's body and a king's head, was a potent symbol of the monarch's power.

Inner chambers of the pyramid of King Unas (Fifth Dynasty) at Saqqara. The walls are covered with Pyramid Texts, the world's oldest collection of religious writings, while the ceiling is decorated with stars to resemble the vault of heaven.

Painted relief from the tomb of the vizier Kagemni (Sixth Dynasty) at Saqqara, showing a mock fight with punt poles. Such scenes illustrate the rarefied and decadent world of the ruling elite in the late pyramid age.

Relief of craftsmen from the tomb of Ankhmahor (Sixth Dynasty) at Saqqara. In the upper section, metalworkers use blowpipes to heat a furnace holding a crucible of molten metal. Below, jewelry makers string bead collars.

Wooden coffin (Twelfth Dynasty) from el-Bersha. The decoration comprises a frieze of objects, extracts from the Coffin Texts and a route map, all designed to assist the deceased in his afterlife journey.

lands," was a base for paramilitary patrols, sent into the surrounding desert to monitor the movement of people and goods. Uronarti, or "re-pelling the tribesmen," served as a command center for the regional garrisons and provided a further campaign palace for the king's use. A common feature of all the forts was their inspired use of the local topography to enhance their defensive capability. Curtain walls ran along the line of rocky ridges, steep cliffs were topped with towering battlements, and covered stairs led to the river to ensure access to a water supply in the case of siege.

Beyond Uronarti, the most impressive group of forts—and the focus of the entire policy—guarded the narrow Semna Gorge, a natural bor-der that was easy to defend. On the east bank, overlooking the main river channel and preventing infiltration from the Eastern Desert, stood Kumma, "opposing the bowmen." Facing it, on the west side of the gorge, was the principal fortress of Semna, "powerful is Khakaura, the justified." Dominated by large barracks, Semna stood ready to seal the gorge and defend Egyptian interests from attack by Kush. In addition to having a permanent garrison of four hundred to five hun-dred men, the commander could also quickly summon reinforcements from Uronarti, Iken, and Buhen, farther downstream, via a system of beacons sited at relay stations within sight of each other. In times of peace, the main role of the Semna garrison was to control traffic along this stretch of the Nile. Vessels would moor in the fort's lower pool while cargoes were off-loaded onto Egyptian ships or overland donkey caravans for the onward journey to Iken. A forward base at Semna South, given the belligerent name "suppressing the Nubians," pro-vided a holding area for native caravans awaiting permission to con-tinue their journeys, as well as a lookout to monitor people and ships approaching the gorge.

Together, the second cataract forts presented an awesome display of Egyptian military and administrative might: an architectural expres-sion of the king's power as well as a logistical support for Egyptian in-terests in the region. No wonder that Senusret III would later be venerated as a god in Wawat, or that Greek historians would dub him "High Sesostris" ("Sesostris" was the Greek rendering of "Senusret"). Just as important as the forts themselves, however, was the system of surveillance they supported. In a remarkable series of documents known as the Semna Dispatches, the patrols that were sent out on a regular basis from Semna South, Semna, Kumma, Uronarti, and Shalfak reported their findings to the local commander. In an atmosphere of nervousness approaching paranoia, the patrols adopted an uncompromising stop-and-search policy. Even small groups of Nubians were intercepted, by force if necessary, and questioned. Those without legitimate business in Egyptian-controlled territory were sent back over the border. A typical dispatch reads: "The patrol who went forth to patrol the desert-edge . . . have come to report to me, saying, 'We have found the track of 32 men and 3 asses. . . .' "[13] Every patrol leader signed off his dispatch with the same words: "All the affairs of the King's Domain (life, prosperity, health!) are safe and sound." One can detect a desperate eagerness to prove that nothing untoward had happened.

The determination of the Egyptian authorities to maintain absolute control was certainly in keeping with the Twelfth Dynasty's obsession

Senusret III WERNER FORMAN ARCHIVE

with security, borne of bitter experience. Rather than their actions being an unnecessarily macho response to a relatively low threat level, it now appears that fear of attack by the kingdom of Kush was well placed. Egypt's rival on the upper Nile was wealthy, powerful, and jealous of its northern neighbor, a dangerous combination. So, as an added incentive to his garrisons to fight the good fight, Senusret III had a monumental stela set up inside the fortress at Semna. Its inscription urged the soldiers to defend the king's conquests with the words "Valorous it is to attack, vile to retreat."[14] Senusret boasted of his own ruthlessness against the Nubians: "I have carried off their women and brought away their dependants, burst forth to [poison] their wells, driven off their bulls, ripped up their barley, and set fire to it."[15] Total warfare was the Egyptian ideal. Finally, the king had a statue of himself installed in a special shrine at Semna, to inspire his men to loyalty and bravery. The inscription read, "My Majesty has had an image of My Majesty made upon this frontier . . . so that you will be steadfast for it, so that you will fight for it."[16] It was impossible to resist such a powerful mix of propaganda and coercion, of encouragement and intimidation.

Indeed, one look at a typical statue of Senusret III would have been enough to convince any soldier to do his duty. Never before in the history of ancient Egypt had a king used sculpture so effectively to project so terrifying an image of royal power. Senusret III's statues—and there are many of them—have a deeply unsettling effect. The torso is always taut, muscular, and virile, presenting the ideal of youthful vigor beloved of Egyptian kings. But it is the face that haunts the viewer: bulging eyes under hooded lids, sunken cheeks, a brooding downturned mouth. This radical departure from the conventions of royal portraiture is at once mesmerizing and terrifying; his is the true face of tyranny. Adding to the effect are the outsize ears, their message being that Senusret was the all-hearing monarch. Those who spoke out of turn were likely to regret their indiscretion.

The Twelfth Dynasty police state continued under the king's iron grip for another half century after Senusret III. His successor, Amenemhat III (1818–1770), favored a meaner style of portraiture alongside archaic forms of sculpture, designed to underline the antiquity of kingship. The achievements of his reign were spectacular: massive reclamation and building works in the Fayum; not one but two pyramids (the first having developed cracks just as it neared completion); and an upsurge in mining and quarrying expeditions to bring back precious stones for the royal workshops (four expeditions to the Wadi Hammamat for graywacke, three to the Wadi el-Hudi for amethyst, and no fewer than twenty-three to the Sinai for turquoise). In cultural terms, his reign marks the high point of the Twelfth Dynasty. Fueled by Nubian gold, trade with the Near East prospered, too. The king rewarded his loyal allies, the princes of Kebny, by showering them with gifts. They, in turn, became increasingly Egyptianized in an attempt to emulate their powerful sponsors.

Close ties between the Egyptians and their Asiatic neighbors were also maintained in the Sinai peninsula, where the local Palestinian rulers provided logistical support to the Egyptian mining expeditions. With friendly relations established, the peaceful immigration of Asiatics into Egypt, especially into the northeastern delta, replaced the forcible resettlement of Asiatic slaves that had taken place earlier in the dynasty. Semitic-speaking Asiatics from the Sinai, with their experience in desert travel, made ideal recruits for Egypt's paramilitary police force patrolling the Western Desert. Interacting with Egyptian military scribes, they developed a hybrid script for writing their own language—the earliest alphabetic script in history. But the steady buildup of an Asiatic population in the Nile Valley and delta would soon make itself felt in other ways as well, with disastrous consequences for Egypt.

At the end of Amenemhat III's long reign of nearly five decades, the unthinkable happened: the dynasty found itself without a youthful male heir to carry the torch for another generation. As an emergency measure, the old king had an aged relative crowned co-regent. But, whether through lack of personal charisma, faltering political support, or merely old age, Amenemhat IV failed to make an impression during his decade on the throne. He was succeeded in turn by a daughter of Amenemhat III, Sobekneferu (1760–1755). The accession of Egypt's first female king—there was no word for "queen," the very notion being anathema to ancient Egyptian ideology—was a sure sign that the Twelfth Dynasty had run out of steam. Desperate to bolster her legitimacy, she emphasized her relationship with her father (virtually ignoring her ineffective predecessor), and concentrated her building activities at Hawara, where Amenemhat III had constructed his second pyramid complex. But after a brief reign of just four years, Sobeknef-eru, too, was gone.

The dynasty that had begun with a bang ended with a whimper. Without the smack of firm government, the forces of disorder, both inside and outside the country, saw their chance.

CHAPTER 9

BITTER HARVEST

"THE MISERABLE ASIATIC"

THE ANCIENT EGYPTIANS HAD A NATURAL SUPERIORITY COMPLEX. They liked to think of themselves as a civilization apart, their beloved country uniquely blessed and protected from less fortunate neighbors by its natural borders of sea and desert. This self-image could not have been further from the truth. Situated at the crossroads of Africa, Asia, and the Mediterranean, Egypt was always a melting pot of peoples and cultural influences. From time immemorial, the fertile fields of the Nile Valley and delta were a magnet for migrants from the harsher, arid lands to the west, east, and south. In turn, the industry, technology, and customs of successive waves of immigrants enriched and renewed Egyptian civilization. On occasions, however, peoples from neighboring lands came to Egypt with less benevolent intentions, bringing notions of conquest along with cultural innovations. Such invasions were rare, and generally repulsed or kept at bay by a strong centralized state. But at times of political weakness, Egypt was more vulnerable, especially along its porous northeastern border. The exhaustion of the Middle Kingdom state at the end of the Twelfth Dynasty offered just such an opportunity to Egypt's envious and ambitious neighbors. The result was very nearly catastrophic for the survival of pharaonic culture.

Obsessive about internal security and border defenses, the Twelfth Dynasty monarchs had taken considerable steps to fortify the frontier along the northeastern delta. Sealing it completely, as had been done at Semna, in Nubia, was impossible because of the nature of the terrain. But the Walls of the Ruler, built by Amenemhat I and strengthened by his successors, established a forbidding line of fortifications to deter foreign aggressors. In addition, the forts themselves supported a regular system of patrols to monitor, intercept, and regulate the movement of peoples across the border. Tjaru (modern Tell el-Hebua) was the linchpin of Egypt's northeastern defenses, and was as impressive a fortress as any in conquered Wawat. Yet despite this iron curtain, migration into the delta by Semitic-speaking peoples from the Near East not only continued but accelerated during the course of the Twelfth Dynasty. Some of the settlers may have been prisoners of war, captured and brought back from the campaigns of Amenemhat II and Senusret III. Others were undoubtedly legal migrants, employed by the Egyptian state to assist the state-sponsored mining expeditions to the Sinai; to work on major construction projects in the Fayum; or to act as guides, desert trackers, and police on the country's desert fringes. By the late Twelfth Dynasty, "the miserable Asiatic" (as one Twelfth Dynasty text put it) formed a significant element in the population, and immigrants from the Near East began to rise through the ranks of Egyptian society, even winning promotion to government positions. In the northeastern delta, where many of these migrants had originally settled, what started life as a small community of foreign workers soon became a magnet for much larger waves of immigration, as people fleeing the harsher climatic and economic conditions of their homelands sought sanctuary and opportunities for betterment with their relatives and compatriots in Egypt.

One site in particular was the focus of this sustained influx. The town of Hutwaret (modern Tell el-Dab'a), on the eastern bank of the Nile's Pelusiac Branch, had been established as a small border settlement by the Herakleopolitan dynasty and had been refounded by Amenemhat I as part of his frontier defenses. However, under the weak rule of his descendants Amenemhat IV and Sobekneferu, the system of surveillance must have broken down, allowing a steady stream of immigrants to cross the border. Once settled at Hutwaret, they built houses in their own tradition and maintained their own way of life. Yet these immigrants were not entirely ignorant of Egyptian customs. Quite the reverse. Many of them were already highly Egyptianized before settling at Hutwaret, suggesting that they had come from the Lebanese port city of Kebny, with its long-standing cultural and political ties to Egypt. Others may have come from Cyprus. Among these long-distance migrants were bedouin tribespeople from southern Palestine, swept up in the great tide of human migration pouring into the Nile delta. It was a heady mix of languages, peoples, and traditions that rapidly transformed Hutwaret into a multicultural town, unlike anywhere else in Egypt.

Since people of Asiatic origin had already attained high office elsewhere in Egypt, it is not surprising that the opportunities for advancement were even greater at Hutwaret. One prominent dignitary chose to express his social standing in quintessentially Egyptian form, by means of a large stone statue for his tomb chapel. But he also emphasized his non-Egyptian background by the style of his portrait—his large, red, mushroom-shaped coiffure marking him out as an immigrant from Kebny, his yellow skin color conforming to the traditional Egyptian convention for depicting Asiatics. The curved throw stick that he held in one hand served as both a symbol of office and an ethnic identifier, since this peculiar object was the very hieroglyph used to write the word "Asiatic." Here was a man proud of his foreign ancestry and willing, it seems, to flaunt it in defiance of Egyptian xenophobia.

After little more than a generation, the Asiatic population of Hutwaret had grown confident in its distinctive hybrid culture, prosperous from Mediterranean trade, and increasingly willing to flex its political muscles. An imposing mansion was built as the official residence for the town governor, the equal of anything at Kahun or Wah-sut; indeed, it was a palace of royal pretensions. In its grounds, high-ranking officials were interred in lavish tombs, each marked according to Asiatic custom by a pair of donkeys buried at the entrance. One of these high-status tombs belonged to a man calling himself the overseer of Retjenu, a title usually borne by the Egyptian official in charge of relations with Syria-Palestine. Another tomb belonged to a chief steward and treasurer. Although these titles seem to demonstrate the continued reach of the central government, it is debatable to what extent the elite of Hutwaret still considered themselves answerable to the king in Itj-tawy. In any case, the royal court had its mind on other problems.

MONARCHY WITHOUT MAJESTY

AFTER TWO CENTURIES OF RULE BY A SINGLE FAMILY, THE GOVERNMENT machine found itself singularly ill-prepared for the succession crisis that followed the brief reign of Sobekneferu. It is as if the elite had simply forgotten how earlier generations had coped when faced with the extinction of the royal line. The result was a rapid turnover in the office of kingship to mirror the chaos at the end of the Old Kingdom. Kings came and went with bewildering rapidity, reigning for periods of mere months or even days as the throne passed from claimant to claimant. Over the course of 150 years, Egypt had no fewer than fifty kings (the so-called Thirteenth Dynasty), compared to just eight in the preceding two centuries. In all likelihood, the most powerful families in the land, unable to agree on a single candidate, opted for the mechanism of a rotating succession. Since the elderly members of each rival lineage were the most likely to command respect at court, Egypt effectively became a gerontocracy, with one aged king after another attempting to make his mark. Despite this travesty of traditional monarchy, the administration continued as before with a surprising degree of efficiency—a reminder, perhaps, that the real business of government fell to viziers and treasurers rather than their royal masters. In official documents, leading bureaucrats were content to pay lip service to the age-old custom of the royal prerogative, even if officials were now appointing the king, rather than the other way around.

In the country at large, it was harder to paper over the cracks. Private individuals stopped invoking the king or the royal residence on their funerary monuments, no longer convinced that it would make any difference to their chances of an afterlife. Now, it seemed, the king was barely around long enough to make provision for his own. Pyramid building all but stalled, many kings making do with a shaft tomb cut inside the pyramid enclosure of one of their Twelfth Dynasty forebears. Expeditions to the Sinai ceased altogether. All the outward trappings of might and majesty disappeared from a beleaguered monarchy. The accession of Sobekhotep III (circa 1680), perhaps the twenty-sixth king of the Thirteenth Dynasty, provides a stark illustration of the changes that had overtaken Egypt in a mere half century. In sharp contrast to many of his predecessors, Sobekhotep openly flaunted his nonroyal origins, making a virtue of the fact that he had no royal blood in his veins. He lauded his nonroyal parents in a series of commemorative inscriptions and confidently publicized his commoner relatives. It all suggests a deep-seated malaise in the very institution of monarchy.

Sobekhotep III's background in the military, with some time in the king's personal bodyguard, would certainly have given him an intimate knowledge of court politics. As king, he turned this to his advantage, increasing the number of key government officials and restarting royal building projects to restore some measure of stability to the administration. But it was not to last. The heartbeat of royal government was faltering; even the odd burst of activity could not mask that reality.

The crisis was felt particularly acutely at Egypt's distant outposts, the fortresses of occupied Wawat. An emasculated administration found itself unable to maintain the system of rotating garrisons that had staffed the forts during their heyday in the Twelfth Dynasty. One by one, the Nubian forts were relinquished by the Egyptian government, which was now incapable of extending its writ beyond the traditional borders of the Two Lands. The forts of the Semna Gorge were the last to be abandoned, as the Thirteenth Dynasty did its feeble best to uphold Senusret III's frontier. Eventually, even Semna itself was handed over to its small resident population as the remaining government envoys packed their bags and departed for the last time. Left to their own devices, and increasingly uncertain of receiving logistical support or provisions from the capital, some of the fortress communities started to think the unthinkable and look southward to another potential sponsor. The kingdom of Kush might have been Egypt's sworn enemy, but at least it had the gold to pay those in its employ.

A similar fate awaited the fortresses of the northeastern delta. With their patrols discontinued and their garrisons recalled home, central control of Egypt's most vulnerable frontier effectively ceased. It did not take long for an ambitious leader to fill the power vacuum. A man named Nehesy not only took charge of the fortresses, but he promptly declared himself king of an independent delta state, with its capital at Hutwaret—in direct challenge to the government at Itj-tawy. Safe within his power base, Nehesy knew exactly what was expected of a legitimate Egyptian king. He upheld the traditional system of administration and put himself under the patronage of his local deity, Seth, lord of Hutwaret. An Egyptian temple founded in the town at this time may have been the concrete manifestation of Nehesy's public piety, although it was dwarfed by an adjacent temple of Asiatic style, indicative of the mixed culture prevalent throughout Hutwaret. With oak trees shading its forecourt and a vivid blue painted exterior, this Asiatic temple on Egyptian soil was one of the largest anywhere in the Near East. It amply demonstrates the confidence and prosperity of Nehesy's royal foundation.

Yet, despite its initial stability, his newly established dynasty was not without difficulties. The deliberate vandalism of earlier tombs (the statue with the mushroom-shaped coiffure was smashed to pieces and its inlaid eyes gouged out) hints at civil unrest, and society was heavily militarized. Soldiers were buried with their weapons at the ready, and the town echoed to the sounds of metalworkers making new armaments.

In earlier times, the secession of a province would have been met with a swift and ruthless response from the center. But the government at Itj-tawy was hardly in a fit state to win back Hutwaret by force. Indeed, Nehesy's declaration of independence dealt the Thirteenth Dynasty regime a body blow, cutting the dynasty's remaining links with the Near East and starving it of trade income. The dynasty limped on, retaining the vestigial trappings of state power, but with little conviction. The end was not long in coming.

Within a few decades, the government at Itj-tawy and the breakaway delta dynasty were both brought down by a combination of natural and man-made disasters. At Hutwaret, famine and plague devastated the population. Whole families of adults and children were buried together, hugger-mugger, without the usual careful preparations. A series of extremely short reigns at the end of the Thirteenth Dynasty suggests a similar calamity farther south. Weakened by disease, the whole of Lower Egypt became easy prey to an outside aggressor. From over the border, a force of well-equipped invaders, armed with the latest military technology—horse-drawn chariots—stormed Egypt, taking beleaguered Hutwaret and sweeping on southward to conquer the ancient capital of Memphis. The Hyksos had arrived.

RULERS OF FOREIGN LANDS

THE HYKSOS WERE A UNIQUE PHENOMENON IN THE HISTORY OF ancient Egypt. For more than a century (1630–1520), a Semitic-speaking elite from coastal Lebanon ruled northern Egypt and were recognized as overlords in the rest of the country. They transformed their capital at Hutwaret into a town wholly Asiatic in culture, worshipped a foreign god (Baal), and were buried following foreign rites. Their very names were alien, and their conquest seemed to later generations, and perhaps to some at the time, to represent the destruction of created order itself. For the century of their rule, their heartland in the northeastern delta prospered as never before, thanks to vibrant trade with other parts of the eastern Mediterranean and more distant lands. Hutwaret expanded to two or three times its previous size, and became the nerve center of a mini-empire that encompassed parts of southern Palestine and the Lebanese coast.

The loss of Memphis to these invaders dealt the Thirteenth Dynasty a fatal blow, both psychological and practical. Egypt's ancient capital symbolized the very concept of national unity, while its location at the junction of the Nile Valley and the delta was the key to controlling the internal movement of goods and people. The Hyksos takeover of such a strategic objective forced the royal court to abandon Itj-tawy and beat a hasty retreat southward. There was not even time, apparently, to gather up precious temple and state archives, with the result that the successors of the Thirteenth Dynasty would have to reinvent the canon of religious texts without reference to the accumulated wisdom of earlier generations. As for the court itself, it swiftly reestablished a government of sorts at Thebes, traditional heartland of Egyptian independence. But the court's writ had collapsed and now extended over just the seven southernmost nomes of Egypt, the old "head of the south" from which the Middle Kingdom had been born six centuries earlier. For a short time, while the government in exile came to terms with the new political reality and consolidated its strictly limited authority, parts of the central Nile Valley experienced a power vacuum. At Abdju, cult center of Osiris, such an absence of divine kingship from the apex of society was particularly calamitous. So the local elite took matters into their own hands and established their own ruling dynasty. But without the usual accoutrements of skilled craftsmen and trained bureaucrats, these "kings" of Abdju presented a dejected picture of monarchy, their crudely fashioned monuments at odds with their royal pretensions. It was a valiant attempt to preserve Egypt's most important institution at the country's most important center of worship. But good intentions were no match for the well-organized and well-resourced Hyksos. After little more than twenty years, the Abdju dynasty was snuffed out, leaving barely a trace in the record.

Farther south, at Thebes, the refugees from Itj-tawy fared somewhat better. For many in Upper Egypt, they were still the only legitimate lords of the Two Lands, and they continued to receive loyal service from the same families who had held office under the old regime. Yet this apparent continuity was an illusion. In reality, the situation had changed utterly. In more settled times, Thebes had been a great city, favored by royal patronage and prosperous from its trade links with every part of Egypt and Nubia. Now, cut off from the Near East by the Hyksos presence in the north, and from southern lands by the loss of the oases and the Nubian forts, Thebes was a shadow of its former self—weak, impoverished, and vulnerable. The gods, too, seemed to have deserted the Egyptians in their hour of need, sending natural disasters to compound the people's misery. Less than a decade after the abandonment of Itj-tawy, the native Egyptians faced a bitter blow when floodwaters overwhelmed the temple of Amun at Ipetsut, sacred epicenter of their Theban realm. The king decided the only course of action was to lead by example, wading into the temple's submerged broad hall to inspect the damage, his bedraggled entourage in dejected attendance.

The next Egyptian monarch faced even worse: a combination of famine, flood, and attack. Neferhotep III claimed to have nourished Thebes during the worst of the food shortage, and to have "protected his city when it was sunk,"[1] but when the weakened population found itself under attack from advancing Hyksos armies, the best Neferhotep could do was steel the resolve of the populace and "make it brave [in its dealings] with foreigners."[2] Stressing the ruler's role as military leader was one way to rally the troops, but Neferhotep's adoption of epithets such as "guide of mighty Thebes" smacks more of hope than expectation.

From the monarch to his humblest subject, there was the gnawing fear that Thebes, like Memphis before it, would fall to the invaders. The most telling royal inscription from the time is the commemorative stela erected at Ipetsut by King Mentuhotepi (a reassuringly old-fashioned Theban name, if written in a curiously provincial manner). In quintessential Egyptian fashion, the text is full of boast and bluster,

Mentuhotepi comparing his army to "crocodiles on the flood."[3] Yet when it came to his own power, his choice of words betrayed the uncomfortable truth: "I am king within Thebes, this my city."[4] Trying to emphasize his legitimacy, Mentuhotepi called himself "one who acts as king."[5] Not even the most ephemeral ruler of the Thirteenth Dynasty would have needed to protest so cravenly about his royal credentials. The Egyptian monarchy was in a piteous state indeed.

Nothing underlined this decline more starkly than the fate of the Nubian fortresses. Abandoned by the central government in the dying days of the Thirteenth Dynasty, the Egyptian inhabitants left behind had looked elsewhere for employment. The kingdom of Kush—the dominant power on the upper Nile, a prosperous trading nation in its own right, Egypt's sworn enemy, and the very reason behind the forts' construction—needed no further bidding. Expanding its territory northward, it assimilated Wawat and took over control of the forts, meeting little if any resistance. During the period of Hyksos control in the north, the Egyptian expatriates living in Wawat, both civilian and military personnel, willingly served their new Nubian masters. At Buhen, a man named Ka boasted, "I was a brave servant of the ruler of Kush."[6] His colleague Soped-her, the fortress commandant, even helped rebuild the temple of Horus at Buhen "to the satisfaction of the ruler of Kush."[7] In the dedication of his commemorative inscription, Soped-her covered all eventualities, invoking the Egyptian funerary god Ptah-Sokar-Osiris; the local deity Horus, lord of Buhen; and even the deified Senusret III; but also the unnamed "gods that are in Wawat." He was clearly hedging his bets. Senusret III would have turned in his grave. The tables were now turned on the Egyptians. It was they, not the Nubians, who had to pay taxes on trade shipments; they, not the Nubians, who could be told where, what, and when they could trade. The heyday of the Twelfth Dynasty must have seemed a distant memory.

The Hyksos Kingdom, by contrast, was flourishing. As existing networks of Asiatic immigrants absorbed more newcomers, settlements and their associated cemeteries sprung up throughout the eastern delta. A large fortified town was founded at Tell el-Yahudiya, complementing the defensive installations taken over by the Hyksos elsewhere in the frontier zone. Confident in their new homeland, the Hyksos rulers gave full expression to their distinctive cultural identity. At Hut-waret, altars blazed with burnt offerings in front of the main temple, which was dedicated to Baal-Zephon, the Syrian storm god, who had rapidly assimilated the cult of the Egyptians' own storm god, Seth. Infants who died young had their remains interred, according to Asiatic custom, in imported Palestinian amphorae—even though Egyptian amphorae were stronger and would have offered better protection. In matters of trade, too, the Hyksos consciously turned their backs on Egypt, eschewing commerce with Middle Egypt or the south (although they continued to secure gold from Kush via the oasis route) in favor of dealings with Palestine and Cyprus. Wine, olive oil, timber, and copper flowed into the bustling harbor at Hutwaret, swelling its coffers and making it one of the greatest royal cities in the entire Near East. To proclaim their economic and political might, the Hyksos rulers built a great citadel on the banks of the Nile. Occupying more than half a million square feet of river frontage on reclaimed land, it was surrounded by a huge curtain wall twenty-five feet thick, fortified with buttresses. Inside the compound, the royal residence was a place of luxury and opulence. Gardens and vineyards provided fresh produce and offered shade from the Egyptian sun, while a carefully constructed stone-lined channel delivered fresh water from the river directly into the heart of the palace.

Surrounded by such affluence, a change came over the Hyksos rulers. The earlier kings had been content to describe themselves as "rulers of foreign lands" (in ancient Egyptian, *"heqau-khasut,"* the derivation of the term "Hyksos"), a moniker that had been used in the Middle Kingdom for the princes of Near Eastern city-states. The accession of King Khyan (circa 1610), however, brought a new outlook and marked the apogee of Hyksos power. Determined to be recognized as a proper Egyptian sovereign, commensurate with his exalted economic status, he sent a diplomatic gift to the Minoan ruler of Crete at Knossos, announcing his arrival on the world stage. For domestic consumption, he adopted a full royal titulary, headed by the Horus name "he who embraces the banks [of the Nile]." It was, as ever, a statement of political intent as much as ideology. Khyan's objective was to break out of the Hyksos heartland and bring all of Egypt within his embrace. A military advance through Middle Egypt cowed the northern two-thirds of the country into submission. It is even possible that the Hyksos armies succeeded in conquering Thebes for a year or two before marching back to their delta base, laying waste to towns and temples as they retreated. Khyan's successor, King Apepi (1570–1530), went one step further in his public pronouncements, taking the Horus name "pacifier of the Two Lands" (redolent of Amenemhat I at the outset of the Twelfth Dynasty) and describing himself on one of his monuments as "beloved of Seth, lord of Sumenu." By claiming the divine sanction of a god within the Thebans' own heartland (Sumenu was a town only a few miles from Thebes), Apepi was thereby claiming the crown of the entire country. Things had never looked darker for the survival of an independent Egyptian kingdom.

DOWN BUT NOT OUT

YET, SOMEHOW, DESPITE ALL THE SETBACKS, THE FLAME OF EGYPTIAN self-determination (or the ambition of the ancien régime to be restored to power) was never quite extinguished. The withdrawal of the Hyksos forces from Upper Egypt, back to their delta power base, offered a glimmer of hope to the Thebans, a chance to reconstruct and regroup. The new king of Thebes, Rahotep (who is identified as the first ruler of the Seventeenth Dynasty), began the program of repairs to shrines devastated by the Hyksos armies. At Gebtu, he ordered restoration work to commence at the temple of Min, noting that "its gates and doors are fallen into ruin."[8] At the holy site of Abdju, the cult of Osiris-Khentiamentiu was revived. Both acts were about symbolism as much as preservation of monuments. By beautifying the temples of the gods and reinstating ancient religious practices, Rahotep was clearly signaling his intention to be a legitimate Egyptian ruler, one who carried out the most important duties of kingship. His successors followed suit, repairing the temple at Abdju and making additions there and at Gebtu. Both sites, key players during Egypt's first civil war, were again at the forefront of Theban strategy. This went beyond religious activity to encompass practical politics as well. Military garrisons were established at both Gebtu and Abdju as forward bridgeheads to be used in any fight against the Hyksos. The groundwork was being laid for a Theban resurgence.

The successors of King Rahotep also set about resuscitating another traditional royal prerogative, pyramid building. While the tombs of Neferhotep III and his ilk had been miserable affairs, little more than burial shafts sunk in the rock, the Seventeenth Dynasty rulers were intent upon recalling the glory days of the Middle Kingdom. So, on the steep hillside of Dra Abu el-Naga, in western Thebes, they founded a new royal necropolis. The tomb of Nubkheperra Intef, fourth king of the dynasty, is the best known. The burial chamber was hewn into the cliff face and was entered via a descending shaft, but this was only the private aspect of the tomb. Marking its location on the surface, for all to see, was a steep-sided pyramid, built against the hillside and contained within a rather shoddily built brick retaining wall. The pyramid was also made from mud bricks. These were early days in the Theban renaissance, and quarrying large amounts of stone was still beyond the means of the fledgling dynasty. But the tomb was plastered and whitewashed to give at least the vague appearance of a stone monument with a smooth casing. At forty-three feet in height, the pyramid barely registered next to the monuments of the Twelfth Dynasty, but the intention was there, even if the resources were not. In a similar vein, Intef had to make do with a reused statue, probably pilfered from the nearby mortuary temple of Mentuhotep II.

Even if Nubkheperra Intef lacked the means to be a great king, he certainly had the resolve. On the obelisks erected in front of his tomb, he made another, highly significant public gesture of his determination to revive Egypt's fortunes. In carefully cut hieroglyphs, he associated himself with some of the most important deities of Egypt: Osiris-Khentiamentiu, the god of Abdju, guarantor of a blessed resurrection and afterlife; Anubis, lord of the necropolis, the jackal god of mummification who presided over burials; and, perhaps curious in such funereal company, Sopdu, "lord of foreign lands." But the inclusion of Sopdu was no mistake. This rather minor deity had two crucial attributes. He was the patron god of foreign lands, especially the hill country of the Sinai and southern Palestine, and his cult center was located in the eastern delta at Per-Sopdu, squarely inside the Hyksos Kingdom. It was a classic instance of theological tit for tat. If Khyan could claim the patronage of a Theban god to bolster his assertion of political hegemony, then Intef could do likewise and put himself under the protection of a delta god with special responsibility for foreign lands. With Sopdu's blessing, the Theban Seventeenth Dynasty might hope to beat the foreigners at their own game and regain control of the lands lost to the invaders.

Divine support was one thing, but practical politics was quite another. Before Nubkheperra Intef could hope to start mobilizing his supporters in a fight against the Hyksos, he had to consolidate his dynasty's grip on power in its own backyard. It was a case of united we stand, divided we fall. A remarkable document attesting to this realignment of power has been preserved at Gebtu. It is a royal decree by Nubkheperra Intef settling an internal dispute that had arisen within the powerful bureaucracy running the temple of Min. The details of the sorry affair are not recorded, but the king's verdict on the perpetrator, Minhotep, was clear and unequivocal:

> Have him cast out from the temple of my father, Min. Have him driven out of that temple office from son to son and generation to generation, and hurled to the ground. His provisions are to be taken away . . . so that his name is not remembered in this temple—as is done to one like him who rebels.[9]

We may suspect that Minhotep's seditious behavior was not an act of sacrilege against the temple itself but a move against Intef's loyal supporters—especially since the beneficiary of Minhotep's excommunication was the mayor of Gebtu, Minemhat, a devoted servant of the Seventeenth Dynasty. By such means, throughout the temples and towns of Upper Egypt, the Theban kings steadily concentrated power in the hands of men they knew they could trust.

The result was a unified and close-knit administration, ready and eager to relearn and restore traditional protocols and modes of government. Nubkheperra Intef's successor, Sobekemsaf II (circa 1560), showed his own aptitude for this program of renewal when he sent a quarrying expedition to the Wadi Hammamat, no doubt with logistical support from the regime's new friends at Gebtu. It was the first such state-sponsored mission in 160 years. True, it may have comprised just 130 men, compared to the 19,000 who took part in an expedition under

Senusret I, and the personnel may have been recruited somewhat haphazardly, but it was a start. Deeper in the Eastern Desert, at the mines of Gebel Zeit, work started up again, assisted by mercenaries recruited from the desert Medjay people. As well as procuring materials for a renaissance in the royal workshops, the Theban administration was beginning to stretch itself, flexing its muscles and honing its responses in readiness for war. In the clearest sign yet that battle plans were being drawn up, Sobekemsaf made a new donation of land to the local temple at Madu (modern Medamud), a few miles outside Thebes. The choice of recipient was no accident, for the god of Madu was none other than Montu, the Theban war god who had inspired the Eleventh Dynasty to victory in the struggle for reunification six centuries earlier. Perhaps Montu would assist a new generation of Theban warriors in their own battle for national salvation.

Just as everything looked ready, fate dealt the Seventeenth Dynasty a cruel blow. From the distant reaches of Nubia, via the Egyptian-built fortresses of Wawat, a great army raised by the ruler of Kush swept northward, attacking towns and villages in Upper Egypt, ransacking temples and tombs, and carrying off the spoils. What was alarming for the Egyptians was that the Kushites were not alone but had recruited allies to their cause: "Kush came . . . having agitated the tribes of Wawat, all the [peoples?] of upper Nubia, Punt, and the Medjay."[10] This was a formidable coalition, embracing the inhabitants of Nubia, who no doubt relished a chance to get even with their erstwhile oppressors, but also the people of the far-off land of Punt and the Eastern Desert Medjay, always ready to offer their services to the highest bidder. The doughty townspeople of Nekheb, at the center of the firestorm, put up stiff resistance under the brave leadership of their governor, repelling the invaders and forcing them back beyond the first cataract. Even so, the governor himself lost property to the pillaging horde, and the Theban side sustained casualties it could ill afford. The Kushite invasion came as a dreadful shock, but provided a salutory lesson to the Seventeenth Dynasty: before they could safely launch their campaign for national reunification (in which loyal soldiers from Nekheb would play a leading role), they would first have to secure their southern flank.

THE FIGHT BACK BEGINS

IN THE HYKSOS CAPITAL AT HUTWARET, KING APEPI MUST HAVE sensed the impending outbreak of hostilities. He took the precaution of strengthening the fortified enclosure wall of the royal citadel, and of forming a strategic military alliance with Kush. Using the desert route via the oases, which the Hyksos had controlled since the early days of their rule, his messengers could communicate with the ruler of Kush without having to pass through Theban territory. Apepi might have to offer Kush a share of the spoils, but carving up Egypt between the two powers would be an acceptable compromise if it meant the end of Egyptian independence for good. Without a hint of irony, Apepi used an age-old Egyptian trick to rally his supporters for the fight ahead. In a barrage of propaganda, the Asiatic king proclaimed his power with new and ever more elaborate epithets: "strong-willed on the day of battle, with a greater name than any [other] king, protector of distant lands who have never glimpsed him."[11] To sum up, he claimed, "There is not his like in any land!"[12]

The new Theban ruler, Seqenenra Taa, was supremely unfazed by this fighting talk. Instead of indulging in a war of words, he made preparations for the real conflict. His first move was to establish a forward campaign headquarters, from which the assault on Memphis and Hutwaret could be planned and directed. The chosen location was Deir el-Ballas, on the west bank of the Nile opposite Gebtu. There he built a fortified palace compound to accommodate the royal family. It was served by a bakery complex and surrounded by a substantial settlement for members of the king's entourage. Overlooking the entire site, atop a high hill, there was a lookout post with commanding views of the Nile Valley. All in all, it was the perfect defensive location.

With his strategic command and control center up and running, Taa launched the first wave of attacks against Hyksos forces. And he was no armchair general: he led from the front, his tall frame, muscular body, and large head topped by thick, curly black hair making him every inch the war hero. Drawing strength from his own sense of destiny, and stiffened by the resolve of his feisty sister-wife, Ahhotep, he engaged the enemy in hand-to-hand combat. Then . . . disaster. In the thick of battle, the king fell—perhaps struck from behind—while riding his

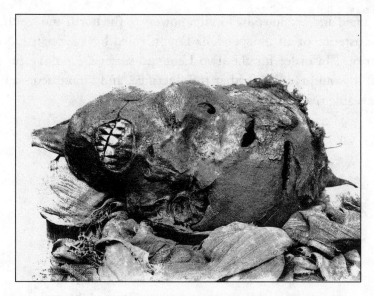

*Mummified head of King Taa, showing the fatal wound inflicted by
an Asiatic axe blade*   G. ELLIOT SMITH, *THE ROYAL MUMMIES*

chariot. Unprotected, he was set upon by his attackers with daggers,
axes, and spears. An Asiatic axe penetrated his skull, causing a massive
head injury and killing Taa outright. In the chaos and confusion, it was
impossible to prepare the corpse properly for burial. Instead, the dead
king was hastily embalmed, without even his limbs being straightened,
and taken back to Thebes. There, before a grieving family and a
stunned populace, "Taa the Brave," as the inscription on his coffin
called him, was laid to rest, his designated successor, Kamose, leading
the mourners.

Taa had been cut down in his prime, after a reign of barely four years
(1545–1541). The mantle of office, and the hopes of the Egyptians,
now rested on Kamose's shoulders. Inexperienced and unsure how to
proceed, the new monarch summoned his war council. In heartfelt and
anguished tones, he bemoaned his and his country's fate: "Why do I
ponder my strength while there is one prince in Hutwaret and another
in Kush, and I sit joined with an Asiatic and a Nubian, each man holding his portion of Egypt and sharing the land with me?"[13] Never before
in the fourteen hundred years since the foundation of the state had
Egypt's fortunes sunk to such a low ebb. The country had experienced
disunity and insurgency in the past, but this was different. With Egypt

threatened and occupied by foreign powers to the north and south, the very existence of an independent Egypt, ruled by Egyptians, looked precarious. In order for the Two Lands to survive, let alone prosper again, it would require further toil, sacrifice, and bloodshed—and an unshakeable resolve to prevail.

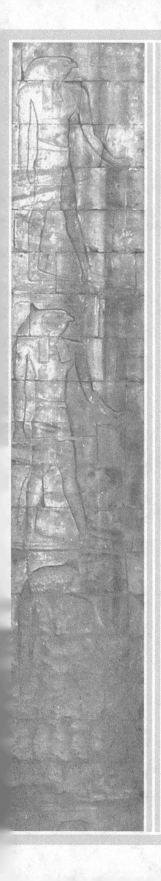

PART III
THE POWER AND
THE GLORY
(1541–1322 B.C.)

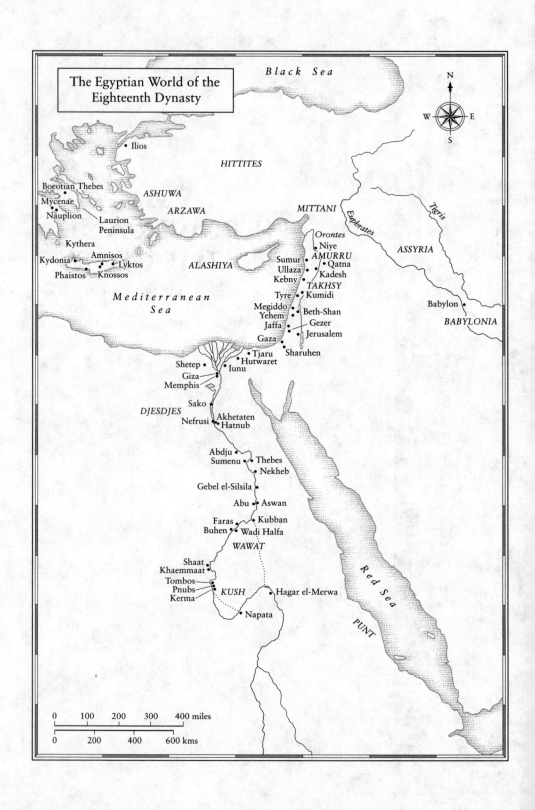

The Egyptian World of the
Eighteenth Dynasty

Black Sea

N
W E
S

• Ilios

HITTITES

Boeotian Thebes
Mycenae •
Nauplion •
Laurion
Peninsula

ASHUWA

ARZAWA

MITTANI

Euphrates

Tigris

Kythera •

Kydonia •
Amnisos •
Lyktos •
Phaistos •
Knossos •

ALASHIYA

Orontes
• Niye
AMURRU
Sumur • • Qatna
Ullaza • • Kadesh
Kebny • *TAKHSY*
Tyre • • Kumidi
Megiddo • • Beth-Shan
Yehem • • Gezer
Jaffa • • Jerusalem
Gaza •
• Sharuhen

ASSYRIA

Babylon •

BABYLONIA

*Mediterranean
Sea*

• Tjaru
• Hutwaret
Shetep • •
Giza • Iunu
Memphis •

Sako •

DJESDJES

Akhetaten
Nefrusi • • Hatnub

Abdju •
Sumenu • • Thebes
• Nekheb

Gebel el-Silsila •

Abu • • Aswan

Faras • • Kubban
Buhen • • Wadi Halfa

WAWAT

Shaat •
Khaemmaat •
Tombos •
Pnubs • *KUSH*
Kerma • • Hagar el-Merwa

• Napata

*Red
Sea*

PUNT

0   100   200   300   400 miles

0   200   400   600 kms

THE VALLEY OF THE KINGS, LUXOR TEMPLE, THE COLOSSI OF Memnon, and the gold mask of Tutankhamun—the dazzling cultural achievements of ancient Thebes conjure up a lost world of breathtaking opulence and artistic patronage on a lavish scale. Created in the space of eight generations, these towering monuments and dazzling treasures are the legacy of a single royal line, the Eighteenth Dynasty, that ruled over the Nile Valley for two centuries. Its period in power represents the high-water mark of pharaonic civilization, when Egypt's confidence and sense of its own destiny seemed to know no bounds.

Casting off the yoke of foreign domination, King Ahmose and his descendants promulgated the cult of monarchy with a renewed vigor. If divine kingship was the drama, Thebes was the stage. With the wealth created by foreign trade and wars of conquest, this modest provincial town in Upper Egypt was transformed into the religious and royal capital of an empire, a "hundred-gated" city with obelisks, temples, and giant statues dominating the skyline in all directions. From its palaces and offices, courtiers and bureaucrats governed the king's realm with ruthless efficiency, controlling every aspect of people's lives and livelihoods. While the king played out the great ceremonies of state, his people continued to labor in the fields, their lot little changed. In the cloistered world of the Eighteenth Dynasty, the only revolutions involved the institution of kingship itself. Although their reigns marked abrupt departures from accustomed practice, neither the female king Hatshepsut nor the heretic pharaoh Akhenaten was able to overturn centuries of accumulated tradition.

Part III charts the rise and fall, the triumph and tragedy, of the Eighteenth Dynasty, from national renewal to decadence and decay. It describes how, with dynamic and determined leadership, and no small measure of self-belief, a band of Theban loyalists succeeded against all odds in expelling the hated Hyksos invaders and reunifying the Nile Valley. Shaking off the dishonor of foreign rule, Egypt extended its reach to emerge as a great imperial power, controlling a territory that stretched more than two thousand miles. Breaking out of their former introspection, the pharaohs discovered a role for themselves on the world stage. Foreign emissaries from distant lands brought exotic tribute to the royal court, while the Egyptian army swept all before it in the hills and plains of the Near East. In the south, the systematic colonization and exploitation of Nubia gave Egypt mineral wealth to match its military might, and provided the royal workshops with the raw materials to manufacture sumptuous and sophisticated works of art. It was truly a golden age.

Yet the steady enhancement of royal authority on top of so much power and prosperity proved disastrous. When a ruler with a penchant for radical theology decided to push the godlike status of the monarchy to its logical extreme, Egypt was turned upside down as hallowed cults and customs were swept away in an orgy of autocratic and puritanical fervor. Only the death of the heretic king and the swift maneuverings of counterrevolutionaries ensured a return to the old ways and a more stable regime. But in the process, the Eighteenth Dynasty itself withered and died, having been weakened and discredited. Its passing paved the way for a new imperial order, one based not upon fine gold but upon cold bronze.

CHAPTER 10

ORDER REIMPOSED

ARMED STRUGGLE

THE LIBERATION OF EGYPT FROM HYKSOS RULE WOULD BE REMEM-
bered by later generations as a moment of national renewal, of cultural
renaissance, the dawn of a new age. The kings who led the fight for
Egyptian independence would be regarded as founders and unifiers on
a par with Menes, the first ruler of Egypt, and the great Mentuhotep,
victor in the country's protracted civil war. Egyptologists, too, share
this view of the struggle between the indigenous Egyptians and their
Asiatic overlords. The expulsion of the Hyksos signals the beginning of
the New Kingdom, that most glorious of eras in the long history of ancient Egypt.

But that was not how it felt at the time. King Kamose's lament on
the state of his country was heartfelt. In 1541, hemmed in between the
Hyksos in the north and the Kushites in the south, Egypt as an autonomous territory occupied barely a third of the area that the great
kings of the Twelfth Dynasty had controlled. For many Egyptians,
even within the Theban heartland, the status quo did not seem such a
bad option. After all, collaboration with the Hyksos ruler in Hutwaret
had its benefits: the Thebans were allowed to cultivate fields and to
pasture herds in lands under Hyksos control, and receive supplies of
animal fodder from the same region, in return for taxes paid to their
foreign masters. Kamose's own officials are reported to have told him
that they were happy with this relationship. While this may be a classic
piece of royal propaganda, designed to portray the king as a resolute
and decisive leader in the face of cowardly and complacent officials, it
probably contains more than a grain of truth. The Hyksos had brought
technological innovations to Egypt (not least the horse and chariot),
opened up the country to Mediterranean commerce on a grand scale,

and shown themselves every bit as adept at administration as the native Egyptians. A policy of peaceful coexistence would certainly have been the easy option. But it held little attraction for a man and a dynasty with ambitions to recapture the glories of the past. For a proud Theban, foreign occupation of any part of the beloved land was anathema, and Kamose expressed his personal determination in the clearest possible terms: "My wish," he told his closest lieutenants, "is to rescue Egypt."[1]

Before Egypt could be said to have been "rescued," however, there were the small matters of continued Hyksos occupation and a growing Kushite menace to deal with. The ruler of Kush had built up a formidable army with a sizeable cavalry, and would lose no opportunity to extend his writ. The raids on Nekheb a generation earlier had taught the Thebans a valuable lesson: securing their southern frontier was an essential prerequisite to engaging the northern enemy. Outnumbered by the Hyksos forces and with inferior military technology, they could ill afford to fight on two fronts simultaneously. The threat from Kush would have to be neutralized first. So in 1540, in only his second year on the throne, and after months of preparation, Kamose led his forces southward. Their immediate mission was to retake Wawat and secure it against Kushite attack, thereby creating a buffer zone on the Thebans' southern flank. Moving through the sparsely populated stretch of valley south of Abu, they seem to have encountered little if any resistance. As they reached the foot of the second cataract, their goal loomed into view: the fortress of Buhen. After serving as one of the main nerve centers of Egyptian military occupation throughout much of the Middle Kingdom, Buhen had fallen easily under Kushite control in the following decades. The fort's Egyptian inhabitants had all too readily switched sides, serving their Nubian masters as dutifully as they had the great kings of the Twelfth Dynasty. But once they saw a new Egyptian army massed in force on the horizon, they appear to have capitulated without a fight, rediscovering their erstwhile allegiance to the lord of the Two Lands. Welcomed as a conquering hero, Kamose oversaw the restoration of Buhen's defenses and its rearmament as a vital forward garrison.

Strategic commander that he was, his vision extended beyond immediate defensive needs. Looking to the future and the long-term occupation of Nubia, he also reestablished Egyptian administration in the region. No king could rely on the vacillating loyalties of fortress commanders. A different mechanism would have to be found to ensure direct royal control of the conquered territories. Kamose's solution was an administrative innovation that would characterize Egyptian control of Nubia for centuries to come. He appointed a trusted official, Teti, to be the first "king's son" of conquered Nubia, a viceroy who would act on the king's behalf and answer directly to his royal master for all Nubian affairs. With Teti firmly installed in the viceregal headquarters at Faras, Kamose and his forces returned to Egypt to prepare for battle with the Hyksos, an altogether more difficult and dangerous proposition.

Kamose's strategy for his northern front was as much psychological as military. His calculation was that a policy of shock and awe directed against the Hyksos-supporting towns of Middle Egypt would have a profound effect on his opponents' morale and soften them up for a final assault. In his own words,

> I sailed downstream as a victor to drive out the Asiatics according to the command of Amun . . . my brave army in front of me like a blast of fire.[2]

His first target was the town of Nefrusi, which lay inside Hyksos territory just to the north of the regional administrative center of Khmun (modern el-Ashmunein). Nefrusi was governed by an Egyptian called Teti, son of Pepi. If Kamose's forces could make an example of him, other collaborators might heed the message and desert to the Egyptian side. After maneuvering into position under cover of darkness, the Theban army struck Nefrusi at first light: "I was upon him like a hawk. . . . My army were like lions carrying off their prey."[3] Showing no mercy, Kamose watched while the town was ransacked, then ordered it to be razed to the ground. A similar fate was dealt the settlements of Hardai and Pershak a few days later. With towns throughout Middle Egypt lying in ruins, Hyksos hegemony in the region had been destroyed. Thebes was on the march.

Then an unexpected stroke of luck delivered Kamose a further propaganda coup. Building on the Thebans' long experience and mastery

of desert routes, honed in the days of civil war, Kamose had regular surveillance missions patrolling the tracks through the Western Desert,
keeping a discreet watch over comings and goings, and reporting on
any unusual movements. For their part, the Hyksos also relied on
desert routes for trade with the kingdom of Kush. (Thebes might have
been subject territory, but sending shipments of Nubian gold by river
through the heartland of the resistance was simply too risky.) Hence
the road between Sako (modern el-Qes) in Middle Egypt and the
Kushite capital at Kerma via the Western Desert oases was a busy high-
way, carrying trade caravans and diplomatic messengers between north
and south. One such envoy had the misfortune of being intercepted by
Kamose's patrol, just south of the oasis of Djesdjes (modern Bahariya).
We can imagine the Thebans' delight when they discovered that the
messenger was carrying a letter from the Hyksos king to the new ruler
of Kush. And the contents of the letter were nothing short of explosive:

> From the hand of the ruler of Hutwaret. Aauserra, the son of Ra
> Apepi, greets the son of the ruler of Kush. Why do you ascend as
> ruler without letting me know? Have you noticed what Egypt has
> done against me? The ruler who is there, Kamose . . . , penetrates
> my territory even though I have not attacked him as he has you. He
> chooses these two lands in order to afflict them, my land and yours,
> and he has ravaged them. Come northward; do not flinch. Look, he
> is here in my grasp. There is no one who will stand up to you in
> Egypt. Look, I will not give him passage until you arrive. Then we
> shall divide up the towns of Egypt.[4]

Despite his pique at not being kept informed about the Kushite succession, Apepi was making an extraordinary offer to his Nubian ally: in
return for military support, he would be willing to share Egypt—a classic case of divide and rule. The Thebans' worst fears were well-
founded. If they did not act, and soon, Egypt risked utter annihilation.

Kamose's response was immediate and intuitive. Instead of killing
the unfortunate messenger, he sent him back to Hutwaret with a message of his own for Apepi: "I will not leave you alone; I will not let you
walk the earth without my bearing down upon you."[5] To drive the
point home, the messenger was also instructed to tell Apepi about

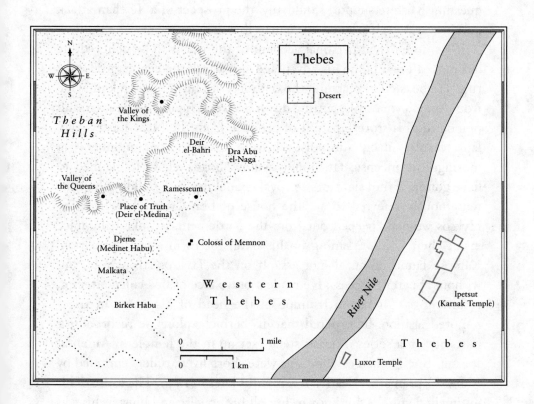

Kamose's recent attacks on towns in Middle Egypt. Not only were the Theban forces brave and determined, they were scoring victories in the Hyksos's backyard. Apepi had fatally betrayed his own weakness by requesting Kushite support. Suddenly, the prospect of a Theban attack on Hutwaret itself seemed more plausible than ever.

If Kamose's vivid personal account of the war is to be believed, he did indeed press home his advantage and attack the center of Hyksos rule. He boasted of reaching the outskirts of Hutwaret, drinking wine from Apepi's vineyards, cutting down his trees, raping his women, and plundering his storeships full of produce from the Near East: "gold, lapis lazuli, silver, turquoise, bronze axes without number . . . , moringa oil, incense, fat, honey, willow, boxwood."[6] He claimed to have gotten within sight of the royal citadel itself—a building he contemptuously referred to as "the house of brave words"—where the Hyksos women "peeped out from the battlements . . . like baby mice inside their holes."[7] Lining up his naval forces in attack formation, Kamose launched an all-out assault on the Hyksos stronghold, but without apparent success. He made a brave face of this failed attempt, returning to Thebes in triumph at the head of his army. In time-honored fashion, he ordered that his heroic exploits be recorded for posterity on a series of great stelae, set up in the temple of Amun at Ipetsut. But Theban celebrations were short-lived, rudely curtailed by Kamose's premature death a few months later in 1539. The cause of his untimely demise is not known. For all his bravery and bluster, his was not a victor's burial. He was interred in a modest, ungilded coffin with two daggers by his side, his life's work unfinished.

As if Kamose's death were not devastating enough for the Egyptians, their sense of loss, frustration, and anxiety must have been compounded by the vagaries of the royal succession. Just three years earlier, Kamose had very likely been chosen as king in place of the heir apparent because he was of an age to carry on the fight that had claimed Seqenenra's life. Now, with Kamose dead as well, the heir could not easily be passed over again . . . even though he was only a boy.

As Thebes waited for the new king, Ahmose, to come of age, ten long years passed in military stalemate. With Buhen in Egyptian hands, Kush was successfully held at bay. Apepi's demoralized forces were in no position to launch an attack, but without a leader, neither were the Thebans. All they could do was sit tight and make preparations.

VICTORY AT ALL COSTS

AFTER A DECADE OF ENFORCED INACTIVITY, EGYPT WAS CHAMPING AT the bit when Ahmose reached adulthood in 1529 and took his place at the head of his army. At last, the final push could begin. The best account comes from a man who was not merely an eyewitness but an active participant in the battle for Hutwaret. Ahmose, son of Abana, as his loyalist name suggests, was one of the Theban king's most eager and devoted foot soldiers. His father before him had served in the Theban forces. Growing up in the town of Nekheb, a staunch ally of Thebes, Ahmose, son of Abana, would have absorbed loyalty to the Theban cause with his mother's milk. Pursuing a military career, he first joined the marines on the ship *Wild Bull*. A few years later, he was transferred to another craft, the *Northern*, which formed part of King Ahmose's fleet for the initial siege of the Hyksos capital. While the Theban navy blockaded Hutwaret, preventing Hyksos forces from breaking out, the king led his army on a carefully planned advance through Middle Egypt toward the apex of the delta. Their first objective was both strategic and highly symbolic: the city of Memphis, traditional capital of Egypt since the foundation of the state. Next came an equally significant target: Iunu, cult center of the sun god Ra. It, too, fell with apparent ease. The Thebans could now claim to be a national army, one with divine support from the creator god.

Back at Hutwaret, Ahmose, son of Abana, joined a new warship, the *Risen in Memphis*, named to celebrate the fall of the capital. Spurred on by their comrades' success, the marines launched a daring assault on the main Nile channel that flowed past the Hyksos citadel, killing several enemy soldiers in the process. The war of attrition seemed to be going Thebes's way. Ahmose, son of Abana, was rewarded for his bravery with the gold of honor, Egypt's highest military decoration—the first of seven such awards during his long and distinguished career.

A second marine assault had to be broken off when the king summoned his forces to join a fierce fight south of Hutwaret. As Theban

Ahmose, son of Abana, with his wife and pet monkey
DR. WILLIAM MANLEY

land forces drew nearer their final objective, they were beginning to meet stiffer resistance. The final piece in King Ahmose's strategy, before the all-out attack on Hutwaret could commence, was the capture of Tjaru, the border fortress that had proved such a vital element in homeland security during the Twelfth Dynasty. Three months after taking Iunu, and after a brief siege, Ahmose's army captured the fort. Theban forces were now in a position to intercept any Hyksos retreat from Hutwaret. Apepi and his followers were caught in a trap.

With such a carefully planned series of moves brilliantly accomplished, the final outcome was never in doubt: "Hutwaret was plundered."[8] This laconic comment from Ahmose, son of Abana, summed up the Theban victory. For most of Hutwaret's Asiatic inhabitants, death came quickly. For those who managed to escape the destruction of their city, Egyptian forces lay in wait at the border. A few Hyksos may have made it to the relative safety of Hyksos-controlled territory in Palestine, but King Ahmose had plans for them, too. Determined that there should be no hiding place for Egypt's erstwhile oppressors (as he saw them), he led his army across the northern Sinai and laid siege to Sharuhen (modern Tell el-Ajjul), the main center of Hyksos political and commercial power in the Near East. For three years, Egyptian forces surrounded the city until it, too, surrendered. A loyal garrison was duly installed, as at Buhen, to secure the surrounding territory for the Egyptian king. And, just to make sure, a backup force was stationed at nearby Gaza, which had been renamed "the town the ruler seized," just to rub it in. Ahmose's victory was total. After a brief tour of coastal Palestine, during which he hacked up a few towns to intimidate the native inhabitants, the king returned in triumph to Egypt. The hated Asiatic had been driven out. National unity had been restored.

Expelling the Hyksos and securing Egypt's northern frontier with a defensive buffer zone were a good start, but Ahmose knew that the country's future prosperity would depend on more than just security. It needed renewed access to gold, and that meant large-scale reconquest and reoccupation of Nubia, especially the gold-bearing region south of the second cataract. This became the major strategic objective for the latter part of Ahmose's reign. Buhen was already safely in Egyptian hands and was a useful forward base for operations, but what Egypt needed, above all, was a fortified headquarters in the immediate vicinity of the gold mines. That meant outdoing the great conqueror Senusret III and setting the border even farther south than Semna.

Fortunately, the perfect geographical location presented itself. The island of Shaat (modern Sai) lay midway between the second and third cataracts, right at the heart of the gold-producing region. One of the largest islands in the Nubian Nile, it was ideal for settlement and fortification. On his only Nubian campaign, Ahmose headed directly for Shaat, occupied the island, and built a military headquarters, enclosed by a massive fortified wall fifteen feet thick, reinforced with buttresses. The site was well chosen, atop a sandstone outcrop that overlooked the east branch of the Nile and a broad section of the east bank. A sandstone quarry was opened up on Shaat to provide building material for the fortress and other royal installations in lower Nubia. And finally, Ahmose had a statue of himself installed in the temple at Shaat to act as a focus for patriotic fervor and to inspire the loyal defense of his new southern headquarters, just as Senusret III had done at Semna. With Egyptian hegemony now firmly established from the coasts of the Near

East to the upper Nile, Ahmose boasted that "his slaughter is in upper Nubia, his war cry in the lands of Phoenicia."[9]

Egypt was great once more, its people free from occupation and the threat of invasion. But not everyone shared in the mood of national euphoria. "Freedom," people might have remembered, meant different things to different audiences. For the monarchy, the restoration of order meant a return to the methods of the past, with the king at the apex of society, supported and served by an uncomplaining populace. For the populace, Egypt's rebirth meant a return to autocratic government. Yet a few people *were* willing to risk their lives to oppose the Theban monarchy and its seemingly unstoppable rise to absolute power. No sooner had Ahmose planted the Egyptian flag on Shaat Island and begun to sail northward to Egypt than a minor rebellion broke out, led by a Nubian insurgent. He seems to have taken the opportunity of the king's temporary absence to launch an attack, but it was woefully underprepared and doomed to failure. Ahmose summoned his forces, engaged the rebel, and seized him as a living captive. His hapless followers were taken prisoner, no doubt to be sent to work in the gold mines of Nubia. Then, inspired perhaps by such a brave but reckless show of defiance, a more serious insurgency flared up. This time it was led by an Egyptian named Tetian, possibly a son or relative of the governor of Nefrusi, who had been the object of Kamose's wrath a generation earlier. Tetian's cause, opposition to Ahmose's rule, had attracted a large number of supporters, and these malcontents clearly posed a real threat to the government and its plans. The king's response was immediate and ruthless. "His Majesty killed him; his gang was annihilated."[10] The dissidents (or freedom fighters) had had their chance and had squandered it. There would not be another open rebellion against the Egyptian monarchy for five hundred years.

Hand in hand with political challenges came natural disasters. To the north of Egypt, the Minoan civilization had recently been devastated by the volcanic eruption of Thera. The ash cloud had completely buried the Minoan colony of Akrotiri, while burning debris falling from the sky had destroyed crops and houses on Crete, 150 miles away. Weakened by the resulting famine and social instability, the Minoan world, which had dominated the Aegean for five centuries, suddenly looked vulnerable, a fact not lost on the small but ambitious city of

Mycenae, on the Greek mainland. At around the same time, though probably unconnected with the Theran cataclysm, a meteorological calamity beset Egypt: a violent rainstorm swept the country, causing major damage to property, including the royal residence. Determined to rectify this show of divine displeasure as vigorously as he had put down Tetian's rebellion, Ahmose ordered the restoration of flood-damaged buildings and the replacement of temple furniture, so that Egypt was "restored to its former state."[11] Recording his pious actions for posterity, the king likened the damage caused by the tempest to the recent ravages of the Hyksos. The message was clear: whatever the source of chaos, Ahmose, the true king and upholder of creation, would impose order in its place.

FAMILY VALUES

BORDERS SECURED, ACCESS TO TRADE AND GOLD REESTABLISHED, IN-ternal opposition silenced—Ahmose's achievements might have been thought sufficient to restore the might and majesty of the Egyptian monarchy. But his vision for the country went beyond practical eco-nomics and politics to embrace ideology as well. Whether by learning or instinct, Ahmose and his advisers realized that ideas could be the most powerful force for national unity, if harnessed appropriately and well tuned to the Egyptian psyche. The king's own experience had taught him the importance of a close-knit family, and the same was un-doubtedly true out there in the towns and villages of Egypt. With the country—or its rulers, at least—enjoying peace and plenty once more, Ahmose set about making his own royal family the primary focus for religious devotion throughout the land. It was perhaps his greatest achievement, and one that was to define his entire dynasty.

Personally, Ahmose had particular cause to give public recognition to key members of his family. Because he had acceded to the throne as a boy, the government had been run during his minority by his grand-mother Tetisheri and his mother, Ahhotep. Indeed, Ahhotep's impec-cable royal credentials gave her unrivaled legitimacy to carry out such a role. She was, after all, a king's daughter, a king's sister, a king's great wife, and, by the end of her life, a king's mother as well. The peculiarly incestuous relationships favored by Ahmose's family meant that his mother and father were full brother and sister, both of them offspring of Tetisheri. Ahmose in turn married his full sister, Ahmose-Nefertari. (The relationships and the frequency of the name Ahmose, for both men and women, must have made life in the royal court either fiendishly complicated or greatly simplified.) Whether keeping it in the family to such an extent was designed to distinguish the royals from ordinary mortals (by copying the brother-sister marriages of the gods) or was intended merely to shut out any potential rival claimants, the result was an exceptionally close group of relatives in which the female members played an unusually prominent role. Ahmose's genius was to turn this family business into a national cult.

At Abdju, ancient burial place of kings and thus a key site for the veneration of royal ancestors, Ahmose erected a pyramid temple for himself, decorated with scenes of his victory over the Hyksos, and a shrine for his grandmother Tetisheri. At its center, a monumental stela recorded that "His Majesty did this because his love for her was greater than anything [else]."[12] We can detect here, perhaps, the enduring bond between a man and his grandmother who brought him up while his own mother was busy with affairs of state. For Ahhotep, Ahmose's thanks and praise were even greater. He had a great stela set up at Ipet-sut in the temple of Amun, which was fast becoming Egypt's national shrine. As well as listing the king's pious donations to the temple (mostly huge quantities of gold from the mines of Nubia), the inscription exhorted the people of Egypt, now and in the future, to remember Ahhotep's considerable achievements:

> Give praise to the lady of the land,
> The mistress of the shores of Hau-nebut,
> Whose reputation is high over every foreign land,
> Who governs the masses,
> The king's wife, the sister of the sovereign (life, prosperity, and
>   health!),
> The king's daughter, the noble king's mother,
> The wise one,
> Who takes care of Egypt.
> She has gathered together its officials
> And guarded them;

She has rounded up its fugitives
And gathered up its deserters;
She has pacified Upper Egypt
And subdued its rebels:
The king's wife, Ahhotep, may she live![13]

It is an extraordinary encomium for an exceptional woman. As well as recording Ahhotep's role in governing the country, the verses more than hint at her involvement in putting down the rebellion of Tetian and reimposing law and order throughout the land. It is no coincidence that Ahhotep's grave goods from her grateful son included a necklace of golden flies, awarded for bravery in battle (the fly was an appropriate symbol of perseverance). She was evidently a force to be reckoned with, and would serve as a powerful role model for other ambitious royal women later in the dynasty.

Ahhotep's curious epithet, mistress of the shores of Hau-nebut, is particularly tantalizing. Much later, in the Ptolemaic Period, the phrase "Hau-nebut" was used to refer to Greece, and it suggests a connection between the Eighteenth Dynasty Egyptian royal family and the Minoan civilization of Crete. It may be no coincidence that, in addition to the golden flies, Ahhotep's burial equipment included two objects, a dagger and an axe, with characteristically Minoan decoration. Recent excavations at Hutwaret lend weight to the theory of a diplomatic alliance between Ahmose's family and the Minoans (the leading naval power in the eastern Mediterranean). The public rooms of the early New Kingdom royal palace, built on the ruins of the former Hyksos citadel, were decorated with frescoes in Minoan style. Scenes of acrobats, bull leaping, and bull wrestling have close parallels on the island of Thera and on Crete itself, at the palace of Knossos. Most suggestive of all is a large griffin, a motif related to Minoan queenship. Its presence at Hutwaret raises the intriguing possibility of a dynastic marriage between the Egyptian and Minoan courts. It might have been the first time that Egypt sought the protection of a foreign power against third-party aggression; it would certainly not be the last.

Having thus honored his grandmother and mother, Ahmose's policy of elevating royal women to the status of national icons now turned to his own generation and his sister-wife, Ahmose-Nefertari. Her rise to prominence coincided with a natural moment of transition in the life of the royal family: the death of the queen mother Ahhotep and the birth of an heir apparent. With this new arrival ensuring the dynasty's future, Ahmose-Nefertari thus became a king's mother as well as a king's daughter, king's sister, and king's great wife, the same collection of titles held by her late mother. But her brother-husband had another title planned for her, one that would give her not just status but considerable wealth and political influence as well. Ahmose-Nefertari was to become god's wife of Amun, the female counterpart to the high priest of Amun and hence effectively joint head of the Amun priesthood. The creation of this new office was part of a wider reorganization of religious administration under Ahmose, and it was a masterstroke. With a flourish, it achieved two goals, giving the dynasty control of a major political and economic institution (the temple of Amun, with its vast wealth and extensive landholdings) and establishing a close theological link between the cult of Amun and the royal family. To confirm his intentions, Ahmose erected another monumental stela at Ipetsut, recording the property and authority vested in Ahmose-Nefertari as god's wife. For her part, she did not disappoint. For the rest of her life, she used the title "god's wife" above all others.

GILDED MONUMENTS

WHEN KING AHMOSE DIED A FEW YEARS LATER IN 1514, STILL ONLY in his thirties, Egypt stood transformed. In the space of a single reign, the country had shaken off the yoke of foreign occupation, confirmed itself as a new and rising power in the Near East, regained mastery of the Nubian gold mines, and quelled internal dissent. The monarchy had triumphantly reestablished itself at the apex of Egyptian society, mastering the political scene and engineering a brilliant symbiosis with the dominant national cult. The foundations had been laid for the power and glory of the New Kingdom. Now all that remained to be done was to build upon those foundations—to give concrete architectural expression to the mystery and majesty of kingship in a manner that would last for eternity. That would be the task for Ahmose's son and heir, Amenhotep I (1514–1493).

Or, rather, for the queen mother, since Ahmose's premature death left Egypt, once again, with an underage monarch. This time the country was at peace, and the court could turn its full attention to a building program the likes of which Egypt had not seen for centuries. Ahmose had already reopened the limestone quarries at Ainu (modern Tura) late in his reign, and had boasted that stone blocks were being hauled from the quarry face by "oxen from the lands of Phoenicia."[14] Under the young Amenhotep I, extraction resumed at all the great quarries—Bosra and Hatnub for alabaster, Gebel el-Silsila for sandstone—and turquoise mining started up again in the Sinai for the first time since the reign of Amenemhat III, 250 years earlier. The length and breadth of Egypt echoed once more to the sounds of quarrymen, masons, and builders. It was as if the Pyramid Age had returned. Only the emphasis this time was on temples for the living, not tombs for the dead.

For the second time in Egyptian history, the focus of royal building activity was the dynastic seat of Thebes. In the centuries since it had first risen to prominence, the settlement had expanded beyond the confines of the Middle Kingdom walls, but conditions were still cramped and squalid for most of the inhabitants. In the absence of planning regulations, districts grew up organically, masking the grid pattern of the earlier town. With agricultural production the city's first priority, building land was at a premium, and tangles of houses were crammed together in a dense maze of alleyways. Space, water, and shade were desirable commodities in ancient Egypt but extremely hard to come by in an urban setting. Families who could afford to do so built upward to gain extra room, escape the risk of flooding during a high Nile, and retreat from the accumulated rubbish and foul odors at street level. Only the wealthiest Thebans could afford to build out of town on the desert margin, where more plentiful land made possible the construction of luxurious villas with their own pleasure gardens. City dwellers had to make do with the occasional breeze coming through window gratings high up in the walls, painted reddish brown to reduce the sun's glare. All in all, life in New Kingdom Thebes was crowded and noisy. For those living closest to the temple of Amun, it was about to get noisier still.

Under the Eighteenth Dynasty, the great temple at Ipetsut (Egyptian for "the most select of places") was the greatest beneficiary of royal largesse. It had been founded by the Theban Eleventh Dynasty in the dark days of civil war, and had been honored by the Theban Twelfth Dynasty. Now, with another dynasty from Thebes on the throne of Egypt, Ipetsut was again the natural focus for royal projects. Although the surviving Middle Kingdom buildings were relatively small in scale, the purity of the architecture and quality of the relief carving evidently had a profound effect on Amenhotep's builders. Inspired, in particular, by the beautiful monuments of Senusret I, they set about creating copies for the new king's grand design. Their replica of Senusret's jubilee pavilion was correct down to the last detail; only the substitution of the name Amenhotep for that of Senusret distinguished the copy from the original. Directly in front of the Twelfth Dynasty temple, a great courtyard took shape, dominated by a giant pylon gateway resembling the hieroglyph for "horizon," the place where the sun rose and set. Amenhotep I's Ipetsut would be nothing less than the act of creation in microcosm. The courtyard walls were decorated with scenes of the king offering to Amun, and priests offering to the king— the quintessential combination of divine and royal cults in a single space. In the center of the court, a magnificent alabaster shrine was erected as a resting place for the sacred barque shrine of Amun when it was carried in procession through the temple. The alabaster shrine's decoration stressed the mystic union between god and king, and depicted the royal jubilee (already being planned, though never actually celebrated). Along two sides of the court, small side chapels housed statues dedicated to the royal cult, their walls decorated with scenes of perpetual offerings. To complete the layout, a sacred abattoir was built next to the temple. It would be used to provide cattle for religious festivals and, of course, for the cults of Amenhotep I and his mother, Ahmose-Nefertari. Ostensibly a magnificent new house for the god Amun, Amenhotep's constructions at Ipetsut were equally a monument to divine kingship. The fact that the two strands could not be disentangled was entirely deliberate. By placing himself as the direct heir to the great royal builders of the Middle Kingdom, Amenhotep was consciously casting a veil over the intervening chaos. His work at Ipetsut seemed to confirm that the sacred essence of kingship had passed directly from the Twelfth Dynasty to the family of Ahmose. Like all great Egyptian rulers, Amenhotep I had a penchant for rewriting history.

The king's ambition, to turn Thebes into a giant open-air temple to kingship, did not stop at Ipetsut. In the sacred theater of the Nile Valley, the west bank was just as important as the east, since the two together formed one of those symbolic dualities through which the Egyptians made sense of the world around them. In the particular case of Thebes, the west bank was the city's main burial ground, where the rulers of the Seventeenth Dynasty had built their modest pyramid tombs, but it also had a deep and ancient connection with kingship. The dramatic embayment in the cliffs at Deir el-Bahri was believed to be a dwelling place of Hathor, mother goddess and protector of monarchs. For this reason, the civil war victor, King Mentuhotep, had chosen it as the location for his mortuary temple and for the national war grave. The symbolism of the place must have been particularly striking for Amenhotep I. Not only had his own Theban dynasty recently emerged triumphant from another war, but the theological relationship between Hathor and the king provided the divine pattern for his own close association with his mother, Ahmose-Nefertari. Their joint rule was not just god-given; it was divinely inspired.

To give these ideas concrete expression, Amenhotep commissioned two chapels at Deir el-Bahri, one of them directly in front of Mentuhotep's temple. He also built a sanctuary to house the barque of Amun when it traveled across the Nile from Ipetsut in a great procession once a year called the Beautiful Festival of the Valley. At Deir el-Bahri, as at Ipetsut itself, the inscriptions and decoration emphasized the royal cult, with particular emphasis placed on the role of Ahmose-Nefertari and on the king's much anticipated jubilee. Finally, Amenhotep erected a temple dedicated to himself and his mother on the plain of western Thebes, directly in front of the Seventeenth Dynasty royal necropolis, where his father and grandmother lay buried. They would have been proud of him. The cult of the royal family was now at the center of the nation's religious life, at Thebes and Abdju, and the family's monuments marked the horizon in every direction.

Long after their monuments had been dismantled and reused by later generations of rulers, Amenhotep I and Ahmose-Nefertari were remembered and revered by the inhabitants of western Thebes as patron deities of the district. Their memory was especially sacred to one small community known as the Place of Truth (modern Deir el-Medina). The community's foundation sums up the religious and architectural program of Ahmose's dynasty and its lasting impact on ancient Egyptian civilization as a whole. By the time Amenhotep I came to the throne, kings had learned from bitter experience that a monumental tomb, especially a pyramid, was more of a curse than a blessing. Advertising the location of the royal burial for all to see merely attracted the attention of tomb robbers and almost guaranteed that the deceased would *not* remain undisturbed for eternity. If the king were to enjoy a blessed afterlife, as intended, the nature of the royal tomb itself had to change.

As part of his wider program of religious remodeling, Amenhotep I implemented just such a radical redesign. From now on, the royal mortuary complex would be split into two distinct elements. A mortuary temple, sited prominently on the plain, would stand as the monarch's permanent memorial and would act as a public focus for the royal cult.

A view of the workmen's village WERNER FORMAN ARCHIVE

Quite separate, hidden away in the cliffs of western Thebes, a royal tomb cut deep into the rock would provide a secure resting place for eternity, without any outward sign to attract unwanted attention. To ensure complete secrecy for the royal burial, it would be necessary not only to conceal the tomb but also to isolate its builders from the rest of the population. The solution was to establish a workmen's village, hidden away in a remote valley in the Theban hills, where those employed on the royal tomb, together with their wives and children, could live in splendid isolation. The secrets of their sensitive work would remain safe. The Place of Truth was duly founded, with Amenhotep I and Ahmose-Nefertari as its royal patrons, and the community remained in use, fulfilling its original purpose, for five centuries. Today it is the single most important source of evidence for daily life in the New Kingdom.

As for Amenhotep I's own tomb, its whereabouts remain a mystery, despite more than a century of archaeological investigation. In contrast to his successors' sepulchres, which have become modern tourist traps, Amenhotep's dwelling place for eternity lies undisturbed. In this, as in the rest of his program for the Egyptian monarchy, his wish was fulfilled.

CHAPTER 11

PUSHING THE BOUNDARIES

FIRESTORM OVER NUBIA

A PARADOX LAY AT THE HEART OF EGYPT'S NEW KINGDOM renaissance. The country's restoration to its former glory had been led by the institution of hereditary monarchy, yet this very system suffered from fundamental weaknesses. For two successive generations, the throne had passed to minors. Although this gave the female members of the royal family an unprecedented opportunity to exercise leadership, having the sacred office of kingship held by a child, dependent on others for direction, was not exactly in accordance with the Egyptian ideal, nor was it a recipe for strong government. Worse still, the inbreeding favored by the Theban rulers of the late Seventeenth and early Eighteenth dynasties had narrowed the gene pool to a dangerous degree. Amenhotep I and his sister-wife were themselves the offspring of a brother-sister marriage, as were their parents. With only two great-grandparents between them, it is perhaps not surprising that Amenhotep I and his queen were unable to have children. Indeed, it is remarkable that they were not afflicted by more serious congenital conditions.

Monarchy is nothing without an assured succession, and the lack of an heir risked undoing all the hard-won achievements of Amenhotep and his dynasty. What the king lacked in fertility he more than made up for in strategic ability. Recognizing the imperative of a legitimate successor, he took the unusual decision late in his reign to adopt one of his most trusted and talented lieutenants, a man named Thutmose, as heir apparent. Thutmose's origins are shrouded in obscurity—the new king hardly wished to publicize his unorthodox path to power—but his selection was inspired. Though already in middle age, and unlikely to enjoy a long reign, he possessed apparently inexhaustable energy and determination. He had a bold vision for Egypt's destiny, one that involved not merely cementing the victories of Kamose and Ahmose but actively extending the nation's borders to forge an Egyptian empire. Under the Thutmoside Dynasty, Egypt would be transformed, at home and abroad, into the most powerful and glittering civilization of the ancient world.

Thutmose I (1493–1481) was the first king for three generations to come to the throne as an adult. He was in a position to begin his program of government straightaway, but only after he had countered any possible rumblings against his claim to the kingship. The continued presence of the royal matriarch, Ahmose-Nefertari, gave his reign a much-needed stamp of legitimacy, but Thutmose decided to take more public steps to underline his right to rule. His first act as king was to issue a decree announcing his coronation and his formal adoption of royal titles—two ceremonies that confirmed a king in power and conferred upon him divine authority. He sent the decree to his viceroy in Nubia, Turi, with express instructions to erect monumental copies in the major centers of Egyptian control—Aswan, Kubban, and Wadi Halfa. The memory of rebellion against King Ahmose was still raw, and Thutmose was determined to browbeat his Nubian subjects into submission from the very start. For the lands south of the first cataract, Thutmose's coronation decree was both a warning and a promise. Within twelve months, Nubia would reel from the most concerted and devastating campaign of conquest ever launched by Egypt.

"Enraged like a panther," Thutmose declared his aim "to destroy unrest throughout the foreign lands, to subdue the rebels of the desert region."[1] The firestorm over Nubia raged for most of his second year on the throne (1492). The rulers of the Middle Kingdom had been content to pursue a defensive strategy, guarding Egyptian interests in Wawat against the threat from the kingdom of Kush through a mixture of economic engagement and political appeasement. The disastrous results of this policy had been visited upon Egypt when the country was at its weakest. Thutmose I was not about to repeat the same mistake. For him, the only long-term guarantee of Egyptian security was the annihilation of the Kushite threat.

From the forward base on Shaat Island, Thutmose ordered a flotilla of ships to be dragged overland around the dangerous rapids of the third cataract, ready for an all-out assault on Kerma, capital of the Kushite Kingdom. The onslaught that followed was unyielding and terrifying in its ferocity. Kerma was sacked and burned, its temple desecrated. The victorious Thutmose set out cross-country with a detachment of his army and a large entourage of officials. Rather than following the river, they took instead the desert route from Kerma to the distant reaches of the Nile beyond the fourth cataract. This had both a practical logic and a symbolic purpose. It achieved the objective of extending Egyptian authority farther than ever before without the need to conquer all the intervening Kushite-controlled territory along the river.

The king and his followers halted at a great quartz rock (modern Hagar el-Merwa, near Kurgus) that rose up from the desert plain next to the Nile. A prominent marker in the landscape, visible for miles around, it was also of great spiritual significance to the local population and was covered in religious carvings. Thutmose ordered a victory inscription to be carved over these native scribblings, obliterating them with a bald statement of pharaonic power that proclaimed the boundaries of his new empire. The inscription also recorded the presence, at this most symbolically charged of occasions, of Thutmose's daughter Hatshepsut. For Thutmose, extending the boundaries of Egypt was not just a personal priority but the destiny of his new dynasty. It was an injunction the impressionable young princess would not forget.

Returning to Kerma, the king looked upon the devastation that his army had wrought and, true to form, resolved to memorialize the crushing victory in yet another monumental inscription. (The power of the written word to render permanent a desired state of affairs lay at the heart of Egyptian belief and practice.) Carved into the side of an imposing, sloping rock just outside the city limits, near modern Tombos, the text gives an extensive commentary on the Nubian campaign. Its bloodcurdling tone surpasses even the ancient Egyptians' accustomed rhetoric, painting a lurid picture of the carnage visited upon the unfortunate inhabitants of Kerma:

> There is not a single one of them left.
> The Nubian bowmen have fallen to the slaughter,

and are laid low throughout their lands.
Their entrails drench their valleys;
gore from their mouths pours down in torrents.
Carrion eaters swarm down upon them,
and the birds carry their trophies away to another place.[2]

In the same breath, the inscription extols (righteous) warfare and pumps up Thutmose I as a glory-seeking conqueror who is ready to roam the earth, taking on all comers: "He trod [the earth's] end in might and victory seeking a fight, but he found no one who would stand up to him."[3] The Tombos text, which describes foreigners as "god's abomination," strikes a particularly uncompromising tone of exultant cruelty and rampant militarism.

Before leaving Nubia, the king ordered a series of fortified towns to be established throughout the conquered territories, to give the Egyptians a permanent foothold in Kush and to deter future rebellions. One of these forts was called, with typical bombast, "no one dares confront him among all the nine bows [the traditional enemies of Egypt]." To facilitate Nubia's administration, it was divided into five districts, each controlled by a governor sworn in fealty to the Egyptian king. In a further measure intended to inculcate loyalty, the sons of Nubian chiefs were forcibly taken to Egypt, to be "educated" at court alongside their masters, in the hope that they would learn Egyptian customs and an Egyptian worldview. They also served as convenient hostages against possible insurrection by their relatives back home in Nubia.

An altogether more gruesome deportation awaited the defeated ruler of Kerma. If the Egyptian sources are to be believed, he was felled in battle by Thutmose I himself. If so, it was a mercifully quick death. On the Egyptians' triumphant journey home, the enemy's corpse was strung up at the bow of Thutmose's flagship, *Falcon*. There it hung, putrefying and flyblown, a gruesome mascot of the king's victory and a dire warning to any other would-be foes. Once back in Egypt, the conqueror thanked the gods for his victory by dedicating a stela at the sacred site of Abdju. At the end of the usual pious formulae, the king reverted to type, reveling in his subjugation of foreign peoples: "I made Egypt the chief, and the whole earth her servants."[4]

Thutmose's empire building had now taken on a religious zeal.

WIDER STILL AND WIDER

CONQUERING NUBIA, A NATURAL EXTENSION OF THE EGYPTIAN NILE Valley and a land easily accessible by boat, was one thing. Extending Egypt's boundaries into Asia, with its multitude of city-states and unfamiliar terrain, was quite another. Yet no sooner had Thutmose finished celebrating bringing Kush to heel than he was busying himself with plans for an equally ambitious foray into the Near East, "to wash his heart [that is, slake his desire] throughout the foreign lands."[5] This time, however, the king's main aim seems to have been a short-term propaganda coup rather than all-out military supremacy. The Egyptian garrisons at Sharuhen and Gaza, established by his predecessors, seemed sufficient to prevent another Hyksos-style invasion by hostile Asiatics. Egyptian economic interests continued to be centered on the entrepôt of Kebny, from which the royal court could obtain all the exotica it desired: timber, aromatic oils, tin, and silver. But this was not enough for Thutmose, scourge of Nubia. He craved international recognition for Egypt as a great power, on a par with the other emergent empires of the Near East. And he knew that the quickest way to win such status was a massive show of force right under the noses of his rivals.

There may also have been a longer-term strategic motive for an armed foray into Asia. Thutmose's predecessors of the late Middle Kingdom had failed to recognize the threat posed by the Hyksos until it was too late. He was determined not to repeat their mistake. His envoys and spies would have told him that in northern Mesopotamia, far beyond the borders of Egypt, another potentially hostile power was growing in strength. The Kingdom of Mittani had been forged from a collection of smaller states by a force of Indo-European–speaking warriors. As well as their strange tongue (reflected in the names of their kings, and some of their gods), they had brought with them from the steppes of Central Asia the horse-drawn chariot and a class of elite charioteers called the *maryannu*. With this highly effective new weaponry, Mittani had grown strong enough in the time of Ahmose to invade Anatolia and inflict a heavy defeat on the Hittite Kingdom. By the reign of Amenhotep I, Mittani had driven the Hittites out of northern Syria, upsetting the delicate political balance in the Near East. Mittani was on the march, sweeping all before it. It seemed only a matter of time before it encroached upon the Egyptian sphere of interest. Faced with such a prospect, Thutmose determined that a preemptive strike was the wisest policy—better safe than sorry.

So, in the fourth year of his reign, he set out for the kingdom of Mittani, known by the Egyptians as Naharin, "the two rivers"—in other words, Mesopotamia. Details of the expedition are sketchy, but it seems likely that to avoid a lengthy and protracted campaign through Palestine, Thutmose opted instead for an amphibious operation, sailing up the coast of the eastern Mediterranean and landing his forces in the friendly harbor of Kebny. From there, it would have been a much shorter overland march into northern Syria and to the banks of the upper Euphrates. Beyond the mighty river lay Mittani proper.

Local intelligence sources confirmed Thutmose's worst fears: Mittani was indeed planning an attack on Syria-Palestine, directly threatening Egypt's economic interests. The king lost no time in engaging the enemy and "made great carnage among them,"[6] capturing some of their prized horses and chariots. To rub salt into Mittani's wounds, Thutmose did what might, by now, have been expected of him: he had a great commemorative inscription carved on the banks of the Euphrates, to mark the ultima Thule of his new empire. From the borders of Mesopotamia, in the north, to the fourth cataract, in the south, Egypt's power had never been so widely felt.

Honor satisfied, the Egyptian army turned for home. All-out conquest of Mittani had never been in the cards, for Egypt had no strategic interest in controlling a land so far from home. But Thutmose had succeeded in firing a warning shot across Mittani's bows and neutralizing its immediate threat. He had also demonstrated Egypt's new superpower status on the world stage, both to Mittani and to its nervous neighbors. Yet rather than heading straight back to Egypt with his victorious forces, Thutmose decided to indulge in a classic display of triumphalist hauteur. Halting his homeward march in the land of Niye, in the valley of the river Orontes (modern Asi), he proceeded to hunt the herds of Syrian elephants that roamed the area. This extraordinary act was no doubt carefully calculated. On a symbolic level, it drew on the ancient ideology of kingship, establishing an explicit parallel between the defeat of Egypt's enemies and the subjugation of untamed nature.

Thutmose the military leader was consciously promoting himself as Thutmose the cosmic avenger. On a more practical level, it must have reinforced the news that by now was spreading throughout the Near East—that a great king had arisen in Egypt who showed as much machismo in his peacetime pursuits as he did on the battlefield.

HER FATHER'S DAUGHTER

WHEN THUTMOSE I DIED IN 1481 AFTER A REIGN OF JUST A DOZEN years, he left as his legacy an Egyptian empire whose boundaries stretched from Syria to sub-Saharan Africa. The great kings of the Near East—the rulers of Babylonia, Assyria, Mittani, and the Hittites— recognized their Egyptian brother as a full member of their select club. Yet this newly won authority was both superficial and vulnerable. At Kerma the local people had rebuilt their town and temple, reaffirming their indigenous traditions in defiance of their Egyptian overlords. As soon as news of Thutmose's death reached upper Nubia, the Kushites revolted, hoping to regain some of the autonomy that their nemesis had so barbarously crushed. Foremost among the rebels were the surviving sons of the very king of Kush whom Thutmose had slain and so gruesomely hung from the prow of his flagship. Revenge was sweet indeed. The Kushite forces attacked the fortresses built by Thutmose, killed their Egyptian garrisons, plundered their cattle, and for a time seemed to threaten Egyptian rule over Nubia. But they had reckoned without the determination of Thutmose's young successor and namesake, who showed himself every inch his father's son. Ordering an immediate military response to the uprising, Thutmose II (1481–1479) commanded that every Nubian male should be put to the sword, save just one of the Kushite princes who would be brought back to Egypt for "education" in time-honored fashion.

In his ruthless determination to defend his father's achievements, Thutmose II was no doubt supported by his half sister and consort, Hatshepsut. Living up to her name (which means "foremost of noblewomen"), Hatshepsut was not merely the king's great wife. As daughter of Thutmose I by his chief consort, Hatshepsut clearly regarded herself as having a stronger claim to the throne than her husband, whose mother had merely been a secondary wife. So, when Hatshep-

Hatshepsut, the female pharaoh   WERNER FORMAN ARCHIVE

sut's young husband succumbed to ill health after only three years on the throne, she seized her chance. No longer content to stand on the sidelines, she set her sights firmly on gaining the top job. As for Ahmose before her, kingship would be the focus of her ambition, Thebes her stage. Just as her father had extended the borders of Egypt, so Hatshepsut would push the boundaries of royal ideology further than ever before.

For a woman to hold the reins of power in ancient Egypt was not unprecedented. At the end of the Twelfth Dynasty, a female king, Sobekneferu, had briefly occupied the throne. More recently, during the upheavals and reconstruction of the late Seventeenth and early Eighteenth dynasties, three successive generations of royal women, Tetisheri, Ahhotep, and Ahmose-Nefertari, had exercised great influence over the affairs of state. On the face of it, Hatshepsut was merely following in this tradition when she ruled as regent for Thutmose II's infant son, her stepson, Thutmose III. As a contemporary inscription makes clear, there was a different tone to Hatshepsut's authority from the very start. After her husband's death,

His son arose in his place as king of the Two Lands, having assumed rule upon the throne of his begetter; while his sister, the god's wife Hatshepsut, conducted the affairs of the land, the Two Lands being in her counsels. She is served; Egypt bows [its] head.[7]

Her position as god's wife gave her some authority, especially in the Theban region, but Hatshepsut and her courtiers must have been acutely aware that she was not the king's mother, merely his step-mother and aunt. For her to exercise full control of the government would require appropriate ideological cover and proper theological justification. Her first bold step was to adopt the equivalent of a royal throne name, which she used alongside her queenly titles. Then, seven years into the new regency, in 1473, Hatshepsut made the determined and irrevocable decision to adopt the full panoply of kingship: the regalia of crowns and scepters and the hallowed titles and styles of Egyptian monarchy. Although she had to share the throne with her young stepson, there was no doubting who was the senior co-regent. Hatshepsut's reign had begun in earnest.

In the wake of such an unorthodox accession, the new female king and her advisers embarked on a concerted program of myth-making to bolster her legitimacy. They promoted the story of her divine birth, and rewrote history to have her elected as heir apparent during her father's lifetime. On monuments and inscriptions, she consciously emphasized her father's achievements, calling herself "the king's firstborn daughter," and studiously ignored the brief reign of her late husband. It was as if Thutmose II had never existed and the throne had passed directly from Thutmose I to Hatshepsut.

This sleight of hand may have convinced some of her detractors, but there was still the awkward question of her gender. The ideology of kingship required—demanded—a male ruler. Yet Hatshepsut, as her very name announced, was female. Her response to this conundrum was deeply schizophrenic. On some monuments, especially those dating from the time before her accession, she had the images recarved to show her as a man. On others, she had female epithets applied to male monarchs of the past, in an apparent attempt to "feminize" her ancestors. Even when portrayed as a man, Hatshepsut often used grammatically feminine epithets, describing herself as the daughter (rather than son) of Ra, or the lady (rather than lord) of the Two Lands. The tension between male office and female officeholder was never satisfactorily resolved. Little wonder that Hatshepsut's advisers came up with a new circumlocution for the monarch. From now on, the term for the palace, *per-aa* (literally "great house"), was applied also to its chief inhabitant. *Peraa*—pharaoh—now became the unique designation of the Egyptian ruler.

While Thutmose I had concentrated his efforts on building an empire, his daughter's greatest desire was to deck Egypt with buildings befitting its new status. Hatshepsut's reign is remarkable for the sheer number and audacity of her monuments, from a rock-cut shrine deep in the mountains of Sinai to a stone-built temple inside the fortress of Buhen, in Nubia. But it was Thebes that benefited most from her plans. The city's sacred landscape, laid out at the very beginning of the New Kingdom, offered Hatshepsut unrivaled opportunities to associate herself ever more closely with the state god Amun-Ra, and hence to silence her critics and doubters once and for all. For generations, Amun-Ra's chief temple at Ipetsut had enjoyed a theological importance belied by its rather modest proportions. Hatshepsut changed all that. She set about transforming it into a true national shrine, adding a "noble pillared hall"[8] between her father's two monumental gateways. At the core of the temple she reshaped the Middle Kingdom sanctuary, while on the south side her architects created a vast new gateway, the largest to date, fronted by six colossal statues of the female king. Nearby, she erected a chapel carved from blocks of red sandstone and black granite, each of them decorated with exquisite scenes of Hatshepsut performing the rituals and duties of kingship. On the north side of the temple, she built a royal residence with the revealing name "the royal palace 'I am not far from him' [that is, Amun-Ra]."

The crowning glory of her additions to Ipetsut were three pairs of obelisks, designed, quite literally, to point the way to the divine. On the base of one pair, she had her masons carve a long text, to record her pious motives for all eternity. It stands to this day as Hatshepsut's principal apologia, the most revealing insight into her character and ambition:

I have done this with a loving heart for my father Amun. . . . I call to attention the people who shall live in the future, who shall consider this monument that I made for my father.. . . It was when I was sitting in the palace that I remembered my maker. My heart directed me to make for him two obelisks of electrum [a natural alloy of gold and silver], their pinnacles touching the heavens. . . .

Now my mind turned this way and that, anticipating the words of the people who shall see my monument in future years and speak of what I have done. . . . He shall not declare what I have said to be an exaggeration. Rather, he will say, "How like her it is, loyal to her father!" . . . For I am his daughter in very truth, who glorifies him and who knows what he has ordained.[9]

HOLY OF HOLIES

BEYOND IPETSUT, HATSHEPSUT TOOK UP WHERE AMENHOTEP I HAD left off, adding yet more architectural props to the great Theban stage set of kingship. From her gateway on the south side of Ipetsut, she set forth a new axis that linked the temple of Amun-Ra with a temple dedicated to the god's consort Mut and, beyond that, with a new shrine for the divine barque at Amun's southern sanctuary (modern Luxor). To make proper symbolic use of this new processional way, Hatshepsut's theologians inaugurated an annual celebration, the Festival of Opet, during which the cult image of Amun was carried from Ipetsut to Luxor, for a period of rest and relaxation. Amun of Opet would journey across the river to visit the west bank (and a small temple specially built by Hatshepsut to receive him), opening up yet another ritual axis. With the Beautiful Festival of the Valley already connecting Ipetsut and Deir el-Bahri, processional routes now demarcated the whole of Thebes. The city and everything in it belonged incontrovertibly to Amun-Ra, thanks to the ministrations of his beloved daughter.

Of Hatshepsut's many constructions in Egypt, none received more care and attention than her temple at Deir el-Bahri. The site's close association with Hathor, mother goddess and guardian of kingship, must have given it a special appeal to a female monarch. The fact that it lay directly opposite her new southern gateway at Ipetsut gave it added symbolic potency. Such a spot demanded a monument of uncommon quality. What Hatshepsut and her architects created at Deir el-Bahri over the course of thirteen years remains one of the most remarkable buildings from ancient Egypt. The uniqueness of its design is striking, even today. Its scale and grandeur overwhelm just as their patron intended. Though devised, first and foremost, as a grand resting place for the barque shrine of Amun-Ra during the Beautiful Festival of the Valley, the temple called by Hatshepsut Djeser-djeseru, "Holy of Holies," also incorporated shrines to Anubis, Hathor, and Ra, as well as a set of chapels for the perpetual celebration of her funerary cult alongside that of her father, Thutmose I. A single building sought to incorporate every aspect of royal ideology, from the monarch's relationship with the ancient deities Hathor and Ra to the celebration of the royal ancestors and the king's eternal destiny.

The entire complex was arranged as a series of huge terraces, with the sheer cliff face as a stunning natural backdrop. It was inspired by the neighboring temple of Mentuhotep, yet it outdid its predecessor in every department and cast Hatshepsut as the founder of a new age. A

Scene from the Egyptian expedition to Punt   WERNER FORMAN ARCHIVE

causeway linked the main temple to a valley temple more than half a mile to the east. The last five hundred yards of this processional route were flanked by more than a hundred sphinxes of Hatshepsut. The temple proper was likewise furnished with magnificent statuary showing the monarch in different guises, offering to the gods or transfigured as Osiris. Behind the pillared façades of each terrace, delicately carved and painted scenes recorded key episodes from Hatshepsut's life, real or imagined: her divine birth; her election as heir apparent; her coronation; the transport of her obelisks to Ipetsut; and, perhaps most famous, the expedition she sent in 1463 to the fabled land of Punt to bring back exotic materials for Amun-Ra. The vivid details of the African landscape, the Puntites' stilt houses, and their obese queen have made this tableau one of the best-known in any Egyptian temple. It seems to capture the freshness, vitality, and innovation that characterize the reign of Hatshepsut, the most effective and powerful of the handful of women ever to rule ancient Egypt.

There is one further, unusual aspect to Hatshepsut's reign—the unprecedented favors bestowed on her most devoted follower, Senenmut. A man of humble origins, Senenmut rose to prominence during Hatshepsut's regency. As tutor to her daughter, he enjoyed privileged access to the royal family's inner sanctum. As overseer of the audience chamber, he effectively controlled who did and did not get to see the regent. While as steward of the queen's estate, he wielded considerable economic influence. The combination of offices made him Hatshepsut's most influential courtier by far. He seems to have had an artistic bent, to judge from the unparalleled quantity, quality, and diversity of his surviving statuary, and his skills were recognized by Hatshepsut, who promoted him to the office of overseer of all the king's works, and chief architect. In this capacity, he masterminded the sculpting and transport of the Ipetsut obelisks, and the construction of "Holy of Holies." His special reward, among many, was royal permission to carve his own devotional reliefs at Deir el-Bahri, Ipetsut, and "in [all] the temples of Upper and Lower Egypt."[10] At Deir el-Bahri, he even had himself depicted in the upper sanctuary, albeit carefully concealed behind the open doors of the shrine. For a commoner to be shown in the most sacred part of the temple was not just unusual but unprecedented.

He was likewise allowed to commission a vast funerary complex, the largest of its time, comprising a public cult chapel and a secluded burial chamber, the latter reaching right underneath the sacred enclosure at Deir el-Bahri and equipped with a stone sarcophagus, another royal prerogative. It is little wonder that Senenmut's jealous contemporaries harbored suspicions about the precise nature of his relationship with Hatshepsut, and little wonder that a cheeky Theban workman illustrated the more scurrilous rumors in a sexually explicit graffito.

Ironically, Hatshepsut's elevation to the kingship did not bring commensurate promotion for Senenmut. He was replaced as tutor to the princess and subsequently disappeared from the official record. Whether he fell out of favor, retired, or simply died from natural causes remains a mystery. What is clear is that he never married and he left no heirs. Such, perhaps, was the price of winning and keeping his mistress's favor.

MIGHTIER YET

WHILE HATSHEPSUT, IN HER MORE AMBITIOUS MOMENTS, MAY HAVE hoped to see her daughter follow in her footsteps, a mother-daughter succession would have stretched the ideology of kingship just too far. In the end, the throne passed to her stepson, nephew, and son-in-law, Thutmose III, who after a decade and a half as junior co-regent finally achieved sole rule in 1458. Whatever his personal feelings toward his stepmother, he certainly shared her idolization of Thutmose I. And it was with his grandfather's energy and zeal that he set about consolidating his imperial inheritance. Just ten weeks after taking over the reins of power, Thutmose III rode out at the head of his army on his first military campaign to the Near East. He was determined, no doubt, to prove himself as brave and resolute a leader as his forebear, but there was also an immediate political imperative. While Hatshepsut's regime had been preoccupied with construction projects at home, Egypt's foreign rivals had not been idle. The kingdom of Mittani, temporarily humbled by Thutmose I, had reasserted itself and was busy stirring up resistance to Egyptian rule among a coalition of Asiatic princes. Chief among them was the prince of Kadesh (modern Tell Nebi Mend), who had holed himself up with his key allies in the fortified town of

Megiddo (the biblical Armageddon). Since Megiddo controlled the Jezreel Valley, the main north-south route through northern Canaan as well as the easiest route between the Jordan Valley and the Mediterranean coast, Egypt ignored such unwelcome developments at its peril. Attack was the best form of defense.

At the end of winter 1458, Thutmose III and his household division of ten thousand men passed through the border fortress of Tjaru, bound for Megiddo. After a march of nine days, they reached Gaza and bedded down for the night in friendly company. But this was no time for relaxation. They were off again at the crack of dawn, setting forth "in valor, victory, power, and vindication."[11] A further eleven days' march through unfamiliar and hostile territory brought the army to the town of Yehem, where the king held a war council. From Yehem, three roads led to Megiddo: one to the north, one to the south, and the most direct route through the narrow Aruna Pass. According to the official campaign record, the king argued for the Aruna road against the advice of his generals. Whatever the truth behind the decision, it was inspired, for as the Egyptian soldiers advanced through the narrow defile, with Thutmose leading from the front, they met no resistance. The enemy had been waiting for them to the north and south, never expecting them to risk the Aruna road. Once the Egyptian rear guard had safely emerged from the pass, the entire force continued down the road toward Megiddo and pitched camp on the bank of the Qina Brook in the early afternoon. Like Shakespeare's Henry V on the eve of Agincourt, Thutmose steeled his men for battle the following morning, telling the soldiers of the watch, "Be steadfast, be steadfast! Be vigilant, be vigilant!"[12]

At daybreak on April 27, the king appeared in the midst of his infantry, standing on a chariot of electrum and clad in shining armor—a dazzling sight to inspire his troops and intimidate the enemy. It seems to have done the trick, for the opposing forces "fled headlong toward Megiddo with faces of fear, abandoning their horses and their chariots of gold and silver, [the men] to be hoisted up into the town by their clothes."[13] Then, to the Egyptians' eternal shame, their discipline cracked, and instead of pressing home their advantage, they set about plundering the possessions the enemy had left behind on the battlefield. Having failed to capture Megiddo before the town could muster

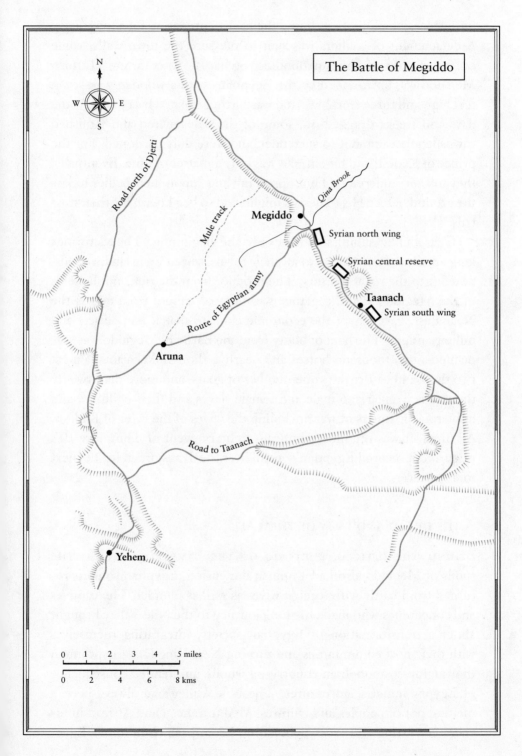

The Battle of Megiddo

N
W · E
S

Road north of Djerti

Mule track

Qina Brook

Megiddo ●

Route of Egyptian army

□ Syrian north wing

□ Syrian central reserve

Taanach

□ Syrian south wing

Aruna ●

Road to Taanach

Yehem ●

0 1 2 3 4 5 miles

0 2 4 6 8 kms

its defenses, the Egyptians found themselves preparing for a long siege. A detachment of soldiers was sent to measure the town walls, while others cut down the surrounding orchards. After a great effort, Megiddo was surrounded by the Egyptians with a wooden wall seven feet high and three feet thick, and was further isolated by a ditch. As the days and weeks dragged on, some of the beleaguered and famished townspeople came out to surrender, and were duly pardoned. For the prince of Kadesh and his allies, it was only a matter of time. Eventually, they too surrendered to Thutmose, crawling "upon their bellies to kiss the ground before His Majesty's might, and to beg breath for their nostrils."[14]

Their public submission was only the beginning. The victorious king appointed new rulers to all their towns, seized their land, and annexed it to the royal treasury. The produce from the rich, arable fields of the Megiddo Plain, together with annual tribute from across the Near East, gave Egypt the economic clout to match its political and military might. The haul of booty from the Battle of Megiddo was stupendous: two thousand horses and nearly a thousand chariots; almost two thousand cattle, the same number of goats, and more than twenty thousand sheep; 1,796 male and female slaves and their children, and numerous prisoners of war, including the wives of the ruler of Kadesh. All in all, it was the most signficant military event of Thutmose III's reign and it secured Egyptian control over the Transjordan for the next four centuries.

THE DREAD AND ENVY OF THEM ALL

BEHIND THE OFFICIAL RHETORIC OF THE CAMPAIGN ANNALS, THE spoils of Megiddo also had a human dimension. Egyptian soldiers returned from battle with foreign wives as well as plunder. The captives and concubines who made the long journey to the Nile Valley brought about a transformation of Egyptian society, integrating themselves with their host communities and turning New Kingdom Egypt into a thoroughly cosmopolitan country—a wholly unintended consequence of Egypt's imperial adventures. The Nile Valley had always been a melting pot of peoples and cultures, Mediterranean and African influences coexisting and cross-pollinating. From prehistoric times Egypt had welcomed immigrants from other lands, as long as they thoroughly integrated themselves and adopted Egyptian customs. Even at the height of the Pyramid Age, when Egyptian chauvinism and self-confidence had known no bounds, a native citizen of Memphis might have rubbed shoulders with a shipwright from Kebny or a mercenary from Nubia, albeit bearing adopted Egyptian names. But the influx of foreigners prompted by Thutmose III's campaigns was on an altogether different scale. Egyptian towns and cities found themselves home to significant foreign populations, and the migrants were quick to make the most of their new opportunities. One particularly talented prisoner of war, named Pas-Baal, rose to become chief architect in the temple of Amun, an office his descendants held for at least six generations. Even the royal palace witnessed changing attitudes toward foreigners. Among the booty brought back from the Near East by Thutmose III were three Syrian women on whom the young king seems to have doted. One of them was named Manuwai, from the Amorite word meaning "to love." Her companions were named Manhata and Maruta (Hebrew "Martha," meaning "lady"). Thutmose showered all three of them with sumptuous gifts: golden armlets, bracelets, and anklets; beaded collars; diadems inlaid with precious stones; vessels of precious metal, and rare glass vases. Barely a century after the expulsion of the hated Hyksos, the Egyptian king had Asiatic wives in his harem. It was a remarkable turnaround.

After Megiddo, Thutmose III led another sixteen military operations in the Near East during the next two decades, at a dizzying frequency of almost one a year. Most were little more than heavily militarized tours of inspection, to cement previous victories and receive tribute from vassal princes. But a few forays into Syria-Palestine had real military objectives. The city-state of Tunip, in northern Syria, posed a particular threat, and was the focus of three consecutive campaigns. Thutmose turned his forces against Tunip's coastal protectorates, conquering them, taking their rulers hostage, and transforming their harbors into fortified supply centers for the Egyptian army. Slowly but surely, Egypt was eliminating the opposition and annexing large swaths of the Near East. Where Thutmose I had been content with a show of force, his grandson was determined to win and hold territory for the long term.

Not that Thutmose III was immune to the attractions of a propaganda coup. For his eighth campaign, he decided to set the seal on his grandfather's achievements, following in his footsteps to the very borders of Mittani. As it had two generations earlier, the Egyptian army journeyed by sea from the delta to Kebny. There, timber was cut and ships were built, which the pharaoh's men proceeded to haul overland to the banks of the Euphrates. Having "crossed the great bend of Naharin in bravery and victory at the head of his army,"[15] Thutmose found the Mittanian forces ill-prepared for battle. Their king fled, and his nobility sought refuge in nearby caves to escape the Egyptian onslaught that devastated the surrounding towns and villages. Thutmose took the enemy's retreat as a surrender, and recorded his triumph on a stela set up right next to Thutmose I's victory inscription. History was repeating itself, just as the king intended. To complete the coup de théâtre, the pharaoh proceeded to Niye, where he killed 120 elephants in direct emulation of his grandfather. He then took time out to visit the local bow-making industry at nearby Qatna and participate in a sporting conquest, before collecting more tribute from the native princes and marching back to Egypt. Altogether, the campaign lasted a record five months. The plaudits from Mittani's fellow enemies came thick and fast. Babylonia sent gifts of lapis lazuli; the Hittites sent shipments of silver, gems, and wood. Assyrian envoys brought tribute, too—as, a little later, did delegations from Ashuwa, on the Ionian coast, and the land of Tanaya (perhaps Mycenae), which provided silver and rare iron. Egypt's reputation was at its zenith, and Thutmose III, Egypt's warrior pharaoh, was the toast and envy of foreign capitals from the Aegean to the Persian Gulf.

There remained only the unfinished business of Nubia. Where brute force had failed to crush Kushite opposition, perhaps a more calculated policy might succeed. Kerma had been rebuilt time and again by its loyal citizens, so rather than razing the city to the ground, Thutmose III took the simpler expedient of founding his own Egyptian settlement next door. Drawn away by opportunities for trade and employment, the population of Kerma slowly but surely migrated the short distance to the new town of Pnubs. Starved of commerce, the old city, talisman of Kushite nationhood, withered and died. Instead of killing the local rulers and hanging them upside down from his bowsprit, Thutmose III brought them and their families back to Egypt for a spell of assimilation, before repatriating them, thoroughly acculturated, to continue administering their homelands on behalf of the Egyptian crown. While Egyptian control was never as strong in Kush as it was in Wawat, Thutmose's policy was a success, and serious rebellions did not trouble the New Kingdom pharaohs again.

Thutmose III was justly hailed in his lifetime as the ruler "who makes his boundary as far as the Horn of the Earth, the marshes of Naharin."[16] In the eyes of posterity, he was, perhaps, the greatest of all pharaohs.

CHAPTER 12

KING AND COUNTRY

ALL THE KING'S MEN

THUTMOSE III'S FOREIGN CONQUESTS LOOM LARGE IN CONTEMPORARY accounts of his reign and still dominate our view thirty-five centuries later. Yet, while the king spent long periods away on campaign, especially during the first two decades of his sole rule, he could not afford to neglect domestic affairs. Egypt was geographically extensive, and a nation of strong local and regional traditions. The forces of decentralization were never far beneath the surface. Bitter experience, twice in Egypt's history, had shown that in the absence of firm central government, the country could easily fall prey to political fragmentation, internal conflict, and foreign invasion.

For the early Eighteenth Dynasty kings, Ahmose and Amenhotep I, rebuilding their shattered realm had been the priority, overseas adventures an unaffordable distraction. That Thutmose III was able to devote his considerable reserves of energy to widening the frontiers of Egypt is a testament as much to his forebears' administrative reforms as to his own leadership skills. For the system of government that the early New Kingdom rulers put in place strengthened the absolute power of the monarch while releasing him from the day-to-day exigencies of running the country. The king might be the sole source of power, simultaneously head of state and government, commander in chief of the armed forces, high priest of every cult and the gods' representative on earth, and the arbiter of policy, but in practice he delegated matters to a small handful of trusted officials. Reveling in their status and wealth, these men (and they *were* all men—Egypt might have accommodated itself to a female pharaoh, but the corridors of power remained an all-male preserve) who ran the country during the New Kingdom commissioned for themselves beautifully decorated sepulchres in the Theban hills. The so-called Tombs of the Nobles are a favorite tourist attraction today, but also a revealing window on the king's inner circle. Look beyond the brightly colored wall paintings, and the murky reality of power politics comes sharply into view.

For practical purposes, the administration of Egypt was divided into separate departments. Central government combined the office of royal construction projects, headed by an overseer of works, with the all-important treasury, under the control of the chancellor. The army had its own overseer, as did the Nubian gold mines, so vital to the prosperity of the Egyptian economy. Provincial government was the responsibility of regional appointees, such as the king's son and overseer of the southern countries, who administered Egyptian-controlled Nubia, while individual towns had their own mayors. Thebes, the monarchy's theological power base, was treated as a special case, with its own devolved administration entrusted to ultraloyalists. Each temple in the land had its own priesthood with economic as well as religious authority. First among equals was the high priest of Amun, who exercised effective control over the vast landholdings and other assets that belonged to the temple of Ipetsut. Finally, there was the department responsible for the royal household and for the estate that supplied its material needs. Here, the royal steward held sway, controlling access to the king's person and enjoying privileged access to the monarch. At the very top of the government machine, filling the role of intermediary between every department and the king, was the office of vizier (effectively prime minister). In the Eighteenth Dynasty, this position was divided into two, with a northern vizier based in Memphis and a southern vizier in Thebes. All in all, it was a highly effective system, giving the king, through his placemen, control over every aspect of the nation's affairs.

In the days of the pyramids, the major offices of state had been reserved for male members of the royal family, but such a system would have provided the king's younger brothers and sons with opportunities to build up rival power bases, and could have proved disastrous. In the late Fourth Dynasty, the upper ranks of the administration had been opened to men of nonroyal birth. Not only did this keep the king's potential rivals away from positions of influence, but it also enabled the government to be run in a more professional way. By the early New

Kingdom, with Egypt engaged in international relations and empire building on an unprecedented scale, the king's male relatives—with the exception of the crown prince—could be safely packed off to join the army (much like the younger sons of British monarchs in more recent times). There, they could find an outlet for their skills (and frustration) in the service of the state. Meanwhile, back at home, an entire ruling class of bureaucratic families had established itself at the pinnacle of ancient Egyptian society. Its members monopolized the best jobs, often passing them down from one generation to another. Within this small and claustrophobic clique, men of talent and ambition jostled for power, currying favor with the king to advance their own careers.

A quartet of high-ranking bureaucrats who served under Thutmose III and his successor illustrate particularly well the nature of authority in ancient Egypt and the atmosphere of sycophancy and suspicion that permeated the king's inner circle. Through them, we may glimpse the inner workings of the Egyptian state at the height of its power and prestige.

CHURCH AND STATE

MENKHEPERRASENEB WAS HIGH PRIEST OF AMUN, IN OVERALL CHARGE of the great temple of Amun-Ra at Ipetsut, the most important religious foundation in Egypt. The string of titles inscribed in Menkheperraseneb's tomb emphasizes his status as occupant of the senior sacerdotal office in the country: superintendent of the priests of Upper and Lower Egypt; administrator of the two thrones of the god; superintendent of advanced offices; superintendent of the double treasuries of gold and silver; superintendent of the temple of Thes-khau-Amun, set over the mysteries of the two goddesses. Typically for a senior member of the ruling elite, Menkheperraseneb's chief qualification for high office was his personal connection with the royal family. "Menkheperra" was the throne name of Thutmose III, and Menkheperraseneb's very name—"Menkheperra is healthy"—expressed his devotion to the monarch, a loyalty born of close family ties. Menkheperraseneb's grandmother had grown up in the royal palace as a foster sister of the young Thutmose I, while his mother had been a royal nurse. It is quite likely that Menkheperraseneb himself grew up

on the fringes of the royal household, and these connections undoubtedly played a part in his rapid promotion through the ranks of the Theban priesthood.

For the ordinary citizens of Thebes, the Eighteenth Dynasty ushered in a new era of public religious spectacle, far removed from the
rarefied and secretive activities that had characterized state cults in earlier periods. The city at large had been transformed into a giant open-
air arena for the celebration of divine kingship, and the gods
themselves had been brought out from behind the high walls of temples to spread their beneficence among the populace. In the privacy of
their humble homes the peasant farmers of Upper Egypt continued to
worship their traditional household deities: Taweret the hippopotamus, protector of pregnant women; Bes the lion-faced dwarf, guardian
of mothers and children; and the cow goddess, Hathor, who watched
over all her devotees with a maternal eye. But these familiar companions were now joined by altogether more exalted members of the state
pantheon, notably the moon god Khonsu; his mother, Mut; and her
consort Amun-Ra, king of the gods. During the great processions that
were a feature of Theban religion in the New Kingdom, this triad of
deities became directly accessible to the common people for the first
time. On high days and holidays—in particular the Beautiful Festival of
the Valley and the annual Festival of Opet—the barque shrines of
Amun, Mut, and Khonsu were borne on the shoulders of priests from
the great temple of Ipetsut through the crowded Theban streets.
Farmers and blacksmiths, as much as scribes and priests, could bask in
the warm glow of the divine presence as it passed by. Not only did these
spectacles bring color and gaiety to humdrum lives, but the rites also
allowed the citizenry to feel more closely allied with the official dogma
of the state. As always, pharaonic religion was as much about politics as
about piety.

From its headquarters at Ipetsut, the cult of Amun dominated
Theban society on every level. To judge from the scenes and texts in
his tomb, Menkheperraseneb's secular duties as high priest were
more important than his sacred role. He took a keen interest in Thutmose III's building projects at Ipetsut, and boasted of having directed
the work on his monuments. More important still was the administration of the temple's economic assets: its extensive herds of cattle,

its landholdings throughout Egypt, and its mining interests in the Eastern Desert and Nubia. Menkheperraseneb spent much of his time inspecting livestock, supervising the delivery of agricultural and mineral revenues, and ensuring that the temple granaries were kept restocked—all, of course, on behalf of the sovereign. Part of the wealth that poured into Ipetsut was destined for the temple work-shops, which employed the finest craftsmen in the land. Their job was to manufacture costly objects not only for the temple itself, but also for the royal household.

Temple and palace—in ancient Egypt the two institutions were in-extricably intertwined and mutually reinforcing. As high priest, Menkheperraseneb's primary duty was to bolster the monarchy, ideo-logically and financially. These twin strands came together most spec-tacularly in the formal presentation of foreign envoys to the king. The parade of colorful foreign emissaries with their exotic goods—Minoans with animal-headed drinking cups, Syrians with tame bears, Hittites and Asiatics with weaponry and metal ingots—served to emphasize the superiority of the Egyptian ruler over all other lands, and also his fab-ulous material wealth.

While Menkheperraseneb ensured that the temple of Amun-Ra and its priesthood remained loyal to the monarch, his colleague Rekhmira was tasked with an even greater responsibility, the smooth running of the civilian administration throughout Upper Egypt. As southern vizier, Rekhmira exercised a combination of courtly, judicial, and ad-ministrative authority, hearing petitioners with a grievance against the authorities, presiding as chief judge in important cases, and receiving daily briefings from other government ministers. In his own words, he was "second [only] to the king."[1] Rekhmira, too, owed his exalted posi-tion more to influence than to innate ability, coming from a long line of viziers. In accordance with the Egyptian concept of *maat* (truth, jus-tice, and righteousness), the vizier was sworn to carry out his duties with impartiality. At Rekhmira's installation, the king himself delivered the admonishment with these words:

These, then, are the teachings: you shall treat just the same the one known to you and the one not known to you, the one near you and the one far away.[2]

For his part, Rekhmira claimed to have observed this injunction scrupulously. Yet there is something rather telling about his protestations. They suggest that the reverse was the norm, and that most ordinary Egyptians received rough justice from those in authority.

The balance of Rekhmira's activities is also revealing. Aside from his tours of inspection and his daily audience when he listened to plaintiffs in the Hall of the Vizier, flanked by the master of the privy chamber on his right and the receiver of income on his left, his schedule was dominated by briefings from subordinates. Alongside reports from the treasury and the royal estate, key intelligence was provided each day by the head of the palace guard, the garrison commanders, and the head of the security service. The king's personal safety seems to have weighed as heavily as the national economy, underlining the autocratic nature of the ancient Egyptian regime. As well as prime minister and first lord of the treasury, the vizier was effectively commissioner of police, minister for the armed forces, and interior minister as well.

Rekhmira also paid regular visits to Ipetsut, no doubt to ensure that the high priest was performing up to the mark—further evidence of the close connection between religious and secular spheres. Having received information from every department of state, Rekhmira relayed this to the king at a daily conference. While the vizier might coordinate government policy, there was no doubt where ultimate authority lay—and where the power to hire and fire senior officials rested. Despite impeccable connections, Rekhmira's family did not succeed in holding on to high office for a further generation. When Thutmose III was succeeded by Amenhotep II (1426–1400), the old vizier's sons, who might have expected to follow in their father's eminent footsteps, were passed over in favor of another family altogether. A new broom, a deliberate break with the past, brought about a decisive change of family at the top of the Upper Egyptian bureaucracy, and reminded the ruling elite of the precariousness of power in an absolute monarchy. The king giveth and the king taketh away—blessed be the name of the king.

PRIDE AND PREJUDICE

THE CHIEF BENEFICIARY OF THE NEW REIGN WAS A FAMILY WITH EQUALLY strong royal connections to Amenhotep II, not his predecessor. As a young prince, Amenhotep II had received instruction from a man named Ahmose-Humay, who was also overseer of the harem palace, the institution that provided a home for the king's wives and children. Ahmose-Humay's two sons grew up, if not side by side with the prince, then certainly in the same milieu. When Amenhotep came to the throne, he lost no time in promoting his childhood companions to high office. The elder brother, Amenemopet, gained the southern vizierate in succession to Rekhmira, while the younger brother, Sennefer (literally "good brother"), was appointed mayor of Thebes. Between them, Amenemopet and Sennefer controlled virtually every aspect of the Upper Egyptian administration. Moreover, both brothers reinforced their membership in the new king's inner circle by marrying women from the same background. Amenemopet married a woman of the harem palace, and Sennefer a royal wet nurse.

Sennefer is one of the few New Kingdom officials whose true character can be seen in the official record, through the carefully chosen biographical details inscribed in his tomb. Although granted the extremely rare privilege (along with his brother) of a burial in the Valley of the Kings, it is his second Theban sepulchre that is the more famous. Dubbed "the tomb of the vines," it is remarkable for its ceiling, which is molded and painted to resemble a fruitful vine, laden with pendant bunches of grapes. It conjures up an image of Sennefer the bon vivant, the mayor "who spends his lifetime in happiness."[3] This is reinforced by a painting in the tomb and a beautifully carved statue of Sennefer and his wife, both of which share the same small detail—a pendant in the shape of two conjoined hearts, worn by Sennefer around his neck. The pendant is inscribed with the throne name of Amenhotep II and must have been a royal gift. It was evidently Sennefer's most treasured possession, talisman and symbol of his king's favor. Not for nothing did Sennefer describe himself as "one who satisfies the heart of the king."[4] The pun may have been intentional. Sennefer's statue is signed by the two sculptors who fashioned it, which is unusual. Amenmes and Djedkhonsu were "outline draftsmen of the temple of Amun." Sennefer seems to have used his contacts at Ipetsut to procure the services of skilled craftsmen for his own personal project. Such arrangements must have happened all the time, and reflect the private face of public office.

Sennefer wearing his favorite pendant, in his Theban tomb WERNER FORMAN ARCHIVE

Another piece of evidence that reveals Sennefer's character is an even more remarkable survival, a sealed and unopened letter addressed by him to a man named Baki, who was a tenant farmer in the town of Hut-sekhem (modern Hu), north of Thebes. The reason for the missive was to give notice of Sennefer's impending arrival at Hut-sekhem, where he intended to take delivery of certain supplies. In imperious tones, Sennefer hectors his subordinate, warning him:

> Do not let me find fault with you concerning your post. . . .
> Now mind, you shall not slack, for I know that you are sluggish and
>   fond of eating lying down.[5]

While Baki may have deserved such a dressing down, it is equally likely that this was the way Sennefer, proud mayor of Thebes, addressed all his underlings. Pomp and circumstance went hand in hand with pride and arrogance—the story of officialdom throughout history.

No member of the Eighteenth Dynasty administration demonstrates this self-satisfied conceit more unashamedly than the fourth member of our high-ranking quartet, Amenhotep II's chief steward, Qenamun. Like Sennefer and Amenemopet, Qenamun grew up in the harem palace, where his mother was wet nurse to the future king. He referred to her, unblushingly, as "the great nurse who brought up the god."[6] Qenamun was effectively the prince's foster brother, and the bond forged between the two boys in childhood endured, paying dividends for Qenamun when his playmate acceded to the throne.

Qenamun's early career in the army included a spell of active service fighting alongside the king on his Syrian campaign. Not only were the ties of friendship strengthened on the battlefield, but Qenamun's loyalty and physical fitness would also, doubtless, have struck Amenhotep II as eminently suitable qualities for preferment. Back from the wars, the king appointed Qenamun to the stewardship of Perunefer, a harbor and naval base in northern Egypt. Further promotion followed swiftly, Qenamun's devoted service eventually landing him one of the plum jobs in the land, that of chief steward, with overall responsibility for the royal estate. It was an important position, supervising the landholdings and other assets that funded the court. On a day-to-day basis, Qenamun had specific responsibility for the royal family's country residence. This seems to have fitted his character perfectly, since the administrative drudgery was more than usually interspersed with lavish entertainments: troupes of dancing girls, musicians, and the presentation of exotic gifts to the king at the New Year.

In characteristic fashion, Qenamun's extravagant Theban tomb was designed to provide as much wall space as possible, the better to trumpet his dignities to posterity. In this everlasting monument to his ego, Qenamun was able to give free rein to his obsessive predilection for titles. The result is a list of more than eighty epithets—even though, in reality, few of them signify real office. Most stress his privileged position at court, as a member of the king's inner circle: member of the elite and high official, royal seal bearer, confidential companion, dearly beloved companion, gentleman of the bedchamber, fan bearer of the lord of the Two Lands, royal scribe, aide to the king, attaché of the king in every place . . . the list is almost endless. Qenamun devised ever more elaborate formulations to vaunt his position: "chief companion of the courtiers; overseer of overseers, leader of leaders, greatest of the great, regent of the whole land; one who, if he gives attention to anything in the evening, it is mastered early in the morning at daybreak." The language becomes most pompous when stressing Qenamun's loyalty to the king: "doing right by the Lord of the Two Lands"; "giving satisfaction to the sovereign"; "inspiring the king with perfect confidence"; and, perhaps most ludicrous of all, "heartily appreciated by Horus."[7] Rarely had an Egyptian official been quite so intoxicated with the exuberance of his own verbosity.

Yet behind all this bombast and vainglory, Qenamun led a secret double life. Because of his privileged access to the inner sanctum of power, he was ideally placed to pick up court gossip, in particular any murmurings against the king. His role as chief steward provided the perfect cover for carrying out clandestine surveillance as master of secrets, the head of the king's internal security apparatus. Qenamun's undercover role was to be "the eyes of the king of Upper Egypt, the ears of the king of Lower Egypt."[8] Like Elizabethan England, Eighteenth Dynasty Egypt had a sophisticated court underpinned by a network of spies and agents who monitored those in positions of authority, as well as the general population, for signs of dissent. Qenamun's relationship to Amenhotep II was as Sir Francis Walsingham's was to Elizabeth I: ultraloyal, devoted to his monarch, confident of his own authority, and unafraid of making enemies. And enemies there clearly were. After Qenamun's death and burial, the gorgeous reliefs in his Theban tomb were systematically defaced. Not a single image of him survived the attackers' chisels. The same posthumous vilification was meted out to Rekhmira, exemplary vizier. Theirs are cautionary tales, suggesting that high office in ancient Egypt could bring great unpopularity. The self-confident image of the official record masked an unpalatable truth.

SCHOOL RULES

THE CAREERS OF SENNEFER AND QENAMUN ILLUSTRATE THE IMPORtance of personal relationships in winning promotion under an absolute monarchy. Amenhotep II in particular surrounded himself with officials he had known since childhood. In ancient Egypt, growing up alongside the future king was a near certain passport to high office. To be a "child of the nursery" was to rub shoulders not only with the royal children, but also with the offspring of Egypt's great and good, in an atmosphere of privilege and power. The country's future leaders were trained from infancy for the responsibilities they would later assume, receiving an education that was practical and vocational rather than narrowly academic. There was also an overtly political dimension. In the New Kingdom, the inhabitants of the nursery—where children lived as well as learned—included the sons of foreign vassals, brought to court for indoctrination into the Egyptian way of life, in the hope that it would inculcate a lifelong loyalty to the pharaoh. The future Amenhotep II and his friends would therefore have come into contact with Nubian and Asiatic princes, which would have given them a much more cosmopolitan outlook than their forebears. Perhaps this explains why Egypt and Mittani, at war for decades, only finally concluded a peace treaty in the reign of Amenhotep II. As Egypt attempted to reeducate its neighbors, the neighbors in turn had an equally profound influence on the host country.

In the Eighteenth Dynasty, the most important royal nursery was at Gurob, a verdant place in the fertile Fayum depression. Here, kings since the dawn of history had built their pleasure palaces. The abundance of birdlife, attracted to the waters of Birket Qarun, made for excellent hunting, while the royal women who lived in the adjoining harem palace busied themselves with the manufacture of textiles, their raw materials supplied by the Fayum's extensive flax fields. Gurob was hence a place of women and children, relaxation and laughter. Royal princesses and the daughters of the elite could expect to learn at their mothers' feet the accomplishments expected of them: weaving, singing, dancing, perhaps a smattering of reading and writing. By contrast, a harsher discipline was enforced when it came to the education of princes and their male contemporaries. Nowhere was this more keenly felt than in the scribal school, for literacy was the key to power in ancient Egypt.

Reading and writing were central elements in the nursery curriculum, under the guidance of the scribe in the house of the royal children. By repeated copying of examples, this scribe taught his pupils to write in cursive script with pen and ink on papyrus. As they progressed, pupils moved on to the study of longer, classic texts, such as the Middle Kingdom *Tale of Sinuhe* and—a particular favorite—the work known as *Kemit*, "the compendium." *Kemit* was a model letter, used as a set text for scribal training, and it was intended to hone its readers' morals as much as their writing skills. By emphasizing the advantages of literacy, it sought to perpetuate the elevated status enjoyed by the elite:

> As for any scribe in any position at court,
> he shall not be poor in it.[9]

A kindred text, *Satire of the Trades*, developed this theme, denigrating every other occupation while eulogizing the work of the scribe:

> Look, there is no job without a controller
> except that of the scribe: he is the controller.
> So if you are literate, it will be good for you,
> unlike these [other] jobs I have shown you. . . .
> Most beneficial for you is a day in the schoolroom.[10]

Making the pupils learn such texts by rote was a mild form of brainwashing. Yet these idealizing sentiments shy away from the harsh reality of the school environment. Ancient Egypt, like Dickensian England, believed wholeheartedly in the maxim "Spare the rod and spoil the child." As one New Kingdom proverb put it, "A boy's ear is on his back: he hears when he is beaten."[11] The discipline of the scribal school was meant to prepare its pupils for the rigors of government service. The harsh and uncompromising style of education accurately reflected the exercise of power in ancient Egypt. The royal court, despite its luxury, was no place for effete intellectuals. Ambition, determination, resilience, and manly vigor—these were the qualities prized by the government machine, and the nursery sought to drum them into its pupils.

Once the young princes and their schoolmates had mastered the Egyptian language, they were introduced to Babylonian cuneiform, the diplomatic lingua franca of the age. Egypt could no longer afford to luxuriate in its own sense of superiority. In a new era of internationalism, power politics demanded a knowledge of foreign languages and cultures. The curriculum also included mathematics and music, for an appreciation of singing and instrumental music, if not the ability to perform, went hand in hand with membership in polite society. Just as important, for the future king if not for his classmates, was a firm grasp of military strategy. The future Amenhotep II would no doubt have studied the accounts of classic engagements (including, perhaps, his father's great victory at the Battle of Megiddo) alongside the literary, mathematical, and musical papyri.

FIGHTING FIT

IN THE MACHO WORLD OF THE EIGHTEENTH DYNASTY, WHERE A KING was expected to lead his troops into battle and display feats of bravery in the face of the enemy, training the body was as important as educating the mind. Energetic and physical pursuits played a particularly important part in the education of future leaders. Running, jumping, swimming, rowing, and wrestling were all part of the weekly routine, designed to develop strength, stamina, and team spirit. While Sennefer and Qenamun may have preferred the life of the mind, physical exploits being conspicuously absent from both men's biographies, their royal schoolmate, the future Amenhotep II, relished his time spent on the training ground. Taller and stronger than most of his contemporaries, he reveled in sport and developed a prodigious talent as a rower and runner. It was archery, however, that held a special appeal. While staying at the royal palace at Tjeni, he took lessons from the local mayor, Min, who was evidently a great shot himself. It was the proudest moment of Min's life, lovingly recorded in his tomb, as he guided the young prince's aim, advising him "Stretch your bow to your ears."[12]

By the time he reached his teens, "a fine youth, with his wits about him,"[13] Amenhotep had matured into such an accomplished archer that he was apparently able to shoot an arrow through a solid copper target while mounted in a chariot. (We might be rightly suspicious of this fabled act of royal strength and skill, were it not for the abundant evidence of Amenhotep's singular ability with a bow and arrow.) Among his prized possessions was a richly decorated composite bow of wood and horn, the very best of its kind. Archery is mentioned or depicted

Amenhotep II shooting arrows at a copper target WERNER FORMAN ARCHIVE

more frequently than any other activity in the monuments of Amenhotep's reign, a clear indication that it was something of a royal obsession. On one notable occasion, eager to demonstrate his superior skill, he challenged the members of his retinue to beat him in an archery competition, declaring, "Anyone who pierces this target as deep as His Majesty's arrow shall have these things [as a prize]."[14] This unique instance of a sporting contest between a supposedly divine king and his mortal followers provides a vivid insight into Amenhotep's competitive character. His exploits helped to establish the motif of the "sporting king" as a central element in New Kingdom royal ideology.

Amenhotep's other favorite pastime was horsemanship. Unknown in the Nile Valley before the Hyksos invasion, horses had been swiftly adopted by Egypt's ruling class in the early Eighteenth Dynasty. In an age of warrior pharaohs, the ability to ride in the saddle and in a chariot were vital military skills. In keeping with his general sporting prowess, Amenhotep displayed a special affinity with horses from an early age:

Now, when he was still a young prince, he loved his horses and delighted in them. He was strong-willed in breaking them in and understanding their natures, skilled in controlling them and learning their ways.[15]

When he was asked as a young man to look after some of the horses in the royal stables, the results spoke for themselves: "He raised horses without equal."[16]

On becoming king, Amenhotep stressed not only his physical prowess but also his credentials as a military ruler. He was determined to prove himself a worthy heir and successor of his father, the great warrior pharaoh. Following in Thutmose III's footsteps, he led two major campaigns in the Near East. The purpose of the first was to extend and consolidate Egypt's imperial possessions by securing the allegiance of various unaligned chiefs and quelling a revolt in Takhsy (modern Syria). The unfortunate rebels should have learned from recent history: Egypt was not about to be humbled on such an important stage. Amenhotep's army easily prevailed against the enemy and meted out a predictably gruesome fate to the ringleaders. The seven defeated chiefs of Takhsy were rounded up and taken back to Egypt, suspended head-down from the masts of the royal flagship. On arrival in Thebes, in a final act of humiliation, six of the rebels were hung up on the walls of Ipetsut, as an offering to the Egyptian gods and a warning to would-be insurgents. The body of the seventh chief was carried all the way to Napata, in upper Nubia, the southernmost outpost of the Egyptian Empire, to be similarly displayed. As it swung, rotting and stinking in the desert sun, the corpse served as a powerful and grim reminder to the local population of the price of rebellion.

Amenhotep II's first Asiatic campaign not only achieved its political and propaganda goals, it was also immensely successful in economic terms, adding vastly to Egypt's wealth. The booty brought back from Takhsy and neighboring lands comprised nearly three-quarters of a ton of gold, a staggering 54 tons of silver, 210 horses, 300 chariots, 550 enemy cavalry, and nearly 90,000 prisoners of war, including more than 21,000 entire families. Little wonder that the kingdom of Mittani, together with the Hittites and Babylonia, may have sued for peace and established diplomatic relations with Egypt. Victory against such a determined opponent was an impossibility.

Amenhotep's second campaign, two years later, ranged closer to home, in Palestine, but was similarly directed against a specific enemy, in this case the rebel leader of a town near Megiddo. There was no way

Amenhotep was going to allow a region so hard won by his father to secede from Egyptian control within a mere generation. The outcome,
once again, was never in doubt. The chief "whose name was Qaqa was
carried off, the wife, his children, and all his dependents likewise."[17]
Their ultimate fate is not recorded, but it is safe to assume it was appropriately unpleasant. As a final act of vengeance, Amenhotep ordered
his army to massacre the town's entire population before returning in
triumph to Egypt, "his desire slaked in all the hill countries, all lands
beneath his sandals."[18]

No further military campaigns would be required for the rest of
Amenhotep's reign. In their place, peace and prosperity ushered in opportunities for building projects at home. His fame established
throughout the foreign lands, it was now time for Amenhotep to secure
his immortal memory among his own people.

TOWARD THE SUNRISE

THE GIZA PLATEAU, WEST OF MEMPHIS, HELD A SPECIAL PLACE IN
Amenhotep II's affections, for it was here that he had first practiced
archery and horse riding. A training gallop lay near the Great Sphinx,
already a thousand years old, and the area was a favorite location for
royal sporting activities. One day, as Amenhotep cantered around the
great necropolis, he marveled at the pyramids of Khufu and Khafra, his
distant forebears from remote antiquity. Inspired by the monuments'
size, splendor, and sheer age, the king decided to record his own
achievements for posterity on a magnificent stela erected between the
paws of the Great Sphinx. Its combination of the usual lofty sentiments
and specific details of the king's sporting achievements reveals much
about his character. In a further gesture of homage to the guardian of
the Giza necropolis, Amenhotep built a temple next to the Sphinx,
which he worshipped as the sun god Horemakhet, "Horus of the horizon." It soon became a favored focus for acts of piety by other members
of the royal family, including Amenhotep's son and heir, Thutmose IV
(1400–1390).

Indeed, Thutmose went one step further in his reverence for the
Sphinx. He claimed Horemakhet as his personal protector, attributing

his very position to the god's favor. His great stela, erected next to his father's, told how Horemakhet spoke to him in a dream when he was still a prince, promising him the kingship if he would clear sand away from the body of the Sphinx. Once safely ensconced on the throne of Horus, Thutmose kept his side of the bargain, completing the re-excavation of the monument from the sand of centuries, and building an enclosure wall to prevent future encroachment by the shifting desert dunes. It is telling that Thutmose's inscription makes no mention the state god Amun-Ra (in sharp contrast to his father's stela), concentrating instead on Horemakhet. Under the Sphinx-blessed king, the northern, solar deity was honored as the primary guarantor of royal legitimacy. Even at Ipetsut, home of Amun-Ra, the king had himself depicted as half human, half celestial falcon, emphasizing his identification with the sun god (Horus and Ra now being closely associated in Egyptian theology). Through such carefully chosen imagery, he sought to underline the divine solar aspects of his office, abandoning the image of the military ruler that had served his forebears so well.

Thutmose IV reaped the benefits of peace with Mittani, dedicating his reign to internal affairs instead of foreign campaigns. Diplomacy likewise replaced military action as the main instrument of overseas policy. The administration of Nubia was reformed, with the appointment of a viceroy of all Egyptian-controlled lands. Looking to the northern part of his empire, Thutmose IV cemented the alliance with Mittani by taking a Mittanian princess as his wife. Just two generations earlier, his forebear and namesake Thutmose III had fought Mittani for supremacy in the Near East. Now the erstwhile foes were united in marriage. With peaceful conditions restored, trade could flourish once more between the great powers, and caravans of luxury goods traveled by land and sea across the eastern Mediterranean, Palestine, Syria, and Mesopotamia. With an almost inexhaustible supply of gold (every ruler's favorite commodity), Egypt benefited most from this upsurge in commerce, exchanging its mineral wealth for metals, timber, precious stones, and other royal desiderata. Another peace dividend from the alliance with Mittani was a rash of new construction projects the length and breadth of Egypt and Nubia. On each monument the king's fascination with solar symbolism loomed large, presaging a new direction in royal ideology.

A country secure in its borders and at peace with its neighbors, and a monarchy resplendent as never before—the scene was set for an aggrandizement of kingship beyond anything Egypt had seen since the days of the Great Pyramid.

CHAPTER 13

GOLDEN AGE

BLAZE HIS NAME ABROAD

ALL EGYPTIAN KINGS HAD A TALENT FOR SELF-PROMOTION; IT WENT with the job. For the ninth ruler of the Eighteenth Dynasty, Amenhotep III (1390–1353), it must have been particularly difficult to restrain the bombastic urgings of monarchy. Descendant of conquerors and heir to a sun-blessed throne, Amenhotep had the added good fortune to inherit from his father, Thutmose IV, a nation of unprecedented wealth and un-accustomed stability. Egypt's domination of the Near East had reached its apogee. Peaceful relations had been established and cemented with the other great powers, Babylonia, Assyria, and Mittani—even the infa-mously belligerent Hittites were prepared to observe the Pax Aegyptica, for the moment at least. For his reign of nearly four decades, Amenhotep III would have the rare privilege of being the only ruler of his entire dy-nasty not to wage a single military campaign in western Asia. Instead, his period of rule was characterized by an upsurge in the arts of peacetime, and by the promulgation of a personality cult of bewildering intensity.

Amenhotep started early. A mere child at his accession, his first taste of royal celebrity came after just two years on the throne in 1389. In what was probably a set-piece encounter rather than a spontaneous act of bravery, the king took part in a hunt of wild bulls at Shetep (modern Wadi Natrun), west of Memphis. A large glazed scarab (the ancient Egyptian equivalent of a commemorative coin) was issued by the court to mark the occasion. Distributed throughout Egypt and its conquered territories, it served to trumpet the young king's achievement to his contemporaries, and record it for posterity:

A wonder that happened to His Majesty. One came to His Majesty saying, "There are wild bulls in the desert in the region of Shetep."

His Majesty sailed downstream . . . making good time, arriving in peace at the region of Shetep in the morning. His Majesty appeared in his chariot with his entire army behind him. . . . Then His Majesty ordered a ditch to be dug to enclose these wild bulls, and His Majesty went forth against all these wild bulls. The number thereof: 170 wild bulls. The number the king took in hunting on this [first] day: 56 wild bulls. His Majesty waited four days to give his horses a rest. His Majesty appeared in the chariot [again]. The number of wild bulls he took in hunting: 40 wild bulls. Total number of wild bulls [killed]: 96.[1]

The repetitious phraseology protests too much. Even for a young king on the cusp of adolescence, it was surely not a difficult task, aided by "his entire army," to slaughter a herd of bulls corralled inside a ditch with no means of escape. But this announcement set the pattern for the reign as a whole. Amenhotep was acting out the primary, most ancient duty of kingship: to uphold order by defeating chaos in all its guises. Another commemorative scarab, issed in the tenth year of his reign, records the total number of lions shot by the king in his first decade on the throne (110, to be precise).

But, after this youthful predilection for blood sports to prove his virility, a change seems to have come over the king as he entered adulthood. The next special issue scarab, dated a year later, celebrates not a hunt but a construction project, specifically the excavation of a lake for the king's great wife, Tiye. This was no mere ornamental pond but a rowing lake measuring more than a mile long and nearly a quarter of a mile wide (thirty-seven hundred by seven hundred cubits). To mark the lake's formal opening, the king duly had himself rowed up and down in the royal barge, prophetically named *The Dazzling Orb*. Both in the nature of the project itself and in the manner of its inauguration, Amenhotep had found his true calling. From now on, for the rest of his reign, the country would reverberate to the sound of workmen digging, hammering, chiseling, and building. Amenhotep III would be Egypt's greatest royal builder since the foundation of the kingdom fifteen hundred years earlier, acting out his fantasy of building monuments "whose like never existed before, since the primeval time of the Two Lands."[2] In another aspect of his wish fulfillment, these same monuments would play host to spectacular festivals and unrivaled pageantry, all focused on the person of the king.

Inscriptions in two of Egypt's biggest limestone quarries show that construction was already under way at the very beginning of Amenhotep III's reign; the reopening of these quarries was his first recorded act. The pace of building accelerated during his second and third decades on the throne, eventually reaching a fever pitch. From the delta to Nubia, there was scarcely a temple in the land where Amenhotep did not leave his mark. At Saqqara he commissioned the first tomb chapel and burial for the Apis, a sacred bull believed to be the incarnation of the Memphite creator god Ptah. On the island of Abu, he oversaw the construction of a new shrine dedicated to another creator deity, Khnum.

The chief beneficiary of royal largesse, however, was the creator par excellence, the sun god Ra. In a brilliantly calculated program, Amenhotep and his theologians systematically reinterpreted each national cult to emphasize its connections with solar beliefs. Hence, to the temple of Thoth in Khmun, Amenhotep added colossal statues of baboons, animals sacred to Thoth but also revered as the heralds of the sun god because of their habit of shrieking at dawn. At Sumenu (modern el-Rizeiqat), near Thebes, the local crocodile god Sobek was rebranded as the hybrid deity Sobek-Ra and honored with a new temple adorned with monumental sculpture. Wherever he built, Amenhotep took pains to associate himself with solar deities, using epithets such as "heir of Ra" and "Ra's chosen one," for the king wished to be seen as the embodiment of solar energy in all its manifestations. He was the maker and sustainer of life; the bringer of fertility and fecundity; and the fierce "eye of Ra" that, when appeased, turned its ferocity on Egypt's enemies, defending created order. Sophisticated theology was being harnessed to the yoke of divine kingship as never before.

One site, above all others, felt the full energy of Amenhotep's building program. From the moment of his accession, the king adopted the epithet "ruler of Thebes," and he soon set out to prove it in deeds as well as words. During his reign, the city dedicated to Amun-Ra, already the focus of royal construction projects from the beginning of the Eighteenth Dynasty, was transformed into Homer's legendary "hundred-gated Thebes," with a forest of massive temple gateways punctuating the landscape on both sides of the river. At Ipetsut, the epicenter of the Amun cult, Amenhotep ordered the construction of a new monumental entrance for the entire complex, at the same time adding a further gateway on the temple's southern axis that led to the temple of the goddess Mut. Here the king beautified and adorned the buildings with a vast array of fine stone sculpture, including more than seven hundred statues of Sekhmet (two for every day of the year), a lioness deity associated with the fiery "eye of Ra." In the northern part of the Ipetsut enclosure, Amenhotep presided over the rebuilding of an earlier temple to Montu, the son of Amun and Mut, and the construction of a new temple to Maat, goddess of truth and justice. Every edifice was further enhanced with prodigious quantities of the finest sculpture. Indeed, more statues survive of Amenhotep III than of any previous king of Egypt, a testament to the feverish activity of the royal workshops throughout his reign.

Amenhotep's constructions at Ipetsut were but a sideshow, however, compared to his principal project at Thebes, a mortuary temple on the west bank of the Nile. Begun early in his reign and greatly enlarged in subsequent building phases, it was destined to become the largest royal temple in the history of ancient Egypt. Today, little remains beyond the bases of columns. Such a vast monument was too tempting a source of building material for later kings, but in its time it dwarfed even the great temple of Amun-Ra at Ipetsut. Covering an area of ninety-three acres, the complex was unprecedented in scale and magnificence, bursting at the seams with colossal sculpture. Statues of Amenhotep III as the god Osiris, more than twenty-six feet tall, stood between the columns of one court. Another part of the temple was dominated by a seated pair statue of the king and his great wife, Tiye, at twenty-three feet high the largest dyad ever carved in Egypt; fragments of two even larger colossi were found nearby. The temple's northern gateway was flanked by a pair of striding figures of the king carved from granite, while processional avenues were lined with enormous sphinxes and jackals. These ceremonial paths linked the temple's three enormous courts, each of which had its own monumental gateway guarded by yet more colossal seated statues of the king. The easternmost pair of statues still stand more than sixty feet tall, flanked by diminutive statues of Amenhotep's mother, wife, and daughter, and are visible for miles around. (Today they are known as the Colossi of Memnon.) Their sheer immensity, looming over every man, woman, and child in western Thebes, led them to be considered deities in their own right, living images of the king as "ruler of rulers." They certainly conveyed Amenhotep's overwhelming authority, and must have evoked a mixture of awe and fear in every observer.

Amenhotep's supersize colossi imparted a subtler message, too. After being partially submerged in the floodwaters of the Nile for several months each year, they would emerge again as symbols of rebirth, underlining the principal rejuvenating purpose of Amenhotep's mortuary temple, his "mansion of millions of years." In a similar vein, many of the statues of deities set up in the temple's courts were carved from granodiorite, the stone's black color symbolic of rebirth. Statues of the king, on the other hand, were more often carved in red granite or golden quartzite, the solar colors emphasizing Amenhotep's close connection with the sun god. The twin themes of creation and rebirth echoed from every corner of the vast complex, proclaiming the king as the essential pivot of the cosmos.

Amenhotep's royal career had thus far delivered a remarkable boost to the institution of kingship and to the status of its current holder. Much more was to come.

DIPLOMATIC RELATIONS

WHILE THE RULER OF RULERS WAS BUSY IN THEBES RAISING THE monarchy and himself to new heights, his emissaries ensured that his fame and fortune were recognized far and wide. Traveling throughout the Near East and the eastern Mediterranean, Amenhotep's envoys guaranteed Egypt's continued presence at the top table, negotiating treaties and securing favorable trading agreements to maintain their master's imperial aspirations. The most remarkable aspect of Amenhotep's foreign policy is suggested by a series of place-names inscribed on statue bases from his mortuary temple. The hieroglyphic writing system struggled to cope with foreign words, and the tortured combinations of signs seem impenetrable at first: *i-am-ny-sha, ka-t-u-na-y, ka-in-yu-sh, m-u-k-i-n-u.* On closer analysis, they turn out to be a comprehensive list of the most important sites in the Greek world of the fourteenth century B.C.: Amnisos, Kydonia, Knossos, and Mycenae. Also listed are Phaistos, Lyktos, Nauplion, Boeotian Thebes, the island of Kythera, and perhaps even Ilios, Homer's Troy. The order of the place-names suggests the itinerary of a diplomatic mission sent by Amenhotep III to the leading city-states of the Minoan and Mycenaean worlds. He would have had good reason for such a charm offensive: Mycenaean trade networks provided Egypt with supplies of precious cobalt, which was used as a dark blue dye in its glassmaking industry. Lead used to make opaque and white glass came from the Laurion peninsula of Greece, within Mycenae's own hinterland. Despite Egypt's instinctive xenophobia, it could not afford to ignore an emerging economic force in the distant Aegean.

Closer to home, diplomacy was an essential tool for maintaining Egypt's imperial conquests in the Near East. Thanks to a remarkable discovery made in A.D. 1887, the relations among Egypt, its vassals, and the other great powers of the day have been revealed in all their internecine complexity. The Amarna Letters are an archive of official correspondence found among the ruins of the "house of correspondence of the pharaoh" (the secretariat of the ancient Egyptian foreign ministry). The 380 surviving documents are in the form of baked clay tablets. They are written in the cuneiform (wedge-shaped) script of Mesopotamia, and in the Babylonian language of Bronze Age diplomacy. Many date to the latter years of Amenhotep III's reign and were sent by vassal princes to the Egyptian pharaoh, whom they addressed with suitable obeisance as "my sun, my lord." Unlike conquered Nubia, where centrally appointed bureaucrats imposed royal authority along Egyptian lines, Egypt's subject territories in the Near East were allowed to retain their own administrative arrangements and their own indigenous rulers, provided they swore oaths of allegiance to the pharaoh and delivered their annual tribute on time. Yet the indignity of being subject to a foreign power clearly riled, and the vassals seem to have spent much of their time plotting and counterplotting as they attempted to play Egypt off against the other great powers, not least Mittani and the Hittites.

The Amarna Letters reveal a highly volatile state of affairs, with bitter rivalries and almost continuous small-scale conflict erupting between the various city-states. Among the more troublesome vassal princes in Palestine were Milkilu of Gezer, Biridiya of Megiddo, and Abdi-Heba of Jerusalem. Generally, Egypt was content not to involve itself in such local disputes, except when its economic interests were threatened. Farther north, however, the problems were altogether more serious, since they had the potential to disrupt the balance of power between Egypt and the Hittites. A quarter of all the Amarna Letters are from a single vassal, Rib-Adda of Kebny, whose city had enjoyed a special relationship with Egypt for more than a thousand years. Rib-Adda was becoming increasingly suspicious of the neighboring state of Amurru, with its ambitious ruler Abdi-Ashirta. Rib-Adda's fears were well founded. Unchecked, Amurru moved to capture the Egyptian garrison town and administrative capital at Sumur (modern al-Hamidiyah) and virtually besieged Kebny. This turmoil gave the Hittites the excuse they had been waiting for to intervene, and Amurru was lost to Egyptian control. It was a salutory lesson in how minor disputes could escalate rapidly to Egypt's detriment.

Where Thutmose III or Amenhotep II would not have hesitated to intervene militarily, Amenhotep III followed a very different policy. His main objective was to exploit his overseas possessions economically and control them politically with the minimum commitment of Egyptian forces. To this end, garrisons were stationed in the most important ports along the coast—Gaza, Jaffa, Ullaza, and Sumur—and at two strategic locations inland, Beth-Shan, at the eastern end of the Jezreel Valley, and Kumidi, in the Beqa Valley. Fortified grain depots along the coast could be called upon as supply centers in case of military action. Egyptian administrative headquarters with resident governors at Gaza, Kumidi, and Sumur completed the network of colonial rule. In general, the system proved highly effective, and the loyalty of vassal princes was further cemented by regular gifts of precious baubles from the Egyptian royal workshops. (The conferment of imperial knighthoods on Indian princes by the British raj is an instructive modern parallel.)

When it came to maintaining amicable relations with the other great powers, however, something more than trinkets was required. In the eyes of his subjects, the pharaoh may have been master of the universe, but in reality he had to share the world stage with six other Near Eastern leaders. In Mesopotamia there were the kings of Babylonia (southern Iraq), Assyria (the upper Tigris Valley), and Mittani (northern Iraq and northern Syria); in Anatolia, the kings of the Hittites (central Turkey) and Arzawa (southwestern Turkey); and in the eastern Mediterranean, the ruler of Alashiya (Cyprus). The members of this elite club called one another "brother," and were not averse to displays of pique or petulance if they failed to get their own way. Among the Amarna Letters, the three dozen or so missives from the great powers to Amenhotep III are largely concerned with the usual diplomatic niceties: the exchange of greetings, polite inquiries after the king's health, and the presentation of gifts. The beginning of a letter from King Tushratta of Mittani gives the general flavor:

> For me all goes well. For you may all go well. . . . For your household, for your wives, for your sons, for your nobles, for your warriors, for your horses, for your chariots, and in your country may all go very well.[3]

But there is also another common theme, one that reflects Egypt's reputation for fabulous wealth. Again, Tushratta sums it up nicely:

> May my brother send me unworked gold in very great quantities . . . and much more gold than he sent to my father. In my brother's country gold is as plentiful as dirt.[4]

Gold was the preferred currency of diplomatic exchange, and abundant supplies from the mines of Nubia gave Egypt unique leverage among the great powers. Little wonder that an insurrection by the people of the gold mining region of Nubia in the thirtieth year of Amenhotep III's reign was brutally suppressed. Without gold, Egypt was nothing.

In return for regular shipments of gold, Amenhotep III sought to extract the ultimate prize from his fellow leaders: their daughters as diplomatic brides. Early in his reign, the young king succeeded in winning the hand of a Mittanian princess, and a commemorative scarab from 1381 records the arrival of Princess Gilukhepa with her retinue of 317 female attendants, aptly and succinctly described as "marvels."[5] Twenty-five years later, the pharaoh sought another Mittanian princess for his harem, both to cement his friendship with the new Mittanian king and also, one presumes, because Gilukhepa had lost her virgin bloom. The negotiations over this second diplomatic marriage were delicate and detailed, involving much reciprocal gift giving. Eventually, King Tushratta sent his daughter Tadukhepa with an appropriate entourage of 270 women and 30 men, and an enormous dowry including forty-four pounds of gold, together with another thirteen pounds of gold as a personal gift for Amenhotep himself.[6] Coals to Newcastle, one might have thought, but the pharaoh was evidently impressed with the gesture, and the entente cordiale was duly secured.

The Babylonians drove a harder bargain altogether. Amenhotep had already taken one Babylonian princess as a bride early in his reign, but when he tried the same trick with the new king of Babylonia, Kadashman-Enlil I, he met unexpected resistance. Kadashman-Enlil complained that nobody had set eyes on his sister since she had entered Amenhotep's harem more than a decade earlier, and he was reluctant to condemn one of his own daughters to the same fate. To make matters worse, he had not been invited to Amenhotep's recent "great festival." Furthermore, he doubted that foreign brides were being treated in the manner to which they had been born:

> My daughters who are married to neighbouring kings, if my messengers go there they speak with them, they send me a greeting gift. But the one with you is impoverished.[7]

As a final insult, Kadashman-Enlil's request for a reciprocal arrangement, whereby he would marry an Egyptian princess, was rebuffed in no uncertain terms. Amenhotep replied haughtily that no daughter of an Egyptian king had ever married a foreigner, and he had no intention of breaking with tradition just to please the king of Babylonia. Altogether, the omens for a second Babylonian marriage did not look good. In the end, Egyptian gold seems to have won the day, and Amenhotep got his girl. The Amarna Letters contain one further discussion of marriage, a discussion between the pharaoh and the splendidly named King Tarkhundaradu of Arzawa, but here the record is silent as to the eventual outcome of negotiations. It is safe, however, to assume they were successful. Amenhotep III was not a man to take no for an answer.

GLORY TO THE NEWBORN KING

As the pharaoh approached his first jubilee, after thirty years on the throne, his program of self-aggrandizement entered a new phase. Since the dawn of history, the culmination of a king's jubilee celebrations had been marked by the *sed* festival, an ancient rite that symbolized the ruler's rejuvenation and the renewal of his contract with the gods. In Amenhotep's mind, this matter of rejuvenation loomed especially large, and he determined to address it more thoroughly than any of his predecessors. Not for him a mere one-off festival, but instead, true to character, a monumental edifice and a program of royal sculpture to guarantee his rebirth for all eternity. The site he chose for his latest massive building project lay on the east bank of the Nile, three miles south of Ipetsut, directly opposite his mortuary temple. Today it lies at the center of the modern city of Luxor. At the start of Amenhotep's reign, it was almost a virgin site, graced only by a small shrine from the time of Hatshepsut and Thutmose III, built as a "southern residence" for Amun-Ra of Ipetsut. Under royal instructions, Amenhotep's builders lost no time in rebuilding his predecessors' little monument, adding a vast open court, surrounded by a double row of columns shaped like bundles of papyrus. This "solar court" reflected the king's growing emphasis on sun worship—for which an open, unroofed space was far more appropriate than a traditional enclosed sanctuary—and he instructed his architects to add a similar feature to nearly all his temples the length and breadth of Egypt. The solar court's realization at Luxor ranks as one of the most beautiful and impressive of all ancient Egyptian temples. And that was exactly what the king intended:

> Its walls are of electrum, its furnishings of silver; all its gates are decorated on their thresholds. Its pylon rises up toward heaven; its flagstaffs are in the stars. When the people see it, they will give praise to His Majesty.[8]

In front of the sun court, an even more impressive edifice started to take shape, a gigantic colonnade hall with columns reaching more than sixty feet into the air, embellished (as always) with six colossal striding statues of the king. Such architectural wonders were entirely for effect, and they worked magnificently. But the real theological significance of Luxor lay out of sight, in the rear parts of the temple.

Perhaps the most important room in the entire complex is a small chamber, tucked away behind a small barque shrine, next to the offering room. On its western wall, a delicate relief shows two goddesses gently supporting the figures of a woman and a man. They are Amenhotep III's parents, Mutemwia and Thutmose IV. Or rather Mutemwia and someone disguised as Thutmose IV, that someone being the god Amun-Ra, as the accompanying text makes clear. The inscription does not shy away from describing, in unexpectedly graphic terms, the god's purpose in sneaking into the queen's bedchamber, and her enthusiastic response to his overtures:

> She awoke because of the god's scent and cried out with pleasure before His Majesty. . . . She rejoiced at the sight of his beauty, and love of him suffused her body.[9]

By now in a state of ecstasy, Mutemwia swooned over the god, exclaiming "How great is your power! . . . Your sweet fragrance stiffens all my limbs."[10] The sexual metaphor was fully intended. After the impregnation came the annunciation:

> Amenhotep-ruler-of-Thebes is the name of this child that I have placed in your womb. . . . He shall exercise potent kingship in this entire land. . . . He shall rule the Two Lands like Ra forever.[11]

The purpose of this elaborate scene, and of the fictionalized events it relates, was of course to perpetuate the myth of the king's divine birth, something Egyptian monarchs had been claiming to a greater or lesser extent for centuries. Earlier in the Eighteenth Dynasty, in her Holy of Holies at Deir el-Bahri, Hatshepsut had been content to aver her divine birth while drawing a discreet veil over the practicalities. Amenhotep III (or his theologians) showed no such reticence, positively luxuriating in the intimate details of Amun-Ra's encounter with the queen. Perhaps that was to be expected of a monarch with countless foreign "marvels" tucked away in his harem, and who numbered among his homegrown concubines a woman with the nickname "she whose nights on the town are numerous."

Having asserted the monarch's divine origins, Luxor Temple made another bold contribution to the ideology of kingship. Indeed, the temple's most remarkable secret is its true purpose. Unlike almost every other temple in Egypt, it was not principally the cult center of a deity at all. Its role as Amun-Ra's southern residence was secondary, an acceptable cover story rather than the deeper truth. The key to understanding the temple's extraordinary part in the mythology of Egyptian kingship lies in the reliefs that decorate Amenhotep's monumental colonnade. They record the most important celebration to take part at Luxor, the annual Festival of Opet. Each year, the cult images of Amun-Ra, Mut, and Khonsu (and perhaps of the king, too) were taken in their barque shrines from Ipetsut to Luxor in a great procession, either by land or by river. As the statues were paraded through the streets on the shoulders of priests, the population thronged to catch a glimpse of these sacred objects and to receive their blessing. The Opet Festival was an occasion for much jubilation and feasting, and a welcome break from the daily grind. But like everything else in ancient Egypt, it was designed not for the people but for the king. Once safely inside the precinct of Luxor Temple, the cult images were taken from their barque shrines and installed in their new quarters. Then the king entered the sanctuary to commune in private with the image of Amun-Ra.

After a time, he emerged into the hall of appearance, to receive the acclaim of priests and courtiers gathered together for the occasion. (Special hieroglyphs at the base of columns directed the "common people" to the sanctioned viewing places.) His transformation was clear for all to see (and one assumes nobody would have dared to remark on the emperor's new clothes). Through his communion with the king of the gods, the monarch himself had been visibly rejuvenated, his divinity recharged. He had become the living son of Amun-Ra.

The key to the whole ceremony was the royal *ka*, the divine essence that passed, unseen, into the mortal body of each successive monarch and made him godlike. It was as inventive a piece of theology as the ancient Egyptians ever devised, for it explained and reconciled the apparent contradiction that a king could be both mortal and divine. The

Opet Festival allowed the king to unite with the royal *ka*, to become "foremost of all the living *ka*s," a god incarnate. Luxor Temple, then, was a temple to the royal *ka*, the mystery at the heart of divine kingship.

True to form, Amenhotep commissioned a magnificent piece of sculpture to immortalize this remarkable transformation wrought by the Opet Festival. The statue of the rejuvenated Amenhotep III is one of the all-time masterpieces of ancient Egyptian art. Life-size, it shows the king striding powerfully forward, his taut, muscular torso and limbs the epitome of youthful manliness. Most remarkable is the treatment of his face. With immense, oversize almond-shaped eyes, enlarged lips, small stub nose, and high cheekbones, its neotonous features convey a deliberate impression of exaggerated juvenility. The statue shows the king quite literally rejuvenated, his age reduced back to childhood through the magical power of the Opet rites. And the symbolism of the statue goes much further. Its very material conveys the king's close relationship with the sun god, for it is fashioned from a deep purplish-red quartzite, the stone known to the ancient Egyptians as *biat* ("wondrous"). Originally, gilded decoration would have been applied to the collar, bracelets, sandals, and crown, making the statue shine like the sun in the daylight of the open court. Close inspection at the back of the statue reveals a feather pattern on the king's buttocks, to indicate

Statue of the rejuvenated Amenhotep III (detail)
WERNER FORMAN ARCHIVE

that he has been partially transformed into a celestial falcon. To reinforce the solar associations still further, the king's kilt is decorated with rearing cobras, each with a solar orb on its head. Amenhotep himself wears the double crown, and stands on a sledge, both motifs emblematic of the creator god, Atum. Through this rich combination of visual metaphors and references, the statue declares that Amenhotep III is reborn, undying, assimilated with Ra and Atum, a god-king for all eternity. The inscription down the back pillar goes further, naming the king as "foremost of all the living *ka*s" and the "dazzling orb of all lands."

The deliberate and systematic enhancement of royal power had reached its zenith. No longer the mere "son of Ra," the king had become consubstantial with the sun, the creator god who illuminates and brings life to the world. His transformation was complete.

EGYPT'S DAZZLING ORB

THE DEIFICATION OF AMENHOTEP III IN HIS OWN LIFETIME, INTIMATELY connected with the celebration of his first jubilee in 1361, broke new ground for the Egyptian monarchy. Earlier kings had certainly come close to claiming divinity, depicting themselves with godlike attributes, but a distinction (albeit a subtle one) had always been maintained between the king as the earthly incarnation of Horus, and Horus himself; between the "chosen one of Ra," and Ra, who did the choosing; between the monarch as *netjer nefer* ("perfected" or "junior god"), and the real thing. No king before Amenhotep III had dared to state, quite so openly and unequivocally, his outright mutation into the creator deity. The final step in this process can be traced most clearly in distant Nubia, at the southernmost extremity of Eighteenth Dynasty power. One of Amenhotep's many building projects involved the foundation of a new temple inside the fortress of Khaemmaat (modern Soleb), an installation designed to protect Egyptian-controlled Nubia against the hostile lands beyond. In keeping with the king's solar ambitions, the temple was built on the west bank of the Nile, facing the rising sun. Originally the temple was a small barque shrine for the king's personal protector, Amun, but it was subsequently enlarged by the addition of two solar courts and a colonnaded hall filled with sculpture. At the same time, coinciding with Amenhotep's thirtieth year on the throne, the temple's dedication was changed to honor "Amun-Ra of Ipetsut re-siding in the fortress of Khaemmaat" and "Nebmaatra [Amenhotep III's throne name], lord of Nubia." The king of the gods (Amun-Ra) and the god-king (Amenhotep III) made the perfect pairing.

Reliefs in the temple of Khaemmaat also record details of the king's first jubilee. The ancient rites of the *sed* festival, with their emphasis on renewal and rejuvenation, held a special appeal for Amenhotep, and he seems to have begun preparations for his own ceremonies years ahead of time. The addition of solar courts to all his major temples in Egypt and Nubia seems to have been undertaken in anticipation of his jubilee, presaging the king's full and final assimilation with the sun god. When it came to preparing for the festival itself, no stone was left unturned to ensure it would surpass all previous celebrations. Scholars were set to work, consulting "the writings of old,"[12] to discover how the *sed* festival had been staged in centuries past. Among their discoveries was a fifteen-hundred-year-old palette, dating to the very beginning of Egyptian history, which was decorated with an abbreviated scene of ju-bilee rites. Its meager, but hallowed, information was added to the dossier.

Since Thebes was the focus of Amenhotep's symbolic world, the epi-center of his theological experiments, it was only fitting that the sacred city should also be the stage for his jubilee rites. Never one to do things by halves, the king ordered the construction of an entire new ceremo-nial city. The chosen location was on the west bank of the Nile, south of his mortuary temple and facing the place of his rebirth, Luxor Tem-ple. In its first phase (it would be extended yet further for the king's sec-ond and third jubilees), the modestly named "Palace of the Dazzling Orb and the House of Rejoicing" (modern Malkata) extended over a distance of nearly a mile. It included an administrative district with spacious villas for the courtiers, a secondary palace, perhaps for Tiye and her household, and the principal royal residence. Its opulently fur-nished audience chambers had floors covered with richly colored tex-tiles, and ceilings decorated with exotic Minoan motifs. The king's bedchamber had flying vultures painted on the ceiling, interpersed with Amenhotep's royal names and titles. Elegant ointment jars and perfume bottles, exquisitely crafted from multicolored glass, stood on tables veneered with ebony and overlaid with gold. Intricate glass vessels were so popular with the king and his consort that a dedicated factory was established alongside the palace to keep pace with demand. Amenhotep's patronage of glassmaking has been compared with Louis XIV's support for Sèvres porcelain—not the only point of similarity between the two sun-kings.

Amenhotep's ceremonial city and mortuary temple were connected by a raised causeway that continued southward for a further mile and a half, terminating at a lonely spot in the desert (modern Kom el-Samak). Here, in accordance with ancient custom, the king appeared enthroned on a raised dais with twin staircases, symbolizing his dominion over Upper and Lower Egypt. Yet more unfinished royal monuments lay beyond, deep in the Theban hills. Quite what Amenhotep had in mind we can only speculate about. The imagination of the king and his advisers seems to have known no bounds.

The "dazzling orb of all lands" planned one final coup de théâtre to set the seal on his great festival of kingship. A ceremonial city and a fantasy palace in a sacred landscape were not quite sufficient for the ultimate jubilee. Amenhotep cast his mind back twenty years to the rowing lake he had presented as a gift to his wife Tiye, and an idea formed in his mind. For a construction project equaling anything he had attempted to date—and that was saying something—the king ordered the excavation of two vast artificial harbors, one on either side of the Nile. Each measured nearly half a mile long by a quarter of a mile wide. The stupendous quantities of earth excavated from the western harbor were spread out over the surrounding plain to form an artificial platform for the construction of the jubilee city. Today, the western harbor (Birket Habu) survives as a depression delineated by a series of spoil dumps, its huge dimensions only appreciable from the air. The eastern harbor has disappeared altogether under the sprawling modern city of Luxor, but it was clearly discernible when Napoléon visited Egypt. He would surely have approved of its original purpose. Amenhotep's vision was to provide the most spectacular setting imaginable for the jubilee's central ceremony.

On the morning of the main celebrations, the courtiers, high officials, royal acquaintances, and other dignitaries were ushered into the palace. There, the king showered them with gifts of gold necklaces, golden ornaments in the shapes of ducks and fish (both potent symbols of fertility), and, as a special jubilee decoration, ribbons of green linen. The guests shared in a great breakfast banquet with their sovereign before being directed to leave the palace and proceed to the artificial harbors. Then, in a spectacular set-piece display of royal power and divine kingship, Amenhotep III and Tiye appeared at the waterside, decked from head to foot in gold, dazzling like the sun itself. At the eastern harbor, they boarded a replica of the sun god's morning barque. The waiting courtiers picked up the prow ropes and pulled the ship gently along, acting out the daily miracle by which the sun god was towed into the heavens at dawn. The scene then shifted to the western harbor, where king and consort appeared once again, but this time in a replica of the sun god's evening barque. Dignitaries grasped the tow ropes, and the scene was repeated, symbolizing the sun god's descent into the underworld at dusk. Well might the master of ceremonies later boast that "generations of people since the time of the ancestors had not celebrated such jubilee rites."[13]

Amenhotep III went on to celebrate a second and a third jubilee, each accompanied by further monumental buildings and yet more rituals. Then, in the thirty-eighth year of his remarkable reign, in 1353, and quite unexpectedly, he died of unknown causes, still only in his late forties. The shock, to a population bombarded by royal propaganda and a court convinced of the king's immortality, must have been profound. Yet nobody could have dreamed of the revolution that was about to sweep the country under Amenhotep's heir.

Egypt's dazzling sun had set. When it rose again, it would shine with an unrelenting, scorching light.

CHAPTER 14

ROYAL REVOLUTION

NEW DAWN

IN THE ANNALS OF ANCIENT EGYPT, ONE FIGURE PROMPTS MORE COM-
ment and speculation than any other. He attracts admiration and
loathing in equal measure. From romantic novelists to opera com-
posers, few have been able to resist his allure. In his relatively brief lifetime he changed Egypt utterly; yet his dramatic reforms were hurriedly
reversed after his death. He took the institution of divine monarchy to
new heights; yet he was never expected to rule. He is Akhenaten, the
heretic king (1353–1336), the most controversial and enigmatic of
pharaohs, the instigator of a royal revolution. His seventeen-year reign
and the tumltuous decade that followed were perhaps the most exhila-
rating, uncertain, dynamic, and bizarre period in Egyptian history. At
its heart was the king's own radical vision, which, if it had survived,
would have changed not just the history of ancient Egypt but, perhaps,
the very future of humanity.

For much of Amenhotep III's glorious reign, the heir apparent was
Prince Thutmose, the king's eldest son, named, following royal tradition, after his grandfather and great-great-grandfather. Of the second
son, Prince Amenhotep (as he was then named), little is known until
Prince Thutmose's untimely death, an event that propelled his younger
brother into the position of crown prince. Thutmose left few monuments other than a stone sarcophagus lovingly carved for his pet cat. By
contrast, his brother's determination would transform Egypt in less
than a generation.

The new heir to the throne must have witnessed firsthand his father's spectacular *sed* festivals, and they'd clearly had a profound effect
on him. Their dazzling solar imagery, in particular, seems to have
burned itself into the young man's fertile imagination. If notions of

radical theology had begun to form in Amenhotep's mind, there is no evidence of them at the beginning of his reign. Instead, having succeeded as Amenhotep IV, he did what was expected of a pious son and completed the decoration of his father's great entrance gateway at Ipetsut. He added his own reliefs, in suitably traditional style, showing him smiting the enemies of Egypt. In Nubia, he founded a new town, just as his father had, with a temple dedicated to Amun-Ra, king of the gods. From distant Cyprus, the king of Alashiya wrote to congratulate Amenhotep IV on his accession, sending him a jar of "sweet oil" as a coronation gift.[1] Everything seemed set fair for another glorious reign in the familiar dynastic mold. Egypt's imperial possessions paid suitable homage, too. A particularly obsequious letter arrived from the vassal ruler of Tyre, full of the usual sycophantic formulations:

> I fall at the feet of the king, my lord, seven and seven times. I am the dirt beneath the sandals of the king, my lord. My lord is the sun who comes forth over all lands day by day.[2]

Such sentiments seem to have given Amenhotep IV ideas. Within a year of becoming king, he showed his true colors, with a construction program to rival his father's. The sandstone quarries at Gebel el-Silsila went into overdrive, manned by record levels of conscript labor that the king raised through a nationwide call-up. Colossal edifices bursting at the seams with royal statuary were nothing new, of course, and Thebes had become well accustomed to monumental building during the last decade of Amenhotep III's reign. But Amenhotep IV had something alternative in mind. His projects would be focused at a single site, the temple of Ipetsut—not inside the sacred enclosure but outside its eastern wall, on a vacant mudflat. The choice of location, beyond the domain of Amun-Ra and facing the sunrise, was quite deliberate. For Amenhotep's eight new monuments at Ipetsut were to be dedicated not to its usual incumbent but to the Aten, the visible orb of the sun, whose imagery his father had adopted at the time of his first jubilee. Reflecting this theological shift, the grandest project was a temple named Gempaaten (Gem-pa-Aten, "the Aten is found"), and it was quite as ambitious as anything Thebes had witnessed in the previous reign. At its heart was a vast open court lined with a colonnade. Against the pillars stood twenty-foot-high statues of Amenhotep IV and his wife, Nefertiti, each carved from a single block of sandstone. Their distinctive crowns—the double crown or a twin-plumed headdress for the king, a flat-topped crown for his consort—identified them as Atum, Shu, and Tefnut, the original triad of creator gods according to the ancient myth of Iunu. Where Amenhotep III had stressed his sunlike role in maintaining the universe, his son wished to be associated with the very act of creation.

This fundamentalist theology found startling expression, too, in the appearance of Amenhotep IV's statuary. To emphasize his oneness with the creator, embodying both masculine and feminine attributes, and at the same time to underline his separateness from the rest of humanity, the king ordered his sculptors to instigate a radical change in the mode of representation. Every aspect of the king's face and body was deliberately distorted: the head was unnaturally elongated with angular and attenuated features including slit eyes, a long nose, and a prominent chin; a long, sinewy neck and prominent collarbones dominated a narrow upper torso, which contrasted with a distended belly and broad hips; plump legs ended in spindly calves. The overall effect, especially when multiplied over and over again at a colossal scale in the harsh, raking light of the open court, was both frightening and surreal. In a further twist, the statues were emblazoned at strategic points (neck, upper and lower arms, waist) with plaques bearing a pair of royal names, but instead of identifying the king, as might have been expected, they proclaimed the newly invented titulary of the Aten, the monarch's favorite god. Under Amenhotep III, the king had become the solar orb; under his son, the solar orb had become king. Amenhotep IV was declaring nothing less than a co-regency, with himself and the sun god as joint sovereigns. In the abundant reliefs that decorated the Gempaaten, the royal family was invariably shown in the presence of the Aten, depicted no longer as the traditional falcon-headed man but in abstract form as a solar orb with rays ending in human hands, caressing and bringing life to the royal family.

The ultimate purpose of Amenhotep IV's entire building program at Gempaaten, like his father's constructions at Malkata, was to provide a grand architectural setting for the celebration of a royal jubilee. Amenhotep IV held his own *sed* festival in the third year of his reign, main-

Colossal statue of Amenhotep IV from Ipetsut (modern Karnak)
WERNER FORMAN ARCHIVE

taining the frequency established by his father's jubilees. In so doing, he was clearly signaling that his father's reign had not really ended. The inscriptions emphasized that the *sed* festival was not so much the king's as the Aten's. It was a radical but entirely logical development of Amenhotep III's theology: the old king had become the solar orb and, as such, would continue to reign for all eternity, endlessly repeating jubilees stage-managed for him by his son, Amenhotep IV. The *sed* festival at Ipetsut thus marked not a culmination but the beginning of a brave new world. Sun god and king would reign together, re-creating the world anew each day.

The jubilee celebrations also pointed the way to a new future for Egyptian religious life as a whole. Gone were the traditional processions of the gods. In their place, the king and other members of the royal family were the focus of attention and reverence as they traveled each day in state from palace to temple and back again, cheering crowds and dignitaries lining the route. A year after the *sed* festival at Gempaaten, the king set the seal on his new theology by changing his own name, an act of the greatest symbolic power. While many a previous ruler had changed his throne name to signify a new direction, it was highly unusual, if not unprecedented, for a king to change the name he had been given at birth. Through the power of the jubilee, Amenhotep IV believed he had been reborn to new life as co-regent of the Aten. In place of Amenhotep, "Amun is content," he would henceforth be known as Akhenaten, "effective for the Aten." (Similarly, his wife, Nefertiti, added an epithet to her name, to become Neferneferuaten, "beauteous are the beauties of the Aten.")

A PLACE IN THE SUN

SO PUBLIC A REJECTION OF THE AMUN CULT MUST HAVE SAT UNEASILY with the king's continued patronage of Thebes, city of Amun par excellence. To be sure, the Gempaaten and the other Aten temples stood outside the sacred precinct of Ipetsut, but the center of Amun worship was still too close for comfort. Amun's monuments on both banks of the Nile dominated the skyline and were a constant reminder of his hegemony over all other cults. If the Aten were to be truly magnified above all other deities, he would need his own domain, his own city, a place where the solar orb (and his son) could reign supreme. The search was on for a new royal capital.

Akhenaten's chosen location was nothing short of inspired. (Indeed, he claimed to have been led there by the Aten.) In Middle Egypt, roughly halfway between the great religious center of Thebes and the traditional administrative capital of Memphis, there was a spot where the towering limestone cliffs forming the east bank of the Nile receded to form a desert embayment, some seven miles long and three miles wide. It was secluded, easily defensible, and conveniently served by a broad expanse of fertile floodplain on the opposite bank. Most important of all, it was virgin territory, previously unoccupied and unclaimed by any other cult. Even the landscape seemed tailor-made for the king's beliefs, the shape of the eastern cliffs forming the hieroglyph for "horizon," the place where the sun rose each morning to bring new life to the world. It was indeed Akhet-Aten, the "horizon of the orb," and the perfect setting for Akhenaten to realize his utopian vision.

In the late spring of his fifth year on the throne, 1349, the king paid his first formal visit to the site (modern Amarna). Appearing in front of his assembled courtiers on an electrum-plated chariot, dazzling like the sun itself, he issued the decree establishing his new city. After making a spectacular open-air offering to the Aten in front of the cliffs, he declared that Akhetaten would belong to his god forever, as his monument "with an eternal and everlasting name."[3] Not even Nefertiti would be able to shake his determination to realize his dream:

> Nor shall the king's great wife say to me, "Look, there is a good place for Akhetaten elsewhere," nor shall I listen to her.[4]

The king further decreed that his model city would contain a suite of principal buildings for the worship of the Aten and the glorification of the royal family. And Akhetaten, not Thebes, would be the king's eternal resting place:

> If I die in any town of the north, the south, the west, or the east in these millions of years, let me be brought back so that I may be buried in Akhetaten.[5]

The whole ceremony and the details of the king's decree were recorded for posterity on three massive tableaux cut into the cliffs at the northern and southern limits of the site and adorned with statues of the king and queen.

Exactly a year later, Akhenaten paid a second visit to inspect progress. After spending the night in a carpeted tent (called "Aten is content"), he once again rode out at sunrise in a golden chariot, made another great offering to his god, and swore an oath by the Aten and by the lives of his wife and daughters that everything in Akhetaten would belong to the Aten and no other, forever. This second decree, establishing the city limits more precisely, was duly carved into a further set of thirteen boundary markers on both banks of the Nile. Construction of the city itself stepped up a pace, too, helped by vast quantities of stone that were transported from a huge quarry cut into the northern cliffs. Stone "bricks" of a standard size (one cubit by half a cubit), small enough to be handled by a single workman, made for rapid building. Two years of feverish activity later and the city was ready to welcome the royal family to their permanent home.

As Akhenaten had intended, "the horizon of the Aten" was carefully laid out to give prominence to the major public buildings. These were linked by the Royal Road, which ran parallel to the Nile and formed the capital's ceremonial backbone. The king's daily chariot ride from the royal residence to the seat of government and back again deliberately recalled the path of the Aten through the heavens, signaling the close connection between celestial and earthly co-regents. It also gave the city and its inhabitants a regular, ritual focus, replacing the religious festivals of old, which the king's new theology had consigned to oblivion.

The principal royal residence was located at the northernmost edge of Akhetaten, hemmed in between the cliffs and the riverbank, a site chosen as much for security as for aesthetic appeal. As well as the palace itself, set within a fortified enclosure, with extensive barracks for guards, there was a large administrative building and a group of impressive mansions for the king's closest advisers.

As the king traveled south each morning, his chariot accompanied by running platoons of soldiers and police—and, no doubt, flunkies trying hard to keep up—his journey took him first past a separate harem palace for the women of the royal family. Richly decorated with painted murals and gilded stonework, it was a haven of luxury and tranquility. In its central courtyard there were gorgeous formal gardens, kept watered from the river by a sophisticated irrigation system, while stalls for cattle and domesticated antelope provided the palace with the finest meats on a daily basis.

Beyond this royal enclave began the city proper, and we may imagine the king's cavalcade speeding up as it passed the homes of ordinary mortals. A northern suburb, one of two main residential quarters, spread eastward from the Royal Road. Akhenaten's formal planning code evidently did not extend beyond the principal public buildings, for the houses of his subjects were arranged higgledy-piggledy. Large villas belonging to wealthy merchants were surrounded by the smaller houses of dependents, a maze of side streets and back alleys adding to the villagelike atmosphere. The neighborhoods were noisy and bustling, and constituted a more or less permanent building site as new dwellings were erected.

Continuing southward along the Royal Road, the king's chariot procession finally entered the central city, the religious and administrative heart of Akhetaten. The largest building of all was the House of the Aten, the god's principal place of worship, with a street frontage of 750 feet and stretching back almost half a mile. Beyond its two massive entrance towers stood vast open courts, filled with mud brick altars. On festival days, these would be piled high with fruit, vegetables, meat, and poultry, offerings to be consumed by the Aten as he passed overhead. Extensive food production facilities and a dedicated slaughterhouse inside the temple kept the altars well stocked.

Next to the temple was the "king's house," Akhenaten's "office," where the business of government was carried out. One of its most prominent features was a balcony for the royal family's public appearances. A covered bridge led over the Royal Road to the Great Palace, the largest residential building in the entire city, with an area of nearly four acres. Principally a setting for grand state receptions and royal ceremonies, the Great Palace also included offices and quarters for members of the royal household. At its center was a massive open courtyard flanked by colossal statues of Akhenaten and Nefertiti, the better to impress visiting ambassadors. The sense of fear and wonder was further heightened by the floor decoration. The main route used by the king had a plastered pavement painted with images of foreigners. This allowed Akhenaten to trample his enemies underfoot as he went about his state business—"the unselfconscious trumpeting of official brutality."[6]

The final major building in the central city was the Mansion of the Aten, a smaller temple designed for the royal family's daily worship. Aligned with the cleft in the hills that led to the royal tomb, it perhaps also took the place of a traditional mortuary temple. In common with the House of the Aten, its architecture was dominated by open courts—to allow the worship of the visible sun—with a sequence of ramps, steps, and balustrades instead of closed rooms to divide up the sacred space. Akhenaten's new religion had spawned a new architectural vocabulary.

A further residential suburb, dominated by the houses of ordinary workers and beyond the area usually frequented by the king, marked the southern end of the main built-up area. But, on the outskirts of the city, five large ritual complexes, each dedicated to a prominent female member of the royal family, ensured a permanent and highly visible royal presence whichever way the inhabitants turned. In his new "sun city," Akhenaten was omnipresent as well as omnipotent.

THE ONE TRUE GOD

IN ONE SENSE, AKHENATEN'S FUNDAMENTALIST THEOLOGY HAD BEEN foreshadowed by his father's apotheosis. It was but a short and logical step from Amenhotep III's celebration of solar power to his son's exclusive exultation of sunlight itself. It is even possible that Akhenaten regarded the Aten as his real as well as his spiritual father—Amenhotep III in deified form. However, in many important respects, Akhenaten's doctrine was entirely unprecedented and radically at odds with the previous seventeen centuries of ancient Egyptian religious tradition. While kings of the past had stressed their role in upholding *maat* (truth, justice, and created order), Akhenaten professed to live on *maat* like the gods themselves. Truth no longer had an existence independent of the king's actions: it was, by definition, whatever he wanted it to be. Traditional rituals of royal renewal, notably the *sed* and Opet festivals, had emphasized the one-off rejuvenation of the king, until the next such occasion. Akhenaten's *sed* festival at Ipetsut (when he was still Amenhotep IV) had had an entirely different agenda, signifying the permanent rejuvenation of the king and the entire cosmos. Through the co-regency of the Aten and the king, the world had been taken back to its pristine state immediately following the moment of creation. Akhenaten's universe enjoyed (or suffered) daily re-creation, reflecting the daily rebirth of the sun itself, under the beneficent guidance of the divine triad, namely the Aten, the king, and his consort.

If the dogma was rarefied, the implications were stark. A deity whose power was transmitted through its rays, through light itself, would have no use for an enclosed, hidden sanctuary—such as had been built for gods and goddesses since the dawn of civilization. Worship of the Aten demanded open-air temples, filled with tables piled high with offerings for the god's direct consumption. Indeed, the entire city of Akhetaten was one great temple to the Aten, since the visible sun could be observed and worshipped overhead at any time of day. This is more than hinted at by the "royal name" given to the Aten at the time of "his" jubilee (1351). Although written inside the classic cartouche (oval name ring) used by kings, the "name" was, rather, a heavily abbreviated statement of the new creed:

> Live! Ra-Horus-of-the-two-horizons who rejoices on the horizon in his name of light, which is the Aten.

Just as Akhenaten took the role of Light (the god Shu), so the king's new city, Akhetaten, "the horizon of the Aten," was the place where the Aten rejoiced—god, king, and holy city in perfect unison.

Although, in theory, the Aten needed no temples and no priesthood (the king being the god's sole interlocutor), in practice Akhenaten could not devote himself to worship—much as he may have wished to—every hour of every day. After all, he was head of state as well as prophet of a new religion. So, in a nod to previous practice, he appointed a high priest of the Aten shortly after taking up residence at Akhetaten. Meryra, "beloved of Ra," seems to have come from nowhere, or at least took pains to ensure that his previous career and background remained hidden. Like most of Akhenaten's inner circle, he probably owed everything to the king. That way, his loyalty was guaranteed. His formal installation as high priest took place at the king's house in the central city. Akhenaten and Nefertiti, accompanied by their eldest daughter, Meritaten, appeared at the royal balcony, which had been decorated for the occasion with a richly embroidered cushion. Wearing a long white gown and a decorative sash, and attended by members of his household, Meryra entered the royal presence and knelt before the king while official scribes recorded every aspect of the proceedings. (Even under Akhenaten, Egypt had not lost its obsession with record keeping.) Behind the pen pushers were the baton wielders, ready to swing into action at the least sign of trouble. Police, like scribes, were an everyday feature of life at Akhetaten. With a formal declaration, the king confirmed Meryra's appointment to universal acclamation. When the hubbub had subsided, Meryra made his own brief speech of acceptance: "Numerous are the rewards that the Aten knows to give, pleasing his heart."[7] It was a model of concision and piety. His friends then raised him up shoulder-high and bore him from the palace.

The other high point of Meryra's career, some years later, was his investiture with the "gold of honor," the ultimate accolade for a loyal servant. Once the king had heaped gold collars around the high priest's neck, everyone present had to listen, attentive and enraptured, while Akhenaten gave a long, verbose, stilted, and legalistic speech. With its ritualized setting and choreographed moves, Meryra's installation as high priest brings us face-to-face with a style of royal audience that has changed little in three and a half thousand years. His subsequent investiture offers a similar reminder that the world of despots and their cringing lackeys follows an equally time-honored pattern.

At about the same time as Meryra's appointment to the high priesthood, the king began to promulgate a more elaborate statement of his faith. It was referred to, rather chillingly, as the Teaching. It used the vernacular language of the day rather than the classical forms of yore, and was probably composed by the king himself. The *Great Hymn to the Aten*, to give it its formal name, has been called "one of the most significant and splendid pieces of poetry to survive from the pre-Homeric world."[8] It is certainly a masterpiece, its rapturous tone and exultant imagery of the creator's power exerting a profound influence on later religious authors, not least the Jewish psalmists. Its careful reproduction in the tombs of Akhenaten's high officials, as a public gesture of loyalty to the regime, ensured its survival, and it merits quoting at length. Nothing better captures the unbridled joy (Akhenaten's joy, at least) of the king's new religion.

> You shine forth in beauty on the horizon of heaven,
> O living Aten, the creator of life!
> When you rise on the eastern horizon,
> You fill every land with your beauty.

Beautiful, great, dazzling,
High over every land,
Your rays encompass the lands
To the limit of all that you have made. . . .

The earth is bright when you rise on the horizon,
And shine as Aten of the daytime.
You dispel the darkness
When you send out your rays.
The Two Lands are in festival . . .
All the herds are at peace in their pastures,
Trees and plants grow green,
Birds fly up from their nests . . .
Fish in the river leap in your presence,
Your rays are in the midst of the sea. . . .

How manifold are your deeds,
Though hidden from sight.
Sole god, apart from whom there is no other,
You created the earth according to your desire, when you were alone.
All people, cattle, and flocks,
All upon earth that walk on legs,
All on high that fly with wings . . .

Your rays nurse every pasture;
When you rise, they live and prosper for you.
You made the seasons to foster everything of your making—
Winter to cool them, heat that they might taste you.[9]

The hymn's emphasis on the richness and abundance of creation found visible expression in the gorgeous painted walls, ceilings, and floors of the royal palaces. But they were a far cry from the experience of ordinary people, even in Akhenaten's new model city. Cheek by jowl with the grand palaces and temples, the poor citizens of Akhetaten lived short, hard lives. Their bones tell of poor diets, high stress, and physical hardship. Some did irreparable damage to their spines by carrying heavy burdens on a daily basis. Others squatted or knelt all day on mud floors, toiling over crucibles of molten metal or glass in the city's workshops. Inadequately fed in childhood, and mocking the mountains of food laid out for the Aten, men and women alike were physically stunted and prone to debilitating conditions such as anemia. More than half the population died while still in their late teens, and only a few survived into their forties. Most were dead by thirty-five. Buried in shallow pits dug directly into the sand, with only a pile of stones for a memorial, they were laid to rest with a few cheap pots and perhaps a couple of pieces of old jewelry. It was a world away from the official dogma of life, light, and beauty. Little wonder, perhaps, that Akhenaten's lowlier subjects continued to put their trust in the traditional gods, even under the noses of the king's thought police. In the safety of humble dwellings, much-loved deities such as Hathor, Bes, Taweret, and even Amun still had a place.

Despite, or perhaps because of, this continued adherence to the old cults, Akhenaten's doctrine turned ever more fundamentalist. In the early years of his reign, when the court was still based at Thebes, it was evidently acceptable for a royal butler to include prayers to Osiris and Anubis in his tomb. But after the move to Akhetaten, the Aten was swiftly elevated from supreme god to sole god. No others would be recognized or tolerated. The king's vision *would* be imposed on the rest of society. Priests found themselves deposed or reassigned and their temples were closed, and all resources were redirected to the Aten cult. The high-water mark of Akhenaten's puritanical fervor was signaled in the eleventh year of his reign, 1341, when the doctrine of the Aten was officially "cleansed," to remove all references to gods other than Aten or Ra—even gods, such as Horus-of-the-two-horizons and Shu, who were themselves solar deities.

This purification of the Aten cult was accompanied by the active proscription of other deities, especially the now hated Amun, whom the Aten had supplanted as supreme creator. To wipe their names from history, Akhenaten launched a systematic program of state-sponsored iconoclasm. Throughout the country, from the marshlands of the delta to the distant reaches of Nubia, armies of the king's henchmen broke open tomb chapels and burst into temples to deface the sacred texts and images. Armed with chisels and cue cards (reference cards that illustrated for illiterate workmen the phrases to be expunged from monuments), they shinnied up obelisks to hack out the figures and names of Amun-Ra. Personal names that included the element "Amun" or "Mut" were also targeted, even though they included Akhenaten's own father (Amenhotep III) and grandmother (Mutemwia). The officially sanctioned desecration extended even to the plural form of the word "god." Terrorized by the king's cultural revolution, individuals scrambled to protect themselves, subjecting treasured personal possessions to self-censorship and changing their own names to escape the iconoclasts' wrath. An army scribe called Ptah-mose hurriedly became Ra-mose; the priest Mery-neith became Mery-ra—and only felt safe readopting his original name after Akhenaten's death. To much of the population, the orgy of vandalism must have felt like the ritual murder of their most cherished hopes and beliefs.

Yet the king remained unshakeable, his Teaching crystal clear. Not only was the Aten the sole god, but the only path to salvation lay through Akhenaten (throne name Neferkheperura) and the members of his family:

> There is none other who knows you,
> Only your son, Neferkheperura, sole one of Ra.
> You have informed him of your plans and your might.
>
> Everyone who has passed by since you founded the earth,
> You have raised them for your son,
> The one who has come from your body,
> The dual king who lives on truth, the lord of the Two Lands,
> Neferkheperura, sole one of Ra,
> The son of Ra who lives on truth, the lord of diadems,
> Akhenaten, whose life is long;
> And the king's great wife, whom he loves,
> The lady of the Two Lands,
> Neferneferuaten-Nefertiti, living and youthful forever and ever.[10]

Never before had the institution of monarchy been elevated to such an absolute position.

FIRST FAMILY

THE CLOSING LINES OF THE *GREAT HYMN TO THE ATEN* (ABOVE) IL-
lustrate one of the most striking elements of Akhenaten's entire
revolution—the unprecedented prominence given to his wife. In one
sense, Nefertiti was merely following in the footsteps of her Eighteenth Dynasty forebears. From Tetisheri, Ahhotep, and Ahmose-
Nefertari to Hatshepsut, royal women had grown accustomed to
playing an important role in the affairs of state. Tiye had taken this one
step further, engaging in her own correspondence with foreign rulers
and appearing side by side with Amenhotep III as the female counterpart to his male divinity. But Nefertiti broke new ground from the outset. At Ipetsut, she had been granted her own temple, the Mansion of
the Benben, where her husband (then still Amenhotep IV) was not
even depicted. She was shown carrying out ritual actions previously restricted to the king, such as smiting a bound captive or inspecting prisoners. On the boundary stelae commissioned to mark the first
anniversary of the royal couple's visit to Akhetaten, Nefertiti is shown
at the same scale as the king, which denoted her equal rank. Akhenaten's accompanying panegyric further underlines her exalted status:

> Great in the palace, fair of face, adorned with the twin plumes, lady
> of joy who receives praises; one rejoices at the hearing of her voice,
> the king's great wife whom he loves, the lady of the Two Lands.[11]

Every public gesture made by Akhenaten to signal his devotion to the
Aten was mirrored by a gesture from Nefertiti. When he changed his
name from Amenhotep, she added an epithet to hers. While Akhenaten was the living incarnation of Shu, the son of the creator, Nefertiti
was Tefnut, his consort. She adopted the goddess's distinctive flat-
topped headdress as her own, and made it the public symbol of her authority. In the tomb of Nefertiti's high steward, the royal couple are
shown side by side, their images almost entirely overlapping. In some
eyes, at least, Nefertiti and Akhenaten were as one, joint rulers on earth
with the Aten in heaven.

The intimacy of their relationship was made a central tenet of
Akhenaten's new doctrine, publicized in statuary and reliefs through-

out the city. In one scene, the couple hold hands during an official ceremony, in another Nefertiti sits on her husband's lap as she ties a bead
collar around his neck. A fragment of temple relief even shows Akhenaten and Nefertiti getting into bed together. The couple's daughters,
too, were brought into the approved iconography. By the time they had
been at Amarna for two years, Akhenaten and Nefertiti had six daughters. (Akhenaten also had at least one son, born of a minor wife, but the
son was notably excluded from the official record, the female principle
being all-important.) A famous stela shows the king and queen relaxing
at home with their three eldest daughters. Akhenaten cradles and kisses
Meritaten; Meketaten sits on her mother's knee, gesturing toward her
father; and little Ankhesenpaaten pulls at Nefertiti's earring. It was unprecedented even to acknowledge, let alone publicize, such expressions
of affection and emotion among members of the royal family.

The reason for this radical departure from tradition was the royal
family's new role in Egyptian religion, for it had become a holy family,
supplanting the traditional groupings of deities. The royal chariot
drive into the central city had taken the place of the gods' processions.
Statues of Akhenaten and Nefertiti had replaced images of deities.
Since the cult of Aten was an exclusive religion, revealed only to
Akhenaten and his family, ordinary citizens wishing to obtain blessings
from the solar orb had to worship its representatives on earth as intermediaries. In the tombs of favored officials, cut into the cliffs ringing
Akhetaten, worship of the king sublimated individual personalities.
The offering formula was no longer addressed to Osiris, god of the
dead, but to the king, and occasionally to Nefertiti as well. The only
eternal existence now on offer was to bask in the Aten's rays during the
day, to receive a share of offerings from the temple, and to return to
one's tomb at night, watched over by Akhenaten. It was a chilling
prospect.

Residents of Akhetaten even kept statues and images of the royal
family in their household shrines. The size of one's shrine—some were
akin to miniature temples—was a public measure of one's loyalty to the
regime, every bit as important a status symbol as a well, granary, or garden. And for the humble citizens barred from the Aten's formal temples, there was at least one public place of worship in the central
city . . . a chapel of the king's statue.

Akhenaten, Nefertiti, and their daughters   WERNER FORMAN ARCHIVE

Not everyone shared this unbridled devotion to the king and all his works. Tantalizing references from the first set of boundary stelae suggest dissent may have erupted in the early years of the reign. Akhenaten's radical policies must have aroused deep unpopularity among certain sections of the population, and the fear of insurgency haunted his regime. Loyal officials warned potential dissidents of the king's determination to root them out: "As soon as he rises, he exerts his power against the one who ignores his teachings."[12] Yet even within his new city, the king's personal safety was clearly a major preoccupation, and Akhetaten crawled with security. As well as the police force, there were the soldiers and "heads of the army who stand in the presence of His Majesty."[13] An armed escort, bristling with spears, accompanied Akhenaten on his daily chariot ride into the city. An entire block behind the king's house was devoted to barracks for paramilitary forces, and there were additional outposts throughout the city. A complex network of tracks crisscrossing the plain allowed systematic policing of the desert behind Akhetaten. Visible by night as well as day, these routes for military chariots facilitated round-the-clock security. The barren wastes of the Eastern Desert provided a ready hiding place for outlaws, and the police were all too aware of dissidents "who would join those of the desert hills."[14]

Roving police patrols monitored the royal residence from high on the plateau above, while the sheer cliffs behind the palace were virtually impossible to scale or descend easily. Like other despots throughout history, Akhenaten relied heavily on the loyalty of his security personnel, not least his chief of police. Mahu, in common with all the king's top officials, owed everything to royal patronage and was at constant pains to demonstrate his devotion. He had the walls of his tomb inscribed with no fewer than four copies of the *Hymn to the Aten*, the official creed of Akhenaten's new religion. Mahu's public expressions of faithfulness in the presence of his monarch were models of sycophancy. However, in such an atmosphere of paranoia, even an archloyalist was not given unfettered control of royal security. The king also had his own elite bodyguard that included foreign soldiers, perhaps less likely to harbor a grudge against the pharaoh. Senior members of the administration, too, may have been drawn from foreign families. The vizier Aper-El, the king's chief physician Pentu, and the royal chamberlain Tutu may all have been of non-Egyptian descent.

Despite being gods on earth and the sole path to salvation, the royal family nonetheless had to look far afield for unquestioned loyalty.

The final public appearance of Akhenaten, Nefertiti, and all six princesses was a magnificent durbar held in 1342, in the twelfth year of the king's reign. Seated together under a sun shade (for a long, hot spectacle in the open air, comfort came before dogma—for the royal family, at least), they watched as lines of foreign dignitaries paraded before them with exotic gifts, symbolizing the king's sunlike dominion over all lands. As the official record of the event put it,

Appearance of the dual king Neferkheperura-sole-one-of-Ra and the king's great wife, Neferneferuaten-Nefertiti, upon the great palanquin of electrum to receive the tribute of Syria and Kush, the west and the east, every foreign land assembled on one occasion, even the islands in the midst of the sea, presenting tribute to the king.[15]

Not that every foreign ruler was impressed with this characteristic display of Egyptian one-upmanship. In a strongly worded letter to Akhenaten, King Asshuruballit of Assyria complained, "Why should [my] messengers be made to stay constantly out in the sun and die in the sun?"[16] How ungrateful of the Assyrian ambassador to resent such unstinting exposure to the Aten's life-giving rays. . . .

THE END OF THE LINE

DIVINE FAVOR HAD ITS LIMITS. THE DELEGATES HAD BARELY LEFT Akhetaten before tragedy struck the royal family. Akhenaten's second daughter, Meketaten, died at the tender age of seven, followed not long afterward by the king's beloved mother, Tiye. Both were interred, as Akhenaten had decreed, in the royal tomb carved into the hillside in a lonely desert valley on the eastern horizon, eight miles beyond the city. Graphic scenes of mourning capture the mood of the grief-stricken relatives.

A mother's tears for her dead child are the final image we have of Nefertiti at Akhetaten, for she disappears from the record immediately afterward. Perhaps the same calamity that had carried off her mother-in-law and daughter took her as well. Or perhaps the intimations of mortality that now descended upon Akhenaten prompted a radical reevaluation of his wife's status. It may be no coincidence that Nefertiti's disappearance was soon followed by the appointment of a (human) co-regent, to reign alongside Akhenaten. The name of this new co-ruler was none other than Neferneferuaten, the first element in Nefertiti's titulary. The queen, it seems, had become king. Who better, who more reliable, to carry on Akhenaten's revolution than its co-instigator and co-beneficiary?

Akhenaten died after the autumn grape harvest of 1336, in the seventeenth year of his reign. He was laid to rest in the royal tomb, accompanied by revealing grave goods. It is unsurprising, perhaps, that his chosen heirloom was a one-thousand-year-old stone bowl inscribed for Khafra, the builder of the Great Sphinx (mother of all solar monuments). Less predictable were the *shabti* figurines inscribed for Akhenaten himself, to serve him in the model of an afterlife that his religion fiercely eschewed. Even religious fanatics, it seems, are prone to deathbed doubts. Akhenaten's body was placed in a stone sarcophagus protected at its four corners not by the four funerary goddesses but by figures of his beloved Nefertiti.

His wife would indeed guard his body, but not his legacy. Graffiti in a Theban tomb, dated to the third year of Neferneferuaten, seem to indicate the beginnings of a rapprochement with the old Amun priesthood—perhaps even the reopening of a temple to Amun in the god's old heartland. Before Akhenaten's body was even cold in its grave, his exclusive cult of the dazzling Aten had begun to fade.

The death of Akhenaten plunged the court and the country into turmoil. Those who owed everything to his patronage—men such as Meryra and Mahu—must have wished devoutly for his revolution, or at least his regime, to continue. Others, including members of the powerful Amun priesthood, who had patiently bided their time while his zealotry ran its course, saw the chance for a return to the old orthodoxy. The royal family, too, seems to have been riven by doubt. An ephemeral ruler named Smenkhkara—perhaps a son of Akhenaten's of whom we are otherwise unaware; more likely Nefertiti in her third incarnation, as sole king—claimed the throne for the briefest of periods (1333–1332), supported by Meritaten, now elevated to the role of king's great wife. But reactionary forces were growing in strength and looked to the coming generation for a suitable candidate, someone with the legitimacy of royal blood but young enough to do their bidding. Shielded from public gaze for most of his life, Akhenaten's nine-year-old son by a minor wife seemed ideal. His (hastily arranged?) marriage to Nefertiti's "heir," her third daughter, Ankhesenpaaten, only strengthened his claim. Courtiers, priests, and the influential army officers all agreed—it had to be the boy. His name: Tutankhaten, "the living image of the Aten."

Within months, the powers behind the throne of the new child pharaoh had set Egypt on the path back to tradition. Under their care-

ful guidance, the king agreed to change his name, thus publically re-
nouncing the Aten in favor of Amun. History had come full circle. Tutankhaten thus became Tutankhamun; his wife Ankhesenpaaten became
Ankhesenamun ("she lives for Amun"). Next, a great restoration decree
was issued in the king's name—though its wording has his mentors' fin-
gerprints all over it—from the traditional capital of Memphis. It exco-
riated Akhenaten's policies, without mentioning the disgraced ruler by
name:

> When His Majesty became king, the temples of the gods and god-
> desses from Abu to the delta marshes . . . had fallen into ruin. Their
> shrines had fallen into decay, having become mounds thick with
> weeds. . . . The land was in distress; the gods had abandoned this
> land. If armies were sent to the Near East to widen the borders of
> Egypt, they had no success. If one made supplication to a god for
> protection, he did not come at all.[17]

The language of the decree made pointed reference to the "gods" in
the plural, and the new king's actions matched his words. Immediate
measures included the restoration of the temples, paying special attention to the cult centers of Amun-Ra; the reinstatement of their priest-
hoods; and the dedication of new cult statues (paid for by the royal
treasury), all so that Tutankhamun could be said to have "rebuilt what
was ruined . . . and driven away chaos throughout the Two Lands."[18]
The court's abandonment of Akhetaten and the return to Thebes set
the seal on the return of the ancien régime. To mark this complete
break with his father's vision, the boy king, like other reunifiers before
him, took the highly symbolic epithet "repeater of births." His reign
would not be a re-creation like Akhenaten's but a renaissance.

So much early promise, so cruelly cut short. Before he was even out
of his teens, Tutankhamun followed his father to the grave in 1322.
Perhaps he had secretly harbored designs to restore Akhenaten's reputation, once he'd reached his majority and could rule by himself. Perhaps the real powers in the land were afraid of just such an outcome,
and took desperate steps to prevent it. Or perhaps the boy king, physically never very strong, simply met the same fate as most of his subjects: an early death from natural causes. His child bride had tried to

perpetuate the royal line, but her tender age and the narrow gene pool of a brother-sister marriage had resulted in miscarriage. Two stillborn daughters were lovingly mummified and interred beside their father in his hastily prepared tomb in the Valley of the Kings, to await their rediscovery—together with the rest of Tutankhamun's burial treasure—3,244 years later.

Tutankhamun's grieving widow knew the dreadful fate that the courtiers had in store for her. She was the last surviving descendant of Akhenaten and Nefertiti, of Amenhotep III and his ancestors. She held the keys to the throne of Egypt. In a final, desperate act, she wrote an extraordinary begging letter to the king of the Hittites. She pleaded with him to send one of his sons to Egypt, to marry her and rule beside her. She explained, "Never shall I take a servant of mine and make him my husband!"[19] The Hittite king was astonished, telling his courtiers, "Nothing like this has ever happened to me in my entire life!"[20] Eventually, he relented and sent a prince southward, bound for Memphis. But Prince Zannanza never arrived, having died—or having been murdered—en route. Ankhesenamun's worst nightmare came to pass, and she had to endure a forced marriage to a superannuated courtier, a man old enough to be her grandfather, with his eyes on the throne. Her duty done, she too disappeared from the scene, fate unknown.

So died the Thutmoside royal line, one of the most glorious dynasties ever to rule Egypt, progenitor of great conquerors and dazzling rulers. The glory days of Amenhotep III seemed but a distant memory. Defeated abroad and dejected at home, what Egypt needed to restore its confidence and luster—although its long-suffering populace might have disagreed—was decisive leadership. As it happened, there was one institution in the country and one man at its head who could provide just that.

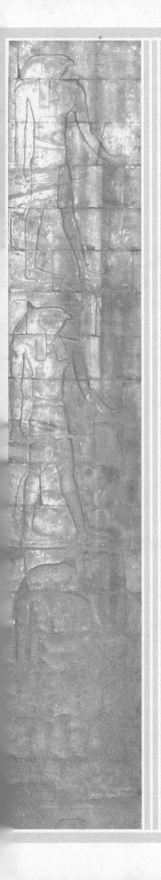

PART IV
MILITARY MIGHT
(1322–1069 B.C.)

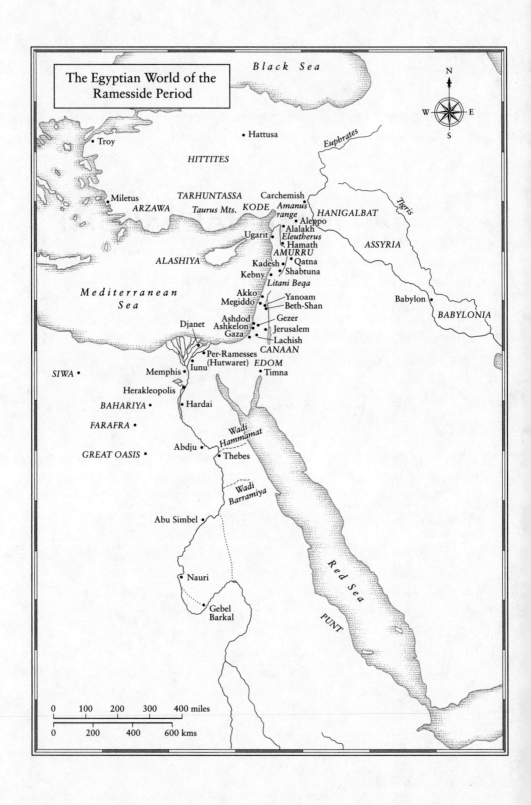

The Egyptian World of the
Ramesside Period

Black Sea

N
W E
S

• Troy

• Hattusa

HITTITES

Euphrates

• Miletus

TARHUNTASSA   • Carchemish
ARZAWA   Taurus Mts.   KODE   Amanus   HANIGALBAT
range
• Aleppo
Ugarit • • Alalakh   Tigris
• Eleutherus
• Hamath   ASSYRIA
AMURRU
ALASHIYA   Kadesh • • Qatna
Kebny • • Shabtuna
Litani Beqa
Mediterranean   Akko •   • Babylon
Sea   Megiddo • • Yanoam
• Beth-Shan   BABYLONIA
Djanet •   Ashdod • • Gezer
Ashkelon • • Jerusalem
Gaza • • Lachish
Per-Ramesses   CANAAN
(Hutwaret)   EDOM
SIWA •   Memphis • Iunu •   • Timna
Herakleopolis •
BAHARIYA • • Hardai
FARAFRA •
Wadi
Hammamat
GREAT OASIS •   Abdju •
• Thebes

Wadi
Barramiya

Abu Simbel •

Red Sea

• Nauri

PUNT

Gebel •
Barkal

0   100   200   300   400 miles

0   200   400   600 kms

IMMORTALIZED BY PERCY BYSSHE SHELLEY'S POEM "OZYMANDIAS," the fallen colossus of Ramesses II in his mortuary temple at western Thebes has come to symbolize the transience of power. Perhaps no other monument better evokes the rise and fall of a great civilization. At once awesome and pathetic, the fallen statue encapsulates the might and majesty of pharaonic Egypt but also its impotence in the face of long-term historic forces. The broader Ramesside Period (the Nineteenth and Twentieth dynasties) likewise holds a mirror to Egyptian civilization, reflecting both its boldness and its inherent weaknesses.

One institution dominates the story of Ramesside Egypt: the army. For a period of two centuries, the influence of the generals was felt, for good and ill, in every aspect of domestic and foreign policy. Military efficiency may have provided an effective short-term solution in times of dynastic turmoil, but over the course of several generations the militarization of politics merely entrenched the power of the army and weakened civil society, with damaging unforeseen consequences. The country's permanent state of readiness for war with the Near East encouraged the development of a new capital in the delta, and this emphasis on Lower Egypt gave the region a political importance that it was to retain for the rest of pharaonic history. At the same time, the progressive alienation of Upper Egypt from the heart of decision-making stoked up fires of resentment that posed a long-term threat to the very cohesion of the state. Above all, war was costly. Ramesside Egypt's interminable battles exhausted both the economy and the government machine. Like the victors in later world wars, Egypt ended up paying a high price.

At the outset of the Ramesside Period, the country was brimming with confidence and imperial ambitions. By its close, the land of the pharaohs had entered a slow but inexorable decline. Part IV charts this crucial turning point in the history of ancient Egypt. In the aftermath of Akhenaten's failed revolution, it took an army officer, Horemheb, to restore order and self-confidence to a shattered realm. His adoption of a fellow general as his heir maintained the influence of the army, and the early Ramessides did not disappoint, showing an inexhaustible determination to regain Egypt's empire. The confrontation between Egypt and its archrival, the Hittite Kingdom, culminated in the famous Battle of Kadesh, an epic if indecisive encounter that eventually paved the way for the first comprehensive peace treaty in world history. Yet Egypt's security was soon threatened by new invaders. Ramesses III, often dubbed "the last great pharaoh," sealed his reputation as victor against the Libyans and the Sea Peoples, but subsequently fell victim to a palace conspiracy. It was the harbinger of things to come.

In the end, internal rather than external factors undermined the pharaonic state. A loss of royal prestige, spiraling food prices, strikes, uncontrolled immigration, widespread corruption, a breakdown in law and order—by the time the eleventh Ramesses came to the throne, Egypt was on its knees. Beleaguered and isolated in his delta residence, the pharaoh did what every Ramesside had done at such times, and appealed to the army for assistance. The result was brutally effective, but not in the way Ramesses XI had hoped. The impotent king was sidelined as an irrelevance, and order was restored by separate military juntas in the north and south of the country. The long-cherished ideal of a unified state ruled by a single divine king was rudely cast aside in the name of control. The rescue of Ramesside Egypt was also its death knell.

CHAPTER 15

MARTIAL LAW

A SOLDIER'S LIFE

EGYPT'S BURGEONING INVOLVEMENT IN FOREIGN AFFAIRS, FROM THE expulsion and pursuit of the Hyksos under Ahmose to the creation of an empire under Thutmose III, had a profound effect on the country at large and the way it was governed. Greater exposure to alien peoples and cultures led to the adoption of exotic ideas and customs in many areas of life, from art and architecture to state and private religion. In keeping with the martial spirit of the age, the iconography of monarchy became strongly militarized, the king appearing on temple reliefs as a great and mighty war leader, and this was reflected in the militarization of society as a whole. The New Kingdom was the age of the soldier, and from humble beginnings the Egyptian army swiftly established itself as one of the most influential groups in society.

For the campaigns of the Old and Middle kingdoms, Egypt's rulers had depended upon conscript armies, raised from the general population on an ad hoc basis and bolstered by mercenaries, often recruited from Nubia. While such a system was adequate for launching sporadic raids to defend Egyptian interests or open up trade routes, it was entirely ill-suited to the demands of an empire. The conquest and annexation of large tracts of foreign territory required permanent garrisons to enforce Egyptian control, backed up by the threat of overwhelming force in case of insurrection. Only a permanent standing army could deliver such a policy. Hence, at the beginning of the New Kingdom, military organization was put on a professional basis, and a full-time army was created for the first time in Egyptian history. By the reign of Akhenaten (1353–1336), the influence of the army was felt throughout the corridors of power. Many of the king's closest followers combined military and civilian office, and these links no doubt served to keep a powerful bloc loyal to the sovereign.

A reorganization of the armed forces in the late Eighteenth Dynasty divided them into two distinct corps, infantry and chariotry. Egypt also had a strong naval tradition (used to great effect in the battles against the Hyksos), but the interdependence of land-based and river-borne fighting was reflected in the interchangeability of military personnel, with men and officers alike alternating between army and navy postings. A major naval base was located at the port of the capital city, Memphis. Another, at the site of the former Hyksos capital, Hutwaret, went under the suitably appropriate name of Perunefer ("bon voyage"). Military garrisons were probably stationed in provincial centers throughout the country for rapid deployment in emergency situations, while a large garrison of reservists just outside Memphis was no doubt a powerful deterrent against would-be insurgents within the Egyptian population.

The principal tactical unit of the infantry was a platoon of fifty men, under a platoon commander, the lowest rank of officer. Each platoon was subdivided into five squads of ten men, each with its own designated squad leader. This arrangement fostered teamwork and a strong esprit de corps, essential to the success of any army. Four or five platoons made up a company, which had its own quartermaster and adjutant and was commanded by a standard-bearer. For operational purposes, several companies could be combined to form a battalion, its precise strength depending on requirements. Major military campaigns saw the consolidation of battalions into regiments or divisions, each under the command of a general and named after one of Egypt's state gods. The chariotry likewise was organized into groups of fifty, and was dominated by officers (like the cavalry in the armies of late-nineteenth-century imperial Europe).

Life as an infantryman in the pharaoh's army might have provided opportunities for adventure and advancement, but it was not a bed of roses. Even for those who joined up voluntarily—as opposed to being conscripted—the training was harsh, and was characterized by indiscriminate beatings. Although there was a specialist cadre of "military scribes" (desk officers) responsible for keeping records and allocating provisions, rations in the field were meager in the extreme, and soldiers were expected to supplement their bread and water by foraging and stealing—little wonder that at the Battle of Megiddo the Egyptian forces were more concerned with pillaging the enemy's possessions than with capturing the town. Many of the soldiers may not have had a square meal in weeks. Nor could an infantryman opt to leave such a life of privation, other than through death in service or promotion. A deserter knew that his relatives were liable for imprisonment until he rejoined his unit. If the treatment meted out to Egyptian recruits was bad, the lot of foreign prisoners of war forcibly conscripted into the army was even worse. They could expect to be branded and registered, and even circumcised to "Egyptianize" them. Only if they survived a lifetime of active service could they look forward to an honorable retirement, cultivating a plot of land allocated to them by the state.

When an Egyptian army marched to war—at a pace of about fifteen miles a day—the basic kit of a soldier comprised a pack, clothing, sandals, and a staff or cudgel for personal protection. More sophisticated weaponry was issued only when the army was ready to engage the enemy. (This was still the era of set-piece battles.) As the weapons were brought on, the shoes came off. Egyptian soldiers fought barefoot. Likewise, body armor was virtually nonexistent, as it impeded movement on the battlefield. Apart from a shield and perhaps a quilted leather jerkin, the infantryman had to rely on his own wits and strength to protect himself. For firepower over long distances, bows and arrows were the weapon of choice. Simple bows came in different sizes, small ones for short-range attack and longbows for use by massed stationary units of archers. Composite bows, a technological innovation of the early New Kingdom, provided even greater penetrating power, and were favored by the officers. Different types of arrows were chosen according to the type of injury the archer wished to inflict: pointed or barbed arrowheads for deep flesh wounds, flat-tipped versions for stunning the enemy. Other long-distance weapons included slings, spears, and javelins. For hand-to-hand combat, clubs and fighting rods were both cheap to produce and brutally effective, delivering crushing blows sufficient to fell even an armored opponent. Battle-axes were good for hacking down enemy forces, scimitars for slashing and slicing. As a weapon of last resort, the short-bladed dagger was invaluable, but also served a more grisly purpose. After each engagement, an Egyptian army counted the enemy dead by severing a hand (or, for an uncircumcised enemy, the penis) from each slain opponent. In a scene from the late Eighteenth Dynasty, a group of victorious Egyptian soldiers is shown leaving the battlefield, three enemy hands skewered on each of their spears.

If the infantry formed the backbone of the Egyptian army, the charioteers were the shock troops. The introduction of the horse and chariot from western Asia at the beginning of the New Kingdom revolutionized warfare in the ancient world, and gave Egypt a highly effective force for use against massed infantry. Each chariot had a two-man crew, comprising a warrior armed with a bow and arrow and a driver-cum-shield-bearer. The chariot's lightweight construction and rear-mounted wheels gave maximum speed and maneuverability, perfect for "softening up" the enemy before a frontal assault, and for harrying defeated forces, to turn a retreat into a rout. The last word in modern weaponry, the chariot was also the ultimate status symbol for the Egyptian elite—even if, like so many other innovations, it had been brought to the Nile Valley by foreigners. Yet the Egyptians of the Eighteenth Dynasty turned this technological triumph against its own inventors, using chariot forces to conquer and overwhelm province after province throughout the Near East. Without the chariot, it is doubtful that Egypt would ever have succeeded in forging an empire.

Chariots, like soft beds on campaign, were the preserve of the officer class. For an ordinary soldier to aspire to such luxuries, he first had to serve his time at the bottom of the hierarchy and work his way up through the ranks. The army certainly offered a passport to prestige and power for determined and ambitious men. Nobody illustrates this better than Horemheb. From a provincial background in Middle Egypt, his glittering military career took him not just to the top of the army but to the very pinnacle of the Egyptian state. Born in the reign of Amenhotep III, Horemheb's early career under Akhenaten is shrouded in mystery—he had no wish in later life to be associated with the royal revolutionary—but there are tantalizing clues that his aptitude and skill had already been recognized with promotion to high office. In the hills of Akhetaten, an unfinished tomb was inscribed for a king's scribe and general named Paatenemheb. Since many ambitious individuals changed their names under Akhenaten's regime to elimi-

A Nubian prisoner with a rope around his neck
WERNER FORMAN ARCHIVE

nate references to the old gods, it is quite possible that Paatenemheb ("the Aten [is] in festival") and Horemheb ("Horus [is] in festival") are one and the same man. Horemheb may have become "Paatenemheb" during Akhenaten's reign and then reverted to "Horemheb" after Akhenaten's death. Certainly, by the time Tutankhamun succeeded to the throne in 1332, Horemheb had come to prominence as commander in chief of the young king's army, a "general of generals."

Horemheb's magnificent private tomb at Saqqara is decorated with lavish scenes showing his activities as great overseer of the army. Vignettes of life in a military encampment show messenger boys running at the double as they carry instructions from tent to tent. Elsewhere, Horemheb receives the supplications of emissaries from hungry foreign lands as they plead for clemency and prostrate themselves "seven times on the belly and seven times on the back." More unsettling still are the scenes of prisoners of war from Horemheb's campaigns in the Near East and Nubia, row upon row of captives lined up before the commander in chief to await their fate. With wooden manacles on their wrists and ropes around their necks, Asiatic prisoners are paraded, pushed, and cajoled by Egyptian soldiers. As a standard part of military policy, entire families of men, women, and children were transported to Egypt as hostages, to ensure the good conduct of their countrymen back home. Even more humiliating treatment was reserved for the Nubian citizens of "vile Kush," ancient Egypt's favorite whipping boy.

The Kushite chief was forced to prostrate himself before Horemheb while armed Egyptian soldiers harrassed and assaulted his men, beating them with sticks and punching them on the jaw in acts of deliberate humiliation. All the while, with customary military efficiency, army scribes recorded every detail.

This ruthlessness found favor beyond the ranks of the army. In pharaonic Egypt, such qualities also provided the perfect springboard for a career in the civil service. Like many senior officers, Horemheb was able to combine both military and civilian roles. At the same time as commanding Tutankhamun's armed forces, he also acted as lord protector to the young king. As "king's deputy in the entire land," "who repeats the king's words to his entourage," Horemheb exercised huge influence over the direction of government policy, and from his office at Memphis he must have been one of the chief architects of the return to orthodoxy. Indeed, the inscriptions in his private tomb conspicuously omit references to Tutankhamun by name, a not-so-coded acknowledgment that the general, not the boy king, called the shots. As the power behind the throne, the commander in chief was already steering Egypt toward military rule as a way of restoring order. As his titles proclaimed, Horemheb was indeed "the two eyes of the king in leading the Two Lands and establishing the laws of the Two Banks." He would not have to wait long to make the ultimate transformation from king's deputy to the top job itself.

MILITARY DISCIPLINE

At the moment of Tutankhamun's untimely death in 1322, Horemheb was in the field in distant Syria, leading Egyptian troops in an unsuccessful campaign to recapture the rebellious city of Kadesh and pry it free from Hittite control. The nature of his involvement in the murky events that ensued—Ankhesenamun's plea to the Hittite king to send her a husband, the murder of Prince Zannanza en route to Egypt, and the accession of the old retainer Ay as pharaoh—remains shrouded in obscurity. Perhaps that was Horemheb's intention. Even if his hopes of election were temporarily thwarted by Ay's intervention, he knew that the new king was an old man with little time left. After a career spent building his power base and biding his time, Horemheb could certainly wait another few years before claiming his prize.

His eventual accession as lord of the Two Lands, after Ay's brief reign of four years (1322–1319), might have seemed inevitable. After all, Horemheb had been designated as Tutankhamun's heir and was merely fulfilling his destiny. That, no doubt, was the spin the royal propagandists put on the general's elevation. In reality, the appropriation of the throne by a commoner with no royal connections represented a complete break with tradition and threatened to undermine the very foundations of a hereditary monarchy. For all intents and purposes, Horemheb's accession was a military coup. He was a skilled enough tactician to realize the dangers, and clearly understood that he would need both to legitimize his own kingship and to put the institution as a whole on a new footing in order to secure his throne. Even with the army behind him, a new program for Egypt would require all his strategic skills.

The first step—as always—was to obtain divine sanction for his regime. This Horemheb achieved by the brilliant but simple expedient of timing his coronation to coincide with the annual Opet Festival at Thebes. As he emerged from the sanctuary of Luxor Temple, both newly crowned and infused with godlike powers through his communion with Amun-Ra, how could anyone doubt or challenge his right to rule? Once securely established on the throne of Horus, the king set his theologians to work to devise a plausible background story that would explain the rise of an army general to the kingship. The result was as ingenious a piece of sophistry as ever flowed from the pen of an ancient Egyptian scribe. The tale told how Horemheb had been marked out from childhood by his local god, Horus of Herakleopolis, who acted as father to him, protecting him until the time came:

A generation and another came and went [and still his father kept him safe], for he knew the day when he would retire to hand him his kingship.[1]

According to this explanation, Horemheb's long career in the military and civilian services was all part of the divine plan. Eventually, when the moment was right (in fact, when the opportunity arose), Horus promoted his chosen candidate and handed him over to the safekeeping of Amun-Ra. A boy from the provinces thus became the lord of the Two Lands.

If both the occasion and the setting for Horemheb's coronation harked back to the glorious reign of Amenhotep III, that was entirely deliberate. Part of Horemheb's program of legitimation involved airbrushing the intervening reigns from history, so that he could present himself as the first rightful pharaoh since Egypt's "dazzling orb." To this end, Akhenaten's temples at Gempaaten were systematically dismantled, their blocks used as fill for Horemheb's own constructions. On his orders, teams of workmen descended upon Akhetaten to expunge all traces of the heretic king. Statues of Akhenaten and Nefertiti were torn down, smashed, and tossed into a heap outside the Great Aten Temple. Also in line for official persecution were Tutankhamun and Ay. The boy king's inscriptions and monuments were recarved with Horemheb's names and titles, so that he could take sole credit for the return to orthodoxy (for which he had, in any case, been largely responsible). As for Ay, the old retainer who had kept Horemheb from the throne, his memory was treated even more harshly. His tomb in the Valley of the Kings and his public monuments were desecrated to extinguish all hopes of immortality. At the end of a lifelong rivalry, Horemheb had the last laugh.

Restoring the temples, reinstating their offerings, and restaffing them "with lay priests and lector priests from the pick of the infantry"[2] were all essential tasks for setting the country back on a traditional path. But Horemheb's counterrevolutionary agenda went far beyond the religious domain. Like other kings since the dawn of history, he had announced his program in the Horus name he adopted at his accession, "mighty bull, whose counsels are penetrating." The emphasis on law as well as order was intentional. Building on his experience of "establishing the laws of the Two Banks" under Tutankhamun, Horemheb now promulgated a series of major legislative reforms, published in the form of an edict. One of the most extensive surviving examples of pharaonic law-making, it was designed both to counteract abuses of power by agents of the state and to reinforce the security of Horemheb's own regime. While the preamble is couched in the usual lofty phraseology—"His Majesty determined . . . to drive out chaos and destroy falsehood"[3]—the detailed measures that follow are wholly pragmatic. They paint a picture of a ruler steeped in military discipline and determined to run Egypt along similar lines. Four of the ten clauses set down new penalties for misuse of authority by agents of the palace. Anyone found guilty of requisitioning boats or workers designated for state projects could expect to receive the harshest of punishments: exile to the desolate border fortress of Tjaru, and facial mutilation. Government employees caught with their noses in the trough could expect to lose them. Also subject to the full force of the law were corrupt palace employees. Fraudulently assessing taxes, collecting too much fodder (thus impoverishing the population at large), or extracting punitive amounts of provisions from local mayors during royal progresses would no longer be tolerated. Nor were members of the armed forces exempt from the same rules. Any soldier found guilty of stealing a hide—even to supplement his basic kit—would be punished severely with one hundred blows and five open wounds, in addition to the confiscation of the stolen items.

Having dealt with official corruption, Horemheb next turned his legislative attention to the law courts. Purging the judiciary has always been a favorite tactic of despots (especially those with a military background), and Horemheb was no exception. He appointed a raft of new judges, men who would be "attentive to the words of the court and the laws of the judgment hall."[4] He further decreed that local officials found guilty of perverting the course of justice would be sentenced to death, adding, "My Majesty has done this to advance the laws of Egypt."[5] And, of course, the king's word *was* the law. The final group of measures in Horemheb's edict are perhaps the most telling, dealing as they do with his own personal security. One clause laid down new restrictions on the activities and movements of employees of the royal harem, always a locus for dissent and possible sedition. The tenth and final clause was even more blatant, decreeing enhanced rewards for members of the king's bodyguard:

It will be like a holiday for them—every man seated with a share of every good thing . . . applauded for all [his] good deeds . . . [rewards] thrown to them from the window and summoning every man by his [own] name.[6]

Royal bodyguards would henceforth receive additional rewards from the king's personal property even while they continued to draw regular rations from the state treasury. The quid pro quo was a new protocol for the innermost chambers of the palace, to ensure that everyone knew and kept his place. Horemheb was not going to take any chances with his own safety. As one who had lived by the sword, he had no intention of dying by it. As the edict made crystal clear, he was "a brave and vigilant ruler."[7]

PASSING THE BATON

BY SUCH MEASURES, HOREMHEB SUCCEEDED IN ESTABLISHING THE authority and legitimacy of his reign, and bringing military discipline to bear on a country weakened by three decades of political upheaval and uncertainty. There was only one fly in the ointment: his lack of an heir. Without children of his own, Horemheb could not risk a disputed succession undoing his hard-won reforms. His solution mirrored his own rise to power. Looking among his closest followers, he identified an ideal successor from the ranks of the army. Paramessu was an army man through and through. The son of a battalion commander, he had started his career as a simple soldier, and had then won an officer's commission and subsequent promotions to fortress commander, aide-de-camp to the king, and finally general. He was a man in the same mold as Horemheb, someone who shared the same background and the same fundamental outlook. Even better, he already had a son, and a grandson was on the way—the perfect ingredients for a new military dynasty. Horemheb proceeded to give Paramessu a series of high civilian offices to prepare him for the eventual succession, appointing him king's deputy and vizier. At the same time, Paramessu had to relinquish his military titles while Horemheb remained in charge of the army. It would have been unwise to hand over such a powerful institution to a subordinate, however trusted. Yet by conferring the titles "king's son" and "hereditary prince" on Paramessu, the pharaoh was clearly signaling his resolve to hand over the kingship itself, in due course. As Horemheb's reign neared its close, his chosen heir changed his name to "Ramessu beloved of Amun" and began to write his name in a royal cartouche. The stage was set for the rise of the Ramessides.

While Horemheb may have promoted the new dynasty, its first member had no doubts that *he*, not his patron, was the real founder. To signal this new beginning, Ramessu—better known as Ramesses I (1292–1290)—deliberately chose his throne name to echo that of Ahmose, founder of the Eighteenth Dynasty. Where Ahmose had been Nebpehtyra, "Ra is lord of strength," Ramesses styled himself Menpehtyra, "Ra is enduring in strength." Yet Ramesses was not to endure in strength for very long. Already an old man at his accession, he entrusted much of the day-to-day running of the country to his son Seti. It was a wise decision. Within eighteen months of coming to the throne, Ramesses was dead. The new king, Seti I (1290–1279), was a vigorous and energetic man, tall and athletic with a distinguished countenance—high cheekbones and the characteristic aquiline nose of the Ramesside males. Horemheb's law code had successfully bolstered royal authority and rooted out corruption, so Seti could now set about restoring Egypt's fortunes, at home and abroad.

The mummy of Seti I
G. ELLIOT SMITH, *THE ROYAL MUMMIES*

Prosperity and security had always been demonstrated through state construction projects, and for the next decade the country echoed to the sound of masons' chisels and the shouts of builders, as Seti commissioned an astonishing series of new monuments at important sites throughout Egypt. Not since the days of Amenhotep III had government architects and artists been kept so busy. Seti's grandest project was a fabulous new temple at Abdju, ancient cradle of kingship and cult center of Osiris. The temple was designed to a bold new plan, and was equally radical in its dedication. At the back of a columned hall fronted by two great courts, there lay not one sanctuary but seven. Each of Egypt's chief deities had a place in this national pantheon: the holy family of Horus, Isis, and Osiris; the solar gods Amun-Ra and Ra-Horakhty; Ptah, the god of Memphis and of craftsmen; and, finally, predictably, Seti himself. A further suite of side rooms provided space for the cults of the Memphite funerary gods Nefertem and Ptah-Sokar, so they wouldn't feel excluded. This bringing together of the greatest deities in the land under one roof, to honor Seti with their presence, was part of a conscious effort to establish the theological credentials of the new Ramesside Dynasty.

The theme of dynastic legitimacy was reinforced in a long corridor that led southward from the columned hall. Its exquisite relief decoration showed Seti's eldest son, Prince Ramesses, reading a papyrus inscribed with the names of sixty-seven royal predecessors, stretching all the way back to Menes, legendary founder of the Egyptian state. The Abdju king list drew upon ancient temple archives, but its primary purpose was religious rather than historical. Designed to stress the unbroken succession of rightful monarchs from the beginning of the First Dynasty down to Seti I and his son, it included the ephemeral kings of the First Intermediate Period but conspicuously omitted the hated Hyksos, the dubious Hatshepsut, the heretic Akhenaten, and his three tainted successors. In the context of a royal ancestor cult, such controversial forebears were best forgotten.

Abdju was the theological center of Seti's regime, and he went to extraordinary lengths to guarantee its proper functioning in perpetuity. First, he endowed it with substantial land and resources, many of them located in the farthest parts of conquered Nubia (where nobody could object). Next, Seti took a leaf out of Horemheb's book and promulgated a wide-ranging decree to protect the assets from improper appropriation by other institutions. Carved into the side of a sandstone hill near the third Nile cataract, in the vicinity of a fortified garrison, the Nauri Decree spelled out the penalty for requisitioning or interfering with the annual shipment of produce sent from Kush to Abdju:

> As for any overseer of the fortress, scribe of the fortress, or agent of the fortress who boards a boat belonging to the temple and takes . . . anything of Kush that is being delivered as revenue to the temple, the law is to be enforced against him in the form of one hundred blows, and he is to be fined . . . at a rate of eighty to one.[8]

Having thus secured regular shipments of produce to fill the coffers of his temple, Seti set about guaranteeing an eternal supply of gold, the commodity above all others that betokened wealth. He ordered new gold mines to be opened up in Egypt's remote Eastern Desert, and took a close interest in the production and transport of the mines' precious ore to the Nile Valley. An inscription at a remote temple in the Wadi Barramiya recounts the king's personal involvement:

> His Majesty surveyed the hill country as far as the mountains, for his heart wished to see the mines from which the fine gold is brought. After His Majesty had walked uphill for many miles, he halted by the wayside to mull things over. He declared, "How irksome is a track without water! What is an expedition to do to relieve their parched throats?"[9]

His answer was to order the stonecutters to leave their mining posts and instead "dig a well in the mountains, so that it might lift up the weary and refresh the spirit of him who burns in summer."[10]

The king's penchant for innovation was also put to great effect in the preparation of his final resting place, a great royal tomb in the Valley of the Kings. Not only is it the longest and deepest of all the royal tombs at Thebes, but it was also the first to be decorated throughout: every wall and ceiling of every passage and chamber is covered with the finest paintings and reliefs. This tomb established the decorative program that would be followed by all subsequent tombs in the valley, until the very end of the New Kingdom. Amid such splendor, one masterwork is justly famed—the magnificent vaulted ceiling of the burial chamber,

painted with astronomical scenes so as to resemble the very vault of
heaven. The Ramesside Dynasty might have been less than a decade
old, but Seti I had no doubts about his immortal destiny.

THE TUMBRELS OF WAR

RESTORING SACRED SITES TO MAGNIFICENCE AND ENDOWING THEM
with dazzling new monuments was a tried and trusted way of rebuilding Egypt's domestic standing, but there was still the question of the
country's international reputation. From his background as an army officer, Seti knew that influence on the world stage came from military
strength. Yet not since the glory days of Amenhotep II had Egypt won
a decisive victory in the Near East. Under Akhenaten and Tutankhamun, attempts to extend or even defend imperial possessions in
Syria had been wholly ineffective. Horemheb had tried to reassert
Egyptian hegemony, but with mixed results. Egypt's reputation as a
great power was seriously compromised, its overseas territories vulnerable to secession or seizure by the Hittites, and its mastery of trade
routes threatened. Action was urgently needed if the Ramessides' inheritance was not to disappear before their very eyes. Seti had lost no
time, launching his first campaign while still crown prince. He had
fought his way along the Phoenician coast to reassert Egypt's traditional sphere of influence and to secure Egypt's continued access to the
Mediterranean harbors, with their garrisons and trading wharfs.

At the start of his sole reign in 1290, he led further campaigns with
similar strategic objectives. The first people to feel Egypt's wrath were
the bedouin of northern Sinai. Struggles between their fractious tribes
were not a hazard to Egyptian security per se, but they did threaten the
country's main supply lines to its imperial possessions in Syria-
Palestine. Seti knew that control of the northern Sinai coastal route
was a necessary prerequisite for more ambitious military maneuvers.
Having reimposed Egyptian authority in his own backyard, he moved
onward into Canaan, regaining control of the key fortified towns of
Beth-Shan and Yenoam. He then set the seal on Egypt's victory by
forcing the chiefs of Lebanon to hew wood in his presence—a public
act of submission to the pharaoh that also emphasized Egypt's claim
over the region's abundant natural resources. In earlier times, small-

scale local actions of this sort would not have required the personal presence of the king at the head of the army. But Seti recognized the need to project a renewed image of royal power abroad, and was fortunate in possessing the appetite for battle. Sustaining such a policy, however, would lead Egypt ever deeper into the quagmire of international politics, with momentous consequences.

The political map of the Near East in Seti's time was radically and irrevocably changed from the confident days of the late Eighteenth Dynasty. Under Thutmose IV and Amenhotep III, Egypt had achieved a lasting peace with the major power of northern Mesopotamia, the kingdom of Mittani, and had secured the new relationship through a series of diplomatic marriages. The two powers had respected each other's spheres of influence and had managed to coexist amicably for half a century. Then, early in the reign of Akhenaten, the accession of a belligerent and ambitious ruler of the Hittites had dealt a body blow to the carefully negotiated balance of power. In a series of swift and devastating campaigns, the Hittite king Shuppiluliuma had succeeded in breaking out of his Anatolian heartland to conquer significant swaths of Mittanian-controlled territory, even raiding the Mittanian capital. Egypt had stuck by its friendship with Mittani, but the Mesopotamian kingdom was by that time all but a spent force. A new superpower had arrived on the scene, and Egypt had been totally unprepared.

Under Akhenaten, the pharaonic government's initial reaction had been not to get involved. This passivity had been a fatal error. The combination of Mittanian weakness and Egyptian hesitancy had then led a number of former vassal states to exploit the power vacuum and push for greater autonomy. Chief among them had been Amurru, a sizeable region of central Syria between the river Orontes and the Mediterranean Sea. As we have seen, the ruler of Amurru, Abdi-Ashirta, had been a shameless wheeler-dealer, quick to take advantage of political rivalries and social instability to advance his own cause. His missives to the Egyptian court form a significant portion of the Amarna Letters archive. Either the Egyptians had not known quite what to make of him or they'd decided a policy of nonintervention was the most sensible course. Yet this disinterest had merely encouraged Abdi-Ashirta in his ambitions, and Amurru had remained outside Egyptian control.

Pharaonic power, once feared and respected throughout the Near East, had had no more success with the wayward state of Kadesh. Its rulers had been a thorn in Egypt's side ever since the reign of Thutmose III, and they had stayed true to character during Akhenaten's reign by going over to the enemy side as soon as the Hittite army had come knocking at their gates. An abortive mission to recapture Kadesh had merely underlined Egypt's weakness. A second attempt on the town during the reign of Tutankhamun had met with similar failure, encouraging the gloating Hittites to consolidate their hold over northern Syria. Aziru of Amurru (Abdi-Ashirta's son), seeing which way the wind had been blowing, had joined Kadesh in pledging allegiance to the region's new Hittite overlords. The attempt by Tutankhamun's widow to engineer a diplomatic marriage to a Hittite prince, to save her from Ay's clutches, could have brought about a lasting peace between the two rival powers. Instead, Prince Zannanza's mysterious death had merely provided yet another excuse for Hittite expansion; the prince's father had vented his wrath on the treacherous Egyptians by attacking Egyptian-held territory in southern Syria.

But the Hittites had not had it all their own way. In a bitter twist of fate, the prisoners of war that had been brought back to the Hittite capital from these punitive raids had carried with them the plague. It had swept through the royal citadel at Hattusa, killing not only the king but his crown prince as well. It was still ravaging the Hittite homeland twenty years later. To the Hittites, it must have seemed that the gods had changed sides. To the Egyptians, these bizarre events far from home seemed to have rekindled the possibility of victory. An uneasy peace had settled over Syria, with Egypt and the Hittites at a stalemate.

So things had stood when Seti I came to the throne. With a soldier's blood in his veins, he was resolute in his determination to restore Egypt's tarnished national pride. After a half century of inglorious retreat, it was time for Amun-Ra to be on the march once again. Having reasserted Egyptian control over Phoenicia and Canaan, Seti set his sights on Amurru and Kadesh. Winning them back would strike a symbolically powerful blow to Hittite aspirations and would go a long way to reviving Egypt's regional reputation. Just a year after recapturing

Beth-Shan and Yenoam, Seti's army struck deep into central Syria. Kadesh was taken, and a triumphant Seti ordered a magnificent victory inscription to be erected in the city. His elation was to be short-lived. As soon as the Egyptian troops had disappeared over the horizon, the perfidious inhabitants of Kadesh returned at once to the Hittite fold. The pharaoh's forces had rather more success with the province of Amurru—once retaken, it remained loyal to its new Egyptian master. At the end of the campaign, a large part of central Syria had changed sides. Seti had erased the humiliations of previous generations and had set Egypt back on the path of imperial greatness. Or so he hoped. In fact, the Hittites were merely regrouping. They had no intention of taking these setbacks lying down. Marshaling their considerable forces high on the Anatolian plateau, they prepared for all-out war. As the skies darkened over the Near East, the looming showdown between the two superpowers would not be long in coming.

Behind the apparent pluck and resolve of Seti I's foreign policy there lurks a conundrum. If Egypt and the Hittites had indeed agreed on some sort of accommodation during the reign of Horemheb, as later sources suggest, then Seti's bold campaigns drove a coach and horses through it. Moreover, his actions set in train a series of increasingly bloody clashes that led not to the restoration of Egyptian supremacy but to long-term losses. In retrospect, Seti's Asiatic wars look rash and foolish. One possible explanation is that his policy was dictated more by political expediency than by a careful calculation of Egypt's strategic interests. Rulers throughout history have resorted to stoking a foreign conflict to deflect attention from problems closer to home. And, indeed, there are tantalizing clues from early in Seti's reign that may suggest an insecurity at the heart of his regime. In the king's battle reliefs at Ipetsut, an enigmatic figure labeled only as "the group marshaler and fan bearer Mehy" is depicted with unusual prominence, as if playing a key role in the battles and in Seti's wider offensive strategy.

To have been given such high status on a royal monument, Mehy (the name is an abbreviation for an unknown longer name) must have been one of the most influential figures at court—perhaps occupying a position akin to that of Horemheb during the reign of Tutankhamun or of Paramessu during the reign of Horemheb. It has even been suggested that the mysterious Mehy was Seti's designated heir, and that the martial king had decided to follow recent precedent by leaving his throne to a fellow army officer.

If so, Seti's son, the adolescent Prince Ramesses, had other ideas. Within a few years of Mehy's figure being carved, every instance was systematically erased from the Ipetsut reliefs, to be replaced by Ramesses's own image. The next generation of the Ramesside Dynasty had no intention of allowing a mere commoner to exercise such influence over the kingdom's affairs. Ramesses, and he alone, would be recognized by posterity as his father's true heir and most steadfast supporter. Ramesses, and he alone, would continue Seti's aggressive foreign policy and fulfill Egypt's destiny as a great imperial power. Ramesses, and he alone, would confront the Hittites directly in a final struggle for international supremacy.

The pharaoh's army readied itself as the country marched onward to war.

CHAPTER 16

WAR AND PEACE

BATTLE ROYAL

ON A CRISP MAY MORNING IN 1274, SHORTLY AFTER DAWN, RAMESSES II broke camp and rode out at the head of his army. Behind him, in the chill morning air, slowly but surely, the massive expeditionary force of more than twenty thousand men inched its way along the dusty track, from the ridgetop vantage point where it had spent the night, down into the valley below. After a month on the march—from the Egyptian border to Gaza, through the hill country of Canaan to Megiddo, and thence along the Litani and Beqa valleys—the army's ultimate destination lay just half a day ahead.

The great town of Kadesh had been a decisive player in the power politics of the Near East for centuries. Situated in the fertile valley of the river Orontes, it commanded one of the few routes that crossed the coastal range to link inland Syria with the Mediterranean coast. It was thus of vital strategic importance for control of the wider region. (Twenty-five centuries later, the Crusaders recognized the same strategic imperative, building the greatest of their castles, Krak des Chevaliers, just a few miles away.)

Back in the days of Thutmose III, the prince of Kadesh had been the leader of the rebels vanquished at Megiddo. In more recent times, Kadesh had successfully played the Egyptians and the Hittites off against each other, switching allegiance from one side to the other. The town's canny rulers had also taken impressive steps to defend themselves. While they might have been quite happy to act as agents provocateurs in the looming confrontation between the two great powers, they had no wish to see their homes reduced to rubble in the process. Nestled in a fork of the Orontes and one of its tributaries, Kadesh was naturally protected on three sides by water. By cutting a channel to the

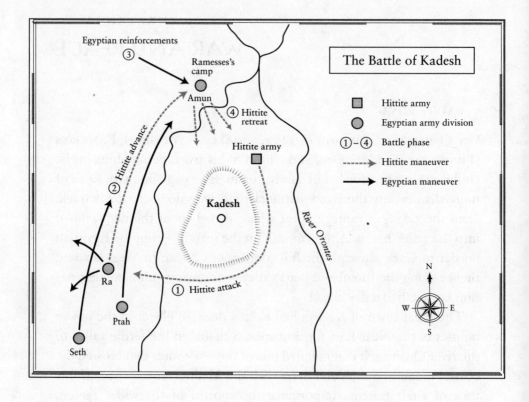

Egyptian reinforcements

③

Ramesses's
camp

Amun

④ Hittite
retreat

Hittite army

Kadesh

River Orontes

② Hittite advance

Hittite attack

① Hittite attack

Ra

Ptah

Seth

The Battle of Kadesh

■ Hittite army

● Egyptian army division

①–④ Battle phase

- - → Hittite maneuver

—→ Egyptian maneuver

N
W · E
S

south of the town, linking the two rivers, the citizens had turned their town, already heavily fortified, into a virtual island, impregnable against attack. Nonetheless, Ramesses had determined to capture Kadesh once and for all, to restore Egypt's imperial reputation in Syria. After a decade of low-level hostilities, the Egyptian and Hittite forces had settled upon Kadesh as the location for a great set-piece battle that would finally decide permanent supremacy over the important terri-tory of Amurru, which had switched sides so frequently during the previous decades. So it was with a combination of resolution and antic-ipation that the pharaoh's army now marched.

The massive force assembled by Ramesses, representing perhaps three-quarters of Egypt's total military strength, was formed of four di-visions, each commanded by a senior royal officer. The king himself was in charge of the lead division, named for the god Amun. Behind him followed the divisions of Ra, Ptah, and Seth. Once on the march, the line of troops stretched for more than a mile, weapons glinting in the sunlight—an awesome sight indeed. As the eldest son and succes-sor of the warrior king Seti I, Ramesses had learned at his father's side the art of military leadership, and he knew that the sight of him tri-umphantly arrayed in his golden chariot would both inspire his own troops and strike fear into the heart of the enemy. Indeed, initial re-ports from the field suggested that the Hittites had taken fright. As the division of Amun marched through dense woods on the south bank of the Orontes, Egyptian scouts intercepted two bedouin tribesmen. Their interrogation yielded astonishing and welcome news: the Hittite army, overawed by Ramesses's resolve and his fearsome war machine, was keeping its distance and was currently 120 miles away in the land of Aleppo. Fearing deliberate misinformation, the Egyptians cross-questioned the nomads, but they stuck to their story. Everything seemed to be going Ramesses's way. Buoyed by this unexpected turn of events, the army pressed on toward Kadesh.

Once out of the woods, the division of Amun forded the Orontes near the village of Shabtuna (modern Ribla) and after another three hours' marching reached their campsite opposite Kadesh. The site was well chosen, with a nearby brook affording welcome refreshment for men and horses alike. While the animals quenched their thirst, the sol-diers began to pitch camp. Chariots were parked, tents erected, and shields set up to form a defensive laager. It was three o'clock in the afternoon. Hazy in the distance, the fortresslike Kadesh dominated the southeastern horizon.

As soon as Ramesses and his forward division reached the campsite, the intelligence corps dispatched scouts into the surrounding countryside, following established practice, to reconnoiter the land and provide information about enemy movements. Almost immediately, they stumbled upon two Hittite spies engaged in similar activities. It was a stroke of extraordinary luck, the first of several strokes that spring afternoon. The enemy agents were subjected not to a mild interrogation but to fierce beatings. What they revealed under torture was a bombshell. Far from being 120 miles away and chary of battle, the Hittite king Muwatalli II and his forces were at that very moment camped behind Kadesh, the town mound concealing their presence from the Egyptians. Moreover, the Hittite commanders had decided to launch a preemptive strike against the Egyptian army and were preparing to attack at any moment.

Having spilled their terrible news, the spies were dragged before an astonished Ramesses, who erupted in fury. He slammed his senior officers for their incompetence and, taking personal charge of events, ordered urgent emergency measures. The royal princes traveling with the king were sent immediately out of danger, fleeing westward, away from the oncoming storm. The vizier was dispatched southward at full speed, to hurry the advance of the division of Ptah, which was only now preparing to ford the Orontes. The message from Ramesses was desperate: "His Majesty is all alone!"[1]

Minutes later, the attack came. A huge detachment of twenty-five hundred Hittite chariots, their warriors fearsome in ankle-length mail coats, swept across the river and struck the division of Ra as it was marching northward toward the Egyptian camp. Unlike the Egyptian battle chariots, which were essentially mobile firing platforms, the Hittite chariots were sturdy war machines. Each carried not two but three crew—a driver and two soldiers—armed with stabbing spears for close-range combat. Used en masse, in an organized charge, the Hittite chariotry was devastatingly effective at demolishing ranks of enemy infantry, as the division of Ra now discovered, to its great cost.

With their dead and dying comrades littering the ground, the surviving Egyptian soldiers panicked and fled headlong toward their camp, the Hittites in hot pursuit. Within moments, the enemy was at the gate. Chariots charged through the unfinished wall of shields to attack the Egyptian generals in their tented headquarters. It was pandemonium. With no time to think, Ramesses acted instinctively, leaping onto his chariot and swinging into action against the Hittite foe. The king was surrounded by his elite bodyguard of Aegean mercenaries, fierce fighting men from the coasts and islands on the western fringes of the Hittite Empire, men whose bravery and resilience had impressed the great powers of the Near East in recent decades. They, not the Nubians of old, were now the hired hands of choice for an Egyptian army. With them at his side, Ramesses darted between his attackers and showed his mastery of the bow and arrow, holding the fort (quite literally) amid chaos and confusion. It would take a miracle to withstand the Hittite onslaught for very long. But then, as if in answer to Ramesses's desperate prayers, help arrived in the nick of time.

It was not a miracle but the result of the Egyptians' tactical genius. While the main Egyptian army had marched overland to Kadesh, a reserve force of elite warriors had been sent by sea, up the Phoenician coast. Its instructions were to land at the Syrian port of Sumur and cut inland via the Eleutherus (modern Nahr el-Kebir) Valley to link up with Ramesses at Kadesh on the day of his arrival. They had done exactly as instructed. As the elite charioteers appeared in a cloud of dust on the horizon, the pharaoh knew help was at hand. Their resolve stiffened by the sudden reinforcements, the Egyptians forced the Hittites to withdraw and made to press home their advantage. Muwatalli, observing the reversal of fortune from a safe distance, sent a second wave of his chariots into the fray. These too were repulsed, and an Egyptian countercharge succeeded in pushing the enemy back toward the Orontes. After falling into the river, many Hittite charioteers were drowned or swept away. Others barely managed to scramble to safety on the opposite bank. The prince of Aleppo, one of Muwatalli's chief lieutenants, was hauled by his men from the bloody waters, barely alive. The Hittites' surprise attack had rebounded on them. In a matter of minutes, a certain victory had turned into an ignominious retreat.

As dusk approached, the Egyptian division of Ptah finally arrived on the scene, in time to round up the surviving Hittite soldiers, make a tally of the enemy dead, and collect the booty abandoned on the battlefield. Egyptian survivors of the carnage limped to their camp, followed, just before nightfall, by the fourth and final army division of Seth. On both sides, it was time to take stock and count the cost. For the Egyptians, dreadful losses on the battlefield had been matched by an equally devastating loss of reputation: their very survival had been in peril, and only the king's personal charisma, combined with the timely arrival of the reserve force, had prevented the army's total annihilation. For the Hittites, the scene was equally bleak. King Muwatalli had lost two of his own brothers in the fighting, together with his secretary, the chief of his bodyguard, four leading charioteers, and numerous officers. With neither side victorious, the Battle of Kadesh was not over yet.

At daybreak, after a fitful night tending the wounded and repairing mangled chariots, the two armies met once more, this time for the planned encounter on the plain in front of Kadesh. Yet the previous day's fighting had fatally weakened both sides. The Egyptians had sustained heavy losses and could not overcome the might of the Hittite infantry. (It had sat out the initial assault, and was thus rested and resolute.) The Hittites, having lost a sizeable proportion of their chariotry, could not inflict a decisive defeat on the Egyptians. After several hours of bloody battle, with no breakthrough in sight, Ramesses withdrew his forces from the field. He realized he would never succeed in his strategic objective of capturing Kadesh, let alone in defeating the Hittites. Muwatalli, too, realized he could not orchestrate a decisive victory. He sued for peace and sent an envoy to the Egyptian camp with terms for a cease-fire. Ramesses had little option but to accept them. Twenty-four hours after arriving at Kadesh, the Egyptians gathered up their matériel and marched homeward. After two months away, Ramesses's once mighty army arrived back in the green fields of the Nile delta in late June, exhausted and despondent.

Yet the king himself seems to have drawn strength from the bruising encounter, not least his own role in saving the day for Egypt. He had snatched, if not victory, then at least survival from the jaws of defeat, and felt ever more certain of his destiny. In keeping with his supremely self-assured—not to say megalomaniac—character, Ramesses now proceeded to turn the whole Kadesh episode to his advantage. In a carefully orchestrated barrage of propaganda—comprising both art and literature—the king broadcast his version of events throughout Egypt. He had the country's finest writers compose a factual prose account of the battle alongside an epic poem, both designed to celebrate the king's "great victory" over the Hittites. The texts were inscribed on temple walls and were, no doubt, recited triumphantly and frequently at court. To complement these literary paeans, Ramesses commissioned his artists to devise a stock set of pictorial scenes to capture the main moments of the battle. Chief among these tableaux, of course, was the oversize figure of the valorous monarch, all alone in the Egyptian camp, fending off the enemy single-handedly. So pleased was the king with the result that he had the same series of images carved on the façades of at least five major temples. Poems and pictures—both allowed Ramesses to contrast the incompetence and vacillation of his senior military officers with his own foresight and ability to be coolheaded under fire. For a king whose birthright could have been threatened by an army insider, this must have been the sweetest revenge.

For modern scholars, the images and words furnish an extraordinary amount of detail, and make the Battle of Kadesh the best-known military encounter in the ancient world. For Ramesses's contemporaries, however, the accounts announced a return to the vainglorious and bombastic kingship of old. After the heresy of Akhenaten, the ephemeral reigns of his immediate successors, and the military junta of Horemheb and the early Ramessides, a resplendent and triumphalist monarchy was back with a vengeance—even if the truth had to suffer in the process.

KING OF KINGS

WHILE STALEMATE AT KADESH HAD SINGULARLY FAILED TO ADVANCE Ramesses II's strategic aims, the standoff and cessation of hostilites did at least allow him to reap a peace dividend. Resources that might have been expended on foreign military adventures could instead be invested in projects at home.

In the first two decades of his reign (1279–1259), Ramesses commissioned major new temple buildings throughout his realm, from the

Lebanese port of Kebny to Gebel Barkal, in distant Sudan. The king seems to have had a particular preoccupation with Egyptian-controlled Nubia, ordering the construction of new shrines at seven different sites. In Egypt proper, architects and masons made impressive additions to the great national temples at Iunu and Herakleopolis, Abdju and Thebes. Today, more standing monuments bear the names of Ramesses II than of any other pharaoh. By a combination of construction and appropriation (taking pains to have his cartouche incised so deeply into the stone that it could never be removed), Ramesses ensured that his name would live forever. He seems to have been driven by a deep desire to surpass all his predecessors, and by a resolute sense of his own uniqueness. One of the king's favorite myths about himself told how the Seven Hathors (the ancient Egyptian equivalent of the Fates) had watched over his infant cradle and devised an extraordinary destiny for him while he was still a babe in arms. Whether this reveals a thoroughgoing monomania or a pathological inferiority complex is open to debate. What is certain is that Ramesses's building projects were characterized more by sheer size and brute strength than by any more refined aesthetic. Only in the exquisite decoration of the Theban tomb prepared for his beloved wife Nefertari did Ramesses allow his craftsmen to give free rein to their artistic sensibilities.

To supply so many simultaneous building projects with the necessary quantities of stone was beyond even Egypt's prodigious quarrying capacity. So Ramesses resorted to the age-old expedient of demolishing his forebears' monuments and requisitioning their stone for his own purposes. The chief victims of this wholesale plunder were the temples built by Akhenaten at Thebes and Akhetaten. The small, regular stone blocks that had enabled the heretic king to build his monuments so rapidly now contributed to the monuments' equally swift demise. Blocks by the thousand were taken from the Aten temples to facilitate the erection of new shrines to the old gods. Ramesses was thus able to kill two birds with one stone: cleansing the land of Akhenaten's heresy and promoting himself as the champion of Egypt's traditional deities.

Since the reign of Amenhotep III ninety years earlier, the greatest stage for the ceremonies of divine kingship had been Luxor Temple, with its gigantic colonnade hall and beautiful open-air courtyard providing a spectacular backdrop to the mysteries of the annual Opet Festival. The temptation to make it yet grander proved irresistible to Ramesses. He added an entire new court and colossal gateway to the temple, decorated with massive scenes of his "triumph" at the Battle of Kadesh. Never shy of improving the monuments of his predecessors, he did not hesitate to change the main axis of Luxor Temple in order to line it up better with Ipetsut and provide a more coherent processional route. Finally, to adorn the new façade of Luxor, Ramesses had installed what would become his trademark—a pair of colossal seated statues of himself, in this case complemented by a pair of towering obelisks. Spectacle, it seems, was all.

Nowhere is Ramesses's taste for the theatrical and self-reverential better demonstrated than in the Temple of Ramesses-beloved-of-Amun (modern Abu Simbel) in lower Nubia. The sheer rock face of a sacred mountain, towering over the Nile just north of the second cataract, was the chosen setting for the king's most remarkable and vainglorious project. The smaller of two temples was officially dedicated to the mother goddess and royal protectress Hathor. Inside, on the back wall of the sanctuary, the Hathor cow is shown emerging from the primeval papyrus swamp, protecting the king in her embrace. Outside, all pretense of piety is dropped, and the decoration concentrates on the king's great wife Nefertari and her doting husband. On either side of the doorway, a standing statue of the queen is flanked by two colossi of Ramesses, thirty feet high. The larger temple develops this theme further, statues and reliefs of Ramesses dominating the interior and exterior. The façade is formed by four vast seated statues of the king, each measuring nearly seventy feet high. On the pedestal, the king's name is shown above rows of foreign captives, emphasizing his mastery of all peoples. Inside the temple, scenes depict Ramesses killing the enemies of Egypt and presenting them to the gods—who naturally include his deified self. Indeed, Ramesses's apotheosis is the dominant theme at Abu Simbel. In desolate, conquered Nubia, where the gods were not watching, the king could give his megalomania free rein.

The true scale of the king's self-aggrandizement is revealed in the innermost parts of Abu Simbel. Beyond the pillared hall—each pillar adorned with a colossal standing statue of Ramesses in the guise of Osiris—and the ubiqitous depictions of the Battle of Kadesh lies the holy of holies, deep inside the mountain. This intimate space is dominated by the statues of Egypt's four chief gods, carved from the living rock. Permanently in the shadows, to one side, sits Ptah, chthonic creator god of Memphis. Next to him are Amun, creator god of Thebes; Ra-Horakhty, the solar deity who combined Ra and Horus; and the deified Ramesses. In his mind and in his monuments, the king was the equal of Egypt's most ancient and revered deities. Moreover, on two

Statues of Ramesses II fronting his temple at Abu Simbel
WERNER FORMAN ARCHIVE

days a year, February 21 and November 21—one of them presumably
Ramesses II's birthday—the first rays of the rising sun penetrated the
entrance of the temple and illuminated the statues in the sanctuary,
bringing them to life. It must have been a stunning spectacle. Few au-
tocrats in human history have conceived a more dramatic expression of
their personality cult.

After Ipetsut, Luxor, and Abu Simbel, Ramesses's greatest project
was his own mortuary temple on the west bank of the Nile at Thebes.
The most ambitious monument of its kind since the reign of Amenhotep III, "Ramesses United with Thebes" (known today as the
Ramesseum) covered an area of more than eleven and a half acres.
Quite unashamedly, every inch of the temple was given over to texts,
reliefs, and statuary celebrating the king. Beyond the first great gateway, decorated with scenes of the Battle of Kadesh, the first courtyard
was dominated by a series of huge pillars along the north side, each of
which had a gigantic statue of Ramesses in front of it. Facing them, on
the south side, was a portico and balcony, where the king could appear
to his loyal followers on high days and holidays. Beyond a second gateway, bearing yet more battle reliefs, lay a second court, likewise
adorned with colossal statues of Ramesses. Dwarfing even these, a vast
granite colossus once stood next to the second gateway, until an earth-
quake felled it in antiquity. Its shattered remains, carved deeply with
the king's throne name, Usermaatra (corrupted to Ozymandias in
Greek), inspired the most famous critique of absolute power in the
English language.

The Ramesseum, perhaps more than any other monument, summed
up its owner's unrivaled status not just in spiritual but also in temporal
matters. Surrounding the temple on all sides, vast storerooms and granaries provided storage for a significant part of Egypt's wealth. It would
have taken 350 boatloads (a quarter of a million sacks) of grain to fill the
granaries completely, enough to support the inhabitants of a medium-size
city (such as Thebes) for a year. In effect, the Ramesseum acted as Upper
Egypt's reserve bank. Both practically and symbolically, the nation's
wealth was under royal control. With such vast resources at his disposal,
Ramesses could afford to indulge his obsession with monumentality,
from the vast colossi of Abu Simbel to the majestic courts of Thebes. Well
might he have uttered the immortal words of Shelley's poem:

"My name is Ozymandias, king of kings:
Look on my works, ye Mighty, and despair!"

HOUSE PROUD

NOT CONTENT WITH ERECTING TEMPLES AND USURPING MONUMENTS
throughout the length and breadth of Egypt, Ramesses II created an
architectural wonder on an even greater scale, one that is now entirely
lost from sight. His father, Seti I, had built a small summer palace near
the old Hyksos capital of Hutwaret, where the Ramesside royal family
had its origins. The young Ramesses must have spent time there,
preparing for battle, and as king he set about transforming it into
something altogether grander. In two decades of nonstop construction,
a vast series of mansions, halls, offices, and barracks grew up around
the royal palace, until Ramesses had created an entirely new city, a dynastic capital equal in splendor to Memphis or Thebes. With customary chutzpah, he named it Per-Ramesses, "the house of Ramesses."

A desirable residence it certainly was, with vast living quarters and
administrative districts full of palaces, temples, and public buildings.
The surrounding countryside was some of the most productive in
Egypt, supplying fruit, vegetables, and wine, and providing pasture for
great herds of cattle. Scribes wrote wondrously of canals filled with
fish, marshlands teeming with waterfowl, fields abundant with green
pasture, and granaries overflowing with barley and wheat. The royal
quarter, covering four square miles, was located in a natural stronghold
on the banks of the Nile, protected by canals and sand promontories.
Court poets penned eulogies on the splendor of Ramesses's palaces, describing pillared halls and decoration of unparalleled richness. Walls,
floors, columns, and doorways—all were encrusted with polychrome
tile work, depicting rivers and gardens, heraldic motifs, and foreign
captives. The steps leading to the throne dais were adorned with prostrate images of the king's enemies, so that he might tread them underfoot each time he ascended or descended.

If the royal residence was dazzling, the elite quarter in the suburbs
was scarcely less so. The area favored by Per-Ramesses's wealthiest citizens resembled a Venetian idyll, with canals, large villas, and water
gardens. The center of the city was dominated by a vast temple dedi-

cated to the divine trinity, Amun–Ra-Horakhty–Atum. Fronted by four colossal statues of the king, it rivaled Ipetsut in size and splendor. The four cardinal points of the city were placed under the symbolic protection of other major deities. In the south was the temple of Seth, lord of Hutwaret, dating back to Hyksos times. In the north, a shrine was built to honor the ancient cobra goddess of the delta, Wadjet. In the west, a temple celebrated Amun of Thebes. Finally, in the east, pointing the way to Egypt's empire in the Near East, a sanctuary was dedicated to Astarte—not an Egyptian deity at all but the Syrian goddess of love and war, appropriated into the Egyptian pantheon and given the special role of protecting the horse team that drew the royal chariot.

Even by the standards of New Kingdom Egypt, Per-Ramesses was a cosmopolitan city. As well as a temple to an Asiatic deity, there were overseas legations and entire quarters for foreign mercenaries. The markets and wharfs played host to merchants from throughout the eastern Mediterranean. With its geographic proximity to Palestine, Per-Ramesses must have been a magnet for immigrants seeking a better life, and it is against such a background that the Bible story of the Exodus came to be written. Exodus 1:11 tells how "Pharaoh" put the enslaved Hebrews to work on two great store-cities, Pithom and Raamses. "Pithom," or Per-Atum, has been identified as modern Tell el-Maskhuta, in the eastern delta, only a day's journey from Per-Ramesses, while "Raamses" can be none other than the new dynastic capital itself. It is highly likely that Semitic-speaking laborers *were* employed in the construction of the city, but they were more likely migrant workers rather than slaves (although the working conditions may have made the distinction somewhat academic). As for any exodus of Hebrews, in the reign of Ramesses II or later, the ancient Egyptian sources are silent. The story may therefore have been a conflation of several unrelated historical events. On the other hand, as we have seen, Ramesses was not one to let the truth stand in the way of his news agenda.

While the court scribes and poets lauded Per-Ramesses as a great royal residence, filled with exuberance and joy, there was also a more menacing side to this most ambitious of royal projects. One of the largest buildings was a vast bronze-smelting factory whose hundreds of workers spent their days making armaments. State-of-the-art high-temperature furnaces were heated by blast pipes worked by bellows. As the molten metal came out, sweating laborers poured it into molds for shields and swords. In dirty, hot, and dangerous conditions, the pharaoh's people made the weapons for the pharaoh's army. Another large area of the city was given over to stables, exercise grounds, and repair works for the king's chariot corps. The royal stud farm provided accommodation for at least 460 horses together with their trainers and grooms. The animals were exercised in a wide, pillared court, while nearby workshops produced and repaired the tack.

In short, Per-Ramesses was less pleasure dome and more military-industrial complex. The city's very foundation had been prompted by an upsurge in military activity in the Near East. It was from here that Ramesses set out for Kadesh, to here that he returned, bloodied but unbowed. For all its pleasures and palaces, Per-Ramesses, with its poly-glot population, must have been a constant reminder of the king's un-finished business in Syria-Palestine. Despite having the largest chariot corps in the entire region, Ramesses remained unable to neutralize the Hittite threat. Yet as he sat in his riverside palace, smarting with frus-tration, the king could have little imagined that events hundreds of miles away were about to deal him the luckiest of hands.

PEACE IN OUR TIME

THE INDECISIVE BATTLE OF KADESH HAD BEEN FOLLOWED BY A DECADE of cold war, with the Hittites and the Egyptians facing off against each other, neither able to achieve hegemony. But the two old rivals were no longer the only powers in the region. Beyond the Euphrates, the king-dom of Assyria was in the ascendant. Barely a year after Kadesh, and emboldened by the Hittites' failure to prevail, an Assyrian army at-tacked the crucial Hittite ally of Hanigalbat (the remnants of the old Mittanian Kingdom) and made it their vassal. It was a warning shot neither the Hittites nor, for that matter, the Egyptians could afford to ignore. Ramesses launched a series of low-level campaigns in the Near East, determined to shore up Egyptian control over its imperial provinces, to crush opportunistic rebellions that had broken out in the aftermath of Kadesh, and to show the Assyrians that Egypt was still a force to be reckoned with.

Having overcome dissidents in the hills of Galilee, and having re-captured the important port of Akko, Ramesses could not restrain his bravado and advanced into the erstwhile Egyptian territory of Amurru, now back within the Hittite fold. First one and then another city-state fell to the pharaoh's army, until Ramesses occupied the middle Orontes Valley, effectively bisecting the Hittites' southernmost province. It looked as if this rash maneuver might provoke another all-out war, but the sudden death of the Hittite king Muwatalli plunged Egypt's enemy into a succession crisis, with major repercussions.

Muwatalli had left the throne to his young son, Prince Urhi-Teshup, who duly acceded as king. But the new monarch's uncle, Hattusili, had other ideas. Before long, two rival courts had developed and the ruling elite was riven by divided loyalties. After much bitter infighting, Hat-tusili prevailed and Urhi-Teshup fled to Egypt, seeking sanctuary at the court of Ramesses II. The pharaoh, who had been watching all these developments from a safe distance, could hardly believe his luck. In his protracted struggle for supremacy with the Hittites, fate had now de-livered him, quite unexpectedly, the ultimate bargaining chip. No sooner had Urhi-Teshup fled to Egypt than Hattusili demanded his immediate extradition. Ramesses refused and put his troops in Syria on high alert, in case the Hittites attacked. But his diplomatic antennae suggested such a course of events was unlikely, for a new ruler had just come to power in Assyria with imperialist ambitions of his own. Ramesses calculated, correctly, that the Hittites would be too preoccu-pied with this threat to their eastern flank to reopen hostilities with Egypt. When the Assyrians invaded Hanigalbat for a second time and liquidated it as a separate territory, the Hittites suddenly found them-selves in greater danger than ever before. Only the river Euphrates sep-arated their kingdom from the belligerent and expansionist Assyria. It was time to put national security before national pride.

An alliance with Assyria was unthinkable, so Hattusili put out dis-creet feelers in Egypt's direction, to explore the possibilities of peace with Ramesses. After a year of fraught negotiations accompanied by much shuttle diplomacy, the details of a treaty were hammered out. So, in early December 1259, a decade and a half after the Battle of Kadesh, a high-level delegation set out from the Hittite capital of Hattusa, high on the Anatolian plateau, bound for Per-Ramesses. Alongside the Hittite envoys traveled a representative from Carchemish, the Hittites' forward base on the banks of the Euphrates; it was a clear indication that cordial relations with Egypt now lay at the heart of Hittite foreign and security policy. After a month traveling the dusty roads of the Near East, the envoys finally arrived in the great delta city and were ushered into the royal audience chamber. Bowing low before Ramesses, the chief Hittite representative presented a great silver tablet, engraved in wedge-shaped cuneiform writing. It was a gift from Hattusili himself, a copy of the comprehensive treaty that from now on would bind the Egyptians and the Hittites in mutual support and friendship. Never to be outdone, Ramesses had the Egyptian version of the treaty engraved on the walls of Ipetsut, to stand as a perpetual record of his diplomatic skill.

And a remarkable document it was, in either language. After declaring a formal end to hostilities between the two kingdoms, the text celebrated the establishment of friendly relations:

> Behold, Hattusili, the ruler of the Hittites, binds himself by treaty to Usermaatra, chosen-one-of-Ra, the great ruler of Egypt, beginning today, so that perfect peace and brotherhood may be created between us forever—he being in brotherhood and peace with me, and I being in brotherhood and peace with him, forever.[2]

The elements of this new relationship were farsighted and wide-ranging: a mutual nonaggression pact, a defensive alliance, an extradition agreement (together with the promise of humane treatment for those extradited), an amnesty for refugees, and, last but by no means least, a clause to safeguard the royal succession and the rights of the monarchy in both kingdoms. With the deposed Urhi-Teshup still on the loose in Egypt, this final measure was a precondition for Hattusili, for it guaranteed his claim to the Hittite kingship and the rights of his heirs. It also played to Ramesses's dynastic concerns, reflected in his radical decision to promote his (many) sons to high office, the first time for a thousand years that such a policy had been adopted. For Hittites and Egyptians alike, honor was thus served, and both sides could claim victory. Egypt reluctantly gave up all hope of winning back Amurru, but kept its other Asiatic province, Upe, and confirmed its trading

Limestone statue of King Mentuhotep III (Eleventh Dynasty) from Thebes. Swathed in mummy wrappings, the king is shown in the guise of the god Osiris, risen from the dead.

Wooden models of infantrymen, from the tomb of Mesehti (Eleventh Dynasty) at Asyut. Part of Mesehti's grave goods, the models capture the militarism of Egyptian society at a time of civil war.

Gold amulet from a Twelfth Dynasty child's tomb at Haraga. According to ancient Egyptian belief, the image of a fish worn in the hair gave protection against drowning.

The pectoral of Princess Mereret (Twelfth Dynasty) is a fine example of Middle Kingdom jewelry. It combines gold, turquoise, carnelian, and lapis lazuli in a highly symbolic, symmetrical design. The piece also carries a political message, showing the king (as a falcon-headed sphinx) protected by the vulture goddess, trampling his enemies.

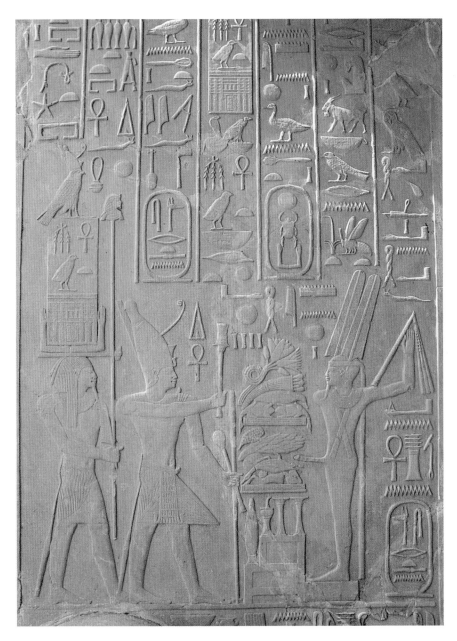

Relief decoration from the "white chapel" of King Senusret I (Twelfth Dynasty) at Karnak. Supported by his *ka* (spirit), the king presents offerings to the god Amun–Ra, shown in ithyphallic form. The white chapel was built to celebrate Senusret I's jubilee.

Aerial view of Thebes. Cult center of the god Amun and stage set for the rituals of monarchy, Thebes became the country's religious capital and a focus of royal patronage from the Middle Kingdom onward.

Obelisk of King Thutmose I (Eighteenth Dynasty) at Karnak. The obelisk, a solar symbol, stands in front of the hypostyle hall in the great temple of Amun-Ra, king of the gods.

Relief block from the "red chapel" of Hatshepsut (Eighteenth Dynasty) at Karnak. To conform with Egyptian theology, the female pharaoh is shown as a king, receiving blessings from the god Amun (enthroned) and his consort, Amunet.

Relief from the festival hall of King Thutmose III (Eighteenth Dynasty) at Karnak. The decoration records the exotic flora and fauna encountered by the king on his expeditions to the Near East.

View over Karnak Temple, the greatest religious building of the ancient world. In the background are the hypostyle hall of Seti I and Ramesses II (center) and the sacred lake (right).

The Colossi of Memnon at western Thebes depict King Amenhotep III (Eighteenth Dynasty). They originally stood in front of one of the gateways of his mortuary temple.

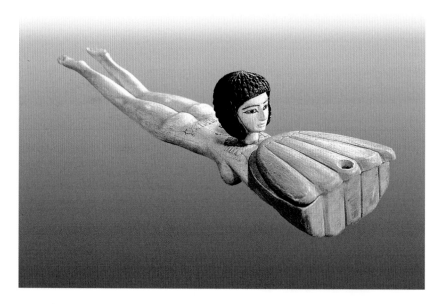

Painted wooden cosmetic box in the form of a swimming girl carrying a pink water lily. It encapsulates the luxury and sophistication of court life during the reign of King Amenhotep III (Eighteenth Dynasty).

Relief block from the "red chapel" of Hatshepsut (Eighteenth Dynasty) at Karnak. As part of the annual Opet Festival, priests carry the barque shrine of the god Amun in procession from Karnak to Luxor.

Statue of Amenhotep, son of Hapu, a favored courtier of the late Eighteenth Dynasty. He is shown in the age-old guise of a scribe, with a papyrus unrolled over his knees, signifying his literacy and hence his political authority. His corpulence symbolizes his wealth and status.

Sandstone bust of King Amenhotep IV/Akhenaten (Eighteenth Dynasty) from the Aten temple at Thebes. Dating to the early part of his reign, it lacks the extreme exaggeration of later representations.

Painted limestone bust of Queen Nefertiti (Eighteenth Dynasty). A sculptor's model, the piece was found abandoned in the workshop of the sculptor Thutmose at the royal capital of Akhetaten. It has become an icon of ancient beauty.

Inlaid lid of a wooden and ivory casket from the tomb of King Tutankhamun (Eighteenth Dynasty). The boy king is shown relaxing in a garden with his young wife Ankhesenamun.

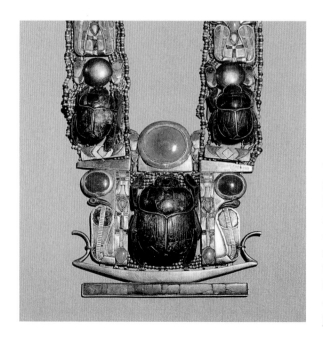

Pectoral from the tomb of Tutankhamun. The scarab beetles, carved from lapis lazuli, are symbolic of rebirth; together with the other elements of the composition, they spell out the king's throne name. The bold, heavy style is typical of Eighteenth Dynasty jewelry.

Gold throne of Tutankhamun. Made for the pharaoh early in his reign, before the abandonment of the Aten cult, it shows the boy king and his young wife in an intimate pose under the rays of the sun disc. Details are inlaid in silver, carnelian, and lapis lazuli.

Gold funerary mask of King Tutankhamun (Eighteenth Dynasty). The treasure of
Tutankhamun has captured the world's imagination ever since its discovery in 1922;
the gold mask, in particular, has come to represent the opulence and mystery of
ancient Egypt.

rights in the Lebanese and Syrian ports, as far north as Ugarit (modern Ras Shamra). With the signing of the treaty, the Near East regained a peace not seen since the heady days of the Egypt-Mittani alliance during the reign of Amenhotep III.

From implacable enemies to the best of friends, Hattusili and Ramesses celebrated the transformation in their relationship with an exchange of congratulatory correspondence. Their wives, too, joined in the love fest, Ramesses's chief consort, Nefertari, sending expensive jewelry and clothes to her "sister" in Hattusa. The only sour note was the continued presence of Urhi-Teshup in Egypt, but Hattusili could not afford to let this spoil the otherwise friendly relations. Indeed, things were going so well between the two rulers that negotiations were opened regarding the possibility of a diplomatic marriage. For Hattusili and his equally forceful wife Pudukhepa, the marriage of their daughter to the great king of Egypt would serve to strengthen the links between the two royal houses and bolster their own position. Ramesses, by contrast, secure on his throne, was principally interested in the enormous dowry that would accompany the Hittite princess. With a beloved Egyptian wife of his own, he showed little personal interest in the bride-to-be. For him it was a transaction, not a marriage.

Whatever misgivings she may have had, the Hittite princess had no choice in the matter, and, in the late autumn of 1246, she set out from the fortified citadel of the Hittite kings. Accompanying her were a great retinue of officials and a vast baggage train of gold, silver, bronze, slaves, horses, cattle, and goats. The procession wound its way slowly through the passes of the Taurus Mountains down into the coastal lowlands of southern Anatolia, then over the Amanus range to the plain of Aleppo, and thence southward, following the valley of the river Orontes, past Kadesh, to the border of Egyptian-held territory. At the frontier, Queen Pudukhepa bade farewell to her daughter for the last time. A messenger was dispatched to Per-Ramesses to tell the waiting pharaoh, "They have traversed sheer mountains and treacherous passes to reach Your Majesty's border."[3] Ramesses immediately dispatched members of his army and officials to meet the cavalcade and escort it through Canaan. The last stop before Egypt itself was a specially built royal palace astride the Sinai coastal road, in which the princess and her attendants could rest and recuperate after their long journey. The brightly colored paintings of flowers and garlands, ornamented with gold leaf, offered a taste of things to come. In February 1245, three months after leaving Hattusa, the procession entered the dazzling city of Per-Ramesses amid scenes of jubilation. After taking delivery of the dowry, Ramesses conferred on his new bride a suitably grandiloquent Egyptian name—Maathorneferura, "she sees [in] Horus [that is, the king] the beauty of Ra"—and then promptly packed her off to one of his harem palaces. Job done.

A few years later, the princess's brother, Crown Prince Hishmi-Sharruma, paid a formal visit to Egypt, spending the winter months in the relatively balmy climate of the eastern delta, a welcome relief from the windswept wastes of his homeland. For a man accustomed to the austere buildings of Hattusa, the gaudy decoration of Per-Ramesses must have made a lasting impression. Indeed, when he eventually became king, Hishmi-Sharruma adorned the sanctuaries of his realm with monumental religious art on a scale far greater than any of his predecessors. Even a Hittite, it seems, could fall under Egypt's unique spell. The crown prince's visit may have been intended to pave the way for an even higher-level encounter, a full-scale summit between Hattusili and Ramesses. A flurry of correspondence between the two capitals certainly discussed the practicalities of such a meeting, and the pharaoh expressed the hope that he and his Hittite counterpart would "see each other face-to-face." The bond of friendship between the two lands was stronger than ever, and would last until the very end of the Hittite Kingdom.

NEW FOES FOR OLD

Throughout his long sixty-seven-year reign (1279–1213), Ramesses II gave a high priority to securing Egypt's imperial possessions in the Near East and neutralizing the Hittite threat. At the same time, his security apparatus was alert to another growing danger, not from the north but from the west. The seminomadic tribes of the Libyan desert and their settled kinsmen along the coast had been a persistant irritant since the earliest days of the First Dynasty. A punitive raid or two had always been sufficient to keep them in check and prevent large-scale infiltration of the western delta. But things had changed. Almost nothing is known about the history and archaeology of Libya before the arrival of the Phoenicians in the eighth century B.C., but from references in Egyptian sources it is clear that an advanced civilization had developed by Ramesside times, at least along the North African coast. Imported artifacts point to close trade links across the Mediterranean with the Mycenaeans, who some two centuries earlier had displaced the Minoans as the main Aegean power. The ships that docked at Libyan coastal harbors brought with them great wealth, boosting the local economy and providing the chiefs with unprecedented resources. From long service as mercenaries in the Egyptian army, the Libyans had also learned a thing or two about modern warfare, acquiring the chariot and gaining considerable skill with the bow and arrow. By late in the reign of Ramesses II, the Libyan tribal rulers had gathered both the financial means and the technology to confront Egypt on equal terms. For the pharaoh, it was a deeply unwelcome prospect.

Ramesses's instinctive response was to fortify the entire Libyan frontier. His defensive system comprised a series of massive fortresses, built at roughly fifty-mile intervals the length of the western delta border. Each fort was within a day's chariot ride of its neighbor, and only a couple of days' ride from Per-Ramesses. Not only did the forts guard the coastal approaches to the delta, but they also enclosed all the major wells in the area, thus denying fresh water to any hostile force. One of the larger forts was even provided with its own temple, to inspire the garrison to feats of courage. In a typically Ramesside gesture, the temple was dedicated to the cult of the deified king.

The pharaoh's western wall did its job for a time, and the Libyans failed to break through the line while Ramesses was on the throne. But in the aftermath of his death and the unexpected succession of his *thirteenth* son, Merenptah (the twelve older sons having predeceased their octogenarian father), the impatient tribal rulers saw their chance. In 1209, the fifth year of the new king's reign,

> one came to say to His Majesty . . . that the vile chief of the Libyan enemies, Mery, son of Dedy, has descended . . .[4]

And the vile enemy had done his homework. Utilizing a wide range of strategic alliances, he had contrived a simultaneous revolt in Nubia, to distract Egypt's southern garrisons, and had augmented his own Libyan army with a large detachment of mercenaries from the Aegean and beyond, "northerners who came from all lands." These Sea Peoples—pirates and raiders in search of plunder and conquest—brought with them an entirely new type of warfare, based upon heavy infantry deploying close combat weapons, small round shields, and body armor. Massed ranks of such well-armed opponents rendered ineffective the chariotry upon which Egypt and the other great powers of the Near East had depended for their military supremacy. Like the Libyans, some of the Sea Peoples had previously served in the Egyptian army—Aegean mercenaries had made up Ramesses II's bodyguard at the Battle of Kadesh—and so knew their enemy's strengths and weaknesses.

Mery's battle strategy was based on the simple expedient of divide and rule. If he could attack Egypt on several fronts simultaneously, causing confusion and disrupting lines of communication, he and his forces might hope to prevail. So, after sending a small raiding party along the coast to keep the border garrisons busy, he and the main assault force set off toward Egypt via the oases of the Western Desert: Siwa, Bahariya, and Farafra. The last oasis commanded a network of desert routes that joined the Nile Valley at different points, so by basing his army here, Mery kept the Egyptians guessing about his ultimate intentions. When he was ready, and sure that the Nubian attack was proceeding as planned, the Libyan chief marched on Egypt in a pincer movement, to prevent a unified counterattack. He led the main force from Farafra, back to Bahariya, and thence to the Fayum, entering the Nile Valley near the pyramids of Dahshur. From there, they headed due north, to the fringes of the western delta. A second detachment left the main army at Bahariya to cross the Nile in Middle Egypt and infiltrate the eastern delta, distracting the Egyptian garrisons at Per-Ramesses and Memphis.

Just a month after receiving the first news of the Libyan invasion, the pharaoh Merenptah arrived with his army near the town of Perirer to engage the foe. It was midsummer, 1208. Just as Ramesses had fought his toughest battle in the fifth year of his reign, so now his son and successor faced the same challenge. This time, however, the Egyptians were leaving nothing to chance. If the Libyans and Sea Peoples understood the Egyptians' tactics, the reverse was also true. Merenptah knew that his archers and chariots could not overcome the massed ranks of the enemy infantry in a head-on fight. Instead, he cleverly drew the opposing forces toward the Egyptian lines while archers positioned on either flank directed volley after volley of raking fire against the advancing soldiers. After six hours of carnage, the Libyan coalition was finished. Then came the Egyptian chariot charge, turning defeat into rout and pursuing the fleeing enemy until all were either dead or captured. The booty was considerable: thousands of metal vessels, livestock, and advanced weaponry. To press home his victory and send a powerful message to other would-be attackers, Merenptah ordered a grim piece of psychological warfare. The defeated Libyans who had survived the battle soon wished they had perished at Perirer, for they were herded together and impaled alive on stakes. By the end of the day, flyblown corpses, their entrails sticky and putrid in the summer heat, lined the main desert route south of Memphis—in full view of any retreating Libyans and of the local populace.

It was a grim warning, but even so barbarous a display could not keep Egypt safe for long. Merenptah knew the Libyans would attack again (as they surely did, just three years later). He knew, too, that their co-conspirators, the Sea Peoples, might arrive at any time, and from almost any direction. So he pursued his own grand strategy, reinforcing Ugarit, sending grain to the Hittites to bolster the northern defenses, and even integrating Hittite infantry into the Egyptian army. (The soldiers were supplied with their own distinctive weaponry from the bronze furnaces of Per-Ramesses.) The old enmities of Kadesh were but a distant memory. In the unsettling new world of the eastern Mediterranean, Egypt needed all the friends it could muster.

The commemorative inscription commissioned by Merenptah to celebrate his second victory over the Libyans, three years after Perirer, is famous today not for the details of the battle, nor for the other elements of his defensive strategy, but for a single, fleeting reference in the penultimate line. After defeating the western invaders, the Egyptian army marched straight across the delta and into Palestine, recapturing the key towns of Ashkelon, Gezer, and Yenoam. To complete the job and impose security over this key buffer zone, Merenptah's forces proceeded to massacre a previously unknown rebel tribe in the hill country of Canaan. The tribe called itself Israel. It is the only reference to Israel in any ancient Egyptian inscription, and it reflects the rise of well-armed bands that, despite being unable to defeat the Egyptians in a pitched battle, could nonetheless pose a serious threat to stability. Israel should have been a headline, not a footnote.

The whole of the Near East was in flux. The old certainties were crumbling, new peoples and polities were in the ascendant, new forms of warfare were tipping the balance of power. Despite its glorious military history and its dynasty of warrior pharaohs, Egypt faced a deeply uncertain future.

CHAPTER 17

TRIUMPH AND TRAGEDY

DISUNITED KINGDOM

IN AN ABSOLUTE MONARCHY, A LONG REIGN COULD PROVE A MIXED blessing. While too rapid a succession of kings could undermine the divine pretensions of the institution and weaken the administration, an extended period of office posed the equal dangers of decadence and atrophy. Ramesses II's extraordinary reign of sixty-seven years certainly had its positive and negative effects on the government of Egypt. On the plus side, the king's determination and charisma enabled him to restore Egypt's reputation as an imperial power, while the plethora of monuments erected during his reign testified to the country's renewed confidence and prosperity. On the down side, Ramesses's longevity combined with his extraordinary fecundity—he fathered at least fifty sons and as many daughters—sowed the seeds for major problems in the royal succession in the following decades.

Although Merenptah's status as the oldest surviving son could scarcely be doubted, and his reign (1213–1204) therefore passed in relative stabililty, no sooner had he died than any number of royal grandchildren came forward to claim the throne. Ramesses II had been determined to reestablish a dynastic model of monarchy after the haphazard succession of the post-Akhenaten era, and had therefore broken with centuries of tradition by granting his many sons influential positions in government. Little wonder that they came to regard themselves as powers in the land, and that their offspring saw the throne as a legitimate goal.

It was no surprise that a major dispute broke out in the senior ranks of the royal family at Merenptah's death in 1204, with two rival claimants attempting to seize control. On one side there was Merenptah's eldest son and appointed heir, Seti-Merenptah. Against him stood another of Ramesses II's many grandsons, Amenmesse. Despite the age-old principle of primogeniture, it was Amenmesse, not Seti-Merenptah, who initially gained the upper hand. He was clearly able to call upon friends in high places, and may even have had a significant section of the army behind him. Amenmesse managed to rule for four years (1204–1200), while Seti-Merenptah sweated it out in some far-flung royal palace, an internal exile in his own kingdom. But the usurper did not have it his own way for long. The balance of power eventually swung back to the legitimate claimant, and Seti-Merenptah was finally able to succeed to his birthright as King Seti II.

The purge began at once. A number of prominent officials who had held office under Amenmesse immediately lost their jobs. Included were two of the highest-ranking men in the kingdom, the high priest of Amun and the vizier. They had backed the wrong man, and now they paid the price. Proscriptions and dismissals swept through the corridors of power, temporarily crippling the administration as Seti removed anyone and everyone who had supported his rival. Nor did he look any more kindly on Amenmesse himself, despite the fact that the two men were first cousins. Every reference to the usurper was ruthlessly expunged. On statues and temple reliefs, the name of Amenmesse was excised and replaced with that of Seti. Since a lasting name ensured immortality, the opposite spelled annihilation. For an Egyptian there could be no worse fate.

Like his father, Merenptah, before him, Seti II was already an old man when he became king, and he was only too aware that he had but a short time to make his mark. The royal quarrymen, masons, and architects went into overdrive as the king sought to leave his legacy in the sacred landscape of Thebes. On the east bank, at Ipetsut, builders began erecting a three-chambered chapel for the sacred barque shrines of Amun, Mut, and Khonsu. It might have been small and insignificant compared to the great columned hall of Seti I and Ramesses II, but it was a monument of sorts, better than nothing. Over on the west bank, the workmen in the Valley of the Kings had never known such a fever of activity as they set to work excavating and decorating not one but three tombs simultaneously—one for Seti, one for his wife Tawosret, and one for his favored chancellor, Bay. With no expansion in the workforce, the pressure was immense, and the valley echoed nonstop with the chisels, shouts, and expletives of the men. It is not surprising that the workmanship was distinctly shoddy.

Time was not on Seti's side. After just two years on his hard-won throne, he went the way of his father and grandfather before him, to join the royal ancestors in the glorious afterlife. His intended heir, a second Seti-Merenptah, was either already dead or unable to assert his rights to the succession. Instead, with the backing of Chancellor Bay (a fickle friend, if ever there was one), the kingship was handed to a sickly teenager with a withered left leg—not exactly the most prepossessing candidate for pharaoh, but amenable to pressure and undeniably royal. For Egypt's new monarch, Siptah, was none other than the surviving son of the usurper Amenmesse.

During Seti II's brief reign, Bay had acted the loyal lieutenant with consummate skill, winning promotion from royal scribe to chancellor, and the rare honor of a tomb in the royal necropolis. It was quite an achievement for any commoner, let alone an outsider of Syrian extraction. Yet, before Seti's mummy had even been laid to rest, Bay switched allegiance to support the polio-stricken son and heir of Seti's arch-nemesis. It was the cruelest betrayal. The kingmaker boasted in public that he "established the king on his father's seat."[1] In reality, Bay's only concern was feathering his own nest. The new king was still underage, so a regency council had to be established; for purposes of legitimacy, it was headed by Seti II's widow Tawosret, but, not very far behind the scenes, Bay pulled the strings.

In the fifth year of the regency, 1193, Tawosret took her revenge. Adopting full kingly titles (as Hatshepsut had done 280 years earlier), she mobilized her band of supporters at court and made her move against Bay. His fall from grace was swift and absolute. He was executed for treason and his name was officially proscribed, so denying him eternal life. Official documents referred to him instead as "the great enemy"[2] or, sarcastically, as "the parvenu from Syria."[3] A year later, his protégé, Siptah, was conveniently dead, too. With her enemies deprived of their last rallying point, Tawosret launched a full-scale persecution of the puppet king's memory. Siptah's names were erased from his royal tomb, and from hers, to be replaced by those of her late husband, Seti II. The triumph of Merenptah's heirs was complete.

But it was a Pyrrhic victory. Egypt had been rocked by more than a decade of internecine fighting among Ramesses II's descendants. The country had been unsettled and undermined by coup and countercoup, purge and counterpurge. The government was paralyzed and power-less. There was no male heir to continue the line. Instead, the throne was occupied by a vengeful widow, a woman, an affront to the hallowed ideology of Egyptian monarchy. Not twenty years after Merenptah's great victory at Perirer, the country had plumbed the depths. And the blame could be laid squarely at the feet of the ruling dynasty. What Egypt needed was a new broom to sweep away the cobwebs of Rames-side rule and reinvigorate the country's sense of purpose and destiny.

Egypt had experienced such moments before. The crisis following the death of Tutankhamun, while no longer within living memory, of-fered a recent parallel to the situation the country now confronted. Then, the solution had been to turn to the army. If then, why not now? For the second time in a century, the power brokers in Thebes and Memphis looked to the ranks of the military for a strongman to estab-lish a new dynasty and put Egypt back on an even keel. The candidate they chose fit the bill perfectly. An army commander, responsible for garrison troops, he had exactly the training and background for a suc-cessful soldier pharaoh. He already had a son (also in the army), and hence offered dynastic continuity. Even his name, Sethnakht ("Seth is victorious"), seemed tailor-made.

He did not disappoint. Marshaling his forces in 1190, Sethnakht set out to restore order and crush all opposition. Within a matter of months, the military coup was complete: "There was no enemy of His Majesty [left] in any land."[4] To set the seal on his triumph, he launched a barrage of propaganda to match his martial prowess. On a victory monument erected at Abu, Egypt's traditional southern border, Seth-nakht conjured up a bleak picture of life before his arrival on the scene: "This land was in desolation; Egypt had strayed from its trust in god."[5] The account went further, alleging a conspiracy by unnamed Egyptian authorities to take over the country with Asiatic help. This veiled ref-erence to Bay played to the Egyptians' oldest and strongest prejudice, their hatred and suspicion of foreigners. Sethnakht was thus able to present himself not as a military thug but as a national savior, whom the supreme deity had chosen "above millions, ignoring hundreds of thou-sands ahead of him."[6] Like Horemheb before him, Sethnakht had his immediate precedessors airbrushed from history; the party line presented him as the legitimate successor of Seti II. It was a sleight of hand, a careful distortion of the truth worthy of a great pharaoh.

Although he was already well past middle age, Sethnakht did not need to worry about his legacy. His son and heir, another Ramesses no less, would see to that. When Ramesses III succeeded as king in 1187, he consciously modeled himself on his great namesake, adopting all the names and royal titles of the victor of Kadesh. He even gave his sons the same names and positions at court as Ramesses II's sons. And he ordered work to begin on a great mortuary temple in western Thebes, in the mold of the Ramesseum. For officials and ordinary Egyptians alike, it must have seemed like a new dawn, a return to the glorious days of Ozymandias.

History was indeed about to repeat itself, but in a way that Ramesses III neither desired nor expected.

FIGHT FOR SURVIVAL

IN THE EARLY YEARS OF RAMESSES III'S REIGN, WORRYING NEWS BEGAN to reach Egypt from the pharaoh's emissaries in the Near East. All along the eastern seaboard of the Mediterranean, cities were being sacked and torched, harbors burned and looted, entire nations laid low. While coastal communities had been harried by pirates for decades, this new onslaught was of an entirely different order of magnitude. Most frightening of all, it had come from out of the blue, the sighting of enemy ships on the western horizon being the first warning of an impending attack. By the time the inhabitants of the Mediterranean ports could muster their defenses, their enemies were upon them. As Egypt watched from afar, great cities and civilizations were reduced to rubble, and the cultural achievements of centuries went up in smoke.

The first to fall was the great maritime city of Ugarit. Its altruism was its undoing. The king of Ugarit had dispatched sizeable military forces to southern Anatolia in response to pleas for urgent assistance from neighboring lands already under attack. Ugarit's soldiers were fighting alongside the Hittites, while its navy was patrolling the coast of Lycia. By being an exemplary ally, Ugarit had unwittingly put itself in the line of fire. Overstretched and underdefended, its remaining forces were hopelessly incapable of defending Ugarit at home when the attack came. In an eleventh-hour attempt to save his entire realm from destruction, the king of Ugarit wrote a desperate letter to his counterpart in Alashiya (Cyprus). Its tone of panic is palpable: "the enemy ships are already here, they have set fire to my towns and have done very great damage in the countryside."[7] It was too late. The clay tablet bearing the king's letter was never sent. It was found much later, still in the kiln where it had been fired, amid the rubble of the devastated city, a vivid firsthand account penned on the eve of destruction. Ugarit was laid waste, never to be reoccupied. One of the great natural harbors of the Mediterranean was reduced to smoldering ruins.

Next to feel the heat (quite literally) was Egypt's close ally, the Hittite Kingdom proper. In a desperate flurry of diplomatic correspondence, the last Hittite ruler spoke of fighting a seaborne enemy—not just on the open seas but on the beaches, on the landing grounds, and in the hills. Fearless and indefatigable, the attackers moved ashore and pushed northward, heading for the Hittite capital at Hattusa. Even with soldiers from Ugarit fighting alongside them, the Hittites could not stop the invaders. In a last-ditch effort to halt the advance, the Hittite king invaded his own neighbor, the coastal territory of Tarhuntassa, seeking to engage the enemy before it could reach the Hittite homeland—but to no avail. First Tarhuntassa and then the Hittite Kingdom were defeated and despoiled. Hattusa itself was plundered and burned; the fortified royal citadel proved no match for the invaders.

Elsewhere in Asia Minor, the glittering cities of Miletus and Troy suffered a similar fate. As the enemy swarmed like a killer horde across the eastern Mediterranean, Mersin and Tarsus were ravaged, and devastation was visited upon northern Cyprus. Next, the hostile forces pressed inland to the Orontes Valley, sacking all the important towns along this strategic thoroughfare. Alalakh, Hamath, Qatna, and even Kadesh—all were obliterated. Farther south, the trading centers of Palestine soon succumbed, places such as Akko, Lachish, Ashdod, and Ashkelon—towns that stood astride the great coast road that led southward and westward . . . to Egypt.

Throughout the Near East, palls of smoke hung in the air where once there had been hubs of commerce and culture. Rich palaces and famous cities lay in ruins. Only Assyria, safe on the far bank of the mighty Euphrates, survived unscathed. By 1179, the eighth year of Ramesses III's reign, the invaders had the last remaining maritime power of the eastern Mediterranean in their sights:

> Countries were simultaneously taken out and devastated. No land could stand before their arms, from the Hittite kingdom, Qode [that is, Cilicia], Carchemish, Arzawa, and Cyprus—they were laid waste, one by one. . . . And on [the enemy] came toward Egypt.[8]

By now, the pharaoh's advisers were well acquainted with the enemy. "The foreign countries plotted together in their islands. . . . Their league comprised Peleset, Tjeker, Shekelesh, Denyen, and Weshesh."[9] Though the names might be strange, the phenomenon was all too familiar. The dreaded Sea Peoples had returned. Thirty years earlier, a different coalition of Aegean and Anatolian peoples had conspired with the Libyans in an attempted invasion of Egypt in the reign of Merenptah. Now new bands had joined together in common cause, sweeping aside all before them. Driven from their homelands (unknown, but possibly the western Mediterranean or Anatolia) by drought, famine, and the desire for a better life, and possessed of a fierce and warlike nature, the Sea Peoples had proved an unstoppable force as they moved steadily southward and eastward, along the Aegean and Mediterranean coasts of Asia Minor, and down the coast of the Near East toward the Sinai and the Nile delta. Alongside battalions of well-armed (and armored) soldiers came women and children in ox-drawn carts, carrying their meager possessions with them. This was a mass migration by desperate and determined people. So far, no city or state had been able to resist. Egypt knew it faced a battle for survival.

At this time of national peril, Ramesses III showed himself the true heir of his great predecessor. As soon as he learned of the impending land invasion that was heading toward Egypt from southern Palestine, he sent orders to the frontier fortresses of the eastern delta to stand firm until reinforcements arrived. Troops were mobilized throughout the country. Their orders were to converge on the eastern border and repel the invaders. But the leaders of the Sea Peoples knew very well that Egypt would be a determined opponent, and had decided to put maximum pressure on the pharaoh's forces by attacking on two fronts.

As the land force moved on the delta from the northeast, a substantial amphibious force of troopships made for the mouth of the main Nile branch, intending to land a second army. This army's orders, no doubt, were to follow the river upstream toward the commercial and military headquarters at Per-Ramesses. Possession of the eastern delta capital would effectively mean control of the whole of northern Egypt—just as it had for the Hyksos 450 years earlier. As Ramesses and his generals pondered the situation, they realized that Egypt faced not merely a hostile invasion, but the threat of permanent occupation.

The response was an immediate nationwide conscription. At its hour of greatest need, the country needed all able-bodied men to stand together. While the professional army dug in at the northeastern border, the conscripts were dispatched to the coast, to blockade the Nile mouth against the enemy fleet. Ramesses's own account of the preparations captures very well the tension, drama, and determination of the moment:

> I had the river mouth prepared like a strong wall, with warships, troop carriers, and merchant vessels. They were all crewed from bow to stern with brave soldiers, fully armed. The infantry comprised every Egyptian recruit. They were like lions roaring on the mountaintops.[10]

In the eastern delta fortresses, the Egyptian army could only watch and wait. Their opponents were slow-moving, covering no more than ten miles a day, but what the Sea Peoples lacked in speed they more than made up for in weaponry and sheer numbers. Their proficiency in close combat fighting had already proved itself, time and again, against the chariot forces of the Near Eastern states. In little more than a generation, advances in military technology had changed the whole nature of warfare, and the great powers had failed to adapt. Egypt knew it had to do better, or go the same way. Merenptah's victory at the Battle of Perirer had shown that it was possible to defeat the Sea Peoples' tactics, if the Egyptians only maintained rigid discipline and used their forces to maximum effect.

The troops did not have to wait long to put the theory into practice. As the dust cloud on the horizon grew in intensity, the enemy came into view—a sheer wall of people, hundreds deep, moving inexorably toward the Egyptian border. The moment of truth had arrived.

The documentary sources are strangely silent on the details of the land battle, recording only the bald fact that the invasion was defeated. Perhaps the Egyptian losses were simply too heavy to acknowledge publicly; certainly, the effort involved in repelling the invaders was stupendous. By contrast, the naval battle off the Mediterranean coast seems to have gone Egypt's way from the start, and provided a much more fitting subject for the official war record. The Sea Peoples' armada, comprising troop carriers rather than warships, had no long-range weapons to pitch against the Egyptian archers on the shore. The pharaoh's generals knew this was their trump card, and realized that if they could only force the enemy inshore, within range, but prevent any landings, victory might be possible. But if just a single troopship managed to break through and disembark its warriors on Egyptian soil, then the tide might turn very quickly.

The great flotilla of strange craft got within sight of the shore, great sailing vessels without oars, their prows and sterns carved to resemble

The Sea Peoples WERNER FORMAN ARCHIVE

the heads of monstrous birds. On board, the enemy warriors looked equally fearsome with their reed helmets and round shields. The Egyptians saw, among the massed ranks of Peleset, Tjeker, Denyen, and Weshesh, a more recognizable opponent—the ubiquitous and treacherous Sherden, with their distinctive horned helmets. Although they had been protectors of Ramesses II at Kadesh, the Sherden were now fighting *against* the forces of another Ramesses.

As planned, the Egyptian navy maneuvered to force the enemy inshore, right into the Nile mouth. If the invaders thought things were going their way, they were sorely mistaken. No sooner were they within a few hundred yards of the shore than the Egyptian archers opened fire, sending a hail of arrows raining down on the attackers' heads. With the troops on board falling like flies, the commanders of the Sea Peoples' ships may have tried to make for open water again, but they found themselves hemmed in by the Egyptian navy. A great sea battle ensued, in which the enemy craft were systematically capsized, and hundreds of Sea Peoples drowned. By the end of the day, the Egyptians had triumphed; their opponents were either dead or captured. Alone among the great powers of the Near East, Egypt had repelled the Sea Peoples and preserved its independence.

Ramesses III had spared his country "the worst disaster in ancient history,"[11] but his victory on the landing grounds of the delta would prove to be the swan song of the New Kingdom. The world was suddenly full of uncertainty; and the accustomed ways of doing things, ways that had served the Egyptians well for centuries, would be found wanting.

OUT OF JOINT

AFTER THE BRUISING ENCOUNTER WITH THE SEA PEOPLES, THE IMMEDIATE reaction of the Egyptian government was to bury its head in the sand and carry on as if nothing had changed. Tradition dictated that a great military victory demanded a monumental commemoration, so that is exactly what the king commissioned. Just as Ramesses II had used the Ramesseum to celebrate his (questionable) victory at Kadesh, so Ramesses III turned his own mortuary temple—closely modeled on his predecessor's—into a war memorial. In the "Mansion of Millions of

Years of King Ramesses, United with Eternity in the Estate of Amun" (known today as Medinet Habu), the entire northern wall of the temple was carved with a vast tableau depicting the land and sea battles against the Sea Peoples. So Egypt's last great royal monument commemorated the country's last great military victory.

Buoyed up by the completion of so grand an edifice, in 1172, Ramesses III ordered the nationwide temple inspection that he had originally planned a decade earlier. After ten years of defending Egypt's borders—not only against the Sea Peoples, but against two attempted Libyan invasions as well—he and his administration finally felt confident enough about national security to turn their attention to the other abiding duty of kingship, honoring the gods. Headed by the chief archivist of the royal treasury (a man with an eye for detail and an interest in historic monuments), the commission started its tour of inspection at Abu, in Egypt's southernmost province, and worked its way northward, slowly but methodically. Every temple in the land was examined with the full panoply of ancient Egyptian bureaucracy. Granaries were audited to assess the extent of temple wealth and the balance of the national grain reserves; buildings were checked for their state of repair; rituals were examined to ensure they were being carried out correctly; and corrupt practices were systematically exposed and rooted out. By the end of the exercise, the king had at his disposal perhaps the most comprehensive survey of the country's religious infrastructure in its long history.

Based upon the commission's findings, Ramesses ordered an extensive program of reorganization, reconstruction, and refurbishment. The ancient temple of Seth at Nubt was restored and a new shrine built alongside it in the deity's honor. The barque shrine at Tod, crafted in the Eighteenth Dynasty, was restored to its former glory, and further beautifying works were carried out at nearby Luxor Temple. At Ipetsut, the country's greatest sacred complex, the king commissioned a new way station and a temple to the god Khonsu. All in all, it was a religious revival, a renaissance of royal patronage to equal the achievements of Ramesses II's reign. Explicitly or implicitly, Ramesses III was trying to turn back the clock and convince Egypt that the glory days of the New Kingdom were still at hand.

As well as restoring the temples' physical fabric, the king also enlarged their endowments of land and personnel. Determined to be recognized and remembered as a great benefactor, he ordered three expeditions to distant lands in a single year (1167), expressly to bring back exotic gifts for the temple treasuries. The first expedition was to the turquoise mines of the Sinai. The second had as its goal the copper mines of Edom. These lay at a place called Timna, about twenty miles north of Eilat, in a desert hollow surrounded by hills. The copper ores here had been exploited by Egypt since the reign of Ramesses II, but pharaonic power had waned in the intervening decades, and the Edomites had reasserted their control. So, before he could send in his miners, Ramesses III had to launch a military campaign to pacify Edom. Mission accomplished: copper extraction was restarted, and at the conclusion of the expedition, the newly smelted ingots were presented to the king at the palace balcony in Per-Ramesses. The third foreign expedition was perhaps the most ambitious of all—a two-month journey to Punt and back, to obtain myrrh and incense for use in temple rituals. It was the first major trading mission to Punt since the reign of Hatshepsut three centuries before, and it was spectacularly successful. The Egyptians returned with their precious commodities, and also with the ingredients for domestic myrrh production: fifteen cuttings from myrrh trees and one hundred seeds.

In his first two decades on the throne, Ramesses III had repelled invasions, restored Egypt's temples, and reestablished national pride. The court now looked forward to the king's thirty-year jubilee, determined to stage a celebration worthy of so glorious a monarch. There would be no stinting, no corners cut. Only the most lavish ceremonies would do.

It was a fateful decision. Beneath the pomp and circumstance, the Egyptian state had been seriously weakened by its exertions. The military losses of 1179 were still keenly felt. Foreign trade with the Near East had never fully recovered from the Sea Peoples' orgy of destruction. The temples' coffers might be full of copper and myrrh, but their supplies of grain—the staple of the Egyptian economy—were gravely depleted. Against such a background, the jubilee preparations would prove a serious drain on resources.

The cracks started to appear in 1159, two years before the jubilee. Of all the state's employees, the most important—and usually the most favored—were the men who worked on the excavation and decoration of the royal tomb. Living with their families in the gated community of the Place of Truth, they had grown used to enjoying better than average working conditions, and better than average remuneration. So, when the payment of their monthly wages (which also included their food rations) was eight days late, then twenty days late, it was clear something was badly wrong. Their scribe and shop steward, Amennakht, went at once to the mortuary temple of Horemheb to remonstrate with local officials. Eventually, he persuaded them to hand over forty-six sacks of corn to distribute to the workers as interim rations. But that was only the start of it.

The following year, as the apparatus of government became increasingly preoccupied with the impending jubilee, the system of paying the necropolis workers broke down altogether, prompting the earliest recorded strikes in history. The crisis erupted just three months before the jubilee was due to begin. Having waited eighteen days beyond their payday and with still no sign of their wages, the workers decided to withdraw their labor. Perhaps then the state would sit up and take notice. Shouting "We're hungry,"[12] they marched en masse from their village and temporarily invaded the sacred enclosure surrounding Ramesses III's mortuary temple. They then set off for the mortuary temple of Thutmose III, just behind the Ramesseum, and staged a sit-in. They weren't going anyhere until their grievances were heard. The beleaguered government officials dispatched from the Ramesseum to reason with the strikers had to listen to their litany of protests, but without the authority to remedy the situation. Only at nightfall did the workers return to their village. Their protest had lasted the whole day. The only gesture by the state was a derisory delivery of pastries. If they have no bread, let them eat cake.

The next morning, with no resolution of the dispute and no wages in sight, the men stepped up their action, installing themselves at the southern gate of the Ramesseum, Thebes's principal storehouse of grain. This time they refused to return to their village at dusk, instead spending the night in uproarious demonstration. At dawn, a few plucky souls broke into the temple itself, hoping to persuade the authorities to give them their dues. The crisis was getting out of hand. Panicked by the angry workers in their midst, the temple administrators called the chief of police, Montumes, who ordered the men to leave immediately. They refused. Unable or unwilling to assert his authority, Montumes was forced to withdraw, tail between his legs, to consult his boss, the mayor of Thebes. When he returned some hours later, he found the workers deep in negotiations with the priests of the Ramesseum and the local government secretary of western Thebes. The men's demands were clear:

> "We have come here out of hunger and thirst. There is no more cloth-
> ing, no more oil, no more fish, no more vegetables. Send [word] to
> the pharaoh, our good lord, and send [word] to the vizier, our
> boss!"[13]

Mention of the vizier and the pharaoh clearly unsettled the Theban authorities. If the situation escalated into a national crisis, they knew their jobs—and necks—would be on the line. So, after several more hours of talking, they capitulated and gave the strikers their overdue rations from the previous month. It helped to diffuse the immediate tension, but the underlying problem had still not been addressed. It was now nearly halfway through the new month, with no sign of the next installment of wages.

On day four of the dispute, news reached the workers that the mayor of Thebes had crossed over to the west bank with more provisions. The chief of police pleaded with them to go with their wives and children to the nearby mortuary temple of Seti I, to await the mayor's arrival. But the strikers were not so easily fobbed off. They had heard such promises before, and had learned not to trust the weasel words of officials. Indeed, it took another four days of protests and marches—including one at night, the men's flaming torches lighting up the sky—to secure the long-overdue rations.

Still the state apparatus proved incapable of carrying out its basic duties. Two weeks after the first series of disputes, the necropolis workers went on strike again, this time taking their protest to the control point leading to the Valley of the Kings. The authorities were beginning to be seriously shaken by these public demonstrations of disobedience, and put pressure on the community leaders to escort the strikers back to their village. Faced with forcible removal, one of the workmen threatened to damage a royal tomb, regardless of the conse-quences. The mood was turning ugly.

The showdown between workers and state authorities culminated just two months before the start of the jubilee year. Striking for a fourth time, the men marched once more from their village, dismissing the shouted pleadings of their superiors with determined obstinacy: "We won't come back. Tell that to your bosses!"[14] This time, they made it clear that their grievances were not just about overdue rations but about the broader failings of the administration:

> "We have gone [on strike], not from hunger but [because] we have a serious accusation to make: bad things have been done in this place of Pharaoh."[15]

For authorities used to a subservient populace, this was dangerous talk indeed. Yet still the ostrich mentality prevailed at the heart of govern-ment. A few weeks later, the vizier himself came to Thebes—not to pla-cate the striking workers but to collect cult statues for the imminent jubilee celebrations. He paid only a fleeting visit to the west bank and incensed the workers with a small handout from his security chief—provoking yet more demonstrations.

When the jubilee arrived, the authorities' indifference was tem-porarily put aside in the interests of national unity. Decorum and basic self-interest demanded that the king's big year should pass off without major incident, so the workers were paid on time and in full. But no sooner had the jubilee passed than the system broke down once more, prompting further, regular strike action. The heart of government was rotten, and the relationship between the state and its workers never fully recovered. Despite the outward show, Egypt's economic vitality and political stability were in serious decline.

TREASON AND PLOT

In the private rooms above the gateway of his mortuary temple, delicate reliefs show Ramesses III in intimate poses with various un-named women in his household. The king relaxes in a comfortable armchair and plays board games with his youthful companions. They offer him fruit and whisper sweet nothings in the royal ear: "Here's to you, Ses!"[16] The royal harem was a venerable Egyptian institution, providing not just a supply of concubines for the king but also residential facilities and gainful employment for all his female relatives. The harem palace had its own landholdings, its own workshops, and its own administration. It was effectively a parallel court, and such a setup was not without its dangers.

As far back as the Old Kingdom, the harem had been a hotbed of plots. There was something about the claustrophobic atmosphere that fed the bitter jealousies and personal rivalries of the king's many wives. With little to occupy their minds besides weaving and idle pleasures, the more ambitious concubines nurtured resentments, angry at the lowly status of their offspring and wondering how they might improve their own and their children's fortunes. When the pharaoh was a strong and successful leader, such murmurings fell away, but when things were going badly in the country at large, the allure of sedition was more tempting.

In 1157, when the temporary euphoria of Ramesses III's jubilee had died away, the gathering storm clouds were clear for all to see. The king was in failing health and Egypt was in a downward spiral. Desperate times seemed to call for desperate remedies. In the seclusion of the harem palace, one of the king's secondary wives, the lady Tiy, decided to take matters into her own hands. She revealed her treacherous plan to the director of the harem and his scribe. Her intention was to remove the heir apparent, Prince Ramesses, and install her own son, Pentaweret, on the throne. Before long, the conspiracy had drawn in many more employees of the harem palace. Even members of the king's inner circle joined the plotters. With the head of the treasury and the royal chamberlain involved, Ramesses III and his heir were in grave danger.

The plan was both complex and devious. While the ringleaders pursued the main objective (the assassination of Ramesses III and the removal of his designated heir), the other harem women would actively spread sedition among their relatives beyond the palace gates, so as to "agitate the people and incite conflict, in order to foment rebellion against their lord."[17] One of the women had written to her brother, who was a commander of Nubian troops, to win his support. A mass mutiny among the ranks of the army, combined with a revolution in the countryside, would surely distract and weaken the authorities. Finally, to give their plot the best chance of success, the conspirators turned to darker means. They enlisted the help of professional magicians, made wax effigies of their opponents, and composed spells designed to paralyze the harem guards. After weeks of careful planning, everything was in place. The stage was set for regicide and revolution.

But the plotters had made a fatal error. With so many people involved, it was virtually certain that someone would blab. Before the plans could be carried through to their fateful conclusion, the authorities were alerted and the conspirators arrested. As the details of the plot became clear, so did the extreme level of the threat to national security. Fearing the repercussions of a full, open trial (with himself as the final court of appeal), the king opted instead for a special tribunal. He appointed a group of twelve trusted officials to investigate, pass judgment, and impose an appropriate sentence. Carefully chosen agents of the state—representing the court, the military, and the civil service—would be judge, jury, and executioner. Ramesses III's only involvement was to give the tribunal carte blanche in dealing with the plotters: "May all that they have done be upon their own heads."[18]

With such a remit, the outcome was never in doubt. In a series of three prosecutions, thirty-eight individuals were tried and found guilty. The ringleaders were allowed to take their own lives. Some were forced to commit suicide inside the courtroom, while others, including Prince Pentaweret, were granted the questionable privilege of doing so outside. All those convicted of treason were further condemned to a second death: their names were hacked out of their monuments and changed in the official court proceedings to deny them a good memory. Hence the commander of Nubian troops Khaemwaset ("arisen in Thebes") became Binemwaset ("evil in Thebes"), Meryra ("beloved of Ra") became Mesedsura ("Ra hates him"), and Paraherwenemef ("Ra is at his right hand") became Parakamenef ("Ra blinds him"). Minor conspirators escaped the death penalty but suffered dreadful mutilations, their noses and ears being cut off to identify them as convicted criminals forever after. As a warning to the population at large, even those who had not been directly involved in the plot but had merely kept silent were punished. Turning a deaf ear to sedition was tantamount to treason.

Finally, to wipe away all evidence of the conspiracy and the tribunal established to investigate it, a prosecution was brought against three of the judges and two officers of the court. On trumped-up charges, they were accused of improper liaison with the plotters. One judge was found innocent. The other two were condemned to mutilation but—conveniently for the state—committed suicide before the sentence could be carried out. With the tribunal report signed off, the authorities hoped that the whole sorry episode could be safely consigned to history.

Except, of course, that it couldn't. It had revealed serious divisions between the ruling dynasty and members of the government, between different factions of the royal family, between the blithe optimism of those in power and the deep malaise in the country at large. The signs could not have been more ominous for the future of Ramesside Egypt.

Whether from wounds inflicted by assailants or from natural causes, Ramesses III died in 1156, a matter of months after the plot was uncovered. His death marked not just the demise of Egypt's last great pharaoh, but the end of the country's confidence in its own destiny. The unwritten contract between rulers and ruled, an arrangement that had secured Egyptian civilization since the dawn of history, was unraveling. So too, before long, would the very fabric of the state.

CHAPTER 18

DOUBLE-EDGED SWORD

SWEAT AND TEARS

FOR THE AVERAGE ANCIENT EGYPTIAN, ONLY TWO THINGS IN LIFE WERE certain: death and taxes. From a baby's first breath, the twin specters of dying and destitution haunted every waking moment. Infant mortality was shockingly high, and of those who made it through the perils of childhood, few could look forward to a life span of much more than thirty-five years. It was not just the combination of poverty and a poor diet that reduced life expectancy. In the unsanitary conditions of Egyptian towns and villages, waterborne and infectious diseases were rife. Bilharzia, hepatitis, guinea worm, and amebic dysentery were inescapable features of everyday life. Those who were not carried off by such unpleasant conditions were often left disfigured or disabled. Visual impairment, caused by illness or injury, was particularly common: "The village was full of the bleary-eyed, the one-eyed, and the blind, with inflamed and festering eyelids, of all ages."[1]

As if the afflictions of disease and premature decease were not bad enough, economic circumstances and the structure of the Egyptian state conspired to keep most ordinary people in a state of permanent penury. Even in a good year, the average farm yield amounted to little more than a subsistence income. If a peasant could have kept the entire crop for his own family, he might just have made a tolerable living. However, since in theory the whole of Egypt belonged to the crown, there were taxes due to the authorities for the privilege of farming the pharaoh's land. Like other governments throughout history, ancient Egypt's rulers were particularly adept at collecting these dues, employing a network of local agents to prevent evasion. Moreover, in a premonetary economy, the taxes were levied in the form of a share of each farm's agricultural produce, and this had to be handed over, come feast or famine. Defaulters could expect to be thrown in prison—a deeply unwelcome prospect that most did their utmost to avoid. As a result, "peasant families always wavered between abject poverty and utter destitution."[2] As in Robin Hood's England, the only escape from overbearing taxation was to abandon the fields completely and go on the run, living as an outlaw on the margins of society. As the New Kingdom progressed, an increasing number of people took this desperate step.

The hard life of a peasant is documented in unusual detail in a papyrus from the late Twentieth Dynasty. The text tells the story of a man named Wermai who fled from his village in Upper Egypt to the great oasis of the Western Desert (modern Dakhla) to seek a better life. Instead, he found himself in even worse circumstances, subject to an uncaring and unscrupulous mayor who had the power to make his people's lives a misery. Not only did the local authorities extract taxation with all their customary ruthlessness, but they feathered their own nests by deliberately reducing the rations doled out to the already hard-pressed peasantry. As a result, the people went hungry while the local bureaucrats prospered.

Despised by the literate elite, Egypt's great mass of agricultural workers were put upon and exploited, yet their unremitting and ill-rewarded labor lay at the base of the country's prosperity. In a very real sense, the sweat of their brows built pharaonic civilization, not that the pharaohs or their advisers seemed either to notice or to care.

Perhaps the most burdensome and loathed of all forms of taxation was the corvée, a tax paid through labor, on demand, by every able-bodied male in the land (and not officially abolished in Egypt until a.d. 1889). The only workers exempt from the corvée were those employed by temples that had been granted immunity from the call-up by royal decree. From the earliest history of the Egyptian state, it was the corvée that provided the labor force required for massive government projects, from the quarrying of stone to the building of pyramids and temples. Conscription into the corvée was organized along military lines and, like other forms of taxation, was carried out by local officials, village and town elders acting on the orders of their regional and national superiors. The recruiting sergeants usually came calling at times of the year when the agricultural economy could manage without a large proportion of the workforce—during the inundation, when the fields were flooded, or in the growing season, when fewer workers were needed on the land.

The draft was indiscriminate and often unfair. Many who were ineligible for duty were nevertheless pressed into service despite their protestations. There was no right of appeal. Fathers found themselves assigned to labor gangs as substitutes for their indigent sons. As peasants were pulled from fields and villages throughout the country, they found themselves locked into a state-run system from which there was little or no chance of escape. Collective punishment was meted out to deserters, with their entire families being held hostage by the authorities against the deserters' eventual return. For deserters who returned or were tracked down, the punishment was a life sentence in a labor gang.

Life on corvée duty was hard and unremitting. Under ancient Egyptian law, serious criminals could be sentenced to hard labor, or even banished to the garrison of Kush to work in the appalling conditions of the Nubian gold mines. For ordinary law-abiding subjects, the prospect of forced labor was scarcely less dreadful. Workers were given few freedoms and no luxuries, while rations were at the subsistence level. Only at the end of their period of service could the men return home, assuming they had survived disease and injury. Unfortunately the standards of health and safety on government projects were abysmally poor, and the casualty rate correspondingly high.

The dangers of the corvée were brought into particularly sharp focus in 1153, early in the reign of Ramesses IV, during an expedition to the quarries of the Wadi Hammamat. Just five months after his accession to the throne, Ramesses decided to revive quarrying activity after a forty-year lull. To prepare the ground, he first sent a 408-strong mission to reconnoiter the area and make arrangements at the quarry site for the resumption of large-scale work. After further visits by various bureaucrats over the following months, everything was finally declared ready. So, in the third year of Ramesses IV's reign, there set out from Thebes a great expedition, the likes of which Egypt had not witnessed for more than seven hundred years. In an indication of its national importance, the mission was led by the most powerful figure in Thebes, the high priest of Amun, Ramessesnakht. Assisting him were officials both civilian and military. The vizier, an overseer of the treasury, the chief tax officer, the mayor of Thebes, and two royal butlers were joined by a lieutenant general of the army, for this was a combined operation. Under their joint control marched a vast conscript army, comprising two thousand civilian workers, eight hundred foreign mercenaries, and five thousand ordinary soldiers. The use of the army for civil projects during the winter months was a pragmatic policy. It kept the soldiers busy and under the watchful eye of the king's advisers at a time when campaigning was undesirable (because of the rainy season in the Near East) and when they might otherwise have been idle. The Ramesside pharaohs appreciated the coercive power of a large standing army but were also wise enough to recognize the political dangers of a military force with too much time on its hands.

Quarrying stone was essentially a hard, manual task, so Ramesses IV's expedition included only a small contingent of skilled workers (just four sculptors and two draftsmen) to supervise the work. By contrast, there were fifty policemen and a deputy chief of police to keep the workers in line and prevent desertion. Once at the quarry face, the men toiled and sweated at their backbreaking work, for long days on end. Their meager rations, brought by oxcart from the Nile Valley, consisted largely of the basics—bread and beer, enlivened by the occasional sweet cake or portion of meat. Natural cisterns hollowed out of the rock were designed to trap rainwater for drinking, but in the parched landscape of the Eastern Desert rain was always in short supply, even in winter. Back in the days of Ramesses II, gold mining expeditions would routinely lose half of their workforce and half their transport donkeys from thirst. Seti I had taken measures to reduce this startling loss of life by ordering wells to be dug in the Eastern Desert, but the incidence of death on corvée missions remained stubbornly high. Hence, the great commemorative inscription carved to record Ramesses IV's Wadi Hammamat expedition ends with a blunt statistic. After listing the nine thousand or so members who made it back alive, it adds, almost as an afterthought, "and those who are dead and omitted from this list: nine hundred men." The statistic is chilling. An average workman on state corvée labor had a one in ten chance of dying. Such a loss was considered neither disastrous nor unusual.

In ancient Egypt, life was cheap.

DOWNWARD SPIRAL

UNWELCOME AS IT MAY HAVE BEEN, FORCED LABOR WAS, IN THEORY, part of the contract between the Egyptian people and their rulers. In return for his subjects' daily toil, the king guaranteed the eternal order of the cosmos, appeasing the gods and ensuring Egypt's continued prosperity. Even in the minds of the hard-pressed and downtrodden peasantry, it could just about be defended as a worthwhile exchange. Except that, after the death of Ramesses III, the country's rulers signally failed to keep their side of the bargain. Following the turmoil surrounding his father's demise, Ramesses IV looked forward to better times: "[Since] Egypt has come into his lifetime, a joyful period has come about for Egypt."[3] As a further sign of his hopes for renewed glory, he modeled his royal titles closely on those of his illustrious forebear Ramesses II, and even planned to outdo the mighty Ozymandias in longevity. On a stela dedicated at Abdju in the fourth year of his reign, Ramesses IV instructed the gods: "Double for me the extended life span and the great reign of King Usermaatra-setepenra [Ramesses II], the great god."[4]

Next to a long life span, every pharaoh's wish was for his heirs to succeed him in an unbroken line. In Ramesses IV's case this desire was made even more acute by bitter experience. Mindful of the harem plot that had so nearly deprived him of the kingship, he hectored Egypt's chief deities, asking—nay, telling—them, "Confer my great office on my heirs; behold, the disaffected are the abomination of your majesties!"[5] If he, Ramesses, carried out his duty to beautify the gods' temples and increase their offerings, then they should deliver the quid pro quo and grant his requests.

But the gods were no longer listening.

To mark his accession, Ramesses IV had authorized a handout of silver to the workmen of the royal tomb, to win their goodwill and ensure conscientious work on his sepulchre. He had also doubled the workforce from 60 to 120 for good measure. Yet his tomb was, in the end, rather small and poorly finished. Despite his wish for glory and his penchant for ambitious projects, none of the king's temple buildings was ever completed. Egypt's economy was faltering, its government ossifying. There was neither the means nor the will, it seemed, to sustain the level of patronage that had characterized the golden age of the New Kingdom. And so much for a long reign: Ramesses IV had asked the gods for 134 years on the throne; fate allotted him just six (1156–1150).

Where Ramesses IV had struggled to keep up the appearance of royal authority, his successors gave up all pretense. While they all took the name Ramesses (so great was its prestige), none of them showed the same determination, resolve, or leadership as their two famous name-sakes. Egypt was fortunate not to face another mass invasion on the scale of the Sea Peoples' attack under Ramesses III, but its borders were far from secure against hostile incursions. Even though there was no longer a superpower in the Near East against which Egypt needed to defend its interests, as it had when facing the Hittites under Ramesses II, there were threats, nonetheless, to Egypt's imperial pos-sessions. Yet none of Ramesses IV's successors was able or willing to give proper attention to the country's foreign or security interests, so preoccupied was the administration with the deteriorating situation at home.

The brief five-year reign of Ramesses V (1150–1145) revealed the depths to which the country had sunk. The pharaoh's accession and coronation ceremonies had barely been completed before the govern-ment uncovered a serious corruption scandal. It transpired that, for nearly a decade, a ship's captain named Khnumnakht had been busy ap-propriating for his own profit substantial quantities of grain destined for the temple of Khnum at Abu. After collecting the grain from one of the temple's estates in the delta, it was Khnumnakht's job to take it hun-dreds of miles upstream to the temple granaries on Egypt's southern border. In fact, during the course of the long voyage, aided and abetted by various farmers, scribes, and inspectors, and encouraged by a cor-rupt priest, he siphoned off a significant proportion of each delivery. By the time he was found out, more than five thousand sacks of barley had been stolen.

The investigation into Khnumnakht's crimes soon revealed the true extent of corruption among the Abu priesthood. One of the priests had not only stolen equipment from the temple treasury, but he had also rustled calves of the sacred Merwer (also known as Mnevis) bull, be-lieved to be an embodiment of the sun god Ra. This was not merely theft; it was sacrilege. Hundreds of miles from the royal residence at

Per-Ramesses, and far from the gaze of government officials, state employees in distant parts of the realm had decided to put their hands into the till, confident that their misdemeanors would go undetected. It was the ultimate indictment of the pharaonic administration, by now so paralyzed that not even its own officials afforded it any respect. Central control over the entire Nile Valley, assisted by reliable and swift communication, had been the sine qua non of the Egyptian state. With local communities now effectively doing their own thing, the prospects for national cohesion looked increasingly grim.

Shaken by such a serious breakdown in economic and political control, Ramesses V determined to restore some measure of order. As earlier pharaohs had recognized, a proper census of national wealth was a prerequisite for effective government, so Ramesses commissioned a survey of landholdings in a ninety-five-mile stretch of Middle Egypt, paying particular attention to grain production and tax collection. The result was a papyrus register some thirty-three feet long, an impressive document indeed. But its royal author, like his administration, was in failing health, and he succumbed to smallpox before the survey's findings could be implemented. In a further sign of government weakness, his pockmarked mummy lay unburied for a year while a modest tomb was hurriedly prepared to receive it. Ramesses V's intended sepulchre had been summarily usurped by his successor. In uncertain times, it was every man for himself.

By now, the situation at Thebes was deteriorating fast. Soaring grain prices reflected the weakness of the economy and the failure of the government to guarantee wages. Contemporary accounts hint at hunger, even starvation, as the peasantry bore the full brunt of the hard times. Hyenas were spotted in the Theban hills, scenting death in the villages below. With tax revenues falling and the court unable to pay for new royal monuments, Ramesses VI (1145–1137) took drastic steps to economize. On the west bank, he halved the workforce of tomb builders to sixty men; on the east bank, at Ipetsut, he simply recarved the additions built by Ramesses IV, to claim them as his own.

The malaise was not just a matter of economic weakness. There was also a security dimension. Ever since the reign of Ramesses III, Egypt had faced repeated incursions by Libyan tribespeople seeking to leave their parched lands and settle in the fertile Nile Valley: "They spend all day marauding the land, fighting daily to fill their bellies; they came to the land of Egypt to seek sustenance for their mouths."[6] In the space of six years, Egypt's last great pharaoh had repelled two attempted Libyan invasions, but had failed to prevent attacks against the Theban region at the end of his reign. Now, with the organs of the state atrophying and the government machine unable to defend Egypt's borders, the Libyan incursions increased in frequency. Under Ramesses V, work on the royal tomb halted altogether for a time as the workers stayed at home for fear of "the enemy"—a foe that had already ransacked and burned at least one Theban village.

In his choice of royal titles and his scenes of military triumph on temple walls, Ramesses VI might have pretended to be Egypt's defender, but the old magic had worn off. The king's protestations were hollow boasts, and they fooled nobody. As garrisons were hastily recalled to maintain national security, Egypt ceased copper mining at Timna, abandoned the "turquoise terraces" of the Sinai, and lost control of its last hard-won possessions in the Near East. So ended the Egyptian Empire, not with a bang but with a whimper. The land of the pharaohs had been reduced from the greatest power in the eastern Mediterranean to a weak and beleaguered nation in just four generations.

Cruel fate dealt pharaonic prestige the final blow. In happier times, a rapid succession of monarchs could have been managed. Now, a series of short reigns seemed to underline the ineffectiveness of Egypt's rulers. Divine kingship looked like an increasingly academic concept. The all too obvious mortality of Ramesses VI, VII, and VIII—all three dying within an eleven-year period—merely emphasized their lack of credit with the gods. Politics abhors a vacuum, and as the influence of the royal court declined, so the stock of the great families of provincial Egypt rose. At Thebes in particular, the most important offices were increasingly concentrated in the hands of a small number of aristocratic dynasties. Offices passed from father to son, in accordance with the Egyptian ideal but ignoring the superior ideal of the royal prerogative. The king exercised less and less real influence as state offices became quasi-hereditary.

Ramessesnakht, high priest of Amun © SANDRO VANNINI

This trend was exemplified by the richest and most powerful figure in Thebes for most of the late Twentieth Dynasty, the high priest of Amun, Ramessesnakht. His loyalist name ("Ramesses is victorious") was all for show. In reality, the high priest and his family were the effective rulers of Thebes and, with it, much of southern Egypt. Ramessesnakht saw off no less than six pharaohs, serving from the last years of Ramesses III into the reign of Ramesses IX. The high priest, not the king, was the new linchpin of the Theban government. Ramessesnakht saw to it that he was succeeded by his two sons in turn, Nesamun and Amenhotep. When the latter had himself depicted at Ipetsut, it was at the same scale as his sovereign. There could be no clearer indication of the hemorrhaging of royal status beyond the temple walls.

CRIME AND COVER-UP

THE SANCTITY OF THE ROYAL TOMB WAS A FUNDAMENTAL TENET OF ancient Egyptian belief from the very beginning of pharaonic history. If the prosperity of the land depended upon divine will, and the well-being of the gods upon the ministrations of the king, then the eternal survival and benevolence of the monarch was in everyone's interests. The royal tomb was designed not merely as a final resting place for an Egyptian ruler but as his passport to the next world and his guarantee of rebirth. As such, it was the single most important structure in the country. The ideal of inviolability had been rudely shattered during the civil unrest of the First Intermediate Period, when the Old Kingdom pyramids had been robbed and desecrated with impunity. A similar fate seems to have befallen the Middle Kingdom pyramids during the dark days of Hyksos rule. So the switch to hidden subterranean, rock-cut tombs under the rulers of the New Kingdom had brought with it a renewed hope that the mummies of Egypt's monarchs would be allowed to rest in peace for all eternity.

However, human nature being what it is, the discord and uncertainty at the end of the Eighteenth Dynasty had prompted opportunistic attempts to rob some of the tombs in the Valley of the Kings. Despite the kings' best endeavors to hide their sepulchres from prying eyes and grasping hands, knowledge of the tombs' whereabouts had clearly leaked out. Horemheb had sought to counter this threat by reforming the workmen's village at the Place of Truth. Out went the transient, even casual workforce of earlier reigns; in came a rigidly controlled and closed community, with death the only means of exit. In return for their vow of perpetual silence, the workmen and their families could expect to be looked after by the state, receiving guaranteed employment and better than usual rations. The most successful workers could even look forward to a degree of prosperity and a tomb of their own in the hillside above the village. It was a contract designed to appeal to the self-interest of both parties.

The strikes of 1158 dealt a blow to this long-standing agreement between the king and the workers of the tomb. If the state was no longer committed to paying the men on time and in full, why should the men protect the state's most jealously guarded secret? Little wonder, then, that amid the economic and political collapse of the late Twentieth Dynasty not even the tombs in the Valley of the Kings were considered sacrosanct.

The first serious incident took place early in the reign of Ramesses IX (1126–1108), when robbers broke into the tomb of Ramesses VI, sealed only a decade earlier. This act of sacrilege was followed a few years later by the wanton vandalism of two of the greatest monuments on the west bank of Thebes, the mortuary temples of Ramesses II and Ramesses III. Fortunately for the government, the thieves and vandals did relatively little damage on these occasions. A formal investigation headed by the high priest of Amun was launched, and security was no doubt tightened. But to little effect. Within a short time, the robbers were back, their soft target the less well guarded royal necropolis of the Seventeenth Dynasty on the hillside behind the Ramesseum. The thieves had little need to case the joint first. As inhabitants of the workmen's village, they knew every inch of the Theban necropolis like the backs of their hands. So, one night in 1114, a stonemason by the name of Amunpanefer set out with his band of accomplices to commit the crime of the century. Entering one of the royal tombs,

> we opened their coffins and their mummy wrappings. We brought back the gold we found on the noble mummy of this god, together with his pectorals and other jewelry that were around his neck.[7]

Having thoroughly pillaged the tomb of Sobekemsaf II for all its valuables, the robbers unceremoniously set fire to the coffins of the king and his consort, reducing their chests of life to smoldering ashes. It was an astonishing act of desecration and blasphemy. The actions of the pharaoh's own employees were now actively undermining the foundations of the state. Not that the robbers were remotely concerned with the theological implications of their actions. For them, all that mattered was the spoils, all thirty-two golden pounds of it. That more than compensated for the state's late rations.

When the robbery finally came to light four years later, all the government could do was punish the ringleaders and set up a royal commission to investigate what had happened (still a convenient substitute for decisive action). But a royal commission in the absence of royal authority was meaningless. It simply served to stoke the bitter rivalry between Thebes's two most important civilian officials. Heading the commission was the mayor of Thebes, Paser. Hampering it by every means at his disposal, fair or foul, was the mayor of western Thebes, Paweraa, whose jurisdiction included the royal necropolis. The two men saw in the investigation a golden opportunity for one-upmanship. While Paser was determined to use the investigation to assert his authority and take his antagonist down a peg or two, Paweraa was equally resolved to eliminate his rival once and for all.

The commission's findings must have made depressing reading back in the government offices of Per-Ramesses. Of the ten royal tombs inspected, only one was still intact. Some had been partly robbed, others completely ransacked. Faced with such a calamity, it was time to find a scapegoat. Yet no sooner had the commission implicated Paweraa than he struck back. Fighting for his political life and for life itself (since the penalty for robbing a royal tomb was death), Paweraa pulled out all the stops and called in every favor. With the help of the vizier Khaemwaset he managed to overrule the commission's findings and emerge unscathed. At the end of the whole process, both Paser and the vizier had mysteriously disappeared from the scene, as had the robbers themselves. No witnesses.

Paweraa survived and prospered. The robberies continued.

Three decades and several high-profile thefts later, a second royal commission was set up by Ramesses XI (1099–1069). This time, to reduce the likelihood of cover-up, the inquiry was led by the vizier himself, as the king's personal representative in Upper Egypt, assisted by the royal treasurer and two royal butlers. If the government was showing how seriously it took the problem, it was little prepared for the scale of the corruption that its investigations uncovered. Once again, most of the men involved in robbing the royal tombs came from the workmen's village. But this time they had not acted alone. The commission found evidence of widespread negligence and complicity among state and temple officials. Some had turned a blind eye to crimes carried out under their noses; others had actively collaborated in theft, sharing in the spoils. One of the suspects questioned by the tribunal had professed innocence, arguing, "I saw the lesson that was meted out to the thieves in the time of the vizier Khaemwaset. Is it likely, then, that I would set out to seek such a death?"[8] But the commission concluded that he was lying. Another robber decided to confess from the outset, recounting how he and four accomplices had emptied a tomb of its silver vessels and divided the spoils among them. The commission was suspicious of this unforced confession, so ordered the man to be "examined with the stick, birch, and screw." But he stuck to his story: "I didn't see anything else; what I saw is what I've said." After a second beating and the promise of many more, he broke down: "Stop, I'll talk . . ."[9] A little light torture worked wonders.

As the net was cast wider, the authorities started to reel in some bigger fish. A theft from the great temple of Amun-Ra at Ipetsut, arguably the most sacred place in the whole of Egypt, had been particularly audacious, striking at the heart of the regime's theological power base. On further investigation, the chief guard of the temple was found to have been behind the robbery.

The conclusion was stark: corruption was now endemic at every level of the priesthood and the government. At Thebes in particular, repeated Libyan incursions combined with food shortages and starvation had led to a complete breakdown of law and order. People no longer felt secure, personally or economically; they no longer trusted in the state's ability to defend them or provide for them. Nor did they fear the state's power to hold them in check or prevent them from taking the law into their own hands. After half a millennium of stability, the edifice of the state was crumbling and collapsing with alarming rapidity. Egypt stood on the brink of anarchy.

DESPERATE REMEDIES

THE GOVERNMENT OF EGYPT DURING THE RAMESSIDE PERIOD WAS DIvided into four broad, functionally distinct units. Supporting the activities of the court was the royal domain, administered by a chancellor and a chief steward. The civil service, headed by two viziers, one for Upper Egypt and one for Lower Egypt, was responsible for taxation, agriculture, and justice. The army, under its commander in chief (often a royal prince), played a relatively minor part in government, despite its prominent role as an instrument of foreign policy. Last but not least there was the religious establishment, led by the overseer of priests of

all the gods of Upper and Lower Egypt. More often than not this exalted post was held by the high priest of Amun. Ever since the latter
years of Ramesses III, the high priest of the country's preeminent cult
had been the most powerful individual in Upper Egypt, wielding more
influence than the mayor of Thebes or even the southern vizier. The
great temple of Amun-Ra at Ipetsut was the largest landowner in the
region, controlling vast estates with thousands of tenant farmers. It also
had extensive workshops employing hundreds of craftsmen, and its
granaries, attached to the mortuary temples of Ramesses II and III,
acted as the main reserve bank not just for Thebes but for Upper Egypt
as a whole. The man who controlled Ipetsut and its economic wealth
controlled Thebes. As kings came and went, this most prestigious
sinecure was monopolized by one family, that of Ramessesnakht. In
troubled times, this local dynasty provided some measure of continuity
and stability, even if it could not bring much succor to the common
people's increasingly blighted lives.

Then, in 1091, the unrest sweeping Thebes came home to roost.
Hungry, desperate, and frustrated by the high priest Amenhotep's in-
transigence, a group of Thebans succeeded in forcibly removing him
from office and replacing him with a new man of their choosing. For
eight months, Amenhotep languished at home, shorn of the trappings
of power, deprived of his accustomed wealth, politically isolated. For a
proud scion of Thebes's leading family, it was quite a comedown.
Worse still, there was only one person in Egypt who could reinstate a
high priest, and that was the king. Groveling to the pharaoh was an unwelcome prospect for Amenhotep, but he knew it was the only path
back to power. So, swallowing his pride, he petitioned Ramesses XI, far
away in the royal residence at Per-Ramesses, to restore him to his
rightful office.

Ramesses was caught between a rock and a hard place. If he failed to
respond to Amenhotep's pleadings and left the usurper in place at Ipetsut, it would be an admission of impotence, effectively signaling the
end of the king's writ in Upper Egypt. If, however, he took steps to restore Amenhotep to the high priesthood, it would merely confirm the
supremacy of a family that had been building its own power base for
generations at the expense of the Ramesside Dynasty. Neither option
was particularly attractive, but restoring the status quo ante seemed

marginally preferable. The only question was how to achieve the desired outcome. Reports from Thebes indicated that the usurper was not going to go quietly; considerable force would be needed to dislodge him from the heavily fortified enclosure at Djeme (modern Medinet Habu). Yet the king was hundreds of miles away in the delta, as were most of Egypt's troops. Sending them southward to unseat a high priest would carry two unacceptable risks, drawing the king into the bitter internal politics of Thebes while leaving the royal residence exposed and vulnerable to attack. There was only one other garrison with enough troops to carry out the operation, and that was stationed in Nubia, under the command of the viceroy of Kush. So Ramesses sent an order to the viceroy, Panehsy, to march north with his Nubian troops as quickly as possible, to suppress the interloper.

It was a fatal error of judgment.

Within weeks, Panehsy had arrived at Thebes in force, and his Nubian soldiers were at the gates of Medinet Habu. An unruly mob stormed the temple enclosure, driving out the usurper and vandalizing the buildings. Other troops rampaged across the west bank, causing damage to its sacred monuments. The operation was a military success but a public relations disaster. Once order had been restored and Amenhotep reinstated as high priest, Panehsy moved swiftly to assess the damage, recover stolen property, and punish those responsible. Some culprits were summarily executed on the viceroy's orders, without waiting for the inconvenience of a trial. In such situations, making an example of a few individuals usually did the job of keeping the rest in line. The inhabitants of Thebes suddenly remembered the roughness of military justice.

Having imposed law and order, Panehsy moved to seize control of the Theban economy, taking charge of the temple granaries. Amenhotep could hardly complain, given that he owed his restoration to the Nubian strongman. By 1087, Panehsy was styling himself as "general and overseer of the granaries of the pharaoh." He, not the high priest of Amun, was now the de facto ruler of Upper Egypt. For a while, the viceroy loyally governed Thebes on behalf of the king, but Ramesses XI was becoming increasingly concerned about his subordinate's growing power. He could sense Thebes and the south slipping away, and was determined to reassert royal authority at all costs. Egypt's empire was no more, its borders were porous, and its people were starving. If he could no longer preserve even the country's territorial integrity, a pharaoh would not be worthy of the name, nor could he call himself a true Ramesses.

From their earliest origins, the Ramessides had been a military dynasty, using military personnel and military solutions to govern Egypt. Now, having unleashed one general and come to regret it, Ramesses XI might have thought twice about doing the same again. Yet, with his options fast running out, all he could do was fall back on his instincts. In 1082, the king duly summoned one of his northern generals, Paiankh, and ordered him to march against Panehsy and drive the upstart viceroy back into Nubia. The result was civil war.

Panehsy was a skilled enough tactician not to sit and wait for the onslaught, but to take the fight to the enemy. He rounded up the Theban garrisons and, bolstered by local conscripts, marched north with his army to engage Paiankh's forces. At first, the viceroy's advance met with considerable success. Reaching Hardai, in Middle Egypt, he stormed and ransacked the town. For a moment, it seemed that the king's army might lose the war. But Paiankh's greater numbers eventually prevailed, and by 1080 Panehsy had been driven out of Egypt. The disgraced viceroy of Kush was back where he belonged, in far-off Nubia.

The conflict may have saved face for Ramesses XI, but it was a disaster for Thebes. The depletion of the local garrisons and the conscription of men of fighting age led to a security vacuum across the city. Widespread looting of temples and tombs broke out and went unchecked for months. The tomb of Ramesses VI was targeted for a second time and its sarcophagus attacked. Worse still, as Panehsy's army retreated, it carried out a scorched-earth policy, ravaging monuments in an orgy of destruction. When the dust finally settled, the pharaoh visited Thebes—in a rare outing from his delta residence—to see for himself the extent of the damage. It was a deeply depressing sight. Not since the dark days of the country's first civil war, a thousand years earlier, had so much devastation been inflicted by fellow Egyptians.

In a vain attempt to turn back the clock and start afresh, Ramesses declared the beginning of a new era. The nineteenth year of his reign was to be known instead as the first year of the renaissance, and subsequent years would follow the new nomenclature. But nobody was fooled, least of all Paiankh—for he, not Ramesses, was the undoubted victor against Panehsy. To prove the point, Paiankh took over the viceroy's titles and dignities, followed by those of the high priest as well. General, overseer of granaries, and high priest of Amun—military, economic, and religious authority were now combined in one person. The "restoration" of pharaonic authority in Thebes had in fact been just another military putsch—except that Paiankh had learned from history. While the viceroy had enjoyed only a brief period of absolute power, Paiankh's regime would be designed to stand the test of time.

An army man through and through, brusque, determined, and ruthlessly efficient, Paiankh ruled Thebes with a rod of iron. He took pains to build a network of influential supporters, surrounding himself with men and women of ability. One such was his wife Nodjmet, a woman of considerable resolve and personal authority. Paiankh's first policy, after imposing martial law in Thebes, was to lead his army into Nubia in pursuit of the renegade Panehsy. Only by securing its southern flank against a repeat attack could the new military junta achieve lasting security. While Paiankh was on maneuvers in Nubia, he left the running of Thebes in his wife's capable hands. The two corresponded regularly, keeping each other informed about major developments. One particular exchange of letters underlines the dark side of military rule. In Paiankh's absence, unease about the regime was growing in Thebes, and Nodjmet wrote to her husband to report on seditious statements made by two policemen. Even the forces of law and order were beginning to mutter against the junta. Paiankh's reply was unequivocal and chilling:

> Have these two policemen brought to my house and get to the bottom of their words in short order. Then have them killed and thrown into the water by night.[10]

Interrogation followed by "disappearance"—the classic fate of dissidents under a military regime.

Political assassinations were not the only murky activities sponsored by Paiankh in his bid to retain power. In another letter from the Nubian front, he ordered two of his Theban henchmen, Butehamun and Kar, to perform an unnamed "task on which you have never before embarked."[11] The euphemistic phraseology was carefully chosen, for the task in question was nothing less than state-sponsored tomb robbery. The war against Panehsy showed no signs of a swift resolution, and Paiankh badly needed funds to finance his military operations and shore up his regime at home. The Theban hills offered a ready treasure trove of gold and silver, buried in the tombs of Egypt's kings, queens, and high officials. So Paiankh's men set out on a deliberate policy of breaking and entering, channeling the proceeds of their crime back to the government coffers. As they roamed the west bank in search of tomb entrances, they marked what they found for systematic future clearance. Butehamun alone left more than 130 graffiti, identifying the repositories of wealth amassed by generations of pious Thebans. Having survived Libyan attack, opportunistic robbery, and civil war, the remaining intact tombs of the New Kingdom pharaohs were now ruthlessly exploited by the rulers themselves. A final taboo had been broken.

After a decade of rule, the junta faced its sternest test when Paiankh died unexpectedly. His sons were too young to take over, and the prospect of an interregnum was deeply unwelcome for a regime that had not yet consolidated its grip on power. So, postponing a dynastic succession in favor of a stopgap solution, Paiankh's supporters moved swiftly and stabilized the situation by choosing another army general, Herihor, as interim leader. He was an inspired choice. A mature and capable leader in Paiankh's mold, Herihor came from the same officer class. He was as vigorous in his private life as he was in military matters, fathering nineteen sons.

Yet none of them was to succeed him. Paiankh's widow saw to that. In a brilliantly calculated move, Nodjmet immediately took Herihor as her new husband, at a stroke bolstering his position and retaining her influence over the eventual succession.

That succession left no room for the Ramesside royal family. While Herihor strengthened the rule of the generals in Upper Egypt, another army man, the king's son-in-law Nesbanebdjedet, took effective power in the north of the country. Egypt was now a nation of two halves, each ruled by a military elite. Though Herihor and Nesbanebdjedet paid lip service to the continued reign of Ramesses XI, there was no denying where real power lay. Isolated and a virtual prisoner in his own royal residence, the last of the Ramessides had seen pharaonic authority slip from his grasp, through a combination of poor decisions and benign neglect. The same army that had brought the Nineteenth and Twentieth dynasties to power was presiding over the country's formal division. Military might had proved a double-edged sword indeed.

As Ramesses XI lay on his deathbed in 1069, after thirty years on the throne, the Nile itself seemed to signal the end of an era. The great river's Pelusiac Branch, on which Per-Ramesses had been founded two centuries earlier, had been silting up for some time. By the end of Ramesses XI's reign, the main channel was so clogged with sediment that ships were no longer able to use the city's harbors. It was a fitting metaphor for the regime's own sclerosis. Starved of commerce and communication, the traders, scribes, and bureaucrats abandoned Per-Ramesses in favor of a new site, Djanet (modern San el-Hagar), some twelve miles to the north. As the old king's funeral cortège wound its way from the royal palace of Per-Ramesses, followed by a clutch of old retainers, the Ramesside Dynasty and its seat of government died together.

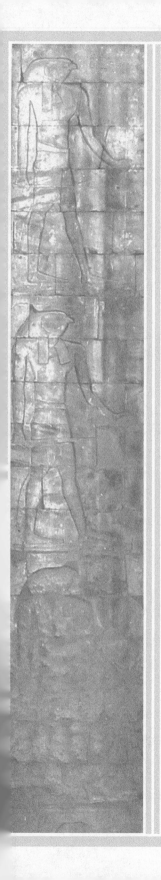

PART V

CHANGE
AND·DECAY

(1069–30 B.C.)

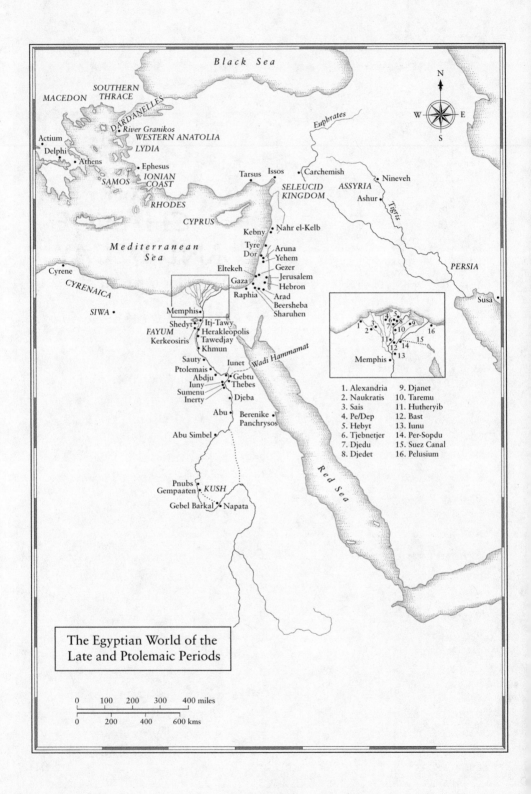

The Egyptian World of the
Late and Ptolemaic Periods

W HEN THE LAST OF THE RAMESSIDES PASSED AWAY IN 1069, little mourned and largely irrelevant, Egypt entered a period of profound change. The death of Ramesses XI was the stimulus for two strongmen, one in the delta and one in Upper Egypt, to assume royal titles and attributes, and to divide and rule the country between them. Whether the formal bifurcation of the Two Lands represented an outright rejection of the pharaonic ideal of national unity, or merely a return to a more natural state of affairs, it ushered in a long-lasting era of political fragmentation, of a kind not seen for a thousand years.

The Egyptians soon discovered that decentralization and regional autonomy could prove a mixed blessing. In the days of old, the consequences of a weak government might have been purely internal. In the first millennium, however, Egypt was surrounded by envious foreign powers, vastly more powerful than in earlier centuries. From the eleventh to the fourth centuries, Egypt's strategic weakness led to repeated invasions. First Libyans, then Assyrians, Kushites, Babylonians, Persians, and finally Macedonians fought over the Nile Valley's agricultural and mineral wealth. Foreign immigrants and nonnative rulers wrought significant changes to Egypt's political organization, society, and culture, transforming pharaonic civilization forever. At the same time, ancient Egyptian religion, the last bastion of traditional culture, sealed itself off from outside influences and became ever more inward-looking. In the face of younger, more dynamic civilizations, Egypt's introspection led in the end to atrophy and extinction.

Part V charts the final tumultuous millennium of ancient Egyptian history, from the Libyan takeover to the Roman conquest. The first three centuries of post-Ramesside rule were relatively peaceful, with collateral branches of a Libyan royal family managing to maintain an uneasy balance of power. But the return of Egypt's old enemy, the kingdom of Kush, in 728 smashed the status quo, and for the next four hundred years the Nile Valley was racked by division, conflict, and foreign occupation. Four successive Assyrian invasions in the space of three decades culminated in the sack of Thebes, delivering a bitter blow to Egypt's national pride. Amid the chaos, a dynasty from Sais maneuvered its way to power, throwing off the Assyrian yoke and repulsing attempted invasions by Babylonia, before finally succumbing to the Persians. Egypt lost its crown to a resurgent Mesopotamia, and never again regained its former supremacy in the Near East.

The ever present Persian threat hung like a dark cloud over the last native dynasties, whose members squabbled over the remains of Egypt, behaving like fractious warlords instead of mighty pharaohs. Alexander the Great's arrival in 332 seemed to offer deliverance, and his brief sojourn in the Nile Valley had as profound an effect on Egypt as it did on the man himself. His successors, the Ptolemies, tried to recapture the glories of the past, albeit with a distinctly Greek flavor. But their constant feuding, coupled with their neglect of Upper Egypt—the crucible of pharaonic civilization—led to political instability, a long-running southern insurgency, and terminal decline. The last act of Egypt's great drama was played out in the streets of Alexandria with a cast of characters as famous as any: Caesar, Mark Antony, and Cleopatra. With her death, in 30, Egypt became a Roman imperial possession and its three-thousand-year-old pharaonic tradition came to an end.

CHAPTER 19

A HOUSE DIVIDED

THE ENEMY WITHIN

PHARAONIC PROPAGANDA MUST SOMETIMES HAVE RUNG RATHER HOL-
low, even for a population fed an incessant and unvarying diet of government spin. By the time of Ramesses XI's death in 1069, Egypt's
kings had been boasting of their famous victories against Libyan invaders for the best part of a century and a half. Back in 1208,
Merenptah had ordered a great commemorative inscription to be set
up in the temple of Amun-Ra at Ipetsut, recounting his crushing defeat
of one such incursion led by the Libyan chief Mery. Just three years
later, the Libyans had returned. Another military victory and another
commemorative inscription had duly followed, but the pharaoh's efforts had bought Egypt barely two decades of peace and security. And
what Merenptah's publicists had failed to mention was that the government had been forced to install a defensive garrison in the southern
oasis to prevent infiltration from the desert—and that the very soldiers
manning the defenses were themselves Libyan mercenaries! Poachers
turned gamekeepers.

Under Ramesses III, the battles against the Libyans in 1182 and
1176 had been nowhere near as conclusive as the official propaganda
had suggested. Behind all the triumphalism, the authorities had felt it
necessary to fortify temples on the west bank of the Nile, including the
king's own Mansion of Millions of Years, with its valuable treasuries
and granaries. Despite the Egyptians' best endeavors, the Libyans who
had been repelled from the western delta had simply turned southward
to infiltrate the Nile Valley in Upper Egypt. The frequent attacks on
Thebes during the later Ramesside Period showed the Libyans' determination and persistence. Ramesses III had also boasted of forcing
thousands of Libyan prisoners to "cross the river, bringing them to

Egypt," where they were settled in fortified camps ("strongholds of the victorious king"),[1] branded with the pharaoh's name, and forcibly acculturated: "He makes their speech disappear and changes their tongues, so that they set out on a path they have not gone down before."[2] Yet the integration had often been only superficial, and sizeable concentrations of Libyans around the entrance to the Fayum and along the edges of the western delta had resolutely hung on to their ethnic identity, forming distinctive communities within the local Egyptian population. By the reign of Ramesses V, a land survey of Middle Egypt noted a substantial proportion of people with foreign names. The Libyans were by now well ensconced. A generation later, a boisterous community that had settled in the central delta near the town of Perhebit (modern Behbeit el-Hagar) was causing the Egyptian authorities particular concern. During the course of the Ramesside Period, Egypt had unintentionally become a country of two cultures, in which a large ethnic minority made its presence increasingly felt.

Of all the country's institutions, the army had felt the impact of Libyan immigration most acutely. The Egyptian military had a long and proud tradition of employing foreign mercenaries, and had therefore proved a natural, and popular, career choice for many Libyan settlers. Whether manning remote desert garrisons or fighting on campaign, Libyan soldiers had served their adopted country with loyalty and distinction throughout the second half of the Twentieth Dynasty. Moreover, some of the more ambitious Libyan soldiers had been able to secure themselves positions of considerable influence at the heart of Egyptian government. Two such individuals were Paiankh and Herihor, the military strongmen who headed the Theban junta in the dying days of Ramesses XI's reign.

By 1069, Libyans in Egypt had not only achieved high office, they stood ready to assume the government itself. With the death of Ramesses XI, and just two centuries after suffering its first Libyan raids, the Nile Valley passed into foreign control—not by invasion or armed conflict but through the discipline and determination of an enemy within. For the first time in Egyptian history, the underdogs had become overlords.

For the next four hundred years, Egypt was dominated by Libyan power brokers, a dramatic twist of fate that had a profound effect on every aspect of society. Although the earliest of these alien rulers, men such as Herihor and Nesbanebdjedet, sported traditionally pious Egyptian names (with their references to Horus and the ram god of Djedet), such outward trappings of pharaonic decorum were an illusion. Beneath a thin veil of tradition, non-Egyptian features flourished. In the predominantly Libyan areas of the delta, local dignitaries openly wore traditional Libyan feather decorations in their hair as a proud marker of their ethnic origin, and Libyan chiefly titles made a comeback. Once the Libyan generals had gained power after the death of Ramesses XI, their kinsmen had even less cause to integrate with the host population, and within a few generations many families reverted to giving their children unashamedly Libyan names that were strange-sounding to the Egyptians, names such as Osorkon, Shoshenq, Iuput, Nimlot, and Takelot. With such a strong sense of their own identity, generations of inhabitants of the western delta regarded themselves as Libyans, not Egyptians—a phenomenon still prevalent enough to be remarked upon by the Greek historian Herodotus five centuries later.

Together with the appearance of Libyan names in official inscriptions, the Egyptian language began to show other signs of the foreigners' influence. Ever since the Middle Kingdom, written Egyptian carved into temple walls in finely executed hieroglyphs had preserved the classic form of the language. Vernacular spoken Egyptian, by contrast, had diverged a long way from this "pure" written form, to the point where the two versions were practically different dialects. While this posed no problem for native Egyptian scribes schooled in the classical script, it must have been a considerable impediment to the Libyan bureaucrats and priests who now ran the country. For them, mastering one form of Egyptian was quite enough. As a result, official inscriptions of the Libyan Period show a marked preference for spoken forms, workaday grammar, and simple vocabulary, in contrast to the more refined formulations of the ruling class.

Language and its precise use had always been of special significance to the Egyptian monarchy, since the choice of royal names and epithets expressed the underlying theology of kingship and set the pattern for a reign. But all this was alien to the Libyan rulers. They adopted the trappings of Egyptian royalty without, perhaps, properly understanding the trappings' nuanced symbolism. Royal titles were simply recycled from one reign to another, repeated ad nauseam. The ancient designation "dual king" lost its sacred exclusivity and became just another handle. In their choice of royal names, too, the kings of the Twenty-first Dynasty seemed to be trying too hard, sporting bizarre and convoluted formulations such as Pasebakhaenniut, "the star rises over the city." Such clumsy attempts at authenticity fooled nobody.

Indeed, the Libyan elite showed their true colors in their obsession with family trees. The recitation of long genealogies is a feature of oral tradition in nonliterate seminomadic societies, and the Libyans of the late second millennium B.C. were no exception. Even after they had gained a written language from their Egyptian hosts, they lost none of their penchant for celebrating long lines of ancestors. For example, one priest from Iunu had a monument carved with the names of thirteen generations of his forebears, stretching back three centuries, despite the fact that the family had been settled in the same Egyptian city and had held the same office for eleven of those generations.

Another carryover from the Libyans' nomadic past was their relative lack of interest in death and the afterlife. Their animal herding ancestors had been used to burying their dead where and when they fell, with little preparation and less fuss. Ancient Egypt, by contrast, had always been punctilious about mortuary provision. Yet the country's new Libyan rulers stayed true to their own cultural instincts and showed a casualness in their approach to the next world that must have been truly shocking to their Egyptian hosts. Individual burials were eschewed as a waste of resources in favor of communal family vaults with little decoration. Even the Libyan pharaohs were content to be buried cheek by jowl with their relatives, in modest stone-built tombs cobbled together from whatever blocks came to hand. Funerary equipment was often recycled from nearby burials, as if equipping the deceased for eternity were a chore, to be accomplished as speedily and cheaply as possible. The construction of splendid royal sepulchres in the Valley of the Kings, and equally magnificent mortuary temples on the Theban plain, came to an abrupt halt, never to be resumed. Tombs lost their special role as a meeting place for the living and the dead, the mortal and the divine. They were now little more than holes in the ground for bodies.

If the Libyans' attitude toward death had an impact on pharaonic culture, their favored model of government had an equally powerful effect on the course of Egyptian history. In their homeland of coastal Cyrenaica, the Libyans had organized themselves along tribal lines, with fairly loose power structures based on family groups, reinforced by marriage ties and feudal allegiances. It was a world away from the strongly centralized absolute monarchy of the Nile Valley. Even before the end of the New Kingdom, Ramesses XI's Libyan generals had shown their disdain for a unified state, with Paiankh and Herihor happily ruling the south while Nesbanebdjedet governed the north of the country.

The administrative division of Egypt into two halves had been a feature of pharaonic government from earliest times, but always with a single king to bind "the Two Lands" together. Once Ramesses XI was dead and gone, his Libyan successors saw no need to maintain this tradition. For them, having two kings ruling concurrently over different parts of the country was not anathema but entirely normal, not anarchy but sensible decentralization. In any case, marriages and alliances maintained the bonds of loyalty between the two branches of the ruling house and served to prevent breakaway dynasties. Yet the subsequent delegation of unprecedented powers to kings' sons—many of whom were put in charge of major cities—and other aspects of Libyan feudalism inevitably weakened the power of the central government and the monarchy, with inevitable long-term consequences.

But all that was in the future. For now, with the last of the Ramesside pharaohs safely interred in the Valley of the Kings, his Libyan successors could count themselves well pleased. One of them was undisputed master of Upper Egypt; the other was lord of the delta. Egypt had entered a new era of foreign domination.

A TALE OF TWO CITIES

ALTHOUGH THE HISTORY OF THE LATE TWENTIETH DYNASTY—THE paralysis and eventual extinction of the New Kingdom—is written in the monuments and machinations of Thebes, the principal seat of government and the main royal residence always remained in the north of the country. Memphis had been the capital of Egypt since the dawn of history, and it retained its role as the headquarters of the national administration right through the Ramesside Period. Thebes may have taken on the mantle of the nation's religious capital, but it was at Memphis that royal decrees were issued, officials appointed, and kings crowned. As for the principal residence of the pharaoh, Per-Ramesses had served that role ever since its founding under Ramesses II. The delta, not the Nile Valley, was the senior political partner in the union of Upper and Lower Egypt. For this reason, when control was formally divided between Herihor and Nesbanebdjedet after the death of Ramesses XI, it was the northern ruler, Nesbanebdjedet (1069–1045), who claimed the first prize, the kingship, while his brother-in-law had to play second fiddle as mere army commander and high priest of Amun. In this way, a convenient fiction of political unity was maintained, even if the reality was a partnership of two quasi-independent kingdoms linked only by ties of marriage.

The division of Egypt into two parallel states was the defining feature of Libyan rule. Each half of the country had its own system of government, its own administration, and its own ceremonial capital. No longer a mere theological conceit, the idea of the Two Lands was now a practical reality.

The delta had borne the brunt of Libyan settlement in the dying days of the New Kingdom, and it was here that the new political order was most keenly felt. The inaccessible marshlands and winding waterways had always favored political fragmentation, and in the heyday of Libyan domination, the delta divided readily into a patchwork of competing centers. Each was ruled by a chief of the Ma or a chief of the Libu (the two main Libyan tribes settled in Egypt), who owed theoretical allegiance to the main royal line. In practice, though, the "king" was only first among equals. Even so, the monarchs based at Djanet (classical Tanis) were conscious enough of their theoretical preeminence to embark upon a grand project worthy of their pharaonic status—the transformation of their royal residence into a ceremonial capital every bit as grand as Thebes.

From humble beginnings as a replacement for Per-Ramesses, Djanet grew rapidly under the patronage of the northern kings into the greatest city in the delta. It was sited on one of the main Nile branches, in an area as favorable for trade as it was for fishing and fowling. To create space for residential quarters and public buildings, the first priority was to raise the banks of the main river and reclaim the land on either side. Only then could construction start in earnest.

If Djanet were to be a northern counterpart to Thebes, it needed an equally magnificent ceremonial centerpiece, a grand temple to the state god Amun-Ra. Unfortunately, many of Egypt's major quarries were under Theban control, and the northern kings' economic power was severely circumscribed. A full-scale royal building project such as might have been undertaken in the glorious days of the New Kingdom was no longer a practical proposition. Instead, Nesbanebdjedet and his two successors Amenemnisu (1045–1040) and Pasebakhaenniut I (1040–985) adopted an altogether simpler expedient, recycling monuments and building materials from nearby Per-Ramesses and other delta sites. The once glittering Ramesside residence was systematically stripped of its stone as obelisks, statues, and building blocks were torn down to be dragged the twelve miles to Djanet and reerected. Often the northern kings did not even bother to reinscribe the plundered monuments—a further sign that they paid only lip service to the age-old traditions of Egyptian monarchy.

On top of a large, sandy hill, where a cemetery for the local rural poor had grown up in the Ramesside Period, Pasebakhaenniut I erected the centerpiece of his "northern Thebes," a suite of temples to the Theban triad of Amun-Ra, Mut, and Khonsu. To underline the sanctity of the complex, he had it surrounded by a great brick wall (in ancient Egyptian, "sacred" and "set apart" were the same word) and he designated one area of the temple precinct as the royal necropolis of his dynasty. Just as Thebes had been rendered sacred by the combination of divine temples and kingly tombs, so, too, would Djanet. By New Kingdom architectural standards, the Libyan royal sepulchres at Djanet were deeply unimpressive—small, irregular chambers built from rough-hewn reused blocks, with little ornament or decoration. But what Pasebakhaenniut's burial lacked in grandeur, it more than made up for in wealth. Within a great granite chest—pilfered, with no little irony, from the Theban tomb of Merenptah, scourge of the Libyans—the king's mummy lay on a silver sheet inside a silver coffin, its face covered with a mask of beaten gold. Around the body lay other

Wendjebaendjedet's cup of gold and electrum
WERNER FORMAN ARCHIVE

costly treasures—inlaid bracelets and pectorals, a chunky necklace of lapis lazuli beads, silver and gold bowls, and a gold scepter. Even the king's fingers and toes were sheathed individually in gold leaf.

Yet this gilded opulence was not used to set the king apart from his subjects, as it would have been in earlier periods. An equally sumptuous set of equipment was provided for the man who shared Pasebakhaen-niut's final resting place. In another sign of the times (and of the feudalism of Libyan rule), this man was not even a royal prince but merely one of the king's chief courtiers. Wendjebaendjedet was a general and army leader, like many of his ilk, and held temple office at Djanet as high steward of Khonsu. In this capacity he may have functioned as the king's deputy in the daily temple rites. But there was no sense of second best in his burial. The amount of gold placed around his body demonstrated his exalted status. There were several magnificent golden cups, including one in the shape of a flower with alternating petals of gold and electrum; a heart scarab on a gold chain; gold pectorals; gold statuettes of deities; a remarkable figurine of the god Ptah, fashioned from lapis lazuli, nestling in a gold shrine; and a series of gold rings, one of them pilfered from the tomb of Ramesses IX.

This last object gives a clue as to the source of such great wealth. The kings of Djanet and their loyal lieutenants derived their grave goods—and the rest of their city—not from trade or conquest but from recycling and outright robbery. To understand the full extent to which the Egyptian monarchy had debased itself, we must turn our gaze southward, to Thebes.

While the delta had concentrations of Libyan settlers and exhibited a tendency toward decentralization, Upper Egypt presented a very different picture. The Nile Valley was ethnically much more homogeneous, with native Egyptians forming the overwhelming majority of the population, and the geography of the valley lent itself to political cohesion. Thebes remained the largest and most important city; whoever ruled Thebes ruled the valley. So, for Upper Egypt in general, the collapse of the New Kingdom state brought not local autonomy but another long spell of Theban domination.

Despite its thoroughly Egyptian character, Thebes had also fallen under Libyan influence during the "renaissance era" of Ramesses XI's reign, due to the presence of Libyan soldiers in the uppermost echelons of the Egyptian army. And, as we have seen, it was under the military junta headed by Paiankh that the state-sponsored theft of valuables from the royal tombs had begun. While campaigning in Nubia, Paiankh had sent one letter to Thebes ordering the scribe of the necropolis, Butehamun, and his assistant Kar to "uncover a tomb amongst the tombs of the ancestors and preserve its seal until I return."[3] The general's instructions to his henchmen marked the beginning of a deliberate policy to strip royal tombs of their gold, to finance the war against Panehsy and to fund Paiankh's wider ambitions. The fact that all this was going on under the ancien régime shows where power really lay. Once Ramesses XI was safely dead, the New Kingdom monarchy consigned to history, and the military rulers of Thebes de facto kings of Upper Egypt, the systematic dismantling of the royal necropolis could be openly pursued as official government policy.

At first, the main targets for the robbers were the tombs of the Seventeenth Dynasty, the burials of royal relatives in the Valley of the Queens, and the kings' mortuary temples at the edge of the cultivation. Then, on the pretext of safeguarding the integrity of all royal tombs, the authorities switched their focus to the Valley of the Kings itself. In the fourth year of Herihor's rule (1066), Butehamun received an order to carry out "work" in the tomb of Horemheb. It was the beginning of the end for the royal necropolis. Over the next decade, the tombs of the

New Kingdom pharaohs were emptied one by one. The workmen who carried out the task even seem to have had a map of the valley (surely provided by the authorities) to assist the clearance. Their main objective was to expropriate the large quantities of gold and other valuables buried in the Theban hills. These were swiftly removed to the state treasury, leaving only the mummies—rudely unwrapped in the search for hidden jewels—to be taken to Butehamun's imposing office at Medinet Habu for processing and rewrapping. Little wonder that Butehamun was proud to call himself, without a hint of irony, "overseer of the treasuries of the kings." So rife was tomb robbery in the Theban necropolis at this time that private individuals designed their interments with an obsessive emphasis on inaccessibility, to make the robbers' job as hard as possible.

Besides larceny, Butehamun's exploratory work in the Valley of the Kings had a second aim—to identify a permanent repository for the royal corpses that had been so rudely removed from their resting places. The tomb of Amenhotep II (next to the tomb of Horemheb) was eventually identified as an ideal location. One fateful day around 1050, the sacred remains of Egypt's divine kings were unceremoniously gathered up and shoved higgledy-piggledy into one of the tomb's chambers. In the process, the great Amenhotep III ended up in a coffin inscribed for Ramesses III, with an ill-fitting lid made for Seti II. Merenptah came to rest in the coffin of Sethnakht, while his own sarcophagus made its way north to Djanet to serve the burial of Egypt's new Libyan ruler (Pasebakhaenniut I). In this unholy mess, the dignified Thutmose IV lay cheek by jowl with the child king Siptah, the military tough guy Sethnakht with the smallpox-ridden Ramesses V. It was a desecration of everything that ancient Egypt had hallowed. An even more illustrious gathering of royal ancestors—including the victors against the Hyksos, Ahhotep and Ahmose; the founders of the workmen's village, Ahmose Nefertari and Amenhotep I; and the greatest of all the warrior pharaohs, Thutmose III, Seti I, Ramesses II, and Ramesses III—were bundled into a secondary cache in the tomb of a Seventeenth Dynasty queen, there to await a more secure, permanent resting place.

The result of all this robbery, officially represented as restoration, was to give the army commanders and high priests of Amun who ruled

Thebes wealth beyond their wildest dreams. Some of the plunder found its way north to their nominal suzerains at Djanet, there to be buried alongside Pasebakhaenniut I and his loyal lieutenant Wendjebaendjedet. (Indeed, the favored chief courtier who ended up with so much gold may have been the king's agent in Thebes, charged with overseeing the clearance of the royal tombs on behalf of his master.) However, for every gold ring or pectoral transported downstream to the northern capital, a great deal more stayed behind in Thebes, to bolster the economic and political fortunes of the southern rulers. Both Herihor (1069–1063) and his successor as high priest Pinedjem I (1063–1033) felt secure enough of their position to claim royal titles, in a direct challenge to their overlords at Djanet. While Herihor seems to have balked at outright confrontation, restricting his claim to the inner parts of the Ipetsut temple, Pinedjem showed no such reticence. Official inscriptions from the second and third decades of his rule were dated to the years of his independent "reign," with scarcely a mention of the kings in Djanet. For his burial in the hills of Thebes, he reused coffins from the tomb of Thutmose I, to add a little Eighteenth Dynasty luster to his own monarchical pretensions.

If the institution of kingship had survived the end of Ramesside rule, it had done so only by cannibalizing the past.

GOD'S WILL

Appropriating the wealth and trappings of monarchy might have been straightforward enough, but buying legitimacy was not so easy. Until the very end of the New Kingdom, the Egyptians had viewed Libyans and all foreigners with customary disdain. For the effortlessly superior natives of the Nile Valley, these hirsute, feather-wearing tribespeople from beyond the Sahara were, at best, mercenaries, and at worst, vile barbarians. Less than a generation later, the same Libyans could scarcely expect to be accepted as legitimate rulers of Egypt, even if they now held all the levers of power.

The solution to the Libyans' dilemma lay, as always, in the subtle application of theology. It was no accident that, at Djanet and Thebes, temples were placed at the symbolic heart of Libyan rule. The great temple of Amun-Ra at Ipetsut had been the religious epicenter of the

New Kingdom monarchy. By replicating the temple in the northern capital of Djanet, Nesbanebdjedet and his successors were pursuing a very deliberate agenda, an attempt to gain divine sanction for their alien regime by placing the supreme god at the apex of society. Conveniently, they could present their policy as a continuation of Ramesses XI's "renaissance," taking Egypt back to its pristine state at the dawn of time when the gods ruled on earth. But in practice, it represented a decisive break with New Kingdom modes of rule. Supreme political authority was now explicitly vested in Amun-Ra himself. In temples and on papyri, the god's name was written in a royal cartouche. One document said that Amun-Ra was "dual king; king of the gods; lord of heaven, earth, the waters, and the mountains."[4] On temple reliefs, Amun was sometimes shown in place of the sovereign, offering to himself or other deities, and he was widely addressed as the true king of Egypt. Nesbanebdjedet's ephemeral successor Amenemnisu went one step further, announcing in his very name that "Amun is king." It was an extraordinary claim.

If the god was monarch, then the king was effectively reduced to the status of his first servant. In Djanet, Pasebakhaenniut I adopted the moniker "high priest of Amun" as one of his royal titles, even enclosing it within a cartouche as an alternative to his throne name. In Thebes, his half brother Menkheperra (1033–990) *was* high priest of Amun, even if his real power came from the sword rather than the censer. This theocratic form of government effectively solved two problems at once. It made it theologically possible to have more than one mortal "ruler" at any one time, since Amun was the only true king. And it helped make Libyan rule more palatable for the native population, especially in Thebes and Upper Egypt, where pious Egyptians still dominated.

In reality, the theocracy was a convenient sleight of hand, a fig leaf to cover the embarrassing reality of a fractured monarchy. But it was important to maintain the fiction, so oracles became a regular instrument of government policy. In both Djanet and Thebes, the god Amun held audiences and issued decrees, like any human monarch. In the southern capital, this trend culminated in the establishment of a regular ceremony, the Beautiful Festival of the Divine Audience, at which the oracle of Amun pronounced on various matters of state. Of course, the people who benefited most from this new type of administration, besides the Libyan rulers themselves, were the priests who staffed and interpreted the oracles. Living in considerable luxury within the sacred precinct of Ipetsut, they helped themselves while serving their divine master.

Their devotion to mammon as much as to god bubbled to the surface in particularly striking form during the pontificate of Pinedjem II (985–960). An acrimonious dispute broke out at Ipetsut between the two classes of priest—the "god's servants" and the "pure ones"—over access to the temple revenues. The god's servants, as the senior of the two cadres, jealously guarded their special access to the inner sanctum, the holy of holies, which was barred to ordinary mortals. This privilege brought with it access to the offerings of food, drink, and other commodities that were placed before the cult statue of Amun during the daily temple office. Once the god had "finished" with them, these offerings were routinely gathered up and redistributed to the god's servants, a nice little bonus. By contrast, pure ones were not allowed into the sanctuary; instead they were employed to carry out ancillary tasks in the outer parts of the temple. One such task involved carrying the barque shrine of Amun when it left the sanctuary to take part in processions, both within the temple enclosure and beyond the walls, through the streets of Thebes. In former times, this portering role would have gone unremarked. But now, with divine oracles taking center stage in the affairs of state, the subtle movements of Amun's barque shrine, as it was borne through the city, were imbued with enormous significance. A sudden lunge, a fleeting tilt—these could be interpreted as indications of god's will, with repercussions for the priesthood, the Theban realm, and the whole of Egypt. The lowly porters recognized that the destiny of the entire nation rested, quite literally, on their shoulders, and they were not slow in turning this influence to their economic advantage. Their demand for a larger slice of the cake brought them into direct conflict with the god's servants. A new political reality had intruded upon ancient privileges.

So great was the material wealth of the Amun priesthood, especially in Thebes, that the Libyan ruling class used every means at their disposal to secure lucrative temple posts. Wives and daughters played a particularly prominent role, helping to secure their clan's economic and political power by putting themselves forward for prestigious positions in the priestly hierarchy. Within a few generations, the office of "god's wife of Amun" came to eclipse even the high priesthood itself.

Although the post-Ramesside rulers of Thebes styled themselves high priests of Amun and claimed to take their orders from the supreme deity, the real basis for their political authority was naked force. The power of the army, not divine sanction, underpinned their regime. Herihor and his successors were experienced enough tacticians to realize that coercive power was the most effective tool of government. So, right from the start, they set about reinforcing their military dictatorship with the architecture of oppression, a string of fortified installations throughout Upper Egypt. The initial links in this chain were five forts in the northern stretch of the Nile Valley—forts that, ironically, had been built by the Ramesside pharaohs to keep the Libyans out of Egypt. By the end of Ramesses XI's reign, these forts had fallen into Libyan hands, to be used as a springboard for the takeover of the whole country. They enabled Egypt's new strongmen to monitor Nile traffic and crush any local insurrections quickly and ruthlessly. Little wonder that the rule of the generals was established with little resistance before the last Ramesses was even cold in his grave.

Chief among the northern forts was Tawedjay (modern el-Hiba), which commanded the east bank of the Nile just south of the entrance to the Fayum. This marked the northern border of the Theban realm and was the principal residence of the army commanders–cum–high priests. It is telling that, from Paiankh onward, the generals who ruled Thebes visited the great city only on high days and holidays, preferring the security of their northern bunker to their city palace surrounded by native settlements. Perhaps they realized just how unpopular their rule was with the traditionally minded population of the south.

The simmering tensions in Upper Egypt exploded early on, at a moment of weakness for the military regime. When Pinedjem I elevated himself to the kingship, he appointed his eldest son, Masaharta, to succeed him as high priest of Amun. For someone with such an overtly Libyan name to stand at the head of the Amun priesthood must have been an affront to many Egyptians, but they had no choice. However, when Masaharta died suddenly in office in 1044, the Theban populace saw its chance and erupted in revolt. Masaharta's successor, his younger brother Djedkhonsuiuefankh, was forced from office after the briefest of tenures. (To the skeptically minded, his rapid fall from grace would have proved the unreliability of divine oracles. Despite bearing a name that meant "Khonsu said he will live," Djedkhonsuiuefankh had his fate sealed by rather more human forces.)

For a moment, it looked as if Upper Egypt might reassert its independence, but the army commanders were not going to give up without a fight. From the safety of Tawedjay, Pinedjem immediately proclaimed his third son, Menkheperra, high priest and sent him southward "in bravery and strength to pacify the land and subdue its foe."[5] With the full backing of the army, Menkheperra quelled the uprising and reasserted his family's authority over Thebes. The ringleaders of the rebellion were rounded up and banished to the Western Desert oases, their death sentences commuted to internal exile, perhaps to avoid stoking further resentment among the local population. Only after an interval of some years, with the flames of resistance well and truly smothered, were the exiles allowed back. However, Menkheperra retained the right to execute any future plotters who threatened his own life.

To drive the message home, he ordered a new series of fortresses to be built much closer to Thebes, at strategic locations on the east and west banks. Like the Norman castles of England, the Libyan strongholds dominated the Nile Valley, a daily reminder to the natives that they were now a subject people in their own land. Throughout the length and breadth of the country, civilian settlements, too, were fortified. The Egyptians were surrounding themselves with high walls to shut out an increasingly frightening and unfamiliar world.

A REPUTATION IN RUINS

IN THE DYING DAYS OF RAMESSES XI's REIGN, THE GENERAL PAIANKH had posed in one of his letters home a heavily loaded rhetorical question: "Of whom is Pharaoh still the superior?"[6] Its answer lay in its very asking. At that very moment, royal power was ebbing away fast, and the age-old pattern of pharaonic government was about to be radically rewritten. The formal division of Egypt between a line of kings at Djanet and their close relatives (the army commanders and high priests of Amun at Thebes) only served to tarnish still further the reputation of the Egyptian monarchy.

Furthermore, Paiankh's protracted war against the viceroy of Kush, Panehsy, signally failed to reestablish Egyptian control of Nubia. With access to the all-important gold mines and the sub-Saharan trade routes lost, Egypt's economy faltered. The loss of the Near Eastern colonies dealt pharaonic prestige another severe blow, reducing the state's revenues from Mediterranean commerce. Even if Herihor and Nesbanebdjedet had been able to mobilize the nation's manpower and resources as in former times, the state's much-reduced coffers would simply not have supported ambitious building projects. It was all the northern kings could do to demolish the monuments of Per-Ramesses and use the secondhand stone to construct their ceremonial capital. Most of them did not even bother to record their achievements at Thebes, as all their New Kingdom predecessors had done.

Herihor's military regime could have tried to win back some international prestige by going on campaign, in traditional pharaonic fashion. But Nubia was too distant and dangerous, and the Near East was separated from Thebes by the northern kingdom. More to the point, the army authorities and garrisons were preoccupied with internal security, which left them little opportunity or appetite for foreign adventures.

Nothing better illustrates the precipitous decline of Egypt's international reputation than the *Report of Wenamun*, a text written in the early years of Herihor's rule. Whether fact or fiction, it takes Egypt's sharply reduced status on the world stage as a leitmotif, at times seeming to revel in the country's embarrassment at the hands of its erstwhile vassals. According to the *Report*, Wenamun, an elder of the portal of Ipet-sut, was sent by Herihor in 1065 to Kebny to bring back a consignment of cedar for the barque shrine of Amun-Ra. The hills of Lebanon had been Egypt's principal source of cedar for two millennia, and a state-sponsored expedition to Kebny was nothing unusual. After stopping off at Djanet to pay his respects to King Nesbanebdjedet and his queen, Tentamun, Wenamun eventually set sail for Kebny, hugging the coastline as countless expeditions had done over the centuries. But no sooner had he dropped anchor in the harbor of Dor, a port in southern Palestine, than he was robbed by his own crew. Wenamun's pleas to the ruler of Dor for compensation fell on deaf ears, and the hapless envoy spent nine days marooned in the harbor before setting sail again. Arriving at Tyre, Wenamun resorted to theft himself, stealing from a ship belonging to the local Tjeker inhabitants (the very same Tjeker who, with the other Sea Peoples, had invaded Egypt a century earlier, in the reign of Ramesses III). After fleeing at dawn to avoid detection and reprisals, Wenamun eventually arrived at his destination, Kebny—only to be refused entry to the harbor by the local ruler. In the changed circumstances of the eleventh century, an Egyptian envoy without documents or gifts could be shown the door just like any other unwelcome visitor. It was a severe embarrassment, both for Wenamun and for his masters back home. He had to wait nearly a month for payment to be sent from Egypt, all the while enduring the taunts of the ruler of Kebny. Eventually, Wenamun received the consignment of timber, narrowly escaped arrest for theft (the Tjeker having caught up with him), and fled once again, this time to Cyprus, where the locals welcomed him by threatening to kill him. At that point, the *Report* breaks off, but the tenor is clear.

In the far-off days of the Twelfth Dynasty, another great literary classic, *The Tale of Sinuhe*, had also taken as its theme an Egyptian abroad. The contrast between Sinuhe's fate and Wenamun's could not be greater. While the former had radiated Egyptian power to his Palestinian hosts, the tables were now well and truly turned. How the mighty had fallen.

A final humiliation awaited Egypt in its dealings with its former imperial possessions in the Near East. If a fragmentary relief of King Siamun (970–950) from Djanet can be taken at face value, this Libyan ruler launched a raid against southern Palestine, perhaps capturing the important town of Gezer. But rather than annexing it to Egypt or giving its treasures to the temple of Amun, as any self-respecting pharaoh would have done in former times, Siamun seems to have used the booty to buy the favors of the local superpower. According to the biblical First Book of Kings, the spoils of Gezer were handed over, together with the pharaoh's own daughter, to Solomon of Israel.[7]

In the prosecution of New Kingdom diplomacy, the pharaoh had frequently taken other kings' daughters in marriage to cement strategic alliances, but he would never have agreed to an *Egyptian* princess being used in this way. Now, in the tenth century, Egypt had to face the uncomfortable truth—a house divided, it was no longer a force to be reckoned with, merely another bit player in the febrile world of Near Eastern power politics. Egypt's star had waned, its reputation was in tatters, and there seemed little prospect of a return to the might and majesty of the New Kingdom.

Yet, at least one Libyan ruler had other ideas.

CHAPTER 20

A TARNISHED THRONE

JERUSALEM THE GOLDEN

THE SEPARATION OF THE TWO LANDS INTO THEIR CONSTITUENT PARTS might have been the new political reality, but it was anathema to traditional Egyptian ideology, which emphasized the unifying role of the king and cast division as the triumph of chaos. As the Hyksos had shown five centuries earlier, the sheer weight and antiquity of pharaonic beliefs had a tendency to win in the end. And, as the Libyan elite became more entrenched, more secure in its exercise of power, a curious thing happened. In certain important aspects, it started to go native.

It was at Thebes, heartland of pharaonic orthodoxy, that the first signs of a return to the old ways manifested themselves. After the "reign" of Pinedjem I (1063–1033), subsequent high priests eschewed royal titles, dating their monuments instead to the reigns of the kings at Djanet. Not that men such as Menkheperra, Nesbanebdjedet II, and Pinedjem II were any less authoritarian or ruthless than their predecessors, but they *were* willing to recognize the supreme authority of a single monarch. This was an important, if subtle, change in the prevailing philosophy. It reopened the possibility of political reunification at some point in the future.

That moment came in the middle of the tenth century. Near the close of the reign of Pasebakhaenniut II (960–950), control of Thebes had been delegated to a charismatic and ambitious Libyan chieftain from Bast, a man named Shoshenq. As "great chief of chiefs," he seems to have been the most forceful personality in court circles. Moreover, by marrying his son to Pasebakhaenniut's eldest daughter, Shoshenq reinforced his connections with the royal family. His calculations paid off. After Pasebakhaenniut's death, Shoshenq was ideally placed to take the throne. The chieftain's accession marked not just the beginning of a new dynasty (reckoned as the Twenty-second), but the start of a new era.

From the outset, Shoshenq I (945–925) moved to centralize power, reestablish the king's political authority, and return Egypt to a traditional (New Kingdom) form of government. In a break with recent practice, oracles were no longer used as a regular instrument of government policy. The king's word had always been the law, and Shoshenq felt perfectly able to make up his own mind without Amun's help. Only in far-off Nubia, in the great temple of Amun-Ra at Napata, did the institution of the divine oracle survive in its fullest form (with long-term consequences for the history of the Nile Valley).

Despite his overtly Libyan name and background, Shoshenq I was still the unchallenged ruler of all Egypt. Moreover, he had a practical method of imposing his will over the traditionally minded south, and reining in the recent tendency toward Theban independence. By appointing his own son as high priest of Amun and army commander, he ensured Upper Egypt's absolute loyalty. Other members of the royal family and supporters of the dynasty were similarly appointed to important posts throughout the country, and local bigwigs were encouraged to marry into the royal house to cement their loyalty. When the third prophet of Amun married Shoshenq's daughter, the king knew he had the Theban priesthood well and truly in his pocket. It was just like the old days.

To demonstrate his newfound supremacy, Shoshenq consulted the archives and turned his attention to the activities traditionally expected of an Egyptian king. He ordered quarries to be reopened and sat down with his architects to plan ambitious building projects. While ordering further removals of New Kingdom pharaohs from their tombs in the Valley of the Kings, he nonetheless took pains to portray himself as a pious ruler and actively sought opportunities to make benefactions to Egypt's great temples. For the first time in more than a century, fine reliefs were carved on temple walls to record the monarch's achievements—even if the monarch in question was unashamed of his Libyan ancestry. But for all the piety and propaganda, the art and architecture, Shoshenq knew that there was still one element missing. In days of yore, no pharaoh worthy of the title would have sat idly by as Egypt's power and influence declined on the world stage. All the great rulers of the New Kingdom had been warrior kings, ready at a moment's notice to defend Egypt's interests and extend its borders. It was time for such action again. Time to reawaken the country's long-dormant imperialist foreign policy. Time to show the rest of the Near East that Egypt was still in the game.

A border incident in 925 provided the perfect excuse. With a mighty army of Libyan warriors, supplemented—in time-honored fashion—by Nubian mercenaries, Shoshenq marched out from his delta capital to reassert Egyptian authority. According to the biblical sources,[1] there was murky power politics at play, too, with Egypt stirring up trouble among the Near Eastern powers and acquiescing in, if not actively encouraging, the breakup of Solomon's once mighty kingdom of Israel into two mutually hostile territories. Whatever the precise context, after crushing the Semitic tribesmen who had infiltrated Egypt in the area of the Bitter Lakes, Shoshenq's forces headed straight for Gaza, the traditional staging post for campaigns against the wider Near East. Having captured the city, the king divided his army into four divisions (with distant echoes of Ramesses II's four divisions at Kadesh). He sent one strike force southeast into the Negev Desert to seize the strategically important fortress of Sharuhen. Another column headed due east toward the settlements of Beersheba and Arad, while a third contingent swept northeast toward Hebron and the fortified hill towns of Judah. The main army, led by the king himself, continued north along the coast road before turning inland to attack Judah from the north.

According to the biblical chroniclers, Shoshenq "took the fortified cities of Judah and came as far as Jerusalem."[2] Curiously, the Judaean capital is conspicuously absent from the roll call of conquests that Shoshenq had carved on the walls of Ipetsut to commemorate his campaign, but it is possible that he accepted its protection money without storming the walls. The city's lament—that "he took away the treasures of the house of the Lord and the treasures of the king's house; he took away everything"[3]—may indeed be a true reflection of events.

With Judah thoroughly subjugated, the Egyptian army continued its devastating progress through the Near East. Next in its sights was the rump kingdom of Israel, with its new capital at Shechem—the site of a famous victory by Senusret III nearly a millennium earlier. Other localities, too, echoed down the centuries as the Egyptians took Beth-

Shan (one of Ramesses II's strategic bases), Taanach, and finally Megiddo, scene of Thutmose III's great victory of 1458. Determined to secure his place in history and prove himself the equal of the great Eighteenth Dynasty warrior pharaohs, Shoshenq ordered a commemorative inscription to be erected inside the fortress of Megiddo. Having thus secured an overwhelming victory, he led his army southward again, via Aruna and Yehem to Gaza, the border crossing at Raphia (modern Rafah), the Ways of Horus, and home. Once safely back in Egypt, Shoshenq fulfilled the expectations of tradition by commissioning a mighty new extension to the temple at Ipetsut, its monumental gateway decorated with scenes of his military triumph. The king is shown smiting his Asiatic enemies while the supreme god Amun and the personification of victorious Thebes look on approvingly.

Yet if all this sword-wielding and flag-waving was supposed to usher in a new era of pharaonic power, Egypt was to be sorely disappointed. Before the work at Ipetsut could be completed, Shoshenq I died suddenly. Without its royal patron, the project was abandoned and the workmen's chisels fell silent. Worse, Shoshenq's successors displayed a lamentable poverty of aspiration. They reverted all too easily to the previous model of laissez-faire government and were content with limited political and geographical horizons. Egypt's temporary renaissance on the world stage had been a false dawn. The country's renewed authority in the Near East withered away just as quickly as it had been established. And, far from being overawed by Shoshenq I's brief display of royal authority, Thebes became increasingly frustrated at rule from the delta.

The specter of disunity stalked the city's streets once more.

TROUBLE AND STRIFE

SHOSHENQ I'S POLICY OF PUTTING HIS OWN SON IN CONTROL OF Thebes had succeeded in its objective of bringing the south under the control of the central government. This achievement, as much as Shoshenq's drive and determination, had made his Palestinian campaign possible. It gave the king the ability to levy troops and supplies from the whole of Egypt, and to recruit mercenaries from Nubia. But the ethnic tensions between the largely Egyptian population of Upper

Egypt and the country's Libyan rulers were never far below the surface, and the capital city of Djanet was a world away from Thebes, both culturally and geographically. It was only a matter of time before southern resentment boiled over.

The king who tempted fate too far was Shoshenq I's great-grandson, Osorkon II (874–835). During his long reign, he lavished attention on his ancestral home, Bast, especially its principal temple dedicated to the cat goddess Bastet. Most impressive of all his commissions was a festival hall to celebrate his first thirty years on the throne. The hall stood at the temple entrance and was decorated with scenes of the jubilee ceremonies, many of them harking back to the dawn of Egyptian history. In conception, it was every inch a traditional pharaonic monument. In execution, too, it stood comparison with the grand edifices of the New Kingdom. But its location—the remote central delta, not the religious capital of Thebes—betrayed its patron's provincial origins. Osorkon II further underlined his loyalty to his home city by building a new temple in Bast, dedicated to Bastet's son, the lion-headed god Mahes. Yet, far from lionizing their sovereign for such pious works, the Thebans looked on in disgust.

Eventually, Upper Egyptian frustration reached the breaking point. The inhabitants of Thebes desperately wanted self-rule and looked for a figurehead to lead the charge. The spotlight, not unnaturally, fell upon the high priest of Amun, Horsiese. The fact that he was Osorkon II's second cousin mattered less than the symbolic potency of his office. As head of the Amun priesthood, Horsiese represented the economic and political strength of Ipetsut and of Upper Egypt in general. So, in the middle of Osorkon II's reign, Horsiese bowed to local opinion and duly proclaimed himself king in Thebes. Two centuries earlier, other high priests had similarly claimed kingly titles and ruled the south as a counterdynasty, separate from the main royal line in the delta but connected to it by family ties. Horsiese and his backers had obviously studied their history.

The declaration of independence by Thebes marked the end of Shoshenq I's united realm, the end of his superpower dream, and a return to the fractured state of the post-Ramesside era. But the current sovereign, Osorkon II, seemed not to mind. For him, the devolution of power to the provinces was an honorable tradition, one that could be safely accommodated within the tribal system of alliances that was his inheritance from his nomadic forebears. He could tolerate breakaway rulers, as long as they were relatives. Keeping it in the family was the Libyan way.

In fact, Horsiese's independent reign was a short-lived affair. Relations with the delta continued much as before, and any notion of real Theban independence was illusory. But the Amun priesthood, having savored the sweet taste of self-determination, had no appetite for a return to centralized control. The principle of southern autonomy had been reestablished, apparently with the tacit approval of the main royal line. The genie was out of the bottle. Henceforth, temple and crown would go their separate ways, with profound consequences for Egyptian civilization.

In 838, the new high priest of Amun, Osorkon II's own grandson Takelot, picked up where his predecessor had left off, proclaiming himself king (as Takelot II) and establishing a formal counterdynasty at Thebes. Osorkon died just three years later, reconciled, it seems, to the explicit division of his realm and the diminution of his royal status. On his grave goods, he had himself shown undergoing the Weighing of the Heart, to decide if he was good enough to win resurrection with Osiris in the underworld. In the past, kings had enjoyed (or presumed) an automatic passport to the afterlife; only mortals had had to face the last judgment. Osorkon was not so sure on which side of the line he stood. In a gesture of farewell, the dead king's faithful army commander carved a lament at the entrance to the royal tomb, but it was a threnody for a fellow traveler, not an elegy for a divine monarch. Within six years of Osorkon II's death, even sporadic recognition of the northern dynasty ceased at Thebes, all monuments and official documents being dated to the years of Takelot II's independent reign (838–812). The whole of Upper Egypt, from the fortress of Tawedjay to the first cataract, recognized the Theban king as its monarch. The future of the south now belonged to Takelot and his heirs.

But not everyone in Thebes rejoiced at this turn of events. Takelot and his family had their detractors, and their effective monopoly of the Amun priesthood's great wealth caused serious resentment, not least among jealous relatives who harbored ambitions of their own. If the Libyan feudal system allowed for regional autonomy, it also encouraged vicious squabbles between different branches of the extended royal clan. Just a decade into Takelot II's rule, one of his distant relations, a man by the name of Padibastet (perhaps a son of Horsiese's), decided to chance his arm. In 827, with tacit support from the northern king, he proclaimed himself ruler of Thebes, in direct opposition to Takelot. There were now two rivals for the southern crown. For a dyed-in-the-wool Libyan such as Takelot, there was only one solution to the crisis—military action. From the safety of his fortified headquarters at Tawedjay—which was named, with characteristic lack of understatement, the "crag of Amun, great of roaring"—he dispatched his son and heir, Prince Osorkon, to sail south to Thebes with an armed escort to oust the pretender and reclaim his birthright.

Force won the day, and "what had been destroyed in every city in Upper Egypt was reestablished. Suppressed were the enemies . . . of this land, which had fallen into turmoil."[4] On reaching Thebes, Prince Osorkon took part in a religious procession to confirm his pious credentials before receiving homage from the entire priesthood of Amun and every district governor. Nervously, they all made a public declaration, swearing that the prince was "the valiant protector of all the gods," chosen by Amun "amongst hundreds of thousands in order to carry out what his heart desires."[5] And well they might, knowing as they did the alternative. Once back in control, Prince Osorkon showed the rebels (some of whom were his own officials) no mercy. In his victory inscription, he callously describes how they were bound in fetters, paraded before him, then carried off "like goats the night of the feast of the Evening Sacrifice."[6] As a brutal warning to others, "Every one was burned with fire in the place of the crime."[7]

With his enemies literally reduced to ashes, Prince Osorkon set about putting Theban affairs in order. He confirmed the temple revenues, heard petitions, presided at the inauguration of minor officials, and issued a flurry of new decrees. And all this administrative activity came with an admonition:

As for the one who will upset this command which I have issued, he shall be subject to the ferocity of Amun-Ra, the flame of Mut shall overcome him when she rages, and his son shall not succeed him.[8]

To this he added, modestly, "whereas my name will stand firm and endure throughout the length of eternity."[9] The stones of Ipetsut must have echoed back their approbation: after all the vicissitudes of recent history, here was a prince in the old mold.

The following year, Prince Osorkon visited Thebes on no fewer than three occasions, to take part in major festivals and present offerings to the gods. He had evidently calculated that more frequent public appearances might win over the doubters and prevent further trouble. He was sorely mistaken. Far from cowing the dissenters, his harsh treatment of the rebels had merely stoked further resentment and hatred among the priesthood. A second, full-scale rebellion broke out in 823, once again with Padibastet as its figurehead. The "great convulsion" precipitated outright civil strife, with families and colleagues divided between the two factions. This time around, Padibastet was the winner, thanks to support from senior Theban officials. He moved quickly to consolidate his position, appointing his own men to important offices. Thebes was lost to Prince Osorkon and his father, Takelot II. They retreated to their northern stronghold to lick their wounds and bemoan their fate. "Years elapsed in which one preyed upon his fellow unimpeded."[10]

But if recent events had shown anything, it was that Theban priests were fickle friends. Another decade later, and Prince Osorkon was back in Thebes, restored as high priest of Amun to the groveling acclamation of his followers: "We shall be happy on account of you, you having no enemies, they being non-existent."[11] It was, of course, all hot air. Padibastet had not gone away, and the death soon afterward of Prince Osorkon's father, Takelot II, merely strengthened the rival faction. A third rebellion in 810 saw Padibastet seize control of Thebes once more, but by 806, Prince Osorkon was back in town and presenting lavish offerings to the gods. A year later, Padibastet had the upper hand again. The prince's faction could not so easily bounce back from this latest setback, and Osorkon once again retreated to the "crag of Amun" to ponder his next move.

Finally, Padibastet's death in 802 shuffled the pack anew, and his successor showed none of the same determination. So, in 796, nearly a decade after his latest expulsion, Prince Osorkon sailed again for Thebes. This time, he took no chances. His brother, General Bakenptah, was commander of the fortress of Herakleopolis, and hence was able to call upon a significant military contingent. Together, the two brothers stormed the city of Amun and "overthrew everyone who had fought against them."[12]

After a power struggle lasting three decades, Prince Osorkon was finally able to claim the kingship of Thebes uncontested. For the next eighty years, under him and his successors, the destiny of Thebes and Upper Egypt did indeed lie with the descendants of Takelot II, just as the old king had hoped. The family's public devotion to Amun of Ipetsut had paid off. However, far to the south of Egypt, in distant upper Nubia, another family of rulers, even more devout in their adherence to the cult of Amun, had been watching the turmoil in Thebes with increasing alarm. In their minds, true believers would never stand for such discord in the supreme god's sacred city. And so they came to a stark conclusion: only one course of action would cleanse Egypt of its impiousness. It was time for a holy war.

THE BLACK CRUSADER

BACK IN THE HEYDAY OF THE EIGHTEENTH DYNASTY, THE CRUSHING victories of Thutmose I and III in Nubia had imposed Egyptian rule as far south as the fourth cataract and had smashed the kingdom of Kush. Smashed, but not obliterated. Time and again throughout history, the Nubian people had shown astonishing resilience, an uncanny ability to hunker down, bide their time, and reassert themselves when the Egyptians' backs were turned. Following the collapse of the New Kingdom, they had done just that, picking up where they had left off. Kush was reborn as the dominant power, and its rulers, once more masters in their own land, grew rich from trade with sub-Saharan Africa. By the middle of the ninth century (just as Thebes was breaking away from delta rule), they were building lavish tombs for themselves in native style, infinitely more impressive than the pathetic sepulchres of their Libyan contemporaries in Egypt.

The rulers of Kush considered themselves superior in another important respect, too. They earnestly believed themselves to be the true guardians of Egyptian kingship. This astonishing conviction was a legacy of New Kingdom imperialism. When Thutmose I had invaded

Kush, he had taken with him not just battalions of Egyptian soldiers but also the high priest of Amun. His objective had been not simply to subjugate "vile Kush" but also to convert its heathen inhabitants to the "true" religion. To the same end, Thutmose III had built a great temple to Amun at the foot of upper Nubia's holiest mountain, Gebel Barkal. The Egyptian propagandists had declared the mountain to be the southern home of Amun and a Nubian counterpart to Ipetsut. Moreover, they had pointed to a towering pinnacle of rock at one end of the mountain that closely resembled a rearing cobra (the protector of Egyptian kings) wearing the white crown of Upper Egypt. The presence of such powerful symbols of kingship allowed the Egyptians to claim that Gebel Barkal was the original birthplace of the Egyptian monarchy and, a crucial piece, that Nubia as far south as the holy mountain was merely an extension of Upper Egypt. Not for the first time, theology provided Egyptian rule with an irrefutable legitimacy. Little did the Egyptians imagine, however, that once they left Nubia, their own propaganda would come back to haunt them.

The cult of Amun and the belief that Gebel Barkal was the origin and source of pharaonic authority were so inculcated in the Nubian elite that these beliefs survived as tenets of faith long after the Egyptian withdrawal. In the tenth century, a Nubian queen could happily cast

Gebel Barkal, the holy mountain of Kush T. KENDALL

herself as a crusading monarch, battling to extend Amun's writ across heathen territories. The early Kushite rulers of the eighth century were similarly ardent devotees of Amun. Around 780, the Kushite chieftain Alara, who called himself a "son of Amun," restored and rebuilt the ruined temple of Amun at Gebel Barkal. His successor, Kashta "the Kushite," went one step further and proclaimed himself the rightful king of the Two Lands. Extending his area of authority as far north as Upper Egypt, he prepared to make his boast a reality.

The waning of Theban power under Prince Osorkon's hapless successors gave the Kushites the excuse and the spur they needed. In the reign of Osorkon's son, King Rudamun (754–735), the chieftain of Kush, Piankhi, pressed his claim to Upper Egypt. Faced with the legendary power of the Nubian military, the Thebans capitulated. Almost without a fight, Piankhi reunited the two Ipetsuts (Nubian and Egyptian) and restored the New Kingdom empire, but under Nubian rule. In a further delicious twist, Piankhi adopted the throne name of Thutmose III, identifying himself as the incarnation of the very pharaoh who had conquered Kush and established Gebel Barkal in the first place. In exchange for recognizing Kushite sovereignty, Rudamun and his heirs were allowed to retain their royal dignity, but they had to agree to retreat to their northern stronghold of Herakleopolis, there to rule over a much reduced territory. Thebes, meanwhile, was handed over to its Nubian conquerors.

Perhaps unexpectedly, Piankhi showed himself the pious and just ruler he claimed to be, graciously allowing Rudamun's relatives to maintain influential positions in the Theban hierarchy. Most prominent of these was Shepenwepet, Rudamun's own half sister. As god's wife of Amun, she was the most senior female member of the Amun clergy and equal to the high priest in the order of precedence. Indeed, it was through her that her father, Prince Osorkon, had continued to control the priesthood once he had elevated himself to the kingship. For Piankhi to leave her in place showed a remarkable degree of tolerance for the old order. Or perhaps it was just practical politics. Looking beyond Thebes, the Kushite ruler could see trouble brewing in the northern Nile Valley, and the last thing he needed was a rebellion in his new Egyptian heartland. Far better to maintain the balance of power for more challenging battles ahead.

They were not long in coming. In the seventy years since Prince Osorkon's final victory over Thebes, the Libyan pattern of collateral dynasties had run riot. Egypt was characterized by a degree of political fragmentation unprecedented in its long history. In Upper Egypt, besides Piankhi himself, there were two kings—at Herakleopolis (the last representative of the old Theban dynasty) and at Khmun. Both had negotiated some sort of compromise deal with Piankhi to retain their thrones, however tarnished. The situation in Lower Egypt was even more extreme. Confined to the family seat of Bast were the lineal descendants of the great Shoshenq I. Elsewhere in the delta, Taremu (modern Tell el-Muqdam) had its own king, Iuput II, while other towns were governed by a bewildering array of great chiefs of the Ma, hereditary princes, and mayors. Piankhi lumped them together, somewhat contemptuously, as "all the feather-wearing chiefs of Lower Egypt."[13] Moreover, he recognized the absurdity of so many different individuals calling themselves "dual king," referring to his rivals simply as "kings" and reserving the full, formal title for himself.

There was one petty ruler, however, who was more concerned with real authority than its outward display. Tefnakht, ruler of the western delta city of Sais, did not claim royal status. He did not need to. As "great chief of the west," he had already expanded his territory to include large parts of Lower Egypt, seizing control of nearby Per-Wadjet by 740 and adding the adjoining delta provinces to his growing realm over the following decade. He, not the jumped up "kings," was the real threat to Kushite control.

Late in 739, as Piankhi was sitting in his palace at Napata, in the shadow of Gebel Barkal, the storm broke. A messenger, ushered through columned halls, past the bodyguards in the waiting room, and finally into the royal audience chamber, brought the news the king had been fearing: "Tefnakht . . . has seized the whole of the west as far south as Itj-tawy."[14] Worse still, the Saite leader was heading south with a large army; towns and cities on both banks of the Nile were opening their gates to him; his forces were besieging Herakleopolis, the gateway to Thebes; and Egyptian officials were rushing to his side "like dogs at his heels."[15] Tefnakht looked unstoppable. To make matters worse, the Libyan ruler of Khmun, Nimlot, had torn up his treaty of friendship with the Kushites and thrown his lot in with the rebels. It was time for Piankhi to act, to protect Thebes and its holy sites from the heathen aggressors.

Pious and pugnacious in equal measure, his response was immediate and decisive. Kushite troops stationed inside Egypt were given the order to advance, engage the enemy, and encircle and capture them. Special ferocity was to be reserved for the traitor Nimlot. His home district was to be besieged and attacked daily. Then Piankhi mobilized the main army, based in Nubia, and sent them forth with a crusading zeal: "You know that Amun, the god, commands us!"[16] Theirs was a divine mission, and Piankhi gave them strict instructions on what do to on their march north. "When you reach the heart of Thebes, in front of Ipetsut, enter the water, purify yourselves in the river, and put on clean linen."[17] Only then they were to make offerings to Amun and kiss the ground in front of his temple, asking for his guidance: "Show us the way, that we may fight in the aura of your strength!"[18]

The Nubian troops did exactly as their sovereign had commanded, before continuing on their way north to engage the enemy. In a fierce naval battle south of Khmun, and on land near Herakleopolis, the Kushites carried the day. Word then reached Piankhi that Nimlot had eluded capture. Enraged, the Kushite ruler decided to go himself to Egypt, to take personal command of the operation, but only after he had celebrated the New Year festival, which he dedicated to his patron deity Amun. In the meantime, his forces threw a security cordon around the entire province of Khmun. Nimlot would not be allowed to escape a second time.

After stopping at Thebes to burnish his fundamentalist credentials, Piankhi arrived on the outskirts of Khmun early in 728. Like Ramesses II on the eve of Kadesh, he appeared in his royal chariot to encourage his troops before giving the order to attack. At his command, missiles rained down on the city, day after day, as the noose was drawn ever tighter. Eventually, "Khmun began to exude a foul odor."[19] It was the stench of death. A short while later, the city capitulated and its treasuries were emptied for Piankhi—even Nimlot's royal crown was offered up as a trophy. In a pathetic gesture of submission, the defeated leader's female relatives came to beg mercy from Piankhi's wives, daughters, and sisters—a plea for clemency, woman to woman. Nimlot's own act of obeisance was to appear before his nemesis with two well-chosen gifts: a sistrum made of gold and lapis lazuli, used in temple rituals to appease a deity, and a horse. Like every other Kushite ruler, Piankhi was a lover of all things equine. (He was so pleased with the gifts, and the gesture, that he had them immortalized in stone at the top of his victory monument, erected on his return home in the temple of Amun at Gebel Barkal.)

Piankhi's fondness for horses showed itself again in an extraordinary episode some hours later, when he went to inspect Nimlot's palace. Two rooms in particular caught his eye, the treasury and the stables. What followed speaks volumes about Piankhi's priorities:

> The king's [Nimlot's] wives and daughters came to him and paid honor to him as women do. But His Majesty did not pay them any attention. [Instead] he went off to the stables, where he saw that the horses were hungry. He said . . . "It is more painful to me that my horses should be hungry than every [other] ill deed you have done!"[20]

The Nubian pharaoh would not be the last monarch in history to prefer horses to people.

The next ruler to submit was the Kushites' erstwhile ally, King Peftjauawybast of Herakleopolis, confirming the total surrender of Upper Egypt. The conquest of Lower Egypt, by contrast, would be an altogether more difficult proposition. The first target in this next phase of the campaign was a group of rebels, including one of Tefnakht's own sons, who had holed themselves up in a fortress at the mouth of the Fayum. On reaching the town walls, Piankhi railed against them, calling them "the living dead"[21] and threatening them with annihilation if they did not surrender within one hour. His bellicose language evidently had the desired effect, and the rebels gave themselves up. Anxious to demonstrate his magnanimity, Piankhi ordered his forces not to kill any of the fort's inhabitants. All the same, its granaries, like those of Khmun, were added to the wealth of the temple of Amun at Ipetsut. It was payback time for Piankhi's divine patron.

Further capitulations followed, as the Kushite forces swept all before them. Next to lay down its arms was the Middle Kingdom capital of Itj-tawy, still an important town in the northernmost Nile Valley. And then, after weeks of campaigning, Piankhi reached the ultimate objective of his holy war, the capital city of Memphis itself. Once again, he urged its citizens not to bar their gates or fight, promising that, if they surrendered, he intended only to honor the local god Ptah and then "continue northward in peace."[22] He pointed to his exemplary record of clemency: "Look at the southern districts. Not a single person was killed there, except for enemies who blasphemed against god."[23] Memphis ignored his blandishments and closed its gates anyway. That night, under cover of darkness, the rebel leader Tefnakht paid a secret visit to the city, to steel its resolve. He knew only too well that without Memphis his cause was doomed. Leaving again before dawn, he slipped past the Kushite army before it realized what had happened. When news of the clandestine visit reached Piankhi, he flew into a rage. Ignoring his commanders' suggestions, he led the charge himself, throwing everything into the capture of the capital. Having won the day, he was as good as his word, taking the earliest opportunity to honor the city's chief god, Ptah. In Memphis, as in every other location he visited, Piankhi was at pains to portray himself as a righteous leader. His was no mere campaign of conquest, but a crusade to purify Egypt and restore its true religion.

Once the capital had fallen and all the citadels in the surrounding province had surrendered, a host of delta rulers came rushing to submit themselves. King Iuput II of Taremu, chief of the Ma Akanosh of Tjebnetjer (modern Samannud), and Prince Padiese of Hutheryib all made formal obeisance to Piankhi. When he visited Iunu to make sacrifices in the temple of Ra, King Osorkon IV of Bast (the lineal descendant of the great Shoshenq I) came "to gaze at His Majesty's splendor."[24] The last, enfeebled representative of the once mighty Libyan Dynasty needed to see for himself the phenomenon that had so forcefully reestablished the majesty of monarchy. Following his lead, the assembled rulers of Lower Egypt pledged their allegiance and a large portion of their wealth to their new suzerain: "Send us back to our towns to open our treasuries to choose according to your heart's desire, and to bring you the choice of our studs and the best of our horses."[25] They had clearly heard about the Nubian's penchant for thoroughbreds, and were desperate to curry favor. Piankhi did not demur.

When a final halfhearted revolt against Kushite rule was swiftly put down, Tefnakht, the leader and the last of the rebels, knew the game was up. He sent an embassy to Piankhi to negotiate terms, not for a surrender but for a cease-fire. Despite his protestations of subservience—"I cannot look at your face in these days of anger, nor stand before your flames!"[26]—Tefnakht knew that he was negotiating from a position of strength. The whole of the western delta was still in his hands, and his troops could keep the Kushites bogged down for months if he so desired. To underline his confidence, he refused to submit in person to Piankhi but cheekily asked for a Kushite delegation to visit *him* in his capital at Sais. It was hardly the outcome Piankhi had been planning for, but if a long, drawn-out war of attrition was to be avoided, it would have to serve. Thus, in the temple of Neith at Sais, and no doubt through gritted teeth, Tefnakht finally swore an oath of loyalty to Egypt's new, undoubted master. The following day, Piankhi witnessed a final, symbolic act of obeisance. The four reigning kings—Nimlot and Peftjauawybast from Upper Egypt and Osorkon IV and Iuput II from Lower Egypt—each wearing the royal uraeus, was ushered into his presence and, prostrating themselves, kissed the ground before him. While Egypt might have had five monarchs, only one was sovereign. The irony of the occasion was not lost on the assembled spectators. It had taken a Nubian to restore the dignity, if not the unity, of kingship.

Before setting sail for Thebes and home, his ships laden with the spoils of victory, Piankhi made one final gesture to underline his zealotry. Of the four kings assembled to pay him homage, all but Nimlot were barred from entering the royal enclosure, not because of their weakness or active opposition, but because they were uncircumcised and had eaten fish—serious affronts to Piankhi's strict interpretation of religious purity laws.

Under Kushite rule, military strength would go hand in hand with moral absolutism. Might and right would prove a dangerous combination.

CHAPTER 21

FORTUNE'S FICKLE WHEEL

UNFINISHED BUSINESS

HAVING COMPREHENSIVELY DEFEATED EVERY OPPONENT AND IMPOSED Kushite hegemony throughout Egypt, Piankhi could have gloried in his newfound status and enjoyed the considerable privileges of pharaonic kingship. However, as his love of horses had already demonstrated, he was a Nubian through and through, and there was no place like home. So, following his tour of conquest and victory in 728, he promptly headed south, stopping only at Thebes to install his daughter as eventual successor to the god's wife of Amun and thereby ensure the continuity of Kushite influence in the god's holy city. Having honored the cult of Amun, the Kushite king and his retinue continued on their way. Four days' sailing brought them to the Nubian border at Abu, and a month later they were back in the familiar surroundings of Napata, their capital city nestled beneath the looming bulk of Gebel Barkal. Safe and sound in his sprawling royal palace, Piankhi reigned another twelve years, years of plenty and prosperity for Kush. But he never set foot on Egyptian soil again.

His attitude toward Egypt reflected his primary concern in going to war in the first place. If the campaign had been politically motivated, he would surely have taken steps to consolidate Kushite power, appointing loyal local governors to carry out orders on his behalf. However, his overriding objective had been religious, to safeguard the holy places of Amun from alien (that is to say, Libyan) interference. In that, he had succeeded. What happened subsequently in terms of Egypt's internal politics was of little or no concern to him. It did not take the Libyan dynasts long to realize this.

As soon as Piankhi's back was turned, his wily Lower Egyptian rivals returned to their old ways. Osorkon IV of Bast carried on playing the rightful monarch, sending a lavish diplomatic gift to the ruler of Assyria when he unexpectedly turned up on Egypt's northeast frontier with a large army in tow. Elsewhere in the delta, Akanosh of Tjebnetjer recovered his injured pride by continuing to rule as before, while Piankhi's archfoe, Tefnakht, now called himself king. It was as if the Kushite conquest had never happened. Indeed, Tefnakht's refusal to submit to Piankhi in person had been a harbinger of things to come: the Kingdom of the West remained the principal player in the shifting politics of the delta, as Tefnakht sought to extend his influence over the whole of Lower Egypt. The Kushites should have learned the lesson the first time around.

Tefnakht died in 720 but his ambitions did not perish with him. His son and successor, Bakenrenef (720–715), was just as determined, just as hungry for power—and just as antagonistic toward Kushite claims on Egypt. To sum up his feelings, he commissioned an extraordinary goblet carved from pale blue faïence. An upper band of decoration showed Bakenrenef being presented with the sign of life by his patron goddess, Neith of Sais, and holding hands with the gods of kingship and wisdom, Horus and Thoth, under the protection of heavenly vultures grasping signs for "eternity." (Wishful thinking, perhaps, but a characteristic display of Saite self-confidence.) In a lower band, captive Kushites—their arms bound behind their backs or above their heads— alternated with monkeys stealing dates from palm trees. It was a cheap racial slur, and a piece of propaganda in the best pharaonic tradition.

The new king of Kush, Shabaqo (716–702), who had only just succeeded Piankhi on the throne, could hardly take such an insult lying down. Unlike his predecessor, Shabaqo resolved to finish the job and bring his adversary to book, once and for all. After launching a second Kushite invasion of Egypt, he did not stop until he had captured Bakenrenef and neutralized him as a focus of insurrection. According to later accounts, the victorious Shabaqo had his opponent burned alive as a sacrificial victim. Certainly, the Nubian showed no hesitation in imposing his rule forcibly throughout the country. At Memphis, he intervened in the burial of a sacred Apis bull, amending the date on the tomb entrance from "year six of Bakenrenef" to "year two of Shabaqo." Within a few months, the Kushite pharaoh was recognized across the eastern as well as the western delta, and he issued a commemorative scarab to celebrate his conquest. In characteristically bloodcurdling tones, it described how "he slew those who rebelled against him in Upper Egypt and Lower Egypt, and in every foreign land."[1]

With the north brought to heel, Shabaqo could turn his attention to the south of the country. Thebes and its hinterland had always been more pro-Kushite—or anti-Libyan. The two amounted to the same thing. But Shabaqo was in no mind to leave things to chance. Although the office of god's wife of Amun was safely in Kushite hands, with one royal relative already in the post (Kashta's daughter, Amenirdis I) and another (Piankhi's daughter, Shepenwepet II) lined up to succeed her, there were other influential positions in the Amun priesthood. Shabaqo decided he needed to control them, too, to be sure of Theban loyalty. As a first step, he installed his own son as high priest of Amun, having shorn the post of all political and military power. Then, favored retainers were appointed to other key posts. In subsequent years, a royal prince was made second prophet of Amun and a royal princess was married off to the mayor of Thebes to secure his allegiance. The Kushites had Thebes all wrapped up, or so it seemed.

Plus ça change, plus c'est la même chose. The Theban desire for self-determination was deep-seated, and the line of mayors of Thebes, while expressing undying devotion to their Nubian monarchs, in fact ran the city and its surrounding region as their personal fiefdom. They maneuvered their relatives into positions of influence in both the civil and religious administrations, and they grew fat on their wealth and status. A case in point was Harwa. Born into a family of priests during the reign of Piankhi, he rose to become head of Amenirdis I's household. After her death, he continued to serve her successor, Shepenwepet II. Rather fancying himself as a man of letters, he described himself on one of his statues as "a refuge for the wretched, a float for the drowning, a ladder for him who is in the abyss."[2] His tomb was equally immodest and was one of the largest nonroyal funerary monuments ever built in Egypt. Moreover, in the privacy of his final resting place, Harwa could give free rein to sentiments that might have cost him his life if expressed in public: one of his *shabti*s held the crook and flail, the most ancient regalia of kingship. Harwa evidently fancied himself as a latter-day king of Thebes, and few among his contemporaries would have disagreed.

The existence of a de facto dynasty ruling Upper Egypt under Shabaqo's overlordship simply reflected the uncomfortable reality of Kushite rule. In practice, it was virtually impossible for a single monarch and a single administration to control a realm stretching more than thirteen hundred miles by river, from the far reaches of Nubia beyond the fifth cataract to the shores of the Mediterranean. Although it must have stuck in Shabaqo's throat, he had little option but to leave the old political structures in place, even as he was loudly claiming to have overthrown them. In the delta, the local rulers bounced back from their latest humiliating surrender. Men openly styling themselves kings continued to reign in Bast and Djanet, the twin centers of Libyan power. Hereditary princes still held sway in Hutheryib, and other local dynasties resumed their rule over the prosperous towns of Djedu, Djedet, Tjebnetjer, and Per-Sopdu. Even in Sais, hotbed and heartland of anti-Kushite resistance, Bakenrenef's grisly end did not extinguish local ambition. A new strongman named Nekau emerged to fill the power vacuum and was soon adopting quasi-royal titles, too.

Behind the façade of a united monarchy, the political map of Egypt encountered by Piankhi in 728 persisted. History was not just repeating itself; time seemed to have stood still.

BACK TO THE FUTURE

IN ANOTHER IMPORTANT RESPECT, TOO, THE KUSHITE MONARCHY represented a return to the past. With piety to Amun a central tenet of their claim to legitimacy, Piankhi and his successors set out to champion other indigenous Egyptian traditions that had been neglected or overturned by the country's recent Libyan rulers. The Kushites saw it as their holy mission to restore Egypt's cultural purity, just as they had saved the cult of Amun from foreign contamination. With active royal encouragement, therefore, priests and artists looked to earlier periods for inspiration, reviving and reinventing models from the classic periods of pharaonic history. An obsession with the past soon influenced every sphere of cultural endeavor.

Shabaqo gave a lead by adopting the throne name of Pepi II, to recall the glories of the Pyramid Age. His successor went one better, dusting off the titulary last used by the Fifth Dynasty king Isesi more than sixteen centuries earlier. High-ranking officials followed suit, adopting long-obsolete and often meaningless titles, just for the sake of their antiquity. The written language was deliberately "purified," taking it back to the archaic form of the Old Kingdom, and scribes were trained to compose new texts in an antiquated idiom. A fine example was the Memphite Theology, a theological treatise on the role of the Memphite god Ptah. Commissioned by Shabaqo himself, the treatise was said to have been copied from an ancient worm-eaten papyrus, preserved in the temple archives for millennia. The authentically archaic language certainly fooled most scholars when the piece was first discovered. But, like much of the Kushite renaissance, the Memphite Theology was a product of the seventh century, cunningly designed to look like a relic of the past—an imagined past of cultural purity that existed only in the minds of the Kushite zealots.

The renewed prominence given to Ptah, alongside Amun, signaled the restoration of Memphis as the principal royal capital, a role it had fulfilled until the division of Egypt at the death of the last Ramesses. Not only was Memphis ideally situated to govern both delta and valley (the original reason for locating the capital at the "Balance of the Two Lands"), but the Kushite kings also had a particular fascination for the monarchs of the Old Kingdom whose monuments dotted the Memphite skyline. On his campaign north in 728, Piankhi had seen the pyramids, and they had clearly made a strong impression. Once back in Nubia, he commissioned one of his own, and in so doing changed forever the form of Nubian royal burials. To complement Piankhi's pyramid, his tomb included other elements of a traditional Egyptian interment, including New Kingdom–style *shabti* figurines and copies of the *Book of Coming Forth By Day* (known today as the *Book of the Dead*), with extracts of the Pyramid Texts included for good measure. But the Egyptianization was not all-embracing. Piankhi still found room in his burial for a team of horses.

This same Egypto-Kushite blend of features gave artists of the period a new and vibrant style in which to work, revitalizing the output of the royal workshops. In statuary, there was a deliberate return to Old Kingdom proportions, the rather squat and muscular treatment of the male body perfectly in tune with the Kushite rulers' self-image. The close-fitting cap crown favored by the Kushite kings also seems to have been chosen for its great antiquity. Yet certain features of royal portraiture were undeniably Nubian—African facial features, thick neck, large earrings, and ram's-head pendants. Splendid but schizophrenic, the royal statuary made for Shabaqo and his successors reflected the contradiction at the heart of Kushite rule. These kings from upper Nubia were determined to present themselves as more Egyptian than the Egyptians, respectful of the ancient traditions. But underneath, they were foreigners all the same, born and bred of a fundamentally different, African culture. It was not always a comfortable mix.

Kushite rule reached its uneasy zenith in the reign of Piankhi's son, Taharqo (690–664). He continued the eclectic archaizing of earlier reigns, copying Old Kingdom models for his Nubian pyramid, but, like his loyal servant Harwa, he based its underground chambers on the New Kingdom tomb of Osiris at Abdju. To recapture the glories of Egypt's past, he ordered extensive renovations and renewals of temples throughout the country, from Meroë, in the far south of Nubia, to Djanet, in the northeastern delta. Of all these projects, the one closest to his heart seems to have been the temple of Gempaaten (modern Kawa), located on the east bank of the Nile at the terminus of a great overland track leading from Napata. Begun by Amenhotep III and extended by Tutankhamun, Gempaaten recalled Egypt's golden age and thus represented the epitome of everything the Kushites wished to restore. As well as reendowing the temple, Taharqo brought the finest artists and craftsmen from Memphis to renovate and beautify it. Their familiarity with the great funerary monuments of the Old Kingdom strongly influenced their

Bronze statuette of a Kushite king
WERNER FORMAN ARCHIVE

work, and this was no doubt the king's intention. For example, a scene of Taharqo as a sphinx, trampling Libyan foes, was heavily based upon a similar scene in the pyramid temple of Pepi II, already sixteen hundred years old. This had itself been copied from the pyramid temple of Sahura, three hundred years older still. Recycling the past was an old tradition.

If Taharqo's intention was to honor Egypt's ancient gods and thus win divine favor for his kingdom and dynasty, his supplications seem to have been answered at an early stage. In the sixth year of his reign, when the king prayed for a good inundation, "the sky even rained in Nubia so that all the hills glistened"[3] and the floodwaters "rose fast, day by day."[4] At Ipetsut, the Nile reached an extraordinary height of twenty-one cubits (thirty-six feet). More miraculous still were the aftereffects of such a great flood: "It made all the fields good; it killed off the vermin and snakes; it warded off the depredations of locusts; and it prevented the south winds from stealing [the harvest]."[5] So impressed was Taharqo with these "four perfect wonders" that he commissioned a commemorative inscription to record them for posterity, with copies erected at Gempaaten and Djanet. To set the seal on the celebrations of this natural miracle, Taharqo's mother made the long journey from Napata to visit him in Egypt for the first time since his accession. For the king, it was a moment of high emotion: "I had left her as a youth of twenty years when I came with His Majesty [King Shabaqo] to Lower Egypt. And now she has come, sailing downstream, to see me after years!"[6] The deep bond between mother and son momentarily transcended the usual royal reserve.

Having inherited the martial instincts of his Kushite forebears, Taharqo lamented the diminution of Egypt's status on the world stage, in particular the fact that tribute from Syria-Palestine was no longer sent to the temple of Amun-Ra at Ipetsut. To right this wrong, what he needed above all was a well-trained and disciplined fighting force that could project Egypt's might beyond its borders as in days of old. The king and his army took great pains to achieve this objective, with long-distance running a favored method of building fitness. On one memorable occasion,

the king himself was on horseback to see his army running when he exercised with them on the desert behind Memphis in the ninth hour

of the night. They reached the great lake [Birket Qarun] at the hour
of sunrise and they returned to the Residence in the third hour of the
day.[7]

In this six-hour nighttime marathon, the recruits covered a distance of
nearly sixty miles, an impressive achievement by any standards. Such
levels of stamina soon paid off. A strike against Libya—the first such
campaign in four centuries—netted a good haul of booty for Ipetsut.
This was followed by a series of military expeditions against Palestine
and Lebanon, in which Taharqo succeeded in extending Egypt's sphere
of influence along the Mediterranean coast as far as Kebny. While not
comparing with the conquests of the great New Kingdom warrior
pharaohs, it was at least a start.

But a full-scale restoration of Egyptian imperial rule would prove an
impossible dream. Unfortunately for Taharqo, another great king in
the region had territorial ambitions of his own, ambitions that allowed
no place for a resurgent Egypt.

LIKE THE WOLF ON THE FOLD

FROM ITS HEARTLAND ON THE BANKS OF THE RIVER TIGRIS, THE KING-
dom of Assyria had first become aware of its Nilotic rival in the early
fifteenth century. Following Thutmose I's efforts to establish an Egyptian empire in the Near East, a wary friendship had developed between
the two powers, the Assyrians sending tribute to Thutmose III in the
wake of Megiddo and maintaining diplomatic, if strained, relations
with the court of Akhenaten. But in Assyria, as in Egypt, a series of
weak rulers had led to a serious decline. By 1000, it was once again reduced to its traditional heartland around the cities of Ashur and Nineveh. The ups and downs of the two great kingdoms mirrored each
other again in the tenth to eighth centuries so that, by 740, just as the
Kushites were beginning to consolidate their rule over the entire Nile
Valley, the Assyrian Empire was being rebuilt by its own determined
ruler (Tilgathpileser III). His tactics were ruthless and uncompromising. Conquered territories were administered directly by centrally appointed governors, who were themselves subject to spot checks by
royal inspectors. To undermine local loyalties and identities, nearly a

quarter of a million people were forcibly resettled across the empire in a concerted campaign of ethnic cleansing. By the time Shabaqo became king of Kush and Egypt, most of the Near East seemed to be smarting under the Assyrian yoke.

Faced with such an intimidating opponent, Shabaqo at first settled for a policy of cautious diplomacy. His first test came when one of the Assyrians' more rebellious vassals, the king of Ashdod, fled to Egypt seeking political asylum. Shabaqo promptly sent him back to face his persecutors. But this entente with the Assyrians did not last long. When the Assyrian ruler Sennacherib began a systematic consolidation of his western territories, Egypt decided that the covert encouragement of local insurgencies would serve its interests better, and began to stir discontent among the fractious rulers of the Near Eastern city-states. The policy backfired disastrously. Sennacherib invaded Palestine to suppress a revolt, whereupon one of the ringleaders, Hezekiah of Judah, turned to Egypt for military support. It was a request Shabaqo could scarcely refuse. He summoned his nephew Taharqo (still just a prince of twenty) north from Nubia to lead the campaign, and the two armies met at Eltekeh, ten miles from Ashdod, in 701. Taharqo's force was besieged, then heavily defeated. Withdrawing to a safe distance, he planned to attack the Assyrians from the rear once they had moved on to Jerusalem to demand Hezekiah's surrender. But Sennacherib was too seasoned a commander to fall for such a ploy. He promptly recalled his troops from the Judaean hills, faced down the Egyptian attack, and forced Taharqo to flee back to Egypt with the remnants of his defeated and dejected army. Kushite military prowess had finally met its match. Egypt was on notice.

The accession of Esarhaddon as king of Assyria in 680 spelled the beginning of the end for Kushite rule. Esarhaddon was every bit as ambitious and ruthless as his predecessor, and determined to incorporate the Nile Valley within his growing empire. He launched a first attack in 674. Taharqo, fresh from his military exercises, repulsed the invaders and won the day. But he knew the Assyrians would not give up so easily, and gave vent to his uneasiness by publicly bemoaning the gods for deserting him in his hour of need. He was right to worry. Three years later, a second invasion force, this time led by Esarhaddon himself, swept down through the Near East, bound for the delta. After wiping out the city of Tyre, Egypt's strongest ally in the region, the force pressed home its advantage and was soon at the gates of Memphis. Taharqo's only option was to flee before the advancing army—leaving his wife and family at the mercy of the Assyrians. After just half a day's fighting, the royal citadel was stormed and plundered for its treasures, which included hundreds of golden crowns "on which were set golden vipers and golden serpents," eight thousand talents of silver, and fifty thousand horses. The Assyrian king could not resist gloating over Taharqo's total humiliation: "His queen, the women of his palace, Ushanahuru [Nesuanhur] his heir, his other children, his possessions, horses, cattle and sheep beyond number, I carried off as booty to Assyria."[8] To rub salt into the wounds, Esarhaddon had an inscription carved to celebrate his victory; it showed the Kushite crown prince with a rope around his neck, kneeling pathetically at his new master's feet. Two more rock inscriptions were cut at key points on the journey home to Assyria, the one at Nahr el-Kelb, in Lebanon, right next to a victory inscription of Ramesses II's. The irony was not lost on either side.

Egypt itself was transformed by the Assyrian invasion. Towns in the delta were assigned Assyrian names, and Esarhaddon appointed "new local kings, governors, officers, harbour overseers, officials and administrative personnel."[9] These included the artful Nekau of Sais, who, within a year, had managed to have himself recognized as king by at least one neighboring delta princeling. Thus, when Taharqo returned to Memphis in 670, he faced rivals both inside and outside his shattered realm. A third Assyrian invasion in autumn 669 was only called off at the last minute because of Esarhaddon's untimely death en route to Egypt. For the hard-pressed Kushites, it was a breathing space, but no more.

Sure enough, the third invasion came just two years later, led by Assyria's latest and most ruthless king, Ashurbanipal. It was almost his first act as king and he had no thought of failure. Egypt was overwhelmed. Taharqo "heard in Memphis of the defeat of his army. . . . He became like a madman . . . and he left Memphis and fled, to save his life, into the town of Thebes."[10] There, he was kept busy putting down an opportunistic rebellion in the southern provinces. Meanwhile, Ashurbanipal imposed his formal overlordship on the whole country, demanding oaths of allegiance from the local rulers in the Nile Valley as well as the delta, and appointing Assyrian governors. Egypt was now a mere province of Assyria.

But the internal politics that had so undermined Kushite efforts to unify Egypt now offered them their only ray of hope. As soon as Ashurbanipal had left the country, many of the dynasts started to plot and scheme with Taharqo to recover Egyptian independence—on their own terms. They might have succeeded, had it not been for the efficiency of the Assyrians' internal security apparatus. Once Ashurbanipal's governors got wind of the plot,

> they arrested these kings and put their hands and feet in iron cuffs and fetters. . . . And they put to the sword the inhabitants, old and young, of the towns of Sais, Pindidi, Djanet and of all the other towns which had associated with them. They hung their corpses from stakes, flayed their skins and covered the town walls.[11]

Public executions were held throughout the delta as a grim warning, and the ringleaders of the insurgency were deported to the Assyrian capital, Nineveh, to be eliminated at Ashurbanipal's pleasure. The only leader to escape with his life was Nekau of Sais, who made a profuse display of loyalty and was duly sent back to Egypt to govern his former fiefdom. As a further sign of Ashurbanipal's trust, Nekau's son and heir, Psamtek, was given a new Assyrian name and appointed to rule the delta town of Hutheryib, whose former prince had been executed along with the other plotters. Not for the first time, the cunning rulers of Sais emerged unscathed from a political maelstrom—unscathed and emboldened. Just as Tefnakht had been the main challenger to Piankhi, and Bakenrenef to Shabaqo, a third and a fourth generation of Saites now squared up against their Kushite adversaries for the mastery of Egypt.

Taharqo died in 664, defeated and dejected. Against the odds, his successor Tanutamun (664–657) made one last stand, a final attempt to seize back the Nile Valley from its Assyrian oppressors. Claiming Amun as his protector, Tanutamun turned his military advance into a public display of piety, ordering the restoration of ruined temples, making divine offerings, and reinstalling priests ejected by the Assyrians. The message was clear: once again, a crusading zeal would deliver the country from the infidels. However, this time the opponent was not a motley collection of minor rulers but a well-resourced, well-equipped, and well-trained occupying force.

Marching on Memphis, Tanutamun gained his first major propaganda coup. "The children of rebellion came out. His Majesty made a great slaughter among them, their number unknown."[12] The arch-collaborator Nekau was captured and executed; his fellow delta rulers simply refused to fight, retreating into their walled towns "like rats into their holes."[13] So Tanutamun returned to Memphis, there to await his opponents' surrender. A few days later, the newly designated spokesman of the rebels, the mayor of Per-Sopdu, presented himself before the king to grovel for his life. As it happened, Tanutamun was in no mood for reprisals. Overcome by a rush of *realpolitik*, he instead released all his rivals to continue governing their respective cities. Hence, on returning home to Napata, he could claim to have restored Egypt's fortunes:

> Now the southerners fare downstream and the northerners upstream to the place where His Majesty is, carrying every good thing of Upper Egypt and every provision of Lower Egypt to please His Majesty.[14]

It was the last such boast any Kushite would make.

SWEET REVENGE

Tanutamun's Egyptian honeymoon was brief in the extreme. Within months, toward the end of 664, Ashurbanipal responded to the Kushite takeover and the execution of his loyal lieutenant Nekau by invading Egypt for a second time. Memphis fell easily, aided by the lingering anti-Kushite tendencies and self-serving duplicity of the delta vassals, but it was not the major goal on this occasion. Instead, Ashurbanipal had his sights set firmly on Thebes, the religious capital and long-term supporter of the Kushite cause. After forty days' march, the Assyrian army reached the gates of the great city. Tanutamun barely had time to flee before the fearsome Mesopotamians were swarming through the streets of Thebes, ransacking the temples, and carrying away fourteen centuries of accumulated treasure: "silver, gold, precious stones . . . linen garments with multicoloured trimmings . . . and two solid-cast electrum obelisks, standing at the door of the temple."[15] The sack of Thebes reverberated through the ancient world as a cultural calamity of epic proportions. Ashurbanipal summed it up succinctly, boasting, "I made Egypt and Nubia feel my weapons bitterly."[16]

The Kushites had been driven back to Kush, there to stay. All of Egypt, from Abu to the shores of the Mediterranean, now recognized the Assyrians as their overlords. But if Ashurbanipal thought this would usher in a long period of Assyrian control in the Nile Valley, he had reckoned without those arch-schemers and most accomplished of political survivors, the rulers of Sais. The western fringes of the delta, with its thin population and low agricultural productivity, had always been relatively unimportant to the Egyptian state, yet, as Tefnakht had shown in the 720s, they could provide a power base for wider ambitions. Now a fourth generation Saite, Nekau's son Psamtek, saw a chance to fulfill the family's destiny and unite not just the entire delta but the whole of Egypt under his rule. After being placed in charge of Hutheryib and Iunu by the Assyrians in 671, Psamtek had inherited control of Memphis and Sais from his father seven years later. These four key dominions gave him jurisdiction over a vast, contiguous swath of territory and made him the unquestioned leader among Assyria's delta vassals. Moreover, during his brief sojourn in Nineveh as Ashurbanipal's prisoner, Psamtek had learned the arts of diplomacy and ruthless ambition from an acknowledged master. He now put the lessons to good use.

Bitter experience—the most devastating being the execution of his father—had taught Psamtek that political resolve was nothing without military supremacy. While still theoretically an Assyrian vassal, he set about building up his own forces. Raising an army in Egypt, right under the noses of the Assyrians, was not an option, and the Egyptians' recent defeats showed how much they lagged behind in military tactics and equipment. Psamtek needed the very best, and he knew where to find it. Using his contacts with the wider Mediterranean world, he recruited Ionian and Carian mercenaries into his army, from the communities of the Aegean coast of Asia Minor, putting them in charge of garrisons at key points along the delta frontier. Alliances with the king of Lydia and the autocratic ruler of the Greek island of Samos enabled Psamtek to boost the size and strength of the Egyptian navy. The presence of Greeks in the upper echelons of the armed forces did not go down well with Egypt's traditional warrior class (of Libyan descent), but for the moment there was nothing they could do about it. Psamtek was a man on a mission.

The results spoke for themselves. Within months, two of the four Libyan chiefdoms that adjoined the kingdom of the west had submitted to Psamtek. The other two followed in short order, giving him most of the central and southern delta. Next to yield were Djedet and Per-Sopdu. Only the king of Djanet, the direct successor of the great Shoshenq I, held out against Saite hegemony, no doubt considering himself every bit as legitimate as his upstart rival from the backward western provinces. Yet by 656, even he had to recognize the inevitable. After eight years of sustained diplomatic and coercive pressure, Psamtek had emerged as the undisputed sovereign of Lower Egypt.

That still left Upper Egypt to be brought to heel.

Following the sack of Thebes, the departing Assyrian army had left the city's mayor, Montuemhat, in control of the south. A close relative of Harwa's and an equally dominant presence, Montuemhat had been a loyal servant of the Kushite Dynasty and was even married to a Kushite princess. In the heyday of Taharqo's reign, none of this had done his career any harm, but it had latterly become something of an embarrassment. However, Montuemhat was a master at bending with the political wind. To strengthen his already considerable local support, he devoted himself to restoring the depradations of the Assyrian army, repairing temples and carrying out extensive building works to return the city's monuments to their former glory. Not least among these was his own tomb, itself the size of an average temple. When it came to the final stages of its decoration, Montuemhat decided, diplomatically, to show his Kushite wife not as a Nubian princess but as the epitome of native Egyptian femininity—just in case his new political masters should suspect him of divided loyalties. It was through such maneuverings that he remained the effective ruler of Upper Egypt, from Khmun to Abu, under three different regimes, Kushite, Assyrian, and finally Saite.

In keeping with such masterful fence-sitting, official Theban documents continued to recognize the moribund Kushite Dynasty for the first eight years of Psamtek's rule. The daughters of the two greatest Nubian kings, Piankhi and Taharqo, still occupied two of the most senior positions in the city's religious hierarchy, god's wife of Amun and "divine adoratrix of Amun," respectively. In the face of such grandeur and tradition, a Libyan princeling from the western delta could hardly compete. Psamtek knew that effective mastery of the south depended upon control of the Amun priesthood. He had an answer to that, too.

On March 2, 656, a magnificent flotilla of ships set out from the quayside in Memphis, bound for Thebes. There were tenders, supply ships, and, at the center of the fleet, a royal barque, shimmering with gold leaf in the bright spring sunshine. In overall charge of the six-hundred-mile expedition was the prince of Herakleopolis and chief harbormaster of Egypt, Sematawytefnakht, Psamtek's relative by marriage and a close confidant. He had been given the responsibility for planning the journey and requisitioning supplies from all the provincial governors through whose domains the flotilla would sail. As with the Following of Horus at the dawn of Egyptian history, this program achieved the dual purpose of sparing the royal exchequer the burden of such a costly undertaking while giving Psamtek's local subordinates the opportunity to outdo one another in demonstrating their loyalty. Among the many exotic provisions under Sematawytefnakht's command, there was one particularly precious cargo: Psamtek's young daughter, Princess Nitiqret. For she was leaving the royal residence to follow a destiny mapped out for her by her father: she was about to be formally adopted as heiress to the god's wife of Amun.

After sixteen days' sailing, the flotilla arrived at its destination and moored at Thebes. Crowds of people lined the riverbank to see the princess come ashore. Before she had a chance to take in her strange new surroundings, she was whisked off by waiting officials to the great temple of Amun-Ra at Ipetsut, to be welcomed by the god's oracle. The formalities completed, Nitiqret was introduced to Shepenwepet II and Amenirdis II. How strange these two dark-skinned African women must have seemed to the delta princess! Yet they were about to become her legal guardians. Psamtek had taken a long-term view. Rather than forcibly ejecting the incumbent god's wife and her designated heir and risk alienating Thebes, he had negotiated the adoption of his own daughter as their eventual successor. This set the seal on his reunification of Egypt and guaranteed that a Saite would eventually succeed to the most important religious office in the south. It was a diplomatic masterstroke.

And an economic triumph. At the heart of the legal agreement, which was drawn up in writing to ensure there could be no backsliding by the Theban authorities, financial concerns loomed large. The contract assigned to Nitiqret (that is, to her father) all the property of the god's wife "in countryside and town." She would receive daily and monthly supplies from the most powerful Theban officials, obligations from which they could not shirk. Heading the list of donors was Montuemhat, who promised to provide bread, milk, cakes, and herbs every day, together with three oxen and five geese per month—all in all, a considerable commitment. Joining him as donors were his (Kushite) wife and eldest son; their loyalty to the new dynasty was thus affirmed. The historic Ipetsut gathering of 656 brought together representatives of all the principal powers in Egypt's recent past. Montuemhat was the last great figure of the old Theban hierarchy. Shepenwepet and Amenirdis, together with the high priest of Amun Harkhebi (Shabaqo's grandson), stood for the old Kushite Dynasty. Sematawytefnakht embodied the altered dispensation in the north; while the young girl at the center of it all, Princess Nitiqret, represented Egypt's new Saite masters. The ceremony was nothing less than a changing of the guard.

To reinforce his newfound authority in Upper Egypt, Psamtek dispatched one of his best generals to Thebes. His mission was to keep a lid on any potential dissent, establish a new garrison at Abu, and maintain a close eye on developments in Nubia. Diplomacy backed by force was the Saite way, and the new dynasty had no intention of allowing Tanutamun, his heirs, or his supporters to stir up renewed trouble in the south.

Yet the proud Kushites were not so easily tamed. After Tanutamun's death in 653, new generations of Nubian rulers looked northward again with greedy eyes. As they rebuilt their forces and perfected their strategy, they waited for the moment to recapture their lost northern kingdom. After a long and patient interval, an opportunity finally presented itself in 593. Psamtek's grandson and namesake, Psamtek II (595–589), had only recently ascended the Egyptian throne and seemed preoccupied with political developments in the Near East. The Kushites assembled their entire army in lower Nubia and prepared to strike. It was a profound miscalculation. Psamtek II differed from his grandfather in one crucial respect: he had neither the need nor the inclination to pander to Kushite pretensions. Upper Egypt had been firmly within the Saite sphere for half a century. Nitiqret had finally succeeded as god's wife, and all the other important posts in the Theban administration had been given to Lower Egyptian loyalists. The Nile Valley was properly unified under central control for the first time in nearly five hundred years. No Kushite army was going to change that.

Warned of the impending invasion, Psamtek II did not hesitate, sending his own expeditionary force southward to Nubia, and accompanying it himself as far as Abu. Ionian, Carian, and Judaean mercenaries led the charge, pausing only at the temple of Abu Simbel to carve their names on the legs of Ramesses II's colossi. On they pressed, razing the town of Pnubs (founded on the site of the ancient Kushite capital, Kerma) in an orgy of savagery worthy of the Eighteenth Dynasty. Walking among the Nubian dead, Psamtek's troops are said to have "waded in their blood as though in water."[17] The army did not stop until it had reached Napata, where it sacked and burned the royal palace and smashed the kings' statues in a symbolic act of vengeance against the Kushite Dynasty. Back home in Egypt, Psamtek II ordered the names of the Nubian pharaohs—Piankhi, Shabaqo, and their successors down to Tanutamun—to be erased from all monuments, even private statues. The aim, through might and magic, was to wipe the Kushites from the pages of Egyptian history. After 135 years of mutual hostility between the Saite and Kushite dynasties, with the Nubians having had the upper hand for more than half that time, revenge was sweet indeed.

A TANGLED WEB

IT WAS NOT IN THE ASSYRIANS' CHARACTER TO LET A HARD-WON province secede. Having launched two invasions to secure Egypt's dominion, Ashurbanipal must have been galled at the Saite expansion. Yet Psamtek I had broken free from Assyrian control with barely a twitch from Nineveh. The reason was a preoccupation closer to home. In southern Mesopotamia, right under the Assyrians' noses, their old rival Babylonia was in the ascendant once again. Within months of Ashurbanipal's death, a vigorous new king came to the throne in Babylonia and set about recapturing the lands lost to Assyria two generations earlier. Assyria decided to swallow its imperial pride and make common cause with its erstwhile vassal, Saite Egypt, in united opposition to this new threat.

At first, the policy was a spectacular success. Psamtek I came to Assyria's support in the Near East, campaigning against Babylonian expansion all the way to Carchemish, on the banks of the Euphrates—the first time an Egyptian army had gone that far since the days of Ramesses II. Babylonia seemed to have been stopped in its tracks. But the tide of history was running against an overstretched Assyrian Empire. Despite Egyptian assistance, Assyria was heavily defeated by the Babylonians in 609 and forcibly absorbed into Babylonia a year later. Now fighting in self-defense, an Egyptian army returned to Carchemish in 605 and launched a spirited attack against a Babylonian force, but was thoroughly routed. Egypt lost its remaining footholds in the Near East and saw its allies fall to Babylonia's sword. First Tyre, and then Jerusalem—one by one, the pharaoh's friends were swept aside by the sheer might of the Babylonian military machine. By 586, despite a number of brave rebellions, the independent states of Syria, Lebanon, and Palestine had been wiped from the map. Judah was enslaved and the Jews deported to Babylon, there to bewail their exile.

Egypt was now the front line. Psamtek II's son and successor, Wahibra (589–570), successfully repulsed an attempted Babylonian invasion in 582, but knew very well that he would need allies to safeguard Egyptian independence. Following his father's example, he looked to the Greek world, and appointed Ionian and Carian mercenaries to positions of prominence in the Egyptian army. They had served with distinction under Psamtek I and II, and might do so again in the cause of freedom. It was a necessary strategy, given the circumstances, but proved deeply unpopular with the native Egyptian military, who felt increasingly marginalized by the high-ranking foreigners in their midst.

For the generals, the last straw came in January 570 when a disastrous campaign in Libya led to a full-scale mutiny by the surviving Egyptian forces. Wahibra sent one of his most experienced commanders, Ahmose, to put down the revolt. But far from reimposing order, Ahmose promptly seized power and was proclaimed king by the rebels. Turning back toward Egypt, he and the renegade army marched on the dynastic seat of Sais, seized it, and forced Wahibra to retreat to his heavily fortified palace in Memphis. By August, the general had been recognized as pharaoh, a second Ahmose, throughout the western delta. In October, after a lengthy standoff during the hot summer months, Wahibra attempted to regain his throne by marching on Sais. Ahmose's army met him head-on and comprehensively defeated the loyalist forces. Wahibra escaped with his life and fled abroad . . . to the court of Babylon. The Babylonian king, Nebuchadrezzar, could scarcely believe his luck. Here was an unmissable opportunity to meddle in Egypt's internal affairs and put a Babylonian puppet on the throne of Horus.

Realizing the impending danger, Ahmose II (570–526) took immediate measures to guard against an invasion. He concluded an alliance with the Greeks of Cyrene, on the North African coast of Libya (founded by colonists in the seventh century), while removing a Greek garrison in the eastern delta thought to harbor sympathies for Wahibra. Pragmatism, not ideology, was the order of the day. In 567, a Babylonian force led by the deposed king attempted to invade Egypt by land and sea, but was roundly defeated. This time, there was no escape for Wahibra. He was captured and killed. Despite the ignominy of his final years, he was nonetheless buried with full royal honors by a victorious Ahmose. The new pharaoh had his finger firmly on the pulse of popular opinion and, although he was happy to be portrayed in satirical texts as "one of the boys" (no doubt to retain the support of the native military), he took pains in public to position himself as a pious and legitimate ruler.

If the army rebels who had put Ahmose II on the throne had been hoping for a reversal of Egypt's recent philhellenic tendencies, they were to be frustrated. As part of his staunchly anti-Babylonian foreign policy, Ahmose actively curried favor with the Greek city-states. In the aftermath of the Sea Peoples' ravages, Greece had been resettled during the ninth century and was now dominated by a series of independent cities that were actively extending their influence by establishing colonies around the Mediterranean and Black Sea coasts. Greek wealth depended above all on free trade, and the city-states were no fans of a Babylonian kingdom whose expansionary ambitions threatened their prosperity. Besides this political alliance, Egypt also had a military interest in the Greek world, for the Aegean mercenaries were famed and prized in equal measure throughout the Near East. The pharaoh made generous donations to Greek shrines (he paid handsomely toward the rebuilding of Delphi after it was gutted by fire) and even married a Greek princess. But his flagship initiative was directed at the Greek traders in Egypt. Ever since the reign of Psamtek I, settlers from the Ionian coast had made their home in the delta. Mercenaries had become entrepreneurs, and many had grown rich from the import-export business, bringing olive oil, wine, and, above all, silver from the Greek world and sending Egyptian grain back in return. It was far too lucrative a business for the Egyptian government not to take an interest, and Ahmose II wanted a share of the profits. Under the guise of granting the Greeks a free trade zone, he passed a law limiting their mercantile operations to the town of Naukratis—conveniently situated just ten miles from Ahmose's royal residence at Sais. This allowed him to regulate and profit from international trade, while posing as its enlightened sponsor.

With royal patronage and protected status, Naukratis swiftly became the busiest port in Egypt. It also developed into an extraordinary cosmopolitan city, where Cypriots and Phoenicians rubbed shoulders with Milesians, Samians, and Chians. Several Greek communities had their own temples—the Chians reverenced Aphrodite, while the Samians preferred Hera—and there was even an ecumenical "Hellenion," where the different communities could come together to worship "the gods of the Greeks." But alongside all this piety, there was also a seamier side to life. Naukratis developed a reputation throughout the Greek world for the attractiveness and looseness of its women. As Herodotus remarked, it was "a good place for beautiful prostitutes." One particularly notorious courtesan had her freedom bought by the brother of the poet Sappho; he no doubt had mixed motives for her emancipation.

By the middle of the sixth century, under Ahmose's wise and wily rule, Egypt was experiencing a minor renaissance. Prosperous and stable at home, respected and valued abroad, it could claim, once again, to be a leading power. In the space of a century it had seen off first the Assyrians, then the Babylonians, and had won its spurs as a key player in the tangled web of international relations. It was also a changed country, more multiethnic and multicultural than in the past. But the Nile Valley had always been a melting pot and a magnet for immigrants, and had successfully absorbed them all. In the end, pharaonic civilization had always emerged stronger, triumphant. For the gods had ordained it, and it would always be the case—or so the Egyptians naively believed.

CHAPTER 22

INVASION AND INTROSPECTION

BATTLING ON

THE RULERS OF THE WESTERN DELTA CITY OF SAIS WERE THE GREAT survivors of ancient Egyptian history. Over the course of two centuries, they plotted, schemed, and muscled their way into a position of dominance, not just in their Lower Egyptian homeland but throughout the Nile Valley. Starting with the prince of the west, Tefnakht, in 728, the canny Saites had refused to kowtow to a rival dynasty from Nubia and had remained a thorn in the side of the Kushites for seventy years. They had then used Assyrian protection to widen their power base in the delta, finally throwing off their vassal status and claiming the prize of a united monarchy. As the ruling dynasty of Egypt, they had proved equally astute, siding with the Assyrians to counter the mutual threat from Babylonia. Honoring the native gods while buying the support of Greek mercenaries, the house of Psamtek succeeded in maintaining Egypt's status and independence in an increasingly uncertain world.

But even the Saites were not invincible. Within a decade of repelling a Babylonian invasion, they found themselves facing an even more determined and implacable foe—an enemy that seemed to come out of nowhere.

In 559, a vigorous young man named Kurash (better known as Cyrus) acceded to the throne of an obscure, insignificant, and distant land called Persia, then a vassal of the powerful Median Empire. Cyrus, however, had ambitions and soon rebelled against his overlord, dethroning him and claiming Media for himself. The Egyptian pharaoh showed little interest in all of this. It was a quarrel in a faraway country between people of whom he knew nothing. Yet Egypt would come to rue its complacency. Within two decades of coming to power, Cyrus had conquered first the Anatolian kingdom of Lydia and then Babylonia, to become the undisputed ruler of an empire stretching from the shores of the Aegean to the mountains of the Hindu Kush. Suddenly, out of the blue, there was a frightening new superpower in the region with a seemingly relentless appetite for conquest.

All Ahmose II could do was hire more Greek mercenaries, build up his naval forces, and hope for the best. Cyrus's death in 530, while fighting the fierce Scythian nomads of Central Asia, seemed to offer a glimmer of hope. However, any thought of a reprieve was swiftly dashed by events in Egypt itself. King Ahmose, with his army background and strategic ability, had successfully held the line for four decades. So his demise in 526 and the accession of a new, untried, and untested pharaoh, Psamtek III (526–525), dealt the country a blow. The death of a monarch was always a time of vulnerability, but with an aggressor on the doorstep, it was nothing short of a disaster for Egypt.

The new great king of Persia, Cambyses, saw an opportunity and seized it. Within weeks of receiving the news of Ahmose's death, he was on the march and heading for the delta. In 525, his forces invaded Egypt, captured Memphis, executed Psamtek III, and forcibly incorporated the Two Lands into the growing Persian realm.

Cambyses lost no time in imposing Persian-style rule on his latest dominion. He abolished the office of god's wife of Amun, denying Ahmose's daughter her inheritance and pushing aside the incumbent god's wife of Amun, Ankhnesneferibra, who had been in office for a remarkable sixty years. There would be no more god's wives to act as a focus for native Egyptian sentiment in Upper Egypt. Not that every Egyptian official saw the Persian takeover as a calamity. Some found it only too easy to change allegiance when faced with the new reality. One such was the overseer of works Khnemibra. Coming from a long line of architects that stretched back 750 years to the reign of Ramesses II, Khnemibra—like his father, grandfather, and great-grandfather before him—bore an overtly loyalist name (in his case the throne name of Ahmose II), and he had served his pharaoh faithfully in the quarries of the Wadi Hammamat. But for all his professed loyalty to the Saite Dynasty, he showed no hesitation in accommodating himself to the Persian invasion. He not only survived the change of regime, he prospered, continuing to serve his new Persian masters and being rewarded for his trouble with a clutch of lucrative priestly offices. For many like Khnemibra, personal advancement trumped patriotism every time.

Others may have had slightly more altruistic reasons for collaborating with the Persians. For the Egyptian elite, nothing embodied their cherished culture and traditions better than their religion. Indeed, every prominent member of society took pains to demonstrate his piety to his town cult, and active patronage of the local temple was a prerequisite for winning respect in one's community. When faced with alien conquerors who worshipped strange gods, some Egyptians decided not to fight but to try to win the Persians over—to the Egyptian way of doing things.

A native of Sais, proudest of delta cities, managed to do just that. Wedjahorresnet had all the right credentials. His father had been a priest in the local temple, and Wedjahorresnet had grown up with a deep devotion to the goddess Neith. Like many a Saite before him, he had pursued a career in the military, rising to the position of admiral under Ahmose II. His naval activities must have included sea battles against the invading Persians. He described the invasion as a "great disaster . . . the like of which had never happened in this land [before]."[1] Yet within months of Cambyses's victory, Wedjahorresnet had ingratiated himself with his new master, winning trust as a senior courtier and being appointed as the king's chief physician, with intimate access to the royal presence. In public, Wedjahorresnet's conversion was as thorough as it was rapid, and he showed no trace of embarrassment in lauding the Persian invasion in glowing terms:

> The great leader of all foreign lands, Cambyses, came to Egypt, the foreigners of all foreign lands with him. When he had assumed rule over this land throughout its length, they settled there and he became great ruler of Egypt, the great ruler of all foreign lands.[2]

Yet there was more than simple collaboration behind this astonishing volte-face. With his knowledge of Egyptian customs, Wedjahorresnet was in a unique position to guide the country's new Persian masters and begin the process of Egyptianization, which would turn them into respectable, even legitimate, pharaohs. An important step in this process was the composition of a royal titulary for Cambyses, which Wedja-horresnet masterminded and no doubt strongly encouraged. Little by little, slowly but surely, the Persians were acculturated, following in the footsteps of previous foreign dynasties—Hyksos, Libyan, and Kushite.

Cambyses seems to have acquiesced to the process. With his vast and polyglot empire, he could ill afford to take a culturally purist view. Instead, he showed great tolerance for the different cultures and traditions within his realm. His predecessor Cyrus had released the Jews from their exile in Babylon, and Cambyses followed suit, protecting the large Jewish community in Egypt on the island of Abu. Elsewhere in the Nile Valley, he was perfectly willing to retain the services of Egyptian officials, and life for many people, especially in the provinces, continued much as before. Only in the military were Egyptian officers replaced and their leadership skills directed anew, as with Wedjahor-resnet.

Having been forced to relinquish his naval command, the erstwhile admiral turned his talents to safeguarding and honoring his local temple. His position at court gave him special influence, and he set about using it to further the cult of Neith at Sais. First, he complained to Cambyses about the "foreigners" who had desecrated the temple by installing themselves inside its sacred precinct, and he persuaded his master to issue an eviction notice. After further lobbying, Cambyses ordered the temple to be purified, and its priesthood and offerings reinstated, just as they had been before the Persian invasion. As Wedja-horresnet explained, "His Majesty did these things because I caused His Majesty to understand the importance of Sais."[3] To set the seal on this "conversion," Cambyses paid a personal visit to the temple and kissed the ground before the statue of Neith, "as every king does."[4] The Persian conqueror was well on the way to becoming a proper pharaoh.

The same pattern was followed at sites throughout Egypt. In the delta city of Taremu, the local bigwig Nesmahes used his influence—he was overseer of the royal harem—to enrich his community and its cult. It may have helped that the Persian kings readily identified with the power of the local lion god, Mahes, but, here as elsewhere, the determination of Egyptian officials to convert their new masters was a key factor behind developments in the First Persian Period. At Memphis, burials of the sacred Apis bulls continued without interruption, and the Egyptian responsible for the cult could even boast of proselytizing the country's new rulers: "I put fear of you [Apis] in the hearts of all people and foreigners of every foreign land who were in Egypt."[5]

The Egyptians might have lost their political independence, but they were determined to maintain their cherished cultural traditions.

AGE OF INVENTION

In reality, the Persian conquest of Egypt was far from being a "great disaster." If anything, the country's new rulers brought a much needed dynamism and energy to the government of the Nile Valley, breathing new life into its institutions and infrastructure. The high point of this renaissance was the reign of Cambyses's successor Darius I (522–486). He took a particularly keen interest in Egypt's repositories of learning, the "houses of life" attached to the major temples. From his royal palace at Susa (built by Egyptian craftsmen with ebony and ivory from Nubia), he ordered Wedjahorresnet, by now an old and trusted retainer living at the Persian court, to return to Sais and restore the house of life after it had fallen into ruin.

Perhaps drawing on the temple records, Darius is said to have codified the laws of Egypt to establish a firm basis for government. He recognized that Egypt was not just another satrapy in his empire. Egypt's great wealth and ancient culture gave it a special significance, and it was simply too important a possession to risk losing. Hence the satrap (Persian governor) based in Memphis was not allowed any control over economic affairs. Instead, these were the responsibility of a separate chancellor, who was also tasked with keeping an eye on the satrap, to prevent him from going native. Satraps were frequently recalled to Persia to account for their activities in person before the great king.

On the whole, though, Darius ruled Egypt with a light touch. Native Egyptians continued to hold high office, the tribute exacted was not excessive, and contemporary documents suggest a degree of prosperity, even in the provinces. The keys to Persian control were excellent communication with the rest of the empire, a good intelligence network, and strategically placed garrisons. From the island of Dorginarti, in lower Nubia, to the deserts of the Sinai, imposing

The Persian great king Darius I in the guise of an Egyptian pharaoh   TOBY WILKINSON

fortresses ringed Egypt's perimeter, giving the Persians the means to put down any signs of insurrection quickly and decisively.

When it came to exploiting Egypt's vast economic potential, Darius's priority was to encourage maritime trade between the Nile Valley and the Persian Gulf. In Upper Egypt, the overland track through the Wadi Hammamat to the Red Sea coast was reopened and was used regularly by Persian expeditions. In Lower Egypt, however, no such route existed, so a different solution had to be found. The answer was one of the greatest engineering projects in ancient Egyptian history, every bit as ambitious as the pyramids at Giza. Back in the heyday of Saite control, Nekau II (610–595) had initiated a scheme to build a canal between the Nile and the Red Sea. Now, a hundred years later, his idea was finally realized. Where the Saites had merely dreamed, the Persians delivered. The result was a canal 150 feet wide that ran for some forty miles from the easternmost branch of the Nile, along the Wadi Tumilat, to the Bitter Lakes and thence southward to the Gulf of Suez.

As ships sailed the four days' journey from one end to the other, they passed massive stelae of pink granite, set up at strategic points along the canal. On each giant slab, ten feet high and seven feet wide, carefully chosen scenes and texts emphasized Darius's dominion over his vast empire. One side of the stelae depicted the great king under the protection of his Persian god Ahura Mazda, with an accompanying text in cuneiform; the other side showed the emblem of Egyptian unification under a winged sun disk, with a laudatory inscription in hieroglyphics. In time-honored pharaonic fashion, the Egyptian version also included a frieze of twenty-four kneeling figures, each perched on an oval ring containing the name of an imperial province. Such scenes would have been a familiar sight to any Egyptian acquainted with the great temples of the land—except that, on Darius's monuments, one of the subject territories was Egypt itself. Little comfort that it was listed alongside such exotic and fabled lands as Persia, Media, Babylonia, Assyria, and even India. Darius drove the message home on the other side of the stela, where he boasted "I, a Persian, with Persians, I seized Egypt. I gave orders to dig a canal from the river that is in Egypt—the Nile is its name—to the bitter river [that is, the Red Sea] that flows from Persia."[6] To celebrate the official opening of his landmark project in 497, the king paid a personal visit to the canal and looked on proudly as a fleet of twenty-four ships laden with Egyptian tribute made its way slowly eastward, bound for Persia.

If the ancient Suez Canal was born of an interest in maritime trade routes, the Persians' desire to control the desert routes across the Sahara, on the other side of Egypt, spawned an equally impressive feat of engineering. Kharga, the southernmost of the four great Egyptian oases, had long been a key nexus in desert communication, where a network of tracks converged, linking the Nile Valley with Nubia, to the south, and the lands beyond the Sahara, to the west. Not since the late Old Kingdom had the Kharga Oasis been permanently settled. The climate had become simply too arid, the annual rainfall insufficient to support even a small population. With their customary ingenuity, the Persians had two answers to the problem. First, they introduced the camel to Egypt. Brought from their Bactrian and Arabian provinces, it revolutionized desert travel, enabling caravans to travel far greater distances without the need to find water. Second, the Persians pioneered an extraordinary technique for bringing the water trapped inside the underground sandstone aquifer to the surface. Throughout the Kharga Oasis, they excavated deep underground rock-cut galleries that ran for miles across the parched landscape. These were, in effect, subterranean aqueducts, enabling gardens and fields on the surface to be irrigated with sweet, fresh artesian water. Thanks to this advanced technology, vast tracts of land were brought into agricultural production for the first time, yielding abundant crops of cereals, fruit, and vegetables, and cotton—another Persian introduction. New villages and towns sprang up around the aqueducts, complete with administrative buildings and temples. Because of the distance of these settlements from the Nile Valley, papyrus was rare and costly, so instead the local inhabitants used shards of pottery as a writing medium for their correspondence. As a result, an extraordinary archive has been preserved that illuminates daily life in this far-flung outpost of Persian imperialism. As might have been expected, individuals and institutions took care to preserve particularly valuable documents. Besides the receipts, household accounts, and everyday jottings, legal contracts feature heavily. They reveal that the basis of the local inhabitants' wealth was not land but water. The water supply from each rock-cut aqueduct was carefully divided into days and fractions of days, and these could be bought and sold, rented, or used to guarantee loans. In this desert oasis, water was, quite literally, money.

There was coinage, too. In 410, the Athenian currency (*stateres*) was introduced as the monetary standard, revealing the pervasive influence of the Greek world on Egyptian commerce. It was yet another sign of the cosmopolitan character of Persian Egypt, a land where people married across the religious and cultural divide; where reliefs in Egyptian temples could depict strange winged creatures from Zoroastrian mythology; and where second-generation Persian immigrants could adopt Egyptian nicknames.

All in all, Egypt under Darius I was a dynamic melting pot of peoples and traditions, a place of cultural innovation, a prosperous trading nation, and a tolerant multiethnic community. But it was not to last.

SURVIVAL OF THE FITTEST

DARIUS'S SUCCESSORS SHOWED MARKEDLY LESS INTEREST IN THEIR Egyptian satrapy. They ceased even to pay lip service to the traditions of Egyptian kingship and religion. Commercial activity began to decline, and political control slackened as the Persians focussed their attention increasingly on their troublesome western provinces and the "terrorist states"[7] of Athens and Sparta. Against such a backdrop of political weakness and economic malaise, the Egyptians' relationship with their foreign masters started to turn sour. A year before Darius I's death, the first revolt broke out in the delta. It took the next great king, Xerxes I (486–465), two years to quell the uprising. To prevent a recurrence, he purged Egyptians from positions of authority, but it could not stop the rot. As Xerxes and his officials were preoccupied with fighting the Greeks at the epic battles of Thermopylae and Salamis, members of the old provincial families across Lower Egypt began to dream of regaining power—a few even went as far as to claim royal titles. After less than half a century, Persian rule was beginning to unravel.

The murder of Xerxes I in the summer of 465 provided the opportunity and stimulus for a second Egyptian revolt. This time, it was led by Irethoreru, a charismatic prince of Sais following in the family tradition, and the revolt was not so easily suppressed. Within a year, he had won supporters across the delta and further afield; even government scribes in the Kharga Oasis dated legal contracts to "year two of Irethoreru, prince of the rebels." Only in the far southeast of the country, in the quarries of the Wadi Hammamat, did local officials still recognize the authority of the Persian ruler. Sensing the popularity of his cause, Irethoreru appealed to the Persians' great enemy, Athens, for military support. Still smarting from the vicious destruction of their holy sites by Xerxes's army two decades earlier, the Athenians were only too glad to help. They dispatched a battle fleet to the Egyptian coast, and the combined Greco-Egyptian forces succeeded in driving the Persian military back to their barracks in Memphis, and in keeping them pinned down there for many months. But the Persians were not going to give up their richest province so easily. Eventually, by sheer force of numbers, they broke out of Memphis and began to take the country back, region by region. After a struggle lasting nearly a decade, Irethoreru was finally captured and crucified as a grim warning to other would-be insurgents.

The Egyptians, however, had enjoyed their brief taste of freedom and it was not long before another rebellion broke out, once again under Saite leadership, and once again with Athenian support. Only the peace treaty of 449 between Persia and Athens brought a temporary halt to Greek involvement in Egyptian internal affairs, and allowed the resumption of free commerce and travel between the two Mediterranean powers. (One beneficiary of the new dispensation was Herodotus, who visited Egypt sometime in the 440s.) Yet Egyptian discontent did not evaporate. The prospect of another major uprising looked certain.

In 410, civil strife erupted across the country, with near anarchy and intercommunal violence flaring in the deep south. At the instigation of the Egyptian priests of Khnum, on the island of Abu, thugs attacked the neighboring Jewish temple of Yahweh. The perpetrators were arrested and imprisoned, but, even so, it was a sign that Egyptian society was in upheaval. In the delta, a new generation of princes took up the banner of independence, led by the grandson of the first rebel leader of forty years before. Psamtek-Amenirdis of Sais was named after his grandfather but also bore the proud name of the founder of the Saite Dynasty, and he was determined to restore the family's fortunes. He launched a low-level guerrilla war in the delta against Egypt's Persian overlords, using his detailed local knowledge to wear down his opponents. For six years, the rebellion continued unabated, the Persians discovering the impotence of a superpower against a determined uprising with popular local support.

Finally the tipping point came. In 525, Cambyses had taken full advantage of the pharaoh's death to launch his takeover of Egypt. Now the Egyptians returned the compliment. When news reached the delta in early 404 that the great king Darius II had died, Amenirdis promptly declared himself monarch. It was only a gesture, but it had the desired effect of galvanizing support across Egypt. By the end of 402, the fact of his kingship was recognized from the shores of the Mediterranean to the first cataract. A few waverers in the provinces continued to date official documents by the reign of the great king Artaxerxes II—hedging

their bets—but the Persians had troubles of their own. An army of reconquest, assembled in Phoenicia to invade Egypt and restore order to
the rebellious satrapy, had to be diverted at the last moment to deal
with another secession in Cyprus. Having thus been spared a Persian
onslaught, Amenirdis might have been expected to welcome the renegade Cypriot admiral when he sought refuge in Egypt. But instead of
rolling out the red carpet for a fellow freedom fighter, Amenirdis had
the admiral promptly assassinated. It was a characteristic display of
Saite double-dealing.

Despite such ruthlessness, Amenirdis did not long enjoy his newly
won throne. By seizing power through cunning and brute force, he had
stripped away any remaining mystique from the office of pharaoh, revealing the kingship for what it had become (or, behind the heavy veil
of decorum and propaganda, had always been)—the preeminent political trophy. Scions of other powerful delta families soon took note. In
October 399, a rival warlord from the city of Djedet staged his own
coup, ousting Amenirdis and proclaiming a new dynasty.

To mark this new beginning, Nayfaurud of Djedet consciously
adopted the Horus name of Psamtek I, the most recent founder of a dynasty who had delivered Egypt from foreign rule. But there the comparison ended. Ever wary of Persian reprisals, Nayfaurud's brief reign
(399–393) was marked by feverish defensive activity. His most significant foreign policy was to cement an alliance with Sparta, sending
grain and timber to assist the Spartan king Agesilaos in his Persian expedition.

In 393, when Nayfaurud's heir Hagar became king, a native-born
son succeeded his father on the throne of Egypt for the first time in five
generations. Despite having a name that meant "the Arab," Hagar was
proud of his Egyptian identity and was determined to fulfill the traditional obligations of monarchy. A favorite epithet at the start of his
reign was "he who satisfies the gods." But piety alone could not guarantee security. After barely a year of rule, the internecine rivalry between Egypt's leading families struck again. This time, it was Hagar's
turn to be deposed, when a competitor usurped both the throne and
the monuments of the fledgling dynasty.

As the merry-go-round of pharaonic politics continued to spin, it
was only another twelve months before Hagar won back his throne,

proudly proclaiming that he was "repeating [his] appearance" as king. But it was a hollow boast. The monarchy had sunk to an all-time low. Devoid of respect and stripped of mystique, it was but a pale imitation of past pharaonic glories. Hagar managed to cling to power for another decade, but his ineffectual son (a second Nayfaurud) lasted barely sixteen weeks. In October 380, an army general from Tjebnetjer seized the throne. He represented the third delta family to rule Egypt in just two decades.

However, Nakhtnebef (380–362) was a man in a different mold from his immediate predecessors. He had witnessed firsthand the recent bitter struggle between competing warlords, including "the disaster of the king who came before,"[8] and understood better than most the throne's vulnerability. As an army man, he knew that military might was a prerequisite for political power. Therefore, his number one priority, with the country living under the constant threat of Persian invasion, was to be a "mighty king who guards Egypt, a copper wall that protects Egypt."[9] But he also appreciated that force alone was not sufficient. Egyptian kingship had always worked best on a psychological level. Not for nothing did Nakhtnebef describe himself as a ruler "who cuts out the hearts of the treason-hearted."[10] If the monarchy were to be restored to a position of respect, it would need to project a traditional, uncompromising image to the country at large. So, hand in hand with the usual political maneuvering (such as assigning all the most influential positions in government to his relatives and trusted supporters), Nakhtnebef embarked upon the most ambitious temple building program the country had seen for eight hundred years. He wanted to demonstrate unequivocally that he was a pharaoh in the traditional mold. In the same vein, one of his very first acts as king was to assign one-tenth of the royal revenues collected at Naukratis—from customs dues on riverine imports and taxes levied on locally manufactured goods—to the temple of Neith at Sais. That achieved the twin aims of placating his Saite rivals while promoting his own credentials as a pious king. Further endowments followed, not least to the temple of Horus at Edfu. Nothing could be more appropriate than for the god's earthly incarnation to give generously to his patron's principal cult center.

Nakhtnebef was not simply interested in buying credit in heaven. He also recognized that the temples controlled much of the country's temporal wealth, agricultural land, mining rights, craft workshops, and trading agreements, and that investing in them was the surest way to boost the national economy. This, in turn, was the quickest and most effective method of generating surplus revenue with which to strengthen Egypt's defensive capability, in the form of hired Greek mercenaries. So placating the gods and building up the army were two sides of the same coin. Yet it was a tricky balancing act. Milk the temples too eagerly, and they might come to resent being used as cash cows.

A wise student of his country's history, Nakhtnebef moved to avoid the dynastic strife of recent decades by resuscitating the ancient practice of co-regency, appointing his heir Djedher (365–360) as joint sovereign to ensure a smooth transition of power. However, the greatest threat to Djedher's throne came not from internal rivals but from his own cavalier domestic and foreign policies. Sharing none of his father's caution, he began his sole reign by setting out to seize Palestine and Phoenicia from the Persians. Perhaps he wished to recapture the glories of Egypt's imperial past, or perhaps he felt the need to take the war to the enemy to justify his dynasty's continued grip on power. Either way, it was a rash and foolish decision. Even though Persia was distracted by a satraps revolt in Asia Minor, it could hardly be expected to contemplate the loss of its Near Eastern possessions with equanimity. Moreover, the vast resources needed by Egypt to undertake a major military campaign risked putting an unbearable strain on the country's still fragile economy. Djedher badly needed bullion to hire Greek mercenaries, and was persuaded that a windfall tax on the temples was the easiest way of filling the government's coffers. Hence, alongside a tax on buildings, a poll tax, a purchase tax on commodities, and extra dues on shipping, Djedher moved to sequestrate temple property. It would have been difficult to conceive of a more unpopular set of policies. To make matters worse, the Spartan mercenaries hired with all this tax revenue—a thousand hoplite troops and thirty military advisers—came with their own officer, Egypt's old ally Agesilaos. At the age of eighty-four, he was a veteran in every sense of the word, and he was not about to be palmed off with the command of a mercenary corps. Only command of the entire army would satisfy him. For Djedher, that meant shunting aside another Greek ally, the Athenian Chabrias, who had first been hired by Hagar in the 380s to oversee Egyptian defense policy. With Chabrias placed in charge of the navy, Agesilaos won control of the land forces. But the presence of three such large egos at the top of the chain of command threatened to destabilize the entire operation. With resentment in the country at large over the punitive taxes, an atmosphere of suspicion and paranoia pervaded the expedition from the outset.

The most vivid account of events surrounding Djedher's ill-fated campaign of 360 is provided by an eyewitness, a snake doctor from the central delta by the name of Wennefer. Born fewer than ten miles from the dynastic capital of Tjebnetjer, Wennefer was just the sort of faithful follower favored by Nakhtnebef and his regime. After early training in the local temple, Wennefer specialized in medicine and magic, and it was in this context that he came to Djedher's attention. When the king decided to launch his campaign against Persia, Wennefer was entrusted with keeping the official war diary. Words had great magical potency in ancient Egypt, so this was a highly sensitive role for which an accomplished magician and archloyalist was the obvious choice. Yet no sooner had Wennefer set out with the king and the army on their march into Asia than a letter was delivered to the regent in Memphis implicating Wennefer in a plot. He was arrested, bound in copper chains, and taken back to Egypt to be interrogated in the regent's presence. Like any successful official in fourth-century Egypt, Wennefer was adept at extricating himelf from compromising situations. Through some astute maneuvering, he emerged from his ordeal as a loyal confidant of the regent. He was given official protection and showered with gifts.

In the meantime, before a shot had been fired, most of the army had begun to desert Djedher in favor of one of his young officers—no less a personage than Prince Nakhthorheb, Djedher's own nephew and the Memphis regent's son. Agesilaos the Spartan reveled in his role as kingmaker and threw his lot in with the prince, accompanying him back to Egypt in triumph, fighting off a challenger, and finally seeing him installed as pharaoh. For his pains, he received the princely sum of 230 silver talents—enough to bankroll five thousand mercenaries for a year—and headed home to Sparta.

By contrast, Djedher, disgraced, deserted, and deposed, took the only option available and fled into the arms of the Persians, the very enemy he had been preparing to fight. Wennefer was promptly dispatched at the head of a naval task force to comb Asia and track down the traitor. Djedher was eventually located in Susa, and the Persians were only too glad to rid themselves of their unwelcome guest. Wennefer brought him home in chains, and was showered with gifts by a grateful king. In a time of political instability, it paid to be on the winning side.

ANIMAL MAGIC

EGYPT'S CAT-AND-MOUSE GAME WITH THE MIGHTY PERSIAN EMPIRE IN the fourth century determined not just its domestic and foreign policies, but also its national psychology. The ever present threat of reconquest and the constant need for defensive vigilance turned Egypt in on itself as it struggled to find the basis for a renewed sense of security. In a world of global forces, change, and uncertainty, the Egyptians looked increasingly to those traditions and values that defined them and set them apart from other cultures. The most enduring and distinctive feature of pharaonic civilization was its religion. Regarded with haughty disdain by the Greeks and with mystified detachment by the Persians, Egypt's plethora of animal deities embodied the best native Egyptian values. Moreover, the gods represented age-old, unchanging forces that promised ultimate salvation, whatever the vicissitudes of real life: "Change and decay in all around I see; O thou who changest not, abide with me."[11]

Sacred animal cults had a long history in the Nile Valley—animals had been buried in funerary enclosures in the early Predynastic Period, and the Apis bull had been worshipped at Memphis since the foundation of the Egyptian state—but their rapid rise in popularity was a defining phenomenon of Egypt's brief period of independence from Persian rule. And it led to some of the strangest practices ever witnessed in the land of the pharaohs.

By the middle of the fourth century, animal cults were ubiquitous. There were sacred cats at Bast, sacred dogs and gazelles at Thebes, sacred bulls at Iunyt, sacred crocodiles at Shedyt, even sacred fish at Djedet. Each cult had its own temple and priesthood, and because of the system of rotation used for temple employees, this meant that a large proportion of the population shared in the wealth of a nationwide phenomenon. One of the greatest concentrations of animal cults was at Saqqara, burial place of kings and nobles since the dawn of history. By the reign of Nakhthorheb (360–343), Egypt's dead elite found themselves joined in their subterranean world by a veritable menagerie of beasts, great and small.

One of the most holy places on the Saqqara plateau was the Serapeum, where temples and workshops on the surface covered a vast underground catacomb for the Apis bulls. Nearby stood a further complex of temple, hypogeum, and administrative buildings serving the cult of the mother of Apis, a sacred cow worshipped as the incarnation of the goddess Isis. After its death, each successive cow was purified, embalmed, wrapped in linen bandages, and adorned with amulets before being interred in a subterranean vault that had taken up to two years to excavate from the living rock. The huge stone sarcophagus carved for every mother of Apis was so heavy that the team of thirty men required to haul it into place could command up to a month's wages for ten days of backbreaking work.

Beyond the catacombs for the sacred bulls and their mothers, there was a vast network of underground galleries for mummified baboons. Brought by river or sea all the way from sub-Saharan Africa (only a few were successfully bred in captivity), the apes were kept in a special compound inside the temple of Ptah at Memphis. There, they were worshipped as manifestations of Thoth, the god of wisdom, and embodiments of "the hearing ear" that acted as intermediary between people and the gods. Animals were thus the saints of ancient Egyptian religion. After death, each baboon was deified as Osiris and buried in a rectangular wooden box, which was placed in a niche cut into the rock walls of the subterranean vault. The niche was sealed with a limestone slab bearing the name of the baboon, its place of origin, and a prayer. A typical inscription read,

May you be praised before Osiris, O you Osiris Marres the baboon. He was brought from the South. His salvation [that is, death] happened and he was placed in his coffin in the temple of Ptah.[12]

Pilgrims came to Saqqara from far and wide seeking advice, insight into the future, cures for sickness, even success in court cases—all in the hope that Osiris the baboon would carry their supplication to the gods in return for a votive offering or for the pious act of mummifying and burying one of the sacred animals. The area thronged with fortune-tellers, interpreters of dreams, astrologers, soothsayers, and purveyors of magical amulets, plying their dubious trades among the countless worshippers. As for the myriad priests and embalmers, they also made a handsome living out of the pilgrims, especially as they often substituted cheaper, smaller monkeys for the rarer, more expensive baboons; because the animal was hidden beneath mummy wrappings, the purchaser could not tell the difference.

Perhaps the most extensive of all the animal cemeteries at Saqqara were the ibis galleries. Ibises, like baboons, were sacred to the god

Mummified falcons WERNER FORMAN ARCHIVE

Thoth, and the desperate search for wisdom led the Egyptians to mummify and bury up to two million birds at Saqqara alone. Each ibis gallery measured thirty feet wide by thirty feet high, and was filled from floor to ceiling with neat stacks of pottery jars, each containing a mummified body part or an entire corpse of a sacred ibis. To keep pace with demand, ibises were bred on an industrial scale, on the shores of nearby Lake Abusir and at other farms throughout Egypt. At Khmun, the principal cult center of Thoth, a vast area was devoted to feeding the flocks of birds. When they died, even the tiniest parts of them— individual feathers, nest material, fragments of eggshell—were carefully gathered up for sale and burial. Indeed, the ibis priests would often bury the birds' dead bodies in the ground to speed up decomposition, making it easier to separate individual bones and turn a quick profit. The use of turpentine, imported from Tyre, accelerated the process still further, but had the unfortunate side effect of scorching the bones inside the mummy package. But by then, the pilgrim had paid the fee and gone home.

The final catacomb at Saqqara was devoted to falcons, sacred to the god Horus. Here, Egyptian ingenuity went a stage further. As well as dedicating mummified falcons, visitors could also purchase and donate Horus statuettes. The hollow base of the statuette, accessed through a sliding panel, could accommodate either an inducement—for example, a mummified scrap of shrew, by way of a snack for the falcon deity—or a prayer, written on a roll of papyrus. By packaging the prayer and offering together, the pilgrim could be sure of delivering request and payment at the same time, for added efficacy.

As a solar deity, Horus enjoyed a special affinity with Thoth (associated with the moon), so ibises and falcons formed a natural pairing. But there was another, less subtle reason for the popularity of the falcon cult at Saqqara. The cult was actively encouraged and sponsored by the state. Not that the government was much interested in popular religion, but it *was* keen to promote the cult of the king. And according to ancient beliefs, the monarch was the earthly incarnation of Horus. More than that, Nakhthorheb's very name alluded to the cult of Horus ("Horus of Hebyt is victorious"), so king and falcon were identified even more closely than usual. The cult of "Nakhthorheb the falcon" was fostered alongside the sacred animal cult, so that the two became virtually indistinguishable. It was a policy carefully calculated to harness popular religion in the service of the monarchy.

Right from the beginning of his reign, Nakhthorheb recognized the power of beliefs and symbols to consolidate support for himself and his dynasty. One of his first orders to his loyal servant Wennefer was to restore the two-thousand-year-old mortuary cults of Sneferu and Djedefra, two kings from the height of the Pyramid Age. The propaganda value in reviving these institutions was considerable, since it publicly associated Egypt's new ruler with two of his most illustrious predecessors. Beyond Memphis, too, Nakhthorheb indulged in a frenzy of building not seen since the reign of Ramesses II. Scarcely a temple in the country escaped some form of royal beautification. Nakhthorheb wanted to be regarded by his contemporaries as well as by posterity as a true pharaoh, not merely the latest in a long line of warlords that were here today, gone tomorrow. But there was also a hint of panic in his orgy of construction. He concentrated much of his effort on gateways and enclosure walls—the most vulnerable parts of temples—and seems to have felt an overriding need to protect Egypt's sacred buildings from malign forces. In this respect, his religious policy was of a piece with his international agenda. Both were focused on safeguarding Egypt from the enemy.

As for the Persians, they never accepted the secession of their most affluent province. No amount of temple building, mummification of sacred animals, or pharaonic posturing would deflect them from their aim of recapturing the Nile Valley. Back in 373, Nakhtnebef had successfully repelled an attempted Persian invasion directed against the delta. Thirty years later, his grandson Nakhthorheb was not so lucky. The forces of the great king Artaxerxes III captured Pelusium, on the Mediterranean coast, with relative ease, and marched southward to Memphis. By the late summer of 343, the Egyptian capital had fallen, resistance had crumbled, and independence had been extinguished. Nakhthorheb, the last native-born Egyptian until the modern era to rule unchallenged over his homeland, fled abroad. In the end, his piety and politicking were no match for the sheer strength of Artaxerxes's army. The clock had been turned back seven decades, and Egypt was once again a satrapy of the mighty Persian Empire.

HOLDING OUT FOR A HERO

IF ANYONE ALIVE DURING THE PERSIAN INVASION OF 343 COULD HAVE remembered Cambyses's conquest 180 years earlier, they would have had an overwhelming sense of déjà vu. Yet, for most, grown accustomed to a precarious independence, the country's forced reabsorption into a foreign realm must have seemed a genuine disaster. Many Egyptians, especially in the provinces, adopted a head-in-the-sand approach to the latest reversal of fortune. They hunkered down and continued with normal life as much as possible, quietly maintaining their native traditions as far as they could, in quiet defiance of their alien masters. A fine example of this tendency was Padiusir, a pious devotee of Thoth who lived in Khmun, the god's principal cult center. Day in, day out, as the thousands of sacred ibises squawked and screeched in the nearby feeding grounds, Padiusir carried out his duties in the temple with exemplary diligence—while, beyond his narrow horizons, the country seethed with unrest:

> I spent seven years as controller for this god, administering his endowment without fault being found, while the ruler of foreign lands was protector in Egypt, and nothing was in its former place, since fighting had started inside Egypt, the South being in turmoil, the North in revolt . . . , all temples without their servants; the priests fled, not knowing what was happening.[13]

Egypt's unshakeable confidence in its own traditions was both its genius and its undoing. What had been the country's greatest strength in happier, more settled times became its fatal weakness in the face of unfamiliar forces. The customs and solutions that had maintained Egyptian civilization in the third and second millennia were no longer up to the job. Egypt had lost its preeminence and was now just another country—albeit a wealthy one—to be fought over by younger, nimbler empires. Padiusir's conscientious resignation was thus a symptom of a wider malaise. Frightened and bewildered by the rapidly changing global situation, most Egyptians preferred to look the other way, put their trust in their old gods, and carry on regardless.

The last, feeble gasp of Egypt's once proud spirit of independence came at the end of 338. The stimulus was the death of yet another Persian great king. As the court in Persepolis mourned the passing of Artaxerxes III and prepared to crown his successor, the last in a long line of Egyptian freedom fighters stepped forward to liberate his country. Little is known for certain about the mysterious Khababash, his obscurity reflecting the hopelessness of his cause. He seems to have been a native of Memphis, or at least to have had a close association with the capital, and the city was one of the first places in Egypt to recognize his "kingship." But Khababash's popularity was not confined to Lower Egypt. Thebes, too, threw its weight behind his attempt to seize the throne. From the upper reaches of the Nile Valley to the shores of the delta, the whole country was anxious to cast off the Persian yoke. Khababash was the best—the only—bet. Recognizing that Persian retaliation was likely to be in the form of a seaborne invasion, he headed straight for the strategically important harbor city of Per-Wadjet, "crossing the marshlands that were in all its districts, penetrating the morass of Lower Egypt, and inspecting every estuary leading to the Great Green [that is, the Mediterranean Sea] in order to repel the Asiatic fleet from Egypt."[14] It was a sensible enough strategy, but a rebel leader, even one with the hopes and aspirations of Egypt riding on his shoulders, was no match for the Persian army at its mightiest and most determined. Khababash's insurrection lasted barely eighteen months. His fate, like most things about him, remains a mystery. The final outcome was renewed Persian control, under a new great king, Darius III (336–332 in Egypt, 336–331 in Persia).

Egypt had never been more vital to the Persians. Its wealth was desperately needed to buy mercenary support for an increasingly embattled empire. For a century and a half, Persia had been grappling with the Greek world for control of the Aegean and Anatolia. Sparta and Athens had proved persistent thorns, putting up heroic resistance and humbling the great king's armies with acts of bravery and defiance. Now attention had swung northward to the mountainous kingdom of Macedon, which had recently taken on the mantle of Panhellenic leadership against the Persians. In the late summer of 336, at precisely the same time that Darius III was being enthroned at Persepolis, the new young king of Macedon, Alexander III, was winning recognition throughout Greece as head of the League of Corinth and commander of the Persian expedition initiated by his father. The world was at a turning point, if only Darius could have sensed it.

By the spring of 334, Alexander had crossed the Hellespont, into Persia's western province, and marched southward to engage the massed ranks of the imperial army. The epic battle at the river Granikos in May that year signaled the beginning of the end for Darius and for Persia. Further campaigns in Anatolia followed during the summer, culminating in the siege of Halicarnassus. Autumn and winter saw Alexander's forces moving along the coast, sweeping all before them. In November 333, a second pitched battle between the two opposing armies was fought at Issos, in Cilicia. Ironically, the Persians counted a sizeable number of Egyptians among their multiethnic forces. Ordinary soldiers no doubt fought for whoever paid them. But the willing collaboration extended also to members of the elite, including the eldest son of the exiled Nakhthorheb, who apparently saw no contradiction in supporting the very army that had defeated his father. As it had shown time and again, the Egyptian military, even in its upper echelons, had one overriding wish—to align itself with the winning side. History is written by the victors, as the Egyptians, with a history longer than most, well knew.

Now, however, history was running out for the Persians. An Egyptian collaborator, Sematawytefnakht, watched from the sidelines as Darius suffered another crushing defeat. Suddenly, Alexander looked unstoppable. Overcome with homesickness, or a powerful desire to save his own skin, Sematawytefnakht fled the battlefield and returned to Egypt, there to await the installation of a new regime and further opportunities for advancement.

As news reached the Nile Valley of Alexander, his thirst for glory and his invincible army, the Egyptians began to wonder whether he could be the strongman they were looking for to rid them of the hated Persians. In the absence of a native-born hero, and faced with a stark choice between Darius and Alexander, the Macedonian looked like the lesser of two evils. For sure, there could be no illusions about his methods. After the seven-month siege of Tyre in the first half of 332, Alexander had shown exemplary cruelty to those who had dared to oppose him, ordering the public crucifixion of the survivors. A few months later, the unfortunate governor of Gaza, a city that had also shut its gates against Alexander, suffered an even worse fate. The governor was tied to a chariot while still alive and driven around the city walls until he died from his wounds in excruciating agony. Nothing and no one would be allowed to stand in Alexander's way. But the Egyptians had always been used to despotic rulers. Authoritarian dictators had been the norm in the Nile Valley for the best part of three thousand years. As the country looked back to its glorious past with increasing nostalgia, it must have seemed that Alexander was a man very much in the traditional pharaonic mold, a ruthless tyrant, to be respected and feared. More important still, he was a proven winner, and Egypt longed for victory, if only by proxy.

In the dying weeks of 332, Alexander marched across the Egyptian border and seized power without a fight. The Persians simply melted away. Here he was, the conqueror of the known world in the land of the pharaohs. Whether by instinct or through careful advice, he knew what was expected of him. One of his first acts on reaching Memphis was to pay his respects to the sacred Apis bull. The great beast was brought out from its stall into the adjoining courtyard for the curious Macedonian to inspect. For Alexander's hosts, it was a sign that the old ways had returned. Here was a king who understood the demands of piety.

Yet, for Alexander himself, an interest in ancient Egypt's religious traditions was more than just a public relations exercise. Like all previous invaders, he was entranced by the country's age-old culture. Egypt was casting its inimitable, irresistible spell. Thus far, nothing had been allowed to delay or detain Alexander in his military crusade. Each victory had been the spur to another, giving the enemy no respite or time to regroup. Now, against all expectation, he deliberately turned his back on the Persians. In the early spring of 331, after founding the city that would bear his name for eternity, Alexander headed not eastward to engage Darius a third time but westward into the sandy wastes of the Sahara. His destination, three hundred miles distant, was the Siwa Oasis with its famed oracle of Amun. Whatever passed between god and king remained a mystery, but Alexander emerged from the encounter a changed man—indeed, no longer a man but a living god, descended from the creator himself. "He put his question to the oracle and received (or so he said) the answer that his soul desired."[15]

Thus did the ruler of Macedon become king of Egypt. The Nile Valley would not be ruled by one of its own sons for another twenty-two centuries, yet the allure of pharaonic civilization was as influential as ever.

Padiusir and his ilk had been proved right.

CHAPTER 23

THE LONG GOODBYE

THE GLITTERING PRIZE

ALEXANDER LEFT EGYPT IN APRIL 331, NEVER TO RETURN. HIS STAY
had lasted barely four months. Yet, in that brief time, he had not merely
added the land of the pharaohs to his growing list of conquests and had
himself recognized as a living god. With an eye on his empire's destiny,
as well as his own, he had also put in place farsighted administrative
arrangements to ensure strong government in the Nile Valley after his
departure. Alexander recognized that, although won by the sword,
Egypt would not flourish under a military junta, so he ensured a clear
separation of powers, leaving the military command in Macedonian
hands, while civil matters were entrusted to two governors, one Egyptian and one Persian. Proud of his Greek inheritance, Alexander was
nonetheless intent on building a multicultural empire, a world of opportunity where talented individuals of all ethnic backgrounds could
rise to the top. The Nile Valley might now be Macedonian territory,
but an Egyptian dignitary such as Sematawytefnakht could still amass
honors and offices, confident of being "blessed by his lord, revered in
his nome."[1] As Alexander's public display of piety to the Apis bull had
been intended to emphasize, he wanted to present himself as a libera-
tor, and an enlightened ruler who respected and honored Egypt's ancient traditions and beliefs. In this spirit, the Macedonian commander
of the occupying forces, Peukestas, had a notice pinned up at the sacred
animal necropolis at Saqqara, forbidding his troops from entering the
ritual area. It survives to this day as one of the oldest known Greek documents on papyrus, and as a vivid demonstration of Alexander's inclu-
sive ethos.

Not everyone in Alexander's retinue, however, shared his broad-
mindedness and his interest in good government. Very soon his care-

fully laid plans began to fall apart as his subordinates' competing ambitions came to the surface. The Egyptian governor resigned, leaving his Persian counterpart in sole charge of the civilian administration. Before long, he was sidelined in turn, as the Greek commander in charge of the eastern border area and the country's finances, Kleomenes of Naukratis, won promotion to the post of satrap, with comprehensive powers. Despite Alexander's best endeavors, Egypt was on its way back to being a dictatorship.

Alexander's untimely death, just eight years later, on June 10, 323, sealed the country's fate. As Alexander's closest lieutenants squabbled over the division of his vast empire, a general named Ptolemy, son of Lagus, succeeded in being allocated the satrapy of Egypt. Since he had accompanied his childhood friend Alexander on the visit to the oracle of Amun, Ptolemy may have been able to argue that he had some claim to the province. He certainly knew that it was the wealthiest and easiest to defend of Alexander's many conquests—ideally suited, in other words, to become, once again, a powerful kingdom in its own right. Without delay, Ptolemy traveled to Egypt, removed the unpopular Kleomenes, and set about consolidating his own authority.

Taking charge of the Two Lands posed a knotty problem. Ptolemy might have held the reins of political and economic power, but he lacked the moral and spiritual authority that Alexander had possessed to reign over Egypt as pharaoh. With the great conqueror dead, the Egyptians might balk at another Macedonian monarch. Ptolemy knew that Alexander's imprimatur would be essential if he, a commoner, were to win recognition as a legitimate ruler. It had been Alexander's dying wish to be buried within the sacred precinct of the temple of Amun at Siwa; but the new regent of Macedon, Perdiccas, had decided for political reasons that the dead hero should be interred in the dynastic necropolis of the Macedonian kings at Aegina. Everyone, it seemed, wanted Alexander's body as a talisman of legitimacy.

Employing all his tactical skills, honed on the battlefields of the Near East, Ptolemy hatched an audacious plan to steal Alexander's corpse from right under Perdiccas's nose. As the funeral cortège made its way from Babylon, bound for the Hellespont, Ptolemy's army hijacked it in Syria and forced it to divert to Egypt. Once the hero's body was safely on Egyptian soil, Ptolemy showed his true colors. Rather than carrying out Alexander's wishes, he had the body buried at Memphis, traditional capital of the pharaohs. With Alexander's aura cast over the seat of government, nobody could now deny Ptolemy his right to rule.

It is not surprising that the deception incensed Perdiccas, provoking an immediate conflict between Macedon and Egypt—the first in a wearying series of internecine wars between Alexander's successors that would drag on for thirty-five years. At the same time, the Greek penchant for deadly family feuds showed itself, laying waste to Alexander's surviving relatives within twelve years of his own death. First, his heir and half brother Philip III was murdered at the behest of Alexander's mother, Olympias. Then, Alexander's posthumous son, Alexander IV, was murdered by his guardian.

In Egypt (where the unvarnished truth had never been allowed to get in the way of decorum), dates continued to be reckoned as if the younger Alexander were still alive and reigning. But it was nothing more than a political fig leaf, designed to conceal Ptolemy's real intentions beneath a veneer of loyalty. A year earlier, Ptolemy had moved his residence to Alexandria, Alexander's city by the sea. When the new capital was ready, the general made his move. On January 12, 304, he proclaimed himself king. One of his first acts as monarch was to have Alexander's body moved to Alexandria and reinterred in a glass-sided coffin in a lavish new tomb. There Alexander would lie for all eternity as a founding father and patron deity, not just of a new city, but also of a new dynasty. The house of Ptolemy had arrived.

The next eighty years, under the first three Ptolemies, were the golden age of Ptolemaic rule. Though elevated to king, Ptolemy I lost none of his general's touch, using the interminable Wars of the Successors to carve out an empire in the eastern Mediterranean. He acquired Cyprus in 313, followed by strategic footholds in Anatolia and the Aegean. These he added to Cyrenaica (coastal Libya), which he had already annexed to Egypt just a year after Alexander's death. In the early 280s, Ptolemy won recognition as head of the Island League, securing his hegemony over the Cyclades. And he made strategic alliances with Macedon through diplomatic marriages to the daughters of two important families. When he died in the winter of 283–282, at the ripe old age of eighty-four, Ptolemy I had succeeded in creating a buffer zone against invasion that would last for another two and a half centuries.

The eventual outcome of the conflict between Alexander's successors was a threefold division of his realm. In the northwest, Macedon, his ancestral homeland, remained an independent kingdom. In the south, the Ptolemies ruled over Egypt, Cyrenaica, and Cyprus. The great central swath of territory, comprising southern Anatolia, the Near East, Mesopotamia, and Persia, had fallen to another of Alexander's generals, Seleucus, and the Seleucid Kingdom emerged as a powerful rival to the Ptolemaic Empire. Territorial disputes between these three Hellenistic monarchies continued under Ptolemy II and III (285–246 and 246–221), erupting into the full-scale Syrian Wars between the Ptolemaic and Seleucid powers. These periodic conflicts provided opportunities for a wealthy and well-defended state such as Egypt to extend its power still further. With the aid of a large naval fleet, Ptolemy II added southern and western Anatolia to his conquests; his successor Ptolemy III won control of the Ionian coast, the Hellespont, and southern Thrace.

This territorial expansion was a means to an end, not an end in itself, for throughout the Ptolemaic lands, trade was at the heart of government policy. As with later world empires, Ptolemaic Egypt grew fabulously wealthy from commercial activity underpinned by extensive natural resources. Early in his reign, Ptolemy II launched a campaign against the Nubian kingdom of Meroë, and succeeded in seizing control of lower Nubia, with its abundant gold reserves. To drive the point home, he founded a gold processing city in the Wadi Allaqi, named Berenike Panchrysos ("all-gold Berenike") in honor of his redoubtable mother. Control of Nubia also had the added bonus of providing Egypt with a supply of African elephants, to pit against the awesome Indian war elephants of the Seleucid army. In another move, Ptolemy II ordered the Suez Canal, built by Darius some 230 years earlier, to be dredged and reopened to shipping. From ports on the Red Sea coast, ships plied the sea routes to India; riverboats sailed up the Nile to sub-Saharan Africa, while camel trains followed the overland routes west across the Sahara and east to Arabia. Under Ptolemaic rule, Egypt was once again at the hub of a great trading empire.

When it came to trumpeting their fabulous wealth and far-flung imperial connections, the Ptolemies were not given to modesty. In the winter of 275–274, Egypt witnessed one of the most magnificent pageants ever staged in the ancient world. From the cushioned comfort of a vast tent, erected within the walls of the royal citadel, Ptolemy II and 130 specially invited guests watched as a great ceremonial procession filed past. First came the statues honoring the dynasty's patron deities, Dionysus, Zeus, Alexander, and Ptolemy I and his wife Berenike. Following them, exotic tribute from Africa, Arabia, and India thundered past: twenty-four elephant wagons, antelope, ostriches, wild asses, leopards, a giraffe, a rhinoceros, and countless camels; then Nubians bearing tribute, colorful Indian women, cattle, and dogs (all of them "fauna" in Ptolemy's eyes). Finally came the military contingent, an essential element of any triumphalist procession, comprising eighty thousand soldiers from the Ptolemaic army. Where the pharaohs of the New Kingdom had merely carved scenes of tribute on the walls of tombs and temples, the Ptolemies staged the real thing.

In a more radical departure from pharaonic precedent, Ptolemy II's astonishing pomp took place not in Thebes or Memphis but in Alexandria, the jewel in the Ptolemaic crown. Since its foundation on April 7, 331, the city had grown into the leading commercial center of the Mediterranean world. Alexander had personally selected the location, and he had chosen well. Since it was fewer than twenty miles from one of the Nile's main mouths, yet unaffected by the annual inundation, Alexandria was ideally situated for maritime trade. A double natural harbor, divided by a causeway, provided deep-water anchorage for merchant shipping, and extensive wharfs were built for loading and unloading goods. As well as warehouses, shipyards, and the emporium, the waterfront also provided the perfect location for a theater and a temple to Poseidon, Greek god of the seas. Inland, the main city was laid out on a grid system (another Hellenistic trait), with two broad, hundred-foot-wide avenues intersecting at right angles. Along these boulevards were ranged the principal public spaces, notably the market square and the major temples. Indeed, as befitted an administrative and dynastic capital, precincts and palaces covered between one-quarter and one-third of the city. The royal mausoleum and colossal statuary, law courts, and a porticoed gymnasium: monuments in Egyptian and Greek styles, in polished granite and dazzling marble, stood cheek by jowl in a mesmerizing blend of Hellenistic and pharaonic cultures.

Alexandria was a place where two worlds met in a rich and heady mix—even if some native Egyptians insisted on referring to it, contemptuously, as the "building site."

No institution better demonstrated the Ptolemies' vision for Alexandria than the Great Library. Ptolemy I had been determined from the outset to steal Athens's crown and promote his capital as the paramount intellectual center of the Greek world. To this end, he established a scholarly academy within the palace quarter, presided over by a priest of the Muses. The Museum swiftly became a powerhouse of research and teaching, as the Ptolemies sought out the best brains from across the Greek world and lured them to Alexandria with the promise of academic freedom and a guaranteed salary—paid directly from the royal treasury. The Museum buildings had all the necessary elements of a scholarly community: covered arcades with recesses and seats for quiet contemplation; a large dining hall, in which the learned members could meet and discuss ideas; and, of course, a library. Not just any library but the greatest collection of books in the ancient world, acquired by fair means or foul from the best book markets of the day. Ptolemy III was so desperate to acquire original editions of Greek literary classics that he even resorted to outright theft. His ruse was to borrow books from the libraries of Athens, in return for a hefty deposit of fifteen silver talents. As soon as the manuscripts had arrived safely in Alexandria, Ptolemy sent his thanks to the Athenians—they could keep the deposit, he was keeping the books.

In its heyday, the Great Library numbered half a million papyrus rolls, representing the sum total of knowledge in every field of inquiry. The wealth of its written holdings was matched only by its glittering array of scholarly talent, as successive directors of the library gathered about them an astonishing array of visiting academics. There were one or two Egyptians—notably Manetho, a priest of Sebennytos (Egyptian Tjebnetjer), who was commissioned to write a history of Egypt—but the vast majority of Alexandria's intellectuals came from across the Greek world. Euclid, the founder of geometry, was brought from the Platonic School in Athens and organized the entire corpus of Greek mathematical knowledge into a unified system. The engineer Archimedes invented his water-lifting device while he was in Egypt, and the astronomer Aristarchus of Samos advanced the theory of a

solar system with the sun at its center. In 245, the geographer and astronomer Eratosthenes was appointed director of the library. During
his stay in Egypt, he accurately calculated the circumference of the
earth by measuring the length of the shadow cast by a stick at the same
time of day in Aswan and Alexandria. His contemporaries in Alexandria
included physicians steeped in the Hippocratic tradition who established the basic workings of the nervous, digestive, and vascular systems, while the court poet Callimachus compiled a painstaking
catalogue of books in the Great Library, laying the foundations for the
survival of Greek learning into later antiquity and beyond.

In a city of such intellectual wonders, one final architectural masterpiece quite literally beamed Alexandria's achievements to the far horizon. On a rocky islet connected to the mainland by a long breakwater
stood the Pharos, towering hundreds of feet into the sky. Commissioned by Ptolemy I and completed by his successor in 280, it was a
miracle of engineering. The great tower was built from blocks of stone
weighing on average seventy-five tons, and the structure rose in three
massive stories, by turns square, octagonal, and cylindrical. At the summit, topped by a gigantic statue of Zeus, was the crowning glory, a beacon that burned day and night. Its light, magnified by mirrors, was
visible a vast distance out to sea—to guide people, goods, and ideas
from across the Mediterranean into the Ptolemies' thriving metropolis.
A practical landmark for shipping and a powerful symbol of Ptolemaic
power, the Pharos epitomized the Greek mastery of Egypt.

ONE COUNTRY, TWO SYSTEMS

THE MARITIME WORLD BEYOND ALEXANDRIA MIGHT HAVE BEEN THOR-
oughly Greek, but the delta and Nile Valley were a different matter.
Ptolemaic law recognized only three autonomous cities (*poleis*) in
Egypt: Alexandria itself; the ancient trading center of Naukratis; and
the new foundation of Ptolemais, established by Ptolemy I near Abdju,
in Upper Egypt, as a counterweight to the traditional hegemony of
Thebes. In each polis, the citizens enjoyed special tax privileges and were
permitted to elect their own magistrates. Immigrants from across the
Greek world came in the thousands to Ptolemaic Egypt, seeing it as a
land of opportunity where there were fortunes to be made in finance and

commerce. But such immigrants—as immigrants tend to do—naturally gravitated to existing Greek communities. Alexandria, Naukratis, and Ptolemais rapidly became multiethnic polyglot cities, where Sicilians, Illyrians, and Thracians rubbed shoulders with Ionians and Carians. By contrast, large tracts of the Egyptian countryside, where the native population was dominant, remained relatively immune to immigration.

This cultural and ethnic divide between the Greek cities and the Egyptian countryside ran like a fault line through Ptolemaic society. The Pharos may have been a beacon to a land of opportunity, but it was no Statue of Liberty. A small class of Greek officials, merchants, and soldiers ruled the roost, while the mass of Egyptian peasantry tilled the fields, as they had always done. The Ptolemies showed no hesitation in adopting the autocratic, authoritarian mode of rule perfected by their pharaonic predecessors, while entrusting the reins of power to a small Greek-speaking coterie of royal favorites. Out went the vizier—the head of the Egyptian administration since the dawn of history—to be replaced by a *dioiketes*. Under him, officials with similarly alien titles controlled every aspect of government, from the chief secretary (*hypomnematographos*) in Alexandria to the chief administrator (*strategos*) in each province, appointed by the king to keep a close eye on the native population. The ruling class had their *gymnasia*, bastions of (male) Greek culture. These men wrote and spoke in Greek, and they continued to think of themselves as Greeks, even after three or four generations in Egypt. They also had their own legal system, imported from their homeland. It operated alongside the native pharaonic system of courts that continued to decide cases between Egyptians. It was quite literally a case of one law for those in power, another law for the rest.

In the towns and villages of rural Egypt, especially in the Fayum, with its concentration of Greek military settlers, the native population had no choice but to accommodate this new, alien culture in their midst. Many in the lower ranks of the bureaucracy adopted double names, using higher-status Greek names in the exercise of their official duties but reverting to their Egyptian names for private matters. In a typical village such as Kerkeosiris, Greek shrines dedicated to Zeus and the two heavenly twins, Castor and Pollux, jostled for space with native shrines where people still worshipped the old deities Isis, Thoth, Bastet, and Amun. Even in Memphis, with its thriving port and its long tradition of cultural mixing, each ethnic group lived in a separate quarter of the city.

The question for the Ptolemies was how to bind together such disparate elements into a unified kingdom, how to prevent the country from fragmenting along ethnic and cultural lines. The answer, as so often in Egyptian history, was religion. Animal cults had been a characteristic feature of ancient Egyptian religion for centuries, and Ptolemy I took great pains to honor them. He paid particular devotion to the most ancient and revered of all such cults, the Apis bull of Memphis, not least because of its strong connection with divine kingship since the First Dynasty. To complement the bull's cult center at Saqqara, Ptolemy I built a second complex at Alexandria, dedicated to Osiris-Apis ("Serapis" in Greek). Pilgrims came from all over the Greek world to visit the two Serapeums. The native Egyptians, however, remained distinctly underwhelmed. They knew traditional deities when they saw them. Serapis, represented as a Greek hero god, was not one of them. Eventually, the Ptolemaic state withdrew its funding for the cult of Serapis, having failed to win over the Egyptian population.

Rather more successful was the Ptolemies' attempt to combine the Hellenistic and Egyptian concepts of monarchy into a single country-wide ruler cult. Alexander's life and death had demonstrated the potency of the Hellenistic version, and the Ptolemies understood the unifying force of Egyptian divine kingship, a doctrine that had been the country's defining belief for most of its history. Combining the two strands—Hellenistic and pharaonic—seemed to promise a result that would be irresistible to both communities. At first, it was the Hellenistic cult of the *basileus*, "king," that took precedence. Ptolemy I deliberately promoted the cult of Alexander, associating himself with it and establishing it in Alexandria to give his dynasty legitimacy. He elevated his former boss to the position of state god and made Alexander's priest—an office denied to native Egyptians—the highest ranking clergyman in the land. Not that Ptolemy was overcome with modesty when it came to self-deification. Beyond the shores of the delta, on the island of Rhodes, he was only too happy to be worshipped as a god during his lifetime. After his death, he was formally deified in Egypt, and a festival in his honor, the Ptolemaia, was celebrated in Alexandria every four years, accompanied by processions, sacrifices, banquets, and sporting competitions.

Ptolemy II went even further, founding cults for numerous members of his family, including his mistresses. His great procession of 275–274 proclaimed the material and military basis of his (Greek) kingship, and at the same time, he took steps to polish his credentials as pharaoh. Soon after his accession, he visited many of Egypt's most important sanctuaries, especially those devoted to the indigenous animal cults, to fulfill his religious duties as an Egyptian ruler. He had images of himself and members of his dynasty placed in the Serapeum at Saqqara, alongside the statues of the Apis bull and other Egyptian gods. Above all, like all good pharaohs before him, he honored the gods by commissioning spectacular new temple buildings. A complex dedicated to Isis was begun on the island of Philae, at the first cataract; work was also undertaken at Ipetsut, Gebtu (Greek Koptos), Iunet (Greek Tentyris), Saqqara, and in the delta at Per-hebit (Greek Iseum).

The native temples were bastions of Egyptian culture, proudly independent institutions that made a point of rejecting external influences, as a way of maintaining pharaonic religion and customs. So, by acting the royal patron, in time-honored fashion, Ptolemy II hoped to reconcile the native population to foreign rule. The temples were also important landowners and centers of economic activity, so they offered the king material as well as spiritual gain. To tap into this vital source of wealth, Ptolemy forced the temple estates to accept crown agents, trusted officials who were tasked with looking after the government's economic interests.

Egypt's famed wealth had always been based upon its agricultural productivity, and from the start, the Ptolemies were determined to exploit their new domain to the full. The founder of the dynasty established his eponymous city, Ptolemais, in an area renowned for its arable cultivation. He launched an even more ambitious project in the Fayum, reclaiming vast tracts through irrigation and trebling the region's cultivable land in the process. Under Ptolemy II, in a miracle of civil engineering, an artificial lake with a capacity of 360 million cubic yards was created in the southern Fayum; it held enough water to irrigate about sixty square miles of arable land. Because these estates had been created anew from barren desert, they lay outside any preexisting land claims, and their produce was channeled straight into the state's ample coffers.

Similarly, in every rural community throughout Egypt, the lowliest official in the government hierarchy, the village scribe, concerned himself first and foremost with land use and farm yields. His main task was to work out how much land could be rented out by the state to tenant farmers and how much revenue it would produce. Scribes were summoned to their provincial capital to meet with the Greek governor in the state records office twice a year—once in February, to prepare for the annual survey of agricultural production, and again four weeks later to report on the survey's findings. Later in the year, in the early summer, village scribes from across Egypt gathered in Alexandria to answer to the *dioiketes*. It was a stark reminder that, whether the country was ruled by an Egyptian or a Greek, the economy remained at the heart of the state's concerns.

Like colonial rulers before and since, the Ptolemies were concerned with squeezing every drop of profit out of their territory, regardless of the consequences. They levied a land tax on Lower Egypt and a harvest tax on Upper Egypt, and charged high fees for holding government office. Even a village scribe had to pay a commission on appointment (and reappointment), and was compelled, as a condition of service, to lease land from the crown at a very high annual rent. Little by little, the state imposed a new economic regime throughout Egypt, turning ever more land over to wheat production, using intermediaries to collect revenue, and maximizing taxation by every means possible. As a result, Ptolemaic Egypt outshone every other Hellenistic state in wealth and power. But these policies also bred instability and insurrection. Subservient in their own country, the native Egyptians would not stay silent and uncomplaining forever.

REBELLION!

THE PTOLEMIES MAY HAVE SOUGHT TO PROJECT AN IMAGE OF DIVINE authority, but their view of themselves as benevolent rulers was by no means universally shared. After only two generations of Greek rule, elements of the Egyptian population decided to vent their frustration at the punitive economic policies imposed by their foreign masters. In 245, Ptolemy III was forced to break off his campaigning during the Third Syrian War to deal with a native revolt. It was a minor and short-lived insurrection but the harbinger of worse to come. Resentment festered for another three decades, kept at bay by the Ptolemies' machinery of repression.

Ironically, the last straw was a famous military victory. In 217, after the Fourth Syrian War had been raging for two years, the forces of Ptolemaic Egypt and the Seleucid Kingdom reached a decisive moment and faced each other across the border near the town of Raphia. To finance the war effort, Ptolemy IV (221–204) had increased taxes still further, imposing a heavy burden on an already hard-pressed population. He had also put aside the Ptolemies' long-standing contempt for non-Greek soldiers by recruiting a large force of Egyptian troops (albeit armed in Macedonian style). On the eve of battle he addressed his forces, acting the part of a traditional pharaoh, but the pretense fooled nobody, especially as he had to use an interpreter to translate from Greek into Egyptian. The Battle of Raphia resulted in a narrow Ptolemaic victory, and Ptolemy IV had himself immortalized on the walls of Egyptian temples as a war hero and "ruler of Syria."[2] It was the last time a Ptolemy would display such confidence in his own sovereignty. Armed and battle-hardened, the twenty thousand Egyptian troops seized the opportunity to mutiny, feeding a widespread revolt throughout the delta. Peasants left their villages in droves and lived as outlaws, roaming the countryside. Bandits attacked a Greek garrison and an Egyptian temple, both symbols of repression. The Macedonian and Seleucid kings offered their assistance to Ptolemy IV, putting aside their dynastic rivalry in face of this native insurrection, but to little effect. Within a few years, civil war raged through Lower Egypt.

Encouraged by the unrest in the north, the citizens of Thebes were the next to rebel. Ever since the fall of the New Kingdom, Upper Egypt in general and the Theban region in particular had harbored secessionist tendencies. The attitude of the Ptolemies, who rarely strayed beyond their northern power base, merely exacerbated Theban resentment at being ruled from distant Alexandria. Sensing the native threat, Ptolemy IV ordered construction to begin on a vast new temple to Horus at Djeba (Greek Apollonos polis), in the far south of Egypt. But it was too little, too late. A contemporary text (the Demotic Chronicle) lambasted the Ptolemaic rulers, accusing them of ignoring *maat*, and prophesied that a native king would rise up to overthrow the foreigners.

The prophecy was soon fulfilled. In 206, a charismatic rebel leader won an initial victory against the state's forces. Within a few months, after taking the sacred city of Thebes, he was proclaimed pharaoh and given official recognition by the priesthood of Amun. Horwennefer, "beloved of Amun-Ra, king of the gods," began his reign in the autumn of 205. From Abdju, in the north, to Inerty (Greek Pathyris), in the south, Upper Egypt was once again under native rule. Land records were destroyed, the hated tax regime was suspended, and Greeks were forced from their homes. Ptolemaic rule was in retreat. For a brief, heady moment, it looked as if the Nile Valley might wrest itself free from foreign domination, as it had at other turning points in its history.

The Ptolemies thought otherwise. At the end of 200, a new king in Alexandria, Ptolemy V (204–180), launched his counteroffensive. Greek troops marched southward from their bases in the delta and the Fayum. By early 199 they had recaptured Ptolemais, and as summer turned to autumn they laid siege to the sacred site of Abdju. Having seized the cult center of the god Osiris-Wennefer from the rebel leader, they pressed on to Thebes, there to win a further victory. Pessimism among the freedom fighters turned to despair as they lost first their capital, then their leader. Horwennefer's death in mid-autumn 199 might have spelled the end of Theban resistance, but a successor, Ankhwennefer, quickly filled his shoes, continuing the same sequence of regnal years as if nothing had happened. However, with Ptolemaic forces in control of Thebes, and another major Greek garrison dug in at Aswan, Ankhwennefer's options were severely limited. Daringly, he chose to march northward, perhaps using the desert routes, and targeted the province of Sauty (Greek Lykopolis), 190 miles north of Thebes. By inflicting maximum damage, plundering towns, and disrupting the normal workings of the rural economy, Ankhwennefer's plan was to isolate the Ptolemaic troops occupying Thebes, deprive them of supplies, and cut their lines of communication with Alexandria. It was a bold move, and a successful one. Before long, the Ptolemaic army was forced to abandon Thebes and retreat southward. The rebel forces were back in the game.

Frustrated by the degree of opposition in Upper Egypt, Ptolemy V decided to direct his firepower against the delta rebels. In 197, his army besieged their fortified and well-stocked headquarters. In the end, the insurgents' idealism proved no match for the superior strength and weaponry of the Ptolemaic forces. The town was captured and the ringleaders of the uprising were brought to Memphis, there to suffer public execution by impalement as part of Ptolemy's coronation festivities. This highly charged occasion on March 26, 196, mixing politics and religion in characteristically Egyptian style, was duly commemorated in a great royal decree, inscribed in the country's two languages (Egyptian and Greek) and three scripts (hieroglyphics, demotic charac-

The Rosetta Stone © THE TRUSTEES OF THE BRITISH MUSEUM

ters, and Greek). This Decree of Memphis survives to this day, more famously known as the Rosetta Stone.

Buoyed by his decisive victory in the delta, Ptolemy V turned his attention, once again, to Thebes. First, the Ptolemaic army drove the rebel forces from the province of Sauty in a bloody battle that ravaged the land. Then, in the autumn of 191, Ankhwennefer abandoned Thebes and fled toward the Nubian border. His options were fast running out. Once back in control of Thebes, the authorities, ever concerned with economic matters, held a public auction of land confiscated from the insurgents. The sooner it was returned to profitable cultivation, the sooner the taxes would start to flow again. With Greek troops now converging on Aswan, well supplied with grain from all over Egypt, Ankhwennefer knew that his cause was doomed. Despite receiving military assistance from Nubia, the Egyptian rebels were finally defeated on August 27, 186. Ankhwennefer's son was killed in battle; he himself was captured and imprisoned. Only the intervention of a synod, held in Alexandria a few days later, spared him an excruciating death. The Egyptian priests managed to persuade Ptolemy V that killing Ankhwennefer would merely create a martyr and that a wiser policy would be to brand him an enemy of the gods but pardon him. The king swallowed hard, accepted the priests' counsel, and issued a great amnesty decree, instructing all fugitives to return to their homes and fields.

In a further attempt to placate native sentiment, Ptolemy V lavished spending on the temples, resuming the work at Djeba that had been suspended at the outbreak of the insurgency in 206. Yet, hand in hand with these conciliatory gestures, he also took steps to impose absolute military control over the south. For the first time, loyalist Greek soldiers were given land grants in Upper Egyptian communities. The governor resident in Ptolemais was given complete control of civil and military matters, and two new army camps were set up at strategic points near Thebes, at Sumenu (Greek Krokodilopolis) and Inerty. Future rebels would not have it so easy.

Ptolemy V reserved his final act of vengeance for the remaining northern rebels who had started the revolt in the first place. In 185, on the pretext of seeking a negotiated settlement, he lured them to the city of Sais—symbolic center of Lower Egyptian resistance since the far-off days of Tefnakht more than five centuries earlier. Too late they realized the trap. On the king's orders, they were stripped naked, harnessed to carts like oxen, and forced to pull the carts through the city streets—watched by the city's terrified inhabitants—before being tortured to death. Ptolemaic mercy had its limits.

The royal family's appetite for internecine rivalry did not. The internal crises affecting the dynasty grew increasingly serious from the late third century onward, exacerbated by the persistent native rebellions. When Ptolemy V had come to the throne in 204, aged barely six, his mother, due to become regent, had been murdered by powerful court officials. They had then fought among themselves to gain the upper hand, weakening the government still further. Riven by conflict at home, the Ptolemaic state had been trounced abroad, losing its overseas possessions in Syria, Anatolia, and Thrace. By the time of Ptolemy V's death in 180, a once mighty empire was fatally weakened.

And with Hellenistic power crumbling across the eastern Mediterranean, an ambitious young state was watching developments with hungry eyes.

THE ROAD TO ROME

THE LATINS WERE ONE OF A NUMBER OF ITALIC TRIBES DESCENDED from settlers who had first migrated into Italy around the time of the Sea Peoples. In 753, according to their own tradition, the Latins had established a city by the banks of the river Tiber. This foundation, Rome, had grown steadily in size and influence until, by 338, it had controlled the surrounding province of Latium and within another eighty years the whole of peninsular Italy, ousting Greek colonists in the process. Little wonder that the Ptolemies had wanted to be on friendly terms. So in 273, following his great procession, flush with pride and more confident than ever of his own importance, Ptolemy II had taken the step of arranging a formal exchange of envoys with the rising star of international politics. The treaty of friendship with Rome was the beginning of a long, tortuous, and ultimately fatal attraction.

From the outset, the Ptolemies regarded the Romans with a mixture of haughty condescension and sycophantic fascination, as is the wont of established superpowers with up-and-coming nations. To curry favor with Rome (and despite having a treaty with the Phoenician city of Carthage, on the North African coast), Ptolemaic Egypt sat on its hands during the First Punic War, and received a delegation of grateful Romans as a reward for its duplicity. Playing the same game, Rome intervened in the endless struggles between the Ptolemaic Kingdom and its Macedonian and Seleucid rivals, posing as a friend of Egypt in order to further its own international ambitions. In such an atmosphere, the Hellenistic dynasties' bitter feuding led inevitably to the emergence of Rome as the key player in Mediterranean politics.

Like his father, Ptolemy VI (180–145) became king at the age of six. For the first four years of his reign, with his mother acting as regent, some degree of stability was maintained. But after her death in 176, those at court who backed the king's siblings broke cover and soon forced the proclamation of a triarchy. Ptolemy VI, his sister, and his younger brother Ptolemy VIII would henceforth reign as joint sovereigns. It was a recipe for disaster. A disastrous Sixth Syrian War, during which Ptolemy VI tried to negotiate terms with the enemy, led to his being deposed by the febrile citizenry of Alexandria. The Seleucid king, Antiochos, claiming to represent Ptolemy VI (but interested only in a land grab of his own), besieged the Egyptian capital, before breaking off his campaign to deal with domestic problems. The situation was a typically Macedonian cocktail of sibling rivalry, territorial ambition, and native unrest.

Enter the coolheaded Romans to restore order. When Antiochos moved against Alexandria again in the spring of 168, having already captured Cyprus and Memphis and begun issuing royal decrees as ruler of Egypt, Rome intervened decisively to prevent a unification of the Seleucid and Ptolemaic kingdoms. A few months later, in early July, the Roman envoy Popilius met Antiochos in a suburb of Alexandria called Eleusis. With showstopping chutzpah, the envoy demanded an immediate cessation of hostilities and the complete withdrawal of Seleucid forces from Egypt and Cyprus without delay. Overawed, Antiochos meekly complied, and left with his tail between his legs. The Day of Eleusis went down in history as the moment when Rome saved Egypt. It was a Faustian pact.

For the remaining 130 years of Ptolemaic rule, Roman, not Greek, power was the key factor in the destiny of the Nile Valley. As family disputes between Ptolemy VI and his siblings wore out the kingdom, Rome was increasingly asked to intervene on one side or another, and the Romans strengthened their stranglehold on the country's fate. To make matters worse, opportunistic rebellions continued to break out in Upper Egypt, insurgents taking advantage of the power vacuum at the center. In 165, Thebes erupted in revolt. Serious clashes spread to the Fayum, where rebels burned land documents in a direct challenge to the authorities; farmers left their villages; and fugitives sought sanctuary in the temples. Ptolemy VI responded with a decree making the leasing and cultivation of land compulsory, but the measure proved so ineffective and unpopular that he was forced to go into exile. It is not surprising that he headed straight for Rome.

Ptolemy VIII fared no better. Within a year, his tyrannical rule led to calls for his brother's return and he found himself turning to Rome for support. Exiled in Cyrenaica, desperate to regain power, and unsettled by an attempt on his life in 156–155, Ptolemy VIII made a will promising his kingdom to Rome if he should die without a legitimate heir. It had the desired effect of frightening his political opponents— better the devil you know, they concluded—but it merely weakened Egyptian independence still further. Only with the death of Ptolemy VI in 145 did the younger brother finally regain his throne.

On returning to Alexandria, Ptolemy VIII married his brother's widow (and his own sister), and it is said that he had her son by Ptolemy VI murdered during the wedding celebrations. It was entirely typical of his wanton barbarity. He carried out harsh reprisals against the Jewish troop commanders who had risen up against his regime, and he banished many Greek intellectuals from Alexandria. As a counterbalance to the many enemies he was making among the immigrant population, Ptolemy VIII deliberately curried favor with his Egyptian subjects, patronizing their temples and issuing amnesty decrees. It was a shameless bribe, but it worked. Well used to brutal rulers, the native population turned a blind eye to Ptolemy's atrocities and rallied to his side.

The dynasty's domestic affairs—never straightforward—then turned increasingly bizarre. Ptolemy began an intimate relationship with his sister-wife's younger daughter, marrying her in 141 and making her queen. As a result, mother and daughter became the fiercest of rivals. Those seeking to oust the despotic king could now count on his older wife's full support. When civil war broke out between the two camps in 132, Ptolemy fled to Cyprus, taking his younger consort with him and leaving his estranged wife to be acclaimed sole ruler in Alexandria. Fearing that his son by her would be proclaimed king, Ptolemy had the young boy kidnapped, brought to Cyprus, and murdered before his own eyes. He then dismembered the body and had the pieces sent back to the boy's mother to arrive on the eve of her birthday celebrations. Never one to put personal grief before political gain, she put the remains on public display in Alexandria, to arouse the people's wrath against the tyrant Ptolemy. But the native Egyptian population remained steadfastly loyal. His cruel calculation had paid off.

Ptolemy VIII's popularity among his Egyptian subjects gave him the perfect springboard, and he recaptured the country from his wife's backers. He further capitalized on his native support by promoting Egyptians to high office for the first time in two centuries. Men such as the royal scribe Wennefer spouted the same self-aggrandizing hyperbole as their predecessors from the golden age of Egyptian civilization—"I was one honoured by his father, praised by his mother, gracious to his brothers. . . . I was one praised in his town, beneficent in his province, gracious to everyone. I was well-disposed, popular, widely loved, cheerful."[3] But alongside the self-congratulation, there was an equal measure of dissipation that signaled the decay of pharaonic mores: "I was a lover of drink, a lord of the feast day . . . singers and maidens gathered together . . . braided, beauteous, tressed, high-bosomed . . . they danced in beauty, doing my heart's wish."[4] Such decadence was a sign of the times. The people of Egypt were taking their cue from their rulers. Once Ptolemy VIII had retaken Alexandria, to teach his opponents a lesson he had the gymnasium surrounded and torched, burning everyone inside alive. Such senseless violence in the pursuit of power, combined with rampant corruption, only accelerated Egypt's decline.

In the summer of 116, Ptolemy VIII breathed his last in Alexandria, leaving his throne to his young wife and whichever of her two sons she preferred. At the same time, seven hundred miles upstream, a group of Romans came to visit the temple of Isis at Philae and carved their names on the temple wall, leaving behind the oldest surviving Latin inscriptions in Egypt. The two incidents nicely summed up the past and future

The Ptolemaic temple of Horus at Djeba (modern Edfu) WERNER FORMAN ARCHIVE

of the Nile Valley. The dynastic strife of an old and tired regime looked increasingly irrelevant in the face of Roman expansionism. Twenty years later, Rome inherited Cyrenaica, leaving Cyprus as the only overseas Ptolemaic possession. History repeated itself as two royal brothers (Ptolemy IX and X) vied for power and there was further unrest in Upper Egypt. A second Ptolemy willed his kingdom to Rome in return for military support, and there were more outrages in the capital.

Of all the old certainties that had given Egypt its self-confidence, only a belief in the traditional gods remained. For that reason, if for no other, great were the celebrations in 70 when the vast new temple of Horus at Djeba was finally consecrated, 167 years after Ptolemy III had performed the foundation ceremony. Thoroughly Ptolemaic in design but undeniably pharaonic in dedication, the towering edifice of sandstone, with its pylon gateways and columned halls, was the epitome of the hybrid Hellenistic-Egyptian culture that successive generations of Greek pharaohs had struggled to create. The crowds who gathered that day to enjoy the colorful pageantry must have hoped, in their heart of hearts, that they were witnessing a new dawn, a promise of future harmony and prosperity.

Similar sentiments, no doubt, accompanied the birth a few months later of the king's newest child. Of mixed ancestry, Ptolemy XII's baby daughter carried on her tiny shoulders the hopes and expectations of her diverse countrymen. Her life would be devoted to maintaining their independence; her death would signal the end of pharaonic Egypt. Her name was Cleopatra.

CHAPTER 24

FINIS

CREDIT CRUNCH

FROM THE BEGINNING OF EGYPTIAN HISTORY, THE HIGH PRIEST OF Ptah had been one of the most important men in the kingdom. Since the unification of the country, Memphis had been the national capital, and Ptah was the city's principal deity. So Ptah's chief officiant was in the very top echelon of clergy, one of a handful of high priests responsible for guarding Egypt's revered religious traditions. In theory, the high priest of Ptah—or the "greatest of craftsmen," to give him his ancient and esoteric formal title—was a royal appointee. But the notion of the royal prerogative had a habit, throughout Egyptian history, of conflicting with the even more deeply ingrained hereditary ideal, whereby fathers passed their offices to their sons. So it was that, under the Ptolemies, the top job in the Memphite priesthood had been held by a single family, son succeeding father in unbroken succession for more than 260 years. As generation followed generation, the high priests of Ptah skillfully combined hereditary office with ultraloyalty to the sovereign, to become the most powerful and influential native family in the land. In the great southern city of Thebes, once the religious capital of the Egyptian Empire, the high priests of Amun had displayed lukewarm enthusiasm toward their Greek rulers. Not so the high priests of Ptah, who had been resolute supporters of the Ptolemies, eagerly bestowing the stamp of divine authority in return for royal favor. Their southern compatriots may have regarded such collaboration with disgust, but in truth nothing could have been more Egyptian.

At the time of Cleopatra's birth in 69, Greatest of Craftsmen Pasherenptah had more cause than most of his ancestors to support the regime. Succeeding to the high priesthood at the age of fifteen, he had dutifully crowned Cleopatra's father, Ptolemy XII, as one of his first of-

ficial acts. He remained a member of the king's trusted inner circle, and
could boast with only a touch of hyperbole of having been "born
Egypt's sovereign."[1] For the forty years after Cleopatra's birth, the fortunes of the two individuals, Pasherenptah and Cleopatra, would be
closely intertwined. Priest and princess—their lives and fates chart the
final chapter in the long history of ancient Egypt.

From the moment of her birth, Cleopatra was regarded as a semi-
divine being. Her royal father had been hailed as the "new Dionysus"
(or, for his Egyptian subjects, the "young Osiris"), and the long-
standing royal cult of the Ptolemies had effectively made him a god on
earth. The Egyptian clergy—with Pasherenptah as their cheerleader—
saw no difficulty in accepting and supporting the divinity of the first
family, since it had been one of the central tenets of pharaonic religion
since the dawn of history. But the reign of Ptolemy XII was no golden
age—quite the reverse. Instead of growing rich from agricultural
bounty and foreign trade, Ptolemy XII presided over an abrupt and
precipitous decline in the nation's fortunes.

It all came down to protection money. Egypt had long ceased to be
a major power in the eastern Mediterranean. Of the once extensive
Ptolemaic lands, only Cyprus remained within the fold, ruled by
Ptolemy's brother. The Mediterranean had a new power, Rome, determined to extend the frontiers of its nascent empire. In the face of such
a ruthless and well-armed opponent, nations had only two options: resist and be eliminated, or collaborate. Ptolemaic Cyrenaica had already
fallen to the Romans in 75, and Ptolemy had no intention of letting
Egypt go the same way. Getting into bed with the enemy was the lesser
of two evils. For its part, Rome was like a lion on the hunt: it could
sense weakness in its quarry, and lost no time in moving in for the kill.
The legal will of Ptolemy X, which had seemed to promise the Nile
Valley to Rome, provided the Romans with the perfect excuse for ex-
torting revenues from what was still the richest country in the region.
For its part, Egypt had no choice. It was a question of pay up, or else.

When Princess Cleopatra was a mere toddler of four years, this
stark reality came into sharp focus. Far away in the Roman senate, the
republic's political leaders, as competitive and disputatious as ever,
began to use Egypt as a tool to further their own ambitions. In 65,
Crassus proposed the formal annexation of the Nile Valley as a Roman

province, a move vigorously opposed by Cicero as detrimental to the stability of the republic. Temporarily thwarted, the hawks on the Capitoline Hill turned their attention instead toward an easier prey, the Seleucid Kingdom of western Asia. At a stroke, the Ptolemies' old rival in the Near East was liquidated by the armies of Pompey the Great and absorbed into the Roman realm. Anxious to back a winner, Ptolemy XII responded to this momentous development by sending eight thousand cavalry to support Pompey's further expansion into Palestine. No matter that his extravagant gesture of goodwill exhausted the crown revenues, forcing tax rises and cuts in public expenditure, and stirring up a minor revolt. Keeping on the right side of Rome was now the number one priority, irrespective of the domestic repercussions. Pompey looked on with customary Roman hauteur, refusing even to help Ptolemy put down the insurrection that the tax rises provoked.

Egypt should have learned its lesson from this unhappy episode, but its naive foreign policy seemed to have a momentum of its own. As the country became progressively indebted to its bullyboy "protector," the Egyptian population came to hate the Romans and everything associated with them. It did not augur well for the Ptolemaic Dynasty.

To make matters worse, Rome had two rival strongmen. Buying off Pompey was not enough, since Julius Caesar was equally powerful. The devil had two faces; both needed appeasing. When in 59 Caesar threatened to raise "the Egyptian question" once more in the senate, Ptolemy resorted to his favored strategy. He paid protection money equal to half of Egypt's annual revenue, in return for official recognition as king of Egypt and a "friend and fellow of the Roman people" (*amicus et socius populi Romani*). Not that it did him much good. Barely a year later, as Ptolemy celebrated the marriage of his close confidant the high priest Pasherenptah to a fourteen-year-old bride, his newfound "friends" went ahead and annexed Cyprus, driving its king (Ptolemy's brother) to commit suicide. Joy thus turned to sorrow within a matter of months, but Ptolemy kept quiet, for fear of angering Rome. The pharaoh was now bankrupt morally as well as financially.

It was all too much for the proud and passionate citizens of Alexandria, who rose up and ousted their craven king, forcing him into exile. A dejected Ptolemy went first to Rhodes, to kowtow before the Roman magistrate who had just accepted the Cypriot surrender. In the ultimate humiliation, Ptolemy was ushered in to see Marcus Porcius Cato while the latter was on the toilet after a particularly effective dose of laxative. In the days of old, the pharaoh had been accustomed to grinding foreigners underfoot; now he was less significant than a barbarian's bowel movements. There was no farther to fall.

Yet, far from seeking a way out of its imperiled position, the Ptolemaic Dynasty continued to behave as before, ever the author of its own ruin. In Alexandria, the throne was offered first to Ptolemy's wife and then, after her untimely death, to Ptolemy's eldest daughter, Berenike. A woman ruling alone was anathema to the Greeks, so attempts began immediately to find her a suitable husband. But Berenike was as recalcitrant and bloodthirsty as her ancestors. The first suitor died en route; the second was stopped at the border by the Romans; the third made it to Alexandria but was strangled after a few days when his bride-to-be declared herself fatally unimpressed.

From Rhodes, Ptolemy wound his way to Ephesus and thence to Rome, arriving in 57 and staying for two years. During that time, he acted the archetypal dictator-in-exile, ordering the liquidation of his domestic opponents while living it up in foreign villas. Eventually, he clinched the deal he had come for. In exchange for a sum of ten thousand talents—equal to Egypt's entire annual income, and borrowed from a banker named Rabirius, who could scarcely believe his fortune—Ptolemy would be restored to his throne by Gabinius, the Roman governor of Syria. On April 15, 55, with Gabinius's army at his side, Ptolemy marched into Alexandria, reclaimed his kingdom, executed his daughter Berenike, and named Rabirius as his new finance minister.

Egypt was not just in Rome's pocket; it was now effectively a provincial branch of the Roman central bank. For Ptolemy XII, restoration equaled utter humiliation.

FRIENDS, ROMANS, COUNTRYMEN

DURING HIS TWO YEARS OF ENFORCED EXILE IN ROME, PTOLEMY XII seems to have received comfort and reassurance from a particularly beloved companion. There is evidence that he took one of his daughters with him on his travels to Rhodes, Ephesus, and Rome, and while her identity cannot be proven with certainty, Cleopatra is the most likely candidate. For the princess had just turned eleven at the time of her father's ousting—old enough to travel, young enough to be allowed out of Egypt without posing a threat to her elder sister Berenike. If Cleopatra did indeed spend her preteen years in Rome, she learned valuable lessons from the experience. No Ptolemaic ruler could afford to pander entirely to Roman wishes, but nor could Roman might be ignored. Keeping one's throne while preserving national sovereignty required the deftest of footwork on the narrowest of tightropes. Cleopatra would soon find herself walking it alone.

Soon after his return from Rome, Ptolemy moved to shore up his position among the priesthood and the native population at large. Since the time of Narmer, kings had burnished their credentials and bolstered their authority by beautifying the gods' shrines and going on tours of inspection. Nearly three millennia later, Ptolemy XII saw no reason to depart from accustomed practice. He therefore ordered construction to commence on a vast new temple to the goddess Hathor, at Iunet, in Upper Egypt; the foundation stone was duly laid on July 16, 54. At the same time, Ptolemy carried out an official visit to Memphis, accompanied by the leading representative of the native aristocracy— Pasherenptah, high priest of Ptah. Both acts were a deliberate show of traditional pharaonic power, and Ptolemy took a further step to secure his dynasty by appointing Cleopatra as his formal co-regent in 52. After nearly three decades on an uneasy throne, perhaps he sensed his days were numbered. On March 7, 51, a solar eclipse over Egypt was widely interpreted as a portent of doom. A few days later, Ptolemy XII was dead, and Cleopatra was proclaimed ruler of Egypt. She was just seventeen.

In accordance with her father's will, she shared the throne with the elder of her two brothers (the ten-year-old Ptolemy XIII), while Rome was appointed as their official protector. Like most of the Ptolemies' previous dynastic arrangements, it was a disaster in the making. At first, Cleopatra tried to go it alone, sidelining her co-regent brother and ruling single-handedly for the first eighteen months of their reign. But a series of natural and political disasters soon turned the public mood against her. In the summer of 50, an unusually low inundation led to crop failure and widespread food shortages. Cleopatra had to enact emergency legislation to prevent outright famine. A pharaoh's first and foremost responsibility was to placate the gods and ensure the continued prosperity of Egypt; for the gods to have deserted Cleopatra so early in her reign was a profoundly worrying development. She compounded her growing unpopularity by bowing to a request to deport some fugitives who had fled Syria after murdering the sons of the Roman governor. By sending them back to their deaths, she confirmed the native Egyptians' worst fears about Rome's unstoppable rise. The tide of opinion now began to turn rapidly against Cleopatra and in favor of her brother.

In the midst of all this domestic turmoil, Cleopatra also had to contend with unwelcome developments abroad. Rome's two military strongmen, Pompey and Caesar, were now embroiled in a bitter civil war. To pay back old debts, Cleopatra sided with Pompey (whose close ally, Gabinius, had restored Ptolemy XII to his throne). But even an alliance with a foreign warlord could not protect her from the wrath of her own people. In the early months of 48, like her father before her, Cleopatra was forced into exile. However, instead of going with cap in hand to Rome, she decided to raise an army closer to home, in her still-loyal province of Palestine. By the late summer, two opposing armies—one backing Cleopatra, the other her brother—faced each other in the eastern Nile delta.

Ptolemy XIII, who had already won recognition by Rome as sole pharaoh, must have felt the more confident of the two siblings. But when Pompey fled to Egypt on August 9, 48, after suffering a crushing defeat by Caesar in Greece, Ptolemy's confidence turned to recklessness. He watched nonchalantly from the harborside at Alexandria as Pompey was ferried ashore and promptly stabbed to death by one of Pompey's own officers (now in Ptolemy's pay), before he could even set foot on Egyptian soil. If Ptolemy had thought that killing Caesar's sworn enemy would win him friends, he was sorely mistaken. When

Bronze coin of Cleopatra
WERNER FORMAN ARCHIVE

Caesar himself arrived in Alexandria four days later, to be presented with Pompey's severed and pickled head, he reacted furiously to this savage treatment of a fellow Roman general. He marched straight to the royal palace, set up residence, and summoned Ptolemy XIII to meet him. Sensing the importance of the moment—with Pompey dead, Caesar was now the undoubted ruler of Rome—Cleopatra seized her chance. Evading detection by her brother's guards, she made her way to Alexandria and smuggled herself into the palace to join the audience with Caesar.

In the humid heat of a mid-August day, in the royal quarter of Alexandria, the legendary meeting took place—the twenty-one-year-old Ptolemaic queen and the fifty-two-year-old Roman general. With her long, aquiline nose and pointed chin, she was not particularly attractive by modern standards. Battle-worn and weather-beaten, he was hardly in the prime of life. But beauty is in the eye of the beholder, and power is a proven aphrodisiac. The chemistry worked.

To the disgust and disbelief of Ptolemy XIII and his supporters, Caesar threw his weight behind Cleopatra and her claim to the throne of Egypt. Ptolemy's army besieged the palace while his Alexandrine allies proclaimed Cleopatra's younger sister Arsinoe queen in her place. Events then moved swiftly. In March 47, Roman reinforcements arrived to liberate Caesar and Cleopatra from their palace prison. Fierce fighting ensued, during which Ptolemy was drowned in the Nile. With her rival out of the way, Cleopatra was restored to the throne with her eleven-year-old brother (yet another Ptolemy) as her co-regent, and Cyprus was returned to Egypt as a further gesture of support by Rome. Arsinoe was taken captive and deported to Italy.

Caesar and Cleopatra sailed up the Nile to celebrate their triumph—although the accompanying flotilla of four hundred Roman troopships hardly gave the Egyptian populace much cause for celebration. Cleopatra had won, but Egypt had lost. The three Roman legions now stationed permanently in the Nile Valley were a testament to that. As Caesar remarked in his later account, he

> thought it beneficial to the smooth running and renown of our empire that the king and queen [Ptolemy XIV and Cleopatra] should be protected by our troops, as long as they remained faithful to us; but

if they were ungrateful, they could be brought back into line by those same troops.[2]

An occupying army was not Caesar's only legacy to Egypt. In the summer of 47, after he had left to continue his campaigning, Cleopatra gave birth to a boy. In no doubt about his paternity, she named him Ptolemy Caesar. At her command, the Cyprus mint issued special commemorative coins to celebrate the arrival of the royal baby. Decorated with the double cornucopia, they proclaimed the abundance and promise of the Romano-Egyptian union.

Another birth to different parents, a year later, was the cause of equal celebration and thanksgiving. This time, both father and mother were present to share the joy. The happy parents were the high priest Pasherenptah and his wife of twelve years, Taimhotep. Their delight at the birth of a son was all the greater because of the anguish that had preceded it. In the early years of their marriage, Taimhotep had born her husband three healthy children, but they had all been daughters. In ancient Egypt, every man wished for a male heir, the more so when he was the high priest of Ptah and the hereditary holder of an office that had been in his family for eleven generations. By the time he turned forty-three, Pasherenptah must have begun to wonder if he would die without a successor. In desperation, his wife turned to the trusty native gods—in particular, to Imhotep. The courtier of Netjerikhet who had lived twenty-six centuries earlier, at the dawn of the Pyramid Age, and whose crowning achievement, the Step Pyramid, still rose majestically on the Memphite skyline, was worshipped throughout Egypt as a god of wisdom, magic, and medicine. His cult was especially strong in Memphis, and Taimhotep herself, as a daughter of the city, carried his name. If any of the gods would answer the couple's prayers for a son, surely Imhotep would. So, Taimhotep "prayed together with the High Priest to the majesty of the god great in wonders, effective in deeds, who gives a son to him who has none: Imhotep, son of Ptah."[3] Wondrously, the prayer was answered. Imhotep appeared to her in a dream, promising her a son if she would arrange for his Memphite shrine to be beautified—you scratch my back, and I'll scratch yours. It helped that Taimhotep's husband was perhaps the most influential man in Memphis and head of the local priesthood. The builders, painters, and decorators must have completed their work in record time. On July 15, 46, at around two o'clock in the afternoon, Taimhotep gave birth to the longed-for son. "There was jubilation over him by the people of Memphis. He was given the name Imhotep and was also called Padibastet. Everyone rejoiced over him."[4]

For Taimhotep, the birth of a son was the culmination of her wifely duties. For Cleopatra, her son's birth had a deeper, religious significance. To mark the birth of her Caesarion, "little Caesar," the queen consecrated a roof shrine at Iunet, a temple dedicated, appropriately, to the ancient mother goddess Hathor. At Iuny (Greek Hermonthis), she built a "birth house" to celebrate the institution of divine procreation. In Ptolemais and Alexandria, the two great Greek cities of Egypt, she actively promoted the cult of Isis, already one of the most popular Egyptian deities and now a goddess with whom Cleopatra felt a special affinity. For, in popular belief, Isis was a divine mother and protector, caring for her worshippers as she did for her infant son Horus. It was not difficult to draw the parallels. The royal propaganda of the time encouraged the association, and statues deliberately blended the iconography of Isis with the features of Cleopatra. Goddess and queen were becoming one.

Cleopatra certainly had more credibility as an Egyptian deity than her forebears, since, unlike every previous Ptolemy, she seems to have taken the trouble to learn the native language. She evidently considered Egypt to be her home, and took pains to honor the traditional cults. She adopted a feminine version of the earliest and purest expression of divine kingship, the Horus title, and at least some of her Egyptian subjects viewed her as a fully legitimate pharaoh. All the stranger, then, that at the height of her popularity she should have left Egypt to travel to Rome as Caesar's guest when he finally returned home from campaigning in 46. For two years, she stayed in his estate across the Tiber. The relationship between them was the subject of much gossip, not least when Caesar dedicated a gold statue of Cleopatra in the Roman shrine of Venus Genetrix. His subsequent preparation of a bill, to be put before the senate, to allow him to marry (bigamously) outside Italy, have children with a foreign wife, and create a second capital city seemed to confirm the Romans' worst fears: under the malign influence of an oriental queen, their war hero was going native.

The assassination of Caesar on March 15, 44, put paid to his exotic ambitions. Within a month, Cleopatra left Rome and returned home to Alexandria. Another month later, her brother and co-ruler, Ptolemy XIV, was conveniently dead. In his place, Cleopatra elevated Caesarion to the throne as Ptolemy XV, "the father- and mother-loving god." In Cleopatra's mind, the parallels between her own life and the life of the gods seemed to grow stronger by the year. Caesar had been murdered, just like Osiris; his son and heir Caesarion was the new Horus. As for the widowed mother, Cleopatra, no one could now doubt her transformation into the living Isis.

DANGEROUS LIAISONS

IF CLEOPATRA HAD ACHIEVED APOTHEOSIS, HER FELLOW MEMBERS OF the pantheon were not impressed. Indeed, the gods seemed to have deserted Egypt. A further series of low Niles in 43–41 led to more food shortages. In the big cities and in the countryside, the Egyptians felt increasingly desperate. Hard-pressed and hungry, they ceased even to look forward to the promise of a more comfortable afterlife. Imagining the hereafter as a continuation of their earthly lot, they turned their backs on two thousand years of faith and began to dread what lay beyond the grave. Nobody expressed this fear of death more movingly than Taimhotep. On February 15, 42, at the age of thirty, she died, leaving her husband, son, and three daughters to mourn. As befitted the wife of a high priest, her funerary stela was beautifully fashioned from a slab of fine pale limestone, carved by the country's finest craftsmen. On its face, underneath a winged sun disk, a delicately carved frieze showed Taimhotep worshipping the cream of Egypt's traditional deities: Anubis, god of mummification; Horus, son of Osiris; Nepthys and Isis, Osiris's sisters and chief mourners; the sacred Apis bull of Memphis; and, finally, Sokar-Osiris, god of the dead. If the divine lineup recalled Egypt's traditional self-confidence, the accompanying inscription, in twenty-one lines of finely cut hieroglyphs, embodied the new, darker zeitgeist:

Oh my brother, my husband, friend, High Priest!
Do not weary of drinking, eating, getting intoxicated and making love!

Make holiday! Follow your heart day and night!
Let not care into your heart otherwise what use are your years upon
  earth?
As for the west, it is a land of sleep; darkness weighs on that place
  where the dead dwell.[5]

Taimhotep's funerary inscription is the longest and most heartfelt
lament from ancient Egypt, a poignant assertion that the old certainties
had well and truly disappeared.

Stela of Taimhotep   © THE TRUSTEES OF THE BRITISH MUSEUM

For the country as a whole, as well as for its individual citizens, the future looked ominous. With the murder of Caesar, Egypt had lost its protector. It was anybody's guess how his killers on the one hand and his heirs on the other would now behave toward Cleopatra and her realm. To make matters worse, her younger sister Arsinoe, freed from captivity in Rome and now living at Ephesus, provided a natural focus for dissenters within the Ptolemaic lands.

Cleopatra's mettle was tested to the full as first Cassius and then Mark Antony and Octavian sought military assistance from Egypt. Deploying all her political acumen, she read the situation correctly and threw her lot in with Caesar's allies. Antony's subsequent victory over Cassius and Brutus at the Battle of Philippi vindicated her decision. Egypt was saved—for the moment—but the country's reprieve came at a price. Its unforeseen, and ultimately tragic, consequence was Cleopatra's entanglement with a second Roman war hero.

She may have met Antony for the first time in 55, when he came to Egypt as a young cavalry officer with Gabinius's army. Antony and Cleopatra must surely have come into contact again during her two-year stay in Rome in 46–44. It was to be a case of third time lucky. In the summer of 41, following the entente between Egypt and Caesar's heirs, Antony summoned Cleopatra to meet him at Tarsus, in southeastern Anatolia. With the wind in his sails after Philippi, Antony had set his sights on defeating the Parthian Empire, Rome's last major enemy in Asia. To mount such a campaign he required a forward base in the eastern Mediterranean, and Egypt was ideal. For her part, Cleopatra was in urgent need of a new protector. Mutual advantage thus brought the two together.

With her instinctive skills of presentation and propaganda, Cleopatra turned a diplomatic and political summit into a religious spectacle, arriving by river in the guise of Aphrodite/Isis coming to meet her divine consort, Dionysus. Antony must have been flattered by the analogy, and beguiled by a queen fourteen years his junior. Like Caesar before him, he offered Cleopatra his support in return for her favors. Not even the news of Pasherenptah's death, on July 14, could cool her ardor. Toward the end of the year, Antony and Cleopatra returned together to Alexandria. Nine months later, their twins were born,

Wall painting from the tomb of King Horemheb (Eighteenth Dynasty) in the Valley of the Kings. In the center, Horemheb faces the goddess Hathor, protectress of western Thebes. Behind him stands the god Horus, son of Isis.

Army life: a wall painting from the tomb of the royal scribe Userhat (Eighteenth Dynasty) at western Thebes. In this scene, military conscripts are addressed by an officer (top), wait to be enlisted (middle), and have their hair cut (bottom).

Battle relief of King Seti I (Nineteenth Dynasty) from the northern wall of the hypostyle hall, Karnak Temple. The scenes record military campaigns against the Libyans and the Hittites. The image of the king in his chariot dominates both sections.

Detail of a wall painting from the magnificent tomb of Queen Nefertari (Nineteenth Dynasty) in the Valley of the Queens. The goddess Isis, wearing cow's horns, leads Nefertari (favorite wife of Ramesses II) gently by the hand.

Monumental sculpture and relief of King Ramesses II (Nineteenth Dynasty) at Luxor Temple. The king had his names carved deeply into the stone to prevent subsequent usurpation of his monuments.

King Ramesses III (Twentieth Dynasty) and his son, Prince Amenherkhepeshef, from the latter's tomb in the Valley of the Queens. The boy wears his hair in the customary "sidelock of youth," while his father is dressed in full royal regalia.

Relief from the mortuary temple of Ramesses III in western Thebes showing the aftermath of the battle against the Sea Peoples. Captured Philistines, with their distinctive feather headdresses, are led away as prisoners of war.

The pharaoh humbles the enemies of Egypt: a relief fragment from the reign of Ramesses II shows the king grasping a Nubian, an Asiatic, and a Libyan by the hair. In fact, Egypt's neighbors remained a constant threat throughout the latter centuries of pharaonic rule.

Papyrus map of the Wadi Hammamat showing the location of gold mines and stone quarries. Dating to the reign of King Ramesses IV (Twentieth Dynasty), it is thought to be the world's oldest surviving topographical map.

Gold funerary mask of King Pasebakhaenniut I (Twenty-first Dynasty) from Tanis. Some of the king's golden treasure may have been looted from earlier royal tombs in the Valley of the Kings.

Gilded wooden statue of the god Osiris (Twenty-second Dynasty). The cult of Osiris, with its promise of resurrection, enjoyed countrywide popularity during the later centuries of pharaonic civilization.

Quartzite statue of the chief lector-priest Padiamenope (late Twenty-fifth/early Twenty-sixth Dynasty) from Karnak. One of the most important priests in the cult of Amun, he was wealthy enough to commission the largest private tomb at Thebes.

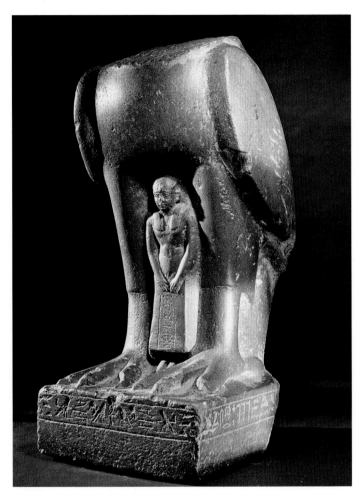

Basalt statue of King Nakhthorheb (Thirtieth Dynasty) protected by the god Horus. The diminutive figure of the king, nestling between the legs of the falcon, emphasizes the reduced status and confidence of the monarchy in the twilight years of Egyptian independence. Compare the statue of King Khafra from two millennia earlier.

Temple of Isis on the island of Philae, near Aswan. One of the most important centers of indigenous Egyptian religion during the Ptolemaic and Roman periods, Philae was also the location of the last-ever inscription carved in hieroglyphics.

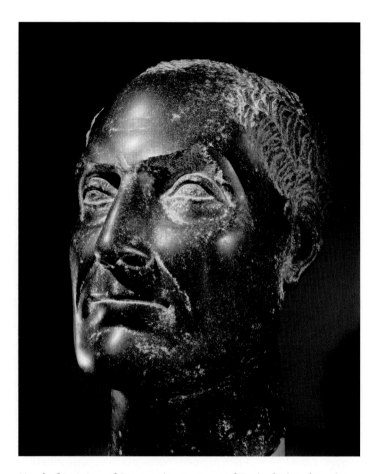

Head of a statue of Penemerit, governor of Tanis during the reign of King Ptolemy XIII. The portrait shows the increasing influence of Greek art in the late Ptolemaic Period, particularly noticeable in the rendering of the hair.

Relief fragment of a Ptolemaic queen, believed to be Cleopatra VII. The vulture headdress was part of the traditional costume of Egyptian royal women. The traces of a grid suggest that the piece was either produced as a sculptor's model or left unfinished.

Alexander Helios and Cleopatra Selene, the sun and the moon—fitting issue for a match made in heaven.

Except that it wasn't. No sooner had the twins come into the world than their father upped and left Egypt. Returning to Rome, he sealed a deal with his great rival by marrying Octavian's sister (Octavia) and spurning Cleopatra. As for the queen of Egypt, she should have learned from bitter experience that a whirlwind romance with a Roman general meant life as a single mother.

For the next three years, with Antony off the scene, Egypt enjoyed a brief respite from the wearying succession of wars, intrigues, coups, and countercoups that had plagued it under the Ptolemies' wayward rule. Imhotep (though only a boy of seven) was appointed high priest of Ptah in succession to his father and forefathers. The Nile inundation returned to accustomed levels, and agricultural production increased. If it had not been for the staggering levels of foreign debt, a legacy of Ptolemy XII's reign, Egypt's economy might have returned to prosperity. As it was, the government coffers were running on empty. Silver coinage was debased from 90 percent to 40 percent precious metal, before virtually disappearing from circulation. In its place, most coins were minted in bronze. Egypt's legendary wealth was going straight into Roman pockets.

Restless to subdue Parthia and win himself even greater renown, by the autumn of 37 Antony had come to the conclusion that Octavian was not going to assist him. Egypt once again seemed the likeliest ally. So he traveled east once more, to Antioch, and called a second summit meeting with Cleopatra. As a sweetener, Antony gave her the contents of the great library of the kings of Pergamum, said to number two hundred thousand volumes—partial compensation for the holdings of the Alexandrian library destroyed a decade earlier during Caesar's war against Pompey. Antony also allocated Egypt a host of Roman territories around the eastern Mediterranean. This allowed Cleopatra to pose as an imperialist pharaoh, a ruler who had restored some of the luster to her forebears' once great empire. To mark this renaissance, she introduced a system of double-dating, proclaiming her sixteenth year on the throne the first year of a new era. But it was all a mirage. The eastern lands were not Antony's to give. Phony title deeds and a collection of books in return for real troops and supplies was hardly a fair exchange. In the far-off days of the Eighteenth Dynasty, Egypt had been respected and feared as the mighty bull of Asia; now, it was Rome's milk cow.

Due to a combination of poor preparation and overconfidence, Antony's first Parthian campaign was a complete disaster. In the space of a few months, he lost a third of his legionaries and nearly half his cavalry to a fierce and determined opponent. The only good news that year was the birth of another son by Cleopatra, Ptolemy Philadelphus. A second Parthian campaign in 34 saw Cleopatra travel with Antony to the banks of the Euphrates. This time, Antony won a limited victory over Armenia, celebrated with quite disproportionate pomp in the "Donations of Alexandria." Before an enormous crowd, Antony and Cleopatra appeared together on silver thrones, she in the guise of Isis. He then boldly proclaimed their children to be the rulers of Rome's eastern provinces. To Cleopatra and Caesarion would be given the traditional Ptolemaic lands of Egypt, Cyprus, and Cyrenaica, together with Coele-Syria; Alexander Helios—attired for the occasion in Persian dress—would be given Armenia, Media, and Parthia (ignoring the inconvenient fact that the last remained unconquered); while the two-year-old Ptolemy Philadelphus, dressed in Macedonian garb, received the provinces of Phoenicia, Syria, and Cilicia (southeastern Anatolia). The boys were hailed as "kings of kings," destined to rule over the entire eastern empire.

It was a complete pipe dream. By acquiescing in it and siding so publicly with Antony, Cleopatra was risking the wrath of Rome, whose senators and citizens took a particularly dim view of orientalist fantasies.

THE END OF THE AFFAIR

A REMARKABLE DOCUMENT ON PAPYRUS SUMS UP EGYPT'S RAPID DE-cline in the last, tragic years of Cleopatra's reign. Dated February 23, 33, it records an Egyptian royal decree granting extraordinary tax privileges to a Roman general. Not just any general, but Antony's right-hand man, Publius Canidius. Cleopatra's edict gave him permission to export ten thousand sacks of wheat from Egypt—not for nothing was the country called the breadbasket of the Roman Empire—and import five thousand amphorae of wine each year, duty free. If that were not enough, Canidius was also exempt from all tax on his Egyptian land-holdings, as were his tenants. In effect, he was declared to be outside the normal tax system. As a political bribe, it must rank as one of the biggest and boldest in history. The decree was addressed to a high-ranking government official in Alexandria, whose job it was to notify other bureaucrats in the administration. To give the measures effect, the Greek word *"ginesthoi,"* "make it happen," was added at the bottom of the papyrus. It may just be in Cleopatra's hand. If so, she was not so much passing a tax measure as signing her own death warrant.

During the course of 33, it had become obvious for a second time that the Roman realm was not big enough for two leaders. Antony, with the eastern provinces at his disposal and friends in the Senate, looked the better bet. But Octavian, Julius Caesar's great-nephew and legal heir, was equally determined. As with Caesar and Pompey sixteen years earlier, the clash of two mighty egos led all too readily to civil war. Cleopatra's close identification with Antony made it easy for Octavian to brand her as public enemy number one, using her to create a distinction between himself, the true Roman, and Antony, the dissolute traitor. No matter that Cleopatra's co-regent (Ptolemy XV Caesarion) was Caesar's own son. In Octavian's eyes, she stood conveniently for everything that was alien and detrimental to Rome's interests. Her fate, and the fate of Egypt, now rested on the outcome of Rome's internal conflict.

As the feud between the two Roman factions intensified, Cleopatra and Antony sailed from Alexandria with an armada of two hundred Egyptian ships. After stopping at Ephesus and Samos, they finally reached Athens. There, Antony publicly repudiated Octavia and cut all ties with his rival's camp. When winter gave way to the milder weather of spring 31, formal hostilities broke out. It soon became apparent that Antony's delusions of grandeur were not matched by his tactical ability. By the beginning of September, his land forces were pinned down in western Greece and his warships were blockaded in a large bay. A naval breakout under fire seemed the only remaining option. The Battle of Actium, on September 2, 31, was more a flight than a military spectacle. Antony and Cleopatra escaped with their lives and 60 of their 230 ships. He fled to Libya, she to Alexandria.

History had taught her that defeated leaders usually did not last long, so she took pains to dress her ships as if she had been victorious. When Antony joined her in the royal palace a few days later, the two of them tried hard to create an impression of normality. A huge festival was organized to celebrate Caesarion's coming of age, royal spectacles always being guaranteed crowd-pleasers and welcome distractions from bad news. On a more mundane level, the wheels of the administration continued to grind, government edicts to be issued, and taxes collected (unless you were Canidius). In the Upper Egyptian town of Gebtu, a guild of linen manufacturers drew up a detailed contract with two local priests to provide for the expenses of the local bull cult. Bureaucracy and animal worship—a quintessentially Egyptian combination. To some, pharaonic civilization must have seemed immortal, impregnable.

But beneath the public display of business as usual, Cleopatra was making feverish preparations for permanent exile. She had the remains of her naval fleet hauled overland from the Nile to the Red Sea, intending to send Caesarion away to India. But the local Nabataean Arabs literally burned her boats, and she found herself trapped in Alexandria with no escape route. As Octavian closed in from Syria and another of his divisions closed in from Cyrenaica, Cleopatra sent him a desperate embassy, offering to abdicate in favor of her children if he would only spare Egypt. Octavian did not reply.

On July 29, 30, the high priest of Ptah, Imhotep, died at age sixteen years and three weeks. He was the casualty either of a weak constitution or, more likely, of a foe determined to eradicate all vestiges of Ptolemaic rule. For three centuries his forebears had successfully safeguarded Egypt's ancient religious traditions, the country's very soul. No more. Three days later, on August 1, Egypt fell to the might of Rome. As Octavian's forces bore down on Alexandria by land and sea, Antony led his own army and navy through the city's gates for one last battle. But, after years of campaigning, he was a spent force. Antony was comprehensively defeated and, as Octavian entered the city, Cleopatra fled to her fortified treasury-cum-mausoleum in the royal quarter of Alexandria. Subsequent events have passed into legend. Misinformed that his lover had already taken her own life, Antony fell on his sword. At Cleopatra's anguished insistence, his weak and almost lifeless body was hoisted up into her apartment, where he expired at her side. She in turn was tricked into leaving the building and promptly incarcerated in the royal palace.

Just ten more golden sunsets over Alexandria and, on August 12, the last queen of Egypt followed her Roman paramour to the grave. In her comparatively short but turbulent life, she had seen one of her sisters overthrown and killed, another paraded as a Roman trophy. Suicide must have seemed a better ending than being lynched or than living the rest of her life in captivity. Whether it was an asp hidden in a basket of figs or a poisoned comb, "the truth about the manner of her death no one knows."[6]

Cleopatra died. Her memory lived on. Four centuries later, a worshipper still lovingly tended her cult statue in Rome. Twenty centuries later, re-creations of her life and loves grip the Western world. She is still with us.

So, too, is her world. In the centuries since her death, the Nile Valley has been fought over by Romans and Arabs, Christians and Muslims. The unrelenting Egyptian sun has bleached the gods' once gaudy temples into romantic sand-colored tumbledown ruins. Tombs have been stripped of their treasures, pyramids of their shimmering capstones. But the allure of pharaonic civilization, embodied in the Western consciousness by its last queen, has proved altogether more resilient.

In physical terms, Cleopatra's enduring monument, her most extravagant architectural legacy, is the temple of Hathor at Iunet. From its porticoed façade, the benign half-human, half-bovine face of the ancient mother goddess still peers down in concerned protection, as it has for two thousand years—as it did over the graven image of Narmer, Egypt's first king, at the dawn of pharaonic history. The iconography and ideology of divine kingship, arguably the ancient Egyptians' greatest inventions, were there at the end, just as they were at the very beginning.

As heir to this extraordinarily ancient tradition, Cleopatra wished, above all, for her dynasty to have a future. On the rear wall of the temple, she was depicted side by side with her son Ptolemy XV Caesarion, making offerings to the gods as her royal forebears had done for three millennia. If she was Isis-Hathor, the divine mother, he would be

Horus—the avenging son of a murdered father who would rise in glory and rule Egypt as a great king.

As with so many of Cleopatra's hopes, fate had other ideas. Caesarion was eliminated by Octavian within days of Alexandria's fall. There would be no future for the Ptolemaic Dynasty—for any dynasty of pharaohs.

Yet alongside the last, bold assertion of divine kingship, the stones of Cleopatra's monument proclaim a deeper, more enduring truth. Next to the figure of the very last Ptolemy are carved four simple hieroglyphs: a sandal strap, a snake, a loaf of bread, and a stretch of alluvial land. The quintessence of pharaonic civilization. Together they form an epithet that had been applied to kings since time immemorial: *ankh djet*—"living forever."

It is a fitting epitaph, not just for Cleopatra but for ancient Egypt.

THE DEATH OF CLEOPATRA DELIVERED EGYPT INTO THE HANDS OF Rome, just as she had feared. With her demise, the proud three-thousand-year-old tradition of pharaonic independence was snuffed out, once and for all, and Egypt became the personal property of a foreign emperor, to be plundered at will. For the next four centuries, Augustus and his successors exploited Egypt's fabled wealth to serve their own interests. Grain ships from Alexandria fed Rome's teeming population; gold from the Eastern Desert filled the imperial coffers; vast columns and architraves of stone were hewn from the Red Sea hills to adorn public buildings in the Roman Forum; and the remote quarry of Mons Porphyrites kept the empire's finest sculptors supplied with the most precious of all materials, the deep purple imperial porphyry.

But Egypt's importance to Rome was not confined to its agricultural and mineral wealth. With unique access to both the Mediterranean and Red seas, the country played a key role in Roman commerce—especially trade with India, source of the oriental luxuries so beloved of the ruling class. Egypt's strategic location, at the nexus of routes linking Arabia, Asia, Africa, and Europe, had been a prime reason for its prosperity as an independent nation; the same geographical advantage now ensured Egypt's subjugation by a succession of foreign empires. Rome, Byzantium, and Persia; the Caliphs, the Ottomans, and the British—all looked upon Egypt as a source of wealth and a trading hub without peer.

Yet the cloud of exploitation had a silver lining. At the end of the eighteenth century A.D., Napoléon launched an expedition to Egypt with the objective of annexing it as a French colony, dominating world trade, and undermining British control of India. The mission is remembered today not for its primary economic and strategic purpose but for an almost incidental outcome—the birth of Egyptology. Although Bonaparte himself was little concerned with the rediscovery of ancient Egypt, he did take 150-odd savants with him when he set sail from Toulon on May 20, 1798. It is to their meticulous observations, published in the monumental *Description de l'Egypte*, that we owe the beginnings of the scientific study of pharaonic civilization.

While the savants are today given star billing in accounts of Napoléon's expedition, at the time they paled into insignificance beside the thousands of infantry and cavalry who journeyed with them to the mouth of the Nile. Moreover, of the learned men who accompanied the invading French army, by far the most important were the surveyors. Their task was to determine the feasibility of cutting a ship canal between the Mediterranean Sea and the Gulf of Suez. Strategic advantage, not scientific knowledge, was uppermost in Bonaparte's mind. And despite British admiral Horatio Nelson's famous victory at the Battle of the Nile—echoing the great naval encounter between the Egyptians and the Sea Peoples three thousand years earlier—the French got their way in the end, and the Suez Canal (modern successor to Darius I's great project) was duly completed in 1869.

The parallels between Egypt's ancient and modern history continued into the twentieth century. Following in Napoléon's footsteps, another expansionary empire, the Third Reich, sought to occupy Egypt in order to dominate Middle Eastern trade routes—this time for the region's oil. As Axis panzer divisions headed for the eastern delta, following the same route used by invading Libyan armies in the late New Kingdom, the Allied offensives at El Alamein in July and October 1942 marked a crucial turning point in the course of the Second World War. In Churchill's famous phrase, El Alamein was "the end of the beginning." How ironic, therefore, that just fourteen years later, the débâcle of the Suez Crisis—which once again saw armies fighting over a small corner of Egypt—signaled the beginning of the end for the British Empire.

From the clash of ancient civilizations to the cold war and beyond, Egypt has found itself at the center of things: "If men could learn from history, what lessons it might teach us!"[1]

Alongside Egypt's geopolitical importance, the country's profound cultural influence has also been felt ever since Caesar sailed up the Nile with Cleopatra. Hand in hand with more material exports, the cult of

Ancient Egyptian imagery on a U.S. one-dollar bill

Isis was carried from Egypt throughout the Roman world, even as far as the shores of Britain. Its impact was significant and long-lasting, especially in Egypt's old stamping ground of the Near East. Despite the proscription of "heathen" cults by the emperor Justinian in A.D. 553, the deep wellspring of ancient Egyptian religion proved a fertile source for the development of early Christianity. For Isis and Horus, substitute Virgin and Child—the iconography (and much of the underlying theology) remained virtually identical.

On a subsconscious level, the allure of pharaonic civilization has proved irresistible to the Romans and their sucessors in the West. Beginning with Hadrian's villa at Tivoli and the Egyptianizing frescoes of Pompeii, and continuing down to the present day with art deco jewelery and the Luxor hotel in Las Vegas, ancient Egypt has continued to exert a powerful influence on Western art and architecture. Individuals and popular movements, too, have appropriated pharaonic ideas in pursuit of their particular cause. Akhenaten, to take just one example, has been co-opted as a role model by Freudian psychoanalysts, Protestant fundamentalists, fascists, Afrocentrists, new age spiritualists, and gay rights campaigners. Hollywood has been especially mesmerized by ancient Egypt's blend of exoticism and antiquity, this fascination giving rise to a succession of hugely popular films, from *The Ten Commandments* and *Cleopatra* to *Raiders of the Lost Ark* and *The Scorpion King*.

In short, through Roman rule, the coming of Christianity, the Arab conquest, and the vicissitudes of the modern world, ancient Egypt as a concept and an ideal has not only survived but prospered. The rulers of the Nile Valley and their hard-pressed subjects succeeded in creating a uniquely powerful culture, one that has fascinated and bewitched all who have come into contact with it—from Alexander the Great to Agatha Christie. Today, in film and literature, and through architecture, design, and tourism, the civilization of the pharaohs is alive and well in the imaginations of people the world over.

The ancient Egyptians could not have wished for more.

ACKNOWLEDGMENTS

THE IDEA OF WRITING A COMPLETE HISTORY OF ANCIENT EGYPT, though perhaps lodged in the back of my mind as a project to undertake in my dotage, would never have come to the fore without the encouragement of my agent, Peter Robinson. To him—and to his colleagues in New York, Emma Parry and Christy Fletcher—I owe an immense debt of gratitude. My thanks are also due to my esteemed academic colleagues Paul Cartledge, Aidan Dodson, Kate Spence, and Dorothy Thompson for giving so generously of their time to read portions of the manuscript, question some of my assumptions, and correct inaccuracies in my understanding of their specialist subjects. Robert Morkot, Kenneth Kitchen, John Coleman Darnell, Colleen Manassa, and Liam McNamara provided invaluable references and stimulating original perspectives on a host of subjects. I am grateful to John Guy for a personal introduction that started the whole ball rolling; to my editors, John Flicker and Bill Swainson, for their belief in the project and attention to detail; and to Kate Spence (again) and Johnny Langridge for assistance with the maps. Finally, for his forebearance and understanding during my long periods of antisocial seclusion while researching and writing this book, I should like to thank Michael Bailey. I hope the finished volume goes some way to atone for his many nights alone in front of the television.

INTRODUCTION

The most accessible account of the discovery of Tutankhamun's tomb and the careers of the main protagonists is Nicholas Reeves, *The Complete Tutankhamun*. Carter's own three-volume publication, *The Tomb of Tut.ankh.Amen*, also makes fascinating reading.

For the decipherment of hieroglyphics by Jean-François Champollion, an entertaining recent study is John Ray, *The Rosetta Stone*. The career of John Gardner Wilkinson is reconstructed from the entry in Warren Dawson and Eric Uphill, *Who Was Who in Egyptology* (pp. 305–307).

The book about Tutankhamun that I read at the age of six was Christiane Desroches Noblecourt, *Tutankhamen*. I have yet to track down my first encyclopedia that piqued my interest in hieroglyphics.

CHAPTER 1: IN THE BEGINNING

The literature on the Narmer Palette is extensive and varied. Besides the valuable original publication by James Quibell, "Slate Palette from Hierakonpolis," among the more interesting recent discussions are Walter Fairservis, "A Revised View of the Na'rmr Palette"; O. Goldwasser, "The Narmer Palette and the 'Triumph of Metaphor' "; Christiana Köhler, "History or Ideology?"; Bruce Trigger, "The Narmer Palette in Cross-Cultural Perspective"; David Wengrow, "Rethinking 'Cattle Cults' in Early Egypt"; and Toby Wilkinson, "What a King Is This." The last also argues that "Narmer" is unlikely to be the correct reading of the name; indeed, the catfish and chisel may not represent a name at all but rather an expression of royal authority. Ian Shaw's *Ancient Egypt: A Very Short Introduction* (passim) and Barry Kemp's *Ancient Egypt: Anatomy of a Civilization* (pp. 83–84) also present some original and important insights. Whitney Davis's *Masking the Blow* is more controversial, though nonetheless stimulating.

Quibell and Green's excavations at Nekhen are summarized in two slim reports, *Hierakonpolis, I* (by Quibell alone) and *Hierakonpolis, II* (by Quibell and Green); these are very usefully supplemented by Green's field notebooks, kept in the Faculty of Asian and Middle Eastern Studies at the University of Cambridge. For an accessible and comprehensive overview of Nekhen and its archaeology, see the historical essay by Barbara Adams in her book *Ancient Nekhen*.

The important material from Nabta Playa has been well documented by the site's excavators, Fred Wendorf and Romauld Schild. Especially useful are their articles "Nabta Playa and Its Role" and "Implications of Incipient Social Complexity." The original announcement of the discovery of the "calendar circle" was made by J. Malville et al., "Megaliths and Neolithic Astronomy."

By contrast, the rock art of the Eastern Desert has been known for a century or more. The most significant early reports are Arthur Weigall, *Travels in the Upper Egyptian Deserts*, and two volumes by Hans Winkler, *Völker und Völkerbewegungen* and *Rock-Drawings of Southern Upper Egypt*, vol. 1. Further discoveries have been documented by Walter Resch, "Neue Felsbilderfunde in der ägyptische Ostwüste"; Gerard Fuchs, "Petroglyphs in the Eastern Desert of Egypt" and "Rock Engravings in the Wadi el-Barramiya"; Pavel Červíček, *Rock Pictures of Upper Egypt and Nubia*; Sharon Herbert and Henry Wright, "Report on the 1987 University of Michigan/University of Assiut Expedition"; Susan and Donald Redford, "Graffiti and Petroglyphs"; David Rohl (ed.), *The Followers of Horus*; and Maggie and Mike Morrow (eds.), *Desert RATS*. The evidence is usefully summarized and interpreted in Toby Wilkinson, *Genesis of the Pharaohs*.

The subject of climatic change in prehistory, and its effects, has received much attention in recent years. See, for example, Kathryn Bard and Robert Carneiro, "Patterns of Predynastic Settlement"; Karl Butzer, "Desert Environments"; and Romauld Schild and Fred Wendorf, "Palaeo-ecologic and Palaeo-climatic Background to Socio-economic Changes." For the closely related topic of prehistoric desert cultures and their influence on the rise of civilization in the Nile Valley, see W. McHugh, "Implications of a Decorated Predynastic Terracotta Model." See also several of the papers in Renée Friedman (ed.), *Egypt and Nubia*, especially Colin Hope, "Early and Mid-Holocene Ceramics"; Deborah Darnell, "Gravel of the Desert"; and Renée Friedman and Joseph Hobbs, "A 'Tasian' Tomb."

The best overview of the geology and topography of the Nile Valley is David Jeffreys, "The Nile Valley." There are strong echoes of the ancient Egyptian creation myth, with its dark and watery abyss, in the Judaeo-Christian creation story: "darkness was upon the face of the deep" (Genesis 1:2). Ancient Egyptian creation myths are considered in detail by James Allen, *Genesis in Egypt*, and are summarized by Vincent Arieh Tobin, "Creation Myths."

Badarian culture was first identified by Guy Brunton and Gertrude Caton-Thompson, *The Badarian Civilisation*, and Wendy Anderson, "Badarian Burials," recognized the presence of social differentiation. The sequence of cultural development during the latter phases of the Predynastic Period has been extensively studied. Authoritative works include Kathryn Bard, *From Farmers to Pharaohs*; Béatrix Midant-Reynes, *The Prehistory of Egypt*; and Toby Wilkinson, *State Formation in Egypt*.

The significance of elite cemeteries for charting the later stages of political unification is discussed by Barry Kemp, *Ancient Egypt* (Chapter 2, especially pp. 73–92), and Toby Wilkinson, *Early Dynastic Egypt* (Chapter 2). "Political Unification," also by Toby Wilkinson, presents a plausible reconstruction of events based on the archaeological evidence. The important new discovery of the Gebel Tjauti victory inscription is published by John and Deborah Darnell, "Opening the Narrow Doors of the Desert" and *Theban Desert Road Survey*. For tomb U-j at Abdju, the royal tomb designed to resemble a miniature palace, see the two volumes of final excavation reports by Günter Dreyer, *Umm el-Qaab I*, and Ulrich Hartung, *Umm el-Qaab II*. The evidence for warfare having played a decisive role in the final stages of unification is discussed by Marcelo Campagno, "In the Beginning Was the War." See also Elizabeth Finkenstaedt, "Violence and Kingship." For cranial injuries at predynastic Hierakonpolis, see Wendy Potter and Joseph Powell, "Big Headaches in the Predynastic."

The surviving Nilometer on Elephantine dates to the Roman Period, but there must have been similar devices from the dawn of history, since the government kept records of the height of the Nile floods from early in the First Dynasty (see Toby Wilkinson, *Royal Annals*). Although more than a quarter century old, John Baines and Jaromír Málek, *Atlas of Ancient Egypt*, still offers the most accessible overview of the geography of the Nile Valley and delta.

1. Herodotus, Book II, Chapter 5.
2. *Book of the Dead*, Chapter 17, section 2.

CHAPTER 2: GOD INCARNATE

Ancient Egyptian kingship has an extensive bibliography. For a good introduction, with further references, see Katja Goebs, "Kingship," and David O'Connor and David Silverman (eds.), *Ancient Egyptian Kingship*. In the latter volume, John Baines, "Origins of Egyptian Kingship," focuses on the early development of kingship ideology, as does Chapter 5 of Toby Wilkinson's *Early Dynastic Egypt*.

The painted beaker from Abdju is published by Günter Dreyer et al., "Umm el-Qaab, Nachuntersuchungen im frühzeitlichen Königsfriedhof" (figures 12.1 and 13). The recently discovered sacred complex of tombs and halls near Nekhen is described by Renée Friedman, "New Tombs and New Thoughts" and "From Pillar to Post." For the Painted Tomb (Tomb 100) at the same site, see H. Case and Joan Crowfoot Payne, "Tomb 100," supplemented by Barry Kemp, "Photographs of the Decorated Tomb at Hierakonpolis." The longevity of the smiting motif is considered by Emma Swan Hall, *The Pharaoh Smites His Enemies*. The iconography of the Battlefield Palette, Gebel Sheikh Suleiman inscription, and Narmer Palette are considered by Bernadette Menu, "L'émergence et la symbolique du pouvoir pharaonique," Winifred Needler, "A Rock-Drawing on Gebel Sheikh Suliman," and Toby Wilkinson, "What a King Is This."

The most detailed discussion of the origins and early development of royal regalia is to be found in Toby Wilkinson, *Early Dynastic Egypt* (pp. 186–199). For the original publication of the wooden staff from el-Omari, see Fernand Debono and Bodil Mortensen, *El Omari* (plates 28 and 43.2). Günter Dreyer, "A Hundred Years at Abydos," includes an excellent color photograph of the royal scepter from tomb U-j (the royal tomb at Abdju).

Palace-façade architecture and its supposed Mesopotamian origins have attracted much comment. Still useful are Henry Frankfort, "The Origin of Monumental Architecture," and Werner Kaiser, "Zu Entwicklung und Vorformen"; the evidence is collated in Toby Wilkinson, *Early Dynastic Egypt* (pp. 224–229). The wider context of cultural interaction between Mesopotamia and Egypt in the late fourth millennium B.C. is addressed by Toby Wilkinson, "Uruk into Egypt," and Ulrich Hartung, *Umm el-Qaab II*.

The best overview of ancient Egyptian royal titles is Stephen Quirke, *Who Were the Pharaohs?*, while Toby Wilkinson, *Early Dynastic Egypt* (pp. 200–208) charts the titles' early development. The latter source (pp. 208–218) also discusses early royal ceremony, a subject dealt with at greater length by Alessandro Jiménez Serrano, *Royal Festivals*.

The Scorpion and Narmer mace heads are examined in detail by Krzysztof Ciakowicz, *Les Têtes de Massues*, and Nicholas Millet, "The Narmer Macehead"; for excellent photographs of both objects by Werner Forman, see Jaromír Málek, *In the Shadow of the Pyramids* (pp. 28 and 29). Liam McNamara is carrying out a thorough reinvestigation and reinterpretation of the Hierakonpolis temple/cult center; for his preliminary conclusions, see "The Revetted Mound at Hierakonpolis." The observation about the severed genitals of Narmer's enemies was first made by Vivian Davies and Renée Friedman, "The Narmer Palette: A Forgotten Member." For Werner Forman's photograph of the statue base of Netjerikhet, with the king trampling the common people underfoot, see Jaromír Málek, *In the Shadow of the Pyramids* (pp. 88–89).

The evidence for possible human sacrifice in early Egypt is discussed in Jean-Pierre Albert and Béatrix Midant-Reynes (eds.), *Le sacrifice humain en Égypte ancienne*, especially the contributions by Éric Crubézy and Béatrix Midant-Reynes, "Les sacrifices humains"; Michel Baud and Marc Étienne, "Le vanneau et le couteau"; and Bernadette Menu, "Mise à mort cérémonielle." Useful summaries include Béatrix Midant-Reynes, "The Naqada Period" (p. 50); Kathryn Bard, "The Emergence of the Egyptian State" (p. 68); Jeffrey Spencer, *Early Egypt* (p. 79); and Toby Wilkinson, *Early Dynastic Egypt* (pp. 227 and 237). Recent evidence for scalping and decapitation at Nekhen is presented by Amy Maish, "Not Just Another Cut Throat"; Sean Dougherty, "A Little More off the Top"; and Xavier Droux, "Headless at Hierakonpolis." The willing death of retainers to accompany their master into the afterlife is not as far-fetched as it may sound. As recently as 1989, a loyal servant of the Japanese emperor Hirohito committed suicide as soon as his monarch's death was publicly announced. The pictorial evidence for human sacrifice in a cultic setting is presented by Toby Wilkinson, *Early Dynastic Egypt* (pp. 265–267).

The subsidiary burials surrounding the First Dynasty royal tombs and funerary enclosures at Abdju were published by Flinders Petrie, *Royal Tombs of the First Dynasty*, *Royal Tombs of the Earliest Dynasties*, and *Tombs of the Courtiers*. Recent fieldwork by the University of Pennsylvania Museum/Yale University/Institute of Fine Arts, New York University expedition has been reported online and by Matthew Adams, "Monuments of Egypt's Early Kings at Abydos." I am indebted to Professor Geoffrey Martin for information about the funerary stelae from the subsidiary burials at

Abdju. The human retainers included dwarfs, trappers of wild game, and a butcher—an entourage redolent of English noble households in the Middle Ages. In a similar vein, the First Dynasty Egyptian kings evidently favored dogs as pets, but one ruler seems to have kept a hyena, while another was buried with donkeys, perhaps to transport his belongings into the next world (see Stine Rossel et al., "Domestication of the Donkey").

CHAPTER 3: ABSOLUTE POWER

The best discussions of the origins and early uses of writing in ancient Egypt are Kathryn Bard, "Origins of Egyptian Writing," and John Ray, "The Emergence of Writing in Egypt." Nicholas Postgate, Tao Wang, and Toby Wilkinson, "The Evidence for Early Writing," compares the Egyptian evidence with early writing from Mesopotamia, Central America, and China. Günter Dreyer, *Umm el-Qaab I*, presents the new evidence from Abdju.

For the early Egyptian presence in southern Palestine, a useful collection of papers is brought together by Edwin van den Brink and Thomas Levy (eds.), *Egypt and the Levant*. An earlier article by Baruch Brandl, "Evidence for Egyptian Colonization," is still useful, while the material from the crucial site of En Besor is presented by Ram Gophna, "The Contacts Between 'En Besor Oasis, Southern Canaan, and Egypt," and (with D. Gazit) "The First Dynasty Egyptian Residency at 'En Besor." The contrast between the reality of Egypt's foreign relations and the institutionalized xenophobia is discussed by Toby Wilkinson, "Reality Versus Ideology." After decades of misattribution, the second inscription at Gebel Sheikh Suleiman was correctly reinterpreted by William Murnane, "The Gebel Sheikh Suleiman Monument," while Toby Wilkinson, *Early Dynastic Egypt* (pp. 175–179), charts the extirpation of the Nubian predynastic A-Group culture by the early Egyptians.

The latter work (Chapter 4) also includes the best treatment to date of early taxation and the workings of the Early Dynastic treasury. A comprehensive publication of the Palermo Stone and its associated fragments may be found in Toby Wilkinson, *Royal Annals of Ancient Egypt*. By the same author, *Early Dynastic Egypt* (pp. 75–78) is now the best source for the reign of Den and, at the end of the First Dynasty, the career of Merka (pp. 148–149). Bryan Emery excavated most of the major First Dynasty mastabas at North Saqqara, and his three-volume *Great Tombs of the First Dynasty* remains indispensable. He also published a separate account of the tomb of Hemaka, *Excavations at Saqqara: The Tomb of Hemaka*, and summarized his findings (with excellent architectural drawings but a now seriously outdated interpretation) in the popular *Archaic Egypt*.

The First Dynasty fortress on Abu is published by Martin Ziermann, *Elephantine XVI*, and its implications are discussed by Stephan Seidlmayer, "Town and State in the Early Old Kingdom."

The history of the Second Dynasty has received less attention than the preceding or succeeding periods, because of the difficulties involved in interpreting the fragmentary evidence. The best summaries are Aidan Dodson, "The Mysterious 2nd

Dynasty," and Toby Wilkinson, *Early Dynastic Egypt* (pp. 82–94). For the cedarwood ships at Abdju, see David O'Connor, "The Earliest Royal Boat Graves" and "The Royal Boat Burials at Abydos"; the earliest bronze vessels in Egypt are published by Jeffrey Spencer, *Early Egypt* (p. 88). Evidence for the early timber trade with Kebny is provided by the recent discovery of coniferous veneers at a predynastic funerary complex at Hierakonpolis. See Renée Friedman, "Origins of Monumental Architecture."

The Gisr el-Mudir has been the subject of recent survey and excavation by a team from the National Museums of Scotland. Their preliminary reports provide the most up-to-date information on this intriguing monument: Ian Mathieson and Ana Tavares, "Preliminary Report"; Elizabeth Bettles et al., *National Museums of Scotland Saqqara Project Report 1995;* and Ana Tavares, "The Saqqara Survey Project."

The late Jean-Philippe Lauer dedicated his entire adult life to excavating and reconstructing the Step Pyramid complex of Netjerikhet, and his three-volume *Fouilles à Saqqarah* remains the unrivaled publication of this monument; his more popular *Saqqara* is more accessible to an English-speaking audience. The careers of Imhotep and other high officials at the court of Netjerikhet are examined in Toby Wilkinson, *Lives of the Ancient Egyptians* (nos. 5, 6, and 7).

For the small step pyramids of the late Third Dynasty, see the preliminary studies by Günter Dreyer and Werner Kaiser, "Zu den kleinen Stufenpyramiden," and Günter Dreyer and Nabil Swelim, "Die kleine Stufenpyramide"; and the interpretations by Stephan Seidlmayer, "Town and State in the Early Old Kingdom," and Toby Wilkinson, *Early Dynastic Egypt* (pp. 277–279).

CHAPTER 4: HEAVEN ON EARTH

The most comprehensive and up-to-date source (with an extensive bibliography) for the Great Pyramid is John Romer, *The Great Pyramid.* Mark Lehner, *The Complete Pyramids,* is essential for understanding Khufu's pyramid as the apogee of a long tradition in ancient Egyptian funerary architecture. José-Ramón Pérez-Accino, "The Great Pyramid," conveniently summarizes some of the more exotic theories concerning the construction of the Giza monument.

For social change at the beginning of the Fourth Dynasty, see Ann Macy Roth, "Social Change." The entry on the Palermo Stone recording the foundation of royal estates by Sneferu is discussed in Toby Wilkinson, *Royal Annals* (p. 143), while Barry Kemp, *Ancient Egypt* (p. 166 and fig. 59), provides a useful discussion of the estates serving Sneferu's mortuary cult. The results of recent excavations at Imu have been published by Robert Wenke, "Kom el-Hisn."

Vivian Davies and Renée Friedman, *Egypt* (p. 74), give a lively account of the building problems at the Bent Pyramid. Calculation of construction rates and different theories about the length of Sneferu's reign are addressed by Rainer Stadelmann, "Beiträge zur Geschichte des Alten Reiches," and Rolf Krauss, "The Length of Sneferu's Reign."

The concentration of political power among a handful of royal relatives during the Fourth Dynasty is discussed by Nigel Strudwick, *The Administration of Egypt in the Old Kingdom*, and Michel Baud, *La famille royale*. For the careers of Hemiunu, Perniankhu, and Hetepheres, see Toby Wilkinson, *Lives of the Ancient Egyptians* (nos. 11, 12, and 9, respectively). Hetepheres's bracelets are beautifully illustrated in the Metropolitan Museum of Art, *Egyptian Art* (pp. 216–217). The best summary of the Great Pyramid's stellar orientation is Kate Spence, "Are the Pyramids Aligned with the Stars?," while her two more specialist articles, "Ancient Egyptian Chronology" and "Astronomical Orientation of the Pyramids," explain and defend her own theory that the Egyptians used two of the circumpolar stars.

The pyramid workforce is discussed in Mark Lehner, *The Complete Pyramids*, which also presents a summary of the material from Gerget Khufu; for a more detailed discussion of the latter, see Zahi Hawass, "The Workmen's Community at Giza." Mark Lehner's publication "The Pyramid Age Settlement" is the definitive source for the pyramid town at south Giza, usefully supplemented by Nicholas Conard and Mark Lehner, "The 1988/1989 Excavation." Richard Bussmann, "Siedlungen im Kontext der Pyramiden," provides a useful synthesis of the evidence to date. For the burials of workers at Giza, see Zahi Hawass, "The Pyramid Builders," and Vivian Davies and Renée Friedman, *Egypt* (pp. 85–87). The physical trauma suffered by the pyramid builders, as well as the medical intervention carried out to treat injuries, is discussed by F. Hussein et al., "Similarity of Treatment of Trauma."

The purpose and symbolism of pyramids has received an enormous amount of attention, and the bibliography is almost endless. A useful starting point is Kate Spence, "What Is a Pyramid For?" but the discussion in the current volume is based upon the author's own unpublished research.

Ann Macy Roth, "The Meaning of Menial Labour," explores the culture of servitude among Fourth Dynasty officials. The evidence for far-flung desert expeditions is presented by Rudolph Kuper and Frank Förster, "Khufu's 'Mefat' Expeditions"; Ian Shaw, "Khafra's Quarries"; and Ian Shaw and Tom Heldal, "Rescue Work in the Khafra Quarries." New excavations at the pyramid of Djedefra are published by Michel Valloggia, "Radjedef's Pyramid Complex," and excavations in the associated necropolis are published by Michel Baud and Nadine Moeller, "A Fourth Dynasty Royal Necropolis."

For the pyramids of Khafra and Menkaura, see, once again, Mark Lehner, *The Complete Pyramids*. Rainer Stadelmann, "The Great Sphinx of Giza," has argued plausibly, on stylistic and topographical grounds, that the Sphinx was carved by Khufu; other scholars have suggested that it was carved in Khufu's likeness, but by his eldest son, Djedefra—or even that it was recarved in the Fourth Dynasty from a lion-headed statue that had first been created in the First Dynasty. But Mark Lehner, "The Sphinx," has made a more convincing case for the generally accepted attribution of the monument to the reign of Khafra, based upon the geological and architectural evidence, and his conclusions have been followed here. For the ivory statuette of Khufu, see, among others, Toby Wilkinson, *Lives of the Ancient Egyptians* (no. 10).

1. Jaromír Málek, "The Old Kingdom," p. 92.
2. Herodotus, Book II, Chapters 124 and 127.

CHAPTER 5: ETERNITY ASSURED

Userkaf's sun temple was excavated and published by Herbert Ricke, *Das Sonnen-heiligtum des Königs Userkaf;* the main elements and decoration of this and other Fifth and Sixth dynasty royal monuments are again usefully summarized in Mark Lehner, *The Complete Pyramids.*

For the administrative reforms at the beginning of the Fifth Dynasty, and later in the Old Kingdom, see Naguib Kanawati, *Governmental Reforms,* and Nigel Strud-wick, *The Administration of Egypt in the Old Kingdom.* Christopher Eyre, "Weni's Career," offers a closely argued and penetrating analysis of political and administrative developments in the late Old Kingdom, as seen through the lens of one individual's career. The standard work on so-called ranking titles is Klaus Baer, *Rank and Title.* Tombs of high officials in the Memphite area are discussed by Jaromír Málek, *In the Shadow of the Pyramids,* and the most famous examples are illustrated in Alberto Sil-iotti, *Guide to the Pyramids of Egypt.* The tomb of Mereruka is comprehensively and beautifully published in the immense two-volume work by Prentice Duell, *The Mastaba of Mereruka.*

The evidence for disease and deformity in ancient Egypt is presented by John Nunn in his book *Ancient Egyptian Medicine* and his article "Disease"; by Joyce Filer, *Disease;* and Eugen Strouhal, "Deformity." Kent Weeks, "Medicine, Surgery, and Public Health," provides a useful overview. The tomb of Ankhmahor at Saqqara shows a fowler in the marshes with a scrotal swelling that might be an inguinal her-nia or a hydrocele, while the tomb of Mehu shows two men with umbilical hernias. See John Nunn, *Ancient Egyptian Medicine,* fig. 8.3.

For the lives and careers of Ptahshepses, Unas, Pepiankh of Meir, Mereruka, Weni, Harkhuf, and Pepi II, see Toby Wilkinson, *Lives of the Ancient Egyptians* (nos. 13–15 and 17–20). For the career of Weni and its wider context, see Christopher Eyre, "Weni's Career"; Eyre argues that the rise of a provincial bureaucracy in the late Fifth and Sixth dynasties signals not the beginnings of local autonomy but quite the reverse, a growing penetration of the state into the affairs of the provinces. For the striking absence of temples dedicated to local gods in the Old Kingdom, see Jaromír Málek, *In the Shadow of the Pyramids* (p. 109).

The standard edition of the papyri from the mortuary temple of Neferirkara at Abusir is Paule Posener-Kriéger, *Les archives du temple funéraire;* Barry Kemp, *Ancient Egypt* (pp. 164–171), also has a useful discussion of some of the documents.

Raymond Faulkner, *The Ancient Egyptian Pyramid Texts,* and James Allen, *The An-cient Egyptian Pyramid Texts,* are the best complete translations of these early religious inscriptions. For the disposition of texts within the pyramid of Unas, see James Allen, "Reading a Pyramid," and for the Cannibal Hymn in particular, see Christopher Eyre, *The Cannibal Hymn.* The famine scene from the causeway of Unas is illustrated in W. Stevenson Smith, *The Art and Architecture of Ancient Egypt* (p. 134, fig. 126).

The existence of an ephemeral king Userkara seems proven by the inscription published by Michel Baud and Vassil Dobrev, "De nouvelles annals." See also Naguib Kanawati, "New Evidence on the Reign of Userkare?"; Naguib Kanawati et al., *Excavations at Saqqara*, vol. 1; and the accompanying illustration (plate 6) in vol. 2 of the same series by Ali el-Khouli and Naguib Kanawati.

Evidence for the conspiracies against the life of Pepi I is presented by Naguib Kanawati, "Deux conspirations." The best discussion of Pepi I's cult chapels remains Labib Habachi, *Tell Basta*. The ongoing French excavations at Ayn Asil are summarized by Georges Soukiassian et al., "La ville d' 'Ayn Asil." For the close links between the central government in Memphis and the Dakhla Oasis, see Laure Pantalacci, "De Memphis à Balat"; and for the watch posts surrounding the Dakhla Oasis, see Olaf Kaper and Harco Willems, "Policing the Desert."

The autobiographical inscriptions of Weni and Harkhuf are translated in Miriam Lichtheim, *Ancient Egyptian Literature* (vol. 1, pp. 18–27). Toby Wilkinson, "Egyptian Explorers," is a convenient source for Harkhuf's expeditions to Yam.

Numerous authors have discussed the causes for the collapse of the Old Kingdom. For two recent examples, see Renate Müller-Wollermann, *Krisenfaktoren*, and Ian Shaw, "The End of the Great Pyramid Age." Various principal factors have been proposed, ranging from adverse climatic conditions to the rise of provincial officials and the progressive alienation of economic resources from the central government. While the last seems unconvincing, compelling evidence for the effect of low Niles at the end of the Sixth Dynasty is presented by James Harrell and Thomas Bown, "An Old Kingdom Basalt Quarry."

1. Pyramid Texts, Utterances 273–274.
2. Weni, autobiographical inscription, lines 3–4.
3. Ibid., lines 10–13.
4. Ibid., lines 6–7.
5. Ibid., lines 27–28.
6. Harkhuf, tomb inscription, right of entrance, lines 8–9.
7. Ibid., left of entrance, lines 4–5.
8. Ibid., far right of façade, lines 6–7.
9. Ibid., far right of façade, lines 15–22.

CHAPTER 6: CIVIL WAR

Although there are some good recent summaries of First Intermediate Period history, notably the articles "First Intermediate Period" by Detlef Franke and "The First Intermediate Period" by Stephan Seidlmayer, there is really no substitute for direct engagement with the primary sources, epigraphic and archaeological. Texts from the period are surprisingly abundant, but scattered and fragmentary. Essential anthologies include Jacques Jean Clère and Jacques Vandier, *Textes de la Première Période Intermédiaire*; Henry Fischer, *Inscriptions from the Coptite Nome* and *Dendera in the Third Millennium B.C.*; Miriam Lichtheim, *Ancient Egyptian Autobiographies*; and, especially, Wolfgang Schenkel, *Memphis-Herakleopolis-Theben*. Ludwig Morenz, "The First Intermediate Period," has suggested that the period should be renamed the "Era of the Regions," to reflect the high degree of political decentralization.

For a reevaluation of the end of the Sixth Dynasty, the identification of Neitiqerty as a male ruler, and the ephemeral kings of the Eighth Dynasty, see Kim Ryholt, "The Late Old Kingdom." The pyramid of Ibi at Saqqara was published by Gustave Jéquier, *La Pyramide d'Aba*, and is summarized in Mark Lehner, *The Complete Pyramids* (p. 164). Hans Goedicke, *Königliche Dokumente* (pp. 163–225) and William Hayes, "Royal Decrees," remain the standard editions of the Gebtu decrees, while Goedicke's "A Cult Inventory" provides useful background information about the temple cult at Gebtu in the late Eighth Dynasty. If, as Goedicke ("A Cult Inventory," pp. 74 and 82) has suggested, Gebtu was a garrison town in the late Old Kingdom, its nomarchs may have provided the Eighth Dynasty kings with military as well as moral support.

Little is known for certain about the Herakleopolitan dynasty; the meager evidence is summarized by Jürgen von Beckerath, "Die Dynastie der Herakleopoliten," while Stephan Seidlmayer, "Zwei Anmerkungen," helps to refine the chronology of the period. The dynasty's rise to power by force may be suggested by the late Old Kingdom tombs at Hagarsa, near Akhmim in Middle Egypt, which seem to show evidence of military activity. See Naguib Kanawati, "Akhmim." For the tomb of "King Khui" at Dara, see Barry Kemp, *Ancient Egypt* (pp. 338–339) and Stephan Seidlmayer, "The First Intermediate Period" (pp. 132–133). Dissent within the Herakleopolitan realm is discussed by Donald Spanel, "The First Intermediate Period." For the inscriptions of Merer and Iti and their references to famine, see Miriam Lichtheim, *Ancient Egyptian Literature* (vol. 1, pp. 87–89). Famine as a leitmotif in First Intermediate Period autobiographies is discussed by Anrea Gnirs, "Biographies." The life and times of Ankhtifi have been treated at length by, among others, Donald Spanel, "The Date of Ankhtifi," and Stephan Seidlmayer, "The First Intermediate Period" (pp. 118–123). The military nature of the conflict between Ankhtifi and his rivals is reflected in the scenes of soldiers, both in the tomb of Ankhtifi himself and in that of his contemporary Setka, from Abu. See Jacques Vandier, *Mo'alla*.

For the conference of nomarchs attended by Intef the Great's representative, see Henry Fischer, *Varia Nova* (pp. 83–90). As well as Intef the Great, nomarch of Thebes, the overseer of his army was also named Intef. Intef the Great's three successors were likewise named Intef (designated Intef I, II, and III, since they claimed royal titles); and one of the Thebans' most loyal lieutenants, who served Intef II, III, and the next king, was another Intef (see John Bennett, "A New Interpretation"). A roll call of the Theban army must have been a confusing exercise! The tradition continued into the reign of Mentuhotep, when the king's chief of police was also named Intef.

The Nubian mercenaries at Inerty were brought to scholarly attention by Henry Fischer, "The Nubian Mercenaries"; more recently, Sabine Kubisch, "Die Stelen der 1. Zwischenzeit," has studied the epigraphy, iconography, and chronology of stelae from the same cemetery. For the hugely important discovery of Tjauti's Western Desert inscription, and a thorough analysis of its significance for the early stages of Theban expansion, see John and Deborah Darnell, *Theban Desert Road Survey*.

The military achievements of Intef II are best traced in the inscriptions of his loyal lieutenants. The Theban annexation of the three southernmost nomes is described in the inscription of Hetepi of Elkab—see Gawdat Gabra, "Preliminary Report on the Stela of *Htpi.*" For the inscription of Djemi, which alludes to the distribution of food aid in the conquered areas, see Hans Goedicke, "The Inscription of *Dmi*"; and for Djari, see Miriam Lichtheim, *Ancient Egyptian Autobiographies* (pp. 40–42). Accounts from the other side in the civil war are preserved in the tombs at Sauty. See Hellmut Brunner, *Die Texte aus den Gräbern der Herakleopolitenzeit von Siut;* and Donald Spanel, "Asyut" and "The Herakleopolitan Tombs." The Herakleopolitan lament over the fate of Abdju appears in the literary work known as *The Instruction for Merikara,* believed to have been written by King Kheti for his son.

For impoverishment and serfdom in the First Intermediate Period, see Juan Carlos Moreno Garcia, "Acquisition de serfs." The carefully calculated imagery used by Intef II in his letter to Khety is discussed by John Darnell, "The Message of King Wahankh Antef II." The letter's subtext is subtly symbolic. By accusing Khety of having "raised a storm" over the Thinite nome, Intef is equating him with Seth, the storm god and enemy of Horus; the implication is that Intef is the true Horus, and hence the legitimate king. The final stages of Intef II's campaign are recorded on the stela of the overseer of scouts of Djari, and on the king's own "dogs stela" inscribed in the last year of his reign. The funerary stela of Intef II and the stela of Tjetji are translated by Miriam Lichtheim, *Ancient Egyptian Literature* (vol. 1, pp. 94–96 and 90–93, respectively).

For the final phase in the civil war and the repressive policies of Mentuhotep, see Henry Fischer, "A God and a General" and "The Inscription of *In-it.f*"; and William Hayes, "Career of the Great Steward Henenu." Scenes in the tomb of Kheti II at Sauty show soldiers marching in formation, holding their shields in preparation for battle, armed with fighting axes; yet, despite such evidence, Hans Goedicke, "The Unification of Egypt" (especially pp. 163–164), argues that the reunification was the result of peaceful negotiations, not of military conquest. His radical reinterpretation has not found general favor, but it illustrates the often slippery nature of the contemporary sources. Graffiti of the soldier Tjehemau at Abisko record Mentuhotep's Nubian campaign; see John Darnell, "The Rock Inscriptions," and "The Route of Eleventh Dynasty Expansion."

Recent archaeological work in the cemetery at Herakleopolis is summarized by Maria del Carmen Pérez-Die, "The Ancient Necropolis at Ehnasya el-Medina." The precise date of formal reunification is uncertain, but Mentuhotep had certainly adopted the title of reunifier by his thirty-ninth year on the throne. Mentuhotep's change of Horus names and the implications of that change are discussed by Sir Alan Gardiner, "The First King Menthotpe"; the king's deification is covered by Labib Habachi, "King Nebhepetre Menthuhotp," and Gae Callender, "The Middle Kingdom Renaissance" (pp. 140–141). The trusted follower appointed by Mentuhotep II to be his personal representative in Herakleopolis was named Intef, son of Tjefi. The war grave (at Deir el-Bahri) was excavated and published by Herbert Winlock, *The Slain Soldiers.* Its alternative dating to the early Twelfth Dynasty, not followed here, is mentioned in Ronald Leprohon, "The Programmatic Use of the Royal Titulary."

1. William Hayes, "Royal Decrees," p. 23.
2. Merer, funerary stela, line 9.

3. Iti, stela, columns 2–3, and 6.
4. Ankhtifi, tomb inscription, section 10.
5. Ibid., section 2.
6. Intef, stela, line 2.
7. Tjauti, false door, right-hand side.
8. Ibid., desert inscription, line 2.
9. Hetepi, funerary stela, line 5.
10. Djemi, funerary stela, columns 3–4.
11. Kheti I, tomb inscription, lines 7–8.
12. Djari, funerary stela, lines 3–4.
13. Intef II, funerary stela, lines 4–5.
14. Tjetji, funerary stela, lines 12–13.
15. Intef, funerary stela from Naga el-Deir, line 4.
16. Henenu, funerary stela, line 3.

CHAPTER 7: PARADISE POSTPONED

The so-called democratization of the afterlife is critically appraised by Stephen Quirke in Werner Forman and Stephen Quirke, *Hieroglyphs and the Afterlife*, which also includes one of the best discussions of the Coffin Texts. The concept of original sin finds perhaps its earliest expression in the Coffin Texts (Spells 1130 and 1031), where Ra says, "I made every man like his fellow; and I did not command that they do wrong. / It is their hearts that disobey what I have said." For the assumption of royal attributes, see also Paul John Fransden, "*Bwt* in the Body." The Sixth Dynasty funerary texts from the Dakhla Oasis survived only as faint impressions on the plaster coating of Medunefer's coffin. Whether they were originally painted on the outer walls of the coffin itself, or on a shroud that covered the coffin, is impossible to determine. Either way, the intention seems to have been to place the protective spells around Medunefer's body.

The definitive study of Middle Kingdom coffins and the origins of the Coffin Texts is Harco Willems, *Chests of Life*. John Taylor, *Egyptian Coffins*, provides a useful and accessible summary; *Death and the Afterlife* by the same author offers a comprehensive introduction to all aspects of ancient Egyptian funerary beliefs, customs, and artifacts. The best translation and commentary on *The Book of Two Ways* is Leonard Lesko's *The Ancient Egyptian Book of Two Ways*. Other useful discussions of this book and the other Coffin Texts include Stephen Quirke, *Ancient Egyptian Religion*; Leonard Lesko, "Coffin Texts"; and Harco Willems, "The Social and Ritual Context of a Mortuary Liturgy." Richard Parkinson, *Voices from Ancient Egypt*, includes some extracts from the Coffin Texts in a modern English translation, while Adriaan de Buck, *The Egyptian Coffin Texts*, is the definitive hieroglyphic edition.

The nature of the *ba* is discussed most thoroughly in Louis Žabkar, *A Study of the Ba Concept*, while the evidence is usefully summarized by James Allen, "Ba."

For the cult of Osiris, John Gwyn Griffiths's article "Osiris" is of key importance, presenting the results of a lifetime's scholarship. Richard Wilkinson, *The Complete Gods and Goddesses* (pp. 118–123), offers an overview of Osiris's iconography, origins, and worship. Geraldine Pinch, *Egyptian Myth*, gives a brief but original interpretation of the Osiris myth. The Osiris mysteries at Abdju are discussed at some length in Toby Wilkinson, *Lives of the Ancient Egyptians* (no. 34), and Osirian festivals elsewhere in Egypt are discussed in Harco Willems, "The Social and Ritual Context of a Mortuary Liturgy." William Kelly Simpson, *The Terrace of the Great God*, is the most comprehensive publication of the Middle Kingdom funerary monuments lining the sacred way at Abdju. Erik Hornung, "Some Remarks on the Inhabitants of the West," dates the mortuary focus on the underworld to the reign of Senusret II, as reflected in the winding passageways beneath the king's pyramid at Lahun.

The best recent investigation of regional and chronological differences in Middle Kingdom funerary customs is Janine Bourriau, "Patterns of Change." *Shabti*s are discussed in most books on Egyptian burial practices, a reliable example being John Taylor, *Death and the Afterlife*. The evolution of the concept of a last judgment is brilliantly traced by Stephen Quirke, "Judgment of the Dead"; while Carol Andrews, *Amulets*, explains the significance of the heart scarab.

1. Coffin Texts, Spell 467.
2. *Book of the Dead*, Chapter 6.
3. *The Instruction for King Merikara*, lines 55–57.
4. Merer, funerary stela, line 7.
5. Coffin Texts, Spell 452.
6. Coffin Texts, Spell 338.
7. Nebankh, heart scarab (translation by Stephen Quirke in Werner Forman and Stephen Quirke, *Hieroglyphs and the Afterlife*, p. 104).

CHAPTER 8: THE FACE OF TYRANNY

Although few syntheses of the Twelfth Dynasty have been published, the specialist literature on the period is extensive, and it is therefore necessary to return to these works and original sources. The inscriptions left by Mentuhotep IV's expeditions to the Wadi Hammamat were published by J. Couyat and Pierre Montet, *Les inscriptions hiéroglyphiques*, although their translations are now out of date. The Eleventh Dynasty royal court was modeled on the court of a provincial governor, with a treasurer and steward taking prominence over other officials. See Wolfram Grajetski, *The Middle Kingdom* (especially pp. 21 and 90).

For the end of the Eleventh Dynasty and possible reasons behind the apparent civil strife, see John Darnell, "The Route of Eleventh Dynasty Expansion into Nubia." The Hatnub inscriptions, a key source for the internal politics of the early Twelfth Dynasty, were published by Rudolf Anthes, *Die Felseninschriften von Hatnub*, and have been carefully studied by Harco Willems, "The Nomarchs of the Hare Nome." Further evidence for dissent at the same period is discussed by William Kelly Simpson, "Studies in the Twelfth Egyptian Dynasty." Dorothea Arnold, "Amenemhat I" (p. 20), suggests that the location of Itj-tawy may have been chosen because it was within the "greater Memphite" capital zone, while affording easy access to the Fayum, an area that had begun to be developed in the early Twelfth Dynasty.

The Horus names of Amenemhat I and his successors are analyzed by Ronald Leprohon, "The Programmatic Use of the Royal Titulary." For Kay's surveillance mission into the Western Desert, see Rudolf Anthes, "Eine Polizeistreife." The important stela of Nesumontu, which alludes to an insurgency against the regime, is published in William Kelly Simpson, *The Terrace of the Great God*, plate 14, and discussed by Dorothea Arnold, "Amenemhat I" (pp. 18–19). For the inscription of Khnumhotep I from Beni Hasan, see Percy Newberry, *Beni Hasan*. Alan Schulman, "The Battle Scenes of the Middle Kingdom," discusses the scenes of warfare from this and neighboring tombs.

The results of recent excavations at the Twelfth Dynasty temple at Ipetsut are published by Guillaume Charloux, "The Middle Kingdom Temple of Amun at Karnak." The construction of Amenemhat I's pyramid is most usefully summarized in Mark Lehner, *The Complete Pyramids* (pp. 168–169). The pyramids of the last two Twelfth Dynasty rulers, Amenemhat IV and Sobekneferu, have not been positively identified, but it is likely that each of the monarchs at least started work on a pyramid complex. For the frontier zone along the northeastern delta and the Walls of the Ruler, see Stephen Quirke, "Frontier or Border?"

The inscriptions published by Zbyněk Žába, *The Rock Inscriptions of Lower Nubia*, constitute the primary evidence for local kings in lower Nubia at the beginning of the Twelfth Dynasty and for the Egyptian military response to their threat. Wolfram Grajetski, *The Middle Kingdom* (pp. 27–28 and 31), summarizes the current consensus. For the chronological position of the Nubian rulers and their relationship with Egypt, see Robert Morkot, *The Black Pharaohs* (pp. 54–55) and "Kingship and Kinship in the Empire of Kush." If we are to believe Mentuhotep II's claim to have annexed Wawat (lower Nubia) to Upper Egypt, then Egyptian control must have been lost again during the ineffective reigns of Mentuhotep's two successors. The name of the Nubian king Intef raises the possibility that he was a direct descendant of the Egyptian Eleventh Dynasty, and as such was a focus of dissent for those opposed to Amenemhat's usurpation of the throne. Barry Kemp, "Old Kingdom, Middle Kingdom and Second Intermediate Period" (pp. 168–169), suggested that the Nubian inscriptions might date to the very end of the Middle Kingdom and represent quasi-autonomous rulers of Egyptian fortified towns abandoned by the central government, but a dating to the early Twelfth Dynasty makes best sense of the evidence.

For the fortress of Buhen, see W. Bryan Emery, H. S. Smith, and A. Millard, *The Fortress of Buhen*, and Barry Kemp, *Ancient Egypt: Anatomy of a Civilization* (pp. 231–235). Until its submergence under the waters of Lake Nasser, Buhen was extremely well preserved and stood comparison with the castles of the Middle Ages; its loss is one of the saddest in the annals of Egyptian archaeology. The forts of Ikkur and Quban, two of the earliest to be built by Senusret I, were deliberately located on either side of the Nile, at the entrance to the Wadi Allaqi. Not only did this wadi lead directly to the ore-rich mountains of the Eastern Desert, but it had also provided the main route for Nubian infiltration into Egypt in earlier periods. Economic exploitation and national security were two sides of the same coin. Stephen Quirke, "State and Labour in the Middle Kingdom," discusses the nature of the "compound" attested in Middle Kingdom sources.

Scholars in favor of a ten-year co-regency between Amenemhat I and his son include William Kelly Simpson, "The Single-Dated Monuments of Sesostris I"; Wolfgang Helck, "Mitregenschaft"; William Murnane, *Ancient Egyptian Coregencies* (pp. 2–5 and 245–253); and Detlef Franke, "Zur Chronologie des Mittleren Reiches." Claude Obsomer has argued against this (though he is something of a lone voice) in "La date de Nésou-Montou" and *Sésostris Ier.* The description of Amenemhat I's assassination is taken from the literary text *The Instruction of Amenemhat I for His Son,* most usefully translated by Miriam Lichtheim, *Ancient Egyptian Literature* (vol. 1, pp. 135–139). Senusret I's chosen Horus name, "[long] live the renaissance," could not have expressed his intentions more clearly. See Ronald Leprohon, "The Programmatic Use of the Royal Titulary."

The classic discussion about propagandist literature in the Middle Kingdom is Georges Posener, *Littérature et politique.* Richard Parkinson, "Teachings, Discourses and Tales," *The Tale of Sinuhe and Other,* and *Voices from Ancient Egypt,* provide important translations and commentaries on the key texts, as does Miriam Lichtheim, *Ancient Egyptian Literature* (vol. 1). The dates of these propagandist texts are still subject to considerable debate. *The Complaints of Khakheperraseneb* cannot predate the reign of Senusret II (since Senusret's throne name, Khakheperra, forms part of the name of the protagonist), and could well be a little later. *The Admonitions of Ipuwer* has been dated to the Thirteenth Dynasty, but this is by no means certain. For a full discussion of the texts and their likely dates, see Richard Parkinson, "Teachings, Discourses and Tales."

For the expedition to the oases under Senusret I, see Heinrich Schäfer, "Ein Zug nach der grossen Oase." The inscriptions in the temple at Djerty/Tod describing civil unrest and Senusret I's response are translated and discussed by Christophe Barbotin and Jacques Jean Clère, "L'inscription de Sésostris Ier à Tôd," and Donald Redford, "The Tod Inscription of Senwosret I." Senusret's jubilee pavilion (the "white chapel") at Ipetsut is published by Pierre Lacau and H. Chevrier, *Une chapelle de Sésostris Ier à Karnak.* For the first phase of Nubian fortresses, built in the reign of Senusret I, see Barry Kemp, "Old Kingdom, Middle Kingdom and Second Intermediate Period" (pp. 130–131).

The Djerty treasure was excavated and published by Fernand Bisson de la Roque et al., *Le Trésor de Tôd.* For translations and commentaries of the annals of Amenemhat II, and discussion of his foreign campaigns, see Sami Farag, "Une inscription Memphite"; Hartwig Altenmüller and Ahmed Moussa, "Die Inschrift Amenemhets II"; and Ezra Marcus, "Amenemhet II and the Sea." The arguments for the identification of Iwa and Iasy as Ura and Cyprus, respectively, are adduced by Wolfgang Helck, "Ein Ausgreifen des Mittleren Reiches"; C. Eder, *Die ägyptischen Motive* (p. 191); Joachim Quack, "*Kft3w and 'I3ssy*"; and Kenneth Kitchen, "Some Thoughts on Egypt, the Aegean and Beyond." The location of Ura directly opposite the northern tip of the island lends credence to the island's identification as Cyprus. Louise Steel, "Egypt and the Mediterranean World," provides an up-to-date summary of Middle Kingdom activity in the eastern Mediterranean. The best discussion of Kahun and Middle Kingdom town planning in general is Barry Kemp, *Ancient Egypt: Anatomy of a Civilization* (pp. 211–221 and 221–231, respectively).

For the end of the nomarchs under Senusret III, see Detlef Franke, "The Career of Khnumhotep III"; the tombs of viziers in the court cemetery have recently been published by Dieter Arnold, "Two New Mastabas of the Twelfth Dynasty." In the case of Khnumhotep III, he left his province to become high steward and vizier—two of the highest offices in the land. Excavations are ongoing at Senusret III's pyramid town at Abdju. For detailed archaeological reports, see Josef Wegner, "The Town of *Wah-sut* at South Abydos" and "Excavations at the Town," with a convenient summary in "A Middle Kingdom Town at South Abydos."

The second cataract forts are brilliantly analyzed by Barry Kemp, "Large Middle Kingdom Granary Buildings" and *Ancient Egypt: Anatomy of a Civilization* (pp. 236–242), and by Stuart Tyson Smith, "Askut and the Role of the Second Cataract Forts." The relay stations were located at Uronarti, Shalfak, Askut, Mushid, Gemai, Mirgissa, and on the rock of Abu Sir. For the ideological and political factors behind their construction, see Kate Spence, "Royal Walling Projects." Paul Smither, "The Semnah Despatches," remains the only detailed publication of these essential documents. Recent discoveries relating to the kingdom of Kush have been reported by Thomas Maugh, "Ancient Kush Rivaled Egypt." The Semna boundary stela is published in facsimile and translation by Richard Parkinson, *Voices from Ancient Egypt* (pp. 43–46).

Janine Bourriau, *Pharaohs and Mortals*, and Felicitas Polz, "Die Bildnisse Sesostris' III. und Amenemhets III," discuss the distinctive royal sculpture of the later Twelfth Dynasty. The reign of Amenemhat III is conveniently summarized by Gae Callender, "The Middle Kingdom Renaissance." Manfred Bietak, "Egypt and the Levant," discusses the evolving relationship between Egypt and Kebny, and the role of Asiatics in the Sinai mining expeditions. The invention of an alphabetic script by Asiatic patrolmen in Egyptian service is published by John Darnell et al., *Two Early Alphabetic Inscriptions*, and G. J. Hamilton, *The Origins of the West Semitic Alphabet*, and summarized by John Darnell, "The Deserts."

For the brief reigns of Amenemhat IV and Sobekneferu and their relationship with Amenemhat III, see Aidan Dodson and Dyan Hilton, *The Complete Royal Families* (p. 95).

1. Mentuhotep IV, Wadi Hammamat inscription, lines 10–11.
2. Hatnub inscriptions, no. 24, lines 7–8.
3. Kay, funerary stela, lines 4–5.
4. Khnumhotep I, biographical inscription, line 5.
5. *The Instruction of Amenemhat I for His Son*, section III.
6. Intefiqer, Wadi el-Girgawi inscription, lines 6–11.
7. *The Instruction of Amenemhat I for His Son*, sections I–II.
8. *The Prophecies of Neferti*, lines 57–67.
9. *The Tale of Sinuhe*, lines 165–168.
10. *The Loyalist Instruction*, section 2, lines 1–6.
11. Dediqu, stela inscription, lines 6–7.
12. Cycle of Hymns to Senusret III, lines 16–21.

13. Semna Dispatch from Serra East (translation by Paul Smither, "The Semnah Despatches," no. 4).

14. Senusret III, Semna stela, line 10.

15. Ibid., lines 14–16.

16. Ibid., lines 20–21.

CHAPTER 9: BITTER HARVEST

The most comprehensive recent study of the Second Intermediate Period is Kim Ryholt's magisterial *The Political Situation in Egypt During the Second Intermediate Period*. However, many of his conclusions, notably the date of the Fourteenth Dynasty secession, are not yet widely accepted. The more conventional chronology, as presented, for example, by Janine Bourriau, "The Second Intermediate Period," Detlef Franke, "The Late Middle Kingdom," and David O'Connor, "The Hyksos Period," is followed here. Despite the arguments of Detlef Franke to the contrary, Ryholt's identification of a separate Abdju dynasty seems to make good sense of the meager evidence, and has been followed here. Ryholt's work remains the best compilation of sources for the Thirteenth to Seventeenth dynasties.

For the fortress at Tjaru, see Mohamed Abd el-Maksoud, *Tell Hebua*. Georges Posener, "Les asiatiques en Égypte," presents some of the textual evidence for Asiatics in Egyptian society during the late Middle Kingdom. Asiatic immigration into the delta during this period, and the site of Hutwaret in all its phases, are discussed by Manfred Bietak, "Egypt and the Levant"; while his articles "Dab'a, Tell ed-" and "The Center of Hyksos Rule" present the results of ongoing excavations at Hutwaret, including the statue of an Asiatic official and the ring bezel naming an "overseer of Retjenu." (The translation is offered by Geoffrey Martin, "The Toponym Retjenu.")

Stephen Quirke's "Royal Power in the 13th Dynasty" is by far the best treatment of a difficult subject. Aidan Dodson, "The Tombs of the Kings," discusses the evidence for the royal tombs of the period. For the career of Sobekhotep III, see Toby Wilkinson, *Lives of the Ancient Egyptians* (no. 37). King Nehesy of the Fourteenth Dynasty is the subject of Manfred Bietak, "Zum Königreich des '3-zh-R' Nehesi." Nehesy is attested both at Tell el-Hebua and at Tell el-Muqdam, which guarded the approach to the Wadi Tumilat. Kim Ryholt, *The Political Situation*, dates the secession of the northeastern delta to the reign of Sobekneferu, making the so-called Fourteenth Dynasty of Nehesy entirely coeval with the Thirteenth Dynasty. However, such an early date is difficult to reconcile with the continuation of the Thirteenth Dynasty's trading relationship with Kebny and has not met with general acceptance. I have followed instead the consensus view, that the rupture took place late in the Thirteenth Dynasty, after the reigns of Sobekhotep IV and Merneferra Ay.

For the channel bringing freshwater into the royal citadel at Hutwaret, see Josef Dorner, "A Late Hyksos Water-Supply System." Initially sixteen feet thick, the citadel's wall was strengethened at a later date, perhaps at the outbreak of hostilities with the Thebans. The Abdju dynasty and the Theban Sixteenth Dynasty are treated at length in Kim Ryholt, *The Political Situation;* the pathetic stela of King Wepwawetemsaf, one of the members of the short-lived Abdju dynasty, is published by Janine Bourriau, *Pharaohs and Mortals* (catalogue no. 58, pp. 72–73). The monuments of Sobekhotep VIII, Neferhotep III, and King Mentuhotepi, together with all the important texts from the Second Intermediate Period, including private inscriptions from Buhen, are translated and discussed by Donald Redford, "Textual Sources for the Hyksos Period." Another invaluable source is Wolfgang Helck, *Historisch-Biographische Texte*. For a more detailed publication of two of the Buhen stelae, see Torgny Säve-Söderbergh, "A Buhen Stela." For the detailed publication of the stela of Mentuhotepi, see Pascal Vernus, "La stèle du pharaon *Mntw-htpi*." Kim Ryholt, *The Political Situation*, makes a convincing case for a temporary conquest of Thebes by Hyksos forces, although this has been refuted by Detlef Franke, "The Late Middle Kingdom."

For the establishment of Theban garrisons at Gebtu and Abdju in the early Seventeenth Dynasty, see Detlef Franke, "An Important Family at Abydos," and Steven Snape, "Statues and Soldiers at Abydos." The Seventeenth Dynasty pyramid complex of Nubkheperra Intef has been excavated and published by Daniel Polz, "The Pyramid Complex of Nubkheperre Intef," with further details supplied by Lisa Giddy, "Digging Diary 2001." For the historical significance of the Seventeenth Dynasty, see Daniel Polz, *Der Beginn des Neuen Reiches*. Vivian Davies, "Sobeknakht of Elkab" and "Egypt and Nubia," presents and discusses the newly discovered inscription describing the Kushite invasion of Upper Egypt. For Seqenenra Taa's campaign headquarters, see Peter Lacovara, "Deir el-Ballas." The life and death of Taa are discussed by Toby Wilkinson, *Lives of the Ancient Egyptians* (no. 39), while Kamose's lament is taken from the Carnarvon tablet, published by Alan Gardiner, "The Defeat of the Hyksos by Kamose."

1. Neferhotep III, Karnak inscription, line 6.
2. Ibid.
3. Mentuhotepi, Karnak stela, line 10 (cf. Donald Redford, "Textual Sources," p. 28, note 75).
4. Ibid., line 5.
5. Ibid., line 4.
6. Ka, funerary stela, lines 6–7.
7. Soped-her, funerary stela, line 9.
8. Rahotep, Coptos stela, line 3.
9. Intef V, Coptos stela, lines 5–7.
10. Sobeknakht, autobiographical inscription, opening lines.
11. Atu, scribal palette, lines 2–3.
12. Ibid., line 4.
13. Carnarvon Tablet no. 1, lines 3–4.

CHAPTER 10: ORDER REIMPOSED

The most detailed source for Kamose's military activities against the Hyksos is his group of three stelae, set up at Ipetsut. For key editions, see Alan Gardiner, "The Defeat of the Hyksos by Kamose," and Labib Habachi, *The Second Stela of Kamose*. Harry and Alexandrina Smith, "A Reconsideration of the Kamose Texts," give a carefully argued interpretation of the sequence of events. Frédéric Colin, "Kamose et les Hyksos dans l'oasis de Djesdjes," presents the evidence for Hyksos influence in the Bahariya Oasis during the Second Intermediate Period. The policy of Kamose and his immediate successors in Nubia is discussed by Dominique Valbelle, "Egyptians on the Middle Nile."

A convenient translation of the autobiographical tomb inscription of Ahmose, son of Abana, is supplied by Miriam Lichtheim, *Ancient Egyptian Literature* (vol. 2, pp. 12–15). For this Ahmose's career, and that of his near contemporary Ahmose-Pennekhbet, see Toby Wilkinson, *Lives of the Ancient Egyptians* (nos. 41 and 42). See also Wolfgang Helck, "Ahmose Pennechbet." The most comprehensive treatment of King Ahmose's battles is Claude Vandersleyen, *Les guerres d'Amosis*, and the relevant section in his book *L'Égypte et la vallée du Nil*. The significance of Sharuhen for the Hyksos is discussed by Eliezer Oren, "The 'Kingdom of Sharuhen' and the Hyksos Kingdom." The early Eighteenth Dynasty's policy of "defensive imperialism" has been expertly analyzed by J. J. Shirley, "The Beginning of the Empire." For the monuments of Ahmose and Amenhotep I on Shaat Island, see Francis Geus, "Sai." The insurgencies of Aata the Nubian and Tetian are referred to, briefly, in the autobiography of Ahmose, son of Abana. The tempest stela is published by Claude Vandersleyen, "Une tempête sous le règne d'Amosis" and "Deux nouveaux fragments," with an English translation by Donald Redford, "Textual Sources for the Hyksos Period." Some scholars have linked the natural disaster described on the tempest stela with the massive volcanic eruption on the Aegean island of Thera, known to have taken place at around the same time; see, for example, Karen Foster and Robert Ritner, "Texts, Storms, and the Thera Eruption." Others, however—most recently Malcolm Wiener and James Allen, "Separate Lives"—have put forward a convincing rebuttal of this theory, interpreting the disaster as a "monsoon-generated Nile flood." The flood hypothesis is followed here.

For Ahmose's monuments at Abdju, see Stephen Harvey, "Monuments of Ahmose at Abydos" and "New Evidence at Abydos." Joyce Tyldesley, *Chronicle of the Queens of Egypt*, discusses the role of Tetisheri and her monument at Abdju. The Ipet-sut stela listing the dignities of Ahhotep and the donation stela installing Ahmose-Nefertari as god's wife are both published by Andrea Klug, *Königlichen Stelen*. For golden flies as military decorations, see Susanne Petschel and Martin von Falck, *Pharao siegt immer* (catalogue nos. 77–80). Scholars dispute whether there were one or two king's wives of the late Seventeenth or early Eighteenth Dynasty named Ahhotep. For the latter view, see, for example, Catharine Roehrig (ed.), *Hatshepsut* (p. 7). The first view, favored by Aidan Dodson and Dyan Hilton, *The Complete Royal Families* (pp. 125, 126, and 128), is followed here. There is similar disagreement about the attribution of the golden flies. Hence, while Ann Macy Roth, "Models of Authority," states that the flies belonged to "Ahhotep I," regarded as the wife of Seqenenra but not a direct ancestor of King Ahmose, William Stevenson Smith, *The Art and Architecture of Ancient Egypt* (pp. 220–221), implies that the flies were part of the burial equipment of King Ahmose's mother. The simplest interpretation is that there was only one senior woman named Ahhotep (daughter of Senakhtenra, sister-wife of Seqenenra, and mother of Ahmose), to whom the golden flies, dagger, and axe belonged.

Jean Vercoutter, "Les Haou-nebout," is the unsurpassed discussion of the problematic term "Hau-nebut." For the Minoan-inspired burial equipment of Ahhotep, see, among other publications, W. Stevenson Smith, *The Art and Architecture of Ancient Egypt* (pp. 220–221). The dagger blade is decorated with the motif of a lion chasing a calf in a rocky landscape, while the axe bears a crested griffin; both objects are inlaid using the niello technique, foreign to Egypt. The Hutwaret frescoes and their implications are discussed in detail by their excavator, Manfred Bietak, in "The Center of Hyksos Rule"; by Manfred Bietak and Nannó Marinatos, "The Minoan Paintings of Avaris"; and by various contributors to Vivian Davies and Louise Schofield (eds.), *Egypt, the Aegean and the Levant*. Most recently, the frescoes have been dated by Manfred Bietak, "Egypt and the Aegean," to the reign of Hatshepsut, rather than earlier in the Eighteenth Dynasty. Bietak seems to base this new dating largely on the circumstantial evidence, namely that "it is during the joint reign of Thutmose III and Hatshepsut . . . that delegations of Keftiu [inhabitants of Crete] are first represented" in Egyptian tombs. However, the strong Minoan connections displayed in the grave goods of Ahmose's mother, Ahhotep, argue for an earlier alliance between the Egyptian royal family and the Minoans, and hence for an earlier dating of the Minoan frescoes at Hutwaret. The archaeological evidence from the palace complex at Hutwaret, notably the pottery, would support a date earlier in the Eighteenth Dynasty than the reign of Hatshepsut (Manfred Bietak, "Egypt and the Aegean," p. 79). The heir, Prince Ahmose, whose birth may have prompted Ahmose-Nefertari's rise to prominence, would not, in fact, succeed to the throne—he predeceased his father, and it was therefore a younger son, Amenhotep (I), who became the next king. For the office of god's wife of Amun, see Michel Gitton, *Les divines épouses de la 18e dynastie*.

For a readable and authoritative description of living conditions in New Kingdom Thebes, T.G.H. James, *Pharaoh's People* (Chapter 8), remains the most convenient source. The monuments of Amenhotep I at Ipetsut are discussed by Gun Björkman, *Kings at Karnak*, and reconstructed by Catherine Graindorge and Philippe Martinez, "Karnak avant Karnak." More than eight hundred blocks and five hundred fragments survive from Amenhotep I's temple, dismantled and reused in later royal constructions. Sadly, nothing remains of the buildings themselves, except for his alabaster chapel, painstakingly reconstructed in the Karnak Open Air Museum. For the king's other building projects in and around Thebes, see Franz-Jürgen Schmitz, *Amenophis I*, and Betsy Bryan, "The 18th Dynasty Before the Amarna Period." Very little is known about the early history of Deir el-Medina, but for a summary, see Frank Yurco, "Deir el-Medina." Aidan Dodson, "The Lost Tomb of Amenhotep I," discusses the mystery of the tomb's whereabouts and the most likely candidates for the king's final resting place.

1. Carnarvon Tablet no. 1, line 4.
2. Ibid., lines 10–11.
3. Ibid., lines 14–15.

4. Kamose, victory stela from Thebes, lines 19–24.
5. Ibid., lines 10–11.
6. Ibid., lines 13–14.
7. Ibid., lines 8–9.
8. Ahmose, son of Abana, tomb inscription, lines 13–14.
9. Ahmose, Karnak stela, line 13.
10. Ahmose, son of Abana, tomb inscription, line 23.
11. Ahmose, Tempest stela, line 21.
12. Ahmose, Tetisheri stela, lines 13–14.
13. Ahmose, Karnak stela, lines 24–27.
14. Ahmose, Tura limestone quarry inscription, lines 5–6.

CHAPTER 11: PUSHING THE BOUNDARIES

The obscure family background of Thutmose I is discussed by Aidan Dodson and Dyan Hilton, *The Complete Royal Families*, p. 128. The background to the beginning of Thutmose I's reign is discussed by Claude Vandersleyen, *L'Égypte et la vallée du Nil* (pp. 247–248). The best recent synopsis of his Nubian campaign is Vivian Davies, "Egypt and Nubia: Conflict with the Kingdom of Kush," together with Vivian Davies and Renée Friedman, *Egypt*, pp. 129–131. The Hagar el-Merwa inscriptions were published in an early study by A. J. Arkell, "Varia Sudanica," and have been the subject of a recent reappraisal by Vivian Davies, "Kurgus 2000," "Kurgus 2002," and "The Rock Inscriptions at Kurgus."

Contemporary evidence for the Asiatic campaign of Thutmose I is extremely scarce but is conveniently summarized by John Darnell and Colleen Manassa, *Tutankhamun's Armies*, pp. 139–141. An important source is a brief reference in the autobiographical tomb inscription of Ahmose, son of Abana (Kurt Sethe, *Urkunden IV*, p. 9, lines 8–10). Undated inscriptions from Ipetsut may record aspects of Thutmose I's Asiatic conquests. See Donald Redford, "A Gate Inscription from Karnak." For the kingdom of Mittani, see Gernot Wilhelm, "The Kingdom of Mitanni," and Michael Astour, "Mitanni," plus the references therein. Betsy Bryan, "The Egyptian Perspective on Mittani," charts relations between the two kingdoms during the Eighteenth Dynasty.

The brief reign of Thutmose II has been studied most carefully by Luc Gabolde, "La chronologie du règne de Thoutmosis II."

For the regency of Hatshepsut and her progressive self-elevation from god's wife to regent to king, see many of the contributions in Catharine Roehrig (ed.), *Hatshepsut*, especially Ann Macy Roth, "Models of Authority," and Peter Dorman, "Hatshepsut: Princess to Queen to Co-Ruler." Peter Dorman, "The Early Reign of Thutmose III," presents a novel explanation for the co-regency. The precipitating factor that led Hatshepsut to declare herself king is unclear. If not the death of Thutmose III's mother, Isis, the death of Hatshepsut's own mother, Ahmose, may have been the spur. If Queen Ahmose was seen as the last link with the early Eighteenth Dynasty royal family, her demise may have forced Hatshepsut's hand, effectively forcing her to claim the kingship in order to defend the legitimacy of her rule.

The tension between male and female personae apparent in Hatshepsut's statuary and inscriptions is discussed by Ann Macy Roth, "Models of Authority," and Cathleen Keller, "The Statuary of Hatshepsut." For Hatshepsut's building works, especially at Ipetsut, see Cathleen Keller, "The Joint Reign of Hatshepsut and Thutmose III" and "The Royal Court." A more popular account of Hatshepsut's regency and reign is Joyce Tyldesley, *Hatchepsut: The Female Pharaoh*, while John Ray, *Reflections of Osiris* (pp. 40–59), provides a lively and provocative account.

The temple of Hatshepsut at Deir el-Bahri is the subject of numerous publications. Among the best recent treatments are Dieter Arnold, "Djeser-djeseru," and Ann Macy Roth, "Hatshepsut's Mortuary Temple." Dorothea Arnold, "The Destruction of the Statues of Hatshepsut," gives an idea of the sumptuous decoration of the temple during Hatshepsut's co-regency. Senenmut's career has been analyzed in detail by Peter Dorman, *The Monuments of Senenmut* and "The Royal Steward, Senenmut"; also useful are Catharine Roehrig, "Senenmut," and Cathleen Keller, "The Statuary of Senenmut."

The most comprehensive recent study of the reign of Thutmose III is Eric Cline and David O'Connor (eds.), *Thutmose III: A New Biography*. Two excellent and detailed studies of the Battle of Megiddo, the king's other Asiatic campaigns, and their impact in the Near East are Donald Redford, *The Wars in Syria and Palestine*, and its summary, "The Northern Wars of Thutmose III." These are supplemented by Claude Vandersleyen, *L'Égypt et la vallée du Nil* (pp. 295–306), and James Allen, "After Hatshepsut: The Military Campaigns of Thutmose III." The strategic location of Megiddo is explained in Michael Roaf, *Cultural Atlas* (p. 133). The political background to the Megiddo campaign is discussed by William Murnane, "Rhetorical History?," while Christine Lilyquist, "Egypt and the Near East," enumerates the booty captured by the Egyptian forces after their victory. For the growing importance of foreigners in Egypt in the middle Eighteenth Dynasty, see Diamantis Panagiotopoulos, "Foreigners in Egypt." The tomb and treasure of the three foreign concubines of Thutmose III have been published in extenso by Christine Lilyquist, *The Tomb of Three Foreign Wives*. The burial of the three princesses may date to early in Thutmose III's sole reign, although many of the objects in the tomb were gifts from the king to the three women during his co-regency with Hatshepsut. The women must therefore have made the journey to Egypt before the Battle of Megiddo, trailblazers for a phenomenon that would later become a feature of the Egyptian royal court.

The foundation of Pnubs and Thutmose III's policy in Nubia is discussed by Vivian Davies, "Egypt and Nubia: Conflict with the Kingdom of Kush."

1. Ahmose, son of Abana, tomb inscription, line 30.
2. Thutmose I, Tombos victory inscription, lines 7–8.
3. Ibid., lines 11–12.
4. Thutmose I, Abydos stela, line 21.
5. Ahmose, son of Abana, tomb inscription, line 36.
6. Ibid., line 37.
7. Ineni, tomb inscription, lines 16–17.

8. Hatshepsut, Karnak obelisk inscription, line 15.
9. Ibid., lines 8–32.
10. Senenmut, Karnak statue inscription, line 26.
11. Thutmose III, Megiddo inscription from Karnak, line 8.
12. Ibid., line 84.
13. Ibid., line 86.
14. Ibid., line 94.
15. Thutmose III, obelisk inscription, left side.
16. Ibid., right side.

CHAPTER 12: KING AND COUNTRY

The structure of the administration in the Eighteenth Dynasty is discussed by Peter Der Manuelian, *Studies in the Reign of Amenophis II*, and Betsy Bryan, "Administration in the Reign of Thutmose III."

Evidence for the career of Menkheperraseneb can be found in the texts and reliefs from his tomb—see James Breasted, *Ancient Records*, vol. 2, pp. 772–776, and Norman and Nina de Garis Davies, *The Tomb of Menkheperraseneb*, respectively. Toby Wilkinson, *Lives of the Ancient Egyptians* (no. 46), offers a useful summary.

At least two earlier generations of Rekhmira's family had held the vizierate. His grandfather Ahmose had been vizier under Hatshepsut, his uncle Useramun during the co-regency of Hatshepsut and Thutmose III. Rekhmira's responsibilities as vizier are described in the texts from his tomb, published by James Breasted, *Ancient Records*, vol. 2, pp. 663–762, with analysis and discussion by G.P.F. van den Boorn, *The Duties of the Vizier*. Convenient digests include Peter Dorman, "Rekhmire," and Toby Wilkinson, *Lives of the Ancient Egyptians* (no. 47).

Primary material relating to Sennefer and his brother has been published by Ricardo Caminos, "Papyrus Berlin 10463"; Howard Carter, "Report upon the Tomb of Sen-nefer"; and Philippe Virey, "La tombe des vignes." For summaries, see William Kelly Simpson, "Sennefer," and Toby Wilkinson, *Lives of the Ancient Egyptians* (no. 51).

Qenamun's tomb was published by Norman de Garis Davies, *The Tomb of Ken-Amun*; his career is reconstructed by Toby Wilkinson, *Lives of the Ancient Egyptians* (no. 49).

Rosalind and Jac. Janssen, *Growing Up in Ancient Egypt*, offer a reliable picture of education in ancient Egypt, while Joann Fletcher, *Egypt's Sun King*, pp. 24–27, deals specifically with the education of a prince.

Amenhotep II's sporting prowess, and other aspects of his reign, are discussed at length by Peter Der Manuelian, *Studies in the Reign of Amenophis II*. His mummy is that of an exceptionally tall and strongly built man. For his campaigns in the Near East, see Betsy Bryan, "The 18th Dynasty Before the Amarna Period," and Bill Manley, *The Penguin Historical Atlas*, pp. 72–73. The growing importance of the sun cult and solar symbolism during the reigns of Amenhotep II and Thutmose IV are analyzed in detail by Betsy Bryan in "Antecedents to Amenhotep III," *The Reign of Thutmose IV*, and "Thutmose IV."

1. Rekhmira, biographical inscription, line 3.
2. Installation of the vizier, from the tomb inscription of Rekhmira, line 15.
3. Sennefer, tomb inscription, burial chamber (section C.4: *Urkunden IV*, p. 1426, line 18).
4. Ibid., sarcophagus chamber (section B.6–7: *Urkunden IV*, p. 1427, line 8).
5. Sennefer, letter (translation by Ricardo Caminos, "Papyrus Berlin 10463").
6. Qenamun, tomb inscription (scene of the young Amenhotep II on his nurse's lap: *Urkunden IV*, p. 1395, line 14).
7. Norman de Garis Davies, *The Tomb of Ken-Amun*, pp. 10–16. The translations are typical of the 1930s milieu in which Davies was working, but they are no less appropriate to the hierarchical and sycophantic world of ancient Egypt.
8. Qenamun, tomb inscription (scene of the young Amenhotep II on his nurse's lap: *Urkunden IV*, p. 1395, line 15).
9. *Satire of the Trades*, section 2e.
10. Ibid., sections 21h–i, 22a,e.
11. *Miscellanies* (quoted in Rosalind and Jac. Janssen, *Growing Up in Ancient Egypt*, Chapter 6).
12. Min, tomb inscription, archery scene, lines 8–9.
13. Amenhotep II, Great Sphinx stela, line 11.
14. Amenhotep II, Medamud inscription, line 2.
15. Amenhotep II, Great Sphinx stela, line 19.
16. Ibid., line 24.
17. Amenhotep II, Memphis stela, line 28.
18. Ibid., line 29.

CHAPTER 13: GOLDEN AGE

Two recent volumes of studies are indispensable for understanding the reign of Amenhotep III. They are Arielle Kozloff et al., *Egypt's Dazzling Sun*, and David O'Connor and Eric H. Cline (eds.), *Amenhotep III: Perspectives on His Reign*. Joann Fletcher, *Egypt's Sun King*, offers an accessible and sumptuously illustrated chronology of Amenhotep's life and reign. All three publications include discussions of the commemorative scarabs. (The bull hunt scarab in particular is published in Arielle Kozloff et al., *Egypt's Dazzling Sun*, p. 70.) Altogether, Amenhotep III issued five different commemorative scarabs; although they are explicitly dated by their content to between the second and eleventh years of his reign, it is possible that they were issued at one and the same time, to highlight the main achievements of his first decade on the throne. The form and material of the scarabs prefigure Amenhotep's later obsession with solar symbolism: the ancient Egyptian name for glazed material was *tjehenet* ("dazzling"), while the scarab represented Khepri, the god of the rising sun.

For Amenhotep III's extensive temple construction projects, see especially Arielle Kozloff et al., *Egypt's Dazzling Sun*, Chapter 4, and Raymond Johnson, "Monuments and Monumental Art." It has been suggested that the statues of Sekhmet from the Mut complex were originally installed in Amenhotep III's mortuary temple on the west bank, only later being moved across the river. However, the close theological association of the two goddesses (Sekhmet and Mut) makes it equally possible that the statues were intended for the Mut complex from the outset. New discoveries of colossal sculpture from the king's mortuary temple at Kom el-Hetan are presented by Hourig Sourouzian, "New Colossal Statues."

Foreign relations, including the significance of the Aegean place-names, are treated at length by James Weinstein et al., "The World Abroad." A fragmentary papyrus from Amarna, which may depict Mycenaean soldiers serving in the Egyptian army of the late Eighteenth Dynasty, is published by Louise Schofield and Richard Parkinson in "Of Helmets and Heretics" and (authors reversed) "Akhenaten's Army?" The most thorough and accessible edition of the Amarna Letters is William Moran, *The Amarna Letters;* Raymond Cohen and Raymond Westbrook's *Amarna Diplomacy* offers a range of scholarly studies on international relations as reflected in the diplomatic correspondence. Samuel Meier, "Diplomacy and International Marriages," discusses the marriages between the great powers attested in the Amarna Letters.

The seminal study of Luxor Temple and its significance in royal theology is Lanny Bell, "Luxor Temple and the Cult of the Royal *Ka.*" Also useful is Richard Wilkinson, *The Complete Temples* (pp. 95–98), and Barry Kemp, *Ancient Egypt* (2nd ed., pp. 261–273); the latter offers a good summary of the Opet Festival and a discussion of the divine birth scene. For the recently discovered statue of Amenhotep III as "foremost of all the living *ka*s" and "dazzling orb of all lands," see Arielle Kozloff et al., *Egypt's Dazzling Sun,* pp. 132–135. The colorful names of Amenhotep III's concubines are analyzed by Nicholas Millet, "Some Canopic Inscriptions."

Amenhotep III's *sed* festivals are discussed by Barry Kemp, *Ancient Egypt* (2nd ed., pp. 276–281). On the occasion of Amenhotep's second *sed* festival in the thirty-fourth year of his reign, the western harbor was enlarged to nearly double its original size; plans for a third phase of expansion were apparently never realized. For the First Dynasty palette apparently consulted by the king's researchers, see Bernard Bothmer, "A New Fragment of an Old Palette." The most accessible publication of the palaces at Malkata and their decoration is William Stevenson Smith, *The Art and Architecture of Ancient Egypt,* Chapter 15. Arielle Kozloff, "The Decorative and Funerary Arts," offers a detailed study of glassmaking at Malkata and elsewhere during the reign of Amenhotep III, with excellent illustrations. Texts and scenes describing Amenhotep III's first and third *sed* festivals feature prominently in the tomb of Tiye's steward Kheruef, published by the Epigraphic Survey, *The Tomb of Kheruef.* The eastern harbor, excavated as a complement to the western "Birket Habu," is clearly marked (labeled "hippodrome") on the map of Thebes from the Napoleonic *Déscription de l'Égypte* (vol. II, plate I, titled "Thèbes: plan général de la portion de la vallée du Nil qui comprend les ruines"), published by Charles Gillispie and Michel Dewachter, *Monuments of Egypt.*

1. Amenhotep III, bull-hunt scarab.
2. Amenhotep III, Kom el-Hetan stela, line 2.
3. Amarna Letters, EA17 (translation by William Moran, *The Amarna Letters*).
4. Ibid., EA19 (translation by William Moran, *The Amarna Letters*).

5. Amenhotep III, marriage scarab.
6. Amarna Letters, EA22 (translation by William Moran, *The Amarna Letters*).
7. Ibid., EA1 (translation by William Moran, *The Amarna Letters*).
8. Amenhotep III, Kom el-Hetan stela, lines 11–12.
9. Amenhotep III, divine birth inscription, Luxor Temple, section 4, lines 2–4.
10. Ibid., section 5, lines 1–2.
11. Ibid., section 5, lines 3–5.
12. Kheruef, tomb inscription, plate 28.
13. Ibid.

CHAPTER 14: ROYAL REVOLUTION

As befits the period of ancient Egyptian history most written about, the reign of Akhenaten and its aftermath have generated a vast bibliography. References up to the end of the 1980s are gathered together in Geoffrey Martin, *A Bibliography of the Amarna Period and Its Aftermath*. For more recent scholarship, the bibliography in Rita Freed et al. (eds.), *Pharaohs of the Sun*, is a good starting point. Rita Freed, "Introduction," provides a useful summary of the main points of interest and the outstanding questions arising from the period. For a thoughtful and provocative recent appraisal, see also John Darnell and Colleen Manassa, *Tutankhamun's Armies* (Chapter 2). The key inscriptions from the period are published in hieroglyphs by Maj Sandman, *Texts from the Time of Akhenaten* (abbreviated elsewhere as *Texts*), and in translation by William Murnane, *Texts from the Amarna Period*.

The most penetrating accounts of Akhenaten himself are Cyril Aldred, *Akhenaten, King of Egypt*; Donald Redford, *Akhenaten, the Heretic King*; and Nicholas Reeves, *Akhenaten: Egypt's False Prophet*. The last two, as their titles suggest, take a rather negative view of their subject and his religious revolution. For the reception and co-option of Akhenaten in modern times, Dominic Montserrat, *Akhenaten*, is exemplary and highly readable.

For the letter from the king of Alashiya to Amenhotep IV at his accession, see Timothy Kendall, "Foreign Relations." Amenhotep IV's constructions at Karnak are in the course of excavation, with the latest results presented in editions of the *Akhenaten Temple Project Newsletter*. For a convenient summary by the project director, see Donald Redford, "The Beginning of the Heresy." The eerie statuary from Gempaaten is illustrated in Rita Freed et al., *Pharaohs of the Sun*. Bak, chief sculptor during the early years of Akhenaten's reign, makes it clear that he was instructed in the new style by the king himself—see Toby Wilkinson, *Lives of the Ancient Egyptians* (no. 59). For the celebration and significance of Amenhotep IV's *sed* festival at Karnak, see Jocelyn Gohary, *The Akhenaten Sed-Festival*; William Murnane, *Texts from the Amarna Period* (p. 5); and John Darnell and Colleen Manassa, *Tutankhamun's Armies* (pp. 25–27).

It has been suggested (John Darnell and Colleen Manassa, *Tutankhamun's Armies*, pp. 37–40) that the proximity of Khmun (classical Hermopolis) was a key factor in the location of Akhetaten because the Hermopolitan creation myth chimed with Akhenaten's religious emphasis. However, it was the creation myth of Iunu (which gave prominence to the triad of creator gods Atum, Shu, and Tefnut) that took center stage in Akhenaten's early doctrine, and Akhenaten himself was adamant that Akhetaten was chosen because it "did not belong to a god nor a goddess." The boundary stelae at Akhetaten are published by William Murnane and Charles Van Siclen, *The Boundary Stelae of Akhenaten*. The discovery of a sixteenth stela is reported by Barry Kemp, "Discovery: A New Boundary Stela." Recent excavations in the main quarry at Akhetaten are described by James Harrell, "Ancient Quarries near Amarna."

For the best accounts of the foundation and layout of the city, and for a description of the principal ceremonial buildings, see Barry Kemp, *Ancient Egypt* (1st ed., Chapter 7); Peter Lacovara, "The City of Amarna"; Michael Mallinson, "The Sacred Landscape"; Barry Kemp and Salvatore Garfi, *A Survey of the Ancient City;* and Barry Kemp, "Resuming the Amarna Survey." Barry Kemp, "The Amarna Story," summarizes the significance of Akhenaten's city as an archaeological site. For the North Riverside Palace (the main royal residence) and associated buildings, see Michael Jones, "Appendix 1: The North City," while Kate Spence, "The North Palace at Amarna," presents the results of recent work at this important complex. Ian Shaw, "Balustrades, Stairs and Altars," discusses the distinctive architecture of the Aten cult. Barry Kemp, "The Kom el-Nana Enclosure," is a good introduction to the outlying royal buildings at the edges of Akhetaten. There was also a workmen's village (Akhetaten's equivalent of the Place of Truth) on the low desert behind the city, for the workers employed on the construction of the royal tomb—and a "stone village," even farther out, the purpose of which remains obscure. See Barry Kemp, "Notes from the Field: The Stone Village."

Akhenaten's radical theology forms a major topic of discussion in all books about the period. John Baines ("How Far Can One Distinguish Between Religion and Politics in Ancient Egypt?") has argued that Akhenaten's doctrine may have been one of monolatry rather than monotheism. For most of the king's subjects, however, such a difference would have been purely academic. Other useful analyses include John Foster, "The New Religion," and Raymond Johnson, "The Setting: History, Religion, and Art." The prayers to Osiris and Anubis early in Akhenaten's reign are found in the tomb of Parennefer at Thebes; see Susan Redford, "Two Field Seasons." The inanimate representation of the Aten, and its consequent relegation to the top of scenes, wittingly or unwittingly directed attention to the figures of Akhenaten, his wife, and his daughters standing below, underlining their godlike status in the new religion; see William Murnane, *Texts from the Amarna Period*, p. 13. Major temples of the Aten were built at Memphis, Heliopolis, and Kawa in upper Nubia, as well as at Akhetaten, while the temple of Amun at Sesebi, in Nubia, was converted to the Aten cult early in Akhenaten's reign.

For the career of Meryra, high priest of the Aten, see Norman de Garis Davies, *The Rock Tombs of El Amarna* (Part I), and Toby Wilkinson, *Lives of the Ancient Egyptians* (no. 58). A convenient translation of the *Great Hymn to the Aten* is in Miriam Lichtheim, *Ancient Egyptian Literature* (vol. 2, pp. 96–100). David Silverman, "The Spoken and Written Word," discusses the use of vernacular language in Akhenaten's religious compositions.

The lives of the poor at Akhetaten have been revealed by recent excavations in the South Tombs cemetery. See Barry Kemp, "Notes from the Field: Lives of the Have-Nots," "Halfway Through the Amarna Season," "How Were Things Made?," and "The Quality of Life"; and Jerry Rose, "Amarna Lives." For the continued observance of traditional cults, see Rita Freed et al. (eds.), *Pharaohs of the Sun* (catalogue nos. 179–181, 183–185). Peter Der Manuelian, "Administering Akhenaten's Egypt," discusses the likely reaction in the country at large to the proscription of the old deities; for a particular example see Maarten Raven, "The Tomb of Meryneith."

Nefertiti has spawned almost as great a bibliography as her husband. One of the best recent analyses of her role in the art and religion of the Amarna Period is Rita Freed, "Art in the Service of Religion and the State." For the monumental statuary of Akhenaten and Nefertiti, see Kristin Thompson, "Amarna Statuary Fragments." Salima Ikram's analysis of household shrines, "Domestic Shrines," is the standard article on this important aspect of Akhenaten's religion. Barry Kemp published the chapel of the king's statue in *Ancient Egypt* (1st ed., pp. 283–285). For the tombs of officials, see Norman de Garis Davies, *The Rock Tombs of El Amarna*. Also, Gwil Owen, "The Amarna Courtiers' Tombs," has some excellent color photographs.

For possible dissent during the reign of Akhenaten and the security response, see John Darnell and Colleen Manassa, *Tutankhamun's Armies*, pp. 189–196. The career of Mahu, chief of police, is profiled by Toby Wilkinson, *Lives of the Ancient Egyptians* (no. 60), based upon the scenes and texts in Mahu's tomb, for which see Norman de Garis Davies, *The Rock Tombs of El Amarna* (Part IV). For foreigners in Akhenaten's bodyguard, see John Darnell and Colleen Manassa, *Tutankhamun's Armies* (pp. 191–193, fig. 25), and Rita Freed et al. (eds.), *Pharaohs of the Sun* (catalogue no. 114). William Murnane, "Imperial Egypt" (p. 109), argues against the foreign extraction of figures such as Aper-El, Pentu, and Tutu. The reception of foreign tribute in the twelfth year of Akhenaten's reign is depicted in the tombs of Meryra II and Huya, published by Norman de Garis Davies, *The Rock Tombs of El Amarna* (Parts II and III).

The royal tomb at Akhetaten, with scenes of mourning at the death of Meketaten, was published by Geoffrey Martin, *The Royal Tomb*; for recent work at the site, see Marc Gabolde and Amanda Dunsmore, "The Royal Necropolis at Tell el-Amarna." Sue D'Auria, "Preparing for Eternity," discusses the afterlife in Akhenaten's theology. Several *shabti*s of Akhenaten are published in Rita Freed et al. (eds.), *Pharaohs of the Sun* (catalogue nos. 219–222).

The identity of Akhenaten's co-regent Neferneferuaten and his ephemeral successor Smenkhkara is one of the most hotly debated questions in Egyptology, with the fragmentary evidence allowing for several plausible solutions. For thorough discussions see any of the books on the Amarna Period listed above, together with Nicholas Reeves, "The Royal Family," and Aidan Dodson, "Why Did Nefertiti Disappear?" (although Dodson has since revised his conclusions). Neferneferuaten's throne name appears in both masculine and feminine versions (recalling Hatshepsut a century earlier) and is accompanied on occasions by the phrase "effective for her husband," both of which make it certain that the new co-regent was a woman. Some scholars identify Neferneferuaten as Meritaten, Akhenaten's eldest daughter, but the correspondence of the name to the first element of Nefertiti's name argues strongly for the identification followed here. Moreover, Neferneferuaten adopts the epithets "beloved of Neferkheperura, sole one of Ra" and "beloved of sole one of Ra, Akhenaten," both of which point to Nefertiti rather than her daughter. William Murnane, *Texts from the Amarna Period* (p. 10), provides further support for this consensus view. The fact that Smenkhkara had the same throne name (Ankhkheperura) as his predecessor Neferneferuaten points heavily in the direction of "Smenkhkara" being yet another name for Nefertiti.

The restoration of traditional cults under Tutankhamun is discussed by William Murnane, "The Return to Orthodoxy." For an overview of Tutankhamun's reign, see Nicholas Reeves, *The Complete Tutankhamun;* John Darnell and Colleen Manassa, *Tutankhamun's Armies;* and Toby Wilkinson, *Lives of the Ancient Egyptians* (nos. 61–65). For the events surrounding the death of Tutankhamun and his widow's desperate appeal to the Hittite king, see Trevor Bryce, "The Death of Niphururiya," who also provides conclusive proof that the widow in question was Ankhesenamun, not Nefertiti. Despite the continuing speculation over the cause of Tutankhamun's death, a CT scan of his mummy in 2002 showed no signs of violence.

1. Amarna Letters, EA34 (translation by William Moran, *The Amarna Letters*).
2. Amarna Letters, EA147 (translation by William Moran, *The Amarna Letters*).
3. Akhenaten, earlier foundation inscription, stela K, line 19.
4. Ibid., stela X, line 15.
5. Ibid., line 20.
6. Kevin Nance, "The Dark Side of King Tut." The quote refers to imagery from the reign of Tutankhamun, but the description is equally applicable to his father.
7. Meryra I, tomb inscription (south wall, west side).
8. John Foster, "The New Religion," p. 99.
9. *Great Hymn to the Aten*, lines 2–11.
10. Ibid., lines 12–13.
11. Akhenaten, later foundation inscription, line 4.
12. Tutu, tomb inscription, west wall, south side, lower part, lines 26–27.
13. Mahu, tomb inscription, front wall, south side.
14. Ibid.
15. Huya, tomb inscription, west wall.
16. Amarna Letters, EA16 (translation by William Moran, *The Amarna Letters*).
17. Tutankhamun, restoration stela, lines 5–9.
18. Ibid., lines 4–5.
19. *The Deeds of Suppiluliuma* (translation after Hans Güterbock, "The Deeds of Suppiluliuma," pp. 94–95).
20. Ibid.

CHAPTER 15: MARTIAL LAW

A work of fundamental importance for understanding the role of the army in New Kingdom society is Andrea Gnirs, *Militär und Gesellschaft*, while the classic account of army organization remains Alan Schulman, *Military Rank, Title and Organization*.

For army life, weaponry, and military tactics, see John Darnell and Colleen Manassa, *Tutankhamun's Armies*. Metal helmets were introduced during the New Kingdom but were not commonplace. The identification of Perunefer with Hutwaret is advocated by Manfred Bietak, "The Tuthmoside Stronghold of Perunefer." For an alternative view, that Perunefer was at Memphis, see David Jeffreys, "Perunefer." The scene showing Egyptian soldiers leaving the battlefield with enemy hands skewered on spears is illustrated in Donald Redford (ed.), *The Akhenaten Temple Project* (plate 14, no. 3).

The key source for the career of Horemheb, as high official and king, is Robert Hari, *Horemheb et la reine Moutnedjmet*. Allan Philips, "Horemheb," discusses an important piece of evidence that suggests, for the Ramesside kings at least, Horemheb was regarded as the founder of their royal house, not the last king of the previous (Eighteenth) dynasty. When it came to the future of the Aten cult, Horemheb may have hedged his bets. There is evidence to suggest that he dedicated two pieces of furniture in the Great Aten Temple at Akhetaten while smashing statues of Akhenaten set up in the same building, thus honoring the Aten as a god (now one of many) while persecuting the memory of the Aten's chief proponent. Horemheb's private tomb, which sheds important light on his military and civilian activities during the reign of Tutankhamun, has been published by Geoffrey Martin, *The Memphite Tomb of Horemheb*. For the likely course of events surrounding the murder of Zannanza and the succession of Ay, see Trevor Bryce, "The Death of Niphururiya." Convenient translations of the coronation inscription and the edict of Horemheb are to be found in William Murnane, *Texts from the Amarna Period*.

The meager evidence for the preroyal career and succession of Ramesses I is gathered together by Daniel Polz, "Die Särge des (Pa-)Ramessu," while Alain-Pierre Zivie, "Ramses I," summarizes what is known of the king's brief reign. Wolfgang Helck, "Probleme der Königsfolge," deals with the general question of royal succession at the end of the Eighteenth and beginning of the Nineteenth dynasties.

For the temple of Seti I at Abdju, see A. M. Calverley and M. F. Broome, *The Temple of King Sethos I at Abydos*. The Nauri Decree is discussed in detail by Francis Llewellyn Griffith, "The Abydos Decree of Seti I at Nauri." For Seti I's sepulchre at Thebes, see Erik Hornung, *The Tomb of Seti I*, with a useful summary in Nicholas Reeves and Richard H. Wilkinson, *The Complete Valley of the Kings* (pp. 136–139).

Seti I's Asiatic wars are documented in a series of reliefs at Ipetsut, analyzed by William Murnane, *The Road to Kadesh*, which is also a good source for the development of Egyptian-Hittite relations, the expansion of the Hittite Kindgom, the role of vassal rulers such as Abdi-Ashirta and Aziru of Amurru, and the role of the mysterious Mehy in the reign of Seti I. For the last, see also William Murnane, "The Kingship of the Nineteenth Dynasty." For the view that Seti I may originally have designated Mehy as his heir, see William Murnane, *The Road to Kadesh* (pp. 163–175); an alternative view is proposed by Morris Bierbrier, "Elements of Stability and Instability."

1. Horemheb, coronation inscription, lines 4–5.
2. Ibid., line 25.

3. Horemheb, edict, preamble, lines 9–10.
4. Ibid., section 9, line 4.
5. Ibid., line 6.
6. Ibid., lines 8–9.
7. Ibid., preamble, line 8.
8. Seti I, Nauri Decree, lines 89–93.
9. Seti I, Kanais temple inscription, text B, lines 1–2.
10. Ibid., line 6.

CHAPTER 16: WAR AND PEACE

As befits his monumental legacy, Ramesses II has been the subject of countless studies, scholarly and popular. The classic text, by the world expert on Ramesside inscriptions, is Kenneth Kitchen, *Pharaoh Triumphant*, supplemented by two accessible summaries, "Pharaoh Ramesses II and His Times" and "Ramesses II." For a good recent account and interpretation of the Battle of Kadesh, see Anthony Spalinger, *War in Ancient Egypt*. The site of Kadesh itself is described by its excavator, Peter Parr, "Nebi Mend, Tell." For Hittite battle tactics and the role of the Hittite chariotry, see J. G. Macqueen, *The Hittites*. William Murnane, "The Kingship of the Nineteenth Dynasty," explores the propaganda value of Ramesses II's accounts of the battle and the reasons for him giving them such prominence on his monuments.

For Ramesses's extensive building projects, a useful summary is Bernadette Menu, *Ramesses the Great*. Gloria Rosati, "The Temple of Ramesses II at El-Sheikh Ibada," publishes the results of recent fieldwork close to Amarna. Ramesside work at Ipetsut and Luxor, together with the Ramesseum, is discussed by William Stevenson Smith, *The Art and Architecture of Ancient Egypt*. The most convenient summary of the temples at Abu Simbel is Lisa Heidorn, "Abu Simbel." For the capacity of the Ramesseum granaries, see Barry Kemp, *Ancient Egypt* (1st ed., fig. 69).

The location of Per-Ramesses offered easy access to the Near East by sea and land, and was ideal as a campaign headquarters. Our knowledge of the city is growing all the time, thanks to ongoing excavations by a German team. For the latest results, see Josef Dorner, "Die Topographie von Piramesse"; Edgar Pusch, "Towards a Map of Piramesse"; and Edgar Pusch, Helmut Becker, and Jörg Fassbinder, "Wohnen und Leben." A reconstruction of the city based upon the ancient sources is presented by Eric Uphill, *Egyptian Towns and Cities*. For industrial installations and workshops at Per-Ramesses, see Thilo Rehren and Edgar Pusch, "Glass and Glassmaking." The bronze foundries are discussed by Edgar Pusch, "Recent Work at Northern Piramesse," and by Edgar Pusch and Anja Herold, "Qantir/Pi-Ramesses." For the chariotry stables, see Edgar Pusch, "'Pi-Ramesse-geliebt-von-Amun,'" and David Aston and Edgar Pusch, "The Pottery from the Royal Horse Stud." The location of the biblical Pithom is confirmed by John Holladay, "Pithom," while the problem of the Exodus is conveniently addressed by John Bimson, "The Israelite Exodus."

Ramesses's campaigns in Syria-Palestine after the Battle of Kadesh are charted by Kenneth Kitchen, *Pharaoh Triumphant*. The most up-to-date works on the Hittite

Kingdom, and specifically the rise and fall of Urhi-Teshup and the reign of Hattusili III, are Trevor Bryce, *The Kingdom of the Hittites*, and Theo van den Hout, "Khattushili III, King of the Hittites." The primary publication of the correspondence between the Egyptian and Hittite courts is Elmar Edel, *Die ägyptisch-hethitische Korrespondenz*, with a useful summary by Ogden Goelet, "Ramesses-Hattusilis Correspondence." A cuneiform tablet from Per-Ramesses that may be part of this diplomatic correspondence was published by Patricia Spencer, "Digging Diary 2003" (pp. 26–27). For details of the royal citadel at Hattusa and the layout of the Hittite capital, see J. G. Macqueen, *The Hittites*. The recent discovery of a Ramesside royal palace in the northern Sinai, perhaps used by diplomatic brides on their way to Egypt, is published by Dominique Valbelle and François Leclère, "Tell Abyad."

For Libyan links with the Mediterranean and the fortresses built by Ramesses II to defend his Libyan frontier, see Steven Snape, "Ramesses II's Forgotten Frontier." Colleen Manassa, *The Great Karnak Inscription of Merneptah*, offers a magisterial account of the Libyan invasion in the fifth year of Merenptah's reign, together with discussions of Mery's strategy, the Battle of Perirer itself, and Merenptah's wider response to the threat posed by the Sea Peoples. The various peoples who made up the mercenary force fighting alongside Mery are listed in the Egyptian account as Akawash (perhaps to be equated with Homer's Achaeans), Turesh (who may have given their name to the Tyrrhenian region of Italy), Lukka (Lycians), Sherden (after whom Sardinia may have been named), and Shekelesh (who may have given their name to Sicily). For the identity of the Sea Peoples, a convenient summary is Anthony Leahy, "Sea Peoples." Robert Drews, *The End of the Bronze Age*, argues for the critical importance of advanced military technology in the military success of the Sea Peoples.

1. Ramesses II, Battle of Kadesh "poem," line 56.
2. Ramesses II, treaty with the Hittites (Karnak version), lines 9–10.
3. Ramesses II, first Hittite marriage inscription, line 34. ("Your Majesty's border" appears only in the Karnak version of the text; the Abu Simbel version gives "His Majesty's border.")
4. Merenptah, great Karnak inscription, line 13.

CHAPTER 17: TRIUMPH AND TRAGEDY

For the disputed succession following the death of Merenptah, see Aidan Dodson and Dyan Hilton, *The Complete Royal Families* (pp. 176–177); Nicholas Reeves and Richard Wilkinson, *The Complete Valley of the Kings* (pp. 150–158); and two articles by Aidan Dodson, "Amenmesse" and "Messuy, Amada, and Amenmesse." Dodson argues that Amenmesse is to be equated with Messuy, viceroy of Nubia under Merenptah. If this is true, Amenmesse would have had a political power base, considerable economic resources, and the Nubian garrisons to support his claim to the throne. For an alternate view, see Frank Yurco, "Was Amenmesse the Viceroy of Kush, Messuwy?" Dodson further suggests that Amenmesse seized power in the area south of the Fayum after Seti-Merenptah had already come to the throne, but the majority of scholars argue that he seized the kingship immediately upon the death of Merenptah. I have followed the majority view.

The reign of Siptah is discussed by Cyril Aldred, "The Parentage of King Siptah." The career of Chancellor Bay is discussed by Pierre Grandet, "L'exécution du chancelier Bay," and Toby Wilkinson, *Lives of the Ancient Egyptians* (no. 77).

The primary source for the beginning of the Twentieth Dynasty is the stela of Sethnakht from Abu, published by Rosemarie Drenkhahn, *Die Elephantine-Stele des Sethnacht*, and which is further analyzed by Donald Redford, "Egypt and Western Asia in the Late New Kingdom," and Stephan Seidlmayer, "Epigraphische Bemerkungen zur Stele des Sethnachte." The stela of Bakenkhonsu, discovered at Karnak in 2006 but not yet fully published, provides the highest known regnal year for Sethnakht, namely a "year four." It also refers to civil disturbances in Thebes that resulted in damage to statues inside the temple of Amun-Ra at Ipetsut. See Mansour Boraik, "Re-writing Egypt's History." Although not certain, Sethnakht's geographical origins are suggested by the fact that, under his son Ramesses III, several men from Bast were promoted to high office; it is tempting to see them as childhood friends of Ramesses III, from the same region of the eastern delta.

The best treatment of Ramesses III's reign, with full references to primary sources, is Pierre Grandet, *Ramsès III*, with a convenient summary by the same author in his article "Ramesses III." For the great battle against the Sea Peoples in the eighth year of the king's reign, see, inter alia, Nancy Sandars, *The Sea Peoples*, and Eliezer Oren (ed.), *The Sea Peoples and Their World*, especially David O'Connor, "The Sea Peoples and the Egyptian Sources." Many attempts have been made to identify the origins of the various groups of Sea Peoples, based upon their distinctive names. For example, the Tjeker (Teucrians) have been associated with the region around Troy and the Weshesh with the city itself, on the assumption that "Weshesh" is an Egyptian corruption of Wilusa/Ilios, the ancient name of Troy. The Denyen have been identified with the Danaoi or mainland Greeks, but are perhaps more likely to have originated in southeastern Turkey or northernmost Syria. If the Peleset originally came from Anatolia as well, they are better known for their subsequent settlement along the coast of the southern Near East, where they became known as the Philistines (and gave their name to modern Palestine). The origins of the Shekelesh are obscure, but it seems likely that later groups of them settled in the western Mediterranean, giving their name to the island of Sicily. If we look beyond names to the military technology of the Sea Peoples, the design of their ships suggests connections with the Mycenaean world but also connections further afield with the Bronze Age Urnfield culture of central Europe (see Shelley Wachsmann, "To the Sea of the Philistines"). The complex origins of the Sea Peoples are discussed by Philip Betancourt, "The Aegean and the Origin of the Sea Peoples," Shelley Wachsmann, "To the Sea of the Philistines," and Louise Steel, "The 'Sea Peoples': Raiders or Refugees?" The Sea Peoples' ultimate destiny is explored by Lucia Vagnetti, "Western Mediterranean Overview." Itamar Singer, "New Evidence on the End of the Hittite Empire," presents vivid evidence for the devastation wrought by the Sea Peoples throughout the eastern Mediterranean.

The reliefs from the mortuary temple of Ramesses III, including the famous scenes depicting the battle against the Sea Peoples, are published by the Epigraphic Survey, *Medinet Habu*. For the inspection of temples in year fifteen of Ramesses III's reign; for Ramesses III's building projects; and for the expeditions to Sinai, Timna, and Punt, see Pierre Grandet, *Ramsès III*. The foreign mining expeditions are described in the Great Harris Papyrus (P. Harris I: 77.8–78.1 and 14a.7–8).

The primary publication of the Turin Strike Papyrus, a contemporary account of the strikes by the necropolis workmen, remains William Edgerton, "The Strikes in Ramesses III's Twenty-ninth Year." Pierre Grandet, *Ramsès III*, gives a useful narrative account (in French). For the original texts, see Kenneth Kitchen, *Ramesside Inscriptions* (vol. V, pp. 529–530, 542; vol. VII, pp. 300–302).

For the harem conspiracy and the tribunal set up to investigate it, see Adriaan de Buck, "The Judicial Papyrus of Turin." The use of black magic by the conspirators is disputed by Hans Goedicke, "Was Magic Used in the Harem Conspiracy," but the evidence of the contemporary papyri seems clear.

1. Bay, Gebel el-Silsila inscription, lines 8–9.
2. Ostracon O.IFAO 1864, recto, line 3.
3. Great Harris Papyrus I, 75, 4.
4. Sethnakht, Elephantine stela, line 15.
5. Ibid., line 4.
6. Ibid., line 5.
7. RS 20.238 (translation after Michael Astour, "New Evidence on the Last Days of Ugarit," p. 255).
8. Ramesses III, great inscription of year eight, Medinet Habu, lines 16–17.
9. Ibid., lines 16–18.
10. Ibid., lines 20–21.
11. Robert Drews, *The End of the Bronze Age*, p. 3.
12. Ramesses III, Turin Strike Papyrus, recto 1, line 2.
13. Ibid., recto 2, lines 2–5.
14. Ibid., lines 14–15.
15. Ibid., lines 15–17.
16. Ramesses III, harem scenes, Medinet Habu.
17. Ramesses III, Turin Judicial Papyrus, 4:2.
18. Ibid., 3:2.

CHAPTER 18: DOUBLE-EDGED SWORD

A vivid, if bleak, picture of peasant life in ancient Egypt is painted by Ricardo Caminos, "Peasants," in stark contrast to the rose-tinted descriptions of other authors. *A Tale of Woe* by the same author offers a translation and commentary on the tale of Wermai from the late New Kingdom. For the institution of corvée labor, see Kathlyn Cooney, "Labour," and Christopher Eyre, "Work and the Organisation of Work in the New Kingdom." For the high death rate on mining expeditions, see John Baines, "Society, Morality, and Religious Practice" (pp. 136–137). The reign and monuments of Ramesses IV, including the Wadi Hammamat expedition and the

Abdju inscription, are discussed in detail by A. J. Peden, *The Reign of Ramesses IV.* The tomb of Ramesses IV is notable chiefly for its sarcophagus. At ten and a half feet in length and seven feet high, it is the largest ever used in the Valley of the Kings. But it, too, was finished in haste.

Despite a relative abundance of documentation, the late Twentieth Dynasty remains one of the least-known periods of ancient Egyptian history, certainly in terms of political developments. For a good summary, see Kenneth Kitchen, "Ramses V–XI." The Turin Indictment Papyrus, detailing the misdeeds of Khnumnakht, is discussed by A. J. Peden, *The Reign of Ramesses IV* (pp. 69–72), and by Pierre Grandet, *Ramsès III* (pp. 218–219).

The survey of landholdings in Middle Egypt commissioned by Ramesses V is known today as the Wilbour Papyrus. The standard edition is Alan Gardiner, *The Wilbour Papyrus,* while Ogden Goelet, "Wilbour Papyrus," offers a helpful summary of the document's salient features. For the mummy of Ramesses V, see John Harris and Edward Wente, *An X-Ray Atlas of the Royal Mummies.* Useful discussions of the titulary and monuments of Ramesses VI include Kenneth Kitchen, "The Titularies of the Ramesside Kings," and Amin Amer, "Reflections on the Reign of Ramesses VI." A papyrus from the late Ramesside Period refers to "the year of the hyenas" as a euphemism for famine. For the Libyan incursions at Thebes, see A. J. Peden, *The Reign of Ramesses IV* (pp. 20–22). The last evidence for Egyptian contact with its former territories in the Near East is a statue base from Megiddo inscribed with the name of Ramesses VI. The career of Ramessesnakht is traced in Toby Wilkinson, *Lives of the Ancient Egyptians* (no. 79).

The tomb robberies of the late Twentieth Dynasty have been discussed by many authors. The essential edition of the original papyrus accounts is Eric Peet, *The Great Tomb-Robberies.* Among other helpful accounts are Cyril Aldred, "More Light on the Ramesside Tomb Robberies," and Ogden Goelet, "Tomb Robbery Papyri."

For the transition between the end of the Ramesside Period and the succeeding Libyan Dynasties, a useful account (though now superseded in several important respects) is Andrzej Niwinski, "Le passage de la XXe à la XXIIe dynastie." The chronology of Ramesses XI's reign, including the suppression and restoration of the high priest Amenhotep, the civil war between the forces of Panehsy and Paiankh, and the proclamation of the renaissance, is a hotly debated topic with two broad schools of thought. The traditional interpretation, which places Herihor before Paiankh, is presented by Kenneth Kitchen, *The Third Intermediate Period in Egypt.* The radical revision, placing Paiankh before Herihor, was originally proposed by Karl Jansen-Winkeln, "Das Ende des Neuen Reiches," and has been taken up by authors such as Jacobus van Dijk, "The Amarna Period" (p. 302), and John Taylor, "Nodjmet, Payankh and Herihor." Despite being refuted in detail by several scholars, notably Jürgen von Beckerath, "Zur Chronologie der XXI. Dynastie," the revision has much to recommend it and has been followed here.

The letters between Paiankh and Nodjmet are translated in Edward Wente, *Letters from Ancient Egypt.* For the systematic plunder of the royal necropolis, which started under Paiankh, see Karl Jansen-Winkeln, "Die Plünderung der Königsgräber des Neuen Reiches." John Taylor, "Nodjmet, Payankh and Herihor," proposes a prominent role for Nodjmet in the succession from Paiankh to Herihor, and from the Twentieth Dynasty to the Twenty-first Dynasty. The abandonment of Per-Ramesses and the foundation of a new capital at Djanet (classical Tanis) are discussed by Geoffrey Graham, "Tanis."

1. Ricardo A. Caminos, "Peasants," p. 24.
2. Ibid., p. 20.
3. Ramesses IV, Wadi Hammamat inscription of year three, line 6.
4. Ramesses IV, great Abydos stela, line 21.
5. Ramesses IV, second Abydos stela, line 35.
6. Merenptah, Libyan inscription, line 22.
7. Papyrus Amherst, p. 2, lines 3–7.
8. Papyrus BM 10052, p. 8, lines 19–20.
9. Ibid., p. 5, lines 8–9.
10. Late Ramesside Letters, no. 35 (translated by Edward Wente, *Letters from Ancient Egypt*, pp. 183–184).
11. Late Ramesside Letters, no. 28.

CHAPTER 19: A HOUSE DIVIDED

The best introduction to the so-called Libyan Period in Egypt (traditionally the Twenty-second to Twenty-fourth dynasties) is Anthony Leahy, "The Libyan Period in Egypt," together with the volume of essays *Libya and Egypt*, edited by the same author. A good introduction to the chronology and rulers of the Twenty-first Dynasty is Kenneth Kitchen, *The Third Intermediate Period* (pp. 255–286), while his article "The Arrival of the Libyans in Late New Kingdom Egypt" discusses the background to Libyan settlement in Egypt during the late Ramesside Period.

The extent of Libyan influence in the Twenty-first Dynasty is still hotly disputed. Karl Jansen-Winkeln, "Der Beginn der libyschen Herrschaft in Ägypten," makes a strong case and his thesis has been largely followed here. However, the alternate view (that the Libyan character really becomes apparent only with the reign of Shoshenq I) is equally strongly held. For discussion of the arguments, see Anthony Leahy, "The Libyan Period in Egypt," and John Taylor, "The Third Intermediate Period." Despite their Egyptian names, there is strong circumstantial evidence to suggest that Paiankh and Herihor were both of Libyan origin. An inscription from the largely Libyan cemetery of the Third Intermediate Period at Herakleopolis has been plausibly connected with Paiankh, and he is known to have had a base in the town that was the heartland of Libyan settlement in Middle Egypt. At least two of Herihor's sons were given Libyan names, and this would have been surprising at the time if there had been no Libyan blood in the family.

A Libyan origin is also likely for the ruler of Lower Egypt at the end of Ramesses XI's reign. The existence of a private statuette naming a "great chief of the Ma Nesbanebdjedet" (Jean Yoyotte, "Les principautés du Delta," p. 127 and plate III) suggests that this name was common among the Libyan population of the delta, and thus helps to reinforce the Libyan identification of the king of the same name. Nesbanebdjedet, "the king, the ram lord of Djedet," is more commonly known by the Greek form of his name, Smendes, but the original Egyptian version better conjures up the labored formulations beloved of the Libyan Twenty-first Dynasty kings. Likewise Pasebakhaenniut, which is usually rendered in its Greek form, Psusennes.

For the undisputed Libyan character of the Twenty-second Dynasty, see, most recently, Eva Lange, "Legitimation und Herrschaft." The importance of genealogies is analyzed by Lisa Montagno Leahy and Anthony Leahy, "The Genealogy of a Priestly Family from Heliopolis." There are numerous examples of throne names being recycled for generations: Pasebakhaenniut I and Osorkon the Elder shared almost identical throne names; Shoshenq I copied the throne name of Nesbanebdjedet, and Takelot I, Takelot II, and Shoshenq IV followed suit; Osorkon II copied the throne-name of Amenemope, as did Padibastet I, Osorkon III, and Rudamun; Shoshenq III copied the throne name of Ramesses II, and Pamay followed suit; Peftjauawybast copied the throne name of Amenemnisu, but had to omit the epithet Heqawaset ("ruler of Thebes") since he had abandoned the city in the face of Kushite expansion. For the change in the conception of the tomb, especially at Thebes, see Takao Kikuchi, "Die thebanische Nekropole der 21. Dynastie."

The classic publications of Djanet and its royal tombs are by the site's principal excavator, Jean Yoyotte; especially useful are "Tanis" and "The Royal Necropolis of Tanis and Its Treasures." For the career of Wendjebaendjedet, see Toby Wilkinson, *Lives of the Ancient Egyptians* (no. 84). For details about the systematic robbery of the Theban royal tombs in the early Twenty-first Dynasty, I am indebted to R. J. Demarée, "The Final Episode of the Deir el-Medina Community." A further useful discussion of the subject is Nicholas Reeves and Richard Wilkinson, *The Complete Valley of the Kings* (pp. 190–207), who pay particular attention to the caches of royal mummies. The mummies reinterred in the tomb of a Seventeenth Dynasty queen were finally removed to the family vault of the Theban high priest Pinedjem II, high in the cliffs above Deir el-Bahri, in the reign of Shoshenq I.

The notion of a "theocratic" government is analyzed in detail by Karl Jansen-Winkeln, "Die thebanische 'Gottesstaat.' " For a key text that has been described as "the credo of the theocracy," see Pascal Vernus, "Choix de textes" (no. 1, pp. 103–104). Jean-Marie Kruchten, *Les annales des prêtres de Karnak*, discusses the role of oracles and gives an account of the dispute between two factions of priests at Ipetsut in the time of Pinedjem II. The classic study of the role of women in the Theban priesthood is Saphinaz-Amal Naguib, *Le clergé féminin d'Amon*.

For the Libyan fortresses in Middle Egypt and the defensive outlook of Twenty-first Dynasty society, John Taylor, "The Third Intermediate Period," provides a useful starting point. The Theban revolt in the reign of Nesbanebdjedet is discussed by Aidan Dodson, "Third Intermediate Period." The original source for this episode is the Banishment Stela, published by Jürgen von Beckerath, "Die 'Stele der Verbannten,' " with further useful observations by Kenneth Kitchen, *The Third Intermediate Period* (pp. 261–262). The fortresses built by Menkheperra were at Gesy (modern Qus), Inerty (Gebelein), and Djeba (Edfu).

John Taylor, "The Third Intermediate Period," discusses the decline of royal power in the Twenty-first Dynasty; and Miriam Lichtheim, *Ancient Egyptian Litera-*

ture (vol. 2, pp. 224–230), provides a convenient translation of the *Report of Wena-mun*, while the journey itself is reconstructed and its implications commented upon by Bill Manley, *The Penguin Historical Atlas of Ancient Egypt* (pp. 98–99). The text has traditionally been dated to the renaissance era of Ramesses XI's reign, but recent scholarship has convincingly argued for a date *after* the death of Ramesses XI, in the reign of his immediate successor. See, above all, Karl Jansen-Winkeln, "Das Ende des Neuen Reiches," together with Ad Thijs, "In Search of King Herihor" (p. 79). Thijs dates the text to the "reign" of the high priest Pinedjem I, arguing that he pre-ceded Herihor as ruler of Thebes, but this particular point seems unlikely. For the likely marriage of Siamun's daughter to Solomon, see Kenneth Kitchen, *The Third Intermediate Period* (p. 280).

1. Ramesses III, Deir el-Medina stela, line 3.
2. Ibid., lines 3–4.
3. Late Ramesside Letters, no. 28 (translation by Vivian Davies and Renée Fried-man, *Egypt*, p. 149).
4. Hymn to Amun—the "credo of the theocracy."
5. Menkheperra, Banishment Stela, line 6.
6. Late Ramesside Letters, no. 21 (translation by Edward Wente, *Letters from Ancient Egypt*, p. 183).
7. 1 Kings 9:16 (revised standard version).

CHAPTER 20: A TARNISHED THRONE

For the accession of Shoshenq I and the historical problems surrounding the reign of Pasebakhaenniut II, see Aidan Dodson, "The Transition Between the 21st and 22nd Dynasties Revisited." It is noteworthy, and typical of the shifting sands of Third In-termediate Period history, that Dodson's previous interpretation of events at the end of the Twenty-first Dynasty (presented in "Psusennes II and Shoshenq I") has been completely overturned by a single new discovery, that of a hitherto unknown in-scribed fragment from Ipetsut (Frédéric Payraudeau, "Des nouvelles annales sacer-dotales"). For Shoshenq's reign and accomplishments, see Anthony Leahy, "Abydos in the Libyan Period" (p. 174), and Kenneth Kitchen, "Sheshonq I." Shoshenq had royal connections of his own, before his marriage to Pasebakhaenniut II's daughter. His uncle, Osorkon the Elder (975–970), had ruled briefly as king at Djanet.

The course of Shoshenq I's Palestinian campaign has been reconstructed by Ken-neth Kitchen, *The Third Intermediate Period* (pp. 432–447), based upon the inscrip-tion on the so-called Bubastite Portal at Ipetsut, published by the Epigraphic Survey, *Reliefs and Inscriptions at Karnak III*. For a convenient cartographic representation of the campaign, see Bill Manley, *The Penguin Historical Atlas of Ancient Egypt* (pp. 102–103). The biblical account of "King Shishak" is difficult to reconcile with the Egyp-tian record of Shoshenq's campaign on two scores. First, Jerusalem is absent from the Ipetsut list of captured and defeated towns—although a portion of the inscription is missing. Second, most of the conquests listed at Ipetsut are in Israel, not Judah. John

Bimson, "Who Was King Shishak of Egypt?," provides a useful discussion of the difficulties in accommodating the two sources. As a result of these discrepancies, there is a growing (if somewhat desperate) view that Shoshenq I must have mounted at least two campaigns in the Near East, one recorded at Ipetsut, the other in the Bible. Shoshenq I's son and grandson were Osorkon I (925–890) and Takelot I (890–874), respectively.

There is as yet no consensus on the precise relationship between the various dynasties and collateral branches of the royal family during the ninth and eighth centuries, although the weight of scholarly opinion seems to be forming around the broad picture suggested by David Aston and John Taylor, "The Family of Takeloth II," and Karl Jansen-Winkeln, "Historische Probleme der 3. Zwischenzeit." It should be noted that the existence of a "Theban Twenty-third Dynasty," founded by Takelot II and running concurrently with the Twenty-second Dynasty at Bast, has been refuted by the doyen of Third Intermediate Period studies, Kenneth Kitchen (*The Third Intermediate Period*, pp. xxviii–xxxiv); but the theory makes best sense of the fragmentary and confusing evidence, and has been followed here. For detailed family trees and a discussion of the relationships between the various rulers and dynasties, *The Complete Royal Families* (pp. 210–231) by Aidan Dodson and Dyan Hilton is invaluable.

The buildings of Osorkon II at Bast are published by Édouard Naville, *The Festival Hall of Osorkon II*, and discussed in summary by Charles van Siclen, "Tell Basta." Pascal Vernus, "Choix de textes" (no. 8, p. 109), publishes the funeral lament for Osorkon II by one of his generals. For the kingship of Harsiese and the declaration of Theban independence during the reign of Osorkon II, see Karl Jansen-Winkeln, "Historische Probleme der 3. Zwischenzeit," and David Aston, "Takeloth II." Both articles are essential to an understanding of the complex chronology of events relating to Prince Osorkon; particularly useful is Karl Jansen-Winkeln's table 1. The primary publication of the prince's travails is Ricardo Caminos, *The Chronicle of Prince Osorkon*. Gerald Broekman, "The Chronicle of Prince Osorkon," offers a recent analysis and commentary.

The history of Nubia during the first part of the Third Intermediate Period remains extremely obscure. One of the best recent studies is John Darnell, *The Inscription of Queen Katimala* (especially pp. 55–63). For the tombs of the early chieftains at el-Kurru, see Timothy Kendall, "The Origin of the Napatan State"; Lisa Heidorn, "Historical Implications"; and a convenient summary by David O'Connor, *Ancient Nubia* (pp. 66–69). Kashta is attested in contemporary inscriptions as far north as Elephantine; if Amenirdis was installed as the future god's wife of Amun not by her brother (Piankhi) but by her father (Kashta), as was the usual practice, Kashta's authority must have extended as far as Thebes. Timothy Kendall, "Kings of the Sacred Mountain" and "Egypt and Nubia" (pp. 409–412), offers up-to-date discussions of the theology associated with the holy mountain of Gebel Barkal. Kendall's suggestion ("Egypt and Nubia," p. 412) that Theban émigrés may have helped to "convert" the Kushite rulers to fundamentalist Amunism seems unnecessary, given the evidence for militant religious fervor among the Nubian elite as early as the tenth century, as demonstrated by the Katimala inscription (John Darnell, *The Inscription of Queen Katimala*, pp. 62–63). Timothy Kendall, "Jebel Barkal," discusses the history of the temples at this important site.

For a long time, the name of Piankhi was rendered as "Piye," but a recent analysis has suggested that "Piankhi" is more accurate. See Claude Rilly, "Une nouvelle interprétation du nom royal Piankhy." For the likelihood of an agreement between Rudamun and Piankhi and friendly relations between the two dynasties, see David Aston and John Taylor, "The Family of Takeloth II." Piankhi's sister Amenirdis was subsequently adopted as Shepenwepet's successor, thus ensuring that a Kushite would eventually become god's wife of Amun.

Iuput II's writ, or at least his influence, seems to have stretched beyond the immediate vicinity of Taremu and as far as Per-Wadjet, in the western delta, judging from the bracelets bearing his name that have recently been excavated at the site. See Ulrich Hartung, "Recent Investigations." The intense political fragmentation of Egypt by 730 and the difficulties of interpretation surrounding rulers such as Iuput II are discussed by Anthony Leahy, "Abydos in the Libyan Period" (Appendix, pp. 177–195), and Patricia and Jeffrey Spencer, "Notes on Late Libyan Egypt." The classic study remains Jean Yoyotte, "Les principautés du Delta." The best original source for the period, and for Piankhi's campaign, is the king's own victory stela, published in full by Nicolas Grimal, *La stèle triomphale*. The four kings shown doing obeisance at the top of the stela are Nimlot and Peftjauawybast from Upper Egypt, and Osorkon IV and Iuput II from Lower Egypt. At the time of Piankhi's campaign, Shepenwepet I (the daughter of Prince Osorkon) may still have been the incumbent god's wife of Amun at Thebes; sometime in the 750s, Kashta had installed *his* daughter (Amenirdis I) as the future god's wife; Piankhi followed suit after his campaign of 728.

For Piankhi's palace at Napata, see Timothy Kendall, "The Napatan Palace." The Kushites' predilection for horses is discussed by László Török, "Iconography and Mentality" (pp. 195–197), while evidence that the predilection predates the rise of Piankhi's dynasty is presented by Irene Liverani, "Hillat el-Arab." A fragmentary victory relief of Piankhi at Gebel Barkal gives particular prominence to the horses he received in tribute from various Egyptian dynasts. See Timothy Kendall, "Kings of the Sacred Mountain" (p. 164, fig. 28).

1. 1 Kings 14.
2. 2 Chr. 12:4–5.
3. 1 Kings 14:25–26.
4. Chronicle of Prince Osorkon, Text A, line 24 (the translations of this text are by Ricardo A. Caminos, *The Chronicle of Prince Osorkon*).
5. Ibid., line 30.
6. Ibid., line 36.
7. Ibid., line 36.
8. Ibid., line 53.
9. Ibid., line 53.
10. Ibid., text B, line 7.

11. Ibid., line 11.
12. Priestly annals at Karnak, fragment 7, line 3.
13. Piankhi, victory stela, line 19.
14. Ibid., line 3.
15. Ibid.
16. Ibid., line 12.
17. Ibid.
18. Ibid., line 14.
19. Ibid., line 32.
20. Ibid., lines 62–67.
21. Ibid., line 78.
22. Ibid., line 85.
23. Ibid., line 86.
24. Ibid., line 106.
25. Ibid., lines 113–114.
26. Ibid., lines 127–128.

CHAPTER 21: FORTUNE'S FICKLE WHEEL

An invaluable starting point for the history of the Kushite Period in Egypt is the collection of contemporary texts, published in transliteration and translation by Tormod Eide et al. (eds.), *Fontes Historiae Nubiorum*. The faïence goblet of Bakenrenef is illustrated and discussed in detail by Günther Hölbl, *Beziehungen der ägyptischen Kultur zu Altitalien* (vol. 1, pp. 81–94, and vol. 2, plates 28–30). For the reign of Shabaqo and the imposition of Kushite rule in Lower Egypt, see the two articles "Shabaqa" and "Twenty-fifth Dynasty" by Kenneth Kitchen.

The career of Harwa is charted by Toby Wilkinson, *Lives of the Ancient Egyptians* (no. 87); for details of Harwa's tomb and the *shabti* with royal attributes, see Francesco Tiraditti, "Three Years of Research in the Tomb of Harwa." The inscription on one of his statues is published by Miriam Lichtheim, *Ancient Egyptian Literature* (vol. 3, pp. 24–28). The persistence of political structures in the delta throughout the Kushite Period is discussed by Kenneth Kitchen, *The Third Intermediate Period* (pp. 395–398). An important new study of the same phenomenon is Olivier Perdu, "La chefferie de Sébennytos."

For the general character of Kushite rule, see Jean Leclant, "Kuschitenherrschaft," plus references. The archaizing trends in Kushite art are discussed by John Taylor, "The Third Intermediate Period" (pp. 350–352 and 354–362), and Gay Robins, *The Art of Ancient Egypt* (pp. 210–229). Barry Kemp, *Ancient Egypt* (1st ed., pp. 26–27), offers an incisive analysis of the Memphite Theology. The text itself (treated as a genuine work of the Old Kingdom or earlier) is published by Miriam Lichtheim, *Ancient Egyptian Literature* (vol. 1, pp. 51–57). For Kushite statuary, see Edna Russmann, *Egyptian Sculpture* (pp. 164–175), and Charles Bonnet and Dominique Valbelle, *The Nubian Pharaohs*. Anthony Leahy, "Royal Iconography and Dynastic Change," examines one particular aspect of Kushite art, namely the cap crown. The reign of Taharqo is discussed by Jean Leclant, "Taharqa," and Donald

Redford, "Taharqa." Taharqo's Near Eastern campaigns, dated to around 670, can be deduced from donation lists in the temple at Kawa. For the importance of the king's mother in African societies, see Jean Leclant, "Kuschitenherrschaft," and E. Y. Kormysheva, "Remarks on the Position of the King's Mother in Kush."

A convenient source for the history of the Assyrian Empire is John Haywood, *The Penguin Historical Atlas of Ancient Civilizations* (pp. 38–39 and 46–47). Dan'el Kahn, "The Assyrian Invasions of Egypt," offers a broad overview of relations between the two countries, with reference to ancient sources. For the diplomatic policy of Shabaqo toward Assyria, see Grant Frame, "The Inscription of Sargon II at Tang-i Var." The Assyrian royal annals, included in James Pritchard (ed.), *Ancient Near Eastern Texts*, give a vivid, if heavily biased, eyewitness account of the invasions by Esarhaddon and Ashurbanipal. For a reconstruction of the Battle of Eltekeh, based on contemporary accounts, see Kenneth Kitchen, *The Third Intermediate Period* (pp. 384–385). An inscription of Esarhaddon that may relate to the plunder of Memphis and the seizure of Kushite royal crowns is published by W. G. Lambert, "Booty from Egypt?" The reference to a rebellion in the southern provinces after the Assyrian invasion of 667–666 is from an inscription of Montuemhat in the Mut temple at Ipetsut. For Taharqo's battles against the Assyrians, see Charles Bonnet and Dominique Valbelle, *The Nubian Pharaohs* (pp. 142–149), while the same authors (pp. 150–154) discuss the brief reign of Tanutamun (including his dream stela) and Psamtek I's takeover. Francis Breyer, *Tanutamani*, offers the fullest discussion yet of the last Kushite pharaoh. For the two obelisks seized by the Assyrians during the sack of Thebes in 664, see Christiane Desroches Noblecourt, "Deux grands obélisques."

Good introductions to the history of the Saite (Twenty-sixth) Dynasty are Kenneth Kitchen, *The Third Intermediate Period* (pp. 399–408); John Ray, "Late Period: An Overview"; and Anthony Spalinger, "Late Period: Twenty-sixth Dynasty." For a rather pessimistic assessment of Saite rule, see Anthony Spalinger, "The Concept of the Monarchy During the Saite Epoch." The extraordinary career of Montuemhat is discussed by Barry Kemp, *Ancient Egypt* (2nd ed., pp. 346–348 and 372), and Toby Wilkinson, *Lives of the Ancient Egyptians* (no. 88). For Montuemhat's Kushite wife, see Edna Russmann, "Mentuemhat's Kushite Wife."

The primary source for the adoption of Nitiqret is the commemorative stela from Ipetsut, published by Ricardo Caminos, "The Nitocris Adoption Stela." For her journey to Thebes and the role of Sematawytefnakht, see Toby Wilkinson, *Lives of the Ancient Egyptians* (nos. 90 and 91). Psamtek I's subsequent Theban policy is analyzed by H. De Meulenaere, "La statue du général Djed-ptah-iouf-ankh." For the Nubian campaign of Psamtek II, see Charles Bonnet and Dominique Valbelle, *The Nubian Pharaohs* (pp. 164–171). Jean Yoyotte, "Le martelage des noms royaux éthiopiens," marshals the evidence for Psamtek II's policy of persecution against the monuments of the Kushite kings.

The background to Babylonian involvement in Egypt is discussed by Dan'el Kahn, "Some Remarks on the Foreign Policy of Psammetichus II," while John Haywood, *The Penguin Historical Atlas of Ancient Civilizations* (pp. 48–49), offers a convenient source for the main developments. For the unsuccessful campaigns of Nekau II against Babylonian expansion in the Near East, see Kenneth Kitchen, *The Third In-*

termediate Period (p. 407). Alan Lloyd, "Apries," refers to the pro-Greek policy of Wahibra. A magisterial analysis of the events surrounding the accession of Ahmose II is Anthony Leahy, "The Earliest Dated Monument of Amasis"; while John Ray, "Amasis," offers a lively and readable account of the pharaoh's pragmatic approach to foreign and domestic policy. For the Greek city of Naukratis, see Barry Kemp, *Ancient Egypt* (2nd ed., pp. 366–370), and John Boardman, *The Greeks Overseas* (Chapter 4).

1. Shabaqo, commemorative scarab.
2. Harwa, statue inscription (translation by Miriam Lichtheim, *Ancient Egyptian Literature*, vol. 3, p. 26).
3. Taharqo, Kawa stela of year six, line 9.
4. Ibid., line 7.
5. Ibid., lines 11–12.
6. Ibid., lines 16–18.
7. Taharqo, desert stela, lines 12–15.
8. Annals of Esarhaddon (the translations of this text are by James Pritchard, *Ancient Near Eastern Texts*, p. 293).
9. Ibid.
10. Annals of Ashurbanipal (the translations of this text are by James Pritchard, *Ancient Near Eastern Texts*, pp. 294–295).
11. Ibid.
12. Tanutamun, dream stela, lines 16–17.
13. Ibid., line 25. The echoes of Kamose's account of his battles against the Hyksos were no doubt deliberate, intended to cast Tanutamun in the same role of national savior.
14. Ibid., lines 41–42.
15. Annals of Ashurbanipal.
16. Ibid.
17. Psamtek II, Shellal stela, column 9.

CHAPTER 22: INVASION AND INTROSPECTION

The Persian Period (or, strictly speaking, the two Persian periods) is one of the most fascinating eras in ancient Egyptian history, yet has received scant attention from Egyptologists. Still the best introduction, and a vital compendium of hieroglyphic sources for the period, is Georges Posener, *La première domination perse*. For administrative purposes, Egypt was joined with the oases and Cyrenaica to form the sixth satrapy of the Persian Empire. For the various (Egyptian and Persian) royal names attested from the period, see Jürgen von Beckerath, *Handbuch der ägyptischen Königsnamen*. Leo Depuydt, "Regnal Years and Civil Calendar," brings much needed clarity to the chronology of the period. Heavily reliant on Greek sources (which have largely been eschewed by the present author), but nonetheless authoritative, is Friedrich Kienitz, *Die politische Geschichte Ägyptens*. A readable account of life in the Persian Period, as reflected in the Petition of Petiese, is John Ray, *Reflections of Osiris* (Chapter 6). Anthony Leahy, "The Adoption of Ankhnesneferibre" (p. 164), touches on the fate of the last god's wife of Amun and the extraordinary longevity of Psamtek I's family. The picture of Cambyses that emerges from the Egyptian sources is in stark contrast to accounts of his reign by Greek historians, who gave him very bad press.

The inscriptions of Khnemibra in the Wadi Hammamat are published by Georges Posener, *La première domination perse* (pp. 98–116); the same work (pp. 1–26) provides the definitive publication of the autobiographical inscription of Wedjahorresnet. Further useful discussions of Wedjahorresnet's career are Alan Lloyd, "The Inscription of Udjahorresnet"; Ladislav Bareš, *Abusir IV;* and Toby Wilkinson, *Lives of the Ancient Egyptians* (no. 93). The activities of Nesmahes at Taremu are put into context by Carol Redmount and Renée Friedman, "Tell el Muqdam."

For the sources of materials and craftsmen employed in the construction of Darius I's palace at Susa, see Paul Cartledge, *Alexander the Great* (pp. 39–40). The outstanding work on the nature of Persian rule in Egypt (and the Egyptian reaction against it) is John Ray, "Egypt: Dependence and Independence." The Persian frontier post on Dorginarti is discussed by Lisa Heidorn, "The Persian Claim to Kush," and the contemporary fortress at Tell el-Herr in the Sinai by Dominique Valbelle, "A First Persian Period Fortress." Barry Kemp, *Ancient Egypt* (2nd ed., pp. 361–363), provides a thoughtful analysis of the Suez Canal stelae of Darius I; for the original publication, see Georges Posener, *La première domination perse* (pp. 48–87) (for the hieroglyphic text) and V. Scheil, "Documents et arguments" (for the cuneiform text). The date of construction can be established quite precisely. From the list of satrapies on the stelae, the canal must have been built after Darius's conquest of Sind in 518 but before his Scythian campaign of 513.

The fascinating story of the Persian water engineers of the Kharga Oasis is told by Michel Wuttmann, "Ayn Manawir." For evidence of intermarriage between Egyptians and Persians, see Ian Mathieson et al., "A Stela of the Persian Period." The inscription of Ariyawrata in the Wadi Hammamat also records this Persian official's adopted Egyptian nickname, Djedher. See Georges Posener, *La première domination perse* (pp. 127–128).

The numerous revolts against Persian rule in the fifth and fourth centuries receive considerable attention in Greek accounts (for obvious reasons), but there are few contemporary Egyptian sources. Ongoing excavations at Ayn Manawir have brought to light an important archive of demotic contracts that seem to corroborate the account of Herodotus on a number of points. See Michel Chauveau, "The Demotic Ostraca of Ayn Manawir." The Jewish community at Abu and the destruction of the temple of Yahweh in 410 are discussed by Bezalel Porten, *The Elephantine Papyri*, and Boulos Ayad Ayad, "From the Archive of Ananiah Son of Azariah."

The purge of Egyptians from positions of authority under Xerxes I can be deduced from the fact that the papyri from Elephantine, dating to his reign and those of his two successors Artaxerxes I and Darius II mention no Egyptians in prominent positions.

For the troubled and tortuous history of the Twenty-ninth Dynasty (Nayfaurud and his successors), see Claude Traunecker, "Essai sur l'histoire de la XXIXe dynastie," and John Ray, "Psammuthis and Hakoris."

Paul Cartledge, *Agesilaos and the Crisis of Sparta*, charts the relations between the Spartan king and his Egyptian contemporaries. The rise of the Thirtieth Dynasty is analyzed by H. De Meulenaere, "La famille royale des Nectanébo"; the Naukratis stela of Nakhtnebef is published by Adolf Erman and Ulrich Wilcken, "Die Naukratisstele," and translated by Miriam Lichtheim, *Ancient Egyptian Literature* (vol. 3, pp. 86–89). John Ray, "Late Period: Thirtieth Dynasty," provides a convenient historical summary of the reigns of Nakhtnebef, Djedher, and Nakhthorheb. For the career of Wennefer, see F. von Känel, "Les mésaventures du conjurateur de Serket," and Toby Wilkinson, *Lives of the Ancient Egyptians* (no. 94). The life and times of Nakhthorheb are examined by John Ray, *Reflections of Osiris* (Chapter 7), and Toby Wilkinson, *Lives of the Ancient Egyptians* (no. 95).

The phenomenon of animal cults in Late Period Egypt has spawned much discussion. Among the best recent analyses is Barry Kemp, *Ancient Egypt* (2nd ed., pp. 373–381), while the fundamental publication is Dieter Kessler, *Die heiligen Tiere*. Kessler looks in particular at the connections between sacred animals and the royal cult. Harry Smith, *A Visit to Ancient Egypt*, is a very readable account of the sacred animal necropolis at Saqqara. For the ibis galleries at Tuna el-Gebel (the necropolis serving ancient Khmun), see Dieter Kessler and Abd el-Halim Nur el-Din, "Inside the Ibis Galleries." One of Nakhthorheb's best preserved temple buildings is published by Neal Spencer, "The Great Naos of Nekhthorheb." The burial of animals to demarcate sacred enclosures at early predynastic Nekhen was reported by Renée Friedman, "Origins of Monumental Architecture."

The stela of Sematawytefnakht, eyewitness of the second Persian conquest, is published by Miriam Lichtheim, *Ancient Egyptian Literature* (vol. 3, pp. 41–44), with additional studies by Paul Tresson, "La stèle de Naples," and Jacques Jean Clère, "Une statuette du fils aîné du roi Nectanebô." Sematawytefnakht's career is summarized by Toby Wilkinson, *Lives of the Ancient Egyptians* (no. 96). For the activities of Padiusir at Khmun, see Miriam Lichtheim, *Ancient Egyptian Literature* (vol. 3, pp. 44–54), and Toby Wilkinson, *Lives of the Ancient Egyptians* (no. 97). The best discussions of the ephemeral reign of Khababash are Friedrich Kienitz, *Die politische Geschichte Ägyptens* (pp. 185–189); Anthony Spalinger, "The Reign of King Chabbash"; and Robert Morkot, "Khababash, the Guerilla King." Alexander's Persian campaign and his conquest of Egypt are analyzed by Paul Cartledge, *Alexander the Great*. (For the significance of the visit to Siwa, see pp. 265–270.)

1. Wedjahorresnet, statue inscription, left side of the statue's garment.
2. Ibid., under the right arm.
3. Ibid., under the left arm.
4. Ibid., left side of naos base.
5. Ahmose, Serapeum stela, lines 4–5.
6. Darius I, Suez Canal stela, cuneiform text (after the French translation by V. Scheil, "Documents et arguments").
7. Tom Holland, *Persian Fire*, back cover.
8. Nakhtnebef, Hermopolis stela.
9. Nakhtnebef, Naukratis stela, lines 2–3.

10. Ibid., line 3.
11. H. F. Lyte, "Abide with Me" (hymn).
12. Inscription from the sacred animal necropolis at Saqqara (translation by Harry Smith, *A Visit to Ancient Egypt*, p. 43).
13. Padiusir, tomb inscription (translation by Miriam Lichtheim, *Ancient Egyptian Literature*, vol. 3, p. 46).
14. Ptolemy (I), Satrap stela, line 8.
15. Arrian, *Anabasis* (quoted by Paul Cartledge, *Alexander the Great*, p. 268).

CHAPTER 23: THE LONG GOODBYE

There is as yet no detailed account of Alexander the Great's time in Egypt, nor of his lasting impact on the country he visited so briefly. Surveys of the Ptolemaic Period generally begin with Alexander, and Günther Hölbl's *A History of the Ptolemaic Empire* is as good an introduction as any. For the notice by Peukestas, see E. G. Turner, "A Commander-in-Chief's Order from Saqqâra."

The career of Ptolemy I is summarized by Toby Wilkinson, *Lives of the Ancient Egyptians* (no. 98). A full discussion of the Wars of the Successors, the Syrian Wars, the expansion of the Ptolemaic Empire, and the procession of Ptolemy II can be found in Günther Hölbl, *A History of the Ptolemaic Empire*. For recent archaeological work at Berenike Panchrysos, see Angelo and Alfredo Castiglioni, "Discovering Berenice Panchrysos."

The foundation and layout of Alexandria are discussed by Jean-Yves Empereur, *Alexandria Rediscovered*, and John Ray, "Alexandria." The Satrap Stela, dated to 311, confirms that Ptolemy had adopted Alexandria as his new capital by this date. The ancient Egyptian name for Alexandria was Ra-qed (Rakhotis in its Greek form). Modern reconstructions of the city's ancient appearance owe much to the description given by Strabo in the first decade of Roman rule, summarized in Alan Bowman, *Egypt After the Pharaohs*. Underwater archaeology in recent years has discovered many of the statues and monuments that once adorned the palace quarters, together with blocks from the Pharos lighthouse. See Jean-Yves Empereur, "Alexandria: The Underwater Site near Qaitbay Fort" and "Raising Statues and Blocks from the Sea at Alexandria." The recognition that the Egyptian name for Alexandria, Rakhotis (Ra-qed), is in fact a euphemism meaning "building site," was made by Michel Chauveau, *L'Égypte au temps de Cléopâtre* (p. 77); see also Mark Depauw, "Alexandria." For a discussion of the intellectuals who studied in Alexandria under the early Ptolemies, see Alan Bowman, *Egypt After the Pharaohs*. A convenient source for the Great Library and the Pharos is Jean-Yves Empereur, *Alexandria: Past, Present and Future*.

Roger Bagnall, "Greeks and Egyptians: Ethnicity, Status, and Culture," provides a recent stimulating discussion of the cultural and ethnic divide between Greek and Egyptian communities in Ptolemaic Egypt. In the earlier Ptolemaic Period, there were in fact three distinct systems of law running in parallel: one for Greeks, one for Egyptians, and a third system to arbitrate between the two communities. The lives of the Greek inhabitants and immigrants are analyzed in detail by Naphtali Lewis,

Greeks in Ptolemaic Egypt. For the structure of the administration and the city of Memphis in the Ptolemaic Period, Dorothy Thompson, *Memphis Under the Ptolemies,* is an unrivaled source. The main features of the cult of Serapis are summarized by Richard Wilkinson, *The Complete Gods and Goddesses* (pp. 127–128). Many works have been written about the Ptolemaic ruler cult; among the most useful is Jan Quaegebeur, "The Egyptian Clergy and the Cult of the Ptolemaic Dynasty."

The economic exploitation of Egypt under Ptolemaic rule is the subject of J. G. Manning's magisterial *Land and Power in Ptolemaic Egypt.* For the role of the village scribe, as attested in the correspondence of one such from Kerkeosiris, see A.M.F.W. Verhoogt, *Menches, Komogrammateus of Kerkeosiris.*

The story of Ptolemy IV addressing his troops through an interpreter before the Battle of Raphia is recounted by Polybius.

Brian McGing, "Revolt Egyptian Style," offers a detailed overview of the native rebellions of the third to first centuries. The Theban revolt of 206–186 is discussed in greater detail by Günther Hölbl, *A History of the Ptolemaic Empire* (pp. 153–159), and Willy Clarysse, "Notes de prosopographie thébaine." For a full publication and analysis of all the contemporary documents, see P. W. Pestman, "Haronnophris and Chaonnophris." An inscription at Philae suggests that Ankhwennefer may have been the son of Horwennefer. John Ray, *The Rosetta Stone,* charts the background to the less well-known delta rebellion of Ptolemy V's reign (centered on a town that was also called Lykopolis in Greek [Shekan in Egyptian]). *The Rosetta Stone* also provides an up-to-date translation of the demotic text of the Rosetta Stone (pp. 164–170). For the aftermath of the insurrections and the imposition of military rule in Upper Egypt, see K. Vandorpe, "City of Many a Gate, Harbour for Many a Rebel."

The incessant internecine fighting within the royal family, Egypt's growing involvement with Rome, and the history of the later Ptolemies are all discussed in detail by Günther Hölbl, *A History of the Ptolemaic Empire* (pp. 181–231). Ptolemy VIII's first wife (and full sister) was Cleopatra II; her daughter, his second wife, was Cleopatra III.

The inscription on the sarcophagus lid of the royal scribe Wennefer is published in translation by Miriam Lichtheim, *Ancient Egyptian Literature* (vol. 3, pp. 54–58). Cleopatra's birth is dated to the end of 70 or the beginning of 69 by some authors (for example, Günther Hölbl, *A History of the Ptolemaic Empire*) and, more precisely, to early 69 by others (for example, Susan Walker and Peter Higgs [eds.], *Cleopatra of Egypt: From History to Myth*). In any case, late 70 and early 69 in modern reckoning fell within the same year in the ancient Egyptian calendar.

Scholars dispute the parentage and ancestry, and therefore the ethnicity, of Cleopatra. While Andrew Meadows, "Sins of the Fathers" (p. 23), argues that she was the daughter of Ptolemy XII and his full sister (Cleopatra V)—a view of which Robert Bianchi, "Cleopatra VII," is certain—W. Huss, "Die Herkunft der Kleopatra," has cast doubts on the identity of Cleopatra's mother. Sally-Ann Ashton, *Cleopatra and Egypt* (p. 1), admits that Cleopatra may have been only "part Egyptian," her foreign blood coming if not through her mother then through her grandmother, a concubine of Ptolemy IX's.

1. Sematawytefnakht, stela inscription (translation by Miriam Lichtheim, *Ancient Egyptian Literature*, vol. 3, pp. 42–43).
2. Temple of Horus at Edfu, innermost rooms.
3. Wennefer, sarcophagus lid inscription (translation by Miriam Lichtheim, *Ancient Egyptian Literature*, vol. 3, pp. 54–58).
4. Ibid.

CHAPTER 24: FINIS

For the high priests of Ptah during the Ptolemaic Period, and especially the last two holders of that office, Pasherenptah and Imhotep, see Jan Quaegebeur, "Contribution à la prosopographie des prêtres memphites," and E.A.E. Reymond and J.W.B. Barns, "Alexandria and Memphis." Reymond's thesis, that Pasherenptah was related to the Ptolemaic royal family (and was Cleopatra's second cousin) is not widely accepted and has not been followed here. The funerary stela of Pasherenptah is published in Susan Walker and Peter Higgs (eds.), *Cleopatra of Egypt* (catalogue no. 192). The reign of Ptolemy XII, including his exile in Rome, is charted in detail by Günther Hölbl, *A History of the Ptolemaic Empire*, and Andrew Meadows, "Sins of the Fathers." The evidence that Cleopatra may have accompanied her father to Rome in 57 is discussed by Guy Weill Goudchaux, "Cleopatra's Subtle Religious Strategy" (p. 131), based on another scholar's interpretation of a Greek inscription.

The history, construction, and decoration of the temple of Hathor at Iunet are analyzed by Jan Quaegebeur, "Cléopâtre VII et le temple de Dendara." The solar eclipse of March 7, 51, presaging Ptolemy XII's death, is thought to be depicted in the roof shrines of the temple. The famous zodiac ceiling, now in the Louvre, shows the positions of the constellations in 50, the first year of Cleopatra's sole reign.

The myriad books on the life, loves, and death of Cleopatra would fill a small library. Two recent studies, Diana Preston's *Cleopatra and Antony* and Joann Fletcher's *Cleopatra the Great*, by a historian and an Egyptologist respectively, illustrate our unending fascination for the last queen of Egypt. One of the better treatments, with a focus on the Egyptian evidence, is Sally-Ann Ashton, *Cleopatra and Egypt*. Evidence that Palestine stayed loyal to Cleopatra after she was driven out of Egypt comes in the form of coins minted in Ashkelon, bearing her portrait, and dated to 49–48. See Susan Walker and Peter Higgs (eds.), *Cleopatra of Egypt* (catalogue no. 220). The story of Cleopatra being smuggled in to see Julius Caesar has been often told; the method varies, according to the author, from a bed-linen sack to a carpet.

The question of Cleopatra's physical appearance is discussed at length by Guy Weill Goudchaux, "Was Cleopatra Beautiful?" It has been suggested that her coin portraits showing her with a long aquiline nose and a pointed chin may have been produced in conscious emulation of Roman portraiture, in a gesture of respect for Julius Caesar. If so, her actual physiognomy may have been somewhat less pronounced, as indicated by some of her statuary. See Susan Walker and Peter Higgs (eds.), *Cleopatra of Egypt* (catalogue nos. 160–164). For the coins minted in Cyprus to celebrate the birth of Caesarion, see Susan Walker and Peter Higgs (eds.), *Cleopatra of Egypt* (catalogue no. 186).

The birth of Imhotep is recounted on the stela of his mother, Taimhotep, published in Susan Walker and Peter Higgs (eds.), *Cleopatra of Egypt* (catalogue no. 193), and translated by Miriam Lichtheim, *Ancient Egyptian Literature* (vol. 3, pp. 59–65). For Cleopatra's activities at native Egyptian shrines, see Sally-Ann Ashton, *Cleopatra and Egypt* (pp. 88–101). A stela showing a male pharaoh in traditional guise but with an inscription naming Cleopatra suggests that she was regarded as a fully legitimate ruler by at least some of her countrymen. Again, see Susan Walker and Peter Higgs (eds.), *Cleopatra of Egypt* (catalogue no. 154). The assertion that Cleopatra could speak Egyptian is from Plutarch, *Life of Antony*, 27.4–5.

For the debasement of silver coinage and the use of bronze during Cleopatra's reign, see Susan Walker and Peter Higgs (eds.), *Cleopatra of Egypt* (p. 177). The Donations of Alexandria were described in detail by Plutarch in his *Life of Antony* (Chapter 54).

The tax decree favoring Canidius is published in Susan Walker and Peter Higgs (eds.), *Cleopatra of Egypt* (catalogue no. 188); some authors question the identification of Cleopatra's own handwriting (see Sally-Ann Ashton, *Cleopatra and Egypt*, p. 76). For the Gebtu contract, see Susan Walker and Peter Higgs (eds.), *Cleopatra of Egypt* (catalogue no. 173). The manner of Cleopatra's demise is discussed, inter alia, by J. Gwyn Griffiths, "The Death of Cleopatra VII"; Griffiths refutes any deliberate religious symbolism in death by snakebite. For the numerous afterlives of Cleopatra, Lucy Hughes-Hallett, *Cleopatra*, is incomparable.

The phrase *"ankh djet"* is enclosed within Ptolemy XV's second cartouche, carved in front of his crown on the rear wall of the Dendera temple; it is clearly visible in the photograph (fig. 3.2) in Susan Walker and Peter Higgs (eds.), *Cleopatra of Egypt* (p. 138), and in the drawings of Dendera published in the Napoleonic *Description de l'Égypte* (Charles Gillispie and Michel Dewachter [eds.], *Monuments of Egypt* [A. vol. IV, plate 28.12]).

1. Pasherenptah, funerary stela (translation by E.A.E. Reymond and J.W.B. Barns, "Alexandria and Memphis," p. 13).
2. Caesar, *The Alexandrian War*, Chapter 33 (quoted by Andrew Meadows, "Sins of the Fathers," p. 25).
3. Taimhotep, funerary stela, lines 8–9 (translation by Miriam Lichtheim, *Ancient Egyptian Literature*, vol. 3, p. 63).
4. Ibid., lines 13–14 (translation by Miriam Lichtheim, *Ancient Egyptian Literature*, vol. 3, p. 63).
5. Ibid., lines 15–16 (translation by Carol Andrews in Susan Walker and Peter Higgs [eds.], *Cleopatra of Egypt*, p. 186).
6. Plutarch, *Life of Antony*, Chapter 85 (quoted by Andrew Meadows, "Sins of the Fathers," p. 31).

EPILOGUE

The character of Roman rule in Egypt, including the country's economic exploitation, is well described by David Peacock, "The Roman Period." For the quarries of

Mons Claudianus that supplied the Roman Forum, see David Peacock, *Rome in the Desert;* and for Mons Porphyrites, see David Peacock and Valerie Maxfield, "On the Trail of Imperial Porphyry." The evidence for Roman trade with India via the Red Sea is presented by Steven Sidebotham and Willemina Wendrich, "Berenike."

The Napoleonic expedition to Egypt is discussed in detail by Charles Gillispie and Michel Dewachter (eds.), *Monuments of Egypt* ("Historical Introduction," pp. 1–29), and in summary by John Ray, *The Rosetta Stone* (Chapter 2).

The recent literature on Egyptomania—the Western fascination with ancient Egyptian culture—is extensive. The standard work is James Curl, *The Egyptian Revival,* while Richard Fazzini and Mary McKercher's "Egyptomania" offers a thoughtful and accessible summary. Jean-Marcel Humbert, Michael Pantazzi, and Christiane Ziegler, *Egyptomania,* provides the catalogue of a landmark exhibition, with superb illustrations. A good recent discussion of Egyptian influences in imperial Rome is Carla Alfano, "Egyptian Influences in Italy."

For the many afterlives of Akhenaten, Dominic Montserrat, *Akhenaten,* is incomparable as well as highly entertaining. The myriad ways in which the modern world appropriates ancient Egyptian culture are analyzed in Sally MacDonald and Michael Rice (eds.), *Consuming Ancient Egypt.*

1. Samuel Taylor Coleridge, *Recollections.*

BIBLIOGRAPHY

SOURCES FOR TRANSLATIONS

In this book, the translations from ancient texts are the author's own, except where stated. The citations below give the publications or editions from which the author translated.

ABBREVIATIONS

FHN: Tormod Eide et al. (eds.), *Fontes Historiae Nubiorum: Textual Sources for the History of the Middle Nile Region Between the Eighth Century BC and the Sixth Century AD*, vol. 1, *From the Eighth to the Mid-Fifth Century BC* (Bergen, Norway, 1994).

KRI: Kenneth Kitchen, *Ramesside Inscriptions, Historical and Biographical*, 8 vols. (Oxford, 1969–1990).

Lesestücke: Kurt Sethe, *Ägyptische Lesestücke* (Leipzig, 1924).

Urkunden I: Kurt Sethe, *Urkunden des ägyptischen Altertums, Abteilung I: Urkunden des alten Reiches*, 2nd ed. (Leipzig, Berlin, 1932–1933).

Urkunden II: Kurt Sethe, *Urkunden des ägyptischen Altertums, Abteilung II: Hieroglyphische Urkunden der griechisch-römischen Zeit* (Leipzig, 1904).

Urkunden IV: Kurt Sethe (later volumes compiled by Wolfgang Helck), *Urkunden des ägyptischen Altertums, Abteilung IV: Urkunden der 18. Dynastie* (Leipzig, Berlin, 1906–1958).

Urkunden V: Georg Steindorff, *Urkunden des ägyptisches Altertums, Abteilung V: Ausgewahlte Texte des Totenbuches* (Leipzig, 1915).

Urkunden VII: Kurt Sethe, *Urkunden des ägyptischen Altertums, Abteilung VII: Historisch-Biographische Urkunden des Mittleren Reiches* (Leipzig, 1935).

TRANSLATED MATERIAL

Ahmose, son of Abana, tomb inscription: *Urkunden IV,* pp. 1–11.

Ahmose, Karnak stela: *Urkunden IV,* pp. 14–24.

Ahmose, Serapeum stela: Georges Posener, *La première domination perse en Égypte* (Cairo, 1946), pp. 41–46.

Ahmose, Tempest stela: Claude Vandersleyen, "Une tempête sous la règne d'Amosis," *Revue d'Égyptologie*, 19 (1967), pp. 123–159.

Ahmose, Tetisheri stela: *Urkunden IV*, pp. 26–29.

Ahmose, Tura limestone quarry inscription: *Urkunden IV*, pp. 24–25.

Akhenaten, earlier foundation inscription (boundary stelae K, X, and M): Maj Sandman (ed.), *Texts from the Time of Akhenaten* (Brussels, 1938), no. CXIX, pp. 103–118.

Akhenaten, later foundation inscription (boundary stelae A, B, J, N, Q, R, S, and U): Maj Sandman (ed.), *Texts*, no. CXX, pp. 119–131; *Urkunden IV*, pp. 1981–1990.

Amenhotep II, Great Sphinx stela: *Urkunden IV*, pp. 1276–1283.

Amenhotep II, Medamud inscription: *Urkunden IV*, pp. 1322–1323.

Amenhotep II, Memphis stela: *Urkunden IV*, pp. 1300–1309.

Amenhotep III, bull-hunt scarab: *Urkunden IV*, p. 1738.

Amenhotep III, divine birth inscription, Luxor Temple: *Urkunden IV*, pp. 1713–1721.

Amenhotep III, marriage scarab: *Urkunden IV*, p. 1738.

Amenhotep III, Kom el-Hetan stela: *Urkunden IV*, pp. 1646–1657.

Ankhtifi, tomb inscription: Jacques Vandier, *Mo'alla: La tombe d'Ankhtifi et la tombe de Sébekhotep* (Cairo, 1950).

Atu, scribal palette: Wolfgang Helck, *Historisch-Biographische Texte der 2. Zwischenzeit und Neue Texte der 18. Dynastie* (Wiesbaden, 1975), no. 85, pp. 57–58.

Bay, Gebel el-Silsila inscription: *KRI*, vol. IV, p. 371.

Bible, Revised Standard Version (London, 1979).

Book of the Dead, Chapter 6: Edouard Naville, *Das Aegyptische Todtenbuch der XVIII. bis XX. Dynastie*, vol. 1 (Berlin, 1886).

Book of the Dead, Chapter 17: *Urkunden V*.

Carnarvon Tablet no. 1: Alan Gardiner, "The Defeat of the Hyksos by Kamose: The Carnarvon Tablet, No. 1," *Journal of Egyptian Archaeology*, 3 (1916), pp. 95–110.

Coffin Texts: Adriaan de Buck, *The Egyptian Coffin Texts*, 8 vols. (Chicago, 1935–1961).

Cycle of Hymns to Senusret III: *Lesestücke*, pp. 65–67.

Dediqu, stela inscription: Heinrich Schäfer, "Ein Zug nach der grossen Oase unter Sesostris I.," *Zeitschrift für Ägyptische Sprache und Altertumskunde*, 42 (1905), pp. 124–128.

Djari, funerary stela: W. M. Flinders Petrie, *Qurneh* (London, 1909), plate II.

Djemi, funerary stela: Hans Goedicke, "The Inscription of *Ḏmi*," *Journal of Near Eastern Studies*, 19 (1960), pp. 288–291.

Great Harris Papyrus I: W. Erichsen, *Papyrus Harris I: Hieroglyphische Transkription* (Brussels, 1933).

Great Hymn to the Aten: Maj Sandman (ed.), *Texts*, no. CXIII, pp. 93–96.

Harkhuf, tomb inscription: *Urkunden I*, pp. 120–131.

Hatnub inscriptions: Rudolf Anthes, *Die Felseninschriften von Hatnub* (Leipzig, 1928).

Hatshepsut, Karnak obelisk inscription: *Urkunden IV*, pp. 356–373.

Henenu, funerary stela: William Hayes, "Career of the Great Steward Henenu Under Nebhepetrē' Mentuhotpe," *Journal of Egyptian Archaeology*, 35 (1949), pp. 43–49.

Herodotus: *The Histories*, translated by Aubrey de Sélincourt, revised by A. R. Burn (Harmondsworth, England, 1972).

Hetepi, funerary stela: Gawdat Gabra, "Preliminary Report on the Stela of *Htpi* from

El-Kab from the Time of Wahankh Inyôtef II," *Mitteilungen des Deutschen Archäologischen Instituts, Abteilung Kairo*, 32 (1976), pp. 45–56.

Horemheb, coronation inscription: *Urkunden IV*, pp. 2113–2120.

Horemheb, edict: *Urkunden IV*, pp. 2140–2162.

Huya, tomb inscription: Maj Sandman (ed.), *Texts*, nos. XXXVI–L, pp. 33–43; Norman de Garis Davies, *The Rock Tombs of El Amarna*, part III (London, 1903–1908).

Hymn to Amun: Pascal Vernus, "Choix de texts illustrant le temps des rois tanites et libyens," in Ministère des Affaires Étrangères/Association Française d'Action Artistique, *Tanis: L'or des pharaons* (Paris, 1987), no. 1, pp. 103–104.

Ineni, tomb inscription: *Urkunden IV*, pp. 59–60.

Installation of the vizier, from the tomb inscription of Rekhmira: *Urkunden IV*, pp. 1085–1093.

Instruction for King Merikara, The: Wolfgang Helck, *Die Lehre für König Merikare* (Wiesbaden, 1977).

Instruction of Amenemhat I for His Son, The: Wolfgang Helck, *Der Text der "Lehre Amenemhets I. für seinen Sohn"* (Wiesbaden, 1969).

Intef, funerary stela from Naga el-Deir: Henry Fischer, *Inscriptions from the Coptite Nome, Dynasties VI–XI* (Rome, 1964), no. 43, pp. 106–111.

Intef, stela: Henry Fischer, *Dendera in the Third Millennium* B.C. (Locust Valley, 1968), p. 200, fig. 39.

Intef II, funerary stela: Gay Robins, *The Art of Ancient Egypt*, fig. 83, p. 85.

Intef V, Coptos stela: Wolfgang Helck, *Historisch-Biographische Texte*, no. 106, pp. 73–74.

Intefiqer, Wadi el-Girgawi inscription: Zbyněk Žába, *The Rock Inscriptions of Lower Nubia (Czechoslovak Concession)* (Prague, 1974), no. 73, pp. 98–109.

Iti, funerary stela: H. O. Lange and H. Schäfer, *Grab- und Denksteine des Mittleren Reichs im Museum von Kairo No. 20001–20780* (Berlin: Reichsdruckerei, 1902), vol. 1, pp. 1–2, and vol. 4, plate 1.

Ka, funerary stela: Torgny Säve-Söderbergh, "A Buhen Stela from the Second Intermediate Period (Khartum No. 18)," *Journal of Egyptian Archaeology*, 35 (1949), pp. 50–58, fig. 1.

Kamose, victory stela from Thebes: Labib Habachi, *The Second Stela of Kamose and His Struggle Against the Hyksos Ruler and His Capital* (Glückstadt, Germany, 1972).

Kay, funerary stela: Rudolf Anthes, "Eine Polizeistreife des Mitleren Reiches in die westlichen Oase," *Zeitschrift für Ägyptische Sprache und Altertumskunde*, 65 (1930), pp. 108–114.

Kheruef, tomb inscription: The Epigraphic Survey, *The Tomb of Kheruef* (Chicago, 1980).

Kheti I, tomb inscription: Hellmut Brunner, *Die Texte aus den Gräbern der Herakleopolitenzeit von Siut* (Glückstadt, Hamburg, and New York, 1937).

Khnumhotep I, biographical inscription: *Urkunden VII*, pp. 11–12.

Loyalist Instruction, The: Georges Posener, *L'enseignement loyaliste: Sagesse égyptienne de Moyen Empire* (Geneva, 1976).

Mahu, tomb inscription: Maj Sandman (ed.), *Texts*, nos. LXII–LXIX, pp. 50–54; Norman de Garis Davies, *The Rock Tombs of El Amarna*, part IV.

Menkheperra, Banishment Stela: Jürgen von Beckerath, "Die 'Stele der Verbannten' im Museum des Louvre," *Revue d'Egyptologie*, 20 (1968), pp. 7–36.

Mentuhotep IV, Wadi Hammamat inscription: J. Couyat and Pierre Montet, *Les inscriptions hiéroglyphiques et hiératiques du Ouâdi Hammâmât*, 2 vols. (Cairo, 1912–1913), no. 110, pp. 77–78 and plate XXIX.

Mentuhotepi, Karnak stela: Pascal Vernus, "La stèle du pharaon *Mntw-htpi* à Karnak: Un nouveau témoignage sur la situation politique et militaire au début de la D.P.I.," *Revue d'Égyptologie*, 40 (1989), pp. 146–161.

Merenptah, great Karnak inscription: Colleen Manassa, *The Great Karnak Inscription of Merneptah: Grand Strategy in the 13th Century BC* (New Haven, Conn., 2003).

Merenptah, Libyan inscription: *KRI*, vol. IV, pp. 2–12.

Merer, funerary stela: Jaroslav Černý, "The Stela of Merer in Cracow," *Journal of Egyptian Archaeology*, 47 (1961), pp. 5–9 and plate 1.

Meryra I, tomb inscription: Maj Sandman (ed.), *Texts*, nos. I–XIV, pp. 1–21; Norman de Garis Davies, *The Rock Tombs of El Amarna*, part I.

Min, tomb inscription: *Urkunden IV*, pp. 976–980.

Nakhtnebef, Hermopolis stela: H. De Meulenaere, "La famille royale des Nectanébo," *Zeitschrift für Ägyptische Sprache und Altertumskunde*, 90 (1963), pp. 90–93.

Nakhtnebef, Naukratis stela: Adolf Erman and Ulrich Wilcken, "Die Naukratisstele," *Zeitschrift für Ägyptische Sprache und Altertumskunde*, 38 (1900), pp. 127–135.

Neferhotep III, Karnak inscription: Wolfgang Helck, *Historisch-Biographische Texte*, no. 62, p. 45.

Ostracon O.IFAO 1864: Pierre Grandet, "L'exécution du chancelier Bay: O.IFAO 1864," *Bulletin de l'Institut Français d'Archéologie Orientale*, 100 (2000), pp. 339–345.

Papyrus Amherst: Eric Peet, *The Great Tomb-Robberies of the Twentieth Egyptian Dynasty* (Oxford, 1930), plates IV–V.

Papyrus BM 10052: Eric Peet, *The Great Tomb-Robberies*, plates XXV–XXXV.

Piankhi, victory stela: Nicolas Grimal, *La stèle triomphale de Pi('ankh)y au musée du Caire JE 48862 et 47086–47089* (Cairo, 1981).

Priestly annals at Karnak: Jean-Marie Kruchten, *Les annales des prêtres de Karnak (XXI–XXIIImes dynasties) et autres texts contemporains relatifs à l'initiation des prêtres d'Amon* (Leuven, Belgium, 1989).

Prophecies of Neferti, The: Wolfgang Helck, *Die Prophezeihung des Nfr.tj* (Wiesbaden, 1970).

Psamtek II, Shellal stela: Charles Bonnet and Dominique Valbelle, *The Nubian Pharaohs* (Cairo and New York, 2005), p. 166.

Ptolemy (I), Satrap stela: *Urkunden II*, pp. 11–22.

Pyramid Texts: Kurt Sethe, *Die altägyptischen Pyramidentexte*, 4 vols. (Leipzig, 1908–1922).

Qenamun, tomb inscription: *Urkunden IV*, pp. 1385–1406.

Rahotep, Coptos stela: Wolfgang Helck, *Historisch-Biographische Texte*, no. 87, pp. 59–60.

Ramesses II, Battle of Kadesh "poem": *KRI*, vol. II, pp. 2–64.

Ramesses II, first Hittite marriage inscription: *KRI*, vol. II, pp. 233–256.

Ramesses II, treaty with the Hittites: *KRI*, vol. II, pp. 225–232.

Ramesses III, Deir el-Medina stela: *KRI*, vol. V, pp. 90–91.

Ramesses III, great inscription of year eight, Medinet Habu: *KRI*, vol. V, pp. 37–43.

Ramesses III, harem scenes, Medinet Habu: *KRI*, vol. V, p. 295.

Ramesses III, Turin Judicial Papyrus: *KRI*, vol. V, pp. 350–360.

Ramesses III, Turin Strike Papyrus: Alan Gardiner (ed.), *Ramesside Administrative Documents* (London, 1948), no. XVIII, pp. 45–58.

Ramesses IV, great Abydos stela: *KRI*, vol. VI, pp. 17–20.

Ramesses IV, second Abydos stela: *KRI*, vol. VI, pp. 20–25.

Ramesses IV, Wadi Hammamat inscription of year three: *KRI*, vol. VI, pp. 12–14.

Rekhmira, biographical inscription: *Urkunden IV*, pp. 1071–1085.

Satire of the Trades: Wolfgang Helck, *Die Lehre des Dw3-Htjj* (Wiesbaden, 1970).

Senenmut, Karnak statue inscription: *Urkunden IV*, pp. 407–415.

Sennefer, tomb inscription: *Urkunden IV*, pp. 1417–1434.

Senusret III, Semna stela: *Lesestücke*, pp. 83–84.

Sethnakht, Elephantine stela: *KRI*, vol. V, pp. 671–672.

Seti I, Kanais temple inscription: *KRI*, vol. I, pp. 65–70.

Seti I, Nauri Decree: *KRI*, vol. I, pp. 45–58.

Shabaqo, commemorative scarab: *FHN*, no. 14, pp. 123–125.

Sobeknakht, autobiographical inscription: Vivian Davies, "Sobeknakht of Elkab and the Coming of Kush," *Egyptian Archaeology*, 23 (2003), pp. 3–6.

Soped-her, funerary stela: Torgny Säve-Söderbergh, "A Buhen Stela," fig. 2.

Taharqo, desert stela: *FHN*, no. 23, pp. 158–163.

Taharqo, Kawa stela of year six: *FHN*, no. 22, pp. 145–158.

Tale of Sinuhe, The: *Lesestücke*, pp. 3–17.

Tanutamun, dream stela: *FHN*, no. 29, pp. 193–209.

Thutmose I, Abydos stela: *Urkunden IV*, pp. 94–103.

Thutmose I, Tombos victory inscription: *Urkunden IV*, pp. 82–86.

Thutmose III, Megiddo inscription from Karnak: *Urkunden IV*, pp. 647–667.

Thutmose III, obelisk inscription: *Urkunden IV*, pp. 586–587.

Tjauti, desert inscription: John and Deborah Darnell, *Theban Desert Road Survey in the Egyptian Western Desert*, vol. 1, *Gebel Tjauti Rock Inscriptions 1–45 and Wadi el-Hôl Rock Inscriptions 1–45* (Chicago, 2002), pp. 30–37.

Tjauti, false door: Henry Fischer, *Inscriptions from the Coptite Name*, plate XIV, no. 14.

Tjetji, funerary stela: Gay Robins, *The Art of Ancient Egypt*, fig. 85, p. 86.

Tutankhamun, restoration stela: *Urkunden IV*, pp. 2025–2032.

Tutu, tomb inscription: Maj Sandman (ed.), *Texts*, nos. XCVII–CIX, pp. 70–87; Norman de Garis Davies, *The Rock Tombs of El Amarna*, part VI.

Wedjahorresnet, statue inscription: Georges Posener, *La première domination perse en Égypte* (Cairo, 1936), pp. 1–29.

Weni, autobiographical inscription: *Urkunden I*, pp. 98–110.

OTHER SOURCES

Adams, Barbara, *Ancient Nekhen: Garstang in the City of Hierakonpolis* (New Malden, 1990).

Adams, Matthew, "Monuments of Egypt's Early Kings at Abydos," unpublished lecture delivered at the colloquium Egypt at Its Origins: Predynastic and Early Dynastic Egypt: Recent Discoveries, British Museum, London, July 28, 2008.

Albert, Jean-Pierre, and Béatrix Midant-Reynes (eds.), *Le sacrifice humain en Égypte ancienne et ailleurs* (Paris, 2005).

Aldred, Cyril, *Akhenaten, King of Egypt* (London, 1988).

Aldred, Cyril, "More Light on the Ramesside Tomb Robberies," in John Ruffle, G. A. Gaballa, and Kenneth A. Kitchen (eds.), *Orbis Aegyptiorum Speculum: Glimpses of Ancient Egypt: Studies in Honour of H. W. Fairman* (Warminster, England, 1979), pp. 92–99.

Aldred, Cyril, "The Parentage of King Siptah," *Journal of Egyptian Archaeology*, 49 (1963), pp. 41–48.

Alfano, Carla, "Egyptian Influences in Italy," in Susan Walker and Peter Higgs (eds.), *Cleopatra of Egypt*, pp. 276–291.

Allen, James P., "After Hatshepsut: The Military Campaigns of Thutmose III," in Catharine H. Roehrig (ed.), *Hatshepsut*, pp. 261–262.

Allen, James P. (trans.), *The Ancient Egyptian Pyramid Texts* (Atlanta, Ga., 2005).

Allen, James P., "Ba," in Donald B. Redford (ed.), *The Oxford Encyclopedia of Ancient Egypt*, vol. 1, pp. 161–162.

Allen, James P., *Genesis in Egypt: The Philosophy of Ancient Egyptian Creation Accounts* (New Haven, Conn., 1988).

Allen, James P., "Reading a Pyramid," in Catherine Berger, Gisèle Clerc, and Nicolas Grimal (eds.), *Hommages à Jean Leclant*, vol. 1 (Cairo, 1994), pp. 5–28.

Altenmüller, Hartwig, and Ahmed M. Moussa, "Die Inschrift Amenemhets II. asu dem Ptah-Tempel von Memphis. Ein Vorbericht," *Studien zur Altägyptischen Kultur*, 18 (1991), pp. 1–48.

Amer, Amin A.M.A., "Reflections on the Reign of Ramesses VI," *Journal of Egyptian Archaeology*, 71 (1985), pp. 66–70.

Anderson, Wendy, "Badarian Burials: Evidence of Social Inequality in Middle Egypt During the Early Predynastic Era," *Journal of the American Research Center in Egypt*, 29 (1992), pp. 51–66.

Andrews, Carol, *Amulets of Ancient Egypt* (London, 1994).

Anthes, Rudolf, *Die Felseninschriften von Hatnub* (Leipzig, 1928).

Anthes, Rudolf, "Eine Polizeistreife des Mittleren Reiches in die westlichen Oase," *Zeitschrift für Ägyptische Sprache und Altertumskunde*, 65 (1930), pp. 108–114.

Arkell, A. J., "Varia Sudanica," *Journal of Egyptian Archaeology*, 36 (1950), pp. 24–40.

Arnold, Dieter, "Djeser-djeseru: The Temple of Hatshepsut at Deir el-Bahri," in Catharine H. Roehrig (ed.), *Hatshepsut*, pp. 135–140.

Arnold, Dieter, "Two New Mastabas of the Twelfth Dynasty at Dahshur," *Egyptian Archaeology*, 9 (1996), pp. 23–25.

Arnold, Dorothea, "Amenemhat I and the Early Twelfth Dynasty at Thebes," *Metropolitan Museum Journal*, 26 (1991), pp. 5–48.

Arnold, Dorothea, "The Destruction of the Statues of Hatshepsut from Deir el-Bahri," in Catharine H. Roehrig (ed.), *Hatshepsut*, pp. 270–276.

Ashton, Sally-Ann, *Cleopatra and Egypt* (Oxford, 2008).

Aston, David A., "Takeloth II—A King of the 'Theban Twenty-third Dynasty'?," *Journal of Egyptian Archaeology*, 75 (1989), pp. 139–153.

Aston, David A., and Edgar B. Pusch, "The Pottery from the Royal Horse Stud and Its Stratigraphy," *Ägypten und Levante*, 9 (1999), pp. 39–75.

Aston, David A., and John H. Taylor, "The Family of Takeloth II and the 'Theban' Twenty-third Dynasty," in Anthony Leahy (ed.), *Libya and Egypt*, pp. 131–154.

Astour, Michael, "New Evidence on the Last Days of Ugarit," *American Journal of Archaeology*, 69 (1965), p. 255.

Astour, Michael C., "Mitanni," in Donald B. Redford (ed.), *The Oxford Encyclopedia of Ancient Egypt*, vol. 2, pp. 422–424.

Ayad, Boulos Ayad, "From the Archive of Ananiah Son of Azariah: A Jew from Elephantine," *Journal of Near Eastern Studies*, 56 (1997), pp. 37–50.

Baer, Klaus, *Rank and Title in the Old Kingdom* (Chicago, 1960).

Bagnall, Roger S., "Greeks and Egyptians: Ethnicity, Status, and Culture," in Robert Bianchi (ed.), *Cleopatra's Egypt* (Brooklyn, N.Y., 1988), pp. 21–27.

Baines, John, "How Far Can One Distinguish Between Religion and Politics in Ancient Egypt?," unpublished lecture delivered at the Spotlight on Egyptian Religion study day, Cambridge, England, September 20, 2008.

Baines, John, "Origins of Egyptian Kingship," in David O'Connor and David Silverman (eds.), *Ancient Egyptian Kingship*, pp. 95–156.

Baines, John, "Society, Morality, and Religious Practice," in Byron E. Shafer (ed.), *Religion in Ancient Egypt* (London, 1991), pp. 123–200.

Baines, John, and Jaromír Málek, *Atlas of Ancient Egypt* (Oxford, 1980).

Barbotin, Christophe, and Jacques Jean Clère, "L'inscription de Sésostris Ier à Tôd," *Bulletin de l'Institut Français d'Archéologie Orientale*, 91 (1991), pp. 1–32.

Bard, Kathryn A., "The Emergence of the Egyptian State (c. 3200–2686 BC)," in Ian Shaw (ed.), *The Oxford History*, pp. 57–82.

Bard, Kathryn A. (ed.), *Encyclopedia of the Archaeology of Ancient Egypt* (London, 1999).

Bard, Kathryn A., *From Farmers to Pharaohs: Mortuary Evidence for the Rise of Complex Society in Egypt* (Sheffield, England, 1994).

Bard, Kathryn A., "Origins of Egyptian Writing," in Renée Friedman and Barbara Adams (eds.), *The Followers of Horus: Studies Dedicated to Michael Allen Hoffman, 1944–1990* (Oxford, 1992), pp. 297–306.

Bard, Kathryn A., and Robert L. Carneiro, "Patterns of Predynastic Settlement Location, Social Evolution and the Circumscription Theory," *Cahiers de Recherches de l'Institut de Papyrologie et d'Egyptologie de Lille*, 11 (1989), pp. 15–23.

Bareš, Ladislav, *Abusir IV: The Shaft Tomb of Udjahorresnet at Abusir* (Prague, 1999).

Baud, Michel, *La famille royale et pouvoir sous l'Ancien Empire égyptien* (Cairo, 2005).

Baud, Michel, and Vassil Dobrev, "De nouvelles annales de l'Ancien Empire égyptien. Une 'Pierre de Palerme' pour la VIe dynastie," *Bulletin de l'Institut Français d'Archéologie Orientale*, 95 (1995), pp. 23–92.

Baud, Michel, and Marc Étienne, "Le vanneau et le couteau: Un rituel monarchique sacrificiel dans l'Égypte de la Ire dynastie," in Jean-Pierre Albert and Béatrix Midant-Reynes (eds.), *Le sacrifice humain*, pp. 96–121.

Baud, Michel, and Nadine Moeller, "A Fourth Dynasty Royal Necropolis at Abu Rawash," *Egyptian Archaeology*, 28 (2006), pp. 16–18.

Bell, Lanny, "Luxor Temple and the Cult of the Royal *Ka*," *Journal of Near Eastern Studies*, 44 (1985), pp. 251–294.

Bennett, John, "A New Interpretation of B.M. Stela 1203," *Journal of Egyptian Archaeology*, 48 (1962), pp. 158–159.

Betancourt, Philip P., "The Aegean and the Origin of the Sea Peoples," in Eliezer D. Oren (ed.), *The Sea Peoples*, pp. 297–303.

Bettles, Elizabeth, J. Clarke, J. Dittmer, C. Duhig, S. Ikram, I. Mathieson, H. Smith, and A. Tavares, *National Museums of Scotland Saqqara Project Report 1995* (Edinburgh, 1995).

Bianchi, Robert S., "Cleopatra VII," in Donald B. Redford (ed.), *The Oxford Encyclopedia of Ancient Egypt*, vol. 1, pp. 273–274.

Bierbrier, Morris L., "Elements of Stability and Instability in Ramesside Egypt: The Succession to the Throne," in Edward Bleiberg et al. (eds.), *Fragments of a Shattered Visage*, pp. 9–14.

Bietak, Manfred, "The Center of Hyksos Rule: Avaris (Tell el-Dab'a)," in Eliezer D. Oren (ed.), *The Hyksos*, pp. 87–139. (Note: This article is cited on the contents page of the Oren volume under a different title, "Avaris, Capital of the Hyksos Kingdom: New Results of Excavations.")

Bietak, Manfred, "Dab'a, Tell ed-," in Donald B. Redford (ed.), *The Oxford Encyclopedia of Ancient Egypt*, vol. 1, pp. 351–354.

Bietak, Manfred, "Egypt and the Aegean: Cultural Convergence in a Thutmoside Palace at Avaris," in Catharine H. Roehrig (ed.), *Hatshepsut*, pp. 75–81.

Bietak, Manfred, "Egypt and the Levant," in Toby Wilkinson (ed.), *The Egyptian World*, pp. 417–448.

Bietak, Manfred, "The Tuthmoside Stronghold of Perunefer," *Egyptian Archaeology*, 26 (2005), pp. 13–17.

Bietak, Manfred, "Zum Königreich des '3-zh-R' Nehesi," *Studien zur Altägyptischen Kultur*, 11 (1984), pp. 59–75.

Bietak, Manfred, and Nannó Marinatos, "The Minoan Paintings of Avaris," in Bill Manley (ed.), *The Seventy Great Mysteries*, pp. 166–169.

Bimson, John J., "The Israelite Exodus: Myth or Reality?," in Bill Manley (ed.), *The Seventy Great Mysteries*, pp. 277–281.

Bimson, John J., "Who Was King Shishak of Egypt?," in Bill Manley (ed.), *The Seventy Great Mysteries*, pp. 289–292.

Bisson de la Roque, Fernand, Georges Contenau, and Fernand Chapouthier, *Le Trésor de Tôd* (Cairo, 1953).

Björkman, Gun, *Kings at Karnak: A Study of the Treatment of the Monuments of Royal Predecessors in the Early New Kingdom* (Uppsala, 1971).

Bleiberg, Edward, Rita Freed, and Anna Kay Walker (eds.), *Fragments of a Shattered Visage: The Proceedings of the International Symposium on Ramesses the Great* (Memphis, Tenn., 1991).

Boardman, John, *The Greeks Overseas* (Harmondsworth, 1964).

Bonnet, Charles, and Dominique Valbelle, *The Nubian Pharaohs* (Cairo and New York, 2005).

Boraik, Mansour, "Re-writing Egypt's History: The Stela of Bakenkhonsu," *Ancient Egypt*, 9.3 (2008–2009), pp. 24–27.

Bothmer, Bernard V., "A New Fragment of an Old Palette," *Journal of the American Research Center in Egypt*, 8 (1969–70), pp. 5–8.

Bourriau, Janine, "Patterns of Change in Burial Customs During the Middle Kingdom," in Stephen Quirke (ed.), *Middle Kingdom Studies*, pp. 3–20.

Bourriau, Janine, *Pharaohs and Mortals: Egyptian Art in the Middle Kingdom* (Cambridge, England, 1988).

Bourriau, Janine, "The Second Intermediate Period (c. 1650–1550 BC)," in Ian Shaw (ed.), *The Oxford History*, pp. 172–206.

Bowman, Alan K., *Egypt After the Pharaohs* (London, 1996).

Brandl, Baruch, "Evidence for Egyptian Colonization of the Southern Coastal Plain and Lowlands of Canaan During the Early Bronze I Period," in Edwin C. M. van den Brink (ed.), *The Nile Delta in Transition*, pp. 441–476.

Breasted, James Henry, *Ancient Records of Egypt* (Chicago, 1906).

Breyer, Francis, *Tanutamani: Die Traumstele und ihr Umfeld* (Wiesbaden, 2003).

Broekman, Gerard P. F., "The Chronicle of Prince Osorkon and Its Historical Context," *Journal of Egyptian History*, 1 (2008), pp. 209–234.

Brunner, Hellmut, *Die Texte aus den Gräbern der Herakleopolitenzeit von Siut* (Glückstadt, Hamburg, and New York, 1937).

Brunton, Guy, and Gertrude Caton-Thompson, *The Badarian Civilisation and Predynastic Remains near Badari* (London, 1928).

Bryan, Betsy M., "Administration in the Reign of Thutmose III," in Catharine H. Roehrig (ed.), *Hatshepsut*, pp. 69–122.

Bryan, Betsy M., "Antecedents to Amenhotep III," in David O'Connor and Eric H. Cline (eds.), *Amenhotep III*, pp. 27–62.

Bryan, Betsy M., "The Egyptian Perspective on Mittani," in Raymond Cohen and Raymond Westbrook (eds.), *Amarna Diplomacy*, pp. 71–84.

Bryan, Betsy M., "The 18th Dynasty Before the Amarna Period (c. 1550–1352 BC)," in Ian Shaw (ed.), *The Oxford History*, pp. 207–264.

Bryan, Betsy M., *The Reign of Thutmose IV* (Baltimore, Md., 1991).

Bryan, Betsy M., "Thutmose IV," in Donald B. Redford (ed.), *The Oxford Encyclopedia of Ancient Egypt*, vol. 3, pp. 403–405.

Bryce, Trevor R., "The Death of Niphururiya and Its Aftermath," *Journal of Egyptian Archaeology*, 76 (1990), pp. 97–105.

Bryce, Trevor, *The Kingdom of the Hittites* (Oxford, 2005).

Bussmann, Richard, "Siedlungen im Kontext der Pyramiden des Alten Reiches," *Mitteilungen des Deutschen Archäologischen Instituts, Abteilung Kairo*, 60 (2004), pp. 17–39.

Butzer, Karl W., "Desert Environments," in Donald B. Redford (ed.), *The Oxford Encyclopedia of Ancient Egypt*, vol. 1, pp. 385–389.

Callender, Gae, "The Middle Kingdom Renaissance (c. 2055–1650 BC)," in Ian Shaw (ed.), *The Oxford History*, pp. 137–171.

Calverley, A. M., and M. F. Broome, *The Temple of King Sethos I at Abydos*, 4 vols. (London and Chicago, 1933–1958).

Caminos, Ricardo A., *The Chronicle of Prince Osorkon* (Rome, 1958).

Caminos, Ricardo A., "The Nitocris Adoption Stela," *Journal of Egyptian Archaeology*, 50 (1964), pp. 71–101 and plates 7–10.

Caminos, Ricardo A., "Papyrus Berlin 10463," *Journal of Egyptian Archaeology*, 49 (1963), pp. 29–37.

Caminos, Ricardo A., "Peasants," in Sergio Donadoni (ed.), *The Egyptians*, translated by Robert Bianchi, Anna Lisa Crone, Charles Lambert, and Thomas Ritter (Chicago, 1997), pp. 1–30.

Caminos, Ricardo A., *A Tale of Woe from a Hieratic Papyrus in the A. S. Pushkin Museum of Fine Arts in Moscow* (Oxford, 1977).

Campagno, Marcelo, "In the Beginning Was the War: Conflict and the Emergence of the Egyptian State," in Stan Hendrickx, Renée F. Friedman, Krzysztof M. Ciałowicz, and Marek Chlodnicki (eds.), *Egypt at Its Origins: Studies in Memory of Barbara Adams* (Leuven, Belgium, 2004), pp. 689–703.

Carter, Howard, "Report upon the Tomb of Sen-nefer Found at Biban el-Molouk near That of Thotmes III No. 34," *Annales du Service des Antiquités de l'Egypte*, 2 (1901), pp. 196–200.

Carter, Howard, and A. C. Mace, *The Tomb of Tut.ankh.Amen*, 3 vols. (London, 1923–1927).

Cartledge, Paul, *Agesilaos and the Crisis of Sparta* (Baltimore, 1987).

Cartledge, Paul, *Alexander the Great: The Hunt for a New Past* (London, 2004).

Case, H., and Joan Crowfoot Payne, "Tomb 100: The Decorated Tomb at Hierakonpolis," *Journal of Egyptian Archaeology*, 48 (1962), pp. 5–18.

Castiglioni, Angelo, and Alfredo Castiglioni, "Discovering Berenice Panchrysos," *Egyptian Archaeology*, 4 (1994), pp. 19–22.

Červíček, Pavel, *Rock Pictures of Upper Egypt and Nubia* (Naples, Italy, 1986).

Charloux, Guillaume, "The Middle Kingdom Temple of Amun at Karnak," *Egyptian Archaeology*, 27 (2005), pp. 20–24.

Chauveau, Michel, "The Demotic Ostraca of Ayn Manawir," *Egyptian Archaeology*, 22 (2003), pp. 38–40.

Chauveau, Michel, *L'Égypte au temps de Cléopâtre* (Paris, 1997).

Ciałowicz, Krzysztof M., *Les Têtes de Massues des Périodes Prédynastique et Archaïque Dans la Vallée du Nil* (Krakow, 1991).

Clarysse, Willy, "Notes de prosopographie thébaine, 7. Hurgonaphor et Chaonnophris, les derniers pharaons indigènes," *Chronique d'Égypte*, 53 (1978), pp. 243–253.

Clère, Jacques Jean, "Une statuette du fils aîné du roi Nectanebô," *Revue d'Egyptologie*, 6 (1951), pp. 135–156.

Clère, Jacques Jean, and Jacques Vandier, *Textes de la Première Période Intermédiaire et de la XIème Dynastie* (Brussels, 1948).

Cline, Eric H., and David O'Connor (eds.), *Thutmose III: A New Biography* (Ann Arbor, 2006).

Cohen, Raymond, and Raymond Westbrook (eds.), *Amarna Diplomacy: The Beginnings of International Relations* (Baltimore, Md., 2000).

Colin, Frédéric, "Kamose et les Hyksos dans l'oasis de Djesdjes," *Bulletin de l'Institut Français d'Archéologie Orientale*, 105 (2005), pp. 35–47.

Conard, Nicholas J., and Mark Lehner, "The 1988/1989 Excavation of Petrie's 'Workmen's Barracks' at Giza," *Journal of the American Research Center in Egypt*, 38 (2001), pp. 21–60.

Cooney, Kathlyn M., "Labour," in Toby Wilkinson (ed.), *The Egyptian World*, pp. 160–174.

Couyat, J., and Pierre Montet, *Les inscriptions hiéroglyphiques et hiératiques du Ouâdi Hammâmât*, 2 vols. (Cairo, 1912 and 1913).

Crubézy, Éric, and Béatrix Midant-Reynes, "Les sacrifices humains à l'époque prédynastique: L'apport de la nécropole d'Adaïma," in Jean-Pierre Albert and Béatrix Midant-Reynes (eds.), *Le sacrifice humain*, pp. 58–81.

Curl, James Stevens, *The Egyptian Revival: A Recurring Theme in the History of Taste* (London, 2005).

D'Auria, Sue H., "Preparing for Eternity," in Rita E. Freed et al. (eds.), *Pharaohs of the Sun* (London, 1999), pp. 162–175.

Darnell, Deborah, "Gravel of the Desert and Broken Pots in the Road: Ceramic Evidence from the Routes Between the Nile and Kharga Oasis," in Renée Friedman (ed.), *Egypt and Nubia*, pp. 156–177.

Darnell, John Coleman, "The Deserts," in Toby Wilkinson (ed.), *The Egyptian World*, pp. 29–48.

Darnell, John Coleman, *The Inscription of Queen Katimala at Semna: Textual Evidence for the Origins of the Napatan State* (New Haven, Conn., 2006).

Darnell, John Coleman, "The Message of King Wahankh Antef II to Khety, Ruler of Heracleopolis," *Zeitschrift für Ägyptische Sprache und Altertumskunde*, 124 (1997), pp. 101–108.

Darnell, John Coleman, "The Rock Inscriptions of Tjehemau at Abisko," *Zeitschrift für Ägyptische Sprache und Altertumskunde*, 130 (2003), pp. 31–48.

Darnell, John Coleman, "The Route of Eleventh Dynasty Expansion into Nubia: An Interpretation Based on the Rock Inscriptions of Tjehemau at Abisko," *Zeitschrift für Ägyptische Sprache und Altertumskunde*, 131 (2004), pp. 23–37.

Darnell, John Coleman, and Deborah Darnell, "Opening the Narrow Doors of the Desert: Discoveries of the Theban Desert Road Survey," in Renée Friedman (ed.), *Egypt and Nubia*, pp. 132–155.

Darnell, John Coleman, and Deborah Darnell, *Theban Desert Road Survey in the Egyptian Western Desert*, vol. 1, *Gebel Tjauti Rock Inscriptions 1–45 and Wadi el-Hôl Rock Inscriptions 1–45* (Chicago, 2002).

Darnell, John Coleman, and Colleen Manassa, *Tutankhamun's Armies: Battle and Conquest During Ancient Egypt's Late 18th Dynasty* (Hoboken, N.J., 2007).

Darnell, John Coleman, C. Dobbs-Allsopp, M. J. Lundberg, B. Zuckerman, and P. K. Carter, *Two Early Alphabetic Inscriptions from the Wadi el-Hôl: New Evidence for the Origin of the Alphabet from the Western Desert of Egypt* (Boston, 2005).

Davies, Norman de Garis, *The Rock Tombs of El Amarna*, 6 parts (London, 1903–1908).

Davies, Norman de Garis, *The Tomb of Ken-Amun at Thebes* (New York, 1930).

Davies, Norman de Garis, and Nina de Garis Davies, *The Tomb of Menkheperraseneb, Amenmose, and Another* (London, 1933).

Davies, W. Vivian (ed.), *Egypt and Africa: Nubia from Prehistory to Islam* (London, 1991).

Davies, W. Vivian, "Egypt and Nubia: Conflict with the Kingdom of Kush," in Catharine H. Roehrig (ed.), *Hatshepsut*, pp. 49–56.

Davies, W. Vivian, "Kurgus 2000: The Egyptian Inscriptions," *Sudan and Nubia*, 5 (2001), pp. 46–58.

Davies, W. Vivian, "Kurgus 2002: The Inscriptions and Rock Drawings," *Sudan and Nubia*, 7 (2003), pp. 55–56.

Davies, W. Vivian, "The Rock Inscriptions at Kurgus in the Sudan," in A. Gasse and V. Rondot (eds.), *Séhel entre Égypte et Nubie: Inscriptions rupestres et graffiti de l'époque pharaonique* (Montpelier, 2004), pp. 149–160.

Davies, W. Vivian, "Sobeknakht of Elkab and the Coming of Kush," *Egyptian Archaeology*, 23 (2003), pp. 3–6.

Davies, W. Vivian, and Renée Friedman, *Egypt* (London, 1998).

Davies, W. Vivian, and Renée Friedman, "The Narmer Palette: A Forgotten Member," *Nekhen News*, vol. 10 (1998), p. 22.

Davies, W. Vivian, and Louise Schofield (eds.), *Egypt, the Aegean and the Levant* (London, 1995).

Davis, Whitney M., *Masking the Blow: The Scene of Representation in Late Prehistoric Egyptian Art* (Berkeley, 1992).

Dawson, Warren R., and Eric P. Uphill, *Who Was Who in Egyptology*, 2nd revised ed. (London, 1972).

de Buck, Adriaan, *The Egyptian Coffin Texts*, 8 vols. (Chicago, 1935–1961).

de Buck, Adriaan, "The Judicial Papyrus of Turin," *Journal of Egyptian Archaeology*, 23 (1937), pp. 152–164.

Debono, Fernand, and Bodil Mortensen, *El Omari: A Neolithic Settlement and Other Sites in the Vicinity of Wadi Hof, Helwan* (Mainz, Germany, 1990).

del Carmen Pérez-Die, Maria, "The Ancient Necropolis at Ehnasya el-Medina," *Egyptian Archaeology*, 24 (2004), pp. 21–24.

Demarée, R. J. "The Final Episode of the Deir el-Medina Community," unpublished lecture delivered at Christ's College, University of Cambridge, England, May 28, 2007.

De Meulenaere, H., "La famille royale des Nectanébo," *Zeitschrift für Ägyptische Sprache und Altertumskunde*, 90 (1963), pp. 90–93.

De Meulenaere, H., "La statue du général Djed-ptah-iouf-ankh (Caire JE 36949)," *Bulletin de l'Institut Français d'Archéologie Orientale*, 63 (1965), pp. 28–32.

Depauw, Mark, "Alexandria, the Building Yard," *Chronique d'Égypte*, 75 (2000), pp. 64–65.

Depuydt, Leo, "Regnal Years and Civil Calendar in Achaemenid Egypt," *Journal of Egyptian Archaeology*, 81 (1995), pp. 151–173.

Der Manuelian, Peter, "Administering Akhenaten's Egypt," in Rita E. Freed et al. (eds.), *Pharaohs of the Sun*, pp. 145–149.

Der Manuelian, Peter, *Studies in the Reign of Amenophis II* (Hildesheim, Germany, 1987).

Desroches Noblecourt, Christiane, "Deux grands obélisques précieux d'un sanctuaire à Karnak," *Revue d'Égyptologie*, 8 (1951), pp. 47–61.

Desroches Noblecourt, Christiane, *Tutankhamen: Life and Death of a Pharaoh* (London, 1967).

Dodson, Aidan, "Amenmesse in Kent, Liverpool, and Thebes," *Journal of Egyptian Archaeology*, 81 (1995), pp. 115–128.

Dodson, Aidan, "The Lost Tomb of Amenhotep I," in Bill Manley (ed.), *The Seventy Great Mysteries*, pp. 80–83.

Dodson, Aidan, "Messuy, Amada, and Amenmesse," *Journal of the American Research Center in Egypt*, 34 (1997), pp. 41–48.

Dodson, Aidan, "The Mysterious 2nd Dynasty," *KMT: A Modern Journal of Ancient Egypt*, 7 (1996), pp. 19–31.

Dodson, Aidan, "Psusennes II and Shoshenq I," *Journal of Egyptian Archaeology*, 79 (1993), pp. 267–268.

Dodson, Aidan, "The Tombs of the Kings of the Thirteenth Dynasty in the Memphite Necropolis," *Zeitschrift für Ägyptische Sprache und Altertumskunde*, 114 (1987), pp. 36–45.

Dodson, Aidan, "The Transition Between the 21st and 22nd Dynasties Revisited," forthcoming.

Dodson, Aidan, "Third Intermediate Period," in Donald B. Redford (ed.), *The Oxford Encyclopedia*, vol. 3, pp. 388–394.

Dodson, Aidan, "Why Did Nefertiti Disappear?," in Bill Manley (ed.), *The Seventy Great Mysteries*, pp. 127–131.

Dodson, Aidan, and Dyan Hilton, *The Complete Royal Families of Ancient Egypt* (London and New York, 2004).

Dorman, Peter F., "The Early Reign of Thutmose III: An Unorthodox Mantle of Coregency," in Eric H. Cline and David O'Connor (eds.), *Thutmose III*, pp. 39–68.

Dorman, Peter F., "Hatshepsut: Princess to Queen to Co-Ruler," in Catharine H. Roehrig (ed.), *Hatshepsut*, pp. 87–89.

Dorman, Peter F., *The Monuments of Senenmut: Problems in Historical Methodology* (London and New York, 1988).

Dorman, Peter F., "Rekhmire," in Donald B. Redford (ed.), *The Oxford Encyclopedia of Ancient Egypt*, vol. 3, pp. 131–132.

Dorman, Peter F., "The Royal Steward, Senenmut: The Career of Senenmut," in Catharine H. Roehrig (ed.), *Hatshepsut*, pp. 107–109.

Dorner, Josef, "A Late Hyksos Water-Supply System at Ezbet Hilme," *Egyptian Archaeology*, 16 (2000), pp. 12–13.

Dorner, Josef, "Die Topographie von Piramesse—Vorbericht," *Ägypten und Levante*, 9 (1999), pp. 77–83.

Dougherty, Sean P., "A Little More off the Top," *Nekhen News*, 16 (2004), pp. 11–12.

Drenkhahn, Rosemarie, *Die Elephantine-Stele des Sethnacht und ihr historischer Hintergrund* (Wiesbaden, 1980).

Drews, Robert, *The End of the Bronze Age: Changes in Warfare and the Catastrophe ca. 1200 B.C.* (Princeton, N.J., 1993).

Dreyer, Günter, "A Hundred Years at Abydos," *Egyptian Archaeology*, 3 (1993), pp. 10–12.

Dreyer, Günter, *Umm el-Qaab I: Das prädynastische Königsgrab U-j und seine frühen Schriftzeugnisse* (Mainz, Germany, 1998).

Dreyer, Günter, Eva-Marie Engel, Ulrich Hartung, Thomas Hikade, E. Christiana Köhler, and Frauke Pumpenmeier, "Umm el-Qaab, Nachuntersuchungen im frühzeitlichen Königsfriedhof, 9./10. Vorbericht," *Mitteilungen des Deutschen Archäologischen Instituts, Abteilung Kairo*, 54 (1998), pp. 77–167.

Dreyer, Günter, and Werner Kaiser, "Zu den kleinen Stufenpyramiden Ober- und Mittelägyptens," *Mitteilungen des Deutschen Archäologischen Instituts, Abteilung Kairo*, 36 (1980), pp. 43–59.

Dreyer, Günter, and Nabil Swelim, "Die kleine Stufenpyramide von Abydos-Süd (Sinki), Grabungsbericht," *Mitteilungen des Deutschen Archäologischen Instituts, Abteilung Kairo*, 38 (1982), pp. 83–93.

Droux, Xavier, "Headless at Hierakonpolis," *Nekhen News*, 19 (2007), p. 14.

Duell, Prentice, *The Mastaba of Mereruka*, 2 vols. (Chicago, 1938).

Edel, Elmar, *Die ägyptisch-hethitische Korrespondenz aus Boghazköi in babylonischer und hethitischer Sprache*, 2 vols. (Opladen, Germany, 1994).

Eder, C., *Die ägyptischen Motive in der Glyptik des östlichen Mittelmeerraumes zu Anfang des 2. Jts v. Chr.* (Leuven, Belgium, 1995).

Edgerton, William F., "The Strikes in Ramesses III's Twenty-Ninth Year," *Journal of Near Eastern Studies*, 10 (1951), pp. 137–145.

Eide, Tormod, Tomas Hägg, Richard Holton Pierce, and László Török (eds.), *Fontes Historiae Nubiorum: Textual Sources for the History of the Middle Nile Region Between the Eighth Century BC and the Sixth Century AD*, vol. 1, *From the Eighth to the Mid-Fifth Century BC* (Bergen, Norway, 1994).

el-Khouli, Ali, and Naguib Kanawati et al., *Excavations at Saqqara North-west of Teti's Pyramid*, vol. 2 (Sydney, 1988).

el-Maksoud, Mohamed Abd, *Tell Heboua (1981–1991): Enquête archéologique sur la Deuxième Période Intermédiaire et le Nouvel Empire à l'extremité orientale du Delta* (Paris, 1998).

Emery, W. Bryan, *Archaic Egypt* (Harmondsworth, England, 1961).

Emery, W. Bryan, *Excavations at Saqqara: The Tomb of Hemaka* (Cairo, 1938).

Emery, W. Bryan, *Great Tombs of the First Dynasty*, 3 vols. (Cairo, 1949; London 1954 and 1958).

Emery, W. Bryan, H. S. Smith, and A. Millard, *The Fortress of Buhen: The Archaeological Report* (London, 1979).

Empereur, Jean-Yves, *Alexandria: Past, Present and Future* (London, 2002).

Empereur, Jean-Yves, *Alexandria Rediscovered* (London, 1998).

Empereur, Jean-Yves, "Alexandria: The Underwater Site near Qaitbay Fort," *Egyptian Archaeology*, 8 (1996), pp. 7–10.

Empereur, Jean-Yves, "Raising Statues and Blocks from the Sea at Alexandria," *Egyptian Archaeology*, 9 (1996), pp. 19–22.

Epigraphic Survey, *Medinet Habu*, 2 vols. (Chicago 1930, 1932).

Epigraphic Survey, *Reliefs and Inscriptions at Karnak III: The Bubastite Portal* (Chicago, 1953).

Epigraphic Survey, *The Tomb of Kheruef* (Chicago, 1980).

Erman, Adolf, and Ulrich Wilcken, "Die Naukratisstele," *Zeitschrift für ägyptische Sprache und Altertumskunde*, 38 (1900), pp. 127–135.

Eyre, Christopher J., *The Cannibal Hymn: A Cultural and Literary Study* (Liverpool, 2002).

Eyre, Christopher J. (ed.), *Proceedings of the Seventh International Congress of Egyptologists* (Leuven, Belgium, 1998).

Eyre, Christopher J., "Weni's Career and Old Kingdom Historiography," in Christopher Eyre et al. (eds.), *The Unbroken Reed*, pp. 107–124.

Eyre, Christopher J., "Work and the Organisation of Work in the New Kingdom," in Marvin A. Powell (ed.), *Labor in the Ancient Near East* (New Haven, Conn., 1987), pp. 167–221.

Eyre, Christopher, Anthony Leahy, and Lisa Montagno Leahy (eds.), *The Unbroken Reed: Studies in the Culture and Heritage of Ancient Egypt in Honour of A. F. Shore* (London, 1994).

Fairservis, Walter A., "A Revised View of the Na'rmr Palette," *Journal of the American Research Center in Egypt*, 28 (1991), pp. 1–20.

Farag, Sami, "Une inscription Memphite de la XIIe dynastie," *Revue d'Égyptologie*, 32 (1980), pp. 75–82 and plates 3–5.

Farout, Dominique, "La carrière du *whmw* Ameny et l'organisation des expéditions au ouadi Hammamat au Moyen Empire," *Bulletin de l'Institut Français d'Archéologie Orientale*, 94 (1994), pp. 143–172.

Faulkner, Raymond (trans.), and Carol Andrews (ed.), *The Ancient Egyptian Book of the Dead* (London, 1989).

Faulkner, Raymond (trans.), *The Ancient Egyptian Coffin Texts*, 3 vols. (Warminster, England, 1973–1978).

Faulkner, Raymond (trans.), *The Ancient Egyptian Pyramid Texts* (Oxford, 1969).

Fazzini, Richard E., and Mary E. McKercher, "Egyptomania," in Donald B. Redford (ed.), *The Oxford Encyclopedia*, vol. 1, pp. 458–465.

Filer, Joyce, *Disease* (London, 1995).

Finkenstaedt, Elizabeth, "Violence and Kingship: The Evidence of the Palettes," *Zeitschrift für Ägyptische Sprache und Altertumskunde*, 111 (1984), pp. 107–110.

Fischer, Henry G., *Dendera in the Third Millennium B.C., down to the Theban Domination of Upper Egypt* (Locust Valley, N.Y., 1968).

Fischer, Henry G., "A God and a General of the Oasis on a Stela of the Late Middle Kingdom," *Journal of Near Eastern Studies*, 16 (1957), pp. 223–235.

Fischer, Henry G., "The Inscription of *In-it.f*, born of *Tfi*," *Journal of Near Eastern Studies*, 19 (1960), pp. 258–268.

Fischer, Henry G., *Inscriptions from the Coptite Nome, Dynasties VI–XI* (Rome, 1964).

Fischer, Henry G., "The Nubian Mercenaries of Gebelein During the First Intermediate Period," *Kush*, 9 (1961), pp. 44–80 and plates X–XV.

Fischer, Henry G., *Varia Nova* (New York, 1996).

Fletcher, Joann, *Cleopatra the Great* (London, 2008).

Fletcher, Joann, *Egypt's Sun King: Amenhotep III* (London, 2000).

Forman, Werner, and Stephen Quirke, *Hieroglyphs and the Afterlife in Ancient Egypt* (London, 1996).

Foster, John L., "The New Religion," in Rita E. Freed et al. (eds.), *Pharaohs of the Sun*, pp. 97–109.

Foster, Karen Polinger, and Robert K. Ritner, "Texts, Storms, and the Thera Eruption," *Journal of Near Eastern Studies*, 55 (1996), pp. 1–14.

Frame, Grant, "The Inscription of Sargon II at Tang-i Var," *Orientalia*, 68 (1999), pp. 31–57.

Frandsen, Paul John, "*Bwt* in the Body," in Harco Willems (ed.), *Social Aspects of Funerary Culture in the Egyptian Old and Middle Kingdoms* (Leuven, Belgium, 2001), pp. 141–174.

Franke, Detlef, "The Career of Khnumhotep III of Beni Hasan and the So-Called 'Decline of the Nomarchs,' " in Stephen Quirke (ed.), *Middle Kingdom Studies*, pp. 51–67.

Franke, Detlef, "First Intermediate Period," in Donald B. Redford (ed.), *The Oxford Encyclopedia of Ancient Egypt*, vol. 1, pp. 526–532.

Franke, Detlef, "An Important Family at Abydos of the Seventeenth Dynasty," *Journal of Egyptian Archaeology*, 71 (1985), pp. 175–176.

Franke, Detlef, "The Late Middle Kingdom (Thirteenth to Seventeenth Dynasties): The Chronological Framework," *Journal of Egyptian History*, 1 (2008), pp. 267–287.

Franke, Detlef, "Zur Chronologie des Mittleren Reiches (12.–18. Dynastie). Teil 1: Die 12. Dynastie," *Orientalia*, 57 (1988), pp. 113–138.

Frankfort, Henry, "The Origin of Monumental Architecture in Egypt," *American Journal of Semitic Languages and Literatures*, 58 (1941), pp. 329–358.

Freed, Rita E., "Art in the Service of Religion and the State," in Rita E. Freed et al. (eds.), *Pharaohs of the Sun*, pp. 110–129.

Freed, Rita E., "Introduction," in Rita E. Freed et al. (eds.), *Pharaohs of the Sun*, pp. 17–37.

Freed, Rita E., Yvonne J. Markowitz, and Sue H. D'Auria (eds.), *Pharaohs of the Sun: Akhenaten, Nefertiti, Tutankhamen* (London, 1999).

Friedman, Renée (ed.), *Egypt and Nubia: Gifts of the Desert* (London, 2002).

Friedman, Renée, "From Pillar to Post at Hierakonpolis," *Nekhen News*, 19 (2007), p. 3.

Friedman, Renée, "New Tombs and New Thoughts at HK6," *Nekhen News*, 18 (2006), pp. 11–12.

Friedman, Renée, "Origins of Monumental Architecture: Investigations at Hierakonpolis HK6 in 2008," unpublished lecture delivered at the colloquium Egypt at Its Origins: Predynastic and Early Dynastic Egypt: Recent Discoveries, British Museum, London, July 28, 2008.

Friedman, Renée, and Joseph J. Hobbs, "A 'Tasian' Tomb in Egypt's Eastern Desert," in Renée Friedman (ed.), *Egypt and Nubia*, pp. 178–189.

Fuchs, Gerard, "Petroglyphs in the Eastern Desert of Egypt: New Finds in the Wadi el-Barramiya," *Sahara*, 4 (1991), pp. 59–70.

Fuchs, Gerard, "Rock Engravings in the Wadi el-Barramiya, Eastern Desert of Egypt," *African Archaeological Review*, 7 (1989), pp. 127–154.

Gabolde, Luc, "La chronologie du règne de Thoutmosis II, ses conséquences sur la datation des momies royales et leurs repercutions sur l'histoire du développement de la Vallée des Rois," *Studien zur Altägyptischen Kultur*, 14 (1987), pp. 61–81.

Gabolde, Marc, and Amanda Dunsmore, "The Royal Necropolis at Tell el-Amarna," *Egyptian Archaeology*, 25 (2004), pp. 30–33.

Gabra, Gawdat, "Preliminary Report on the Stela of *Ḥtpi* from El-Kab from the Time of Wahankh Inyôtef II," *Mitteilungen des Deutschen Archäologischen Instituts, Abteilung Kairo*, 32 (1976), pp. 45–56.

Gardiner, Alan H., "The Defeat of the Hyksos by Kamose: The Carnarvon Tablet, No. 1," *Journal of Egyptian Archaeology*, 3 (1916), pp. 95–110.

Gardiner, Alan H., "The First King Menthotpe of the Eleventh Dynasty," *Mitteilungen des Deutschen Archäologischen Instituts, Abteilung Kairo*, 14 (1956), pp. 42–51.

Gardiner, Alan H. (ed.), *The Wilbour Papyrus*, 4 vols. (Oxford, 1948).

Geus, Francis, "Sai," in Derek A. Welsby and Julie R. Anderson (eds.), *Sudan: Ancient Treasures*, pp. 114–116.

Giddy, Lisa, "Digging Diary 2001," *Egyptian Archaeology*, 20 (2002), pp. 29–33.

Gillispie, Charles Coulston, and Michel Dewachter (eds.), *Monuments of Egypt: The Napoleonic Edition: The Complete Archaeological Plates from La Déscription de l'Égypte* (Princeton, N.J., 1987).

Gitton, Michel, *Les divines épouses de la 18e dynastie* (Paris, 1984).

Gnirs, Andrea M., "Biographies," in Donald B. Redford (ed.), *The Oxford Encyclopedia of Ancient Egypt*, vol. 1, pp. 184–189.

Gnirs, Andrea M., *Militär und Gesellschaft: Ein Beitrag zur Sozialgeschichte des Neuen Reiches* (Heidelberg, 1996).

Goebs, Katja, "Kingship," in Toby Wilkinson (ed.), *The Egyptian World*, pp. 275–295.

Goedicke, Hans, "A Cult Inventory of the Eighth Dynasty from Coptos (Cairo JE 43290)," *Mitteilungen des Deutschen Archäologischen Instituts, Abteilung Kairo*, 50 (1994), pp. 71–84.

Goedicke, Hans, "The Inscription of *Ḏmi*," *Journal of Near Eastern Studies*, 19 (1960), pp. 288–291.

Goedicke, Hans, *Königliche Dokumente aus dem Alten Reich* (Wiesbaden, 1967).

Goedicke, Hans, "The Unification of Egypt Under Monthuhotep Neb-hepet-re' (2022 B.C.)," *The Journal of the Society for the Study of Egyptian Antiquities*, 12 (1982), pp. 157–164.

Goedicke, Hans, "Was Magic Used in the Harem Conspiracy Against Ramesses III?," *Journal of Egyptian Archaeology*, 49 (1963), pp. 71–92.

Goelet, Ogden, "Ramesses-Hattusilis Correspondence," in Donald B. Redford (ed.), *The Oxford Encyclopedia of Ancient Egypt*, vol. 3, p. 122.

Goelet, Ogden, "Tomb Robbery Papyri," in Donald B. Redford (ed.), *The Oxford Encyclopedia of Ancient Egypt*, vol. 3, pp. 417–418.

Goelet, Ogden, "Wilbour Papyrus," in Donald B. Redford (ed.), *The Oxford Encyclopedia of Ancient Egypt*, vol. 3, p. 501.

Gohary, Jocelyn, *Akhenaten's Sed-Festival at Karnak* (London, 1992).

Goldwasser, O., "The Narmer Palette and the 'Triumph of Metaphor,' " *Lingua Aegyptiaca*, 2 (1992), pp. 67–85.

Gophna, Ram, "The Contacts Between 'En Besor Oasis, Southern Canaan, and Egypt During the Late Predynastic and the Threshold of the First Dynasty; a Further Assessment," in Edwin C. M. van den Brink (ed.), *The Nile Delta in Transition*, pp. 385–394.

Gophna, Ram, and D. Gazit, "The First Dynasty Egyptian Residency at 'En Besor," *Tel Aviv*, 12 (1985), pp. 9–16.

Goudchaux, Guy Weill, "Cleopatra's Subtle Religious Strategy," in Susan Walker and Peter Higgs (eds.), *Cleopatra of Egypt*, pp. 128–141.

Goudchaux, Guy Weill, "Was Cleopatra Beautiful?," in Susan Walker and Peter Higgs (eds.), *Cleopatra of Egypt*, pp. 210–214.

Graham, Geoffrey, "Tanis," in Donald B. Redford (ed.), *The Oxford Encyclopedia of Ancient Egypt*, vol. 3, pp. 348–350.

Graindorge, Catherine, and Philippe Martinez, "Karnak avant Karnak: Les constructions d'Aménophis Ier et les premières liturgies amoniennes," *Bulletin de la Société Française d'Égyptologie*, 115 (1989), pp. 36–64.

Grajetzki, Wolfram, *The Middle Kingdom of Ancient Egypt* (London, 2006).

Grandet, Pierre, "L'exécution du chancelier Bay: O.IFAO 1864," *Bulletin de l'Institut Français d'Archéologie Orientale*, 100 (2000), pp. 339–345.

Grandet, Pierre, "Ramesses III," in Donald B. Redford (ed.), *The Oxford Encyclopedia of Ancient Egypt*, vol. 3, pp. 118–120.

Grandet, Pierre, *Ramsès III: Histoire d'un règne* (Paris, 1993).

Griffith, Francis Llewellyn, "The Abydos Decree of Seti I at Nauri," *Journal of Egyptian Archaeology*, 13 (1927), pp. 193–208.

Griffiths, John Gwyn, "The Death of Cleopatra VII," *Journal of Egyptian Archaeology*, 47 (1961), pp. 113–118.

Griffiths, John Gwyn, "Osiris," in Donald B. Redford (ed.), *The Oxford Encyclopedia of Ancient Egypt*, vol. 2, pp. 615–619.

Grimal, Nicolas, *La stèle triomphale de Pi('ankh)y au musée du Caire JE 48862 et 47086–47089* (Cairo, 1981).

Güterbock, Hans Gustav, "The Deeds of Suppiluliuma as Told by His Son, Mursili II," *Journal of Cuneiform Studies*, 10 (1956), pp. 41–68, 75–98, and 107–130.

Habachi, Labib, "King Nebhepetre Menthuhotp: His Monuments, Place in History, Deification and Unusual Representations in the Form of Gods," *Mitteilungen des Deutschen Archäologischen Instituts, Abteilung Kairo*, 19 (1963), pp. 16–52.

Habachi, Labib, *The Second Stela of Kamose and His Struggle Against the Hyksos Ruler and His Capital* (Glückstadt, Germany, 1972).

Habachi, Labib, *Tell Basta* (Cairo, 1957).

Hall, Emma Swan, *The Pharaoh Smites His Enemies: A Comparative Study* (Munich, 1986).

Hamilton, G. J., *The Origins of the West Semitic Alphabet in Egyptian Scripts* (Washington, D.C., 2006).

Hari, Robert, *Horemheb et la reine Moutnedjemet, ou la fin d'une dynastie* (Geneva, 1964).

Harrell, James A., "Ancient Quarries near Amarna," *Egyptian Archaeology*, 19 (2001), pp. 36–38.

Harrell, James A., and Thomas M. Bown, "An Old Kingdom Basalt Quarry at Widan el-Faras and the Quarry Road to Lake Moeris," *Journal of the American Research Center in Egypt*, 32 (1995), pp. 71–91.

Harris, John E., and Edward F. Wente, *An X-Ray Atlas of the Royal Mummies* (Chicago, 1980).

Hartung, Ulrich, "Recent Investigations at Tell el-Fara'in (Buto) in the Western Nile Delta," unpublished lecture delivered at the colloquium Egypt at Its Origins: Predynastic and Early Dynastic Egypt: Recent Discoveries, British Museum, London, July 28, 2008.

Hartung, Ulrich, *Umm el-Qaab II: Importkeramik aus dem Friedhof U in Abydos (Umm el-Qaab) und die Beziehungen Ägyptens zu Vorderasien im 4. Jahrtausend v. Chr.* (Mainz, Germany, 2001).

Harvey, Stephen, "Monuments of Ahmose at Abydos," *Egyptian Archaeology*, 4 (1994), pp. 3–5.

Harvey, Stephen, "New Evidence at Abydos for Ahmose's Funerary Cult," *Egyptian Archaeology*, 24 (2004), pp. 3–6.

Hawass, Zahi, "The Pyramid Builders," in Alberto Siliotti, *Guide to the Pyramids of Egypt* (Cairo, 1997), pp. 86–89.

Hawass, Zahi, "The Workmen's Community at Giza," in Manfred Bietak (ed.), *Haus und Palast im alten Ägypten* (Vienna, 1996), pp. 53–67.

Hayes, William C., "Career of the Great Steward Henenu Under Nebhepetre' Mentuhotpe," *Journal of Egyptian Archaeology*, 35 (1949), pp. 43–49.

Hayes, William C., "Royal Decrees from the Temple of Min at Coptus," *Journal of Egyptian Archaeology*, 32 (1946), pp. 3–23 and plates 2–5.

Haywood, John, *The Penguin Historical Atlas of Ancient Civilizations* (London, 2005).

Heidorn, Lisa A., "Abu Simbel," in Kathryn A. Bard (ed.), *Encyclopedia of the Archaeology of Ancient Egypt*, pp. 87–90.

Heidorn, Lisa A., "Historical Implications of the Pottery from the Earliest Tombs at El Kurru," *Journal of the American Research Center in Egypt*, 31 (1994), pp. 115–131.

Heidorn, Lisa A., "The Persian Claim to Kush in Light of Evidence from Lower Nubia," in Janet H. Johnson (ed.), *Life in a Multi-cultural Society: Egypt from Cambyses to Constantine and Beyond* (Chicago, 1992), pp. 147–148.

Helck, Wolfgang, "Ahmose Pennechbet," in Wolfgang Helck and Eberhard Otto (eds.), *Lexikon der Ägyptologie*, vol. 1 (Wiesbaden, 1975), p. 110.

Helck, Wolfgang, "Ein Ausgreifen des Mittleren Reiches in den Zypriotischen Raum?," *Göttinger Miszellen*, 109 (1989), pp. 27–30.

Helck, Wolfgang, *Historisch-Biographische Texte der 2. Zwischenzeit und Neue Texte der 18. Dynastie* (Wiesbaden, 1975).

Helck, Wolfgang, "Mitregenschaft," in Wolfgang Helck and Wolfhart Westendorf (eds.), *Lexikon der Ägyptologie*, vol. 4 (Wiesbaden, 1982), columns 155–161.

Helck, Wolfgang, "Probleme der Königsfolge in der Übergangszeit von 18. zu 19. Dyn.," *Mitteilungen des Deutschen Archäologischen Instituts, Abteilung Kairo*, 37 (1981), pp. 203–215.

Helck, Wolfgang, *Urkunden der 18. Dynastie* (Berlin, 1955–1958).

Herbert, Sharon, and Henry Wright, "Report on the 1987 University of Michigan/University of Assiut Expedition to Coptos and the Eastern Desert," *Newsletter of the American Research Center in Egypt*, 143–144 (1988–1989), pp. 1–4.

Hölbl, Günther, *Beziehungen der ägyptischen Kultur zu Altitalien*, 2 vols. (Leiden, Netherlands, 1979).

Hölbl, Günther, *A History of the Ptolemaic Empire* (London and New York, 2001).

Holladay, John S., Jr., "Pithom," in Donald B. Redford (ed.), *The Oxford Encyclopedia of Ancient Egypt*, vol. 3, pp. 50–53.

Holland, Tom, *Persian Fire* (London, 2005).

Hope, Colin A., "Early and Mid-Holocene Ceramics from the Dakhleh Oasis: Traditions and Influences," in Renée Friedman (ed.), *Egypt and Nubia*, pp. 39–61.

Hornung, Erik, "Some Remarks on the Inhabitants of the West," unpublished lecture delivered at the Spotlight on Egyptian religion study day, Cambridge, England, September 20, 2008.

Hornung, Erik, *The Tomb of Pharaoh Seti I* (Zurich, 1991).

Hughes-Hallett, Lucy, *Cleopatra: Queen, Lover, Legend* (London, 1990).

Humbert, Jean-Marcel, Michael Pantazzi, and Christiane Ziegler, *Egyptomania: Egypt in Western Art, 1730–1930* (Paris and Ottawa, 1994).

Huss, W., "Die Herkunft der Kleopatra Philopator," *Aegyptus*, 70 (1990), pp. 191–204.

Hussein, F., A. Sarry El Din, R. El Banna, and W. Kandeel, "Similarity of Treatment of Trauma in Workers and High Officials of the Pyramid Builders," unpublished paper delivered at the conference Pharmacy and Medicine in Ancient Egypt, University of Manchester, September 1–3, 2008.

Ikram, Salima, "Domestic Shrines and the Cult of the Royal Family at el-'Amarna," *Journal of Egyptian Archaeology*, 75 (1989), pp. 89–101.

James, T.G.H., *Pharaoh's People: Scenes from Life in Imperial Egypt* (London, 1984).

Jansen-Winkeln, Karl, "Der Beginn der libyschen Herrschaft in Ägypten," *Biblische Notizen*, 71 (1994), pp. 78–97.

Jansen-Winkeln, Karl, "Das Ende des Neuen Reiches," *Zeitschrift für Ägyptische Sprache und Altertumskunde*, 119 (1992), pp. 22–37.

Jansen-Winkeln, Karl, "Historische Probleme der 3. Zwischenzeit," *Journal of Egyptian Archaeology*, 81 (1995), pp. 129–149.

Jansen-Winkeln, Karl, "Die Plünderung der Königsgräber des Neuen Reiches," *Zeitschrift für Ägyptische Sprache und Altertumskunde*, 122 (1995), pp. 62–78.

Jansen-Winkeln, Karl, "Die thebanische 'Gottesstaat,' " *Orientalia*, 70 (2001), pp. 153–182.

Janssen, Rosalind, and Jac. J. Janssen, *Growing Up in Ancient Egypt* (London, 1990).

Jeffreys, David, "The Nile Valley," in Toby Wilkinson (ed.), *The Egyptian World*, pp. 7–14.

Jeffreys, David, "Perunefer: At Memphis or Avaris?," *Egyptian Archaeology*, 28 (2006), pp. 36–37.

Jéquier, Gustave, *La Pyramide d'Aba* (Cairo, 1935).

Jiménez Serrano, Alejandro, *Royal Festivals in the Late Predynastic Period and the First Dynasty* (Oxford, 2002).

Johnson, W. Raymond, "Monuments and Monumental Art Under Amenhotep III: Evolution and Meaning," in David O'Connor and Eric H. Cline (eds.), *Amenhotep III*, pp. 63–94.

Johnson, W. Raymond, "The Setting: History, Religion, and Art," in Rita E. Freed et al. (eds.), *Pharaohs of the Sun*, pp. 38–49.

Jones, Michael, "Appendix 1: The North City," pp. 15–21 in Barry J. Kemp, "Preliminary Report on the El-'Amarna Expedition, 1982–3," *Journal of Egyptian Archaeology*, 69 (1983), pp. 5–24.

Kahn, Dan'el, "The Assyrian Invasions of Egypt (673–663 B.C.) and the Final Expulsion of the Kushites," *Studien zur Altägyptischen Kultur*, 34 (2006), pp. 251–267.

Kahn, Dan'el, "Some Remarks on the Foreign Policy of Psammetichus II in the Levant (595–589 B.C.)," *Journal of Egyptian History*, 1 (2008), pp. 139–157.

Kaiser, Werner, "Zu Entwicklung und Vorformen der frühzeitlichen Gräber mit reich gegliederter Oberbaufassade," in P. Posener-Kriéger (ed.), *Mélanges Gamal Eddin Mokhtar*, vol. 2 (Cairo, 1985), pp. 25–38.

Kanawati, Naguib, "Akhmim," in Donald B. Redford (ed.), *The Oxford Encyclopedia of Ancient Egypt*, vol. 1, pp. 51–53.

Kanawati, Naguib, "Deux conspirations contre Pépy Ier," *Chronique d'Égypte*, 56 (1982), pp. 203–217.

Kanawati, Naguib, *Governmental Reforms in Old Kingdom Egypt* (Warminster, England, 1980).

Kanawati, Naguib, "New Evidence on the Reign of Userkare?," *Göttinger Miszellen*, 83 (1984), pp. 31–38.

Kanawati, Naguib, Ali el-Khouli, Ann McFarlane, and Naguib V. Maksoud, *Excavations at Saqqara: North-west of Teti's Pyramid*, vol. 1 (Sydney, 1984).

Kaper, Olaf E., and Harco Willems, "Policing the Desert: Old Kingdom Activity Around the Dakhleh Oasis," in Renée Friedman (ed.), *Egypt and Nubia*, pp. 79–94.

Keller, Cathleen A., "The Joint Reign of Hatshepsut and Thutmose III," in Catharine H. Roehrig (ed.), *Hatshepsut*, pp. 96–98.

Keller, Cathleen A., "The Royal Court," in Catharine H. Roehrig (ed.), *Hatshepsut*, pp. 101–102.

Keller, Cathleen A., "The Statuary of Hatshepsut," in Catharine H. Roehrig (ed.), *Hatshepsut*, pp. 158–164.

Keller, Cathleen A., "The Statuary of Senenmut," in Catharine H. Roehrig (ed.), *Hatshepsut*, pp. 117–119.

Kemp, Barry J., "The Amarna Story," *Horizon*, 1 (October 2006), pp. 2–3.

Kemp, Barry J., *Ancient Egypt: Anatomy of a Civilization*, 1st and 2nd eds. (London and New York, 1989, 2006).

Kemp, Barry J., "Discovery: A New Boundary Stela," *Horizon*, 1 (October 2006), p. 7.

Kemp, Barry J., "Halfway Through the Amarna Season, March 2007," privately circulated informal newsletter, on file with the author.

Kemp, Barry J., "How Were Things Made? Amarna's Small-Scale Metal Industry," *Horizon*, 2 (July 2007), p. 7.

Kemp, Barry J., "The Kom el-Nana Enclosure at Amarna," *Egyptian Archaeology*, 6 (1995), pp. 8–9.

Kemp, Barry J., "Large Middle Kingdom Granary Buildings (and the Archaeology of Administration)," *Zeitschrift für Ägyptische Sprache und Altertumskunde*, 113 (1986), pp. 120–136.

Kemp, Barry J., "Notes from the Field: Lives of the Have-Nots," *Horizon*, 2 (July 2007), pp. 2–3.

Kemp, Barry J., "Notes from the Field: The Stone Village," *Horizon*, 2 (July 2007), pp. 8–9.

Kemp, Barry J., "Old Kingdom, Middle Kingdom and Second Intermediate Period c. 2686–1552 BC," in Bruce G. Trigger, Barry J. Kemp, David O'Connor, and Alan B. Lloyd, *Ancient Egypt: A Social History* (Cambridge, England, 1983), pp. 71–182.

Kemp, Barry J., "Photographs of the Decorated Tomb at Hierakonpolis," *Journal of Egyptian Archaeology*, 59 (1973), pp. 36–43.

Kemp, Barry J., "The Quality of Life," *Horizon*, 4 (September 2008), p. 5.

Kemp, Barry J., "Resuming the Amarna Survey," *Egyptian Archaeology*, 20 (2002), pp. 10–12.

Kemp, Barry J., and Salvatore Garfi, *A Survey of the Ancient City of El-'Amarna* (London, 1993).

Kendall, Timothy, "Egypt and Nubia," in Toby Wilkinson (ed.), *The Egyptian World*, pp. 401–416.

Kendall, Timothy, "Foreign Relations," in Rita E. Freed et al. (eds.), *Pharaohs of the Sun*, pp. 157–161.

Kendall, Timothy, "Jebel Barkal," in Derek A. Welsby and Julie R. Anderson (eds.), *Sudan: Ancient Treasures*, pp. 158–160.

Kendall, Timothy, "Kings of the Sacred Mountain: Napata and the Kushite Twenty-fifth Dynasty of Egypt," in Dietrich Wildung (ed.), *Sudan: Ancient Kingdoms of the Nile*, translated by Peter Der Manuelian and Kathleen Guillaume (Paris and New York, 1997), pp. 161–171.

Kendall, Timothy, "The Napatan Palace at Gebel Barkal: A First Look at B1200," in W. Vivian Davies (ed.), *Egypt and Africa*, pp. 302–313.

Kendall, Timothy, "The Origin of the Napatan State: El Kurru and the Evidence for the Royal Ancestors," in Steffen Wenig (ed.), *Studien zum antiken Sudan*, pp. 3–117.

Kessler, Dieter, *Die heiligen Tiere und der König* (Wiesbaden, 1989).

Kessler, Dieter, and Abd el-Halim Nur el-Din, "Inside the Ibis Galleries of Tuna el-Gebel," *Egyptian Archaeology*, 20 (2002), pp. 36–38.

Kienitz, Friedrich, *Die politische Geschichte Ägyptens vom 7. bis zum 4. Jahrhundert vor der Zeitwende* (Berlin, 1953).

Kikuchi, Takao, "Die thebanische Nekropole der 21. Dynastie—zum Wandel der Nekropole und zum Totenglauben der Ägypter," *Mitteilungen des Deutschen Archäologischen Instituts, Abteilung Kairo*, 58 (2002), pp. 343–371.

Kitchen, Kenneth A., "The Arrival of the Libyans in Late New Kingdom Egypt," in Anthony Leahy (ed.), *Libya and Egypt*, pp. 15–27.

Kitchen, Kenneth A., "Pharaoh Ramesses II and His Times," in Jack M. Sasson (ed.), *Civilizations*, vol. 2, pp. 763–774.

Kitchen, Kenneth A., *Pharaoh Triumphant: The Life and Times of Ramesses II, King of Egypt* (Warminster, England, 1982).

Kitchen, Kenneth A., "Ramesses II," in Donald B. Redford (ed.), *The Oxford Encyclopedia of Ancient Egypt*, vol. 3, pp. 116–118.

Kitchen, Kenneth A., *Ramesside Inscriptions, Historical and Biographical*, 8 vols. (Oxford, 1969–1990).

Kitchen, Kenneth A., "Ramses V–XI," in Wolfgang Helck and Wolfhart Westendorf (eds.), *Lexikon der Ägyptologie*, vol. 5 (Wiesbaden, 1984), columns 124–128.

Kitchen, Kenneth A., "Shabaqa," in Donald B. Redford (ed.), *The Oxford Encyclopedia of Ancient Egypt*, vol. 3, p. 277.

Kitchen, Kenneth A., "Sheshonq I," in Donald B. Redford (ed.), *The Oxford Encyclopedia of Ancient Egypt*, vol. 3, pp. 280–281.

Kitchen, Kenneth A., "Some Thoughts on Egypt, the Aegean and Beyond of the 2nd Millennium BC," in Panagiotis Kousoulis (ed.), *Foreign Relations and Diplomacy in the Ancient World: Egypt, Greece, Near East* (forthcoming), pp. 3–14.

Kitchen, Kenneth A., *The Third Intermediate Period in Egypt (1100–650 BC)*, 3rd ed. (Warminster, England, 1996).

Kitchen, Kenneth A., "The Titularies of the Ramesside Kings as Expression of Their Ideal Kingship," *Annales du Service des Antiquités de l'Égypte*, 71 (1987), pp. 131–141.

Kitchen, Kenneth A., "Twenty-fifth Dynasty," in Donald B. Redford (ed.), *The Oxford Encyclopedia of Ancient Egypt*, vol. 3, pp. 457–461.

Klug, Andrea, *Königliche Stelen in der Zeit won Ahmose bis Amenophis III* (Turnhout, 2002).

Köhler, E. Christiana, "History or Ideology? New Reflections on the Narmer Palette and the Nature of Foreign Relations in Pre- and Early Dynastic Egypt," in Edwin C. M. van den Brink and Thomas E. Levy (eds.), *Egypt and the Levant*, pp. 499–513.

Kormysheva, E. Y., "Remarks on the Position of the King's Mother in Kush," in Steffen Wenig (ed.), *Studien zum antiken Sudan*, pp. 239–251.

Kozloff, Arielle P., "The Decorative and Funerary Arts During the Reign of Amenhotep III," in David O'Connor and Eric H. Cline (eds.), *Amenhotep III*, pp. 95–123.

Kozloff, Arielle P., Betsy M. Bryan, and Lawrence M. Berman, *Egypt's Dazzling Sun: Amenhotep III and His World* (Cleveland, 1992).

Krauss, Rolf, "The Length of Sneferu's Reign and How Long It Took to Build the 'Red Pyramid,' " *Journal of Egyptian Archaeology*, 82 (1996), pp. 43–50.

Kruchten, Jean-Marie, *Les annales des prêtres de Karnak (XXI–XXIIImes dynasties) et autres textes contemporains relatifs à l'initiation des prêtres d'Amon* (Leuven, Belgium, 1989).

Kubisch, Sabine, "Die Stelen der 1. Zwischenzeit aus Gebelein," *Mitteilungen des Deutschen Archäologischen Instituts, Abteilung Kairo*, 56 (2000), pp. 239–265.

Kuper, Rudolph, and Frank Förster, "Khufu's 'Mefat' Expeditions into the Libyan Desert," *Egyptian Archaeology*, 23 (2003), pp. 25–28.

Lacau, Pierre, and H. Chevrier, *Une chapelle de Sésostris Ier à Karnak*, 2 vols. (Cairo, 1956 and 1969).

Lacovara, Peter, "The City of Amarna," in Rita E. Freed et al. (eds.), *Pharaohs of the Sun*, pp. 61–71.

Lacovara, Peter, "Deir el-Ballas," in Kathryn A. Bard (ed.), *Encyclopedia of the Archaeology of Ancient Egypt*, pp. 244–246.

Lambert, W. G., "Booty from Egypt?," *Journal of Jewish Studies*, 33 (1982), pp. 61–70.

Lange, Eva, "Legitimation und Herrschaft in der Libyerzeit. Eine neue Inschrift Osorkons I. aus Bubastis (Tell Basta)," *Zeitschrift für Ägyptische Sprache und Altertumskunde*, 135 (2008), pp. 131–141.

Lauer, Jean-Philippe, *Fouilles à Saqqarah: La Pyramide à Degrés*, 3 vols. (Cairo, 1936–1939).

Lauer, Jean-Philippe, *Saqqara: The Royal Cemetery of Memphis: Excavations and Discoveries Since 1850* (London, 1976).

Leahy, Anthony, "Abydos in the Libyan Period," in Anthony Leahy (ed.), *Libya and Egypt*, pp. 155–200.

Leahy, Anthony, "The Adoption of Ankhnesneferibre," *Journal of Egyptian Archaeology*, 82 (1996), pp. 145–165.

Leahy, Anthony, "The Earliest Dated Monument of Amasis and the End of the Reign of Apries," *Journal of Egyptian Archaeology*, 74 (1988), pp. 183–199.

Leahy, Anthony (ed.), *Libya and Egypt c. 1300–750 BC* (London, 1990).

Leahy, Anthony, "The Libyan Period in Egypt: An Essay in Interpretation," *Libyan Studies*, 16 (1985), pp. 51–65.

Leahy, Anthony, "Royal Iconography and Dynastic Change, 750–525 BC: The Blue and Cap Crowns," *Journal of Egyptian Archaeology*, 78 (1992), pp. 223–240.

Leahy, Anthony, "Sea Peoples," in Donald B. Redford (ed.), *The Oxford Encyclopedia of Ancient Egypt*, vol. 3, pp. 257–260.

Leahy, Lisa Montagno, and Anthony Leahy, "The Genealogy of a Priestly Family from Heliopolis," *Journal of Egyptian Archaeology*, 72 (1986), pp. 133–147.

Leclant, Jean, "Kuschitenherrschaft," in Wolfgang Helck and Wolfhart Westendorf (eds.), *Lexikon der Ägyptologie*, vol. 3 (Wiesbaden, 1980), columns 893–901.

Leclant, Jean, "Taharqa," in Wolfgang Helck and Wolfhart Westendorf (eds.), *Lexikon der Ägyptologie*, vol. 6 (Wiesbaden, 1986), columns 156–184.

Lehner, Mark, *The Complete Pyramids* (London, 1997).

Lehner, Mark, "The Pyramid Age Settlement of the Southern Mount at Giza," *Journal of the American Research Center in Egypt*, 39 (2002), pp. 27–74.

Lehner, Mark, "The Sphinx," in Zahi Hawass (ed.), *The Treasures of the Pyramids* (Vercelli, 2003), pp. 173–187.

Leprohon, Ronald J., "The Programmatic Use of the Royal Titulary in the Twelfth Dynasty," *Journal of the American Research Center in Egypt*, 33 (1996), pp. 165–171.

Lesko, Leonard H., *The Ancient Egyptian Book of Two Ways* (Berkeley, Los Angeles, and London, 1972).

Lesko, Leonard H., "Coffin Texts," in Donald B. Redford (ed.), *The Oxford Encyclopedia of Ancient Egypt*, vol. 1, pp. 287–288.

Lewis, Naphtali, *Greeks in Ptolemaic Egypt* (Oxford, 1986).

Lichtheim, Miriam, *Ancient Egyptian Autobiographies Chiefly of the Middle Kingdom* (Göttingen, Germany, 1988).

Lichtheim, Miriam, *Ancient Egyptian Literature*, 3 vols. (Berkeley, 1973–1980).

Lilyquist, Christine, "Egypt and the Near East: Evidence of Contact in the Material Record," in Catharine H. Roehrig (ed.), *Hatshepsut*, pp. 60–67.

Lilyquist, Christine, with James E. Hoch and A. J. Peden, *The Tomb of Three Foreign Wives of Tuthmosis III* (New York, 2003).

Liverani, Irene, "Hillat el-Arab," in Derek A. Welsby and Julie R. Anderson (eds.), *Sudan: Ancient Treasures*, pp. 138–140.

Lloyd, Alan B., "Apries," in Donald B. Redford (ed.), *The Oxford Encyclopedia of Ancient Egypt*, vol. 1, pp. 98–99.

Lloyd, Alan B., "The Inscription of Udjahorresnet, a Collaborator's Testament," *Journal of Egyptian Archaeology*, 68 (1982), pp. 166–180.

MacDonald, Sally, and Michael Rice (eds.), *Consuming Ancient Egypt* (London, 2003).

Macqueen, J. G., *The Hittites and Their Contemporaries in Asia Minor* (London, 1986).

Maish, Amy, "Not Just Another Cut Throat," *Nekhen News*, 15 (2003), p. 26.

Málek, Jaromír, *In the Shadow of the Pyramids: Egypt During the Old Kingdom* (Norman, Oklahoma, 1986).

Málek, Jaromír, "The Old Kingdom (c. 2686–2160 BC)," in Ian Shaw (ed.), *The Oxford History*, pp. 83–107.

Mallinson, Michael, "The Sacred Landscape," in Rita E. Freed et al. (eds.), *Pharaohs of the Sun*, pp. 72–79.

Malville, J. McK., F. Wendorf, A. A. Mazar, and R. Schild, "Megaliths and Neolithic Astronomy in Southern Egypt," *Nature*, 392 (1998), pp. 488–491.

Manassa, Colleen, *The Great Karnak Inscription of Merneptah: Grand Strategy in the 13th Century BC* (New Haven, Conn., 2003).

Manley, Bill, *The Penguin Historical Atlas of Ancient Egypt* (London, 1996).

Manley, Bill (ed.), *The Seventy Great Mysteries of Ancient Egypt* (London and New York, 2003).

Manning, J. G., *Land and Power in Ptolemaic Egypt* (Cambridge, England, 2003).

Marcus, Ezra S., "Amenemhet II and the Sea: Maritime Aspects of the Mit Rahina (Memphis) Inscription," *Ägypten und Levante*, 17 (2007), pp. 137–190.

Martin, Geoffrey T., *A Bibliography of the Amarna Period and Its Aftermath* (London, 1991).

Martin, Geoffrey T., *The Memphite Tomb of Horemheb, Commander-in-Chief of Tut'ankhamun, I: The Reliefs, Inscriptions, and Commentary* (London, 1989).

Martin, Geoffrey T., *The Royal Tomb at El-'Amarna*, 2 vols. (London 1974, 1989).

Martin, Geoffrey T., "The Toponym Retjenu on a Scarab from Tell el-Dab'a," *Ägypten und Levante*, 8 (2000), pp. 109–112.

Mathieson, Ian J., and Ana Tavares, "Preliminary Report on the National Museums of Scotland Saqqara Survey Project, 1990–91," *Journal of Egyptian Archaeology*, 79 (1993), pp. 17–31.

Mathieson, Ian J., Elizabeth Bettles, Sue Davies, and H. S. Smith, "A Stela of the Persian Period from Saqqara," *Journal of Egyptian Archaeology*, 81 (1995), pp. 23–42.

Maugh, Thomas H., "Ancient Kush Rivaled Egypt, Experts Say," *Los Angeles Times*, June 19, 2007.

McGing, Brian C., "Revolt Egyptian Style: Internal Opposition to Ptolemaic Rule," *Archiv für Papyrusforschung*, 43 (1997), pp. 273–314.

McHugh, W., "Implications of a Decorated Predynastic Terracotta Model for Saharan Neolithic Influence in the Nile Valley," *Journal of Near Eastern Studies*, 49 (1990), pp. 265–280.

McNamara, Liam, "The Revetted Mound at Hierakonpolis and Early Kingship: A Re-interpretation," in B. Midant-Reynes and Y. Tristant (eds.), *Egypt at Its Origins 2: Proceedings of the International Conference "Origins of the State: Predynastic and Early Dynastic Egypt," Toulouse (France), 5th–8th September 2005* (Leuven, Belgium, and Dudley, Mass., 2008), pp. 901–936.

Meadows, Andrew, "Sins of the Fathers: The Inheritance of Cleopatra, Last Queen of Egypt," in Susan Walker and Peter Higgs (eds.), *Cleopatra of Egypt*, pp. 14–31.

Meier, Samuel A., "Diplomacy and International Marriages," in Raymond Cohen and Raymond Westbrook (eds.), *Amarna Diplomacy*, pp. 165–173.

Menu, Bernadette, "L'émergence et la symbolique du pouvoir pharaonique, de la palette de Narmer aux textes des pyramides," *Méditerranées*, 13 (1997), pp. 29–40.

Menu, Bernadette, "Mise à mort cérémonielle et prélèvements royaux sous la Ire dynastie (Narmer–Den)," in Jean-Pierre Albert and Béatrix Midant-Reynes (eds.), *Le sacrifice humain*, pp. 122–135.

Menu, Bernadette, *Ramesses the Great: Warrior and Builder* (London, 1999).

Metropolitan Museum of Art, *Egyptian Art in the Age of the Pyramids* (New York, 1999).

Midant-Reynes, Béatrix, "The Naqada Period (c. 4000–3200 BC)," in Ian Shaw (ed.), *The Oxford History*, pp. 41–56.

Midant-Reynes, Béatrix (translated by Ian Shaw), *The Prehistory of Egypt: From the First Egyptians to the First Pharaohs* (Oxford, 2000).

Millet, Nicholas B., "The Narmer Macehead and Related Objects," *Journal of the American Research Center in Egypt*, 27 (1990), pp. 53–59.

Millet, Nicholas B., "Some Canopic Inscriptions of the Reign of Amenhotep III," *Göttinger Miszellen*, 104 (1988), pp. 91–93.

Montserrat, Dominic, *Akhenaten: History, Fantasy and Ancient Egypt* (London and New York, 2000).

Moran, William L. (ed. and trans.), *The Amarna Letters* (Baltimore, 1992).

Moreno Garcia, Juan Carlos, "Acquisition de serfs durant la Première Période Intermédiaire: Une étude d'histoire sociale dans l'Égypte du IIIe millénaire," *Revue d'Égyptologie*, 51 (2000), pp. 123–139.

Morenz, Ludwig D., "The First Intermediate Period—A Dark Age?," in Bill Manley (ed.), *The Seventy Great Mysteries*, pp. 228–231.

Morkot, Robert, *The Black Pharaohs* (London, 2000).

Morkot, Robert, "Khababash, the Guerilla King," in Bill Manley (ed.), *The Seventy Great Mysteries*, pp. 146–147.

Morkot, Robert, "Kingship and Kinship in the Empire of Kush," in Steffen Wenig (ed.), *Studien zum antiken Sudan*, pp. 179–229.

Morrow, Maggie, and Mike Morrow (eds.), *Desert RATS: Rock Art Topographical Survey in Egypt's Eastern Desert* (London, 2002).

Müller-Wollermann, Renate, *Krisenfaktoren im ägyptischen Staat des ausgehenden Alten Reichs* (Tübingen, 1986).

Murnane, William J., *Ancient Egyptian Coregencies* (Chicago, 1977).

Murnane, William J., "The Gebel Sheikh Suleiman Monument: Epigraphic Remarks," *Journal of Near Eastern Studies*, 46 (1987), pp. 282–285.

Murnane, William J., "Imperial Egypt and the Limits of Power," in Raymond Cohen and Raymond Westbrook (eds.), *Amarna Diplomacy*, pp. 101–111.

Murnane, William J., "The Kingship of the Nineteenth Dynasty: A Study in the Resilience of an Institution," in David O'Connor and David P. Silverman (eds.), *Ancient Egyptian Kingship*, pp. 185–217.

Murnane, William J., "The Return to Orthodoxy," in Rita E. Freed et al. (eds.), *Pharaohs of the Sun*, pp. 177–185.

Murnane, William J., "Rhetorical History? The Beginning of Thutmose III's First Campaign in Western Asia," *Journal of the American Research Center in Egypt*, 26 (1989), pp. 183–189.

Murnane, William J., *The Road to Kadesh: A Historical Interpretation of the Battle Reliefs of King Sety I at Karnak* (Chicago, 1985).

Murnane, William J., *Texts from the Amarna Period in Egypt* (Atlanta, Ga., 1995).

Murnane, William J., and Charles C. Van Siclen III, *The Boundary Stelae of Akhenaten* (London, 1993).

Naguib, Saphinaz-Amal, *Le clergé féminin d'Amon thébain à la 21e dynastie* (Leuven, Belgium, 1990).

Nance, Kevin, "The Dark Side of King Tut," *Chicago Sun-Times*, May 26, 2006.

Naville, Edouard, *The Festival-Hall of Osorkon II in the Great Temple of Bubastis (1887–1889)* (London, 1892).

Needler, Winifred, "A Rock-Drawing on Gebel Sheikh Suliman (near Wadi Halfa) Showing a Scorpion and Human Figures," *Journal of the American Research Center in Egypt*, 6 (1967), pp. 87–92.

Newberry, Percy E., *Beni Hasan*, I (London, 1893).

Niwinski, Andrzej, "Le passage de la XXe à la XXIIe dynastie: Chronologie et histoire politique," *Bulletin de l'Institut Français d'Archéologie Orientale*, 95 (1995), pp. 329–360.

Nunn, John F., *Ancient Egyptian Medicine* (London, 1996).

Nunn, John F., "Disease," in Donald B. Redford (ed.), *The Oxford Encyclopedia of Ancient Egypt*, vol. 1, pp. 396–401.

O'Connor, David, *Ancient Nubia: Egypt's Rival in Africa* (Philadelphia, 1993).

O'Connor, David, "The Earliest Royal Boat Graves," *Egyptian Archaeology*, 6 (1995), pp. 3–7.

O'Connor, David, "The Hyksos Period in Egypt," in Eliezer D. Oren (ed.), *The Hyksos*, pp. 45–67.

O'Connor, David, "The Royal Boat Burials at Abydos," in Bill Manley (ed.), *The Seventy Great Mysteries*, pp. 38–41.

O'Connor, David, "The Sea Peoples and the Egyptian Sources," in Eliezer D. Oren (ed.), *The Sea Peoples*, pp. 85–102.

O'Connor, David, and Eric H. Cline (eds.), *Amenhotep III: Perspectives on His Reign* (Ann Arbor, 1998).

O'Connor, David, and David Silverman (eds.), *Ancient Egyptian Kingship* (Leiden, Netherlands, 1995).

Obsomer, Claude, "La date de Nésou-Montou (Louvre C1)," *Revue d'Égyptologie*, 44 (1993), pp. 103–114.

Obsomer, Claude, *Sésostris Ier: Étude chronologique et historique du règne* (Brussels, 1995).

Oren, Eliezer D. (ed.), *The Hyksos: New Historical and Archaeological Perspectives* (Philadelphia, 1997).

Oren, Eliezer D., "The 'Kingdom of Sharuhen' and the Hyksos Kingdom," in Eliezer D. Oren (ed.), *The Hyksos*, pp. 253–283.

Oren, Eliezer D. (ed.), *The Sea Peoples and Their World: A Reassessment* (Philadelphia, 2000).

Owen, Gwil, "The Amarna Courtiers' Tombs," *Egyptian Archaeology*, 17 (2000), pp. 21–24.

Panagiotopoulos, Diamantis, "Foreigners in Egypt in the Time of Hatshepsut and Thutmose III," in Eric H. Cline and David O'Connor (eds.), *Thutmose III*, pp. 370–412.

Pantalacci, Laure, "De Memphis à Balat: Les liens entre la résidence et les gouverneurs de l'oasis à la VIe dynastie," in Catherine Berger and Bernard Mathieu (eds.), *Études sur l'Ancien Empire et la nécropole de Saqqâra: Dédiées à Jean-Philippe Lauer* (Montpellier, 1997), pp. 341–349.

Parkinson, Richard B. (trans.), *The Tale of Sinuhe and Other Ancient Egyptian Poems, 1940–1640 BC* (Oxford, 1997).

Parkinson, Richard B., "Teachings, Discourses and Tales from the Middle Kingdom," in Stephen Quirke (ed.), *Middle Kingdom Studies*, pp. 91–122.

Parkinson, Richard B. (ed.), *Voices from Ancient Egypt: An Anthology of Middle Kingdom Writings* (Norman, Oklahoma, 1991).

Parkinson, Richard B., and Louis Schofield, "Akhenaten's Army?," *Egyptian Archaeology*, 3 (1993), pp. 34–35.

Parr, Peter J., "Nebi Mend, Tell," in Eric M. Meyers (ed.), *The Oxford Encyclopedia of Archaeology in the Near East* (New York and Oxford, 1997), vol. 4, pp. 114–115.

Payraudeau, Frédéric, "Des nouvelles annales sacerdotales des règnes de Siamon, Psousennès II et Osorkon Ier," *Bulletin de l'Institut Français d'Archéologie Orientale*, 108 (2008), in press.

Peacock, David, "The Roman Period (30 BC–AD 395)," in Ian Shaw (ed.), *The Oxford History*, pp. 414–436.

Peacock, David, *Rome in the Desert: A Symbol of Power* (Southampton, England, 1992).

Peacock, David, and Valerie Maxfield, "On the Trail of Imperial Porphyry," *Egyptian Archaeology*, 5 (1994), pp. 24–26.

Peden, A. J., *The Reign of Ramesses IV* (Warminster, England, 1994).

Peet, T. Eric, *The Great Tomb-Robberies of the Twentieth Egyptian Dynasty* (Oxford, 1930).

Perdu, Olivier, "La chefferie de Sébennytos de Piankhi à Psammétique Ier," *Revue d'Égyptologie*, 55 (2004), pp. 95–111.

Pérez-Accino, José-Ramón, "The Great Pyramid," in Bill Manley (ed.), *The Seventy Great Mysteries*, pp. 61–66.

Pestman, P. W., "Haronnophris and Chaonnophris: Two Indigenous Pharaohs in Ptolemaic Egypt (205–186 B.C.)," in S. P. Vleeming (ed.), *Hundred-Gated Thebes*, pp. 101–137.

Petrie, W. M. Flinders, *The Royal Tombs of the Earliest Dynasties, II* (London, 1901).

Petrie, W. M. Flinders, *The Royal Tombs of the First Dynasty, I* (London, 1900).

Petrie, W. M. Flinders, *Tombs of the Courtiers and Oxyrhynkhos* (London, 1925).

Petschel, Susanne, and Martin von Falck, *Pharao siegt immer: Krieg und Frieden im Alten Ägypten* (Bönen, 2004).

Philips, Allan K., "Horemheb, Founder of the XIXth Dynasty? O. Cairo 25646 Reconsidered," *Orientalia*, 46 (1977), pp. 116–121.

Pinch, Geraldine, *Egyptian Myth: A Very Short Introduction* (Oxford, 2004).

Polz, Daniel, *Der Beginn des Neuen Reiches: Zur Vorgeschichte einer Zeitenwende* (Berlin and New York, 2007).

Polz, Daniel, "The Pyramid Complex of Nubkheperre Intef," *Egyptian Archaeology*, 22 (2003), pp. 12–15.

Polz, Daniel, "Die Särge des (Pa-)Ramessu," *Mitteilungen des Deutschen Archäologischen Instituts, Abteilung Kairo*, 42 (1986), pp. 145–166.

Polz, Felicitas, "Die Bildnisse Sesostris' III. und Amenemhets III. Bemerkungen zur königlichen Rundplastik der späten 12. Dynastie," *Mitteilungen des Deutschen Archäologischen Instituts, Abteilung Kairo*, 51 (1995), pp. 227–254.

Porten, Bezalel, *The Elephantine Papyri in English* (Leiden, New York, and Cologne, 1996).

Posener, Georges, "Les asiatiques en Égypte sous les XIIe et XIIIe dynasties," *Syria*, 34 (1957), pp. 145–163.

Posener, Georges, *Littérature et politique dans l'Égypte de la XIIe dynastie* (Paris, 1956).

Posener, Georges, *La première domination perse en Égypte* (Cairo, 1936).

Posener-Kriéger, Paule, *Les archives du temple funéraire de Néferirkarê-Kakaï (Les Papyrus d'Abousir)*, 2 vols. (Cairo, 1976).

Postgate, Nicholas, Tao Wang, and Toby Wilkinson, "The Evidence for Early Writing: Utilitarian or Ceremonial?," *Antiquity*, 69 (1995), pp. 459–480.

Potter, Wendy E., and Joseph F. Powell, "Big Headaches in the Predynastic: Cranial Trauma at HK43," *Nekhen News*, 15 (2003), pp. 26–27.

Preston, Diana, *Cleopatra and Antony* (London, 2008).

Pritchard, James B. (ed.), *Ancient Near Eastern Texts Relating to the Old Testament*, 3rd ed. (Princeton, N.J., 1969).

Pusch, Edgar B., " 'Pi-Ramesse-geliebt-von-Amun, Hauptquartier deiner Streitwa-gentruppen'—Ägypter und Hethiter in der Delta-Residenz der Ramessiden," in Anne Eggebrecht (ed.), *Pelizaeus-Museum Hildesheim—Die ägyptische Sammlung* (Mainz, Germany, 1993), pp. 126–144.

Pusch, Edgar B., "Recent Work at Northern Piramesse: Results of Excavations by the Pelizaeus-Museum, Hildesheim, at Qantir," in Edward Bleiberg et al. (eds.), *Fragments of a Shattered Visage*, pp. 199–220.

Pusch, Edgar B., "Towards a Map of Piramesse," *Egyptian Archaeology*, 14 (1999), pp. 13–15.

Pusch, Edgar B., Helmut Becker, and Jörg Fassbinder, "Wohnen und Leben: Oder: Weitere Schnitte zum einem Stadtplan der Ramses-Stadt," *Ägypten und Levante*, 9 (1999), pp. 155–170.

Pusch, Edgar B., and Anja Herold, "Qantir/Pi-Ramesses," in Kathryn A. Bard (ed.), *Encyclopedia of the Archaeology of Ancient Egypt*, pp. 647–649.

Quack, Joachim F., "*Kft3w and 'I3ssy*," *Ägypten und Levante*, 6 (1996), pp. 75–81.

Quaegebeur, Jan, "Cléopâtre VII et le temple de Dendara," *Göttinger Miszellen*, 120 (1991), pp. 49–72.

Quaegebeur, Jan, "Contribution à la prosopographie des prêtres memphites à l'époque ptolémaïque," *Ancient Society*, 3 (1972), pp. 77–109.

Quaegebeur, Jan, "The Egyptian Clergy and the Cult of the Ptolemaic Dynasty," *Ancient Society*, 20 (1989), pp. 93–116.

Quibell, James E., *Hierakonpolis, Part I* (London, 1900).

Quibell, James E., "Slate Palette from Hierakonpolis," *Zeitschrift für Ägyptische Sprache und Altertumskunde*, 36 (1898), pp. 81–84.

Quibell, James E., and Frederick W. Green, *Hierakonpolis, Part II* (London, 1902).

Quirke, Stephen, *Ancient Egyptian Religion* (London, 1992).

Quirke, Stephen, "Frontier or Border? The Northeast Delta in Middle Kingdom Texts," in *The Archaeology, Geography and History of the Egyptian Delta in Pharaonic Times* (Oxford, 1989), pp. 261–275.

Quirke, Stephen, "Judgment of the Dead," in Donald B. Redford (ed.), *The Oxford Encyclopedia of Ancient Egypt*, vol. 2, pp. 211–214.

Quirke, Stephen (ed.), *Middle Kingdom Studies* (New Malden, England, 1991).

Quirke, Stephen, "Royal Power in the 13th Dynasty," in Stephen Quirke (ed.), *Middle Kingdom Studies*, pp. 123–139.

Quirke, Stephen, "State and Labour in the Middle Kingdom: A Reconsideration of the Term *hnrt*," *Revue d'Égyptologie*, 39 (1988), pp. 83–106.

Quirke, Stephen, *Who Were the Pharaohs? A History of Their Names with a List of Cartouches* (London, 1990).

Raven, Maarten, "The Tomb of Meryneith at Saqqara," *Egyptian Archaeology*, 20 (2002), pp. 26–28.

Ray, John D., "Alexandria," in Susan Walker and Peter Higgs (eds.), *Cleopatra of Egypt*, pp. 32–37.

Ray, John D., "Amasis: The Pharaoh with No Illusions," *History Today* 46.3 (1996), pp. 27–31.

Ray, John D., "Egypt: Dependence and Independence (425–343 B.C.)," in Heleen

Sancisi-Weerdenburg (ed.), *Sources, Structures and Synthesis: Proceedings of the Groningen 1983 Achaemenid History Workshop* (Leiden, Netherlands, 1987), pp. 79–95.

Ray, John D., "The Emergence of Writing in Egypt," *World Archaeology*, 17 (1986), pp. 307–316.

Ray, John D., "Late Period: An Overview," in Donald B. Redford (ed.), *The Oxford Encyclopedia of Ancient Egypt*, vol. 2, pp. 267–272.

Ray, John D., "Late Period: Thirtieth Dynasty," in Donald B. Redford (ed.), *The Oxford Encyclopedia of Ancient Egypt*, vol. 2, pp. 275–276.

Ray, John D., "Psammuthis and Hakoris," *Journal of Egyptian Archaeology*, 72 (1986), pp. 149–158.

Ray, John D., *Reflections of Osiris: Lives from Ancient Egypt* (London, 2001).

Ray, John D., *The Rosetta Stone and the Rebirth of Ancient Egypt* (London, 2007).

Redford, Donald B., *Akhenaten, the Heretic King* (Princeton, N.J., 1984).

Redford, Donald B. (ed.), *The Akhenaten Temple Project*, vol. 2, *Rwd-Mnw, Foreigners and Inscriptions* (Toronto, 1988).

Redford, Donald B., "The Beginning of the Heresy," in Rita E. Freed et al. (eds.), *Pharaohs of the Sun*, pp. 50–59.

Redford, Donald B., "Egypt and Western Asia in the Late New Kingdom: An Overview," in Eliezer D. Oren (ed.), *The Sea Peoples*, pp. 1–20.

Redford, Donald B., "A Gate Inscription from Karnak and Egyptian Involvement in Western Asia During the Early 18th Dynasty," *Journal of the American Oriental Society*, 99 (1979), pp. 270–287.

Redford, Donald B. (ed.), *The Oxford Encyclopedia of Ancient Egypt* (New York, 2001).

Redford, Donald B., "The Northern Wars of Thutmose III," in Eric H. Cline and David O'Connor (eds.), *Thutmose III*, pp. 325–343.

Redford, Donald B., "Taharqa," in Donald B. Redford (ed.), *The Oxford Encyclopedia of Ancient Egypt*, vol. 3, pp. 346–347.

Redford, Donald B., "Textual Sources for the Hyksos Period," in Eliezer D. Oren (ed.), *The Hyksos*, pp. 1–44.

Redford, Donald B., "The Tod Inscription of Senwosret I and Early 12th Dyn. Involvement in Nubia and the South," *The Journal of the Society for the Study of Egyptian Antiquities*, 17.1–2 (1987), pp. 36–55.

Redford, Donald B., *The Wars in Syria and Palestine of Thutmose III* (Leiden, Netherlands, and Boston, 2003).

Redford, Susan, "Two Field Seasons in the Tomb of Parennefer, No. 188 at Thebes," *KMT*, 6 (Spring 1995), pp. 62–70.

Redford, Susan, and Donald Redford, "Graffiti and Petroglyphs Old and New from the Eastern Desert," *Journal of the American Research Center in Egypt*, 26 (1989), pp. 3–49.

Redmount, Carol A., and Renée Friedman, "Tell el Muqdam: City of Lions," *Egyptian Archaeology*, 3 (1993), pp. 37–38.

Reeves, Nicholas, *Akhenaten: Egypt's False Prophet* (London and New York, 2001).

Reeves, Nicholas, *The Complete Tutankhamun* (London, 1990).

Reeves, Nicholas, "The Royal Family," in Rita E. Freed et al. (eds.), *Pharaohs of the Sun*, pp. 81–95.

Reeves, Nicholas, and Richard H. Wilkinson, *The Complete Valley of the Kings* (London and New York, 1996).

Rehren, Thilo, and Edgar B. Pusch, "Glass and Glass-Making at Qantir-Piramesses and Beyond," *Ägypten und Levante*, 9 (1999), pp. 171–179.

Resch, Walter F. E., "Neue Felsbilderfunde in der ägyptische Ostwüste," *Zeitschrift für Ethnologie*, 88 (1963), pp. 86–97.

Reymond, E.A.E., and J.W.B. Barns, "Alexandria and Memphis: Some Historical Observations," *Orientalia*, 46 (1977), pp. 1–33.

Ricke, Herbert, *Das Sonnenheiligtum des Königs Userkaf*, 2 vols. (Cairo, 1965 and 1969).

Rilly, Claude, "Une nouvelle interprétation du nom royal Piankhy," *Bulletin de l'Institut Français d'Archéologie Orientale*, 101 (2001), pp. 351–368.

Roaf, Michael, *Cultural Atlas of Mesopotamia and the Ancient Near East* (Oxford, 1990).

Robins, Gay, *The Art of Ancient Egypt* (London, 1997).

Roehrig, Catharine H. (ed.), *Hatshepsut: From Queen to Pharaoh* (New York, 2005).

Roehrig, Catharine H., "Senenmut, Royal Tutor to Princess Neferure," in Catharine H. Roehrig (ed.), *Hatshepsut*, pp. 112–113.

Rohl, David (ed.), *The Followers of Horus: Eastern Desert Survey Report*, vol. 1 (Basingstoke, England, 2000).

Romer, John, *The Great Pyramid: Ancient Egypt Revisited* (Cambridge, England, 2007).

Rosati, Gloria, "The Temple of Ramesses II at El-Sheikh Ibada," *Egyptian Archaeology*, 28 (2006), pp. 39–41.

Rose, Jerry, "Amarna Lives: Reading People's Bones," *Horizon*, 1 (October 2006), p. 7.

Rossel, Stine, Fiona Marshall, Joris Peters, Tom Pilgram, Matthew D. Adams, and David O'Connor, "Domestication of the Donkey: Timing, Processes, and Indicators," *Proceedings of the National Academy of Sciences*, 105.10 (2008), pp. 3715–3720.

Roth, Ann Macy, "Hatshepsut's Mortuary Temple at Deir el-Bahri: Architecture as Political Statement," in Catharine H. Roehrig (ed.), *Hatshepsut*, pp. 147–151.

Roth, Ann Macy, "The Meaning of Menial Labour: 'Servant Statues' in Old Kingdom Serdabs," *Journal of the American Research Center in Egypt*, 39 (2002), pp. 103–121.

Roth, Ann Macy, "Models of Authority: Hatshepsut's Predecessors in Power," in Catharine H. Roehrig (ed.), *Hatshepsut*, pp. 9–14.

Roth, Ann Macy, "Social Change in the Fourth Dynasty: The Spatial Organization of Pyramids, Tombs, and Cemeteries," *Journal of the American Research Center in Egypt*, 30 (1993), pp. 33–55.

Russmann, Edna R., *Egyptian Sculpture: Cairo and Luxor* (London, 1989).

Russmann, Edna R., "Mentuemhat's Kushite Wife (Further Remarks on the Decoration of the Tomb of Mentuemhat, 2)," *Journal of the American Research Center in Egypt*, 34 (1997), pp. 21–39.

Ryholt, Kim, "The Late Old Kingdom in the Turin King-List and the Identity of Nitocris," *Zeitschrift für Ägyptische Sprache und Altertumskunde*, 127 (2000), pp. 87–100.

Ryholt, Kim S. B., *The Political Situation in Egypt During the Second Intermediate Period, c. 1800–1550 B.C.* (Copenhagen, 1997).

Sandars, Nancy K., *The Sea Peoples: Warriors of the Ancient Mediterranean* (London, 1978).

Sandman, Maj (ed.), *Texts from the Time of Akhenaten* (Brussels, 1938).

Sasson, Jack M. (ed.), *Civilizations of the Ancient Near East* (New York, 1995).

Säve-Söderbergh, Torgny, "A Buhen Stela from the Second Intermediate Period (Khartum No. 18)," *Journal of Egyptian Archaeology*, 35 (1949), pp. 50–58.

Schäfer, Heinrich, "Ein Zug nach der grossen Oase unter Sesostris I.," *Zeitschrift für Ägyptische Sprache und Altertumskunde*, 42 (1905), pp. 124–128.

Scheil, V., "Documents et arguments. 10: Inscription de Darius à Suez," *Revue d'Assyriologie et d'Archéologie Orientale*, 27 (1930), pp. 93–97.

Schenkel, Wolfgang, *Memphis, Herakleopolis, Theben: Die epigraphischen Zeugnisse der 7.–11. Dynastie Ägyptens* (Wiesbaden, 1965).

Schild, Romuald, and Fred Wendorf, "Palaeo-ecologic and Palaeo-climatic Background to Socio-economic Changes in the South Western Desert of Egypt," in Renée Friedman (ed.), *Egypt and Nubia*, pp. 21–27.

Schmitz, Franz-Jürgen, *Amenophis I.* (Hildesheim, Germany, 1978).

Schofield, Louise, and Richard Parkinson, "Of Helmets and Heretics: A Possible Egyptian Representation of Mycenaean Warriors on a Papyrus from el-Amarna," *The Annual of the British School at Athens*, 89 (1994), pp. 157–170.

Schulman, Alan R., "The Battle Scenes of the Middle Kingdom," *The Journal of the Society for the Study of Egyptian Antiquities*, 12 (1982), pp. 165–183.

Schulman, Alan R., *Military Rank, Title and Organization in the Egyptian New Kingdom* (Berlin, 1964).

Seidlmayer, Stephan Johannes, "Epigraphische Bemerkungen zur Stele des Seth-nachte aus Elephantine," in Heike Guksch and Daniel Polz (eds.), *Stationen: Beiträge zur Kulturgeschichte Ägyptens; Rainer Stadelmann gewidmet* (Mainz, Germany, 1998), pp. 363–386 and plates 20–21.

Seidlmayer, Stephan, "The First Intermediate Period (c. 2160–2055 BC)," in Ian Shaw (ed.), *The Oxford History*, pp. 108–136.

Seidlmayer, Stephan, "Town and State in the Early Old Kingdom: A View from Elephantine," in Jeffrey Spencer (ed.), *Aspects of Early Egypt* (London, 1996), pp. 108–127 and plates 22–23.

Seidlmayer, Stephan, "Zwei Anmerkungen zur Dynastie der Herakleopoliten," *Göttinger Miszellen*, 157 (1997), pp. 81–90.

Shaw, Ian, *Ancient Egypt: A Very Short Introduction* (Oxford, 2004).

Shaw, Ian, "Balustrades, Stairs and Altars in the Cult of the Aten at el-Amarna," *Journal of Egyptian Archaeology*, 80 (1994), pp. 109–127.

Shaw, Ian, "The End of the Great Pyramid Age," in Bill Manley (ed.), *The Seventy Great Mysteries*, pp. 224–227.

Shaw, Ian, "Khafra's Quarries in the Sahara," *Egyptian Archaeology*, 16 (2000), pp. 28–30.

Shaw, Ian (ed.), *The Oxford History of Ancient Egypt* (Oxford and New York, 2000).

Shaw, Ian, and Tom Heldal, "Rescue Work in the Khafra Quarries at Gebel el-Asr," *Egyptian Archaeology*, 23 (2003), pp. 14–16.

Shirley, J. J., "The Beginning of the Empire," unpublished lecture delivered at the

Egypt Exploration Society 125th Anniversary Conference, London, June 23, 2007.

Sidebotham, Steven, and Willemina Wendrich, "Berenike: Roman Egypt's Maritime Gateway to Arabia and India," *Egyptian Archaeology*, 8 (1996), pp. 15–18.

Siliotti, Alberto, *Guide to the Pyramids of Egypt* (Cairo, 1997).

Silverman, David P., "The Spoken and Written Word," in Rita E. Freed et al. (eds.), *Pharaohs of the Sun*, pp. 151–155.

Simpson, William Kelly, "Sennefer," in Wolgang Helck and Wolfhart Westendorf (eds.), *Lexikon der Ägyptologie*, vol. 5 (Wiesbaden, 1984), pp. 855–856.

Simpson, William Kelly, "The Single-Dated Monuments of Sesostris I: An Aspect of the Institution of Coregency in the Twelfth Dynasty," *Journal of Near Eastern Studies*, 15 (1956), pp. 214–219.

Simpson, William Kelly, "Studies in the Twelfth Egyptian Dynasty III: Year 25 in the Era of the Oryx Nome and the Famine Years in Early Dynasty 12," *Journal of the American Research Center in Egypt*, 38 (2001), pp. 7–8.

Simpson, William Kelly, *The Terrace of the Great God at Abydos: The Offering Chapels of Dynasties 12 and 13* (New Haven, Conn., 1974).

Singer, Itamar, "New Evidence on the End of the Hittite Empire," in Eliezer D. Oren (ed.), *The Sea Peoples*, pp. 21–33.

Smith, Harry S., *A Visit to Ancient Egypt: Life at Memphis and Saqqara (c. 500–30 BC)* (Warminster, England, 1974).

Smith, Harry S., and Alexandrina Smith, "A Reconsideration of the Kamose Texts," *Zeitschrift für Ägyptische Sprache und Altertumskunde*, 103 (1976), pp. 48–76.

Smith, Stuart Tyson, "Askut and the Role of the Second Cataract Forts," *Journal of the American Research Center in Egypt*, 28 (1991), pp. 107–132.

Smith, W. Stevenson, *The Art and Architecture of Ancient Egypt*, revised with additions by William Kelly Simpson (New Haven, Conn., 1981).

Smither, Paul C., "The Semnah Despatches," *Journal of Egyptian Archaeology*, 31 (1945), pp. 3–10.

Snape, Steven, "Ramesses II's Forgotten Frontier," *Egyptian Archaeology*, 11 (1997), pp. 23–24.

Snape, Steven, "Statues and Soldiers at Abydos in the Second Intermediate Period," in Christopher Eyre et al. (eds.), *The Unbroken Reed*, pp. 304–314.

Soukiassian, Georges, Michel Wuttmann, and Daniel Schaad, "La ville d'‘Ayn Asil à Dakhla. État de recherches," *Bulletin de l'Institut Français d'Archéologie Orientale*, 90 (1990), pp. 347–358.

Sourouzian, Hourig, "New Colossal Statues at Kom el-Hettân," *Egyptian Archaeology*, 21 (2002), pp. 36–37.

Spalinger, Anthony J., "The Concept of the Monarchy During the Saite Epoch—An Essay of Synthesis," *Orientalia*, 47 (1978), pp. 12–36.

Spalinger, Anthony J., "Late Period: Twenty-sixth Dynasty," in Donald B. Redford (ed.), *The Oxford Encyclopedia of Ancient Egypt*, vol. 2, pp. 272–274.

Spalinger, Anthony J., "The Reign of King Chabbash: An Interpretation," *Zeitschrift für ägyptische Sprache und Altertumskunde*, 105 (1978), pp. 142–154.

Spalinger, Anthony J., *War in Ancient Egypt* (Oxford, 2005).

Spanel, Donald B., "Asyut," in Donald B. Redford (ed.), *The Oxford Encyclopedia of Ancient Egypt*, vol. 1, pp. 154–156.

Spanel, Donald B., "The Date of Ankhtifi of Mo'alla," *Göttinger Miszellen*, 78 (1984), pp. 87–94.

Spanel, Donald B., "The First Intermediate Period Through the Early Eighteenth Dynasty," in Gay Robins (ed.), *Beyond the Pyramids* (Atlanta, Ga., 1990), pp. 17–22.

Spanel, Donald B., "The Herakleopolitan Tombs of Kheti I, *Jt(.j)jb(.j)*, and Kheti II at Asyut," *Orientalia*, 58 (1989), pp. 301–314.

Spence, Kate, "Ancient Egyptian Chronology and the Astronomical Orientation of Pyramids," *Nature*, 408 (2000), pp. 320–324.

Spence, Kate, "Are the Pyramids Aligned with the Stars?," in Bill Manley (ed.), *The Seventy Great Mysteries*, pp. 71–73.

Spence, Kate, "Astronomical Orientation of the Pyramids," *Nature*, 412 (2001), pp. 699–700.

Spence, Kate, "The North Palace at Amarna," *Egyptian Archaeology*, 15 (1999), pp. 14–16.

Spence, Kate, "Royal Walling Projects of the Second Millennium BC: Beyond an Interpretation of Defence," *Cambridge Archaeological Journal*, 14 (2004), pp. 265–271.

Spence, Kate, "What Is a Pyramid For?," in Bill Manley (ed.), *The Seventy Great Mysteries*, pp. 50–53.

Spencer, A. Jeffrey, *Early Egypt: The Rise of Civilisation in the Nile Valley* (London, 1993).

Spencer, Neal, "The Great Naos of Nekhthorheb from Bubastis," *Egyptian Archaeology*, 26 (2005), pp. 21–24.

Spencer, Patricia, "Digging Diary 2003," *Egyptian Archaeology*, 24 (2004), pp. 25–29.

Spencer, Patricia, and A. Jeffrey Spencer, "Notes on Late Libyan Egypt," *Journal of Egyptian Archaeology*, 72 (1986), pp. 198–201.

Stadelmann, Rainer, "Beiträge zur Geschichte des Alten Reiches. Die Länge der Regierung des Snofru," *Mitteilungen des Deutschen Archäologischen Instituts, Abteilung Kairo*, 43 (1987), pp. 229–240.

Stadelmann, Rainer, "The Great Sphinx of Giza," in Zahi Hawass (ed.), *Egyptology at the Dawn of the Twenty-first Century: Proceedings of the Eighth International Congress of Egyptologists, Cairo, 2000* (Cairo and New York, 2002), vol. 1, pp. 464–469.

Steel, Louise, "Egypt and the Mediterranean World," in Toby Wilkinson (ed.), *The Egyptian World*, pp. 459–475.

Steel, Louise, "The 'Sea Peoples': Raiders or Refugees?," in Bill Manley (ed.), *The Seventy Great Mysteries*, pp. 176–180.

Strouhal, Eugen, "Deformity," in Donald B. Redford (ed.), *The Oxford Encyclopedia of Ancient Egypt*, vol. 1, pp. 364–366.

Strudwick, Nigel, *The Administration of Egypt in the Old Kingdom* (London, 1985).

Tavares, Ana, "The Saqqara Survey Project," in Christopher J. Eyre (ed.), *Proceedings of the Seventh International Congress of Egyptologosts*, pp. 1135–1142.

Taylor, John H., *Death and the Afterlife in Ancient Egypt* (London, 2001).

Taylor, John H., *Egyptian Coffins* (Princes Risborough, England, 1989).

Taylor, John H., "Nodjmet, Payankh and Herihor: The End of the New Kingdom Reconsidered," in Christopher J. Eyre (ed.), *Proceedings of the Seventh International Congress of Egyptologosts*, pp. 1143–1155.

Taylor, John H., "The Third Intermediate Period (1069–664 BC)," in Ian Shaw (ed.), *The Oxford History*, pp. 324–363.

Thijs, Ad, "In Search of King Herihor and the Penultimate Ruler of the 20th Dynasty," *Zeitschrift für Ägyptische Sprache und Altertumskunde*, 132 (2005), pp. 73–91.

Thompson, Dorothy J., *Memphis Under the Ptolemies* (Princeton, N.J., 1988).

Thompson, Kristin, "Amarna Statuary Fragments," *Egyptian Archaeology*, 25 (2004), pp. 14–16.

Tiraditti, Francesco, "Three Years of Research in the Tomb of Harwa," *Egyptian Archaeology*, 13 (1998), pp. 3–6.

Tobin, Vincent Arieh, "Creation Myths," in Donald B. Redford (ed.), *The Oxford Encyclopedia of Ancient Egypt*, vol. 2, pp. 469–472.

Török, László, "Iconography and Mentality: Three Remarks on the Kushite Way of Thinking," in W. Vivian Davies (ed.), *Egypt and Africa*, pp. 195–204.

Traunecker, Claude, "Essai sur l'histoire de la XXIXe dynastie," *Bulletin de l'Institut Français d'Archéologie Orientale*, 79 (1979), pp. 395–436.

Tresson, Paul, "La stèle de Naples," *Bulletin de l'Institut Français d'Archéologie Orientale*, 30 (1930), pp. 369–91.

Trigger, Bruce G., "The Narmer Palette in Cross-Cultural Perspective," in M. Görg and E. Pusch (eds.), *Festschrift Elmar Edel* (Bamberg, Germany, 1979), pp. 409–419.

Turner, E. G., "A Commander-in-Chief's Order from Saqqâra," *Journal of Egyptian Archaeology*, 60 (1974), pp. 239–242.

Tyldesley, Joyce, *Chronicle of the Queens of Egypt* (London and New York, 2006).

Tyldesley, Joyce, *Hatchepsut: The Female Pharaoh* (London, 1996).

Uphill, Eric P., *Egyptian Towns and Cities* (Princes Risborough, England, 1988).

Vagnetti, Lucia, "Western Mediterranean Overview: Peninsular Italy, Sicily and Sardinia at the Time of the Sea Peoples," in Eliezer D. Oren (ed.), *The Sea Peoples*, pp. 305–326.

Valbelle, Dominique, "Egyptians on the Middle Nile," in Derek A. Welsby and Julie R. Anderson (eds.), *Sudan: Ancient Treasures*, pp. 92–99.

Valbelle, Dominique, "A First Persian Period Fortress at Tell el-Herr," *Egyptian Archaeology*, 18 (2001), pp. 12–14.

Valbelle, Dominique, and François Leclère, "Tell Abyad: A Royal Ramesside Residence," *Egyptian Archaeology*, 32 (2008), pp. 29–32.

Valloggia, Michel, "Radjedef's Pyramid Complex at Abu Rawash," *Egyptian Archaeology*, 23 (2003), pp. 10–12.

van den Boorn, G.P.F., *The Duties of the Vizier: Civil Administration in the Early New Kingdom* (London and New York, 1988).

van den Brink, Edwin C. M. (ed.), *The Nile Delta in Transition: 4th.–3rd. Millennium B.C.* (Tel Aviv, Israel, 1992).

van den Brink, Edwin C. M., and Thomas E. Levy (eds.), *Egypt and the Levant: Interrelations from the 4th Through the Early 3rd Millennium BCE* (London and New York, 2002).

van den Hout, Theo P. J., "Khattushili III, King of the Hittites," in Jack M. Sasson (ed.), *Civilizations*, vol. 2, pp. 1107–1120.

van Dijk, Jacobus, "The Amarna Period and the Later New Kingdom (c. 1352–1069 BC)," in Ian Shaw (ed.), *The Oxford History*, pp. 265–307.

van Siclen, Charles, "Tell Basta," in Kathryn A. Bard (ed.), *Encyclopedia of the Archaeology of Ancient Egypt*, pp. 776–778.

Vandersleyen, Claude, "Deux nouveaux fragments de la stèle d'Amosis relatant une tempête," *Revue d'Égyptologie*, 20 (1968), pp. 127–134.

Vandersleyen, Claude, *L'Égypte et la vallée du Nil, Tome 2: De la fin de l'Ancien Empire à la fin du Nouvel Empire* (Paris, 1995).

Vandersleyen, Claude, *Les guerres d'Amosis* (Brussels, 1971).

Vandersleyen, Claude, "Une tempête sous le règne d'Amosis," *Revue d'Égyptologie*, 19 (1967), pp. 123–159.

Vandier, Jacques, *Mo'alla: La tombe d'Ankhtifi et la tombe de Sébekhotep* (Cairo, 1950).

Vandorpe, K., "City of Many a Gate, Harbour for Many a Rebel: Historical and Topographical Outline of Greco-Roman Thebes," in S. P. Vleeming (ed.), *Hundred-Gated Thebes*, pp. 203–239.

Vercoutter, Jean, "Les Haou-nebout," *Bulletin de l'Institut Français d'Archéologie Orientale*, 46 (1947), pp. 125–158; 48 (1949), pp. 107–209.

Verhoogt, A.M.F.W., *Menches, Komogrammateus of Kerkeosiris: The Doings and Dealings of a Village Scribe in the Late Ptolemaic Period (120–110 B.C.)* (Leiden, New York, and Cologne, 1998).

Vernus, Pascal, "Choix de textes illustrant le temps des rois tanites et libyens," in Ministère des Affaires Étrangères/Association Française d'Action Artistique, *Tanis: L'or des pharaons* (Paris, 1987), pp. 102–111.

Vernus, Pascal, "La stèle du pharaon *Mntw-htpi* à Karnak: Un nouveau témoignage sur la situation politique et militaire au début de la D.P.I.," *Revue d'Égyptologie*, 40 (1989), pp. 145–161.

Virey, Philippe, "La tombs des vignes à Thèbes," *Recueil des travauz relatifs à la philologie et à l'archéologie égyptiennes et assyriennes*, 20 (1898), pp. 211–223; 21 (1899), pp. 127–133 and 137–149; 22 (1900), pp. 83–97.

Vleeming, S. P. (ed.), *Hundred-Gated Thebes* (Leiden, New York, and Cologne, 1995).

von Beckerath, Jürgen, "Die Dynastie der Herakleopoliten (9./10. Dynastie)," *Zeitschrift für Ägyptische Sprache und Altertumskunde*, 93 (1966), pp. 13–20.

von Beckerath, Jürgen, *Handbuch der ägyptischen Königsnamen* (Mainz, 1999).

von Beckerath, Jürgen, "Die 'Stele der Verbannten' im Museum des Louvre," *Revue d'Egyptologie*, 20 (1968), pp. 7–36.

von Beckerath, Jürgen, "Zur Chronologie der XXI. Dynastie," in Dieter Kessler and Regine Schulz (eds.), *Gedenkschrift für Winfried Barta* (Frankfurt, 1995), pp. 49–55.

von Känel, F., "Les mésaventures du conjurateur de Serket Onnophris et de son tombeau," *Bulletin de la Société Française d'Egyptologie*, 87–88 (1980), pp. 31–45.

Wachsmann, Shelley, "To the Sea of the Philistines," in Eliezer D. Oren (ed.), *The Sea Peoples*, pp. 103–143.

Walker, Susan, and Peter Higgs (eds.), *Cleopatra of Egypt: From History to Myth* (London, 2001).

Weeks, Kent R., "Medicine, Surgery, and Public Health in Ancient Egypt," in Jack M. Sasson (ed.), *Civilizations*, vol. 3, pp. 1787–1798.

Wegner, Josef, "Excavations at the Town of *Enduring-are-the-Places-of-Khakaure-Maa-Kheru-in-Abydos:* A Preliminary Report on the 1994 and 1997 Seasons," *Journal of the American Research Center in Egypt*, 35 (1998), pp. 1–44.

Wegner, Josef, "A Middle Kingdom Town at South Abydos," *Egyptian Archaeology*, 17 (2000), pp. 8–10.

Wegner, Josef, "The Town of *Wah-sut* at South Abydos: 1999 Excavations," *Mitteilungen des Deutschen Archäologischen Instituts, Abteilung Kairo*, 57 (2001), pp. 281–306.

Weigall, Arthur E. P., *Travels in the Upper Egyptian Deserts* (Edinburgh and London, 1909).

Weinstein, James M., Eric H. Cline, Kenneth A. Kitchen, and David O'Connor, "The World Abroad," in David O'Connor and Eric H. Cline (eds.), *Amenhotep III*, pp. 223–270.

Welsby, Derek A., and Julie R. Anderson (eds.), *Sudan: Ancient Treasures: An Exhibition of Recent Discoveries from the Sudan National Museum* (London, 2004).

Wendorf, Fred, and Romuald Schild, "Implications of Incipient Social Complexity in the Late Neolithic in the Egyptian Sahara," in Renée Friedman (ed.), *Egypt and Nubia*, pp. 13–20.

Wendorf, Fred, and Romuald Schild, "Nabta Playa and Its Role in North-eastern African Prehistory," *Journal of Anthropological Archaeology*, 17 (1998), pp. 97–123.

Wengrow, David, "Rethinking 'Cattle Cults' in Early Egypt: Towards a Prehistoric Perspective on the Narmer Palette," *Cambridge Archaeological Journal*, 11 (2001), pp. 91–104.

Wenig, Steffen (ed.), *Studien zum antiken Sudan* (Wiesbaden, 1999).

Wenke, Robert J., "Kom el-Hisn," in Kathryn A. Bard (ed.), *Encyclopedia of the Archaeology of Ancient Egypt*, pp. 415–418.

Wente, Edward F. (trans.), and Edmund S. Meltzer (ed.), *Letters from Ancient Egypt* (Atlanta, Ga., 1990).

Wiener, Malcolm H., and James P. Allen, "Separate Lives: The Ahmose Tempest Stela and the Theran Eruption," *Journal of Near Eastern Studies*, 57 (1998), pp. 1–28.

Wilhelm, Gernot, "The Kingdom of Mitanni in Second-Millennium Upper Mesopotamia," in Jack M. Sasson (ed.), *Civilizations*, vol. 2, pp. 1243–1254.

Wilkinson, Richard H., *The Complete Gods and Goddesses of Ancient Egypt* (London and New York, 2003).

Wilkinson, Richard H., *The Complete Temples of Ancient Egypt* (London and New York, 2000).

Wilkinson, Toby, "Did the Egyptians Invent Writing?," in Bill Manley (ed.), *The Seventy Great Mysteries*, pp. 24–27.

Wilkinson, Toby, *Early Dynastic Egypt* (London and New York, 1999).

Wilkinson, Toby, "Egyptian Explorers," in Robin Hanbury-Tenison (ed.), *The Seventy Great Journeys in History* (London and New York, 2006), pp. 29–32.

Wilkinson, Toby (ed.), *The Egyptian World* (Abingdon and New York, 2007).

Wilkinson, Toby, *Genesis of the Pharaohs* (London and New York, 2003).

Wilkinson, Toby, *Lives of the Ancient Egyptians* (London and New York, 2007).

Wilkinson, Toby, "Political Unification: Towards a Reconstruction," *Mitteilungen des Deustchen Archäologischen Instituts, Abteilung Kairo*, 56 (2000), pp. 377–395.

Wilkinson, Toby, "Reality Versus Ideology: The Evidence for 'Asiatics' in Predynastic and Early Dynastic Egypt," in Edwin C. M. van den Brink and Thomas E. Levy (eds.), *Egypt and the Levant*, pp. 514–520.

Wilkinson, Toby, *Royal Annals of Ancient Egypt: The Palermo Stone and Its Associated Fragments* (London and New York, 2000).

Wilkinson, Toby, *State Formation in Egypt: Chronology and Society* (Oxford, 1996).

Wilkinson, Toby, "Uruk into Egypt: Imports and Imitations," in J. Nicholas Postgate (ed.) *Artefacts of Complexity: Tracking the Uruk in the Near East* (Warminster, England, 2002), pp. 237–245.

Wilkinson, Toby, "What a King Is This: Narmer and the Concept of the Ruler," *Journal of Egyptian Archaeology*, 86 (2000), pp. 23–32.

Willems, Harco, *Chests of Life: A Study of the Typology and Conceptual Development of Middle Kingdom Standard Class Coffins* (Leiden, Netherlands, 1988).

Willems, Harco, "The Nomarchs of the Hare Nome and Early Middle Kingdom History," *Jaarbericht van het Vooraziatisch-Egyptisch Genootschap Ex Oriente Lux*, 28 (1983–1984), pp. 80–102.

Willems, Harco, "The Social and Ritual Context of a Mortuary Liturgy of the Middle Kingdom (*CT* Spells 30–41)," in Harco Willems (ed.), *Social Aspects of Funerary Culture in the Egyptian Old and Middle Kingdoms* (Leuven, Belgium, 2001), pp. 253–372.

Winkler, Hans A., *Rock-Drawings of Southern Upper Egypt*, vol. 1 (London, 1938).

Winkler, Hans A., *Völker und Völkerbewegungen im vorgeschichtlichen Oberägypten im Lichte neuer Felsbilder funde* (Stuttgart, 1937).

Winlock, Herbert E., *The Slain Soldiers of Neb-hep-et-Rē' Mentu-hotpe* (New York, 1945).

Wuttmann, Michel, "Ayn Manawir," *Egyptian Archaeology*, 22 (2003), pp. 36–37.

Yoyotte, Jean, "Le martelage des noms royaux éthiopiens par Psammétique II," *Revue d'Égyptologie*, 8 (1951), pp. 215–239.

Yoyotte, Jean, "Les principautés du Delta au temps de l'anarchie libyenne," *Mémoires publiés par les membres de l'Institut Français d'Archéologie Orientale du Caire*, 66 (1961) (*Mélanges Maspero* 1/4), pp. 121–181.

Yoyotte, Jean, "The Royal Necropolis of Tanis and Its Treasures," in Herbert Coutts (ed.), *Gold of the Pharaohs* (Edinburgh, 1988), pp. 31–33.

Yoyotte, Jean, "Tanis," in Herbert Coutts (ed.), *Gold of the Pharaohs* (Edinburgh, 1988), pp. 10–27.

Yurco, Frank J., "Deir el-Medina," in Kathryn A. Bard (ed.), *Encyclopedia of the Archaeology of Ancient Egypt*, pp. 247–250.

Yurco, Frank J., "Was Amenmesse the Viceroy of Kush, Messuwy?," *Journal of the American Research Center in Egypt*, 34 (1997), pp. 49–56.

Žába, Zbyněk, *The Rock Inscriptions of Lower Nubia (Czechoslovak Concession)* (Prague, 1974).

Žabkar, Louis V., *A Study of the Ba Concept in Ancient Egyptian Texts* (Chicago, 1968).

Ziermann, Martin, *Elephantine XVI: Befestigungsanlagen und Stadtentwicklung in der Frühzeit und im frühen Alten Reich* (Mainz, Germany, 1993).

Zivie, Alain-Pierre, "Ramses I," in Wolfgang Helck and Wolfhart Westendorf (eds.), *Lexikon der Ägyptologie*, vol. 5 (Wiesbaden, 1984), columns 99–108.

Page numbers in *italics* indicate maps or illustrations.

Abdi-Ashirta, 246, 297
Abdi-Heba, 246
Abdju
    Ahmose erects pyramid temple, 194
    attempt to preserve against Hyksos,
        168–69
    as burial ground for early kings,
        48–49, 54
    conquered by Intef II, 116
    defined, 13, 22
    desecrated in battle, 116
    earliest Egyptian example of writing,
        40, 41–42
    funerary monuments of Khasekhem,
        52
    as holy city, 111
    Huni's small pyramid at, 56
    importance as royal burial ground,
        22, 27, 30, 37–38, 39, 40, 41–42,
        48, 50, 52
    Intef II's stela, 138
    as jewel in Herakleopolitan crown,
        111
    Osiris-Wennefer cult center at, 456
    Pepi commissions cult chapel
        dedicated to himself, 91
    Ramesses II's construction projects,
        308

    reinstatement as royal burial ground,
        50
    revival of cult of Osiris, 172
    Senusret III's nearby pyramid town,
        156
    as theological center of Seti I's
        regime, 294–95
    Thutmose dedicates stela, 205
    tomb of Osiris, 404
    two elements of early royal burials,
        54
    vulnerability during civil war, 113,
        115, 116–17
Abu
    as border post, 20, 48, 94, 145–46
    corruption among temple priesthood,
        346–47
    garrison in fortress, 119
    Huni builds "diadem," 56
    significance of location, 20, 21, 48,
        94, 115
    temple desecration during reign of
        Senusret I, 150
    temple of Khnum, 242, 346, 429
Abu Simbel, 309–11, *310*, 415
Abusir, 78, 79, 85–87
Abydos. *See* Abdju
Actium, Battle of, 479

The Admonitions of Ipuwer, 140, 155
Aegina, 445
afterlife
    becomes more important after civil
        war, 124
    democratization, 127
    last judgment, 137–39
    magical funerary objects, 134–37
    in peaceful and prosperous times,
        125–26
    role of Osiris, 127–28
    role of Ra and Horus, 129
    ruling class view, 125–26
    universal changes in burial customs,
        128–31
Agesilaos, 430, 432–33
agriculture, Egyptian
    as basis for Egyptian wealth, 453–54
    reorganization of land in Lower
        Egypt, 46–47
    Roman exploitation, 483
    taxes as proportion of farm produce,
        45–46, 62
    workers, 342
Aha, xiii, 44
Ahhotep
    as Ahmose's mother, 193, 194–95,
        196
    burial goods, 195
    influence over affairs of state, 194–95,
        209, 271
    remains desecrated, 374
    as sister-wife of Seqenenra Taa, 176
Ahmose, son of Abana, 189, 190, *190*
Ahmose I
    in timeline, xvi
    as boy king, 188
    comes of age, 189–96
    makes royal family focus for religious
        devotion, 193–96
    as rebuilder of realm, 222
    remains desecrated, 374
Ahmose II, xix, 417–18, 419, 421
Ahmose-Humay, 228
Ahmose-Nefertari
    presence during reign of Thutmose I,
        203
    remains desecrated, 374
    as sister-wife of Ahmose I, 194,
        195–96, 199, 209, 271
Ahura Mazda, 426
Akanosh of Tjebnetjer, 400
Akhenaten. *See* Amenhotep IV/
    Akhenaten
Akhetaten (Amarna)
    abandoned by royal court after death
        of Akhenaten, 277
    description, 263–65
    founding of city by Akhenaten,
        261–62
    lives of residents, 268, 272
    role of Aten, 262, 263, 266, 269
    traces of Akhenaten expunged,
        290
Akko, 315, 328
Akrotiri, 192
Alalakh, 328
Alara, 393
Alashiya, 247, 258, 328
    See also Cyprus
Aleppo, 303, 305
Alexander Helios, 477, 478
Alexander III (the Great)
    in timeline, xx
    battles Persians, 441–43
    cult promoted by Ptolemy I, 452
    death and burial, 445–46
    as deity, 446, 448, 452
    Egyptians' early view of, 441–42
    founding of Alexandria, 442
    interest in Egypt's age-old culture,
        442–43
    as new young king of Macedon,
        440–42
    role in Egyptian dynastic kingship,
        26, 452
    seizes power in Egypt, 442
    time spent in Egypt, 444
Alexander IV, xx, 446
Alexandria
    as administrative and dynastic capital
        city, 448–50
    Cleopatra promotes cult of Isis,
        473

cult center dedicated to Osiris-Apis, 452

as final burial place of Alexander the Great, 446

founding by Alexander the Great, 442

Great Library, 449, 450, 477

as intellectual center, 449–50

as leading commercial center of Mediterranean world, 448

Museum for scholarly community, 449

Pharos tower, 450

Ptolemy establishes as capital, 446

Ptolemy VIII flees, then returns, 462

as recognized polis, 450, 451

al-Hamidiyah. See Sumur

Amarna, xxix

See also Akhetaten (Amarna)

Amarna Letters, 245–46, 247, 248, 297

Amenemhat I

in timeline, xv

assassination, 147–48

defends Egypt's territorial integrity, 145–47, 162, 163

founder of Twelfth Dynasty, 141–42, 147

inaugurates new Egyptian capital, Amenemhat-Itj-Tawy, 144

makes son co-regent during his reign, 147

orders pyramid, 144–45

as renaissance ruler, 143–47

rise in state-planned construction, 143–45

self-proclaimed king, 141–42, 147

transition from Mentuhotep IV's right-hand man to monarch, 141–42

Amenemhat II, xv, 152–53

Amenemhat III, xv, 159–60

Amenemhat IV, xv, 160, 163

Amenemhat-Itj-Tawy, 144

Amenemnisu, xviii, 371

Amenemope, xviii

Amenemopet, 228

Amenhotep (high priest of Amun), 349, 354–55

Amenhotep I

in timeline, xvi

construction projects, 197–201, 222

location of tomb, 201

as product of inbreeding, 202

remains desecrated, 374

rethinking of royal mortuary complex, 200–201

as underage monarch, 196–97

Amenhotep II

in timeline, xvii

affection for Giza, 237

change of family at top of bureaucracy, 227–31

education and physical training, 232, 234–36

inner circle, 227–31

as military ruler, 236–37

remains of other kings unceremoniously moved to his tomb, 374

reverence for Great Sphinx, 237

Amenhotep III

in timeline, xvii

characteristics of reign, 240–56

commissions largest royal temple in ancient Egypt, 243–44

commissions Luxor Temple construction project, 249–53

commissions temple inside Nubian fortress of Khaemmaat, 253–54

deification in his lifetime, 251–53

foreign relations, 244–48

as greatest royal builder, 241–44

heir apparent, 257

jubilee celebrations for, 249–56

length of reign, 240, 249, 256

life-size sculpture, 252, 252–53

relationship to Amun-Ra, 249–51, 254

remains moved, 374

Amenhotep IV. See Amenhotep IV/ Akhenaten

Amenhotep IV/Akhenaten
in timeline, xvii
Amenhotep IV changes name to
Akhenaten, 261
appoints Neferneferuaten as co-
regent, 275
background, 257
builds new monuments at Ipetsut
dedicated to Aten, 258–59, 260
builds new royal capital apart from
Amun cult, 261–65
children of, 272, 274, 275
colossal statues at Akhetaten, 264
comparison of his theology with
Amenhotep III's, 265
co-opted as role model by certain
groups, 485
as crown prince, 257–58
death, burial, and aftermath, 275–77
devotion to Nefertiti, 271–72
foreign relations, 297, 298
foreigners in administration, 274–75
fundamentalist religious doctrine,
258, 259, 265–66, 267–68, 269–70
holds *sed* festival at Gempaaten,
259–60
influence of army throughout
administration, 283–84
jubilee celebrations, 260–61
meaning of name, 261
omitted from Ramesside list of
rightful monarchs, 294
opposition to, 273–74
personal safety and security issues,
273–74
promulgates the Teaching, 267–70
rejects Amun cult, 258–61
royal family as religious figures, 272,
273
sees himself as co-regent with sun
god, 259, 260
statuary in Gempaaten temple, 259,
260
temples at Thebes and Akhetaten
plundered by Ramesses II, 308
traces of reign erased, 276–77, 290
Amenirdis (king), xx, 414, 429–30

Amenirdis I (god's wife of Amun), 401
Amenirdis II (legal guardian of
Nitiqret), 413, 414
Amenmes, 228
Amenmesse, xvii, 324, 325
Amennakht, 335
Amnisos, 245
Amun/Amun-Ra
at Abu Simbel, 310
Amenhotep as high priest, 349,
354–55
Amenhotep III's relationship with,
249–51, 254
barque shrine, 213, 377, 380
and coronation of Horemheb,
289–90
god's wife, defined, 196
and Horwennefer, 456
as instrument of government policy
under Libyans, 376–77
Kushite attitude toward, 399, 402
Libyan rulers erect temple at Djanet,
371, 375–76
and Luxor Temple, 249, 250, 251
Menkheperraseneb as high priest,
224–26
name expunged from monuments by
Akhenaten, 269–70
oracle at Siwa Oasis, 442–43, 445
at Per-Ramesses, 313
Prince Osorkon's directive, 389–90
problem of usurper as high priest
under Ramesses XI, 354–56
in Ptolemaic Period, 451
Ramessesnakht as high priest,
343–44, 349, *349*, 354
rapprochement with priesthood after
death of Akhenaten, 276–77
relationship to Aten, 261, 269–70
role in Festival of Opet, 251
role of priesthood, 224–26, 354,
377–78, 387, 388, 465
and Seti I, 294, 298
temple at Napata in Nubia, 384
as Theban state god, 211, 212
Thebes as city dedicated to, 225–26,
242

See also god's wife of Amun; high priest of Amun; Mut (consort of Amun-Ra); temple of Amun at Ipetsut

Amunpanefer, 351

Amurru, 246, 297, 298, 299, 315, 316

Anatolia, 206, 247, 327, 440, 441, 446, 447, 459, 478

Anedjib, xiii

animal cults
  Apis bulls, 424, 434, 435, 442, 444, 452, 474, 480
  baboon, 435–36
  background, 434–35
  falcons, 437–38
  ibises, 436–37
  in Ptolemaic Period, 452

Ankh, 55

Ankhesenamun (formerly Ankhesenpaaten), 277–78, 288, 298

Ankhesenpaaten (daughter of Akhenaten), 272, 276, 277
  See also Ankhesenamun (formerly Ankhesenpaaten)

Ankhnesneferibra, 421

Ankhtifi, 108–9, 114

Ankhwa, 55

Ankhwennefer, 456, 458

Antiochos, 460

Antony, Mark, 476, 477, 478, 479–81

Anubis, 173, 213, 474

Apepi, xvi, 172, 176, 186, 188

Aper-El, 274

apes. *See* baboon cult

Aphrodite, 476

Apis bulls, 424, 434, 435, 442, 444, 452, 474

Apollonopolis Magna, 21

archaeology
  discovery of King Tut's tomb in 1922, xxv–xxviii, *xxvi*
  discovery of Narmer Palette and King Narmer, 6, 7, 14–15
  significance of Rosetta Stone, xxviii, *457*, 457–58
  tombs compared with ancient settlements, 124

Archimedes, 449

architecture, and dynastic kingship, 31

Aristarchus of Samos, 449–50

armaments. *See* weaponry, Egyptian military

Armenia, 478

army, Egyptian
  chariotry operations, 284, 286, 314
  development from conscription to professional organization, 283–86
  division into infantry and chariotry, 284
  garrisons, 206, 246, 284
  infantry operations, 284–86
  soldier's life in, 285–86
  as springboard to career in civil service, 288
  weaponry, 285–86
  See also conscription; fortresses; military, Egyptian

Arses, xx

Arsinoe, 471, 476

Artaxerxes I, xix

Artaxerxes II, 429

Artaxerxes III, xx, 438, 440

Arzawa, 247, 248

Ashdod, plundered by Sea Peoples, 328

Ashkelon, 321, 328

Ashur, 406

Ashurbanipal, 408–9, 410, 411

Ashuwa, 220

Asi River. *See* Orontes River (Asi)

Asia Minor. *See* Anatolia; Turkey

Asiatics, 89, 150, 160, 163, 164, 185, 226

Askut, 156

Asshuruballit, 275

Assyria
  ascendance, 314, 315
  conquest of Kushite Egypt, 363, 407–11
  escapes plunder by Sea Peoples, 328–29
  historical relations with Egypt, 220, 240, 275, 406–7

Astarte, 313

Aswan (city), 20, 456, 458

Aswan Dams, 15–16
Asyut, 22–23
Aten
    Akhenaten commissions new
        monuments at Ipetsut dedicated to,
        258–59, 260
    Akhenaten commissions new royal
        capital for, 261–65
    Akhenaten elevates from supreme
        god to sole god, 269–70
    Akhenaten's temples at Gempaaten
        dismantled, 290
    Great Hymn to the Aten, 267–68, 274
    high priest appointed for, 266–67
    open-air temples for worship of, 266
    reflected in Amenhotep IV's name
        change to Akhenaten, 261
    relationship to Amun, 261, 269–70
Atum (creator god), 17, 18, 26, 253,
    259, 313
Augustus, 483
Ay
    in timeline, xvii
    marries Tutankhamun's widow,
        288–89, 298
    succeeds Tutankhamun as king,
        288–89
    tomb and public monuments
        desecrated by Horemheb, 290
Ayn Asil, 93, 103
Aziru, 298

ba (soul), 129–30, 135, 136
Baal-Zephon, 171
baboon cult, 435–36
Babylonia
    attempted invasion of Egypt, 363,
        364, 416, 419, 420
    historical relations with Egypt, 220,
        236, 240, 248, 416, 417
Badarian society, 11–12, 13
Bahr Yusuf, 23
Bakenptah, 391
Bakenrenef, xix, 400, 402
Baki, 229
Bast, 91, 387, 394, 397, 402, 434–35

Bastet, 387, 451
Battlefield Palette, 28
Bay, Chancellor, 325
Beautiful Festival of the Divine
    Audience, 376
Beautiful Festival of the Valley, 199,
    212, 213, 225
Behbeit el-Hagar. *See* Per-hebit
Bent Pyramid, *63*, 63–64, 65
Beqa Valley, Egyptian garrison in, 246
Berenike (daughter of Ptolemy XII),
    468, 469
Berenike (wife of Ptolemy I), 447, 448
Berenike III, xxi
Berenike IV, xxi
Berenike Panchrysos (city), 447
Bes (deity), 225
Beth-Shan, Egyptian garrison at, 246,
    386
Biga Island, 21
Biridiya, 246
Birket Habu, 255
Birket Qarun, 23
Boeotian Thebes, 245
Book of Coming Forth By Day, 403
Book of the Dead, 403
Book of Two Ways, The, 129, 137
British Empire, 484
Buhen, fortress of, *151*, 157, 170, 184,
    191, 211
bureaucracy
    divisions of government in Ramesside
        Dynasty, 353–54
    role of viziers, 165, 223, 353
    system of government in Eighteenth
        Dynasty, 222–24, 231
    unintended consequences, 85
Butehamun, 358, 373, 374
Byblos. *See* Kebny

Caesar, Julius
    assassination, 474, 476
    Octavian as legal heir, 479
    relationship with Cleopatra, 471–72,
        473
    relationship with Pompey, 467, 470

relationship with Ptolemy XIII,
470–71
as Roman strongman, 467
Caesarion. *See* Ptolemy XV Caesarion
(Cleopatra's son)
Cairo, 23
Callender, Arthur "Pecky," xxv, xxvii,
xxxi
Callimachus, 450
Cambyses, xix, 421–24, 429, 439
camel, Persians introduce to Egypt,
426–27
Canaan, 296, 298, 317, 321
Canidius, Publius, 478–79
Carchemish, 316, 416
Carnarvon, George Herbert, Earl of,
xxv–xxviii, *xxvi*, xxx, xxxi
Carter, Howard
background, xxix–xxx
discovery of King Tut's tomb in 1922,
xxv–xxviii, *xxvi*
follow-up to initial discovery,
xxx–xxxii, *xxxii*
Carthage, 460
Cassius, 476
Castor, 451
cat deity. *See* Bastet
Cato, Marcus Porcius, 468
cemeteries, court, 47, 59–61, 122, 156
Chabrias, 432–33
Champollion, Jean François, xxviii, xxix
chariots
Egyptian military, 284, 286, 314
Hittite military, 304, 305
Christianity, 29, 102, 126, 137, 481, 485
Churchill, Winston, 484
Cicero, 467
Cilicia, 478
Cleopatra
in timeline, xxi
appointed co-regent to Egyptian
throne, 469–70
birth, 464, 465
birth of son, Ptolemy Caesar, with
Julius Caesar, 472, 473
birth of son, Ptolemy Philadelphus,
with Mark Antony, 478

birth of twins with Mark Antony,
476–77
bronze coin, *470*
claim to Egyptian throne backed by
Caesar, 471
as daughter of Ptolemy XII, 464, 465,
466, 469
early difficulties as Egyptian ruler,
469–71
Egypt's rapid decline in her last years,
478–82
end of life, 480–81
forced into exile, 470
last tragic years of reign, 478–81
legendary meeting with Julius Caesar,
471
prepares for permanent exile, 480
promotes cult of Isis, 473, 474,
481–82
Ptolemy XII appoints as co-regent,
469
queen and deity start to become one,
473
regarded from birth as semi-divine
being, 466
relationship with Julius Caesar,
471–72, 473
relationship with Mark Antony, 477,
479–81
restored to Egyptian throne, 471–72
Rome appointed as protector,
469–70
Rome's view of, 478, 479
summoned by Mark Antony to meet
with him, 476, 477–78
and temple to Hathor at Iunet, 473,
481
Cleopatra (movie), 485
Cleopatra II, xx, 535
Cleopatra III, xx, 535
Cleopatra Selene (daughter of
Cleopatra and Mark Antony), 477
Cleopatra VI, xxi
Coele-Syria, 478
Coffin Texts, 129, 130, 131, 134
coinage, 427, 477
Colossi of Memnon, 244

commoners
economic circumstances, 341–44
infant mortality, 341
necropolis, 80
See also workers
Complaints of Khakheperraseneb, The, 155
conscription
as contract between Egyptian people
and their rulers, 345
into corvée, 342–43
military, 93, 283, 284, 285, 330, 344,
356
Ramesses IV's Wadi Hammamat
expedition, 343–44
for state labor, 147, 258, 342–43, 344
threat of Sea Peoples invasion, 330
Coptic language, xxviii
corvée, 342–43
court cemeteries, 47, 59–61, 122, 156
Crassus, 466
creation myth, 15, 17–18
creator gods
Atum as, 17, 18, 26, 253, 259, 313
original triad, 259
Ptah as, 242, 310
Shu as, 259, 266, 269, 271
Tefnut as, 259, 271
Crete, 152, 171, 192, 195
crowns, as Egyptian invention, 30–31
Crusades, 301
Cyclades, 446
Cycle of Hymns, 154–55
Cyprus
annexed by Romans, 467
and Cleopatra, 471, 472, 478
plundered by Sea Peoples, 328
and Ptolemies, 446, 447, 462, 463,
466, 478
Ptolemy VIII flees to, 462
relationship with Egypt, 430
returned by Rome to Egypt, 471
and Rome, 460, 467
Wenamun flees to, 381
See also Alashiya
Cyrenaica, 446, 447, 463, 466, 478
Cyrene, 417
Cyrus (Kurash), 420–21

Dahshur pyramid, 62–64
Dakhla Oasis, 93, 96, 103, 127
Darb el-Arba'in, 20, 23
Darius I, xix, 424–27, *425*
Darius II, xix, 429
Darius III, xx, 440, 441, 442
Decree of Memphis. *See* Rosetta
Stone
Deir el-Bahri, 199, 212–14, 215, 250
Deir el-Ballas, 176–77
Deir el-Medina. *See* Place of Truth
(Deir el-Medina)
delta, Nile
characteristics, 23–24
comparison with Nile Valley, 23–24
exposure to invasion, 24
geography, 23–24
Mediterranean links, 24
See also Lower Egypt
Demotic Chronicle, 456
Den, xiii, 46
Dendera. *See* Iunet
Denyen, 329, 332
Description de l'Egypte, 484
desert routes. *See* trade, international
Deshret, defined, 20
Dionysus, 448, 476
Dispute Between a Man and His Soul,
101, 140
Djanet
base for Libyan ruler of Lower
Egypt, 370–73, 379, 402, 412
becomes greatest city in delta,
370–71
comparison with Thebes, 376, 387
favored by bureaucrats and others
over Per-Ramesses, 359
Libyan construction of necropolis,
371–72, 374, 375
Libyan construction of temples to
Amun-Ra, Mut, and Khonsu, 371,
376
Taharqo commissions
commemorative inscription for
Ipetsut, Gempaaten, and Djanet,
405
Djau, 91

Djeba (Edfu)
  Ankhtifi annexes, 108–9
  Huni pyramid at, 56
  as provincial capital, 56, 59
  Ptolemaic temple of Horus, 455, 458,
    463, *463*
Djebaut, 14
Djedefra
  in timeline, xiv
  mortuary cult restored by
    Nakhthorheb, 438
  relationship to sun god Ra, 74, 79
  as successor to Khufu, 74
Djedet, 367, 402, 412, 430, 434
Djedher, xx, 432–34
Djedkara Isesi, xiv, 403
Djedkhonsu (sculptor), 228
Djedkhonsuiuefankh, 379
Djedu, 131, 402
Djeme. *See* Medinet Habu
Djer, xiii, 38
Djerty (Tod)
  desecration of temple by rebels, 150
  restoration of temple during reign of
    Senusret I, 152
  rich hoard of treasures discovered,
    152
Djeser-djeseru, 213
Djet, xiii, 38
Djoser. *See* Netjerikhet
dollar bill, ancient Egyptian imagery
  on, *485*
Dra Abu el-Naga, 173
dual king, 33–34, 96, 118, 270, 368,
  376, 394
durbar, 274–75
dynastic kingship
  aggrandizement of monarchy,
    72–76
  and architecture, 31
  brutality of, 36–37
  and construction of pyramids, 70–71
  co-regency becomes feature in
    Twelfth Dynasty, 147
  as cornerstone of pharaonic
    civilization, xxxiii
  dark side, xxxiii–xxxiv

development of artistic expression,
  28–31
  as doctrine, 26–27
  at end, 348, 481
  Hellenistic compared with Egyptian,
    452–53
  iconography, 27
  importance in history of ancient
    Egypt, 26–27
  royal ceremonies, 34–39
  royal regalia, 29–31
  royal titles, 32–34
  succession crisis after death of Pepi
    II, 103–4
  system of taxation, 44, 45–46
  tombs of early rulers, 37–39
  weakening after civil war, 124–25

Early Dynastic Period, xiii, 40–57
Eastern Desert
  geography, 10, 12, 27, 105, 111, 157,
    274, 344
  mining interests, 12, 27, 105, 151,
    175, 226, 295, 344
  rock art, *9*, 10, 27
Edfu, 431
  See also Apollonopolis Magna; Djeba
    (Edfu)
Edom, 334
education. *See* scribal school; training,
  physical
Eighteenth Dynasty
  in timeline, xvi–xvii
  description, 181–82
  map, *180*
  security issues, 231
  system of government, 222–24, 231
Eighth Dynasty, xiv–xv, 104–6, 127
El Alamein, 484
el-Badari, 11
Elephantine Island. *See* Abu
elephants, African, 447
Eleutherus Valley, 305
Eleventh Dynasty, xv, 138–39, 140, 141
el-Hiba. *See* Tawedjay fortress
Elkab. *See* Nekheb (Elkab)

el-Kula, 56
Eloquent Peasant, The, 101
el-Rashid, xxviii
el-Rizeiqat. *See* Sumenu
En Besor, 42
Ephesus, 468, 476
Eratosthenes, 450
Esarhaddon, 407–8
Euclid, 449
Exodus, 313
eye of Ra, 242, 243

falcon cult, 437–38
farming. *See* agriculture, Egyptian
Fayum
    concentrations of ethnic settlers, 163,
        366, 451, 456
    defined, 23
    irrigation and land reclamation
        projects, 23, 160, 163, 453–54
    military interests, 320, 378, 396, 451
    site of royal pleasure palaces and
        monuments, 23, 55, 56, 59, 232
female kings, 160, 209, 210–11
    See also Hatshepsut (female king);
        Sobekneferu (first female king)
Festival of Opet
    and Horemheb's coronation, 289
    inaugurated by Hatshepsut, 212
    Luxor Temple as backdrop, 308
    as public religious spectacle
        celebrating divine kingship, 225, 251
    recorded in reliefs in Luxor Temple,
        251–52
    as ritual of royal renewal, 251–52, 265
Fifteenth Dynasty, xvi
Fifth Dynasty
    in timeline, xiv
    architectural legacy, 84, 85–89
    comes to power, 77
    sun temples in, 78–79
First Dynasty, xiii, 44, 45–46
First Intermediate Period, xv, 102, 148,
    350
First Persian Period, xix, 423–24
Following of Horus, 44–45, 413

forced labor. *See* conscription
foreign relations
    under Amenhotep III, 244–48
    under Amenhotep IV/Akhenaten,
        297, 298
    decline of Egypt's international
        reputation under Libyans, 380–82
    relationship to military, 152, 153, 283
    under Seti I, 296–97, 298–99
    under Thutmose I, 206–8
    See also trade, international
fortresses
    Egyptian army garrisons, 206, 246,
        284
    Libyans control throughout Nile
        Valley, 378, 379, 389
    in Nubia, 150–52, 156–59, 166, 170,
        191, 192, 193
    Ramesses fortifies Libyan frontier
        along western delta border, 319
    Walls of the Ruler fortifications, 145,
        162
    See also military, Egyptian
Fourteenth Dynasty, xvi
Fourth Dynasty, xiv, 57–60, 66, 72–76,
    223
funerary customs
    Libyans' relative lack of interest, 368
    means of overcoming death, 88, 102,
        124, 125–31
    rise of Osiris, 131–37
    royal cults in Old Kingdom, 86–89
    shabti, 135–37, 276, 401, 403
    Taimhotep's stela, 474–75, 475
    See also royal tombs and mortuary
        temples

Gabinius, 468, 470, 476
garrisons, army, 206, 246, 284
Gaza, 191, 206, 216, 246, 385
Gebel Barkal, 308, 392, 393
Gebel el-Silsila, 21, 258
Gebel Sheikh Suleiman, 28, 43
Gebel Zeit, 175
Gebtu
    dissolves alliance with Thebes, 112

encompassed by expansionist Thebes, 114

example of bureaucracy and animal worship, 480

Pepi I commissions cult chapel dedicated to himself, 91

Ptolemy II commissions new temple construction, 453

royal decrees from, 105–6

strategic importance of province, 111

temple of Min, 105, 106, 172

User appointed governor of province, 111

Gempaaten temple
built by Amenhotep IV, 258–59
dismantled by Horemheb, 290
as expression of fundamentalist theology, 258–59, 260
site of *sed* festival, 259–60

Gezer, 246, 321, 381

Gilukhepa, 247

Gisr el-Mudir monument, 52–54

Giza, pyramids. *See* pyramids

Giza plateau, 3, 65, 66, 69–70, 237

god's wife of Amun, 196, 210, 278, 393, 401, 413–14, 421

gold, as preferred currency of diplomatic exchange, 247

gold mines. *See* mining and quarrying

Great Hymn to the Aten, 267–68, 274

Great Library of Alexandria, 449, 450, 477

Great Pyramid at Giza
background, 57–58
cannibalized by Amenemhat I, 144–45
construction work, 67–70
divine kingship as purpose, 70–71
orientation, 67, 71–72
project as ultimate projection of absolute power, 71
site selection and preparation, 65–67
statistics, 57
uniqueness, 72–73

Great Sphinx, 75, 237–38, 276

Greek world
Ahmose II curries favor with city-states, 417–18

Athenian currency as monetary standard, 427

Athenians assist Egyptians in battling Persians, 428, 429

free trade with Egypt, 418

Greek pharaohs seek hybrid Hellenistic-Egyptian culture, 452–53, 463

mercenaries appointed to Egyptian army, 411–12, 416, 420, 421, 432

peace treaty between Persia and Athens, 429

place names inscribed in Amenhotep III's mortuary temple, 244–45

Ptolemaic takeover of Egyptian culture, 450–54

relationship with Persia, 429, 440

Green, Frederick, 5–6

Gurob, 232

Hadrian's Villa, Tivoli, 485

Hagar, xx, 430–31

Hagar el-Merwa, 204

Halicarnassus, Battle of, 441

Hamath, 328

Hanigalbat, 314, 315

Hardai, 356

harem, royal, 92, 337–38

Harkhuf, 94–96

Harwa, 401, 404, 412

Hathor, 199, 212, 213, 225, 469, 473, 481–82

Hatshepsut (female king)
in timeline, xvii
construction of monuments, 211–14
as daughter of Thutmose I, 204
favors bestowed on Senenmut, 214–15
omitted from Ramesside list of rightful monarchs, 294
path to power, 208–11
question of divine birth, 250
succeeded by Thutmose III, 215, 250
succeeds Thutmose II as ruler, 208–14, *209*

Hattusa, 315, 328
Hattusili, 315, 316, 317
Hau-nebut, 195
health, 83
Hebrew exodus, 313
hedgehogs, as magical tomb objects,
    134, 135
Hefat, 108
Heliopolis. *See* Iunu
Hemaka, 47, 48
Hemiunu, 66, 67, *67*
Herakleopolis, 107, 109, 111,
    116–17, 119, 123, 308, 391,
    393, 394
Herbert, George. *See* Carnarvon,
    George Herbert, Earl of
Herbert, Lady Evelyn, xxv, xxvi, *xxvi*,
    xxvii, xxxi
hereditary monarchy, 202–3
Herihor
    in timeline, xviii
    as Libyan general in Egyptian
        government, 366, 369, 370, 373,
        375, 378, 380
    as military strongman, 358, 366,
        367
    succeeds Paiankh, 358–59
Hermonthis. *See* Iuny
Herodotus
    observations about Egypt, 15
    view of Egyptian port of Naukratis,
        418
    view of Khufu, 71
    view of western delta inhabitants as
        Libyans, 367
    visits Egypt in 440s, 429
Hesira, 55
Hetepheres, 73–74
Hetepsekhemwy, xiii, 49
Hezekiah of Judah, 407
Hierakonpolis. *See* Nekhen (Kom
    el-Ahmar)
hieroglyphics, xxviii, xxxii–xxxiii, 32, 41,
    367
    See also writing
high priest of Amun
    Amenhotep as, 349, 354–55

Menkheperraseneb as, 224–26, 376,
    379, 383
    problem of usurper under Ramesses
        XI, 354–56
    Ramessesnakht as, 343–44, 349, *349*,
        354
    role of, 223, 224–26, 354, 377–78,
        387, 388, 465
hippos, as magical tomb objects,
    134–35
Hishmi-Sharruma, 318
Hittites
    Assyrian threat to, 315
    cold war with Egypt, 314
    consolidate Syrian hold, 298
    diplomatic marriage of princess to
        Ramesses II, 317–18
    driven out of northern Syria, 206
    establishes diplomatic relations with
        Egypt, 236
    gifts to Egyptians, 220, 226
    invaded by Sea Peoples, 328
    make peace with Ramesses II,
        315–18
    ravaged by plague, 298
    during reign of Amenhotep III, 240,
        245, 246, 247
    showdown with Egypt in Battle of
        Kadesh, 282, 288, 298, 299, 301,
        302, 303–7
    under Shuppiluliuma, 297
    Tutankhamun's widow makes appeal
        for husband to, 278
Horemakhet, 237–38
Horemheb
    in timeline, xvii
    accession to throne, 289–90
    in aftermath of Tutankhamun's death,
        288–89
    background, 282, 286–87
    civil service career, 288
    designated as Tutankhamun's heir,
        289
    legislative reforms, 290–92
    as military officer, 282
    obtains divine sanction for
        coronation, 289–90

orders all traces of Akhenaten
  expunged, 290
personal safety and security,
  291–92
prepares successor, 292, 293
private tomb, 287, 288, 373
reforms workmen's village at Place of
  Truth, 350
relationship to Akhenaten, 286–87
tomb robbed, 373
treatment of prisoners of war, 287,
  287–88
Horsiese, 387, 388
Horus
  defined, 6, 32
  and falcon cult, 6, 32, 126, 437–38
  Horemheb's relationship to, 287,
    289–90
  monarch as earthly incarnation,
    32–33, 51, 79, 126, 131, 437–38
  place in Seti I's temple at Abdju,
    294
  relationship to Egyptian monarchy, 6,
    253
  relationship to Ra, 74, 129, 238,
    310
  as son of Isis, 473, 485
  as son of Osiris, 474
  temple at Buhen, 170
  temple at Djeba, 431, 455, 463, 463
  See also Following of Horus
Horus of Herakleopolis, 289
Horwennefer, 456
Hu. See Hut-sekhem
Huni, xiv, 55–56
Hutheryib, 56, 397, 402, 409, 411
Hut-sekhem, 114, 229
Hutwaret
  as capital of independent delta state,
    166–67
  as Hyksos' capital, 168, 176
  immigrant settlers, 163–64
  military base established, 284
  Thebans siege against, 189–90
Hyksos
  acculturation to Egyptian life,
    423

attempts by Kamose to reclaim
  Middle Egypt from Hyksos,
    185–86, 188
  background, 167–69
  establish capital at Hutwaret, 168,
    176
  form military alliance with Kush, 176
  kingdom flourishes in Egypt,
    170–71
  liberation of Egypt from, 183,
    189–93
  Theban siege of capital, 189–90
  Thebes' collaboration with, 183–84
  threatens Thebes, 172
Hymn to the Aten, 267–68, 274

Ibi, xv, 104–5, 127
ibis cult, 436–37
Idy, 106
Ihnasya el-Medina. See Herakleopolis
Iken, 156
Ilios, 245
Imhotep
  as architect of Step Pyramid,
    54–55
  namesake, son of Pasherenptah, 473,
    477, 480
  worshipped as god of wisdom, magic,
    and medicine, 472, 473
Imu, 62
inbreeding, 202
Inerty, 59, 121, 458
Instruction of Amenemhat I for His Son,
    140
Intef I, xv, 109, 111, 112, 113, 114
Intef II
  in timeline, xv
  as Eleventh Dynasty ruler, 140
  funerary stela, 117, 117–18, 138
  as leader and warrior, 114–15,
    116–17
  as successor to Intef the Great, 113,
    114
Intef III, xv, 118
Intefiqer, 146
Iny, xviii

Ipetsut (Karnak)
administration of temple, 223
Ahmose erects stela for Ahhotep in
temple of Amun, 194–95, 196
Ahmose erects stela for Ahmose-
Nefertari in temple of Amun, 196
Amenemhat I's temple to Amun,
143–44
Amenhotep I's focus on construction
projects, 198
Amenhotep III's construction
program for temple complex, 243
Amenhotep IV/Akhenaten
commissions new monuments
dedicated to Aten, 258–59
Amun-Ra's chief temple, 120, 211
cult of Amun dominates Theban
society, 225–26
floodwaters overwhelm temple of
Amun, 169
Hatshepsut's monuments at, 211–12
high priest of temple of Amun, 223,
224–26, 354, 387, 388, 465
Libyans replicate temple of Amun-Ra
at Djanet, 376
Mentuhotepi's commemorative stela
at, 169–70
Meremptah's commemorative
inscription in temple of Amun-Ra,
321–22, 365
Nefertiti's temple, 271
Ptolemy II commissions new temple
construction, 453
Ramesses III commissions new
construction, 333
Senusret I's jubilee pavilion for
temple of Amun, 150, 198
Shoshenq commissions extension to
temple of Amun, 386
site of Amenhotep IV's new
monuments to Aten, 258–59, 260
Taharqo commissions
commemorative inscription, 405
temple of Amun-Ra, 120, 211, 212,
224, 226
theft from temple of Amun-Ra,
353

Thutmose IV's depiction of himself,
238
Irethoreru, 428–29
Iri, 94
Irtjet, 94, 95
Irukaptah, 84
Isesi. See Djedkara Isesi
Iseum. See Per-hebit
Isis
Cleopatra promotes cult, 473, 474,
476, 478, 481–82
complex on island of Philae, 453, 462
cult, 435, 473, 484–85
as mother of Horus, 473
place in Seti I's temple at Abdju, 294
Israel, 321–22, 381, 385–86
Issos, Battle of, 441
Iteru, defined, 20
Iti, 104, 108
Itibi, 116
Itj-tawy, 144, 164, 166, 167, 168,
169–70, 396
Iunet
Cleopatra dedicates roof shrine to
Hathor, 473, 481
displaces Tjeni as regional
administrative capital, 59
encompassed by expansionist Thebes,
114
monument to Mentuhotep, 121
Ptolemy II commissions new temple
construction, 453
support for Intef the Great, 111
temple to deity Hathor, 469, 481, 482
Iunu
ancient creation myth from, 17, 259
falls to Thebans led by King Ahmose,
189
governed by Assyrian delta vassal,
411
Libyan priest from, 368
as principal cult center of sun god Ra,
74, 189, 397
Ramesses II's construction projects,
308
Iuny, 48, 108, 109, 473
Iunyt, animal cults at, 434–35

Iuput I, xviii
Iuput II, 394, 397, 398
Iushenshen, 111, 112
Iyemhotep, 104

Jaffa, Egyptian garrison at, 246
Jerusalem, 246, 385, 416
Jews
  exiled to Babylon and then released,
    416, 423
  temple of Yahweh on Abu, 423, 429
  troop commanders rise up against
    Ptolemy VI, 461
Jezreel Valley, Egyptian garrison in, 246
Jubayl. See Kebny
Judah, 385, 416

ka (eternal spirit), 61, 130, 135, 136,
  251–52
Kadashman-Enlil I, 248
Kadesh (place), 298, 299, 301, 303, 328
Kadesh, Battle of
  Abu Simbel decorated with scenes
    from, 309
  ends in stalemate, 306–7
  Luxor Temple decorated with scenes
    from, 309
  map, 302
  as showdown between Egyptians and
    Hittites, 282, 299, 301, 303, 307
Kadesh, prince of, 215–16, 218
Kagemni, 84, 90
Kahun, 153–54
Kamose
  in timeline, xvi
  desire to rescue Egypt, 183, 184
  efforts to reclaim Middle Egypt from
    Hyksos, 185–86, 188
  efforts to reclaim Nubia from Kush,
    184–85
  successor to Taa, 177
Kar, 358, 373
Karnak. See Ipetsut (Karnak)
Kashta, 393, 401
Kay, 142

Kebny, 51–52, 160, 163, 164, 206, 246,
  308, 380–81
Kemet, defined, 20
Kemit (model letter text), 233
Kerma, 204–5, 208, 220
Khaba, xiv, 55
Khababash, 440
Khabausokar, 55
Khaemmaat, fortress at, 253–54
Khaemwaset, 339, 352
Khafra
  in timeline, xiv
  orders creation of Great Sphinx, 75
  pyramid at Giza, 75
  stone bowl among Akhenaten's grave
    goods, 276
  as successor to Djedefra, 74–75
Khakaura, 156, 157
Khamudi, xvi
Kharga Oasis, 426–27, 428
Khasekhem, xiii, 50–51, 52, 53, 58
Khasekhemwy. See Khasekhem
Khentika, 84
Kheti, house of, 107, 111, 113, 115,
  117, 119
Kheti I, xv
Kheti II, xv, 118
Khmun (place), 394, 395–96, 437, 439
Khnemibra, 421–22
Khnum, 20, 242, 346, 429
Khnumhotep (manicurist), 84
Khnumhotep I (regional governor),
  142–43
Khnumhotep III (regional governor),
  155
Khnumnakht, 346
Khonsu, 225, 251, 372
Khozam. See Iushenshen
Khufu
  in timeline, xiv
  as builder of Great Pyramid, 57
  death and burial, 74
  ivory statuette, 76
  mother, Hetepheres, 73–74
  opulence of court, 73
  viewed by Herotodus, 71
  See also Great Pyramid at Giza

Khuu, 108–9
Khyan, xvi, 171–72, 173
Kleomenes of Naukratis, 445
Knossos, 171, 195, 245
    See also Crete
Kom el-Ahmar. See Nekhen (Kom el-
    Ahmar)
Kom el-Hisn. See Imu
Kor (island), 156
Krokodilopolis, 458
Kumidi, Egyptian garrison at, 246
Kumma, 157, 158
Kurash. See Cyrus (Kurash)
Kushites
    acculturation to Egyptian life, 423
    attack Upper Egypt with help of
        Nubians, 175, 184
    believe themselves to be guardians of
        Egyptian kingship and culture,
        391–92, 402
    capital sacked and burned, 204–5
    defeat Libyans and impose hegemony
        throughout Egypt, 363, 364,
        391–98, 399
    Egypto-Kushite blend of features in
        art, 403–4, 404
    form military alliance with Hyksos,
        176
    influence of Egyptian theology,
        392–93
    rebellion upon death of Thutmose I,
        208
    Senusret III builds fortresses against
        threat, 156, 166, 170
    Thutmose I wages campaign against,
        203–5, 391–92
    Thutmose III's policy toward, 220–21
    treatment as prisoners of war, 287–88
Kydonia, 245
Kythera (island), 245

labor. See conscription; workers
Lachish, 328
language, Egyptian, 367–68
    See also hieroglyphics; personal
        names; writing

last judgment, as aspect of afterlife,
    137–39
Late Period, xix–xx
    map, 362
Latins (Italic tribe), 459
Lebanon, falls to Babylonia, 416
libraries. See Great Library of
    Alexandria
Libu, 370
Libyans
    acculturation to Egyptian life, 423
    apply Egyptian theology to rule of
        Egypt, 375–78
    attitude toward death and burial,
        368–69
    decline of Egypt's international
        reputation, 380–82
    division of Egypt into two parallel
        states, 370–71
    domination of Lower Egypt, 369,
        370–73, 394
    domination of Upper Egypt, 369,
        373–75, 378–79, 394
    effective monopoly of Amun
        priesthood, 388–89
    and Egyptian language, 367–68
    Egyptian view of foreigners, 375
    favored model of government, 369
    generals gain power after death of
        Ramesses XI, 367
    move to centralize power in divided
        Egypt, 383–86
    move to renew Egyptian authority in
        Near East, 385–86
    nomadic characteristics, 368–69
    nomadic tribes as recurring threat to
        Egypt, 318–21, 333, 347–48, 353,
        365
    as settlers in Egypt, 365–69
    steal valuables from tombs, 358,
        373–75
    take over Egyptian government after
        Ramesside period, 366–69
lion deity. See Mahes
literature
    Admonitions of Ipuwer, The, 140, 155
    Book of Coming Forth By Day, 403

Book of the Dead, 403
Book of Two Ways, The, 129, 137
Complaints of Khakheperraseneb, The,
  155
Cycle of Hymns, 154–55
Dispute Between a Man and His Soul,
  101, 140
Eloquent Peasant, The, 101
flowering in Twelfth Dynasty, 101,
  148–50
golden age, 101, 140
Great Hymn to the Aten, 267–68, 274
Instruction of Amenemhat I for His Son,
  140
Loyalist Instruction, The, 149–50
Prophecies of Neferti, The, 101, 148–49
Satire of the Trades, 101, 233
Shipwrecked Sailor, The, 101
Tale of Sinuhe, The, 101, 149, 233, 381
Lower Egypt
  construction of ancient Suez Canal,
    425–26
  contrast with Nile Valley, 23–24
  defined, 18
  delta characteristics, 23–24
  as "flooded land," 24
  junction with Upper Egypt, 23, 144,
    168
  Libyan domination, 369, 370–73, 394
  Psamtek becomes undisputed
    sovereign, 412
  Ptolemaic victory over rebels, 457–58
  red crown, 30
  reorganization of agricultural lands,
    46–47
  surrenders to Kushites, 396–98
  symbolic relationship to Upper
    Egypt, 23, 33–34, 281
Loyalist Instruction, The, 149–50
Luxor (modern city), 212, 255
Luxor hotel, Las Vegas, 485
Luxor Temple
  Amenhotep III's massive construction
    project, 249–53
  beautified under Ramesses III, 333
  Horemheb's coronation, 289
  Ramesses II adds to, 308–9

shrine for Amun-Ra's barque, 212,
  213
Lyktos, 245

Ma (Libyan tribe), 370, 394, 397
Maat (deity), 97, 138, 243
maat, defined, 58, 226, 265
Maathorneferura, 318
mace heads, 34, 35, 36–37
Macedonian Dynasty
  in timeline, xx
  importance of dynamic kingship, 26
  internecine wars between Alexander's
    successors, 446, 447
  necropolis, 445
  new young king, Alexander III,
    440–43
Madu, 175
Mahes, 387, 423
Mahu, 274, 276
Malkata. See Palace of the Dazzling Orb
  and the House of Rejoicing
Manetho, 26–27, 91, 107, 449
Manhata, 219
Mansion of Millions of Years, 332–33,
  365
Mansion of the Aten, 264
Mansion of the Benben, 271
Manuwai, 219
maps
  ancient Egyptians conception of their
    world, 19
  Battle of Kadesh, 302
  Battle of Megiddo, 217
  Early Dynastic Period, 2
  Eighteenth Dynasty, 180
  Late and Ptolemaic Periods, 362
  Memphite necropolis, 60
  Middle Kingdom, 100
  Nile Valley and surrounding regions,
    xxxv
  Old Kingdom, 2
  Ramesside period, 280
  Thebes, 187
  Upper Egypt, 110
  Valley of the Kings, 187

Maruta, 219

Masaharta, 378

mastaba, 47, 54

Medamud. *See* Madu

Median Empire, 420, 478

Medinet Habu, 333, 355, 374

Medjay, 175

Medunefer, 127

Megiddo (place), 246, 386

Megiddo, Battle of, 215–16, 217, 218, 285

Mehu, 96

Mehy, 300–301

Meidum, 59, 61, 64

Meketaten, 272, 275

melting pot, ancient Egypt as, 162, 163–64, 218–19

Memphis
  as apex of delta, 23
  base of northern vizier, 223
  as capital, 369–70
  captured by Persian king Cambyses, 421
  compared with Thebes, 369–70
  as initial burial place of Alexander the Great, 446
  loss to Hyksos, 168
  loss to Kushites, 397
  Memphite necropolis, 60, 74
  national capital of Egypt after unification, 465
  Persian satrap in, 424
  Ptah as principal deity, 465
  in Ptolemaic Period, 451–52
  restoration by Kushite kings as principal royal capital, 403
  royal compound architecture, 31
  temple of Ptah, 435
  tombs at North Saqqara, 47–48
  White Wall, 31, 47, 54

Memphite Theology, 403

Menes, 15, 26, 183, 294
  See also Narmer

Menkauhor, xiv

Menkaura
  in timeline, xiv

commissions last of pyramids at Giza, 75
  succeeded by Shepseskaf, 77
  as successor to Khafra, 75

Menkheperra (throne name of Thutmose III), 224

Menkheperraseneb (high priest of Amun), 224–26, 376, 379, 383

Mentuhotep II
  in timeline, xv
  descendents, 140
  monuments to, 121, 122
  mortuary temple, 122–23, 199
  Nubian campaign, 152
  reunification of Egypt, 118–22, 135, 140
  significance of name, 118
  temple, 213
  victor in civil war, 183
  war graves near his own tomb, 123

Mentuhotep III, xv, 140

Mentuhotep IV, xv, 140, 141

Mentuhotepi, xvi, 169–70

mercenaries
  Greek, 411–12, 416, 420, 421, 432
  Nubian, 93, 112, 145, 385

Merenptah
  in timeline, xvii
  commemorative inscription, 321–22, 365
  remains moved, 371–72, 374
  responds to Libyan invasion, 320–21
  succeeded by Seti-Merenptah, 323, 324
  successor to Ramesses II, 319
  threat by Sea Peoples, 329, 330

Merenra, xiv, 94, 95, 96

Merer, 108

Mereruka, *81*, 82–83, 90–91

Merikara, xv, 118–19, 137

Meritaten, 266, 272, 276

Merka, 47–48

Meroë, 447

Mersin, 328

Merwer bull, 346

Mery, 318, 319, 365

Meryra, 266–67, 339

Mesopotamia
  cultural exchange with ancient Egypt, 28–29, 31
  first to develop palace-façade architecture, 31
  kingdom of Mittani, 206–8
  mode of rule, 27
  Near Eastern leaders in, 246–47
  as part of Seleucid Kingdom, 447
  role in invention of writing, 41
  as source of lapis lazuli, 152
  writing found in Amarna Letters, 245
  See also Mittani
Metjen, 55
Middle Egypt, defined, 23
Middle Kingdom
  in timeline, xv–xvi
  background, 101–2
  beginning, 122
  flowering of court culture, 235
  map, 100
Miletus, 328
military, Egyptian
  Amenhotep II's Near East operations, 236–37
  chariotry operations, 284, 286, 314
  defeat of Sea Peoples, 330–32
  division of army into infantry and chariotry, 284
  garrisons, 206, 246, 284
  Greek mercenaries in, 411–12, 416, 420, 421, 432
  infantry operations, 284–86
  influence throughout Amenhotep IV/Akhenaten's administration, 283–84
  making of weaponry, 313–14
  New Kingdom development of army from conscription to professional organization, 283–86
  relationship to foreign relations, 152, 153, 283
  soldier's life in, 285–86
  as springboard to career in civil service, 288
  Thutmose III's Near East operations, 215–21
  types of weaponry, 285–86
  See also conscription; fortresses
Milkilu, 246
Min (deity), 105, 106, 172, 174
Minhotep, 174
Minimhat, 174
mining and quarrying
  for construction projects, 21, 53, 66, 68–69, 75, 97, 104, 141, 173, 174–75, 191, 197, 258, 263, 308, 324, 342, 343, 344, 483
  in Eastern Desert, 12, 27, 105, 151, 175, 226, 295, 344
  gold mines, 12, 22, 191, 192, 196, 223, 247, 295, 343, 380
  Nubia as gold mining region, 191, 192, 196, 223, 247, 343, 380, 447
  Ptolemy II seizes lower Nubia for gold reserves, 447
  Ramesses III orders foreign expeditions to bring back treasures for temples, 334
  Sinai turquoise mines, 160, 334, 348
  at Wadi Hammamat, 12, 104, 141, 160, 174–75, 343–44, 425, 428
Minoan civilization, 192, 195, 245
Mirgissa. See Iken
Mittani
  achieves lasting peace with Egypt, 240, 297
  achieves peace with Egypt, 232, 236, 238–39
  diplomatic brides from, 247–48, 297
  as kingdom within Mesopotamia, 206–8, 246–47, 297
  reasserts itself, 215
  Thutmose I makes preemptive strike against, 206–8
  See also Megiddo, Battle of
Moalla. See Hefat
monarchy, hereditary, 202–3
  See also dynastic kingship
Montu, 118, 175, 243
Montuemhat, 412, 414
Montumes, 336
mummification, 124, 128, 129, 293

Mut (consort of Amun-Ra), 212, 225, 251, 270
Mutemwia, 250–51
Muwatalli, 315
Muwatalli II, 304, 305, 306
Mycenae, 193, 220, 245, 319

Nabta Playa, 8–10, 11, 58
Nagada. *See* Nubt
Nahal Tillah, 42
Naharin, 220
  See also Mittani
Nahr el-Kebir Valley. *See* Eleutherus Valley
Nahr el-Kelb, 408
Nakhthorheb, xx, 26, 433, 435, 437–38, 441
Nakhtnebef, xx, 431–32, 438
Napata, 236, 384, 394, 399, 405, 410, 415
Napoléon Bonaparte, 71, 483–84
Narmer
  in timeline, xiii
  depictions, 28, 29, 30, 34, 36
  discovery by archaeologists, 6, 7, 14–15
  as first ruler of united Egypt and founder of Egyptian state, 6, 14–15, 17, 25, 26
  as one of three regional rulers, 12–13
  regalia, 30
Narmer Palette
  approximate age, 6
  decoration, 7, 28–29
  defined, 5
  depictions of Narmer, 28, 29, 30, 34, 36
  discovery by archaeologists, 6, 7
  early kingship imagery, 27
  hieroglyphs, 32
  illustrated, 7
  king's regalia, 30
  Mesopotamian motifs, 29
nation-state concept, xxxiv, 25
Naukratis, 418, 450, 451
Nauplion, 245

Nauri Decree, 295
Nayfaurud I, xx, 430
Nayfaurud II, xx, 431
Near East
  Amenhotep II's military operations, 236–37
  Amenhotep III's diplomacy in, 245–48
  ancient Egypt's relationship with, 42–44
  leaders in Mesopotamia, 246–47
  Libyans move to renew Egyptian authority, 385–86
  as part of Seleucid Kingdom, 447
  plundered by Sea Peoples, 328–29
  Thutmose seeks recognition for Egypt in, 206–8
  Thutmose III's military operations, 215–21
  trade with Hyksos Kingdom in Egypt, 171
  See also Alashiya; Anatolia; Mesopotamia
Nebet, 106
Nebra, xiii, 49
Nebuchadrezzar, 417
necropolis
  for commoners and professional bureaucracy, 80
  Memphite, 60, 74
  royal, at Djanet, 371–72, 374, 375
  royal, tomb robbing, 351–52
  See also royal tombs and mortuary temples
Nectanebo II (Nakhthorheb). *See* Nakhthorheb
Neferefra, xiv, 85, 86, 87
Neferhotep III, xvi, 169, 173
Neferirkara (Fifth Dynasty ruler), xiv, 85, 86, 106
Neferirkara (Eighth Dynasty ruler), xv, 106
Neferkara Pepi II. *See* Pepi II
Neferkauhor, xv, 105–6
Neferkaura, xv, 105
Neferkheperura. *See* Amenhotep IV/ Akhenaten

Neferneferuaten (Nefertiti), xvii, 261,
    270, 275, 276
    See also Nefertiti (wife of Amenhotep
    IV/Akhenaten)
Nefertari (wife of Ramesses II), 308,
    317
Nefertem, 294
Nefertiti (wife of Amenhotep IV/
    Akhenaten)
    adds epithet to name, becoming
        Neferneferuaten, 261
    at Akhenaten's installation of high
        priest of Aten, 266
    and cult of Aten, 270, 271–72
    relationship with Akhenaten, 262,
        271–72, 273, 274–75, 276
    statue in Gempaaten temple, 259
    statue in Great Palace at Akhetaten,
        264
    statues smashed, 290
Nefrusi, 185
Nehesy, xvi, 166–67
Neith (deity), 33, 126, 400, 422, 423,
    431
Neith-hotep (wife of Narmer), 33
Neitiqerty Siptah, xv, 103
Nekau II, xix, 425
Nekau of Sais, 402, 408, 409, 410
Nekhbet, 33, 51
Nekheb (Elkab), 33, 175, 184, 189
Nekhen (Kom el-Ahmar)
    background, 5–6
    discovery of mace heads, 34, *35*
    discovery of Narmer Palette, 6, 14
    early kingship practices, 34–35
    as early provincial capital, 56
    eclipsed by Djeba, 59
    history, 12, 13, 14
    Khasekhem's cult enclosure, 52
    Khasekhem's monuments, 51
    nineteenth century excavation, 5–6
    Painted Tomb, 27
    recent reexamination, 34–35
Nelson, Horatio, 484
Nemtyemsaf II, xiv, 103
Nephthys, 474
Nesamun, 349

Nesbanebdjedet
    in timeline, xviii
    attempts to gain divine sanction for
        Egyptian regime, 376
    Libyan ruler of Lower Egypt, 367,
        369, 370, 371, 380
    recycling of Egyptian monuments,
        371
    takes power in north of Egypt from
        last of Ramessides, 358–59
Nesbanebdjedet II, 383
Nesmahes, 423
nesu bity (dual king), 33–34
Nesuanhur, 408
Netjerikhet
    in timeline, xiv
    as autocrat, 37, 54, 78
    first pyramid built for, 37, 53, 58
    measure of achievements, 55
    Step Pyramid at Saqqara, 53–55, 61,
        78, 87, 472
New Kingdom
    in timeline, xvi–xvii
    beginning, 183, 196
    system of government, 222–24
Niankhkhnum, 84
Nile Valley
    comparison with Nile delta, 23–24
    constriction at Asyut, 22–23
    diversity of landscapes, 20
    and Egyptian creation myth, 15
    first cataract, 20, 21, 42
    geography, 16–23, 106–7
    Herotodus' view, 15
    insufficient water, 16, 97, 107, 474
    inundations, 16, 20, 107–8, 405, 477
    maps, *xxxv*
    as metaphor, 17
    migration to, 11, 163–64
    as one of Two Lands, 18, 20
    Persians build canal to Red Sea,
        425–26
    Qena bend in river, 22
    second cataract, 28, 150, 156–59, 309
    significance to Egyptian life, 15
Nimlot, 394, 395–96, 398
Nineteenth Dynasty, xvii

Ninetjer, xiii, 49–50
Nineveh, 406, 409, 411, 416
Ninth/Tenth Dynasty, xv
Nitiqret, 414, 415
Niuserra Ini, xiv, 85
Niye, 207, 220
Nodjmet, 357–58
nomarchs, defined, 46, 107
North Saqqara (cemetery), 47–48
Nubia
    border with Upper Egypt, 20, 48, 94,
        145–46
    conquered by Amenemhat I, 146–47
    Egyptian fortresses in, 150–52,
        156–59, 166, 170, 191, 192, 193
    Egyptian treatment of Kushites as
        prisoners of war, 287, 287–88
    formally annexed to second cataract,
        150
    Gebel Sheikh Suleiman, 28, 43
    geography, 21, 42
    as gold mining region, 191, 192, 196,
        223, 247, 343, 380, 447
    influence of Egyptian theology,
        392–93
    Kamose reestablishes Egyptian
        administration, 185
    Kushites defeat Libyans and impose
        hegemony throughout Egypt,
        391–98, 399
    mercenaries from, 93, 112, 145, 385
    political developments in, 94–96
    Ptolemy II seizes lower portion, 447
    Ramesses II builds shrines in, 308
    under Senusret III, 156–59
    Shaat Island, 191, 192, 193
    temple of Amun-Ra at Napata, 384
    Thutmose campaign of conquest,
        203–5
    See also Kushites
Nubkheperra Intef
    in timeline, xvi
    efforts to revive Egypt's fortunes
        against Hyksos, 173–74
    royal decree preserved at Gebtu, 174
    tomb, 173–74
Nubt, 12, 13, 14, 27, 31, 42, 59

Nun (deity), 15, 17
nursery, royal, 232–34

oases. See Kharga Oasis; Siwa Oasis
Octavia, 477, 479
Octavian, 476, 477, 479, 480, 482
Old Kingdom
    in timeline, xiv–xv
    defined, 3
    end, 3, 22, 98, 124
    map, 2
Opet Festival. See Festival of Opet
Orontes River (Asi), 207, 301, 303, 305,
    328
Osiris
    background, 127–28
    deification of baboons as, 435–36
    as god of the underworld, 127–28,
        129, 130, 130–31
    place in Seti I's temple at Abdju,
        294
    rise to universal god of the dead,
        131–34, 136
    statues of Amenhotep III as, 243
Osiris-Apis, 452
Osiris-Khentiamentiu, 172, 173
Osiris-Wennefer, 456
Osorkon, Prince (son of Takelot II). See
    Osorkon III
Osorkon I, xviii
Osorkon II, xviii, 387–88
Osorkon III, xviii, 389–91, 393
Osorkon IV, xviii, 397, 398, 399–400
Osorkon the Elder, xviii
"Ozymandias," ix, 281, 311–12

Paatenemheb, 286–87
Padibastet (I), xviii, 389, 390
Padibastet (II), xviii
Padibastet (son of Taimhotep), 473
Padiese, Prince (of Hutheryib), 397
Padiusir, 439, 443
Paiankh, 356, 357–58, 366, 369, 373,
    379, 380
Painted Tomb, 27

Palace of the Dazzling Orb and the
House of Rejoicing, 254–56
palace-façade architecture, 31, 48
Palermo Stone, *43*, 44, 45, 46, 49, 51,
52, 62
Palestine
Amenemhat I guards against
incursions, 145
Amenhotep II's military campaign to
secure hold, 236–37
bedouin tribespeople as immigrants
into Nile delta, 163–64
falls to Babylonia, 416
Libyan ruler in Egypt launches attack
against, 381–82
loyalty to Cleopatra, 470
mention of Israel in Merenptah's
commemorative inscription, 321–22
Pompey's expansion into, 467
proximity to Per-Ramesses, 313
trade with Egypt, 42
trading centers plundered by Sea
Peoples, 328
palette, defined, 6
Pamay, xviii
Panehsy, 355–56, 357, 380
Paraherwenemef, 339
Paramessu
changes name to Ramessu, 292
chosen by Horemheb as successor,
292
See also Ramesses I
Parthia, 476, 477, 478
Pas-Baal, 219
Pasebakhaenniut I, xviii, 371–72, 375,
376
Pasebakhaenniut II, xviii, 383
Paser, 352
Pasherenptah, 465–66, 467, 469,
472–73, 476
Pashermut, xx
Paweraa, 352
Peftjauawybast, xviii, 396, 398
Peleset, 329, 332
Pentaweret, 338, 339
Pentu, 274
Pepi I, xiv, 91–92, 94, 105

Pepi II
in timeline, xiv
adds to temple of Min, 105
death, 103
economy weakens during reign, 107
ineffectual as king, 97–98
throne name of Kushite Shabaqo, 402
as underage monarch, 95, 96
waning of royal authority, 126
Pepiankh of Meir, 97
Per-Atum, 313
Perdiccas, 445, 446
Pergamum, great library, 477
Per-hebit
Libyan community settles nearby in
central delta, 366
Ptolemy II commissions new temple
construction, 453
Peribsen, xiii, 50
Perirer, Battle of, 320–21, 330
Perniankhu, 73
Per-Ramesses
created by Ramesses II, 312–14
description, 312–14
deserted at end, 359
faces invasion by Sea Peoples, 330
Libyans recycle building materials for
new ceremonial capital at Djanet,
371, 380
role as pharaoh's residence, 370
Pershak, 185
Persians
acculturation to Egyptian life, 423–24
battles against Alexander the Great,
441–43
comprise Thirty-first Egyptian
Dynasty, 26
construction of ancient Suez Canal,
425–26
Darius I encourages trade between
Egypt and Persia, 425–27
introduce camel to Egypt, 426–27
invade Egypt and incorporate into
realm, 363, 364, 421–24, 438
leadership after Darius I, 428–34
need for Egypt's wealth, 440
as part of Seleucid Kingdom, 447

Persians (cont'd):
  relationship with Greek world, 428,
    429, 440
personal names, 72–73, 104
Per-Sopdu, 402, 410, 412
Perunefer, 230, 284
Per-Wadjet (Tell el-Fara'in), 33, 394,
    440
Petrie, Flinders, xxix
Peukestas, 444
Phaistos, 245
pharaoh, origin of term, 211
pharaonic state. See dynastic kingship
Pharos lighthouse, 450
Philae (island), 453, 462
Philip Arrhidaeus (Philip III of
    Macedon), xx, 446
Philippi, Battle of, 476
Phoenicia, 296, 298, 319, 430, 478
phyles, defined, 68
Piankhi, xix, 393, 394–98, 399, 400,
    403, 415
Pinedjem I, xviii, 375, 378, 379, 383
Pinedjem II, xviii, 383
Place of Truth (Deir el-Medina),
    199–200, 201, 335, 350
Pnubs, 220, 415
Pollux, 451
Pompeii, 485
Pompey, 467, 470, 471, 479
Poseidon, 448
prehistoric kingdoms, 3, 12–14
private tombs, 80–85
Prophecies of Neferti, The, 101, 148–49
protection money, 385, 466, 467
Psamtek I, xix, 409, 411–14, 416, 430
Psamtek II, xix, 415, 416
Psamtek III, xix, 421
Psamtek-Amenirdis. See Amenirdis
    (king)
Ptah
  at Abu Simbel, 310
  Apis bull as incarnation, 242
  and Battle of Kadesh, 303, 304,
    305–6
  figurine in Pasebakhaenniut I's tomb,
    372

Imhotep succeeds father as high
    priest, 477
Pasherenptah as high priest, 465–66,
    467, 469, 472–73, 476
place in Seti I's temple at Abdju, 294
as principal Memphis deity, 294, 310,
    397, 403, 435, 465
Ptahshepses, 84–85
Ptah-Sokar, 294
Ptolemaia (festival), 452–53
Ptolemaic Period, xx–xxi, 23, 26, 362,
    445–64
Ptolemais (city), 450, 451, 453, 458, 473
Ptolemies, background, 364, 446–50,
    451, 452–54
  See also names of individual rulers
Ptolemy Caesar, 472
  See also Ptolemy XV Caesarion
    (Cleopatra's son)
Ptolemy I, xx, 445–47, 448, 449, 452–53
Ptolemy II, xx, 447, 448, 453–54, 459
Ptolemy III, xx, 447, 449, 455, 463
Ptolemy IV, xx, 455–56
Ptolemy V, xx, 456–59
Ptolemy VI, xx, 460, 461
Ptolemy VIII, xx, 460, 461–62
Ptolemy IX, xx, xxi
Ptolemy X, xx, 463, 466
Ptolemy XI, xxi, 463
Ptolemy XII (Cleopatra's father), xxi,
    464, 465, 466, 467–68, 469, 477
Ptolemy XIII (Cleopatra's brother), xxi,
    469, 470–71
Ptolemy XIV (Cleopatra's brother), xxi,
    471–72
Ptolemy XV Caesarion (Cleopatra's
    son), xxi, 473, 474, 478, 479, 480,
    481–82
Ptolemy Philadelphus, 478
Pudukhepa, 317
Punic Wars, xx, 460
Punt, Egyptian trading missions to,
    175, 213, 214, 334
Pyramid Texts, 88–89, 97, 127, 129, 403
pyramids
  administrative effort for constructing,
    55

at apex of Nile delta, 23
first, 37, 53, 58
at Giza, 3, 57–58, 65–72, 144–45
Ibi's attempt, 104–5
Imhotep as first builder, 54–55
reason for, 124
resurgence of constructing in
  Seventeenth Dynasty, 173
small, built by Huni, 56
as surviving wonder of ancient world,
  57
as symbol of unification and royal
  omnipotence, 48
See also Great Pyramid at Giza

Qaa, xiii, 48–49, 50
Qaqa, 237
Qatna, 220, 328
Qenamun, 230–31
Qift. *See* Gebtu
Quibell, James, 5–6

Ra (sun god)
  Amenhotep III builds shrines to, 242
  eye of Ra, 242, 243
  relationship to Aten, 266, 269
  relationship to Egyptian monarchy,
    253
  relationship to Horus, 74, 129, 238,
    310
Rabirius, 468
Ra-Horakhty
  at Abu Simbel, 310
  as combination of Ra and Horus, 310
  in Ramesses II's temple at Per-
    Ramesses, 313
  in Seti I's temple at Abdju, 294
Rahotep, xvi, 172
Raiders of the Lost Ark (movie), 485
Ramesses, Prince (son of Seti I), 294,
  301
Ramesses I, xvii, 293
Ramesses II
  in timeline, xvii
  Abu Simbel, 309–11, *310*

additions to Luxor Temple, 308–9
Battle of Kadesh, 300, 301, *302*,
  303–7
commissions new dynastic capital,
  Per-Ramesses, 312–14
construction projects, 307–14
diplomatic marriage to Hittite
  princess, 317–18
immortalized by "Ozymandias," 281
length of reign, 318, 323
makes peace with Hittites, 315–18
mortuary temple, 311, 351
new relationship with Hittite king,
  317–18
pairs of colossal seated statues
  installed, 309, *310*
plunders forebears' monuments, 308
remains desecrated, 374
successor in dispute, 323–24
surviving monuments of, 308, 309–11
victory inscription at Nahr el-Kelb,
  408
Ramesses III
  in timeline, xvii
  achievements, 282, 334
  assassination plot against, 338–40
  battles increasing Libyan presence in
    Egypt, 365–66
  death, 340
  early years of reign, 327–32
  faces invasion by Sea Peoples, 329–32
  mortuary temple, 327, 332–33, 351
  orders foreign expeditions to bring
    back treasures for temples, 334
  orders nationwide temple
    refurbishment, 333–34
  remains desecrated, 374
  royal harem, 337–38
  thirty-year jubilee, 334, 335, 337
Ramesses IV
  in timeline, xvii
  accession, 345–46
  period of decline, 345–46
  revives quarrying activity, 343–44
  unfinished temple buildings, 345
Ramesses V, xvii, 346–47, 348, 374
Ramesses VI, xvii, 347–48, 356

Ramesses VII, xvii, 348
Ramesses VIII, xvii, 348
Ramesses IX, xvii, 351
Ramesses X, xvii
Ramesses XI
  in timeline, xvii
  death, 359, 365
  declares renaissance, 356–57
  length of reign, 359
  Libyans claim to continue
    renaissance, 376
  loses power, 358–59
  problem of usurper as high priest of
    Amun, 354–56
  sets up commission to investigate
    tomb robberies, 352–53
  sidelined as irrelevant, 282
Ramessesnakht, 343–44, 349, *349*, 354
Ramesseum, 311
Ramesside Period, defined, 281–82
Raphia, Battle of, 455
Ras Shamra. *See* Ugarit
red crown, 30
Red Pyramid, 64–65
Red Sea, 22, 425–26
regalia, royal, 29–31
Rekhmira, 226–27, 231
religion, Egyptian
  afterlife, 124, 125–31, 134–39
  Amenhotep IV/Akhenaten's
    fundamentalist doctrine, 258, 259,
    265–66, 267–68, 269–70
  animal deities, 434–38
  era of public spectacle in Thebes, 225
  household deities, 225
  pantheon of gods, 294, 313
  relationship of Egyptian kings to sun
    god, 73, 74–75, 78–79, 85, 117,
    129, 130, 134, 237, 238, 242, 244,
    252, 254, 256, 259, 260
  See also Amun/Amun-Ra; Ipetsut
    (Karnak); Ra (sun god)
Report of Wenamun, 380–81
Rhodes, 467–68
Rib-Adda, 246
Ribla. *See* Shabtuna
rock art, *9*, *10*, 27

Rome
  conquest of Egypt, 480–81, 483
  emerges as key player in
    Mediterranean politics, 460,
    462–63
  extorts revenues from Egypt, 466,
    467
  intervenes to prevent unification of
    Seleucid and Ptolemaic kingdoms,
    460
  origins, 459
  Ptolemy XII's two-year exile, 468
  succeeds Egypt as power in
    Mediterranean, 466
  treaty of friendship with Ptolemies,
    459
  view of Cleopatra, 478, 479
Rosetta Stone, xxviii, *457*, 457–58
royal tombs and mortuary temples
  Amenhotep I's, 201
  construction and decoration, 125–26,
    334–37, 350
  decline of craftsmanship, 128–29
  defacing, 231
  end of mortuary temple custom, 368
  exploited by rulers themselves, 358
  Horemheb's, 287
  magical objects, 134–35
  Mentuhotep II's mortuary temple,
    122–23, 199
  North Saqqara cemetery, 47–48
  Nubkheperra Intef's, 173–74
  Old Kingdom construction and
    decoration, 80–85
  place names inscribed in Amenhotep
    III's mortuary temple, 244–45
  in prehistoric kingdoms, 13
  Qenamun's tomb, 230–31
  Ramesses II's mortuary temple, 311,
    351
  Ramesses III's mortuary temple, 327,
    332–33, 351
  Rekhmira's tomb, 231
  robbing of tombs, 200, 350, 351–53,
    358, 373–75, 384
  sanctity of, 350
  Sennefer's tomb, 228, 229

separating mortuary temple from
  tomb, 200–201
Seti I's tomb, 295–96
subsidiary graves, 37–39
Thutmose I's tomb, 375
Tutankhamun's tomb, xxv–xxviii, *xxvi*,
  278
worker discontent, 350–53
See also Abdju; necropolis; pyramids;
  Saqqara; Valley of the Kings
Rudamun, xviii, 393

Sahura, xiv, 85–86, 405
Sai. *See* Shaat Island
Sais (western delta city)
  background, 414, 420
  defined, 402, 458–59
  Irethoreru leads revolt against
    Persians, 428–29
  Khnemibra accommodates himself to
    Persians, 421–22
  relationship with Assyria, 415–16
  Wedjahorresnet collaborates with
    Persians, 422–23
  See also Bakenrenef; Nekau of Sais;
    Psamtek I; Psamtek II; Tefnakht
Salamis, 428
Samannud. *See* Tjebnetjer
San el-Hagar. *See* Djanet
Sanakht, xiv, 55
Saqqara
  Amenhotep III commissions tomb
    chapel and burial for sacred bull,
    242
  animal cults at, 435–38
  Horemheb's tomb, 287
  Khasekhemwy's enclosure, 52–53
  Macedonian papyrus notice, 444
  Ptolemy II commissions new temple
    construction, 453
  site of new royal burial ground, 49,
    77
  Step Pyramid of King Netjerikhet,
    53–54
  See also North Saqqara (cemetery)
Satire of the Trades, 101, 233

Satju, 94, 95
Sauty, 115–16, 118–19, 456, 458
scarabs, 139, 240–41, 247, 401
scepters, as Egyptian invention, 30
school. *See* scribal school
Scorpion (early king), 34, 35, *35*, 36–37
Scorpion King, The, (movie), 485
scribal school, 232–34
Sea Peoples, 320, 321, 328–32, *331*, 333
Second Dynasty, xiii, 49–51
Second Intermediate Period, xvi
sed festival, 249, 254, 259–60, 265
Seila, 56
Sekhemkhet, xiv, 55
Sekhmet, 243
Seleucid Kingdom, 447, 455, 467
Seleucus. *See* Seleucid Kingdom
Sematawytefnakht, 441, 444
Semerkhet, xiii
Semna
  as Nubian fortress, 157, 158, 159, 166
  reminders of Senusret III at, 159
Semna Dispatches, 158
Senenmut, 214–15
Sennacherib, 407
Sennefer, 228, 229
Senusret I
  in timeline, xv
  adds jubilee pavilion to temple of
    Amun at Ipetset, 150, 198
  political unrest during reign, 150
  as ruler, 148–52
  son of Amenemhat, 147
Senusret II, xv, 153
Senusret III
  in timeline, xv
  authoritarian rule, 154–59
  likeness, *158*, 159
  victory at Shechem in Israel, 385
Sepa, 55
Seqenenra Taa, xvi, 176–77, *177*
Serapeum
  at Alexandria, 452
  at Saqqara, 435, 452, 453
Serapis, 452
Sesostris. *See* Senusret III
Seth, 50, 171, 313, 333

Sethnakht, xvii, 326–27, 374
Seti I
    in timeline, xvii
    description, 293
    foreign relations, 296–97, 298–99
    initiates construction projects,
        293–96
    mummy, 293
    remains desecrated, 374
    tomb, 295–96
Seti II
    in timeline, xvii
    construction projects, 324–25
    heir to Merenptah, 323–24
    length of reign, 325
Seti-Merenptah. See Seti II
Seventeenth Dynasty, xvi, 172
Seventh Dynasty, as spurious, xiii, 104
Shaat Island, 191, 192, 203
Shabaqo, xix, 400–401, 402, 403, 407,
    415
Shabitqo, xix
shabti (funerary figurines), 135–37, 276,
    401, 403
Shabtuna, 303
Shalfak, 156–57, 158
Sharuhen, 191, 206, 385
Shechem, 385
Shedyt, animal cults at, 434–35
Shekelesh, 329
Shelley, Percy Bysshe, ix, 281, 311–12
Shemai, 105–6
Shepenwepet I (god's wife of Amun),
    393
Shepenwepet II (daughter of Piankhi),
    401, 413, 414
Shepseskaf, xiv, 77
Shepseskara Izi, xiv, 85
Sherden, 332
Shetep, 240
Shipwrecked Sailor, The, 101
Shoshenq I, xviii, 383–85
Shoshenq II, xviii
Shoshenq III, xviii
Shoshenq IV, xviii
Shoshenq V, xviii
Shoshenq VI, xviii

Shu (creator god), 259, 266, 269, 271
Shuppiluliuma, 297
Siamun, xviii, 381
Sinai turquoise mines, 160, 334, 348
Sinuhe, The Tale of, 101, 149, 233, 381
Siptah
    in timeline, xvii
    as puppet ruler, 325
    remains desecrated, 374
Siwa Oasis, 442, 445
Sixteenth Dynasty, xvi
Sixth Dynasty, xiv, 90–91
slaves, Asiatic, 153–54
Smenkhkara, xvii, 276
Sneferu
    in timeline, xiv
    Horus name, 58
    mortuary cult, 438
    new model of kingship, 58–59
    as pyramid builder, 59, 61–65
Sobekemsaf II, xvi, 174–75
Sobekhotep III, xvi, 165–66
Sobekneferu (first female king), xv,
    160–61, 163
Sokar-Osiris, 474
solar court, Luxor Temple, 249
Soleb. See Khaemmaat, fortress at
Solomon, 381, 385
Sopdu, 173–74
Soped-her, 170
soul. See ba (soul)
Sphinx. See Great Sphinx
sports. See training, physical
Step Pyramid, Saqqara
    architect, 54–55
    background, 53–54
    compared with Meidum pyramid, 61
    Unas's tomb nearby, 87–89
    Userkaf's tomb nearby, 78
stone carving, 7, 7–10, 9, 27
Stonehenge. See Nabta Playa
strikes, among workers, 334–37, 350
Suez Canal (ancient), 425–26, 447
Suez Canal (modern), 484
Suez Crisis, 484
Sumenu, 172, 242, 458
Sumur, 246, 305

sun god, relationship of Egyptian kings to, 73, 74–75, 78–79, 85, 117, 129, 130, 134, 237, 238, 242, 244, 252, 254, 256, 259, 260
  See also Amun/Amun-Ra; Ra (sun god)
Susa, 434
Syria, 296, 416, 478
  See also Hittites
Syrian Wars, 447, 455, 460

Taa. *See* Seqenenra Taa
Taanach, 386
Tadukhepa, 248
Taharqo
  in timeline, xix
  builds fighting force to project Egypt's strength, 405–6
  commands force against Syria, 407–8, 409
  orders Egyptian temple renovations, 404–5
  as zenith of Kushite rule in Egypt, 404–6
Taimhotep
  funerary stela, 474–75, *475*
  prays for son, 472–73
  as wife of high priest Pasherenptah, 472–73
Takelot I, xviii
Takelot II, xviii, 388–89, 390
Takelot III, xviii
Takhsy, 236
  See also Syria
Tale of Sinuhe, The, 101, 149, 233, 381
Ta-Mehu ("flooded land"), 24
Tanaya, 220
Tanis. *See* Djanet
Tanutamun, xix, 409–11, 414, 415
Taremu, 394, 423
Tarhuntassa, 328
Tarkhundaradu, 248
Tarsus
  Cleopatra and Mark Antony meet, 476
  plundered by Sea Peoples, 328
Tawedjay fortress, 378, 379, 389
Tawer, 115, 116–17, 119

Taweret, 225
Tawosret
  in timeline, xvii
  head of regency council for Siptah, 325
  wife of Seti II, 324, 325
taxation
  Cleopatra grants privileges to Roman general, 478–79
  corvée, 341–43
  as proportion of farm produce, 45–46, 62
  by Ptolemies, 454, 467
  recorded on Palermo Stone, 44–45
Tefnakht, xix, 394, 396, 397–98, 400, 411, 420
Tefnut (creator god), 259, 271
Tel Erani, 42
Tell Atrib. *See* Hutheryib
Tell el-Ajjul. *See* Sharuhen
Tell el-Dab'a. *See* Hutwaret
Tell el-Fara'in, 14
  See also Per-Wadjet (Tell el-Fara'in)
Tell el-Hebua. *See* Tjaru fortress
Tell el-Maskhuta, 313
Tell el-Muqdam. *See* Taremu
Tell el-Yahudiya, 170
temple of Amun at Ipetsut
  administration, 223
  Ahmose erects stela for Ahhotep, 194–95, 196
  Ahmose erects stela for Ahmose-Nefertari, 196
  Amenemhat I's grand plans for, 143–44
  as Amun-Ra's chief temple, 120, 211
  flooded, 169
  high priest, 223, 224–26, 354, 387, 388, 465
  Libyans replicate at Djanet, 376
  Merenptah's commemorative inscription, 321–22, 365
  Senusret I adds jubilee pavilion, 150, 198
  Shoshenq commissions extension, 386
  size and scale, 143–44
  theft from, 353

temple of Min, 105, 172, 174

Temple of Ramesses-beloved-of-Amun.
See Abu Simbel

temples. See Luxor Temple; royal tombs
and mortuary temples; temple of
Amun at Ipetsut

Ten Commandments, The, (movie), 485

Tentamun, 380

Tentyris. See Iunet

Teti, xiv, 90–91, 185

Tetian, 192

Tetisheri, 193, 194, 209, 271

Thebes
administration of, 223
Amenhotep III's construction
projects, 242–44
animal cults, 434–35
ascendancy, 109–18
base of southern vizier, 223
becomes focus of royal construction
activity under Amenhotep I,
197–99
as city dedicated to Amun-Ra,
225–26, 242
civil war with Herakleopolis,
112–19
collaboration with Hyksos,
183–84
Colossi of Memnon, 244
commission to investigate tomb
robbing, 351–53
compared with Memphis, 369–70,
465
comparison with Djanet, 387
declares independence from Libyan
rule, 387–88
description, 119–20
dissolves alliance with Gebtu, 112
in Eighteenth Dynasty, 225
established as Egyptian national
capital, 120
Hatshepsut's monuments in,
211–14
Horwennefer takes rule from
Ptolemies, 456
Hyksos threaten, 172
invaded by Assyria, 410–11
under Kushite control, 401
as launchpad for campaign of
national reunification, 109
under Libyan control, 365, 373–75,
391
map, 187
Nile as factor, 21
period of decline, 345–49
processional routes, 212
province attacked by Ankhtifi, 109
Ptolemaic cities as counterweight to,
450–51
Ptolemy V reclaims from Egyptian
rebels, 458
public religious spectacle, 225
Ramesses II's construction projects,
308
resents being ruled from Alexandria,
455
royal court establishes government
after abandoning Itj-tawy to
Hyksos, 168, 169, 170
as stage for Amenhotep III's jubilee
rites, 254–56
Tombs of the Nobles, 223
See also Ipetsut (Karnak)

Thera (volcano), 192, 195

Thermopylae, 428

Third Dynasty, xiv

Third Intermediate Period, xviii–xix

Third Reich, 484

Third Syrian War, 455

Thirteenth Dynasty, xvi, 165, 167

Thirtieth Dynasty, xx, 26

Thirty-first Dynasty, xx, 26

Thoth, 400, 435, 437, 439, 451

Thutmose I
in timeline, xvi
characteristics, 202–3
extends Egyptian authority south of
fourth cataract, 204
foreign relations, 206–8
foster sister, 224
heir apparent to Amenhotep I by
adoption, 202
invades Kush, 203–5, 391–92
legacy, 208

path to power, 202–3
preemptive strike against Mittani,
206–8
tomb robbed, 375
wages campaign to conquer Nubia,
203–5
Thutmose II, xvi, 208
Thutmose III
in timeline, xvii
Asiatic wives, 219
commissions temple at Gebel Barkal,
392
inner circle, 224–27
military operations, 215–21
as perhaps greatest pharaoh, 221
policy toward Nubia and Kushites,
220–21
remains desecrated, 374
stepmother's rule as regent for,
209–14
throne name adopted by Kushite
chieftain Piankhi, 393
widens frontiers of Egypt, 222
Thutmose IV
in timeline, xvii
as father of Amenhotep III, 250
peaceful reign, 238–39
remains desecrated by Libyans,
374
reverence for Great Sphinx,
237–38
Tilgathpileser III, 406
Timna, 348
Tiy (secondary wife of Ramesses III),
338
Tiye (wife of Amenhotep III), 241, 243,
254, 255, 256, 271, 275
Tjaru fortress, 163, 190, 216, 291
Tjauti, 113
Tjebnetjer, 397, 402, 431
Tjeker, 329, 332, 381
Tjemeh, 95
Tjeni
base for overseer of Upper Egypt,
108
conquered by Intef II, 116
large tomb, 13–14

as one of three prehistoric Egyptian
kingdoms, 12, 13, 14, 17, 42, 59
prehistoric rulers, 14
prominence during prehistoric
period, 22
Tjetji, 118
Tod, barque shrine, 333
See also Djerty (Tod)
Tombos, 204–5
tombs, royal. See royal tombs and
mortuary temples
Tombs of the Nobles, 223
trade, international
earliest Egyptian examples, 41–42
between Egypt and Persia,
425–27
in Greek world, 418
impact of writing on, 41–42
under Khasekhem, 52
under Ptolemy I, 447
under Senusret I, 152
trade routes, 20, 21, 23, 186–87
training, physical, 234–36
Troy, 245, 328
Tukh, 56
Tunip, 219
Turi, 203
Turkey, 153, 247
See also Anatolia
Tushratta, 247, 248
Tutankhamun
in timeline, xvii
breaks with late father's religious
vision, 277
death and burial, 277–78
discovery of his tomb, xxv–xxviii,
xxxii, 278
funerary mask, xxxi–xxxii
monuments recarved by Horemheb,
290
name changed from Tutankhaten,
277
opening of sarcophagus, xxxi–xxxii,
xxxii
as underage monarch, 276–77
Tutankhaten. See Tutankhamun
Tutu, 274

Twelfth Dynasty
  in timeline, xv
  characteristics of, 140–41
  co-regency becomes feature of royal
    succession, 147
  cultural high point under
    Amenemhat III, 160
  end, 161
  flowering of literature, 140,
    148–50
  internationalism during, 152–54
  new, stable line of kings, 140–61
  period following, 164–65
  security issues, 159, 162–63
Twentieth Dynasty, xvii
Twenty-first Dynasty, xviii
Twenty-second Dynasty, xviii
Twenty-third Dynasty, xviii
Twenty-fourth Dynasty, xix
Twenty-fifth (Kushite) Dynasty, xix
Twenty-sixth (Saite) Dynasty, xix
Twenty-seventh Dynasty, xix
Twenty-eighth Dynasty, xx
Twenty-ninth Dynasty, xx
Two Lands
  junction of Upper Egypt with Lower
    Egypt, 23, 144, 168
  Nile as unifying thread, 18, 20
  See also delta, Nile; Lower Egypt;
    Nile Valley; Upper Egypt
Ty, 84
Tyre, 381, 408, 416

Ugarit, 317, 327–28
Ullaza, Egyptian garrison at, 246
Unas, xiv, 87–89, 90, 126
Upe, 316
Upper Egypt
  boundaries, defined, 388
  defined, 18
  Horwennefer takes rule from
    Ptolemies, 456
  junction with Lower Egypt, 23, 144,
    168
  under Kushite rule, 396,
    401–2

Libyan domination, 369, 373–75,
    391, 394
  map, 110
  Montuemhat as effective ruler under
    Kushites, Assyrians, and Saites,
    412, 414
  Nile characteristics, 20–23
  Ptolemies wage counteroffensive to
    reclaim from rebels, 456–58
  recessionist tendencies after fall of
    New Kingdom, 455
  symbolic relationship to Lower
    Egypt, 23, 33–34, 281
  white crown, 30–31
Urhi-Teshup, 315, 316, 317
Uronarti, 157, 158
U.S. dollar bill, ancient Egyptian
    imagery on, 485
User, 111, 112
Userkaf
  in timeline, xiv
  chosen location of tomb, 78
  commissions monument at Abusir,
    78, 79, 85
  first ruler in Fifth Dynasty,
    77–79
  opens offices of state to nonroyals,
    79–80
  relationship with sun god, 78
Userkara, xiv, 91
Usermaatra, 311
Ushanahuru, 408

Valley of the Kings
  discovery of King Tutankhamun's
    tomb, xxv–xxviii, 278
  Horemheb's tomb, 290
  last of splendid royal sepulchres, 368,
    369
  map, 187
  Seti I's tomb, 295–96
  tomb robberies, 350–51
  tombs of New Kingdom pharaohs
    emptied under Libyan rule,
    373–75, 384
viziers, role in government, 165, 223,
    353

Wadi Allaqi, 447
Wadi Barramiya, 295
Wadi el-Hudi, 160
Wadi Hammamat, 12, 104, 141, 160,
    174–75, 343–44, 425, 428
Wadi Natrun. *See* Shetep
Wadi Umm Salam, 10
wadis, defined, 10, 21
Wadjet, 33, 313
Wahibra, xix, 416–17
Wah-sut, 156
Walls of the Ruler, 145, 162
water, as currency, 427
Wawat
    Egyptian expatriates in, 170
    Egyptian treatment of Nubians, 154
    gold, copper, and precious stones,
        152
    Kush army sweeps northward via
        Egyptian-built fortresses, 175
    political unrest in, 145–47, 150,
        151–52
weaponry, Egyptian military
    making of, 313–14
    of Sea Peoples, 320
    types of, 285–86
Wedjahorresnet, 422–23
Wenamun, 380–81
Wendjebaendjedet, 372, 372, 375
Weni, 91–92, 93, 94
Wennefer, 433, 434, 438, 462
Wermai, 342
Weshesh, 329, 332
Western Desert
    Libyans as threat to Egypt, 318–21
    Nabta Playa, 8–10, 11, 58
    routes through, 13, 111, 113, 186
    See also Fayum; Kharga Oasis; Siwa
        Oasis
white crown, 30–31
Wilkinson, John Gardner, xxviii–xxix

workers
    agricultural, 342
    and corvée tax, 342–44
    discontent among, 334–37, 350
    Great Pyramid example, 68–71
    at Per-Ramesses, 313–14
    relationship to problem of tomb
        robbing, 350–53
    on royal tomb construction and
        decoration, 125–26, 334–37,
        350
    rules for agents of the palace, 291
    strikes by, 335–37, 350–51
    suburban houses for, 265
    See also conscription
World War II, 484
writing
    as cornerstone of pharaonic
        civilization, xxxiii
    earliest examples in Egypt, 14, 40,
        41–42
    Egyptian belief in power of written
        word, 204–5
    hieroglyphics as Egyptian act of
        invention, 40–41
    transformative power, 40, 41–42
    See also hieroglyphics; literature

xenophobia, xxxiii, 42
Xerxes I, xix, 428

Yam (place), 94, 95–96
Yehem, 216
Yenoam, 321

Zannanza, Prince, 278, 288, 298
Zawiyet el-Meitin, 56
Zeus, 448, 450, 451

DR. TOBY WILKINSON is a Fellow of Clare College, University of Cambridge, and an Honorary Research Fellow in the Department of Archaeology, University of Durham. An acknowledged expert on ancient Egyptian civilization, he has lectured around the world and is a contributor to major international collaborative projects. He is a member of the editorial board of the *Journal of Egyptian History* and broadcasts regularly on radio and television. His books include the critically acclaimed *Thames & Hudson Dictionary of Ancient Egypt* and *Lives of the Ancient Egyptians*.

ABOUT THE TYPE

The text of this book was set in Janson, a misnamed type-
face designed in about 1690 by Nicholas Kis, a Hungarian
in Amsterdam. In 1919 the matrices became the property
of the Stempel Foundry in Frankfurt. It is an old-style
book face of excellent clarity and sharpness. Janson serifs
are concave and splayed; the contrast between thick and
thin strokes is marked.